W9-ADF-999

MAJOR FIGURES OF TURN-OF-THE-CENTURY AUSTRIAN LITERATURE

Studies in Austrian Literature, Culture, and Though

Major Figures of Modern Austrian Literature
Edited by Donald G. Daviau

Introducing Austria. A Short History
By Lonnie Johnson

Austrian Foreign Policy Yearbook
Report of the Austrian Federal Ministry
for Foreign Affairs for the Year 1988

The Verbal and Visual Art of Alfred Kubin
By Phillip H. Rhein

From Wilson to Waldheim
Proceedings of a Workshop on
Austrian-American Relations 1917-1987
Edited by Peter Pabisch

Austria in the Thirties
Culture and Politics
Edited by Kenneth Segar and John Warren

Arthur Schnitzler and Politics
By Adrian Clive Roberts

"What People Call Pessimism":
Sigmund Freud, Arthur Schnitzler and
Nineteenth-Century Controversy at the University
of Vienna Medical School
By Mark Luprecht

Quietude and Quest
Protagonists and Antagonists in the Theatre,
on and off Stage
As Seen through the Eyes of Leon Askin
Written by Leon Askin with C. Melvin Davidson

MAJOR FIGURES OF TURN-OF-THE-CENTURY AUSTRIAN LITERATURE

Edited and with an Introduction

by

Donald G. Daviau

ARIADNE PRESS

Library of Congress Cataloging-in-Publication Data

Major figures of turn-of-the-century Austrian literature / edited
and with an introduction by Donald G. Daviau. -- 1st ed.
p.   cm. -- (Studies in Austrian literature, culture,
and thought)
Includes bibliographical references and index.
ISBN 0-929497-30-9
1. Austrian literature--19th century--History and criticism.
2. Austrian literature--20th century--History and criticism.
I. Daviau, Donald G. II. Series.
PT3817.M35 1990
830.9'9436'09041--dc20   90-893
                                                          CIP

TABLE OF CONTENTS

ACKNOWLEDGEMENTS

I would like to thank all those who assisted in bringing this volume into being. First and foremost my appreciation goes to the colleagues who contributed the individual essays. In addition I wish to express my gratitude to Professors Harvey I. Dunkle, Jorun B. Johns, and Richard M. Lawson for reading the manuscript and making valuable suggestions for improvement.

EDITORIAL NOTE

German titles are used throughout the book after being rendered in English following the first mention. If the work has been published in an English translation, the official translated title is presented in italics or quotation marks. If the English title is given in Roman, this indicates that the work in question has not been translated. Both German and English titles have been listed alphabetically in the index to assist the reader in locating discussions of specific works.

Preface

Major Figures of Turn-of-the-Century Austrian Literature represents the fourth volume in this series that will eventually comprise seven volumes. *Major Figures of Contemporary Austrian Literature* and *Major Figures of Modern Austrian Literature* have already appeared, and "Major Figures of the Austrian Interwar Years" and "Major Figures of the Austrian Nineteenth Century" as well as two additional volumes on the twentieth century are in preparation. When the series is completed it will provide biographical studies of 105 authors from Grillparzer to the very contemporary writers.

As in the previous volumes, each article here has been written by an expert on the specific author and follows a life and works approach. The contributors of the essays have been asked to accomplish the difficult task of producing a study informative and accessible to an introductory audience with no presumed background in Austrian literature and yet possessing sufficient breadth of coverage, depth of analysis, and original insight to be of value to the academic community from students of Austrian literature to specialists. The bibliographies of primary works in German in chronological sequence, of translations into English, and of secondary works in English and German provide a useful reference tool.

The Introduction is intended to provide a general overview of the period from 1880 to 1933, with particular emphasis on the years up to 1918, for the next volume will cover the timespan from 1918 to 1938. I have focused primarily on the so-called Jung-Wien writers because they dominated this era and set the tone for Austrian literature as long as they lived. Within this group I have featured Hermann Bahr partly because he is unjustly ignored by almost every other critic and largely because I am convinced that he represents the main driving force of the 1890s and that one cannot understand this period correctly without placing Bahr in the center.

I have tried to cover the main political and cultural developments that formed the context in which these writers and other artists functioned, although space does not permit more than a bare suggestion of this vibrant, complex, and seminal literary era. In addition I have attempted to address some of the myths and misconceptions that have become part of the literary canon in almost all discussions of the fin de siècle. Most accounts view this period as a rich, guilded, opulent era devoted to a carefree, beautiful life, while in reality life for the majority of the populace was lived at or close to the poverty level under severe conditions. The Jung-Wien writers are still described as aesthetes, decadents and dandies, terms which apply to the characters they created but not to the authors themselves. They are further portrayed as passive introverts fleeing into literature and the arts to avoid reality, while in truth these highly gifted young artists strove to become involved in life, with the avowed purpose of bringing literature and the other arts back into a truthful relationship with their contemporary world.

The mood of decline perceived in the fin de siècle derives mainly from the error of viewing this era in terms of the abolishing of the monarchy, an event applied retroactively, while in actuality no one at the turn of the century had any inkling that the monarchy could end any more than anyone today anticipated even the day before it happened that the Berlin wall would come down overnight. Scholars continue to belabor the issue of a language crisis in Hofmannsthal and in the period around 1900 in general, while neither Hofmannsthal nor any other writer suffered from a language crisis but only from language skepticism.

Individual authors are still misconstrued despite all the current available evidence. Recent accounts still present Hofmannsthal as an unworldly aesthete, Schnitzler as a writer uninterested in politics, Bahr as a dishonest intellectual quick-change artist, and Kraus as the incorruptible, infallible critic who knew no compromise. None of these clicheed stereotypes, formed early in each author's career, is still valid today. Clearly there remains much work to be done before we arrive at a reasonably accurate understanding of this unique literary generation.

The fin de siècle emphasized the sense of totality. It is hoped that the individual essays in this volume will add up to something approximating a sense of the wholeness of this period, the most unique era in modern cultural history.

Introduction

Turn-of-the-century, or as it is often called, fin-de-siècle Vienna, remains, a hundred years after its beginnings, one of the most glamorous, exciting, and significant periods of Austrian literary and cultural history. The phenomenon of the transition into the twentieth century was shared by other nations of the western world, but nowhere do we witness the unique set of circumstances that existed in Vienna during this period. Much of the thinking and many of the issues and developments dominating society today were introduced during this uniquely fertile era which gave birth to the spirit of modernity animating, driving, and transforming societies from the relatively stable nineteenth to the explosive twentieth century. The dramatic changes that took place in Europe during the second half of the nineteenth century—the rapid expansion of industrialization and the concomitant shift from an agrarian to an urban society, the breakthroughs and advances in the sciences, the change from a belief in absolute to relative values, the replacement of the aristocracy by the monied bourgeoisie as the dominant economic class, and the gaining of voting privileges which propelled the move toward democratization—produced the ferment and set the stage for the "transformation of all values" (Nietzsche) that occurred during the transitional building years (*Gründerjahre*) from the founding of the unified German state under Bismarck in 1870 to the outbreak of World War I in 1914.

Every area contributed discoveries, inventions, and innovations. The population shift from the country to the city caused immediate urban blight because of the lack of housing, and Vienna, which experienced burgeoning growth during this period, witnessed severe housing shortages for the workers and the poor, who often had to live in squalor as subtenants and were sometimes reduced to renting a bed.[1] The advent of the railroad, the automobile, and the airplane quickened the pace of life and changed

stable, settled societies into mobile ones. In the sciences Darwin had revolutionized thought about human behavior with his *On the Origin of
Species* (1859), which contained his views of the survival of the fittest and
the importance of heredity and environment in shaping human beings.
Breakthroughs in medicine by Billroth, Rokitansky, and Semmelweis[2]
included new views on hygiene in the operating room and the cure for
syphilis (1907), so rampant and dangerous at that time—claiming
Nietzsche as a victim. Freud expanded the fields of psychology and psychiatry. In physics Einstein and Planck proved the role of relativity operating in the physical world. In philosophy Auguste Comte, among others,
emphasized the primacy of determinism and causality operating in the
empirical world, while Nietzsche challenged the role of traditional reli-
gions by proclaiming that "God is dead." Earlier, Ludwig Büchner had
attempted to prove scientifically that God did not exist, in his seminal
book *Kraft und Stoff* (1880, *Energy and Matter*), which went through
numerous printings and was widely read at the time. The successful
Franco-Prussian war (1870-1871) brought German national pride to the
fore, which was celebrated in a work like Julius Langbehn's *Rembrandt
als Erzieher* (1890, Rembrandt as Educator) and further reinforced by that
English champion of German supremacy, Houston Stewart Chamberlain,
in *Die Grundlagen des neunzehnten Jahrhunderts* (1899, *The
Foundations of the Nineteenth Century*). Young Austrians following
German progress with keen interest and lamenting that nothing stirred in
Austria clamored for Anschluss, and when that failed, determined to work
for equal progress.

Industrialization brought in its wake the strengthening of the bourgeoisie, as the aristocracy weakened to a more honorary than practical
role, and the exponential growth of the proletariat, which found a
spokesman to address its exploitation in Karl Marx. An alternative for the
proletariat was offered by Viktor Adler, who in 1888 founded the Social-
Democratic party, which was banned almost immediately but later laid the
foundation for Austro-Marxism.[3] The move toward greater democracy
and increased human rights, begun in the brief revolution of 1848, finally
bore fruit in 1907 in Austria with the male franchise to vote.

These sweeping economic, political, and social changes influenced
the course of literature and the other arts. In addition to Nietzsche[4] and
Wagner, foreign authors such as Ibsen, Strindberg, Taine, Barrès,
Huysmans, Zola, Maeterlinck, Tolstoy, and Dostoyevsky contributed to a
new conception of the form and meaning of art, the role of the artist, the

relationship of art and life, and the conflict between spirit and nature (*Geist und Natur*), which served as the dominant theme of literature between 1885 and 1914. The confluence of all of these ideas resulted in a revolution of the spirit, a reaction against the past, and a call by the sudden profusion of young writers, artists, and intellectuals for a regeneration of the arts and culture in the name of truth. They wanted their own art in tune with their own time and repudiated the flight into the historical past or to exotic regions, as found in the writings of Heyse, Scheffel, Ebers, Dahn, and Wildenbruch.

The new program designed to bring art and life back into harmony took different forms in Germany and Austria: Berlin Naturalism was based on strict observation of the empirical world, on determinism, causality, and the repudiation of the metaphysical, while Viennese Impressionism stressed the truth of the moment and the unity of the universe, of the seen and the unseen worlds, and allowed the possibility that chance influences human activities. These two movements, running concurrently, represent different branches from the same root: the desire to create an art serving the truth of their day. The approach differed primarily because of the sympathy of the Naturalists for the plight of the workers—a concern that surfaced again after 1910 among the Berlin Expressionists and because of the short-sighted decision of the Naturalists to ignore the metaphysical side of life. The socially motivated desire of the Naturalists to approach truth by rendering a photographic and phonographic reproduction of proletarian life in the slums of Berlin or in rural settings, or by portraying suffering and disadvantaged human beings struggling against ignorance and inherited defects such as dipsomania, insanity, and persecution complexes, along with ill health from the effects of malnutrition and overwork held no appeal for the young Viennese writers of the same generation.

Not that Vienna could not rival Berlin in numbers of unemployed, poor, and disadvantaged people. For all the glitter of the monarchy, the aristocracy, and the wealthy bourgeoisie during the expansion years, the underprivileged majority suffered a hard and harsh life at a survival level.[5] The Viennese writers were well apprised of the artistic trends in Berlin but, unlike their Berlin counterparts, preferred not to dwell on grim reality and the severity of life at its lowest level, but rather to focus on the problems of life in general or of their own class. In contrast to Gerhart Hauptmann's attempts to stir the public's conscience to alleviate the plight of the exploited workers in a play like *Die Weber* (1892, *The Weavers*), the

Viennese writers—also in the name of truth—devoted their attention to the moral and ethical issues of their society, that is, of people who were financially secure and enjoyed every material advantage. While the Berlin Naturalists learned from the Goncourts, Taine, and Zola, the Viennese generation preferred to follow Barrès, Huysmans, and the French symbolist and decadent writers such as Baudelaire and Mallarmé. The Viennese writers are often accused of fleeing reality because of their choice of depicting their own class, but in truth their motivation in choosing their direction and focus was just as positive as the decision of the Berlin writers to concentrate on the lower classes. The goal of these young writers, all of whom knew each other—Hauptmann was highly respected by all of the Viennese authors—remained the same: to reconcile art and life and write in the name of truth.

A major difference between Berlin and Vienna has always been the attitude toward the past. While German literary history shows a series of jagged, abrupt shifts of direction, Austrian literature proceeds in a smooth, progressive line. At the end of the century the Berlin writers reacted sharply against the previous generation, even against the classical writers Goethe and Schiller, while the Viennese continued to respect older authors like Ferdinand von Saar and Eauard von Bauernfeld, as well as earlier authors like Grillparzer, Raimund, and Nestroy. The same situation held true in the political sphere. While in Germany the aristocrats had been under attack and losing ground to the bourgeoisie since the 1850s, the aristocrats in Austria retained their privileged position within society by the acquiescence of the wealthy bourgeois entrepreneurs, who respected the hierarchy and seemed content to run their businesses and proclaim their status as the new wealthy and powerful class through their opulent mansions and furnishings. In Vienna this sense of hierarchy remained a key factor in the organization of society, and Schorske, who has contributed so fundamentally to our understanding of this period, errs when he attributes the cultural renaissance at the turn of the century to the liberal bourgeoisie's compensating for its political weakness by adopting the aristocratic culture:

> In brief, the Austrian aesthetes were neither as alienated from their society as their French soul-mates nor as engaged in it as their English ones. They lacked the bitter anti-bourgeois spirit of the first and the warm melioristic thrust of the second. Neither dégagé nor engagé, the Austrian aesthetes were alienated not

from their class, but with it from a society that defeated its expectations and rejected its values. Accordingly, young Austria's garden of beauty was a retreat of the beati possidentes, a garden strangely suspended between reality and utopia. It expressed both the self-delight of the aesthetically cultivated and the self-doubt of the socially functionless.[6]

It is true that these young writers were not alienated from their class in any kind of generational conflict, but neither were they alienated from society. They were very much engaged—who of any generation anywhere could be considered more activist than Hermann Bahr or Karl Kraus? The other writers of the generation aligned around these writers may have been socially involved to a lesser degree but they were involved nevertheless.

The main reason for viewing this Viennese literary and cultural renaissance in falsely negative terms of aestheticism, decadence, and flight from reality derives from the mistake of commentators who accept the works written during this period as identical with the thinking of the authors themselves. This fallacy that equates Hofmannsthal with Claudio in *Der Tor und der Tod* (1893, *Death and the Fool*), and Schnitzler with *Anatol* (1891) misses the point that in these and in all other cases the writers have not produced works extolling and endorsing aestheticism and decadence, as contemporary critics were only too willing to believe, but rather condemning these tendencies as bankrupt approaches to life. Once this fundamental error is eliminated, the literary generation of the fin de siècle can be seen as the positive moral force that it was. The introduction of morality cancels out any possibility of decadence, for the two approaches are diametrically opposed.

Furthermore, to continue to designate these writers as aesthetes or decadents is no longer appropriate as we know them today. Such appellations continue the errors of earlier scholarship, some of it rooted in anti-Semitism against this generation of predominantly Jewish writers, and perpetuate the fundamental mistake of identifying these young authors with the characters they created in their writings. Schorske wrongly interprets this generation's turn to the arts as a means of seeking refuge from reality: "If the Viennese burgers had begun by supporting the temple of art as a surrogate form of assimilation into the aristocracy, they ended by finding in it an escape, a refuge from the unpleasant world of increasing political reality. . . The life of art became a substitute for the life of action."[7] The renaissance in the arts took place because of the sudden presence of so many talented young people, not out of compensation for the political weakness of their class. These young writers consciously chose the arts over politics from the beginnings of their careers. Only Bahr, whom Schorske and the other critics ignore although he dominated the turn of the century as its central figure, first tried economics and then politics with Schönerer, Pernerstorfer, and Adler before he discovered the arts in Paris in 1887 and determined that they would serve society better. He began to propagate this message from Paris in the essays of *Zur Kritik der Moderne* (1890, On the Criticism of Modernity). He had published his programmatic essay "Die Moderne" (1890, Modernity) in E. M. Kafka's journal *Moderne Rundschau* in 1890, and thus his views were known in Vienna prior to his return in 1891, when he assumed the role of the catalyst of modernity.[8]

None of the other writers had any experience with politics, nor did they experience any conflict with their parents. Even Bahr, who after joining Schönerer had proclaimed to his father in 1881 that the age of liberalism was over, remained a liberal in his thinking. The sole program of this generation was to bring truth into art and culture by making literature once again a reflection of the contemporary social reality. Beyond that aim they pursued their own individual interests in their own preferred techniques and forms. These young men and women embraced the arts not out of a negative but out of a positive motivation: they were convinced that the arts offered a better, more rewarding path to the future than politics both for themselves and for society. To continue to view these writers and this period in negative terms of introversion, passivity, and fear of life is to ignore the abundance of documentation to the contrary now available, showing that their goal was precisely the contrary: to develop a sense of reality, progress, and unity among Austrians.

The young generation of writers, artists, and intellectuals at the turn of the century, all coming from well-to-do or extremely affluent families, all educated professionals and immensely talented, were imbued with tremendous self-confidence and the highest expectations in life. They felt no desire or need to flee reality because their world was a very pleasant one. They chose a different reality than the writers in Berlin, but their concern with ethical and moral values, their sense of social responsibility was no less real in their writings than in works addressing matters of workers' wages or other everyday issues. The young Viennese writers were not avoiding social responsibility, simply addressing it in a context more to their liking. One must ask why a slum should be regarded as more real than a rose garden, why the investigation of the bankruptcy of aestheticism, of the relationship of art and life, the examination of epistemology and the moral problems of society, are less vital or real than a slice of Berlin life featuring inherited diseases or complexes. Even Hauptmann had to reply to critics of the love scene in *Vor Sonnenaufgang* (1889, *Before Sunrise*) that life could sometimes be beautiful.

Austrian literature and culture had lapsed into a hiatus in the second half of the nineteenth century; the prevailing aristocratic culture consisted of German classicism—Goethe and Schiller—and the Romantics. In Austria, Grillparzer, the nation's greatest writer, who had fallen silent in 1838 after the debacle at the première of his comedy *Weh dem, der lügt* (1838, *Woe to Him Who Lies*), had died embittered and relatively unheralded in 1872. Few artists of the earlier generation had escaped the "Austrian fate," being ignored, attacked, and possibly broken in spirit by the misunderstanding of critics and public alike.[9] It was in fact the absence of any strong culture that enabled the young generation to assume dominance so easily and quickly. Anzengruber, the most realistic of any Austrian writer, produced plays portraying life in the provinces, while Bauernfeld churned out light-weight, entertaining comedies of manners. Ferdinand von Saar, the retired army officer, who resembles Theodor Fontane in Berlin through his transitional role between generations and his realistic technique, described life in the garrison towns and created a gallery of genuine Austrian types. He also introduced social criticism into such works as *Die Steinbrecher* (1874, *The Stone Breakers*), as did Marie von Ebner-Eschenbach, also a transitional figure, in works such as *Dorf- und Schloßgeschichten* (1883, *Tales of Village and Manor*). She featured the Austrian upper classes, but described also the life of the peasants and the middle class with a realism that rivaled Anzengruber's and Rosegger's. Rosa Mayreder's work on behalf of women's liberation, and Bertha Suttner's contribution to the cause of pacifism with her novel *Die Waffen nieder* (1889, *Down with Arms*), for which she received the Nobel prize for peace in 1905, furnish additional examples that serve to refute the charge that turn-of-the-century literature avoided or neglected reality.

The major initial link between Berlin, Paris, and Vienna was Bahr, who had studied and worked in each of these cities and had become acquainted with the major writers and trends. Hence on the basis of first-hand observation he could "overthrow" German Naturalism as early as 1891 in his book of essays *Die Überwindung des Naturalismus* (The

Overthrow of Naturalism), and play a key role in introducing literary decadence to Vienna. When he returned to Vienna from Berlin in 1891, he became the central figure by virtue of his broader experience and greater number of publications as well as by virtue of his energy, outspokenness, and personal charisma. It must be understood that no formal group called Jung Wien ever existed. The appellation was invented by commentators as a convenient term for the young friends who met in the Café Griensteidl: Andrian, Bahr, Beer-Hofmann, Hofmannsthal, Salten, and Schnitzler. Later the group was augmented by Auernheimer and Wassermann, who, like the others, often spent his summers in picturesque Alt Aussee.[10] They never entered into any formal organization, formulated no charter or code of principles and goals, and—in sharp contrast to the Naturalists—wrote no literary manifestos. According to a quip of Beer-Hofmann, who kept his reserved distance, they were not exactly friends but people who did not get on each other's nerves. However, Salten comments that despite the distance they all maintained, they were and remained good friends all their lives.[11] They were all single and met socially in the Café Griensteidl—the institution of the coffee house played an important role as a meeting place for writers and artists. They discussed their literary plans, occasionally read their latest works to each other, and were mutually supportive. The group made one joint effort to form a theater analogous to Brahm's *Freie Bühne* (Free Theater) in Berlin, formed to avoid censorship, but after one attempt the idea was dropped. That they shared ideas about themes and literary technique can be seen in the parallel development of their works from 1891 to 1906; a comparison of works year by year reveals how the progression of ideas follows a similar course among the writers.

The fundamental driving force behind Bahr's decision to work in Vienna was the same idea that had motivated his political activity in the 1880s: the desire to help break Austria out of its stagnation so that it could emulate the progressiveness of Germany and take its place alongside the other developing and prospering European nations. He set the tone for the arts in his programmatic essay "Die Moderne" (1891, Modernity), in which he contended that the world had changed fundamentally but the writers and artists had lagged woefully behind. It now behooved the writers and the cultural scene in general, he insisted, to catch up with life and to record accurately how it was then being lived rather than to create idealized, romanticized notions of what the world should be like or had been in the past. His program was not a flight from reality but precisely the opposite, a demand for literature to become truthful by reflecting contemporary reality. He argued that the world proceeds in a state of continuous flux, and human beings must stay attuned to change through their nerves in order to stay abreast of their age and thus stay truthful, that is, modern. By preaching a "nervous" art and a "nervous" approach to life Bahr advocated Impressionism and abolished the idea of the fixed ego. Not until 1903 did he find his views confirmed by Ernst Mach's *Analyse der Empfindungen* (1888, *Analysis of Perceptions*) after they had become acquainted in the salon of Bertha Zuckerkandl. The concept of the ego in flux became the basis of turn-of-the-century thought with ramifications influencing all areas of life.

A major result of discovering the constantly changing ego was the realization that all human values including the good, the true, and the beautiful were relative rather than fixed; the concept of relativity became the accepted standard and affected everything, even the perception of time. The new ideas in art and literature were shaped accordingly. The young writers accepted the notion that, since life and the human being are constantly changing, only the moment is true. Thus was born the cardinal tenet of Impressionism: what was true for this moment might be false in the next. Impressionism, which was already known from the French painters of the 1860s—Manet, Monet, Pissarro, Renoir, Seurat—now became adopted in literature. As a result the Viennese writers feared the grand universal truth and specialized in short works capturing the truth of a given moment. They could write works showing how the same preconditions would, with the slightest change often caused by chance, lead to opposing results. Few great novels came out of this generation, and of those some of the best remained fragments: Musil's *Der Mann ohne Eigenschaften* (1930-1943, *The Man Without Qualities*) and Hofmannsthal's *Andreas* (1932). Instead, the aphorism, as had been the case in German Romanticism around 1800, became a favorite form, as did the short lyric drama, the one-act play, the novella, the tale, the diary, the essay, and the feuilleton. Life was viewed as a mosaic with each aspect an independent truth; the length of time depended on perception rather than on measurement. The notion of "eine heile Welt," a harmonious universe, was generally accepted by these writers, as reflected in Hofmannsthal's saying that in the world "alles kommt zu allem" (everything leads to everything else). Later they discovered in the baroque idea of the coincidence of opposites further justification for the world view and literary approach they had been employing.

Bahr carried his campaign of modernity to art and architecture by publicizing the need for these fields to reflect their society. The dominant tendency practiced by the artists of the Künstlerhaus was historicism, lavish paintings of historical events, attractive buildings, and nature scenes, all in academically accepted, realistic fashion. The boldest and most representative painter of the time was Hans Makart, who, like Saar in literature, served as a transitional figure. In music the waltzes of Strauss and Lehár prevailed, and the major composers were Mahler, Zemlinsky and, soon to arrive on the scene, Schoenberg, Berg, and Webern. But for the aristocratic culture the dominant musicians were Brahms, Beethoven, and Schubert.

Architecture offers perhaps the best example of the prevalent historicism that had created the division between life and art and concomitantly a sense of artificiality in the culture of Vienna. When the defensive wall surrounding the inner city had been torn down at the order of Emperor Franz Joseph in 1848—somebody had taken a shot at him from the wall—Michael Etienne, the editor of the prestigious newspaper the *Neue Freie Presse* proposed the idea of building a broad boulevard around the city, the Ringstrasse, and lining it with impressive buildings as a showcase for the city.[12] Work began in 1857, and lavish buildings were constructed, each in a different architectural style chosen to correspond to the purpose of the building, i.e., the city hall in neo–gothic, the parliament building in Greek, and the university, the Burgtheater, the art and natural science museums, the concert hall, and the opera house in renaissance style. People might like the historical approach or deride its artificiality, but everyone noticed and rejoiced in the attention that the new street brought to Vienna. The Viennese continue to admire the Ringstrasse today as much as the majority did at the time. The devastation of a number of the buildings during World War II allowed the possibility of removing these structures and creating new ones. Instead the old plans were brought out, and buildings such as the Burgtheater and the opera were restored with modern building materials and techniques but retaining the original interiors and exteriors. Buildings that once may have been artificial in the sense of not corresponding to the art of its own time have now taken on the patina of age and stand as legitimate cultural monuments, a source of pride to Austrians and a perpetual delight to visitors.

Because of the rapid growth of Vienna and the presence of a great deal of money, interest in the arts and in architecture increased to fill the demand for new homes with luxurious decorations and furnishings. In the growth environment at the turn of the century the arts found room to flourish as never before in Austria. The public was not disappointed at what it found in the arts, for a new generation of writers, artists, and intellectuals had emerged, all young, well educated professionals, all voracious readers and keen observers alert to the changes taking place all over Europe and all determined to contribute to the development of their homeland to make it stronger, more vital, more progressive, and equal in achievement and status to the other major nations of Europe. Austria, and particularly Vienna, which lies so far to the east, had up to then been perjoratively considered "Halbasien" (Ferdinand von Kürenberger), the gateway to the east. Metternich, the dictatorial chancellor forced out of power in 1848, considered that the Orient began on the Landstrasse, the main artery leading out of Vienna to the east.

Austrian progress had been restrained by Metternich, who sealed the borders to prevent an open exchange of information. The young Franz Joseph, whose program consisted of maintaining the status quo, also impeded change and progress. Because historical Austria had been established under the Babenbergers in the eleventh century as an outpost to keep the Turks from invading Germany, a role performed twice, in the sixteenth and seventeenth centuries, Austria was always considered a province of Germany and suffered from an inferiority complex as a result. This feeling was exacerbated by the breakup of the Holy Roman Empire of the German Nation in 1809 and the eventual expulsion of Austria from its alliance with Germany in 1867 after losing the Battle of Königgrätz the previous year. The call for Anschluss or annexation with Germany arose immediately and escalated into one of the major political problems of the 1880s with the formation of the German National Party of Georg von Schönerer; it continued to be a problem until Hitler forcibly fulfilled the idea in March 1938.

Numerous other difficulties plagued the monarchy, particularly problems with the minority nations comprising the multi-national state. Austria had been forced to recognize Hungarian sovereignty in 1867 by establishing the dual monarchy. The country's fortunes had been declining since the rule of Maria Theresia in the eighteenth century, and the conservative program of Franz Joseph was welcomed by the aristocrats and not strongly opposed by the wealthy bourgeoisie, which had been shaken by the stock market crash of 1873. Only the younger generation wanted to see a more progressive Austria, however one gained through enlightenment and reason, not revolution. By the turn of the century the combination of prosperity, talent, a strong sense of security, and a desire of the young generation for self-fulfillment overcame everything difficult and unpleasant—until the outbreak of World War I. The nation's best and brightest young people adopted a positive attitude and devoted their attention to an examination of life's beauty, complexity, and mystery.

It is this positive, life-affirming feature of the fin de siècle that makes it as appealing and popular today as it was in its own time. Recent exhibits such as "Traum und Wirklichkeit" (Dream and Reality)[13] at the Vienna Künstlerhaus in 1985 attracted great attention as did the exhibit "L'Apocalypse Joyeuse" at the Centre Pompidou in Paris in 1986, "Vienna 1900: Art, Architecture, and Design," at the Museum of Modern Art in 1986, and other smaller exhibits in Philadelphia and St. Louis.[14] Such art movements as Jugendstil, Art Nouveau, the Viennese Secession[15] and the Wiener Werkstätte remain as popular as ever and continue to influence artistic styles. Painters like Klimt and Schiele rank at the top of the list in popularity, and motifs from their works, trivialized to the maximum, adorn everything from calendars and clothes to coasters, playing cards, and shopping bags. The enthusiasm for this period, which shows no sign of abating, can be attributed to its attractiveness and beauty on the one hand and to its significant contributions and achievements on the other.

For ultimately, if the fin de siècle consisted of nothing more than ephemeral surface beauty, glamor, and charm, if it were only a beautiful façade or "Schlagobers," covering nothing of substance, as Michael Frayn's film "The Mask of Gold" tries to demonstrate, it would never have lasted a hundred years and still command the enthusiastic interest it continues to enjoy today. In truth it is the last attractive period in modern cultural history; for with the demise of the monarchy and the advent of the republic Austria became a grimmer, more serious place, as did the rest of Europe. Part of the continued charm and appeal of this period clearly reflects nostalgia for a less politicized, more beautiful world; but to regard the fin de siècle as nothing more than a sensuous, aesthetic period devoted to the good life for those who could afford it, is to misunderstand the serious underlying conditions that added depth, substance, and significance to the surface beauty. These writers, artists, musicians, theater directors, architects, scientists, philosophers, and intellectuals contributed importantly to their society, and this complex of new ideas, forms, and styles infused with an unvarying moral and ethical basis, has enabled this era to retain its importance to the present day. If it had consisted only of decadent art for art's sake, it would have been forgotten, the fate of such movements in Germany, France, and England. Hofmannsthal's poems remain vital, while those of Stefan George have been relegated to the past. The Viennese artistic contributions in all of the arts rank with the best of their time anywhere, and Hofmannsthal, Kraus, Schnitzler, Klimt, Schiele, Otto Wagner, Loos, Joseph Hoffmann, and Mahler compare with the best in the world in their respective arts.

This period was no "Gay Apocalypse" lacking in any sense of moral and ethical responsibility, as Herman Broch has described it in his much quoted essay "Hugo von Hofmannsthal und seine Zeit" (1951, *Hugo von Hofmannsthal and His Time*).[16] Broch fell prey to the same error as other commentators in viewing the fin de siècle as the harbinger of the end of the monarchy. He also misconceived the period as a completely aesthetic one, overlooking the moral and ethical dimension present from the beginning. Aestheticism and decadence played major roles during the decade of the 1890s, but only in the negative sense of condemning these lifestyles and only in their writings, not in the lives of the authors themselves. Claudio, Anatol, and Georg are aesthetes and decadents, Hofmannsthal, Schnitzler, and Beer-Hofmann were not. Bahr affected the pose of decadence, but he could not sustain it for long and repudiated decadence in 1896. Aesthetes avoid moral and ethical responsibility, and decadents adopt a lifestyle with a reversal of normal values, preferring night over day, death over life, passivity over action, enjoyment over creativity, evil over good, atheism over religion, artificiality over nature, and homosexuality over heterosexuality. These attributes fit Count Robert de Montesquiou,[17] Oscar Wilde, or the group around the *Yellow Book* in England, but not the Jung-Wien writers, who exhibited no desire to live artificial lives and whose works were produced in a moral and ethical context throughout their careers and aimed at the betterment of society. These writers loved nature, bicycle-riding, tennis, swimming, and, with the exception of Andrian, the opposite sex—completely the contrast of decadence. Their repudiation of decadence can be further seen in their rejection of D'Annunzio and endorsement of Isadora Duncan and her natural dancing style.

Because of its appeal and importance the fin de siècle has become one of the most investigated periods of literary history; critics never weary of examining and re-examining the turn of the century in its totality and in its individual features and ideas, which are juxtaposed in ever new contexts and combinations. And yet, for all of the intensive investigation of this period, one about which we perhaps have more documentation than any other, primarily because of the tendency of all of these writers, painters, and musicians to preserve their literary estates and to keep correspondences and diaries—they were all convinced of their importance and of the uniqueness of their generation—a great deal of work still needs to be done before we will have properly understood and correctly nuanced all of its implications. A considerable body of unpublished and in some cases unreleased material exists in the national and city libraries in Vienna as well as at the literary archive in Marbach am Neckar in Germany. When all of this information becomes available, it will be possible to recreate the period from 1890 to 1933 virtually on a day-by-day basis from the perspective of a number of individuals. The detailed diaries of Bahr and Schnitzler, which are in the process of being published, cover the period from 1887 to 1933 and provide a solid basis that is being steadily augmented by other accounts together with their and other correspondences.

Despite all of the information that we possess, much of what has been written about the fin de siècle is based on fundamental misconceptions that were established early and have continued to be repeated as myths that are still perpetuated although current evidence dispels them. Literary history is prone to myth-making, and once a myth becomes established, its eradication is extremely difficult, if it is possible at all. Writers like Bahr, Hofmannsthal, Kraus, and Schnitzler all suffer from false images that were introduced at the beginnings of their careers and continue to be perpetuated today: Bahr the intellectual quick-change artist, Hofmannsthal the unworldly aesthete, Kraus the incorruptible man of no compromise, and the apolitical Schnitzler. The effects of such early judgments color our understanding of almost every phase of the turn of the century and render it inaccurate. In some cases it is a question of changing the nuances, while in others the problems are of a more fundamental nature.

One of the basic misconceptions derives from the illogical tendency to view the fin de siècle retroactively in terms of the abolition of the monarchy in 1918. Because the monarchy undeniably ended as one of the casualties of World War I, commentators adopted the stance that the great flourishing at the end of the century represented an Indian summer, a final, artificial deceptive blossoming just prior to the demise of the monarchy, analogous to the state of euphoria often experienced before death. Knowing that the monarchy ended, critics searching for causes have believed to detect the mood of melancholy and resignation, lassitude and passivity, languor and yearning in the fin de siècle to a degree that has been exaggerated out of all proportion. This imposition of a retroactive explanation for the grandeur of the turn of the century has caused critics to overlook the fundamental nature of the artistic and literary life in its own terms and instead to search for the signs of decay and decline that will buttress their theory about the imminent demise of the monarchy. Thus this period is conceived as an end rather than as the beginning that it represented to this generation.

The myth is attractive and appealing, and even seems plausible; thus it continues to survive despite its inaccuracy. The monarchy did not have to end in 1918;[18] its demise was a political decision promulgated by Woodrow Wilson and the terms of the Versailles Treaty partly to prevent Austria and Germany from rising again to cause another war and partly because of Wilson's avowed interest in supporting individual rights for the member nations of the multi-national state.[19]

Franz Joseph died in 1916, the longest reigning monarch in Europe, and his grandnephew Karl assumed the throne. However, when President Wilson advocated that the monarchy should be abolished and the member states granted their independence, Austria was immediately reduced to a "Rumpfstaat" (torso or rump state) of approximately 8,000,000 people, to a republic referred to as "the state that no one wanted" (Der Staat, den keiner wollte).[20] Thus the ending of the monarchy was a political decision which the victors imposed upon the losers and not the result of normal historical processes. Had Wilson not demanded its abolition, the monarchy would have continued in Austria, just as has been the case in England and Holland. Perhaps pressures for independence would have caused its eventual demise, but at the time most Austrians, if given the choice, would have preferred to retain the monarchy rather than to be transformed into a republic. Indeed, most Austrians feared that the small state would not be economically viable, once again raising calls for Anchluss with Germany, a move denied by the terms of the treaty.

But beyond these facts one must understand that Austria did not end even though the monarchy no longer existed. Indeed, most of the writers took little notice of its passing and generally ignored the republic, continuing to write in terms of the Habsburg myth as if nothing in Austria had changed.[21] Finally, it is important to recognize that even the possibility that the monarchy could end was an idea far removed from the minds of the young writers and artists of the generation of 1890. They fully believed that they represented a new beginning, and everything that they undertook was carried out in this spirit and with the feeling of security that the monarchy provided. Their perception, formed by a comparison with the changes and developments occurring in other European nations, must be regarded as the prevailing reality of the time. Certainly the Austro-Hungarian Monarchy had been beset by a multitude of problems ever since 1848 because Austrian politicians and bureaucrats, dedicated and loyal as they were, pursued misguided policies in dealing with the member states of the *Vielvölkerstaat* (multi-national state), spurring strong unrest and a growing desire for nationalism in the various member nations—Czechoslovakia, Hungary, Poland, Romania, Yugoslavia—comprising some 50,000,000 people, speaking diverse languages and held together artificially by an elaborate, unimaginative, and unresponsive bureaucratic system heavy on protocol and short on understanding.[22] The monarchy may have been faltering in the face of growing demands for national independence, but as yet no overwhelming push existed among the satellite states to overthrow it, and certainly none from the gifted young generation in Austria to whom the future belonged and who displayed no inkling that the demise of the monarchy was imminent. Nor did anyone else anticipate the end, including the emperor, the aging Franz Joseph, who had taken the throne in 1848 as a callow youth and devoted his strictly regimented Spartan life to serving his nation as a fatherly and then as a grandfatherly image in this "goldenes Zeitalter der Sicherheit" (golden age of security), as Stefan Zweig termed it.

While the young generation wanted to introduce progressiveness to Austria, it felt comfortable with the monarchy and respected the emperor for the most part, even though it wanted to override his tenacious determination to maintain the status quo. These young people loved the world in which they lived, loved Vienna to such a degree that many of them felt they could not live anywhere else. They rarely traveled far outside of Austria beyond the almost obligatory travels of every educated person; early trips to France, an "italienische Reise" à la Goethe, and a trip to Greece. Otherwise travel consisted usually of trips in connection with performances of their plays in theaters in Berlin, Munich, Dresden, and Prague. In most cases their dramas had to be sanctioned by performance elsewhere before being premiered in Vienna. They were conscious that theirs was a unique period, and at the same time they wanted to improve upon their world to make it even better and to help it continue forever. When the fin-de-siècle world with its special values and lifestyle disappeared irretrievably in the Anchluss of 1938, a writer like Stefan Zweig preferred to commit suicide (in exile in Petropolis, Brazil in 1942) rather than face the brutal reality of the Third Reich that had destroyed his *Welt von Gestern* (1942, *World of Yesterday*), as he titled his biography of his age. The works, letters, diaries, and activities of these young men and women all brimmed over with the promise of the better world that they envisioned and hoped to help create through the agency of the arts. The thought that doom and disaster were lurking in the wings never entered their thinking. The normally prescient Bahr, who was called the man of the day after tomorrow, failed to foresee the end of the monarchy because he was much too engrossed in building for the future, nor did the vigilant, perceptive Kraus, who continuously warned about the dire effects of the rampant amorality he saw in Vienna on all levels of society but particularly among the writers, journalists, and artists. But he predicted the collapse of society for its hypocrisy and dishonesty, not of the monarchy. When the end arrived, it came from an unexpected source that no one could have predicted, took a different form, and occurred for different reasons than Kraus had predicted.

An example of the kind of confusion that prevails about this generation may be seen in the following:

> These, then, are the historical circumstances surrounding the emergence around 1890 of what can be called Viennese decadence: longing for renewal, which peters out into a sterile aestheticism exclusively preoccupied with the individual psyche; an enjoyment of loneliness and simultaneously a suffering from isolation, which it is hoped can be overcome by mystical myths of "life"; and a feeling of being those who have "come afterwards," whose "modern nervosity" is in strange contrast with the world of their fathers, a world they no longer feel any obligation towards but from which they nevertheless never feel quite free. The "lost generation," conscious of its privileged position, floats with Nietzsche, but not with Baudelaire, on the mere surface of aesthetic beauty.[23]

Virtually every statement here contains an error caused by confusing the works of these young writers with their personal lives. The young Viennese authors were not a lost generation in any sense of the word any more than the generation before them; they had firm convictions about what they wanted to achieve and even about how they wanted to achieve it, namely, through art. In the author's defense, it must be pointed out that in the next paragraph he retracts most of what he has just stated to produce a more accurate appraisal:

> It has to be said, however, that the outline that we have here drawn is only a rough and ready one and is valid only for a short period [which he does not specify]. Even during the brief time around 1890 when they were meeting in the Café Griensteidl, the young Viennese were already searching for new norms and goals; indeed they could almost be described as tentative anti-decadent moralists, feeling their way nervously towards various new exits. Ultimately they will each find their own particular answer, while together they will realize the whole spectrum of spiritual avenues that their age offered them.[24]

It cannot be overemphasized that these young writers all possessed enormous self-confidence and had every reason to do so as members of an affluent, privileged class with every opportunity handed to them, and blessed with intelligence and literary gifts. Above all, they were all driven by an ambition to be creative and to achieve success, both good liberal values. They described melancholy, lonely, introverted characters in order to portray the negative features and to denounce the bankruptcy of decadence, but they themselves shared neither those problems nor those values.

If one examines the generation of 1890 in its own context, one has to be struck by the fact that this was a youth movement, with the ebullience, energy, idealism and promise of youth movements in general. Youthfulness and new beginnings were emphasized in the very names given to the groups. The young university students in the fraternities (*Burschenschaften*) attracted to Schönerer's German National Party in the 1880s, were commonly referred to as *Die Jungen*. The group of six literary friends received the appellation Jung Wien or Young Vienna. Bahr's book of essays describing his generation was entitled *Renaissance* (1896). The journal of the Secessionist art movement, founded in 1897 and headed by Gustav Klimt, was called *Ver Sacrum* or Sacred Spring. Rebirth in the form of enlightened evolution, not revolution inspired the program endorsed by these authors and other artists. They represented a generation in transition, to be sure, moving between tradition and innovation, but it was a gradual, orderly transition.

While the liberalism of their fathers' generation came under attack in the 1870s and 1880s, the Jung-Wien writers continued to believe in the liberal ideas of progress through enlightenment and education (*Bildung*). They all revered Adalbert Stifter, the representative author of nineteenth-century liberalism. They also remained on good terms with their parents, even Bahr, whose radical political apprenticeship as a Schönerer follower brought his father to despair. However, he soon saw the error of his ways and broke with radical politics, turning instead to art and to working within the system. It is noteworthy that there are no writings by the Jung-Wien authors dealing with the generational conflict. This development was reserved for the following Expressionist generation. The nearest thing to a generation conflict in Austria in the 1880s occurred when the socialist Viktor Adler held meetings in his parents' home to plan the overthrow of their values. A follower of Schönerer and a member of the German National Party until it turned anti-Semitic in 1885 and cast him out, Adler carried out his political ideas through the founding of the Socialist party in 1888. But even his opposition to his parents' values was expressed in peaceful terms, not in the bitter combative tone found in the later Expressionists' lives and writings.

The Jung-Wien writers felt no interest in politics nor in bringing about political change in the 1890s, nor was there any reason for such an interest in the secure environment of the time. They were at a point in life when they were working to establish themselves in their various careers, Beer-Hofmann as a lawyer, Schnitzler as a medical doctor, Bahr and Salten as journalists, and Hofmannsthal hoping for an appointment to teach French at the University of Vienna; they were content to follow their personal interests while working within the system. Of these writers only Bahr had taken an active part in politics, belonging to the radical German National Movement in the 1880s, during which time he had advocated the overthrow of the Emperor and Anschluss with Germany. At a student rally to commemorate the death of Richard Wagner in 1883, he had given a fiery speech calling for Anschluss, which caused his dismissal for life from the University of Vienna. His future in politics was planned for him by Schönerer and Pernerstorfer and, when he broke with them, by Viktor Adler, with whom he worked on his Social Democratic weekly *Gleichheit* in 1886. His discovery of literature during his year in Paris in 1887 changed his direction from politics to literature, which henceforth remained his primary concern. The contempt he felt for politicians who talked but never acted is reflected in his early naturalist play *Die große*

Sünde (1887, The Big Sin). None of the other writers except Kraus concerned themselves with politics until the advent of World War I, and even Kraus treated politics more in aesthetic than in real terms, that is, he remained a commentator critiquing language usage rather than becoming an active political leader. His public read each new issue of the flaming red journal *Die Fackel* (1899-1936, The Torch) not for political guidance but to revel in Kraus's language and in his attacks on leading figures of the day that were often as unfair as they were brilliant.

The interest of this generation was not in politics but in life, which became the highest value and which they sought to understand in order to be able to live it to the fullest. Inspired by Nietzsche's *Lebensphilosophie* (philosophy of living) and Bergson's *élan vital*,[25] the goal of these young men was to maximize their personal development. Their positive emphasis featured life, not death, progress, not the status quo, action, not passivity, accomplishment and deeds, not a feeling of helplessness and melancholy, building a better future, not seeking refuge in the past or in fleeing from reality. Death was constantly invoked, but only in the sense of *memento mori*, with the aim of reminding people to live. And when these authors turned to the Austrian past and to the values of Goethe, as they began to do as early as 1896, it was with the intention of using the strength of the Austrian and German traditions as a foundation for the future of the country. In answering the question of how best to approach life and fulfill their goals for the future, they all agreed that the arts offered a more promising means of achieving their goals than politics.

In the eternal search for an answer to the question of the meaning of life and how best to approach life, the nineteenth century had pursued various possibilities: religion, politics, enlightenment, liberalism, the new religion of Marxism, Social Democracy, materialism, and science. But for the young Austrian writers and artists at the turn of the century there was only one answer: the arts, which would enhance life by making it more beautiful, by bringing understanding and unity in terms of a meaningful, relevant culture, and by contributing to a better future and a "new man" (*neuer Mensch*). They carried on the traditional liberalist view of enlightenment by their intention of bringing the arts to all of the people and of creating a new vital culture that would make possible a richer, more attractive environment and a better life for everyone. While the Berlin Naturalists and later the Expressionists (1910-1925) attempted to improve social conditions by writing works describing the plight of the workers, the Impressionists in Vienna envisioned workers enjoying life more by

sharing in the arts. Energized by the optimistic, irrepressible, indefatigable Bahr, the young writers who gathered in the Café Griensteidl discussed their society and culture, and shared and developed their views on
literature, the arts, and life as a group. They were not writing in an introverted manner to delve into their own psyches, but from the time Bahr
arrived on the scene in 1891, they were influenced by his program of creating a more truthful art, one in tune with the real world, and one which
would help to produce the new culture that they felt Austria needed to
become the equal of other European nations, which had progressed at a
more rapid rate than Austria.

Hofmannsthal, the greatest writer of this generation and of the
Austrian twentieth century, began by trying to fathom the nature of existence in such early poems as "Was ist die Welt?" (1890, "What is the
World?") or "Terzinen über Vergänglichkeit" ("Terzinas on
Transitoriness"). He then proceeded to grapple with major problems of
existence such as how one passes from the state of what he called preexistence into existence or life, and once there how one copes with such
major problems as that of fidelity, that is, how one can remain true to oneself while changing steadily to stay in tune with the changing world and
remaining true to one's commitments. Finally he devoted great attention
to the issue of what it means to be a human being. Schnitzler, the medical
doctor, attempted to diagnose the interpersonal relationships of his day, to
dissect the round dance of life to show the centrality of sexuality in human
existence and the myriad of psychological problems it could cause. Bahr
delved into epistemology to track the sources of human thought,[26] discovered that the human being has no fixed ego but remains a personality in
constant flux, and stressed the necessity of staying "modern" by constantly changing to remain abreast of the ever-changing world. Beer-Hofmann,
who was acculturated rather than assimilated as were Andrian,
Hofmannsthal, and Schnitzler, embraced Zionism and regarded the
strength of Judaism as the best means of approaching social problems.
The overriding principle regardless of approach was truthfulness—to oneself and to reality by changing in harmony with the world outside.
Hofmannsthal's guiding principle, Addison's statement "The whole man
must move at once," can serve as the motto of the whole generation. The
search for authenticity in life, this basic tenet of modernity, was the major
tie binding this group together, along with their shared belief in the integrity, that is, wholeness of the individual, the desirability of personal fulfillment, and the acceptance of the unity of the seen and unseen worlds. This

stress on totality of experience makes clear why this group embraced Wagner's idea of the *Gesamtkunstwerk* (total work of art) as its dominating artistic approach.

The major writers in Vienna in the 1890s were not part of an art-for-art's-sake movement, as Stefan George discovered when he tried to woo the young Hofmannsthal and make the eighteen-year-old prodigy a disciple of his circle. Even at that early age Hofmannsthal instinctively possessed a sense of social responsibility and was searching for depth and meaning in his life, qualities that provide a measure of his youthful genius. These young writers read voraciously, a practice they continued throughout their lives, and were thoroughly in tune with the happenings in the world about them, not only in Austria but in other European countries as well; this international dimension serves as another argument against the alleged introversion of these so-called aesthetes and decadents. With the gifts given to them they aimed at delving into the nature of human existence in a way and with a refinement never achieved earlier, with the aim of rivaling the literature in other countries.

Viennese Impressionism or Neo-Romanticism derives from the same root as Berlin Naturalism. It followed the same influences but interpreted these sources differently. Bahr was convinced as early as 1890 that the Berlin writers had fundamentally misunderstood French Naturalism, which did not eschew the metaphysical as the Berlin Naturalists had done. A work like Zola's *Thérèse Raquin* is a prime example of French Naturalism, showing the metaphysical and the psychological along with the naturalistic descriptions of character based on determinism, heredity, and enviroment. In short, Zola remained true to human nature and to scientific observation in his naturalistic approach, while the Berlin writers interpreted Zola in a way too limited to last more than a short time. Gerhart Hauptmann had already outgrown the German theory in *Bahnwärter Thiel* (1887, *Flagman Thiel*) and broke with it definitively in *Hanneles Himmelfahrt* (1893, *The Ascension of Hannele*). The major differences between Berlin and Vienna were not of kind but of approach. Whereas the Berlin writers stressed realistic description and attempted to produce a phonographic and photographic reproduction of external life, the Viennese supplied the same meticulous, detailed attention to the inner workings of the mind, to the psychological processes or *Seelenstände* (states of mind). Both groups took their main impetus from France, but the Berlin Naturalists followed the theoretical Zola of *Roman experimental* (1880, *The Experimental Novel*), while the Viennese were influenced more by the French Symbolists, Baudelaire and Mallarmé, and by Barrès, Bourget, and Huysmans, whose novel *A rebours* (*Against the Grain*) was hailed as the breviary of decadence.

While the Viennese writers attempted to establish moral and ethical guidelines for living, the artists and architects were contributing to the same goals of improving the quality of life by creating a more beautiful environment. It is important to understand how small and how centralized the world of the arts was in Vienna at this time (and still is). People lived in close proximity, saw each other almost every day either in the Café Griensteidl until it was torn down in 1896 to make room for a bank, or at the offices of Bahr's newspaper *Die Zeit* (1894), which he founded with Isidor Singer and Heinrich Kanner to carry his message to the public without the intervention of timid editors who feared reactions by the government against his writings. It was a time when writers, artists, architects, musicians, philosophers, politicians, and scientists all knew each other and shared their thinking. They met either in the coffee houses or in the salons of Bertha Zuckerkandl, Frau von Wertheimstein, and later of Alma Mahler. Earlier Caroline Pichler's salon was renowned. Bahr, for example, was a close personal friend of the architect Joseph Olbrich and the painter Gustav Klimt. Olbrich designed Bahr's house in Ober St. Veit in 1900, and Klimt painted the "Nuda Veritas" for Bahr. Through his articles in *Die Zeit* Bahr had begun in 1894 to lay the groundwork for the eventual founding of the Austrian Secession, which was established in 1897 to break with the traditional painters of the Künstlerhaus.

To show their respect for the past the Secessionists named the respected Rudolph von Alt honorary president, while Gustav Klimt was appointed as the presiding officer. It is no accident that the charter of the Secession parallels Bahr's program of modernity, including the need to achieve rapprochement with the rest of Europe. Foreign artists were invited to become members and exhibit, and Rodin among others accepted the invitation.

The desire of the young writers and artists to achieve the maximum of personal development and to approximate in art the totality of existence caused a turn to the *Gesamtkunstwerk*. The aesthetic principles of Lessing, who in *Laokoon* (1766) had carefully separated art forms, were obliterated in the desire to capture or at least to convey the experience of life as accurately as possible. Just as Wagner had blended all of the arts in his operas to create his own world on the operatic stage, the writers worked with the painters, scene designers, dancers, and musicians, to strive for a sense of wholeness, of totality. Max Reinhardt was the director who best exemplified this approach to the theater, and Alfred Roller the stage designer most sought after for his imaginative creations. This belief in the unity of the world and the desire to approximate this totality in their works further demonstrate that these young writers did not feel separated from the reality around them and provide additional evidence of why the idea of their fleeing from reality is a misconception. This same idea of totality inspired the architect Joseph Olbrich, who designed the classically simple, functional Secession building capped by a large decorative, golden grill intended as a laurel wreath crown for art. He dreamed of constructing an entire city with a harmonious design, a concept that was partially carried out when he was commissioned by the Grand Duke of Hesse to build an artists' colony in Darmstadt. Unfortunately Olbrich died in 1908 before he was able to complete more than two buildings of the project, and no one continued his work. At the same time Otto Wagner, who believed that only functional designs could be beautiful, enriched Vienna with Jugendstil buildings that were useful as well as decorative. His efforts to blend beauty and practicality were adopted by the Wiener Werkstätte, founded in 1903 by the wealthy Viennese entrepreneur Fritz Wärndorfer with the idea of combining art and craft, of uniting artists with artisans, a variation of the *Gesamtkunstwerk* idea.[27] This enterprise was influenced strongly by the English movement, led by the pre-Raphaelites, including William Morris, Dante Gabriel Rossetti, Edward Burne Jones, and Walter Crane and the Glasgow School of Charles Rennie Mackintosh, who exhibited regularly at the Secession. The Secession building carried the motto "Der Zeit ihre Kunst, der Kunst ihre Freiheit" (To the age its art, to art its freedom)—the last part a plea against censorship—demonstrating that the aim of both the Secession and the Wiener Werkstätte contradicts the notion of the arts fleeing reality.[28] When the Secession no longer fulfilled those ideals after 1900 but began to imitate itself, Bahr turned away from it as did Klimt.

Led by Joseph Hoffmann, the Wiener Werkstätte produced glassware, lamps, chairs, tableware, furniture, and housewares as well as the houses to hold these furnishings. The highpoint of their efforts was the Palais Stoclet, perhaps the forerunner of modular housing in the sense that it was assembled in Vienna, dismantled, and reassembled in Brussels for the millionaire Stoclet. Expense was no object, and to this day no one knows the cost of the project. The best artists of the day, including Klimt, combined their talents under the supervision of Hoffmann, to produce this finest example of Wiener Werkstätte creativity. Today the house is a museum. Another venture of the Wiener Werkstätte, the Wittgenstein house in Vienna, today serves as the Bulgarian consulate and also as a museum. The Wiener Werkstätte still exists but only as a shadow of its original uniquely innovative beginnings. It stands as one of the major examples of the trend toward unity among the arts and the goal of creating a new cultural environment for the broad public. The buildings designed by Olbrich, Hoffmann, and Otto Wagner have been preserved as major landmarks in present-day Vienna. No large-scale attempt has been made to continue their ideals, although Friedensreich Hundertwasser has created one apartment house to show what could be done in a contemporary context.

Music has always been a central artistic force in Vienna, not only the waltzes of Johann Strauss and Richard Lehár, which are featured so prominently in tourist ads, but first and foremost Gustav Mahler, who directed the Vienna Opera, and Richard Strauss who though a Bavarian, conducted frequently in Vienna and composed six operas along with incidental ballets and dances in collaboration with Hofmannsthal. These operas perhaps come closest to emulating the Wagnerian idea of the *Gesamtkunstwerk*, blending as they do all of the arts. However, the inspiration behind these works was not only the *Gesamtkunstwerk*, but also the Austro-Bavarian baroque tradition, which Hofmannsthal discovered and invoked in his operas and dramas alike.

Each of the arts reached a high point of importance and prominence during the 1890s, but none of the other arts approached the importance of the theater, which dominated the contemporary scene in a manner never witnessed before. The new Burgtheater on the Ringstrasse opened in 1888, and it became the aim of every young writer to have a play performed there. As Auernheimer described, the theater was everything: "At the peak of the social pyramid, which at times elevated one over the divinely ordained class distinctions, stood the artist, the musician, the painter, the poet—if he wrote for the theater—above all the actor. Vienna, which was always a theater-going city, became one in those days to a degree never witnessed before."[29] Even Theodor Herzl, the brilliant feuilletonist and Paris correspondent for the *Neue Freie Presse*, the leading Viennese newspaper of its day, began his career as a playwright. He continued to strive for success in the theater to the end of his life while earning his living as a journalist, a not uncommon occurrence at this time when few writers were able to support themselves from their writings alone. Although he was and is still renowned as the founder of Zionism, he remained to his death disappointed that he had never achieved success as a dramatist. Fritz Mauthner, another journalist who earned his laurels as a critic of language, strove also for success in the theater. It was simply the thing to do, according to the standards of the time, and everyone who could write made the attempt. For success in the theater could bridge every social barrier, could overcome class, financial standing, or anti-Semitism and bring entry into the reigning salons and thereby into the best society. To have a play performed in the Burgtheater brought prestige, recognition, and financial reward that could not be gained in any other way.

The theater has always been a major institution in Viennese life, both the aristocratic court theater and the Volkstheater, which flourished in the first half of the nineteenth century with the plays of actors turned writers such as Nestroy and Raimund. The poor people enjoyed their own theaters and performers just as much as the more affluent public who flocked to the Burgtheater. According to Bahr, the public went to the Burgtheater to see famous actors like Girardi, Novelli, Kainz, Hohenfels, and Duse in order to learn how to speak, to move, and to act. They followed the lives and adulated the famous performers the way people today idolize movie stars. Escapism played a part in the theater's importance, but its role went deeper than that. Because of its state subsidy the Burgtheater served social and political interests through the choice of directors and the selection of plays. This function can be seen in the 1890s in the directorship of Max Burckhardt, another of Bahr's close friends, who with the latter's guidance modernized the method of acting and the repertoire, introducing the newest authors from other countries to Viennese audiences.

Bahr played an important role in the Burgtheater again in 1918. Supported by the efforts of Hofmannsthal and Andrian, who held the position of General-Intendant of the theater and opera in Vienna, Bahr was appointed dramaturge and director of the Burgtheater. He planned to use the repertoire to create a sense of unity in Austria in the last months of the war and to help avoid chaos after the fall of the monarchy and the establishment of the republic. The devastation from the war made it impossible to carry out any cohesive program, and Bahr departed after six months, in April 1919, without having fulfilled his purpose. But the attempt shows how the Burgtheater's prestige was conceived and how politically-minded these writers were. In Bahr's view the Burgtheater served as a primary school where the public could learn how to become a nation. This turn to politics was taken also by the other writers of Bahr's generation in their later years.

The approach of the Viennese writers was heavily psychological rather than physiological because of their early fascination with tracing the inner processes of the mind. Whether it is Bahr tracking the search for perfect color envisioned in the mind of a young painter in Paris in *Die gute Schule* (1890, The Good School), or Hofmannsthal presenting the inner thoughts of a young aesthete at the moment before death in *Der Tor und der Tod* or Schnitzler portraying the thinking of a young soldier in stream-of-consciousness technique in *Leutnant Gustl* (1900, *Lieutenant Gustl*), the intent is the same, to try to trace the psychological workings of the mind to the subconscious level, to let the characters reveal themselves with minimal intrusion of the author. With the exception of Schnitzler, who read and reviewed medical literature and had studied recent psychological innovations by Charcot in France, these writers were not scientifically trained. They intuited the psychological processes by attempting to stay as truthful as possible while delving into the inner recesses of the mind. It is not a question of their being influenced by Freud, at least initially, for all of these writers employed psychological principles in their works before Freud had completed his medical degree and several years before Freud had discovered the central importance of sexuality in contributing to psychological hysteria, as he described in his *Studien über Hysterie* (1895, *Studies in Hysteria*), which he wrote with Dr. Josef Breuer. Like the other intellectuals of this time, Freud shared the interdisciplinary interests that were so prominent, and he has always been considered a hybrid. Members of the scientific community view him as a writer more than as a scientist because his theories, based on intuition, were not always rigorously documented and thus not capable of duplication and verification by other scientists. Freud is another example of how the dividing lines between fields were blurred during this period. In a much publicized letter of 1926 Freud admitted that he regarded Schnitzler as his literary alter ego.

All of these writers utilized dreams in their works, and Schnitzler was particularly fond of chronicling his dreams in his diaries, occasionally attempting an interpretation. Freud's *Traumdeutung* (1900, *Interpretation of Dreams*) one of the influential books of its time, was again a case of parallel development. Freud not only called attention to the importance of dreams, but also influenced the attraction to abberational behavior and personalities by these writers shortly after 1900.

Bahr's play *Die Andere* (1906, The Other Woman) utilizes ideas of Freud, Mach, and Ribot's *Les Maladies de la Personalité*. Hofmannsthal was fascinated by Morton Prince's study of multiple personalities in *The Dissociation of a Personality* (1907) and incorporated some of these ideas into his novel *Andreas*, which he unfortunately was never able to finish.

Even before Freud the young generation in Vienna had centered on the themes of eros and thanatos, not surprising in view of their goal to live life to the fullest. As mentioned, they did not glorify death in decadent fashion but wished to celebrate life as Austrians had been doing for generations, especially in reaction to such a disaster as the plague of the seventeenth century, which spawned the popular song, "Ach du lieber Augustin." Because the field of focus was the morals and ethics of interpersonal relationships, sex and eroticism played a prominent role in the concerns of this generation and serve as predominant themes in their writings. There are several reasons for this prominence: this is a youthful generation at an age when sexual exploration is a major interest, the entire period is a celebration of life with self-fulfillment a main goal, and the erotic is an area in which such freedom is usually expressed most pronouncedly. Ultimately these writers, like Frank Wedekind in Germany, consciously wanted to remove the lid from the hypocrisy which surrounded sexuality in their society, as Zweig has detailed in his autobiography.[30] On the one hand the young authors were engaging to a degree in *épater le bourgeois*, and on the other they were fighting against the prevalent double standard of their male-dominated society. For this combination of reasons love, sexuality, and eroticism played a major role in the life, literature, and art of the times.[31] The works of Bahr and Klimt contain a celebration of eroticism.[32] From the beginnings of his career, Schnitzler was accused of having only two themes—love and death—and although it has long since been proven that his oeuvre displays considerably more variety,[33] critics continue to see him in the clichéd terms of the early misconception.[34] He concentrated on diagnosing the games people play in their interpersonal relationships and described the variations and combinations that he had witnessed or could imagine. His *Reigen* (1903, *Round Dance*), showing how mindless sexual drives tie all levels of society together, has never been surpassed as an objective analysis of the role of sex in society, of the tyranny of sex in human existence.

Hofmansthal too made eros rather than sex a central theme, usually on the more ethereal and elevated level of romantic love, posing the dilemma of interpersonal relations, which Schnitzler described in realistic terms, in the form of the problem of fidelity (*Treue*). Twenty-four of Hofmannsthal's works from 1891 to 1929 deal with the problem of fidelity, as Hofmannsthal tried to resolve basic human problems resulting from the Machian view that life was constantly in flux. Despite his genius Hofmannsthal was never able to resolve this problem in any but the most artificial way in works like *Ariadne auf Naxos* (1912) and its sequel *Die Frau ohne Schatten* (1919, *The Woman without a Shadow*). His solution was to combine transformation into a new person, brought about by suffering and renewed love, with selective forgetting so that the new persona would not be crippled by guilt feelings toward earlier commitments. But he could never develop his solution into one of universal application although he struggled with this problem to his last work, *Arabella* (1929).

The eccentric bohemian Altenberg glorified women and never wearied of singing their praises in his short prose works, so-called "extracts of life," and letters. His amatory exploits were well known, and he kept a gallery of women's pictures on the walls of his room. Rilke too celebrated love and eros in his writings and produced some of the most powerful love poems of his day. His youthful work *Die Weise von Leben und Tod des Cornets Christoph Rilke* (1906, *Lay of the Love and Death of Cornet Christopher Rilke*), every young man's wish dream—the gift of romantic love with an unknown woman followed by an equally romantic heroic death in battle—was one of the most popular works of its time and was carried in the knapsacks of many soldiers in World War I. On the other end of the scale stands Felix Salten's pornographic novel *Josephine Mutzenbacher* (1903), which rivals his *Bambi* in durability, remaining available today in book form and in film.

The fin de siècle revealed a curious ambivalence toward women, idolizing them on the one hand as the "femme fragile" and demeaning them on the other as the "femme fatale" or woman of the demimonde.[35] Even those who idealized and glorified women in their writings, like Hofmannsthal, whose works with few exceptions feature women protagonists, failed to treat women as equals in their own lives. Bahr once made the caustic statement about Hofmannsthal that he did not even know what his wife Gerty looked like. Klimt created lavish pictures of women but often reduced them to a face completely overwhelmed by the extravagantly ornamental costumes enveloping and concealing every trace of a body. In contrast his sensuous painting of Judith captured the spirit of the time, with its penchant for the beautiful wanton women of the demimonde, suggesting lacivious pleasures. Other paintings such as "Medizin" and the

"Nuda Veritas" as well as his pencil sketches of nudes reveal his glorification of the female form. Bahr worshipped Anna Mildenburg, with whom
he had one of the great love affairs of this period before they were married
in 1909, but he too generally held women in low regard. In his most
famous comedy, *Das Konzert* (1909, *The Concert*), he tries to gain sympathy for the protagonist, who cannot control his sexuality and resist the
advances of his adoring female students who insist on his accompanying
them on "concerts." He cannot change his image or his nature, much as
he would like to. Auernheimer's play *Casanova in Wien* (1924, Casanova
in Vienna) similarly shows how women will not allow the great lover to
change his image. Kraus defended prostitutes' rights but generally had little respect for women and never married. His early love, the actress
Annie Kalmar, died young, and his proposal to Baroness Sidonie von
Nadhérny was rejected after Rilke dissuaded her from accepting it.
Schnitzler had great difficulties with women in his personal life, but nevertheless he succeeded better than most of his colleagues in adopting a
fairer attitude toward women's emancipation and equality in his later
years.[36]

The women's emancipation movement in Vienna had been initiated
in 1870 by Marianne Hainisch. But even though it was supported by
women like Rosa Mayreder and Bertha von Suttner, it still had not progressed very far in Austria by the turn of the century. Women of the time,
unless they were an Alma Mahler, Lou Andreas-Salome, or Bertha
Zuckerkandl, strong and secure enough to live their lives on their own
terms, usually had to subordinate their talent and intelligence to the masculine world that controlled every sphere of life. Even educated and talented women like Marie von Ebner-Eschenbach, Eugenie delle Grazie,
and Emil Marriot, who wrote under a pseudonym, could not escape the
strictures of their society. The masculine view that a woman must remain
under male protection (domination) at all times, being passed from the
father's home to her husband's, was firmly entrenched. Arranged marriages to protect family wealth were standard, and young girls generally
married men twice their age without any voice in determining their fate
and future. Ebner-Eschenbach wrote *Unsühnbar* (1890, Unexpiable), a
novel of adultery growing out of such a marriage, portraying the tragedy
for the woman, similar to the classic depiction of this situation in Theodor
Fontane's *Effi Briest* (1895).

Because men deferred marriage until they were established financially, they spent their time either with prostitutes or "sweet girls" (*süsse*

Mädel), the term Schnitzler invented to characterize those young working women from the suburbs who were willing to trade sexual favors for the opportunity to taste the life of the privileged rich before settling into marriage within their own class. They were the women with whom the young men about town (*Lebemänner*) whiled away their time before they married and took their place in society. Sometimes they did not grow out of this phase and developed into adventurers (*Abenteurer*), exploiting women either because they loved them as Casanovas or hated them as Don Juans. Both figures became topois of the time and figured as models in many of the works. In all instances such figures were condemned, for these writers fought against the double standard in their works to a much greater degree than in their own lives. In a provocative work entitled *Die tiefe Natur* (1907, The Profound Nature), Bahr has the wife ask her husband why men reserve their most adventurous love-making for their mistresses, while their wives received only polite and perfunctory attention. Schnitzler had suggested the problem of the "respectable woman" (*anständige Frau*) in the scene "Weihnachtseinkäufe" (1891, *Christmas Shopping*) in *Anatol*, where Gabriele states that she could love just as well as the "sweet girl" from the suburbs if only she had the courage to do so. Schnitzler illustrated this point also in the central scene of *Reigen*, where the young husband reveals his hypocrisy by lecturing his young "respectable" wife on the dangers of consorting with loose women who engage in affairs. The dangers for women who violated the male imposed code of morality were real enough, as so many writings of the time demonstrate.

While all the writers of this generation opposed the double standard in their works and in principle—none more than Kraus, who repeatedly defended prostitutes from the injustice of not being able to resort to the courts when they were cheated, even though prostitution was a legally recognized profession—they were also realistic enough to show the difficulties women faced in seeking equal rights. Schnitzler demonstrates in *Das Märchen* (1893, *The Fairy Tale*) and in *Freiwild* (1896, *Free Game*), that the concept of true equality between men and women and the ability of men to allow women the same sexual freedom that they themselves enjoyed remained an idealistic theory not yet ready to be put into practice. Women who took the same freedom as men and were discovered paid a heavy price.

There was a perceptible shift in attitude toward women in the later writings of this generation. Schnitzler came out strongly in support of the marriage contract,[37] as did Hermann Bahr in his novel *Der inwendige*

Garten (1927, The Inner Garden). Schnitzler, who underwent the greatest
change of attitude, portrayed women who had developed sufficient self-
assurance to lead independent lives. In *Spiel im Morgengrauen* (1926,
Play at Daybreak) and particularly in *Der Gang zum Weiher* (1927, The
Way to the Pond), Schnitzler introduced independent women who took
control of their own lives, made their own choice of companions, and
were not dependent upon men for their well being. Hofmannsthal too had
changed his earlier view that women were imbued with a spirit of self-sacrifice and portrayed strong, independent women in the Marschallin in
Der Rosenkavalier (1911), Helene in *Der Schwierige* (1921, *The Difficult
Man*), and Helena in *Die ägyptische Helena* (1926, The Egyptian Helen).
Nevertheless, all of these writers, including Kraus, did little to assist the
women's movement actively and generally continued to have difficulties
accepting women as equals in their personal lives.

     None, however, was as radical as Otto Weininger, the most outspo-
ken voice against women, whose dissertation and subsequent book,
Geschlecht und Charakter (1903, *Sex and Character*), stimulated great
controversy when it was published. Weininger was a disturbed individual
who completed his book and then committed suicide in despair over the
fact of his Jewishness, which he could not change despite his conversion
to Protestantism in 1902. A misogynist, Weininger considered women
second-class citizens incapable of escaping their femininity and rising to
the intellectual heights of men. Because women were victims of their sexuality, he felt that men and women could never overcome the differences
between them.

     The second aspect of Weininger's book, his self-hatred over being
born Jewish, struck a theme that was as dominant a topic at this time as
the double standard and one that has remained a major problem throughout the twentieth century to the present day: anti-Semitism. Despite its
long history in Austria anti-Semitism had been held within reasonable
bounds until the 1880s. Jews had been released from the ghettos in 1848,
and Jewish merchants and wine dealers had been granted a special dispensation by the Emperor in the eighteenth and nineteenth centuries to carry
on trade.[38] Having grown wealthy, they requested and were granted permission to move to Vienna, where they assumed prominent positions
under the protection of their special franchises awarded by the royal
house. The success of the Jewish businessmen brought a backlash that
found expression in Eugen Dühring's book *Die Judenfrage als Racen-
Sitten-und Culturfrage* (1881, The Jewish Question as a Question of Race,

Morals, and Culture), complaining about Jews' domination of the business world. Much more damaging, however, was the Schönerer plank added in 1885 to the Linz Program of the German National Movement (1882), which introduced the notion that being Jewish was a matter of race rather than of religion. People with Jewish blood could never assimilate because they would always remain Jews by virtue of their blood. With this definition Schönerer turned Jews into outsiders and scapegoats for the ills of the country. This proclamation was soon followed by the Waidhofer decree in 1887, a ruling by the German National Burschenschaften that declared Jewish students *satisfaktionsunfähig*, that is, not worthy of being given the opportunity to seek satisfaction in a duel if they were insulted. At the time men like Theodor Herzl, Viktor Adler, and Heinrich Friedjung were all Jewish members of Schönerer's German National Party, Herzl as a fraternity brother of Bahr in the Albia. After Schönerer's proclamation all Jews were unceremoniously ejected from the party. As an alternative to Schönerer, Adler in 1888 founded his own Social Democratic Party, which later developed into Austro-Marxism after 1900. Herzl, deeply affected by the anti-Semitic basis of the Dreyfus trial in Paris, went on to found the Zionist movement.

Bahr was put into a crisis of conscience by this ejection of his Jewish friends, one of whom committed suicide in despair, and he soon broke with Schönerer. He learned about anti-Semitism from Adler as well as from Herzl. Like Weininger, Adler suffered from Jewish self-hatred, as did also Karl Kraus. Adler had converted to Protestantism in 1879 and Kraus to Catholicism in 1911, although he left the church again in 1921 to express his displeasure with its policies. Bahr changed his views about anti-Semitism radically and in 1894 published *Der Antisemitisms*, a volume of interviews devoted to anti-Semitism, which he called "the opium of the public." For the rest of his life he fought against anti-Semitism in his writings and contributed to an understanding of the Jewish problem and Zionism.[39] His book *Die Rotte Korahs* (1919, Korah's Cohorts) ranks alongside Schnitzler's *Der Weg ins Freie* (1908, *The Way to Freedom*) as one of the best portrayals of the Jewish question in all of its ramifications. Regardless of whether they had fully assimilated through religious conversion or had acculturated, all Jewish writers and other artists regarded themselves as Austrians.

Hofmannsthal's Jewish heritage stemmed from his great- great-great grandfather, Isaak Löw, a successful silk merchant wealthy enough to lend money to the Emperor and to receive the patent of nobility for services rendered. Hofmannsthal was raised a Catholic and retained no ties to the

Jewish religion, tradition, or culture. Auernheimer was Protestant, like his German father, and likewise maintained no connections to a Jewish heritage. In most cases a Jewish background played little role in their lives until the rise of National Socialism in the 1930s. Zweig, for example, had his consciousness raised and his Jewish ties reawakened only when in the safety of England he was besieged by requests for assistance by friends who wanted to escape from Germany. Similarly, for all of the others, their Jewishness did not play a significant role in their lives until the Anschluss on 11 March 1938 made it a matter of life and death. Friedell (Vienna, 1938) and Ernst Weiss (Paris, 1942) preferred to commit suicide rather than to be taken prisoner and sent to a concentration camp. Auernheimer was sentenced to Dachau in 1938 but managed to be released after six months through the intervention of Emil Ludwig and the American Chargé d'Affairs, Prentiss Gilbert.

Schönerer eventually self-destructed in 1888 when he lost his parliamentary immunity and was sent to jail for a brawl, but by that time the poison of anti-Semitism on the basis of blood had taken firm root. At the time there were approximately 250,000 Jews in Vienna, many of them holding prominent positions as bankers, businessmen, doctors, journalists, musicians, painters and writers. Their percentage was small, but the visibility was high, causing Zweig to suggest in the 1930s that Jews should step down from positions of leadership in order to keep as low a profile as possible.[40]

Attention to the Jewish question was increased considerably by Herzl's program of Zionism, which caused a sharp division among the Jews, who regarded themselves as Austrians and were placed in a quandary of conscience by the call to return to Palestine. The situation for the Jews in Vienna was not helped by the presence of Karl Lueger, or "Handsome Karl," as he was called, the mayor of Vienna and Schönerer's successor as the leading anti-Semite in Vienna. Three times the people elected Lueger mayor until finally in 1897 the Emperor had to overcome his distaste for the man and ratify his appointment. Lueger gained his popularity by making himself the champion of the lower middle classes, courting their support by pandering to their prejudices in denouncing Jewish capitalists. He was first and foremost a politician who pursued his own interests over any other consideration. He had Jewish personal friends, and when questioned about them, he glibly and cynically retorted that he determined who was a Jew. Anti-Semitism, the debate over Zionism, and the Jewish question were rife in Vienna in 1908, when the young Adolf Hitler tried to enroll in the academy of applied arts to learn to paint but was not accepted.

While anti-Semitism was a major presence on the scene in Vienna, it was not a crippling one for this generation of artists and writers. Certainly Jews still had difficulty obtaining teaching positions at the University, and there were also conflicts in the medical profession, as Schnitzler showed in his outstanding play *Professor Bernhardi* (1912) and as his father, Freud, and Semmelweis could attest. In general the writers and artists were able to surmount prejudice by virtue of their secure financial position and their literary success, which enabled them to rise above most of the unpleasantness. When Schnitzler was dishonorably discharged from the army for his unsparing exposure of the military mentality and outdated code of honor in *Leutnant Gustl*, he could refuse to appear at the hearing and shrug off the insult.

Since the writers of this generation had all been educated in the traditional classical curriculum of the Gymnasium, stressing rationality and deterministic causality, the discovery of the limitations of thinking and speaking caused language itself to become problematical and a major concern of the time. Not since the days of German pietism had language been extended to its limits, as these young writers were attempting to do in their works. Then it was a matter of creating new words to express religious visions; now the need arose for a language that could capture the nuances of thinking, of states of mind, and above all express the simultaneity of ideas and the interconnectedness of the world.

About few other topics at the turn of the century has so much been written as about the problem of language, and no other problem of the time has been so fundamentally misunderstood. Literary history has canonized the myth that the Jung-Wien generation experienced a "language crisis" around 1900. This crisis was supposed to have been mainly experienced by Hofmannsthal and Andrian, although it is found in Schnitzler and most other writers as well. The litany runs as follows: because of his "language crisis" Hofmannsthal could no longer write lyric poetry and turned to other forms such as drama, libretto, and essay after writing "Ein Brief" (1902, "A Letter"), more popularly known as the Chandos Letter, to describe his "crisis." This inaccurate formulation about Hofmannsthal's life and career and the equally misconstrued term "language crisis" are still widely accepted views despite all the current evidence to the contrary. These ideas found in published dissertations are still being passed on from professors to students, who then pass them on in turn to their students. Such is the way myths in our profession are perpetuated, and that is why it is so difficult to eradicate them, if it is possible at all.

The term "language crisis," would seem to indicate a problem that reaches such a critical state that a radical change has to take place one way or the other. A crisis in a sick person, say, means that the patient will either get better or worse, live or die, but cannot stay the same. The definition does not appropriately characterize Hofmannsthal's situation at the end of the century, nor does it fit anyone else. For if Hofmannsthal cannot be said to have suffered a "language crisis," then no one else comes into question either. This loose misapplied term has wrenched the problematic of language into an erroneous context, and it should be eliminated from future scholarly discussion of the language problem, which is complex enough without the added confusion of such a sensationalizing and misleading formulation.

The term "language crisis," was brought into currency in connection with Hofmannsthal in Ernst Naef's book *Hugo von Hofmannsthal* (1938), where he titled the chapter on "Ein Brief" "Die Krise." From its specific application to the Chandos Letter the term was gradually applied to other writers, not only in Austria but in Germany as well, and then to the whole period. Naef not only misdated "Ein Brief"—it was written in August 1902, not in 1901— but he also misunderstood its meaning and its position in Hofmannsthal's overall writings. This is not to fault Naef; he did not enjoy the advantage of the quantity of material available today on Hofmannsthal gathered for the purpose of the new forty-volume edition of his works. Nevertheless, the misconception that he initiated has caused a major disservice to the discussion of Hofmannsthal's life and work by dividing them artificially into two halves, while on the contrary they are a seamless unity from beginning to end. In his autobiographical *Ad me ipsum*, where he attempted to show the interconnectedness of his writings, Hofmannsthal stressed " The formidable unity of my work."[42]

Hofmannsthal never underwent any unusual crisis around 1900, and certainly not a language crisis. Beginning in 1892 and proceeding throughout his life he experienced times when writing became difficult. The period around 1900 was no isolated event and one that he attributed to normal problems of maturing, as he himself described his situation.[43] At no point during these (or any other years) did he suffer from an inability to write, as the numerous texts and letters from this period attest. It must also not be overlooked that Hofmannsthal was recognized as one of the greatest conversationalists of his day, as well as a prolific letter writer,[44] additional facts that contradict the idea of equating him and Chandos as well as the notion that he ever experienced impediments with language. He did encounter problems in completing works—he struggled for almost two years in an attempt to adapt Browning's *The Ring and the Book* and finally had to concede defeat; but this problem derived from his lack of an understanding of dramatic structure, not from any difficulty with words. He encountered the same problem with his adaptation of Otway's *Venice Preserved* in *Das gerettete Venedig* (1904). It is illogical and defies common sense to assume, as critics have done, that an author suffering from an inability to write because of a language crisis could then proceed to describe his problem in such sophisticated, elegant, polished form. The confusion stems from the same problem alluded to earlier, namely, the tendency of critics to equate writers with the characters they create and to interpret them interchangeably. Chandos is a fictional persona who reflects autobiographical traits of Hofmannsthal, but he cannot be equated with Hofmannsthal anymore than Hofmannsthal can be considered Chandos.

A recent book has argued that Chandos was able to overcome his difficulties in writing because of the demands of etiquette;[45] specifically his sense of "Anstand" or politeness demanded that he write a reply to Bacon describing his problem, which he was able to do one last time in Bacon's ornate rhetorical style prior to lapsing into permanent silence as far as writing is concerned. Again this view is misconceived, for if Chandos is suffering from an impairment, a psychological disturbance that has caused him "to have utterly lost the faculty to think or speak coherently about anything," as he states, and further prevents him from even conversing on subjects that involve value judgments, then it is unlikely that fulfilling the expectations of politeness would help him to overcome the psychological block from which he suffers. Clearly "Ein Brief" was written by Hofmannsthal, not by Chandos. It was written for a volume to be entitled "Erfundene Gespräche und Briefe" (Invented Conversations and Letters), and was conceived as the letter that Chandos would have written, had he been able to do so.

As I have argued elsewhere,[46] "Ein Brief" was written primarily as a "letter" to Stefan George, whose friendship Hofmannsthal wished to keep, just as Chandos wishes to keep the friendship of Bacon, while at the same time conveying to him that he could no longer pursue the direction of their earlier writings in which they had shared many points of view.

Since George was pursuing Hofmannsthal to become a member of his circle, Hofmannsthal was forced into this expedient, which he hoped would enable him to walk the tightrope of maintaining his independence while at the same time retaining a friendship he valued. Hofmannsthal caused Chandos to lapse into silence as a fictional rhetorical device for not being able to oblige the older writer's wishes to continue writing as they had in the past, while he himself continued on his own path to what he called "the social." The very fact that Hofmannsthal printed this essay in a Berlin newspaper in two installments served as a clear message to George, who abominated literary works printed in the newspaper and believed strictly in art for art's sake, that Hofmannsthal had grown up, was his own person, and knew clearly the direction he wished to follow, namely, that of social responsibility. It is part of the misconception of Hofmannsthal that he was an unworldly aesthete with little practical sense. In truth he was a tough-minded pragmatist, certain of his own mind, a man of independent spirit who followed his own inclinations regardless of any other considerations. His handling of George, his break with Bahr in 1908, and his ability to work with Richard Strauss demonstrate these qualities of Hofmannsthal persuasively.

One aspect of Hofmannsthal that seems to be little recognized was his desire to be wealthy. His family had lost its money in the stock market crash of 1873 and had never recovered its fortunes. Although his father held a good position as director of the Boden-Credit-Anstalt bank in Vienna, Hofmannsthal's mother always suffered from insecurity as a result of the loss of the family wealth, and this feeling carried over to Hofmannsthal, who was always concerned about money and seeking ways to earn more. He recognized by the turn of the century that writing lyric poetry and lyric dramas was never going to bring him the kind of income he desired. Certainly his experimentation with prose forms, his adaptations of classics to learn how to write a full-length drama, and his turn to writing libretti for Richard Strauss, were steps taken out of artistic considerations. At the same time the desire to write a play that would be successful in the Burgtheater and in other major theaters, the income from the operas with Strauss—he complained that Strauss received a greater share than he did—and other projects such as the planned series *Ehrenstätten Österreichs*, and the *Österreichische Bibliothek* (1915-1918) were motivated partly by practical as well as political considerations. In later life Hofmannsthal was envious of the financial success of the works of Zweig.

Hofmannsthal's gradual transition, which encompassed the years from 1899 to 1906, resulted from the normal process of maturing and was determined as much by pragmatic as artistic considerations. This is not to say that language did not become problematic around the turn of the century. But the term language skepticism more reasonably describes the phenomenon of the growing mistrust of language. In this case, as in other matters it is impossible to generalize. One must differentiate between writers and consider them as individuals, for there was little unity among them, particularly after 1900, not only in the direction and themes of their works, but also in lifestyle and outlook. It is one of the major troublesome features of commentaries about the turn of the century that critics attempt to generalize as if these writers thought and acted as a group, while in fact they rarely acted in any collective manner that would permit generalizations.

All the writers at the turn of the century discussed language in one way or another, but usually from different standpoints. Hofmannsthal believed in the totality of existence. The writer's command of language was simply inadequate to trace the interconnectedness of the universe and to convey it in all of its ramifications. Maurice Maeterlinck, a writer much admired by Hofmannsthal and the other Viennese writers, created memorable images that aptly describe the feeling toward language that prevailed at the time:

> How strangely do we diminish a theory as soon as we try to express it in words! We believe we have dived down to the most unfathomable depths, and when we reappear on the surface, the drop of water that glistens on our trembling finger-tips no longer resembles the sea from which it came. We believe we have discovered a grotto that is stored with bewildering treasure; we come back to the light of day, and the gems we have brought are fake—mere pieces of glass—and yet does the treasure shine on unceasingly, in the darkness. There is something between ourselves and our soul that nothing can penetrate.[47]

George later expressed an analogous view in a poem called "Das Wort" (1930, The Word), where he describes a poet with an idea waiting for "the gray Norn" to provide the words in which to present it, only to learn that there were none available. The thought must remain unsaid: "There is nothing where the word fails." One can immediately see the similarity to the later Wittgenstein, who stated that "the limits of my language signify the limits of my world," and also that "One must be silent about what one cannot express."[48] Being silent, however, remains a rich, not an impoverishing experience. Hofmannsthal, George, Maeterlinck, and Wittgenstein all believe that even though the most important matters in life cannot be expressed, they are nevertheless present and affect one's life.

To solve the problem of the inadequacy of words to describe some of the basic experiences of life, Hofmannsthal turned away from attempting to describe the actual process of inner change to showing what had taken place, invoking the assistance of the spectator or reader in recognizing the psychological change that had occurred to bring about the transformation of a character from one state to another. Perhaps the best illustration of this technique is to be found in *Ariadne auf Naxos* (1912), in which Hofmannsthal presented the miracle of existence, transforming Ariadne from the nadir of her life and her readiness for death, through suffering and renewed love, to a new self and life as a full human being. Hofmannsthal could not find the words to describe the psychological transformation within Ariadne, but he recognized that he could demonstrate that this inexpressible "miracle of existence" had happened by allowing the spectator or the reader to witness its occurrence.

Schnitzler too was persuaded of the limitations of words, and of the inter-connectedness of life, an idea that he attempted to convey in "Die dreifache Warnung" (The Threefold Warning), which shows how a trifling incident can cause major repercussions far away from the original scene and without any awareness of the original cause. Bahr, the journalist par excellence, who could argue any side of any question, never experienced any difficulties with language, nor did language become problematic for him. The closest that he came to discussing language was in the reprinted version of his early novel *Die gute Schule*, where he stated in a preface that words meant more to him in 1898 than they had originally when the novel was published in 1890. Beer-Hofmann, Mayreder, and Rilke also expressed a mistrust of language or lamented its limitations, but none of these authors felt impaired in their ability to write. Rilke endeavored to refurbish overused words and restore their luster.

All of the Jung-Wien writers followed parallel lines utilizing the same themes and forms throughout the 1890s, including Kraus who although adopting a negative stance toward his contemporaries was nevertheless linked to them by his criticism of their writings and because he resembled them more than he would ever admit. Around the turn of the century all except Kraus experimented with the pantomime form as an aspect of their questioning of language. Although all of the works were minor and the interest in pantomime was short-lived, the implications for their subsequent writings and for their attitude toward language were significant. The turn to pantomime was an attempt to convey immediacy of feeling in the most direct and universal manner as the best means of conveying truth, of conveying the wholeness they were striving for. Pantomime replaced naturalistic description with universal symbols, replaced the detailed analysis of psychological states of mind with actions, and replaced words with mime, gestures, body movements, and dance supplemented by music, lighting, and staging. In short, works influenced by the Japanese theater—the Japanese craze reached its height at this time—exemplify the experimentation attempted during the transitional period around 1900, as these writers sought new ways to expand their literary range.

Bahr wrote three pantomimes—*Pantomime vom braven Manne* (1901), *Der Minister* (1902), and *Der liebe Augustin* (1902). None of these works has ever been set to music or performed. Since they were all minor works and he wrote no further pantomimes, it is evident that the form was too constrictive for him despite his enthusiasm for its theoretical possibilities and potential. Yet the idea of pantomime in placing the actor in the center of the theater, of stressing universal symbols that fit a living tradition, of creating a theater based on symbol and the concept of the *Gesamtkunstwerk* to produce a direct emotional reaction in the audience all played a role in his later dramas.

Hofmannsthal, who learned a great deal from Bahr, his close personal friend in the 1890s, followed a parallel development with regard to pantomime. He too believed in universality in the theater, in the *Gesamtkunstwerk*, and in the capability of the theater to unify the public. He too was influenced by the Japanese theater and was strongly convinced of the importance of tradition, especially the Austro-Bavarian baroque theater tradition. Hofmannsthal wrote the ballet *Der Triumph der Zeit* (The Triumph of Time) in 1900 and *Der Schüler* (The Student) in 1901, his only true pantomime that was ever published. Other works which reflect pantomime techniques and interest are *Vorspiel für ein Puppentheater* (1906, Prologue for a Puppet Theater), *Leda und der Schwan* (1900), *Jupiter und Semele* (1901), *Amor und Psyche* (dance, 1911), *Das fremde Mädchen* (dance, 1911, The Strange Girl), *Jedermann* (1911, Everyman), *Josephslegende* (ballet, 1914), and *Die grüne Flöte* (ballet-pantomime,

1916, The Green Flute). Finally there are three later unpublished and unperformed pantomimes written to accompany the *Salzburger großes Welttheater Axt-Pantomime* (1922, The Salzburg Great World Theater Axe Pantomime), *Christianus der Wirt* (1927, Christianus the Innkeeper), and *Gott allein kennt die Herzen* (1928, God Alone Knows Human Hearts), which show that the interest in pantomime was not merely a temporary one.

The experimentation with pantomime around 1900 reflects Hofmannsthal's determination not only to minimize words, but also to master the techniques of writing effective vital drama. Through his understanding of the possibilities of pantomime, of gesture, and mimicry Hofmannsthal was able to move away somewhat from the excessive psychological examination that in effect reduced the effectiveness of a work like *Das gerettete Venedig*, to produce texts with greater reliance on action and conveying their meaning through other means than words. In this learning process he was aided not only by Bahr's critical writings, but also by his personal friendship with performers. Above all, his collaboration with Richard Strauss taught him economy of text as well as reliance on other methods of expression. The correspondence of Hofmannsthal and Strauss represents a major document of twentieth-century letters, providing valuable insights into both men as well as into their creative processes.

As is true for Bahr, Hofmannsthal's pantomimes, dances, and ballets form a union of past and present, leading back through the baroque to the very origins of the theater and ahead to the revival of the festival idea to make the theater once again a living cultural force uniting all levels of society. Hofmannsthal shared Bahr's view of the theater as a moral and social force and lent his support to help Bahr's appointment as director of the Burgtheater in 1918.

In turning to Schnitzler one finds a different motivation for the interest in pantomimes, of which he wrote only two. The first, *Der Schleier der Pierrette* (The Veil of Pierrette), was begun in 1892 and completed in 1910 with a musical setting by Hans von Dohnányi. Schnitzler also used the theme in 1902 in the drama *Der Schleier der Beatrice* (The Veil of Beatrice). The second pantomime, *Die Verwandlungen des Pierrot* (1908, The Transformations of Pierrot), has never been performed. Unlike Bahr's pantomimes which describe in precise detail the gestures and movements of the actor as well as the motifs for the musical accompaniment, Schnitzler writes an almost straightforward play in dialogue form with the notation that the dialogue is not to be spoken but is to be translated by the actor into the appropriate pantomimic gestures.

Despite the fact that Schnitzler designated only two works as pantomimes, it is possible to see the influence of pantomime in other works beginning with *Paracelsus* (1897). However, in contrast to Bahr and Hofmannsthal this tendency in Schnitzler becomes a matter of theme rather than of technique. In this period Schnitzler conceives of his characters as puppets under the control of a higher, mysterious power. Such works as *Reigen* (1903, *Round Dance*), *Marionetten* (1902-1904, *Marionettes*), *Der Puppenspieler* (1903, The Puppeteer), *Der tapfere Cassian* (1904, *Brave Cassian*), and *Zum großen Wurstel* (1905, At the Sign of the Great Harlequin), while not strictly pantomimes, closely resemble the pantomime tradition in outlook and to some degree in form.

In his letters to Otto Brahm, Schnitzler often stressed that his characters, once he had created them, assumed a life of their own which he could no longer control. Thus, while he, the author, believed he was pulling the strings of his characters, ultimately he discovered that he too was only a puppet in the hands of a higher power. This conclusion becomes most apparent in the final scene of *Zum großen Wurstl*, where the mysterious gray figure appears with a drawn sword, waves his blade over the stage as if to cut the puppet strings of each figure, causing everyone, including the author, to collapse. The lights go out, extending the implications of death to the audience and demonstrating the subservience of all individuals to a higher power. When the lights return, the play resumes at the beginning. Life is a continuous puppet show.

Since the pantomime form is ideal for rendering this puppetlike condition of man, for showing human beings as marionettes, it is a logical choice for Schnitzler to demonstrate his deterministic Weltanschauung. This purpose motivated his interest in pantomime. It should be noted that both Bahr and Hofmannsthal were also strongly influenced at this time by the idea of an overpowering fate. Bahr's comedy *Josephine* (1898), the dramas *Der Athlet* (1899, The Athlete), *Der Meister* (1904, The Master), the novel *Theater* (1897), and the prose works in *Wirkung in die Ferne* (1902, Remote Effect) all reflect the role of fate in determining the course of human actions. In this same period Hofmannsthal utilizes the idea of fate in the dramas *Die Hochzeit der Sobeide* (1899, Sobeide's Wedding) and *Das Bergwerk zu Falun* (1900, The Mine at Falun) as well as to some extent in the narratives *Reitergeschichte* (1899, Tale of the Cavalry) and *Das Erlebnis des Marschalls von Bassompierre* (1900, The Experience of Marshall von Bassompierre). Schnitzler, however, unlike Bahr and Hofmannsthal, was neither reacting against words nor experimenting with new dramatic forms.

Beer-Hofmann, whose language skepticism led him to prefer pantomime to spoken drama in his later life, had produced an early pantomime: *Pierrot Magus* (1892), translated into French the same year under the title *Pierrot Hypnotiseur* but never published in either version. Later he published the pantomime *Das goldene Pferd* (1921-1922, The Golden Horse). He served as the director of his own plays and provided lengthy stage directions which rival the text in length, in an attempt to provide a complete interpretation of each character by indicating the appropriate mimicry, gestures, and vocal intonations. Beer-Hofmann believed that the more the pantomimic element in drama is strengthened, the more universally understandable it becomes and the greater the audience to which it can speak. Language, he felt, led to over-subtlety, a tendency of art he wished to counteract. His efforts to reach audiences directly resemble the turn to the baroque theater that Bahr and Hofmannsthal underwent at the same time.

While the experiments with pantomime enriched their understanding of the theater and dramatic presentation, the writers recognized that the avoidance of language, even with all of its limitations, represented a substantial loss. Therefore they tried another approach: they shifted from trying to trace the psychology of the characters to describing actions and allowing the spectators or readers to determine through empathy the psychological processes that had occurred. While it was not possible to delve into the subconscious to trace the thinking that motivated the characters' actions, the results could be shown. For example, Schnitzler adopted the technique of employing a gesture instead of attempting to describe in detailed psychological terms how the inner transformation of attitude takes place. At the end of *Der blinde Geronimo und sein Bruder* (1900, *Blind Geronimo and His Brother*), when the estranged brothers are stopped by the policeman, Geronimo intuits spontaneously without a word being spoken, that Carlo had not been robbing him, as he had assumed, but that he had robbed for him to prove his innocence. He shows his renewed love and trust by embracing Carlo silently. The author merely concludes, gratuitously, "He had his brother again, no he had him for the first time."

One important ramification of this change of approach was to change the reader from a spectator into a partner in the construction of the work, an approach to literature that continued to develop in the course of the twentieth century until it has become the standard technique of most contemporary authors. These writers helped to break down the concept of the omniscient author, which dominated the prose of the nineteenth century, and thus played an important role in transforming the role of the author, as did Schnitzler's introduction of the stream-of-consciousness technique in *Leutnant Gustl*. Schnitzler also added the dimension of ambiguous endings, forcing readers to carry the work forward in their minds and choosing the conclusion they felt most appropriate from their interpretation of the text. Another dimension of literary experimentation to expand what could be conveyed despite the limitations of words invoked the mysterious metaphysical world, the supernatural, and the occult. These elements were continued in the works of Kubin, Meyrinck, and Perutz.

Hofmannsthal eventually worked his way through some of his language skepticism, by recognizing that the antidote for the paralysis stemming from concern about language was action. Just as Schnitzler produced works with opposing endings, Hofmannsthal repeated much of the problematic of the Chandos letter in the comedy *Der Schwierige* with a happy ending. The romance of Hans Karl Bühl and Helene Altenwyl suffers through a number of trials because of their mutual mistrust of language, their conviction that words are indecent and cause more problems than they solve. By the end of the play, however, they not only find each other in allomatic love, that is, a love that mutually transforms each partner to a new self and level of existence. Their union also represents their connection with the world.[49] Hans Karl finds his voice and will take a socially responsible position in society. Contrary to his former mistrust of words, he will now make a speech in parliament. Hofmannsthal himself had been striving for such a position of social responsibility when he broke away from George and worked to reach the broad public rather than simply a narrow circle of like-minded artists. He had used his voice during World War I, when he was authorized to give lectures in Switzerland and in Sweden about the role of Austria in the war. Hofmannsthal had come to recognize the importance of language despite its limitations.[50]

Schnitzler too maintained a healthy language skepticism, but basically his approach to the problem of language differed from Hofmannsthal's. Being even more pragmatic than Hofmannsthal, as one would expect in a scientifically trained observer—a good case can be made for considering Schnitzler a Naturalist, and it is not surprising that he enjoyed close ties to Otto Brahm, who performed all of his plays in Berlin—Schnitzler worried less about the limitations of language and more about how words were being used or misused, about the use of language in role playing and in the hypocrisy rampant in the society of the time. Schnitzler, like Hofmannsthal, enjoyed opening the ground beneath the feet of the smug philistines who felt so secure in life by showing them the abyss that could appear at any time through the intervention of chance. Hofmannsthal, in *Idylle* (1897, Idyll) and Schnitzler in *Paracelsus* (1897) shatter the world of the bourgeois protagonists in a way that they will never forget. Schnitzler insisted that people were always engaged in play acting with the dividing line between play and reality not always apparent. Role playing runs throughout most of Schnitzler's works, nowhere more pronouncedly than in "Die kleine Komödie" ("The Little Comedy") and in the *Komödie der Worte* (1915, Comedy of Words).

It is a curious matter that, while most writers lamented their difficulties with language in one form or another, the one writer who devoted more attention to the problem of language than any other, Karl Kraus, never complained of difficulties with his own use of language, only with the misuse of words by others. He never doubted his own ability to use language, nor did he express any skepticism that language was inadequate to convey his meaning. The son of a wealthy family, Kraus enjoyed the same background and upbringing as the other writers, went to the same schools, frequented the Café Griensteidl, and simply adopted a different course during the 1890s, preferring to become the "conscience" of his generation. His very lifestyle of sleeping days and working nights reflects his contrary nature and Weltanschauung. He embarked upon the mission of destroying what was amoral and criminal in his society, believing that by removing the corruption and evil, the good qualities of society would flourish and the country would be restored to the purity of its "origins." He made a career of attacking language misusage, particularly by his *bête noire*, the *Neue Freie Presse*, because for Kraus misuse of language reflected slipshod thinking and lack of character, not the limitation of words to convey meaning. Language misuse served him as an indicator of an individual's morality. Measuring an individual's linguistic expression against his actions enabled Kraus to demonstrate hypocrisy. Working in terms of this discrepancy between word and deed is the method of satire, which Kraus raised to a fine art and employed with the most telling effect of any writer of his time and perhaps of any time. Language and deed, word and meaning, had to coincide for Kraus, a viewpoint analogous to Hofmannsthal's view that "the whole man must move at once."

Since Kraus equated language and morality, one of his favorite techniques was to allow his victims to express themselves, sometimes with commentary, sometimes without, in order to reveal their hypocrisy and corruption. He did not see how "a whole line could be written by half a man," or how "a work could be built on the quicksand of character." He felt that his language was "the whole world's whore that I turned back into a virgin," clearly an expression of his faith in language and his confidence in his ability to use it. Kraus actually believed that he did not use language, but that language made itself available to him, serving as the "divining rod that refines the sources of thought." "Because I take an idea by the word, it comes," he boasted. Kraus paralleled the turn to the past of the Jung-Wien writers not only with his idea of returning the world to what he called "the origin," (*der Ursprung*), an earlier, more harmonious, less corrupt time—an early version of the Expressionist dream of returning to a more primitive, pristine culture—but also in matters of language, calling himself "One of the epigones who live in the old house of language."[51]

Kraus attacked almost all of the other Viennese writers except Altenberg for alleged offenses against his standards, but his severest ire was reserved for the institution of the feuilleton, a favorite form of the time. With the exception of Schnitzler, who was loath to write for the newspaper, all of the contemporary writers employed this vehicle as a direct means of reaching the general public. The Austrian popular philosopher Popper-Lynkeus considered the feuilleton of the *Neue Freie Presse* "a people's university." Auernheimer, a leading practitioner of the form which he, like Ludwig Speidel, defined as "the immortality of one day," regarded Speidel as the Goethe and Herzl the Heine of the feuilleton.[52] But while most writers utilized this light form, in which graceful, polished style received the major emphasis and ideas were secondary, Kraus viewed it as anathema precisely because of this discrepancy between form and content. He never forgave Heine for his role in popularizing what Kraus considered a shallow, deceitful form, which featured the kind of ornamentation Loos denounced in architecture.

While Kraus followed his own technique of employing language as a measure of the character of his contempories, Fritz Mauthner, a journalist and would-be dramatist turned philosopher, devoted the most intensive analysis to the problems of language at the turn of the century. He shifted the emphasis of philosophy from analysis of thought to a critique of language. Like Kant, he believed that it was not possible to know the world through language, but Mauthner felt that art was possible because of the emotive content of words. The ambiguity of words, which causes problems for science and philosophy, serves as an enrichment for literature. Throughout Mauthner's essays on language, as in all other discussions of language, a basic paradox prevails: even while philosophers and writers insist that language is inadequate to render truth, they nevertheless feel that we should believe their particular truth. Fortunately, in the practical world of everyday reality we are able to suspend our disbelief about what we "know" philosophically and logically so that the world can still function in terms of the only reasonable agency that we possess for communication: language. Authors, too, after registering all their protests about language skepticism, wisely suspend their theoretical reservations about the efficacy of language and continue to write "as if" language can possess meaning.

Mauthner, whose *Beiträge zu einer Kritik der Sprache* (1901, Contributions to a Critique of Language) Hofmannsthal read prior to writing the Chandos Letter, was known to the young writers of the time, another instance of how close the intellectual and artistic worlds of Vienna were at the turn of the century. He knew Hofmannsthal and Zweig and became a particularly close friend of Bahr in the 1920s in Munich, where the two visited frequently and took walks in the English garden. Bahr considered Mauthner one of the true leaders and guiding forces of Germany. The line from Mauthner leads directly forward to Wittgenstein, who in his *Tractatus*, a collection of individual propositions, attempted to construct with rigorous logic a philosophical description of the limits of language. Although he concluded that one must be silent, if one cannot express a thought, being silent does not mean to be without thought. The individual can still directly intuit the world, as Hofmannsthal had shown in the epiphanies Chandos experienced, Schnitzler in the revelation of Geronimo, and Bahr in the religious transformation of Count Flayn in *Himmelfahrt* (1914, Ascension). This turn to inner illumination which transcends reason and causes inner transformation became a European-wide phenomenon: Paul Claudel, August Strindberg, Tolstoi, and all the German Expressionists—a reaction against positivism or other mechanistic systems. In the growing dominance of science and materialism, the conflict between reason and feeling or reason and faith grew into a major theme, often connected to the problem of language as in Musil's *Die Verwirrungen des Zöglings Törless* (1906, *Young Törless*), Rilke's *Die Aufzeichnungen des Malte Laurids Brigge* (1910, The Notebooks of Malte Laurids Brigge), and in Kafka's *Beschreibung eines Kampfes* (1903, *Descriptions of a Struggle*). Musil described the conflict between reason and faith most eloquently in his narrative tale *Tonka* (1924) while Bahr, who lamented the national trend toward "Betrieb" (business), and had returned to Catholicism in 1914, discussed the problem in his essay *Vernunft und Glaube* (1917, Reason and Faith).

To attempt to compensate for the perceived inadequacies of language, the writers turned to the *Gesamtkunstwerk* and found further reinforcement for their total approach in art in the rediscovery of the baroque, which not only united all of the arts, but also added the dimension of the broad public, precisely the audience that these writers were determined to reach after 1900. As in the case of Mach, Mauthner, and Freud the verification for their ideas on the baroque came belatedly with the third volume of Josef Nadler's *Deutsche Literaturgeschichte der deutschen Stämme und Landschaften* (1918, Literary History of German Tribes and Lands). Bahr first conceived the idea of establishing an outdoor theater in Salzburg in 1903 in a letter to Max Reinhardt, but the idea did not come to fruition until 1920, when the first Salzburg Festival took place under the auspices of Hofmannsthal, Reinhardt, and Strauss, without Bahr's involvement.

Hofmannsthal had already discovered that works like his opera *Der Rosenkavalier* (1908) fit into the Austro-Bavarian baroque tradition. This connection led him in turn to *Jedermann* which became the centerpiece of the Salzburg Festival and has remained so to the present day. Hofmannsthal also embraced the baroque religious play in his adaptation from Calderon that became *Das Salzburger große Welttheater.* In later years he based his admiration for writers like Max Mell and Richard Billinger on their blending of provincial nature plays with religious themes and Germanic mythology. He did not live long enough to see how these tendencies led them into the Nazi orbit.

The baroque idea dominated the thinking of Bahr and Hofmannsthal after 1900. The baroque concept of art corresponded to their desire to involve the broad public in cultural activities, and it also fulfilled their ideal of including the provinces in order to create a sense of national unity. Throughout the 1890s Vienna had claimed all of the emphasis, although provincial writers like Rosegger, Greiner, and later Bartsch and Schönherr found more than local success. As early as 1897, through the impetus of Rosegger and Greiner, Bahr ran a series entitled "Discovery of the Provinces." Partly he intended to confront hypocritical Vienna with the wholesomeness of the countryside; but more importantly he wished to contribute to the creation of a unified Austrian and not simply a Viennese culture. Only in this way could Austria become the strong flourishing nation that could fulfill its role as the heart of a loose-knit federation of

European states. Bahr envisioned a second baroque wave uniting north and south, east and west, with Austria as the center. While his vision may not materialize precisely as he predicted, the concept of an economically united Europe will be fulfilled in 1992.

During the years 1899-1906, the Jung-Wien generation underwent a transition attributable to the normal process of maturing and their modernist ideal of staying abreast of the changing external world. The transition, extending as it did over seven years, was gradual and not on the order of a dramatic crisis. Up to this point these authors had concentrated on condemning aestheticism and decadence; now they felt that the time had come to turn their attention to life itself in positive terms. In *Bergwerk zu Falun* Hofmannsthal had bid a final farewell to the aestheticism he had been condemning throughout the 1890s, by burying Elis Fröbom in a mountain, showing the dead end that the worship of beauty for its own sake represented. The Chandos Letter merely reiterates in clearer language what he had already portrayed symbolically in the earlier work. He now clearly knew the future direction of his life: a commitment to the social.

Kraus, born in 1874, the same year as Hofmannsthal, founded his journal *Die Fackel* in 1899, which shaped the course of his future life as a major critic of society. Beer-Hofmann, who changed least among these writers, likewise portrayed the death of the aesthete in *Der Tod Georgs* (1900, George's Death) and found his mission in Zionism. Schnitzler also condemned the aesthete and the *Literat*, the hack writer, in *Der einsame Weg* (1904, The Lonely Way), the last act of which, as he wrote to Bahr, he considered a summing up, not only of that topic, but also of the first forty-two years of his life.[55] Bahr too underwent a major change in 1903, the year that he almost died. When he recovered, he declared his affirmation of life over art in the *Dialog vom Marsyas* (1905, Dialogue of Marsyas). In 1906, having grown weary of the continuous battle in Vienna and suffering the "Austrian fate" of most Viennese writers and artists, a lack of appreciation by the public as well as by colleagues and critics, Bahr departed to work as dramaturge and director with Reinhardt in Berlin, signaling the end of his campaign of modernity begun in 1891. The group had already dispersed, for they had never adopted another meeting place such as they had enjoyed in the Café Griensteidl, which was demolished in 1896. When they had first met in 1891, they were all young and in the process of sowing their wild oats while they gained their education and began their professional life. Now Hofmannsthal, Bahr,

Beer-Hofmann, and Schnitzler were married and settling into the careers they had chosen.

The most powerful influence on the urge for life felt by these writers was Nietzsche with his attacks on stultification, his preaching of the *Übermensch*, and above all his espousal of the *Lebensphilosophie*. His injunction to live life to the fullest, even to live dangerously regardless of the consequences, to develop oneself to the maximum, were messages accepted eagerly by this young generation and served as a major antidote to cultural pessimism. It would be difficult to overestimate Nietzsche's influence on a generation which had been raised in a school system dedicated to the idea of maintaining the status quo and of training malleable citizens for the state. These schools, in collusion with the parents, allowed little or no room for individual growth or development. As a result most of the members of this generation who commented on their school years claimed that they had been crippled to some degree by the school system.

Nietzsche taught this generation to believe in itself. His call to break free of society's shackles and live life intensively found a particularly strong response in Bahr, who had proclaimed himself a Nietzschean in 1888. In 1900 Bahr proposed an independent school in Salzburg where people could develop freely to the maximum of their potential. He continued to stress this message of independence of spirit to the younger generation in all of his writings after 1900, most explicitly in *Dialog vom Tragischen* (1904, Dialogue of Tragedy) and in *Buch der Jugend* (1908, Book of Youth). It became the accepted view that not the length, but the quality of life mattered. This idea formed the basis of Bahr's early Expressionist play *Der arme Narr* (1907, *The Poor Fool*). This same message is found in Hofmannsthal's *Idylle* (1897) and in Schnitzler's *Der Ruf des Lebens* (1905, *The Call of Life*), which appropriately he dedicated to Bahr.

By 1906 the battle for modernity had clearly been won. New ideas, new developments, and new artists had entered the scene and hastened the change,[56] although again the transition was a smooth one. The new artists did not condemn their predecessors but paid homage to them. Schoenberg recognized the contribution of Mahler, and Loos praised the work of Otto Wagner. Functionalism became one of the new trends, not only in art and architecture, but also in language.[57] The *Wiener Werkstätte* blending art and craft, and Otto Wagner, who believed that only architecture or furnishings that were practical could lay claim to beauty, fit into this transition. The appearance of the architect Adolf Loos with his condemnation of historicism and ornamentation in *Ornament und Verbrechen* (1908, *Ornament and Crime*) signaled that a new phase had begun. His "house without eyebrows," so-called because the windows lacked decorative frames, inspired controversy and raised the ire of the Emperor, who henceforth avoided the exit to the Michaelerplatz in order not to have to look at this building. Loos became an ally of Kraus, who also derided his generation for its penchant for superfluous decoration, revealing that it did not know the difference between an urn and a chamberpot. Ties were formed with Ludwig Ficker and the group in Innsbruck around the journal *Der Brenner*, as well as with Oskar Kokoschka, the multi-talented painter-dramatist who created one of the earliest Expressionist plays in *Mörder, Hoffnung der Frauen* (1908, *Murderer, the Hope of Women*), and led painting into Expressionism. Their views were shared by the composer/painter Arnold Schoenberg, Alban Berg, and Anton Webern, all of whom stripped music to its essence in developing the twelve-tone technique. These writers, artists, architects and musicians were all forerunners of Expressionism, which in 1908 was appearing on the scene also in Germany.

Expressionism in Austria has never received the same attention as in Germany, for despite the number of adherents—including Theodor Däubler, Georg Trakl, Hans Kaltneker, Jakob Haringer, Anton Wildgans and the painter/writer Gütersloh—the movement, while important, never dominated the literary scene in Vienna as it did in Berlin.[58] The lack of prominence in Vienna stemmed primarily from the fact that many of the Austrian writers took part in the Expressionist movement in Berlin, particularly the young generation of Prague writers, who, led by Max Brod, preferred to function within the literary scene in Berlin, which had suddenly become so vital, rather than to work in Vienna. Kraus had initially visited Prague and tried to court them, but one by one his friendships with Brod, Werfel, and others ended in lengthy, bitter polemics. Brod played a leading role in the early days of Expressionism in Berlin, and through his reading of Werfel's poetry he launched Werfel there as a major poet of Expressionism. Brod also introduced Oskar Baum and Kakfa to Berlin but, modest as he was, Kafka failed to create the immediate sensation that Werfel did. Other Prague writers who contributed in Berlin were Albert Ehrenstein, Paul Kornfeld, and Johannes Urzidil. Kraus also tried to establish himself in Berlin, where his good friend and admirer Elsa Lasker-Schüler was an established figure. He attempted to publish a Berlin edition of *Die Fackel* in collaboration with Herwarth Walden, but the project failed. More polemics in Berlin, with Alfred Kerr among others, ended Kraus's contacts there. Both Kraus and Bahr admired Expressionism, which the latter in his book *Expressionismus* (1915) considered a more vital movement than Impressionism.

Concerns about language, aestheticism, the double standard, women's emancipation, self-fulfillment, and the nature and role of the artist, as well as the conflict of spirit and nature or art and life, were interrupted by the outbreak of World War I in August 1914. The assassination of the headstrong archduke Franz Ferdinand, more highly regarded than the Emperor in some circles and a possible heir apparent, in Sarajevo prompted the ambitious general Conrad von Hötzendorf to advise the emperor to teach the upstart Serbs a lesson and thus send a warning to other nations rebelliously flirting with thoughts of independence and national self-determination which were much in the air. This latest tragedy was only one in a series that plagued the royal house. Franz Joseph's only son and the heir apparent, Crown Prince Rudolf, had committed suicide at Mayerling in 1889.[59] The Empress Elisabeth suffered as an unhappy consort for Franz Joseph, and helped arrange some consolation for him in the company of the actress Katharina Schratt,[60] while she, Elisabeth, drifted aimlessly from one vacation spot to another until her trials were ended abruptly when she was assassinated by an Italian Irredentist in Geneva. Franz Joseph's brother Maximilian had been executed in Mexico. The Emperor acceded to the delivery of an ultimatum that the Serbs would have to reject in the belief that a brief war would take place. Instead the war spread quickly throughout Europe, which had enjoyed a generation of peace and was poised like a row of dominoes. The atypically incautious military move tipped the first domino and caused a reaction that quickly developed into the major conflagration of World War I.

The declaration of war was greeted with almost universal acclaim, followed quickly by a turn to opposition and pacifism by the writers and artists when the initial euphoria wore off and the ugly reality of the conflict became known. The Jung-Wien writers were too old or otherwise unfit for military service except for Hofmannsthal, who was nine years younger than the others. He joined his regiment of dragoons, but his literary importance kept him out of any war zone. He remained in Vienna, where he could follow the war through conversations with his friend Joseph Redlich, the Minister of Finance. Although he was for a time assigned to give lectures in Switzerland and Sweden on Austria's mission,

Hofmannsthal had ample opportunity to continue his literary endeavors. He not only revised the opera *Ariadne auf Naxos*, but also completed the sequel, the opera *Die Frau ohne Schatten* (1919, *The Woman without a Shadow*). Schnitzler continued to write in the same vein but, as has been documented in a recent study by Clive Roberts, with much greater concern for political matters than critics had recognized.[61] He collected his views on war and peace in the essay *Über Krieg und Frieden* (1939, *Some Day Peace Will Return*), which was published only posthumously. His diaries also contain numerous references to the war and politics. Bahr remained a political commentator in his published diaries, remaining informed not only through his reading, but also by carrying on an active correspondence with Joseph Redlich.[61] Other younger writers, including Rilke, Zweig, Franz Ginskey, Rudolf Hans Bartsch, Musil, Franz Blei, Egon Erwin Kisch, Felix Braun, Franz Theodor Csokor, Hans Müller, Emil Lucka and Franz Werfel, who first served and was injured, were assigned to the press corps or to the Royal Archives in lieu of military service. Eventually the pacifist Zweig wearied even of this involvement in the war, not to mention the infringement on his personal life, and when granted a furlough to attend the première of his pacifist play *Jeremias* in Switzerland in 1917, he remained there for the remainder of the war. A tragic casualty of the war was the poet Georg Trakl, who was driven to commit suicide when as a medical orderly he was placed in charge of wounded soldiers whose sufferings he could not alleviate. By and large, however, the war had little appreciable effect on the Austrian writers' lives or productivity, because their age, reputation, and degree of affluence protected them. The situation contrasts sharply with the young generation of Expressionist writers in Germany, many of whom were killed in action during the first year of the war.

Having survived the war, the Jung-Wien writers also surmounted the difficulties of the peace, which included a loss of the monarchy and the transformation of Austria into the First Republic under the Socialists Karl Renner and Otto Bauer. The writers and artists generally ignored the change of political systems and continued to pursue essentially the same themes, interests, forms, and lifestyle as earlier, modulated slightly with their evolving views of the role of art and the artist but basically proceeding as if no external political change had occurred. These writers, so often falsely accused of fleeing reality in the 1890s, actually did so more in the 1920s by turning conservative and retreating into the historical past, although to their credit, for the purpose of making the country's heritage relevant to their own time, as Hofmannsthal described in 1927 in his call for a "Conservative Revolution." If one were restricted solely to the literature of the post-World-War-I period as an indication of social and political events, one would not know virtually until 1938 that Austria was no longer a monarchy.

Schnitzler too turned to the past and continued to write tales and plays about the world that essentially no longer existed, although he introduced recent thinking about women's equality, psychology, and war. His late prose works, *Fräulein Else* (1924), *Traumnovelle* (1936, *Rhapsody: A Dream Novel*), and *Flucht in die Finsternis* (1931, *Flight into Darkness*) represent the pinnacle of his narrative writing. Similarly his last major drama, *Der Gang zum Weiher* (1927, The Way to the Pond), containing an amalgamation of his early ideas (the genesis began in 1907) with the form of Grillparzer's Habsburg dramas, serves as a capstone to his dramatic writing. This play is set in the eighteenth century, and is written in verse, an intentional choice to combat the realism that dominated literature but as untimely a choice of form as can be imagined, when one considers that Hitler was making inroads at the polls in Germany, National Socialism was beginning to take root in Austria,[62], and that the world was already on a collision course with the disaster of World War II. However, just as everyone had been oblivious to the sudden end of the monarchy, no one in 1927 had the slightest inkling of the war and the holocaust to come despite Hitler's *Mein Kampf.*

All of the Austrian writers and intellectuals dismissed Hitler as an uneducated, ignorant lightweight who would soon self-destruct because of his extremist views. For such perceptive and knowledgeable writers with their extremely refined sensitivity to the psychology of human nature, the appraisal of Hitler represented the worst misjudgment of their careers. They refused to consider Hitler and his writings seriously, and their comforting views to each other, which represented the consensus, were based far more on hope than on fact. All of the usual seismographic voices with the keen antennae failed in this instance. Kraus recognized the danger more than anyone else, but was severely restricted in what he could report without censorship. Eventually he found the grotesqueness of the National Socialists movement so monstrous that it exceeded his satiric capabilities and gave him no alternative other than to fall silent—at least temporarily. Bahr trivialized Hitler in his last novel "*Österreich in Ewigkeit*" (1928, Austria in Eternity) and avoided mentioning him in his published diaries. Although he continued to comment on current events, his topics increasingly featured Goethe, the baroque, eulogies for friends, and recollections of the glory days of Jung Wien.

The other writers of their generation paid little attention to the emergence and growing domination of National Socialism, until the book burnings in Germany in May 1933 forced all writers to take a stand. Salten was thrust into the spotlight at the International P.E.N. Club meeting in Ragusa in 1934, when a resolution was introduced to condemn the book burnings, which included works of Austrian authors. He declined to support the motion because he feared that the loss of the German book market would harm Austrian writers and publishers and withdrew from the meeting in protest with Grete Urbanitski, head of the Austrian delegation, and the German representatives. His support of the German position did not help him in 1938, when he too had to flee into exile in Switzerland, where he died in 1945.

The generation of 1890 was mercifully spared the final disastrous confrontation of their ideal and idealized world of art with that of political reality that occurred with the Anschluss on 11 March 1938. Rilke died in 1926, followed by Hofmannsthal (1929), Schnitzler (1931), Bahr (1934), and Kraus (1936). Musil died in exile in Switzerland in 1942, supported by his publisher and by friends who still believed in him, while he struggled to achieve the impossible task of completing *Der Mann ohne Eigenschaften*. Andrian found his voice to speak against the idea of Anschluss in *Österreich im Prisma der Idee* (1937, Austria in the Prism of the Idea), before he too had to flee into exile in Brazil. Auernheimer, Beer-Hofmann, and Broch were among those who escaped to the United States. Zweig committed suicide in exile in Petropolis, Brazil in 1942. The turn-of-the-century generation had experienced the severe inflation of the 1920s, the turning of Austria into an armed camp of rival political factions, the burning of the Palace of Justice in 1927, and in some cases the civil war of 1934; yet all of them died still preserving the values and ideals of the world in which they had grown up, the world that had changed before their eyes irretrievably into the world of yesterday.

Notes

1. For a description of the life of the poor and underprivileged, see Hubert Ch. Ehalt, Gernot Heiss, Hannes Stekl, eds. *Glücklich ist, wer vergisst...? Das andere Wien um 1900* (Wien: Böhlau, 1986).
2. Ralph D. Parks, "The Impact of the Viennese School of Medicine on Modern American Medicine," in Peter Pabisch, ed., *From Wilson to Waldheim* (Riverside: Ariadne Press, 1989), pp. 110-111.
3. Cf. Anson Rabinbach, ed., *The Austrian Socialist Experiment, Social Democracy and Austromarxism, 1918-1934* (Boulder and London: Westview, 1985).
4. Bruno Hilldbrand, ed. *Nietzsche und die deutsche Literatur* (Tübingen: Niemeyer, 1978).
5. J. Robert Wegs, *Growing Up Working Class.* Continuity and Change Among Viennese Youth, 1890-1938 (University Park and London: The Pennsylvania State University Press, 1989).
6. Carl E. Schorske, *Fin de siecle Vienna* (New York: Knopf, 1980), p. 304. It is necessary to recognize that Schorske's book, for all of its positive qualities, consists of a collection of his essays, some of which date back more than a decade and were not updated for republication. Consequently, while they accorded with the information of their day, these views, in a number of instances, have been overtaken by recent findings.
7. Ibid, pp. 8-9. Schorske's view is echoed by Robert Waissenberger: "The absence of any apparent relation between contemporary social conditions and the rarified qualitative standards set by art leads us to assume that art...represented in some degree a reaction to the disquieting nature of reality." *Vienna 1890-1920* (New York: Rizzoli, 1984), p. 7.
8. Cf. Donald G. Daviau, "Herrmann Bahr, Catalyst of Modernity and Cultural Mediator," in *Hermann Bahr* (Boston: Twayne, 1985), pp. 35-55.

9.   Hans Weigel, *Flucht vor der Größe* (Wien: Morawa, 1960).

10.   Cf. Viktor Suchy, "Ausseerland—Zuflucht der Dichter. Eine `Seelenlandschaft' der Literatur," *Literatur in der Steiermark* (1976), pp. 369-411.

11.   Felix Salten, "Aus den Anfängen. Erinnerungsskizzen," *Jahrbuch deutscher Bibliophilen und Literaturfreunde*, 18./19. Jg. (1932-1933), p. 45.

12.   Cf. Elisabeth Springer, *Geschichte und Kulturleben der Wiener Ringstrasse* (Wiesbaden: Franz Steiner, 1979).

13.   *Traum und Wirklichkeit. Wien 1870-1930.* 93. Sonderausstellung des Historischen Museums der Stadt Wien. 28. März bis 6. Oktober 1985 (Wien: Eigenverlag der Museen der Stadt Wien, 1985).

14.   Beth Bjorklund, "Museum of Modern Art's Vienna 1900: Conception and Reception," *Modern Austrian Literature*, Vol. 22, No. 1 (March 1990), 99-107.

15.   "Within the hundred years from 1860 to the present day, the Secession forms a peak of international importance in the arts." Kristian Sotriffer, *Modern Austrian Art* (New York: Prager, 1965), p. 8.

16.   Hermann Broch, *Hugo von Hofmannsthal and His Time.* Michael P. Steinberg, trans. and ed. (Chicago: University of Chicago Press, 1984).

17.   Cf. Phillip Jullian, *Prince of Aesthetes. Count Robert de Montesquiou. 1855-1921* (New York: Viking, 1968).

18.   Joachim Remak, "How Doomed the Habsburg Empire?" in *The Journal of Modern History*, XLI (1969), 142ff.

19.   Cf. Charles E. McClelland, "President Woodrow Wilson and the Austrian Monarchy," in Peter Pabisch, *From Wilson to Waldheim* (Riverside: Ariadne Press, 1989), pp. 33-51.

20.   Cf. Helmut Andics, *Der Staat, den keiner wollte* (Wien: Molden, 1968).

21.   Claudio Magris, *Der Habsburgische Mythos in der österreichischen Literatur* (Salzburg: Otto Müller, 1966).

22.   Cf. John-Paul Himka, *Galician Villagers and the Ukrainian National Movement in the Nineteenth Century* (Edmonton: University of Alberta, 1988).

23.   Wolf Wucherpfennig, "The `Young Viennese' and their Father. Decadence and the Generation Conflict around 1890." *Journal of Contemporary History*, Vol. 17, No. 2 (January 1982), 29.

24. Ibid.
25. Cf. Günter Martens, *Vitalismus und Expressionismus* (Stuttgart, Berlin: Kohlhammer, 1971), pp. 32-54.
26. Manfred Diersch, *Empiriokritizismus und Impressionismus* (Berlin: Rütten & Loening, 1977).
27. Cf. Jane Kallir, *Viennese Design and the Wiener Werkstätte* (New York: Galerie St. Etienne/ George Braziller, 1986).
28. James Shedel, *Art and Society. The New Art Movement in Vienna 1897-1914* (Palo Alto: Sposs, 1981).
29. Raoul Auernheimer, *Das Wirtshaus zur verlorenen Zeit* (Wien: Ullstein, 1948), pp. 68-69.
30. Stefan Zweig, "Eros Matutinus," in *Die Welt von gestern* (Stockholm: Bermann-Fischer, 1944), pp. 70-91.
31. Nike Wagner, *Geist und Geschlecht, Karl Kraus und die Erotik der Wiener Moderne* (Frankfurt a.M.: Suhrkamp, 1982).
32. Alessandra Comini, *Gustav Klimt, Eros and Ethos* (New York: Braziller, 1975).
33. Frederick J. Beharriel, "Arthur Schnitzler's Range of Theme," *Monatshefte*, Vol. 43, No. 7 (November 1951), 301-311.
34. When Alistaire Cook presented a television series of five of Schnitzler's works, the program was entitled "Games of Love and Death." The book containing the stories used in the dramatizations was likewise so named: Arthur Schnitzler, *Vienna 1900: Games with Love and Death* (New York, Baltimore: Penguin, 1974).
35. Cf. Bram Dijkstra, *Idols of Perversity. Fantasies of Feminine Evil in Fin-de-Siècle Culture* (New York, Oxford: Oxford University Press, 1986); also Gudrun Brokoph-Mauch, "Salome und Ophelia: Die Frau in der österreichischen Literatur der Jahrhundertwende," *Modern Austrian Literature*, Vol. 22, Nos. 3/4 (1989), 241-255.
36. Barbara Guth, *Emanzipation bei Arthur Schnitzler* (Berlin: Volker Spiess, 1978).
37. Robert O. Weiss, "Schnitzler's Ideas on *Schmutzliteratur* and the Marriage Contract," *Modern Austrian Literature*, Vol. 9, No. 2 (1976), 50-54.
38. Miriam J. Levey, *Governance and Grievance.* Habsburg Policy and Italian Tyrol in the Eighteenth Century (West Lafayette, Indiana: Purdue University Press, 1988) and William O. McCagg Jr., *A History of Habsburg Jews, 1670-1918* (Bloomington, Indiana: Indiana University Press, 1989).

39. Donald G. Daviau, "Hermann Bahr und der Antisemitismus, Zionismus und die Judenfrage," *Literatur und Kritik*, No. 221/222 (1989), pp. 21-41.
40. Stefan Zweig, "Keep out of Politics," *Query*, Book 2, London, 1938, p. 77.
41. John Heller, *Memoirs of a Reluctant Capitalist* (New York: Aaris Books, 1983).
42. Hugo von Hofmannsthal, "Ad me ipsum," *Aufzeichnungen* (Frankfurt am Main: Fischer, 1959), p. 237.
43. Hugo von Hofmannsthal, *Briefe 1900-1909* (Wien: Fischer, 1937), p. 67.
44. Erhard Buschbeck, "Bahr und Hofmannsthal im Gespräch," in: *Hugo von Hofmannsthal. Der Dichter im Spiegel der Freunde*, Helmut A. Fiechtner, ed. (Bern: Francke, 1963), pp. 232-235.
45. Andreas Härter, *Der Anstand des Schweigens*. Bedingungen des Redens in Hofmannsthals "Brief" (Bonn: Bouvier, 1989).
46. Donald G. Daviau, "Hugo von Hofmannsthal, Stefan George und der *Chandos Brief*. Eine neue Perspektive auf Hofmannsthals sogenannte Sprachkrise," in *Sinn und Symbol*. Festschrift für Joseph P. Strelka, ed. Karl Konrad Pohlheim (Bern: Peter Lang, 1989), pp. 219-248.
47. Maurice Maeterlinck, *The Treasure of the Humble* (New York: Dodd, Mead, 1911), pp. 61-62.
48. Ludwig Wittgenstein, *Tractatus logico-philosophicus. Logischphilosophische Abhandlung* (Frankfurt am Main: Suhrkamp, 1969), Propositions 5, 6 and 7.
49. "Union with the world through the union of two individuals," in "Ad me ipsum," *Aufzeichnungen*, p. 222.
50. "Language, yes, it is everything; but beyond it, behind it there is still something: the truth and the mystery." Hugo von Hofmannsthal, "Neue deutsche Beiträge," *Prosa IV*, (Frankfurt am Main: Fischer, 1957), p. 142.
51. Karl Kraus, *Half-Truths & One-and-a-Half Truths*. Selected Aphorisms. Edited and translated by Harry Zohn (Montreal: Engendra, 1976), pp. 63-65, 68f.
52. Raoul Auernheimer, *Das Wirtshaus zur verlorenen Zeit* (Wien: Ullstein, 1948), p. 87.
53. Ibid., p. 88.
54. Donald G. Daviau, "Hermann Bahr, Josef Nadler und das Barock,"

Vierteljahresschrift des Adalbert-Stifter-Instituts, Vol. 35, Nos. 3/4 (1986), pp. 171-190, and George C. Schoolfield, "Nadler, Hofmannsthal und 'Barock,'" ibid., pp. 157-170.

55. Donald G. Daviau, ed., *The Letters of Authur Schnitzler to Hermann Bahr* (Chapel Hill: The University of North Carolina Press, 1978).

56. Jay F. Bodine, "Paradigms of Truthful Literary and Artistic Expressivity—Karl Kraus and Vienna at the Turn of the Century," *Germanic Review*, Vol. 56, No. 2 (Spring 1981), pp. 41-50.

57. Katherine Arens suggests the term functionalism to describe Mauthner's language criticism. *Functionalism and Fin de siècle, Fritz Mauthner's Critique of Language* (New York: Lang, 1984), pp. 258-259.

58. Theodor Sapper, *Alle Glocken der Erde*. Expressionistische Dichtung aus dem Donauraum (Wien: Europa, 1974).

59. Frederic Morton, *A Nervous Splendor*. Vienna 1888/1889 (Boston/Toronto: Little, Brown and Company, 1979).

60. Jean de Gourgoing ed., *The Incredible Friendship*. The Letters of Emperor Franz Joseph to Frau Katharina Schratt (New York: State University of New York, 1966).

61. Adrian Clive Roberts, *Arthur Schnitzler and Politics* (Riverside: Ariadne Press, 1989).

62. Bruce F. Pauley, *Hitler and the Forgotten Nazis*. A History of Austrian National Socialism (Chapel Hill: The University of North Carolina Press, 1981).

Additional Bibliography

I.   Works in English:

Ilsa Barea, *Vienna. Legend and Reality* (London: Secker and Warburg, 1966).

Jean Cassou, Emil Langui, Nikolaus Pensner, *Gateway to the Twentieth Century. Art and Culture in a Changing World* (New York, Toronto, London: McGraw Hill, 1962).

Edward Crankshaw, *The Fall of the House of Habsburg* (New York: Viking, 1963).

Gerald Chapple and Hans Schulte, eds. *The Turn of the Century. German Literature and Art 1900-1915* (Bonn: Bouvier, 1983).

Amos Elon, *Herzl* (New York: Schocken, 1986.).

Jodef Fraenkel, ed. *The Jews of Austria: Essays on their Life, History and Destruction* (London: Valentine, Mitchell, 1967).

Friedrich Funder, *From Empire to Republic.* An Austrian Editor Reviews Momentous Years (New York: Albert Unger, 1963).

Wallace Dace, *National Theaters in the Larger German and Austrian Cities* (New York: Richards Rosen Press, 1980).

Allan Janik and Stephen Toulmin, *Wittgenstein's Vienna* (New York: Simon & Schuster, 1973).

William A. Jenks, *Vienna and the Young Hitler* (New York: Columbia University Press, 1960).

Lonnie Johnson, *Introducing Austria.* A Short History (Riverside: Ariadne, 1989).

William M. Johnston, *The Austrian Mind* (Berkeley: The University of California Press, 1972).

William M. Johnston, *Vienna, Vienna.* The Golden Age 1815-1914 (New York: Clarkson N. Potter, 1981).

Robert A. Kann, *A History of the Habsburg Empire 1526-1918* (Berkeley, Los Angeles, London: University of California Press, 1977).

Klemens von Klemperer, *Ignaz Seipel*. Christian Statesman in a Time of Crisis (Princeton, New Jersey: Princeton University Press, 1972).

Inge Lehne and Lonnie Johnson, *Vienna—The Past in the Present. A Historical Survey* (Wien: Bundesverlag, 1985).

Arthur J. May, *Vienna in the Age of Franz Josef* (Norman: University of Oklahoma Press, 1966).

Erika Nielsen, ed., *Focus on Vienna 1900. Change and Continuity in Literature, Music, Art and Intellectual History* (München: Fink, 1982).

William J. McGrath, *Dionysian Art and Populist Politics in Austria* (New Haven and London: Yale University Press, 1986).

Nicolas Powell, *The Sacred Spring*. The Arts in Vienna 1898-1918 (London: Casell and Collier MacMillan, 1974).

Marsha L. Rozenblit, *The Jews of Vienna 1867-1914*. Assimilation and Identity (Albany: State University of New York Press, 1983).

Carl E. Schorske, *Fin-de-siècle Vienna. Politics and Culture* (New York: Knopf, 1980).

Henry I. Schvey, *Oskar Kokoschka*. The Painter as Playwright (Detroit: Wayne State University Press).

Hilde Spiel, *Vienna's Golden Autumn* (London: Weidenfeld and Nicholson, 1987).

A. J. P. Taylor, *The Habsburg Monarchy 1809-1918* (London: Hamish Hamilton, 1960).

Peter Vergo, *Art in Vienna 1898-1918* (London: Phaidon, 1975).

Robert Waissenberger, *Vienna 1890-1920* (New York: Rizzoli, 1984).

Joseph Wechsberg, *The Vienna I Knew*. Memories of a European Childhood (Garden City, New York: Doubleday, 1979).

Richard Weininger, *Exciting Years*. Ed. by Rodney Campbell (Hicksville, N.Y.: Exposition Press, 1978).

C. E. Williams, *The Broken Eagle. The Politics of Austrian Literature from Empire to Anschluss* (New York: Harper & Row, 1974).

II. **Works in German**

Klaus Amann and Albert Berger, eds. *Österreichische Literatur der dreissiger Jahre* (Wien: Böhlau, 1985).

Maria Auböck, et al. *Wien um 1900. Kunst und Kultur* (Wien: Brandstätter, 1985).

Roger Bauer et al., eds., *Fin de siècle. Zur Literatur und Kunst der Jahrhundertwende* (Frankfurt am Main: Klostermann, 1977).

Erich Alban Berg, *Als der Adler noch zwei Köpfe hatte: ein Florilegium 1898-1918* (Graz: Styria, 1980).

Peter Berner, Emil Briggs and Wolfgang Mantel, eds. *Wien um 1900. Aufbruch in die Moderne* (Wien: Verlag für Geschichte und Politik, 1986).

Otto Breicha und Gerhard Fritsch, eds. *Finale und Auftakt. Wien 1898-1914* (Salzburg: Otto Müller, 1964).

Franz Endler, *Österreich zwischen den Zeilen* (Wien, München, Zürich: Molden, 1973).

Jens Malte Fischer, *Fin de siècle. Kommentar einer Epoche* (München Winkler, 1978)

Otto Friedländer, *Letzter Glanz der Märchenstadt: das war Wien um 1900* (Wien: Gardena Verlag, 1969).

Albert Fuchs, *Geistige Strömungen in Österreich 1867-1918* (Wien: Löcker, 1978).

Ulrich Greiner, *Der Tod des Nachsommers* (München: Hanser, 1979).

Ernst Haeusserman, *Das Wiener Burgtheater* (Wien, München, Zürich: Molden, 1975).

Johannes Hawlik, *Der Bürgerkaiser.* Karl Lueger und seine Zeit (Wien, München: Herold, 1985).

Fred Hennings, *Die Ringstrasse.* Symbol einer Epoche (Wien: Amalthea, 1977).

Franz Kadrnoska, ed. *Aufbruch und Untergang österreichischer Kultur zwischen 1919 und 1938* (Wien: Europa, 1981).

Jacques Le Rider, *Der Fall Otto Weininger.* Wurzeln des Antifeminismus und Antisemitismus (Wien: Löcker, 1985).

Heinz Lunzer, *Hofmannsthals politische Tätigkeit in den Jahren 1914-1917* (Frankfurt am Main: Peter Lang, 1981).

Lucian O. Meysels, *In meinem Salon ist Österreich: Berta Zuckerkandl und ihre Zeit* (Wien, München: Herold, 1984).

Jens Rieckmann, *Aufbruch in die Moderne. Die Anfänge des Jungen Wien* (Königstein/Ts: Athenäum, 1985).

Hartmut Scheible, *Literarischer Jugendstil in Wien* (München, Zürich: Artemis, 1984).

Hans Tietze, *Wien: Kultur/Kunst/Geschichte* (Wien: Dr. Hans Epstein, 1931).

Gotthart Wunberg, ed., *Das junge Wien. Österreichische Literatur- und Kunstkritik 1887-1902*, 2 vols. (Tübingen: Niemeyer, 1976).

Peter Altenberg

Andrew W. Barker

"Ein Spiegel sie der Dinge um sich her!"

"Be a mirror of the things around you!"

"Die Kunst ist Kunst, das Leben ist das Leben, aber das
Leben künstlerisch zu leben ist die Lebenskunst"

"Art is art, life is life, but to live life artistically is the art of life"

Despite the intensive revival of interest in fin-de-siècle Vienna the name of Peter Altenberg seemingly remains consigned to the periphery of literary history and critical attention. Yet in his own day he attracted the interest of many leading progressive figures not only in literature but also in the fields of art, architecture, and music. In 1903/4 he worked in close association with Adolf Loos, editing the pioneering art journal *Kunst, Monatsschrift für Kunst und alles Andere* (Art. Monthly for Art and Everything Else). In 1909 Oskar Kokoschka painted Altenberg's portrait; in 1912 Alban Berg set five of his texts to music. The performances of two of these so-called "Altenberg Lieder" brought about one of Vienna's most notorious musical riots at a concert organized by Arnold Schoenberg on March 31, 1913. Thomas Mann said of Altenberg that reading his work was like "love at first sound" ("Liebe auf den ersten Laut").[1]

Karl Kraus, the most acutely perceptive and unforgiving of men, never lost his admiration for Altenberg, putting up with his wildly extravagant behavior as he did for few others. The measure of Kraus's early esteem for Altenberg may be judged from the fact that Altenberg alone of the "Young Vienna" writers escaped inclusion in Kraus's mordant attack on their foibles and mannerisms in *Die demolierte Literatur* ("Literature demolished") of 1896. A list of Altenberg's contemporary admirers reads like a roll call of Central Europe's most gifted and innovative creators and would appear to provide the poet with impeccable credentials. Indeed, such was his standing that in 1914 he was nominated jointly with Arthur Schnitzler for the Nobel Prize for literature. The outbreak of war, however, led to the suspension of the award for that fateful year, and when it was resumed it went instead to Romain Rolland. Yet for all the esteem in which Altenberg was held by the great and the good, he has still to find anything more that a marginal place in the twentieth century repertoire.

What, one is forced to wonder, are the reasons behind the comparative neglect of a once highly esteemed author? To answer this question fully in Altenberg's case would require a longer essay than possible here, but it may be in order to dwell briefly upon the possible causes of Altenberg's eclipse before embarking upon a survey of the life and work of this eccentric figure once dubbed the "Verlaine of the Ringstraße."

That the judgements and opinions of academic critics and literary historians play a crucial part in determining the nature of the literary canon is now widely accepted. One needs only to look at the work of F.R. Leavis to perceive how one man's espousal of certain writers can effect the re-assessment of a literary corpus as wide-ranging and diverse as the English novel of the 19th and 20th centuries. That Altenberg has had short shrift from the people who help determine the nature of literary merit may stem from a number of seemingly divergent but often related reasons. First of all he is an Austrian, and Austrian literature has often made slower headway in the academic consciousness than "German" literature. Compare, for example, the relative attention paid to the Austrian realists Saar and Eschenbach and to the Germans Raabe and Storm. This may be a reflection of comparative worth, but it may also reflect the fact that the historiography of literature written in German was for long conditioned by the concerns of frequently (North) German (Protestant) scholars. Be that as it may, a fairly typical latterday example of the still inconsistent treatment of major Austrian figures may be found in the pseudo-authoritative *Handbuch des deutschen Romans,* which despite the inclusion of such "honorary Germans" as Kafka and Musil makes no mention of a novelist of the stature of Heimito von Doderer.[2]

Although he became a Roman Catholic in 1900, probably under the influence of Karl Kraus, Peter Altenberg was born a Jew, and his work was consigned to the flames by the Third Reich as an example of "degenerate art." Now it could be objected that other Jewish writers have not suffered such a permanent eclipse, but it was Altenberg's lot to be not only an

Austrian and a Jew but also to write almost exclusively in forms which tend to resist the classifying urges of the academic critic and arbiter of taste. Altenberg's preferred form is neither dramatic nor lyrical nor narrative but often a mélange of all three, the prose poem, the fragmentary conversation, the aperçu. His chosen style is what he terms the "telegram style of the soul" ("Telegramm-Stil der Seele"), a style which will portray a person in one sentence, a spiritual experience on one page, a landscape in one word.[3] Egon Friedell, the renowned cultural historian and friend of Altenberg, believed that Altenberg's style contained the essence of his appeal to the modern age, an age which has so little time to spare: "For him it is never a question of saying something as beautifully as possible but of saying it as precisely and as succinctly as possible. What he wants is not beauty but truth, for he is convinced that the truth also always contains beauty."[4]

Altenberg usually referred to his more extended pieces as "Sketches" or "Studies," but such labels do little to convey adequately the range and flavor of the best of his intense miniatures. Perhaps they are best seen not in the context of conventional literary classification at all but rather in the context of extreme precision, expressiveness, and wit which we find in such a work as Arnold Schoenberg's *Three Little Orchestral Pieces* of 1910. In his attempts to capture the "substance of the novel" while at the same time suppressing the "long-winded analyses" and "superfluous descriptions" associated with the genre in its nineteenth century guise,[5] Altenberg produced his own "Rustic Novel," the "Roman am Lande" which appeared in 1896 in his first collection entitled *Wie ich es sehe* ("How I See Things"). Karl Kraus was of the opinion that one piece of Altenberg's was worth as much as an entire Viennese novel;[6] there can be few shorter novels than this in any language:

> George, the exceedingly handsome gardener's lad at the market garden loves Frau R of the villa R with its linden park.
>
> He has not left the place for four years, which lies vis-à-vis.
> Mornings and evenings the winds come laden with limes.
> The job is bad, the food is bad, the master is bad - -.
> George sleeps in the greenhouse. Everything is open and the night scents are good - -.
> Damnation! His mistress cannot sleep and in the greenhouse youth blossoms and breathes- - -.

He has but one thought: "Linden Princess" and "when" and "how" - - - !?
Then the greenhouse-door rattles - - - - damnation! The mistress!
But she, the princess in the Linden park, rushes unstoppably towards him, on the path of disappointments, of wisdom, of time - - -.
"She gave me cigarettes," he once said, " I kissed her hand - -."
Then he looks out again "from the garret of life" and sees the long endless road - - -.
Damnation! The mistress cannot sleep and in the greenhouse youth blossoms and breaths - - -.
Frau R. sleeps, sleeps - - -.
Damnation - - -!
Mornings and evenings the winds come laden with limes.

If his being an Austrian Jew working in a medium which it is hard to classify has contributed to Altenberg's neglect, how is it, one might object, that Robert Walser, the Swiss writer of prose miniatures who like Altenberg suffered mental disorder (and who, incidentally, had no high opinion of Altenberg), has fared so much better in terms of critical acclaim? There is no easy answer to this except to adduce what is perhaps a further determining factor in Altenberg's failure to attract widespread critical attention. That factor may well be a certain fastidiousness on the part of the critics, for what could have brought Altenberg lasting fame had he lived in Paris has brought a rather different response from the sober-sides who so often write on things Germanic. Peter Altenberg was an extremely bizarre man indeed. He was unable to regulate his intake of either drugs or alcohol and is reported by Adolf Loos to have required 24 bottles of Pilsner to enable him to sleep at night.[7] He presumably possessed a cast iron bladder. He had a life-long regard for women of ill repute and took what many will feel as an unhealthy interest in pubescent girls, even though he was attracted to them precisely because he felt that their beauty had not yet been tainted by sexual activity. Although he abused his body with toxic potions, Altenberg was paradoxically obsessed from an early age with dietary matters. This preoccupation, one he shared with Nietzsche, Wagner, and Mahler, reached its most sustained literary expression in *Pròdrŏmŏs* (1906), where Altenberg touchingly demonstrated his passion for the Greek notion of the healthy mind in the healthy body. He followed faddish diet after faddish diet and was convinced of the merits of strong purgatives. As he announced without undue bashfulness in *Fechsung* (1915): "I would rather die of diarrhoea than of constipation." He even made his father a birthday present of a laxative named Kurella. His mind, always likely to become overheated, grew increasingly unstable as he aged and as the abuse of his senses through narcotics increased. Altenberg was also rather unscrupulous in his regard for the money which well-meaning friends (especially Karl Kraus) raised for him. Indeed, writing in 1912 about his literary origins, Altenberg considered himself to be nothing more than a "Schnorrer."[8] Be that as it may, people always seemed willing to provide P.A. (as he was universally known) with regular sums of cash to finance his wayward life, knowing that it was given ultimately in the service of art or to finance his frequent contributions to children's charities. The great actor Josef Kainz, for instance, subsidized Altenberg to the tune of 50 Crowns per month while the poet's brother Georg allotted him the highest monthly sum, money taken from the family firm which he ran. Unfortunately the firm went bankrupt in 1905 and Peter Altenberg was reduced to applying for a hawker's license to peddle the jewelry which he had designed and produced.

Despite his frequent lapses from the highest standards of decorum Altenberg's personal appeal caused his friends to stand by him. Moreover, as an artist he was always taken most seriously by his own best contemporaries. Even they, however, could only smile and shrug when he tried to actualize his theory that if he ran really fast and flapped his arms strongly enough he could take off and fly like a bird. A critic of the 1970s might complain that Altenberg uses language with "criminal neglect"[9] but Karl Kraus, a linguistic purist if ever there was one, found nothing to cavil at in his handling of the German language. The love which Altenberg inspired received a lasting memorial in the commemorative *Das Altenbergbuch*, which Egon Friedell brought out in 1921 and which contains tributes not only from the Mann brothers, Thomas and Heinrich, but also from Hofmannsthal, Georg Kaiser, and Adolf Loos as well as a letter purporting to come from a barely literate Viennese prostitute lamenting the fact that never again would she hear the voice of her "dear, good Mr Peter." Altenberg was a Viennese celebrity of the first order, recognized and pointed out wherever he ventured, the subject of instantly recognizable caricatures in popular magazines and newspapers. As early as 1896 the critic Rudolf Strauß had characterized Altenberg as this "décadent par excellence,"[10] a man, who like Joseph Roth a generation later, lived out his alcoholic life at coffeeshop tables with no fixed abode beyond a cramped hotel room. Unlike Roth's, the walls of Altenberg's room were plastered with the nude pictures of ladies of his acquaintance, all in oak frames and bearing signatures. In Altenberg's view, the only indecent thing about nudity was to find nudity indecent. "Es gibt nur eine Unanständigkeit des Nackten - - - das Nackte *unanständig zu finden.*"[11] In the winter Altenberg's favorite haunt was the Café Central, while in summer he would frequent one of the street cafés on the Graben, dressed in his favorite suit with its loud checks, trousers at half mast, in sandals and with a pince-nez on a long cord dangling around his neck.

Altenberg's chosen life-style was thus noticeably at odds with the bourgeois norm, but his roots were in the comfortable ambience of the well-off Viennese middle classes. His tenuous relationship with the realities of his origins is nowhere better illustrated than in the rejection of his given name Richard Engländer in favor of the literary persona of Peter Altenberg. The change of name marked the writer's ultimate dissociation from his personal past: he took his nom de plume from a girl nicknamed Peter whom he met in the village of Altenberg on the Danube, a few miles upstream from the city of Vienna. The high incidence of literary pseudonyms is a marked feature of Viennese culture around the turn of the century, and much might be inferred from the reluctance of writers and artists to confront the public under their given names. A factor which must not be overlooked is the desire of Jewish authors to hide their racial identity behind less obviously Jewish-sounding names, but the ambivalent relationship of so many of the "Young Viennese" writers to "reality" in general has become a cliché of literary scholarship, and nowhere is this ambivalence so overtly announced as in the regard of such writers for the shifting nature of their public identity. Apart from the example of Peter Altenberg one could cite from the world of letters in Vienna Felix Biedermann, Siegmund Salzmann, und Egon Friedemann who become respectively Felix Dörmann, Felix Salten, and Egon Friedell. In the case of Richard Engländer it would seem that he disappeared totally into the literary persona of Peter Altenberg, never to re-emerge. The escape from the bourgeois past became a reality far more tangible and recognizable than the "real" Richard Engländer had ever been.

Richard Engländer had never been really at home in the world of the affluent circles which he came from. Unlike Hofmannsthal or Andrian, he was no prodigy but a late-comer to literature who did not publish his first book until 1896 when he was already 37 years of age. Until then his life had been one of increasing alienation from his background although his respect for French language and culture was something tangible which he brought with him from his respectable family home. Herr Moriz Engländer, the writer's father, was a well-off businessman and a devoted reader of Victor Hugo, whose picture adorned the wall over his bed. Like so many of the other writers of "Young Vienna" Altenberg was thus a typical merchant's son without the financial acumen of the father. Perhaps in Altenberg's case the love of French civilization he found in his family home fired in him the wish to devote his life to art and beauty regardless of the comforts and demands of respectable society. His espousal of "la Bohème" certainly stands in marked contrast to the often thoroughly bourgeois lifestyle and aspirations of so many of his artistic contemporaries in Vienna around the turn of the century. Not for him the safe haven of the Austrian diplomatic corps ultimately sought by Leopold von Andrian, otherwise perhaps the most consistent "aesthete" among his contemporaries in the "jeunesse dorée." In the late 1870s and early 1880s Altenberg did certainly make some attempts at a socially acceptable mode of living: he followed his father's wishes and studied law, later attempting medicine, but returning to law after making nothing of medical studies. There was also an interval in Stuttgart, where he attempted with no visible success to learn about the book trade. Nevertheless, the Stuttgart interlude taught him the merits of acquiring what in those days was termed "a good hand," that is to say, clear and legible handwriting. Indeed, Altenberg's stylish calligraphy was to remain a feature of his mode of working even amid the growing chaos of his later life. So clear were his manuscripts that his publisher Fischer always gave them to apprentice printers to set, but for Altenberg this only produced more anguish because their stumbling attempts led to galley proofs littered with errors. As he ruefully noted in *Vita ipsa* at the very end of his life, even here he was thus the victim of his own merits. Any merits which the young Richard Engländer possessed were not immediately apparent to his father, who was much aggrieved at his son's failure to adapt to the life of the bourgeoisie. As early as 1882 he had sought medical opinion about his son's "condition," the doctor diagnosing "Berufsunfähigkeit," the constitutional inability to pursue a career. This failure to settle down and espouse a career helped bring about the termination of Altenberg's relationship with his mother, whom he adored. Despite the rupture in his life which this caused she always remained his ideal of feminine beauty, and her image recurs in one guise or another on innumerable occasions in his writing. She remained the ultimate inspiration for the many "wunderschöne Frauen" who people the pages of his books with their delicate limbs, graceful hands and feet. The same type of beauty is instantly recognizable in the female portraits of Altenberg's good friend Gustav Klimt, a beauty which proclaims there is no such thing as too slim, only too fat.

One day in 1894 Arthur Schnitzler lighted upon Altenberg as he sat in the Café Central, busily engaged in writing notes. Demanding to see them, Schnitzler must have appreciated their worth quickly, for before long at a literary soirée at the home of Richard Beer-Hofmann some of Altenberg's work was declaimed to great effect. Many years later an account of this literary début by Altenberg appeared in the collection *Semmering 1912* entitled "So wurde ich." Looking back, the author recalls how he had before him a newspaper account of the disappearance of a young girl on her way to a music lesson. Affected deeply by her unaccountable fate, he wrote down the sketch entitled "Lokale Chronik," at which point, he remembers, Schnitzler entered the room accompanied by Hofmannsthal, Salten, and Beer-Hofmann. The gathering at Beer-Hofmann's home took place on the following Sunday, though it would appear from Altenberg's account that he himself was possibly absent from the party, for on the following Wednesday Hermann Bahr, who had been present, wrote to Altenberg requesting material for his newly established magazine *Die Zeit*. Peter Altenberg's literary career was now underway although his first efforts did not come out in Bahr's journal but in the ephemeral journal *Liebelei*. Richard Engländer would soon have disappeared forever, and the stream of prose poems, sketches, and aphorisms had begun to flow. It would flow unabated until the poet's sad and debilitated end in January 1919.

Important though Hermann Bahr's original encouragement was, of perhaps even greater significance was the role played by Bahr's greatest foe, the satirist Karl Kraus. According to Altenberg in "So wurde ich" it was Kraus, the scourge of the Viennese aesthetes and all their works, who sent a packet of Altenberg's sketches to the prestigious publishing house of Samuel Fischer in Berlin, recommending Altenberg to him as an "original, a genius." Out of this series of apparently chance meetings there finally appeared Altenberg's first and possibly finest collection of prose miniatures entitled *Wie ich es sehe* (1896). As was the case with most of the young generation of Austrian writers Altenberg's work was thus published not in his own country but in Berlin. Many questions remain unanswered, however, about the time between Beer-Hofmann's soirée in 1894 and the emergence to considerable acclaim of Altenberg's first book. In an early English-language contribution Randolph Klawiter asserts that Kraus "happened to read some of Altenberg's vignettes" and then "sent a bundle of them to Dr. Samuel Fisher," a statement which hardly accounts for the clear sense of formal progression which marks much of *Wie ich es sehe* and which from the outset has generally failed to engage critical attention.[12] In his biographical essay Camillo Schaefer urges caution with respect to Kraus's role in helping to establish Altenberg's literary career,[13] but Altenberg clearly had certain things in common with Karl Kraus: his view of nature, the longing for the harmonious unity of man, plants and animals and an openness towards feminine sensuality and sexuality at odds with the hypocrisies of the age. Like Karl Kraus Altenberg also displays a fundamental distrust of the notion of technological "progress" which marks him as yet another Austrian writer whose work betrays what Karl Mannheim would term a "conservative style" of thought. Karl Kraus was convinced above all that Altenberg was an *honest* writer, that there was nothing phony, affected, or sham about him. Peter Altenberg believed that, come what may, truthfulness ("Wahrhaftigkeit") would always prevail over a sham existence ("Lebenslüge.")[14]

The reading public took instantly to Altenberg's work, and in the opinion of the critic Jost Hermand he stood higher in public esteem than Thomas Mann at the turn of the century.[15] Initial critical reaction to Altenberg was swift and favorable too with positive evaluations of *Wie ich es sehe* coming from both Bahr and Hofmannsthal. If anything, Hofmannsthal appears somewhat bemused by the work and he also tends to condescend towards Altenberg in a manner which has persisted among critics until the present day. Because Altenberg led a life which seemed devoid of profession, order, a life devoted to the art of observation and the preservation in words of the flavor of a moment, the view has arisen, fostered by Hofmannsthal's original review, that Altenberg is a totally haphazard, naive and willful writer, who above all is representative of some hazily construed "Viennese Impressionism." There is, to be sure, a good measure of truth in such an assessment of Peter Altenberg, but this is by no means the whole story. Egon Friedell certainly tried as early as 1909 to dispel such notions in his postscript to *Bilderbögen des kleinen Lebens* ("Illustrated Broadsheets of Humble Life"). Though he does not mention Bahr's name specifically, it is clear that Friedell sees Altenberg as fulfilling to the letter Hermann Bahr's notion of modernity as the synthesis of Romanticism and Naturalism, for he dubs him "der erste naturalistische Romantiker" (the first naturalistic Romantic).[16] Altenberg's discomfort at the failure of a writer such as Hofmannsthal to grasp the significance of his book is evident if one compares the second edition of *Wie ich es sehe* with the first. The collection is now prefaced by a long quotation, suitably adapted without any acknowledgment by Altenberg, from Huysmans' seminal novel of 1884 *A Rebours (Against the Grain)*. The passage selected by Altenberg for his new Preface concerns the prose poem and is clearly to be understood as a conscious attempt by the author to reinforce the reader's perception of the work's formal qualities. Huysmans' Duc Des Esseintes is tired of a "literature attacked by organic diseases, weakened by intellectual senility, exhausted by syntactical excesses, sensitive only to the curious whims that excite the sick."[17] His literary heroes are Baudelaire and Mallarmé, both past masters of the prose poem which is Des Esseintes' favorite form, containing within "its small compass and in concentrated form the substance of a novel while dispensing with the latter's long-winded analyses and superfluous description."[18] It demands the utmost precision and care in the choice of every word; every adjective must be "sited with such ingenuity and finality that it could never be legally evicted and would open up such wide vistas that the reader could muse on its meaning, at once precise and multiple, for weeks on end."[19] This is not literature for the masses but "an intellectual communion between a hieratic writer and an ideal reader, a spiritual collaboration between a dozen persons of superior intellect scattered across the world, an aesthetic treat available to none but the most discerning."[20] For Huysmans' Duke, and for Peter Altenberg also, the prose poem thus represents "the dry juice, the osmazome of literature, the essential oil of art."[21]

At his best Altenberg can live up to the demands set by Huysmans' trend-setting hero, in whose literary manifesto is revealed a dissatisfaction with prevalent narrative forms and a sober skepticism which might surprise those who regard him (and Altenberg too) purely as examples of literary decadence. The dissatisfaction with ornament for ornament's sake, the desire for an aesthetic functionalism which returns artistic form to basic principles reveals very clearly why Altenberg should prove such an attractive figure to Karl Kraus, Adolf Loos, and the composers of the "Second Viennese School." who sensed in him a reformatory zeal akin to their own. Indeed, Altenberg can justifiably be seen as probably the earliest example of that aesthetic minimalism which was to become such a marked feature of Viennese art in the early part of the 20th century and which was to have world-wide repercussions.

Peter Altenberg was obsessed with watching people, places, events, the natural world. He was obsessed with recording his observations and reproducing them in such a way as to form a comment (and often a very direct one) upon the age and place in which he lived. Nevertheless, his art is often oblique, fleeting, elusive, though sometimes it can appear silly, trivial, grindingly repetitive, and ultimately pointless. Often, however, it is remarkable concrete and politically aware and always tries to confront rather than evade reality as Altenberg saw it. Despite his alcoholism and drug-addiction his clear-sightedness sometimes permitted him a vision of the late Habsburg society granted to few others at a time when most of the Austrian bourgeoisie still basked in Stefan Zweig's "Golden Age of Security." In the words of Egon Friedell, Peter Altenberg was a "seer in the double meaning of the word: a seer of things present and a seer of things to come."[22] In the piece "Coming to a close" ("Es geht zu Ende") Altenberg displays his social and political awareness in a way totally mis-understood by Hofmannsthal, who contended that Altenberg's work lacked any sense of historical awareness.[23] Altenberg's critics from Bahr and Hofmannsthal onward have all been struck by his unique voice, his own special "tone," which is especially difficult to catch in translation, for so often Altenberg's transparency comes across as childish superficiality. Yet even in translation, inadequate though this may be, there is no mistak-ing the menace in the narrative voice of "Es geht zu Ende."[24] It is a barely veiled threat to the old order, the autumn of whose ascendancy is placed in the context of an autumnal landscape:

A sunny day - - -, In the sunny spots warmth, heat - - in shady spots cellar-cold. In the air there is the scent of withered leaves and fresh moist earth. In the river meadows stand short thin heliotrope strips, colchium autumnale. Brown damsel flies bathe in the sunlight - - -.
On the white road between the dark brown pear trees the Duke drives with his son in an open carriage. A tiger skin lies over their feet. As they pass by the small sundrencned cemetery they remove their hats with a deep sweep.
The servant on the box makes the sign of the cross.
Only the fat coachman sits unmoving - - he is on duty.
He stares at the white sunny road with the autumn leaves - - -.
In the garden of a villa red and yellow dahlias are in bloom. On a bench in the autumn sun there sits a young girl. She is dreaming: "Will the ball-gowns have round necklines this year?!"
The dahlias are grown in all colours - those are the harmonies of culture.
In the ducal garden they stand in thick clumps, mottled red and yel-low, white and mauve, pink and rust-red, like claret and saffron, like shimmering alps and the colour of cinnamon - - -.
The carriage draws in through the cast-iron trellised gate with the gold rosettes. The servant springs from the box. The old duke and the young duke climb out. The servant bows low. Only the fat

coachman sits unmoving. He stares at the white sunny avenue with its autumn leaves - - -.

The bright birches tremble. The crows caw in the skies "kraa - - - kraa!"

The dahlias stand there all colors, the bright ones gleam like butter, the dark ones are as dull as velvet.

Aristocrats and villa dwellers! Still you sit in the gardens in the autumn sun and travel the roads in your open carriages - - -!

Still you may drink the golden lights of the last autumn days, you, the dahlias and the crows - - - kraa!

Here death and decay are in the air, the late flowering of the autumn only half masks the signs of finality in this piece. Egon Friedell, who knew Altenberg so well that he ironically dubbed himself the Eckermann in Altenberg's life, believed that there was an almost religious quality to that side of his nature which was not that of the impassive observer but of an ethically motivated reformer. As Altenberg's career progressed he became increasingly obsessed with the notion of helping to create a new and better species of humankind through a carefully controlled diet and through man's emulation of the example set by woman. Women, he felt, were ideally higher creatures than men, who needed to be redeemed from the grossness of male sexual lust. They could not, however, redeem themselves; that was the function of the "higher" man whom Altenberg envisaged. Altenberg's life, he believed, was devoted to an extraordinary enthusiasm for the divine work of art which is the female form: "Gottes Kunstwerk 'Frauenleib,'"25 while Friedell commented that he had "a heightened and hitherto unparalleled ability to place himself in the spiritual life of the woman.... There has never before been a poet who even came close to him in this respect. He is the first real psychologist of those mysterious creatures who unceasingly accompany and determine our lives but who always remain foreign and incomprehensible to us."26

Inevitably regarded by many as no more than a harmless eccentric fool, Altenberg was often happy to exploit the immunity lent him by his public image to express with freedom his analysis of what we now know with the hindsight of history to be a doomed way of life. Nowhere does the sharpness of Altenberg's vision show through more than in the piece entitled "At Home," the last of the "Lake-side" ("See-Ufer") cycle in *Wie ich es sehe*, written some twenty years before the world of the aristocrats and villa dwellers vanished forever. Here alienated servants wait sullenly upon a class which lives in blissful ignorance of the true feelings of the people who service their every whim and who, in the vision of the future which emerges from this item, will be the ultimate victors in the looming battle: "And when everything has collapsed in ruins and ashes the little light brown clouds of steam will still curl peacefully upwards from the servants' coffee."[27] Altenberg might not have had any great degree of contact with the industrial proletariat, but he knew intimately the lives of that great swath of the population which was "in service." Moreover, he foresaw the way of the future in *Pròdròmòs* when he proclaimed: "There will come a time when all working people will withdraw their labor unless they can do their work in an area with first-class ventilation and well-oxygenated clean air."

Peter Altenberg's dissatisfaction with the present, so clearly articulated in *Wie ich es sehe*, is also apparent in his next work *Ashantee* (1898). In this collection he idealizes the primitive unspoiled freedom of the African savage: a "savagery" which on closer inspection turns out to be a prejudiced figment in the imagination of an overripe culture. In this work the author makes no secret of his erotic response to the ebony-skinned beauties who not only titillate his senses but who also, he feels, with their instant attractiveness act as mediators between very different cultures. The inspiration for Altenberg's observations was the visit to Vienna of an entire village from the African Gold Coast, erected in the city as a "tableau vivant" for the inspection and appraisal of a curious Viennese public. This fundamentally insulting notion was neatly turned on its head by Altenberg to reveal the crass voyeurism of the supposedly superior and more "civilized" Austrians.

In *Was der Tag mir zuträgt* (1901) ("What the day brings me") he responded to the widespread curiosity aroused by his writing by providing his readership with a "Selbstbiographie" which, apart from falsifying his age by three years, provides valuable insights into Altenberg's conception of himself as an author. He stresses in particular the importance of the perceptive subjective self and the overriding importance of the faculty of sight; he compares this sense with the riches of the Rothschild family: "*Auge, Auge, Rothschild-Besitz des Menschen!*" He is also noticeably modest about his achievements, denying their status as works of literary art by dubbing them simply "extracts of life." If in this often exquisite collection Altenberg continued along the lines which had earlier brought him considerable acclaim but no real financial certainty, his next work *Pròdròmòs* (Greek = precursor) brought a certain change of tone and subject matter. Though still a compilation of short studies and sketches as before, the book also tried to present his reading public with an outline of his "philosophy," which he somewhat arcanely summarizes as "ein erster Versuch einer physiologischen Romantik" ("an initial attempt at physiological Romanticism"). Heavily indebted to Nietzsche (whom Altenberg denied ever having read), it is often a chaotic book, as Altenberg cheerily acknowledges in one of the main asides which are a constant feature of his work here: "'But put some system and order into your insights,' a well-wisher said to me. To put system and order into insights is like wanting to drown a few vital truths in a dead sea of deceit."

In a thoroughly random and aphoristic fashion *Pròdrŏmŏs* promulgates Altenberg's visions of the better life, one which will reflect the age's new-found enthusiasm for the Olympic ideal of the healthy mind in the healthy body. Although it is a vision which must have struck many of his Austrian contemporaries as bordering upon lunacy, it is one which our era with its ever-growing awareness of health foods, proper exercise, and the ecology of the planet will not find so bizarre. Although we may not share Altenberg's obsession with laxatives and processed foods which require no digestive effort, he is nonetheless recognizably of our own age in his insistence upon proper sleep, fresh air, sensible footware, and the purposeful exercise of the body: "Luft und Haut sind Liebesleute. Sie wollen sich vermählen, trotz aller Fährlichkeiten!" ("Air and skin are lovers. They wish to be joined together despite all the dangers")."

What is so touching about Altenberg is his almost complete failure to live up to his ideals despite his best efforts. His view of alcohol as "a weapon of life in the hands of the mature connoisseur" will find a ready acceptance among the many who enjoy it and can cope with it, but for him it merely contributed to the miseries of his existence. Though Altenberg's practice was so at odds with his ideals, in certain respects he stuck tenaciously to his views on hygiene and diet. He refused to wear underclothes and adopted a type of dress notably at odds with the modish restrictions and constrictions of a corseted age. His hostility to the exigencies of fashion is most forcefully expressed in the piece entitles "Mode" ("Fashion") in *Märchen des Lebens* (1908), where he dismisses those who follow fashion as profoundly uncultured and servile to boot: "*Sich nach der Mode richten, ist bereits tiefste Unkultur. Es beweist die Sklavennatur.*" Ultimately, what Altenberg propagates with respect to food and clothing is also a counsel of despair in the knowledge that he has abused his own body (and mind) to an already intolerable degree. For *Pròdrŏmŏs* is the expression of the author's melancholy at his own condition, as when he writes of alcohol not as a positive force but as a substance "which fills in the dreadful abyss between what we are and what we should like to be, ought to be." Altenberg's existence, dominated by sleeping draughts, alcohol dependency, and the knowledge that the real world would always disappoint him was increasingly beset by melancholy. Yet in the face of this melancholy, which was heightened by the financial cares ensuing from the bankruptcy of the family firm, Altenberg could still shake a defiant fist. We read in *Pròdròmòs* :

> Melancholy is the appreciation of the distance between one's being and one's own possible, attainable ideals! Woe betide the man who does not suffer from melancholy! To find peace and contentment prematurely is to sign one's own surrender at Sedan! Melancholy is the voice of God within us, endlessly calling us to our duty to become God-like! This dark endless voice which sounds forth and prevents any coming to rest. Woe betide those who live their lives away in peace. Only when the summits have been conquered is there any lasting peace.

Altenberg continued to suffer spiritual torment, unable to still his fascination for the "eternally feminine" through an attachment to any single woman. Yet as a critic has pointed out,[28] Altenberg's "erotomania" remained essentially that of an onlooker, a voyeur even, despite his deep attachments to the actress Annie Kalmar, whom he "bequeathed" to Karl Kraus, to Lina, the estranged first wife of Adolf Loos, to Helen Nahowitz, who later married Alban Berg, and to a young, "moderately pretty"[29] girl from Hamburg, Helga Malmberg, whom he met in 1906 and who many years later wrote some vivid memoirs of her days with the aging and increasingly unstable poet.[30] In the collection entitled with considerable irony *Märchen des Lebens* ("Life's Fairytales") there appears a nightmarish passage dominated by insomnia and disillusion where Altenberg writes: "My hotel room grows light, my soul grows dark . . . now would be the fitting hour to go and hang myself from the window."

One has increasingly the impression of the clown singing out his torment to a public which can see only the figure of fun, the mask and not the reality. In "Ein Brief" ("A Letter") the writer tries bravely to make public his insight into the sort of women who fascinate him and humiliate him and who, he knows, are quite unworthy of his idealization of them:

> I wrote an impassioned letter to a sweet girl of low repute, portraying her in all her perfection from head to toe - - -.

> In the evening she had the waiter call me to her table at the Café L.
> "Yer wrote me a letter?!?"
> "Yes, yes indeed, I was so bold, Miss - - -"
> "Wot for?!?"
> Later on she learned who this letter writer was.
> Then she said to her gentlemen friends: "Yer'll never believe this,
> Peter Altenberg's wrote me this great passionate letter. Come 'ome
> wiv me, I'll show it yer - - -."
> And thus my letter did, in a certain respect, have some point.

At times the mood of this gloomy collection with its recurring motifs of sickness and the sanatoria with which the writer was already acquainted, comes close to the open misogyny of Otto Weininger, whose work was making a considerable impact upon the intellectual circles around Kraus and Loos, in which Altenberg constantly moved. Altenberg was, however, often accredited with a courtly attitude to women; Adolf Loos called him "the last troubador."[31], for the actress Anni Mewes he was "the last of the Knights," a "troubador amidst machines"[32], and here he laments that fate of man at the hands of the latterday "belle dame sans merci": "There is only one real delusion of grandeur: the belief of a man in the faithfulness of a beloved woman!"

Altenberg also laments his own fate, the fact that he has become a prisoner of the image he has so consciously and for so long cultivated; he rails against having to wear "the yoke of a poseur or a madman."[33] *Märchen des Lebens* bears witness then to a melancholy and disenchantment generally unperceived in Altenberg's writing, a man who has been duped just once too often: "ein vertrauender Mann ist ein Idiot" ("a trusting man is an idiot").[34] This collection is thus the product of a mind already stretched to the limit; it is obsessed with failure, rejection, and sickness to an extent studiously ignored by Karl Kraus when he came to make his collection of Altenberg's work in the late 1920s.[35] The publication of *Märchen des Lebens* did nothing to solve Altenberg's pecuniary worries, and his fiftieth birthday in 1909 was marked by the second of the Berlin critic Alfred Kerr's public collections for him (the first had been in 1904), but the sum raised was negligible. This merely served to confirm Altenberg's somewhat self-pitying view of himself as the archetypal neglected and misunderstood genius. His fiftieth birthday was also marked by Egon Friedell's postscript to Altenberg's sixth collection *Bilderbögen des kleinen Lebens*, an evaluation of his work which can still be read today with profit. (Friedell later incorporated the study into *Ecce*

Poeta (1912), his larger study of the poet.) Like Hugo von Hofmannsthal before him, Friedell sets too little store by the conscious aspect of Altenberg's creativity, regarding him as someone who writes utterly mechanically, much as a telegraph responds to an invisible electric current.[36] Above all, however, he views Altenberg as the artistic equivalent of the scientific researcher, as a passionate searcher after the hidden truths of existence. Friedell acknowledges the fragmentary and disparate impression which a superficial reading of Altenberg's work is almost bound to impart, but he explains it by referring to the extraordinary brevity and concision of Altenberg's which registers material just as a photographic plate responds to a fragmentary moment's exposure to light. He is thus eminently a writer for the modern age (here he takes up a theme broached by the writer himself in a section of the *Bilderbögen* headed simply "Peter Altenberg"). Altenberg is thus reminiscent both of modes of modern communication in their technical guise - photography, telegraphy - and of the tempo of "modern life" with its inability to devote space and time to expansive gesture but needing rather to communicate with minimum effort and maximum effect.[37] Altenberg's chosen forms combine brevity with precision and accuracy; he does not seek beauty for its own sake but rather truth, being convinced that truth by definition encompasses beauty. As we noted earlier, Hermann Bahr believed that truly "modern" art would ensue as a synthesis of Naturalism and Romanticism, a notion here taken up by Friedell, who regards Altenberg as a writer who supremely combines these apparently antithetical approaches to literary production. Above all else though he believes he is a *writer* par excellence, "He is not lyric poet, not a novelist and not a philosopher, he is a writer; a writer and nothing else."[38]

Although *Bilderbögen des kleinen Lebens* is the product of one of the most difficult periods in Altenberg's life, it is among his most impressive works and made an especially profound impact upon Karl Kraus. If in *Wie ich es sehe* Altenberg produced one of the (if not the) shortest novels in German, then in the *Bilderbögen* he wrote what must be among the shortest of dramas too, entitled "Alles geht seine Wege" (All things go their ways") and subtitled "A five-minute scene which actually lasts a year":

Courtroom.
The President of the Court rises:
"The industrialist Anton Romangshorn is hereby sentenced to 10 years hard labor for the murder of his wife Sartypa!"

In the public gallery the young Lieutenant Zarsky collapses unconscious.

One year earlier.
Cozy dining-room in red. Red lampshade, red silk stripes on the
table cloth and serviettes, red tulips on the table in red vases before
each plate.
Romangshorn: "You have made a Symphony in Red out of the dining-room, my dear romantic Sartypa - - -."
She: "You asked me to do something special for your new friend.
Quite honestly, I feel that our home has been desecrated by someone
who is a stranger to me. Every room speaks so marvelously and
clearly of our peace, the closeness of our hours together - - -. Then
suddenly someone is staring in at us with ice-cold unfeeling eyes!"
R.: I wouldn't have burdened you with it. But I have never known
two men in such different walks of life to be so much of one mind
as Zarsky and I. I am an industrialist but also a bit of a Romantic,
he is a Romantic yet also a serious soldier."
A bell rings.

The maid announces Lieutenant Zarsky.
R.: "My friend Lieutenant Zarsky - - - Sartypa!"
Z.: "I am only a soldier, but I feel a deep, deep friendship for your
husband."

They sit down to supper. The maid begins to serve - - -.

Z.: "A Symphony in Red, this table - - -."
She: "Should you find it amenable here with us, Lieutenant, then
next time I will make one in your favorite color! Which is it then?!"
Z.: "Green - - -."
She: "Fine, then instead of taking flowers I shall use ferns. I have
chosen Sole Mornay for the supper. It is one of our favorite dishes -
I hope it's one of yours . . ."
R.: "I do not wish to flatter the Lieutenant, but once you have got to
know him better - - -."
She: "Marie, pour the Lieutenant some more of our famous
'Chateau Romangshorn'."
As he drinks, bowing slightly towards Sartypa, the curtain falls.

Semi-debilitated and drug-dependent Altenberg was now to embark upon an extensive period of traumatic stays in nursing homes, mental hospitals, and eventually, worst of all, the "Steinhof" asylum for the severely mentally ill. In 1910 Altenberg's devoted friend Helga Malmberg conveyed to Karl Kraus a message from Altenberg, then in the "Nervenheilanstalt Inzersdorf," as a result of which there appeared in the *Fackel* of 22/9/1910 an appeal on behalf of the sick poet. The appeal was taken up by the whole of the popular Viennese press (an institution normally despised by Kraus), and this time the response was overwhelming. Yet only a couple of months prior to this Arthur Schnitzler had noted in his diary for 4/7/1910 that according to Kraus's nieces Peter Altenberg was reputed to be rich, and that his mendicant manner was simply a sign of his nervous disorder.

Whatever the truth about Altenberg's financial plight, it is clear that his creativity was not totally extinguished by his incarceration because in 1911 there appeared a further collection entitled *Neues Altes* ("Something New, Something Old"). As the title indicates, the mixture is much as before, even to the extent of material from *Märchen des Lebens* being reintroduced in the new collection. This, however, was by now a well-established practice of Altenberg's, as is obvious if one examines succeeding editions of *Wie ich es sehe* which by 1905 had incorporated many new pieces as well as much of the material from *Ashantee*. In the case of *Wie ich es sehe* this addition of extra material destroyed the balance of the book and vitiated the formal sense of progression and integration which distinguished the editions of 1896 and 1898. An examination of these editions will demonstrate evidence of both discrimination and formal cohesion, but by the time of *Neues Altes* it is hard to perceive any real ordering behind the items, many of which display all too clearly the author's self-obsession during these appallingly difficult years. Helga Malmberg relates in her book that Altenberg did not concern himself with the order in which his texts were eventually published, leaving it all to an official of Fischer, his Berlin publisher. *Neues Altes*, however, is notable as the source from which Alban Berg drew the textual inspiration for his revolutionary *Altenberg Lieder*, written in 1912 and first performed at the riotous concert on March 31, 1913. Arthur Schnitzler was at this concert, and reports on the rowdy scenes in the laconic style typical of his diaries.[39] He obviously disliked Berg's "silly songs," although Igor Stravinsky numbers them among our century's most perfect works of art.[40] Berg knew Altenberg, of course, and visited the sick writer in Steinhof. He appears in the sketch "Bekanntschaft" (Acquaintance") in *Neues Altes*, while his wife Helene, née Nahowski, is the inspiration for an ecstatic poem in the same volume entitled simply "H.N."[41] It is obvious from the poem that Altenberg was deeply attracted to Helene, a woman who clearly corresponded closely to his ideal of feminine beauty with her willowy tallness and her ash-blond hair falling almost to her waist. In addition to this love poem Altenberg also writes about the later Frau Berg in the impassioned "Besuch im einsamen Park" ("Visit to the lonely park"), a piece which first appeared in *Märchen des Lebens* before turning up again in *Neues Altes*, by which time Helene was already married to the composer. In spite of Altenberg's amorous inclinations the friendship of Berg and his wife with the poet lasted till his death in 1919.

That there were close ties between the Altenberg/Kraus/Loos set and Schoenberg and his acolytes has been succinctly pointed out by the musicologist Mosco Carner, who refers to Altenberg as "a kind of literary Erik Satie translated to the Vienna scene at the turn of the last century . . . Altenberg's credo was: 'Artist, remain true to yourself! Have the courage to confess to your nakedness!' (This might be Schoenberg speaking to his pupils)."[42] Carner sees this "emphasis on absolute truth and fidelity in art and on the prerogative of the modern artist to allow his private personality to saturate his work" as the "motto of all Viennese artists in the two decades before the First World War."[43] Carner even believes that Altenberg influenced Alban Berg's literary style with its plethora of meaningful dots and dashes and the simultaneous use of question and exclamation marks.[44] That Karl Kraus was clearly aware of the more than superficial links between Altenberg's art and that of the musical innovators in Vienna is evidenced by *Die Fackel* No 300 of 1910, where on opposite sides of the page he reproduces one of the songs from Schoenberg's cycle *Das Buch der hängenden Gärten* and Peter Altenberg's "Widmung (Sommerabend in Gmunden)" ("Dedication [Summer evening in Gmunden])."

Peter Altenberg's health remained at a low ebb for most of 1911, toward the end of which he had to face up to the end of his relationship with Helga Malmberg, the mainstay of his life in the sanatorium. In the autumn he left Inzersdorf and went to recuperate in the mountainous Semmering region south of Vienna; there, twenty years previously, he had enjoyed an intense but probably platonic relationship with Olga Waisnix, who was soon afterwards to become probably the greatest love in the life of Arthur Schnitzler. Altenberg spent the winter and early spring of 1912 on the Semmering, collecting material for the volume *Semmering 1912* which appeared in 1913. Much of the summer of 1912 was also passed there, high up in the easternmost reaches of the Alps. Financially cushioned by the considerable sum of money raised by the newspaper appeal, Altenberg revelled in the marvels of his natural surroundings and in his newly regained liberty. At the same time he was undergoing treatment for his alcoholism, but by November money was apparently running short once more, and the poet went back into the abyss from which for a time at least he seemed successfully to have emerged. By December 1912 Altenberg's condition was such that at the instigation of his brother Georg he was committed to the asylum "Am Steinhof," where he remained until the spring of 1913. Altenberg remained unconvinced of the necessity of this further incarceration as was also Arthur Schnitzler, a qualified doctor of medicine. He noted in his diary for April 20th, 1913 that Altenberg was as little, or as much, of a madman as he had ever been. During this period Altenberg wrote despairing letters to Karl Kraus and to his brother, but to little avail until Adolf Loos procured his release. In May 1913 Loos took Altenberg off to Venice, where he gave every impression of being cured. Altenberg spent the summer in Venice surrounded by caring friends like the Loos family and Karl Kraus, and moving in a circle which included his publisher Fischer, Ludwig Ficker, the editor of the Expressionist periodical *Der Brenner*, and Georg Trakl. Money problems continued to beset Altenberg, however, and the drinking cure appeared to have been unsuccessful. In a letter which Loos penned to Kraus in Vienna in October he reports that Altenberg was downing 18 bottles of beer a day.[45] Altenberg was nevertheless still undeniably productive, converting his impressions into instant art, as the second edition of *Semmering 1912* reveals with its cycle of sketches devoted to Venice. Moreover, his well-publicized physical and mental difficulties did little to diminish the esteem in which he was held. The writer may have felt spurned and unfulfilled, but the fact remains that when Altenberg's fortunes were so low he was nevertheless nominated for the Nobel literature award. The money from the prize, even though split between Altenberg and Schnitzler, would have helped him enormously, but as we saw, the outbreak of the Great War cancelled the award for 1914.

At the end of July 1914 Kaiser Franz Josef declared war on Serbia and inaugurated the chain of catastrophies which would fulfill the poet's prophesies about the future of his society. Only too soon the world of the villa owners and the landed gentry would crumble about them. Yet at this awesome juncture in world history Schnitzler's diary makes revealing reading, for his main concern on August 1st was not with the outbreak of war but with his wife's sense of disquiet at his sharing the Nobel Prize with Altenberg.[46]

The enthusiasm for war was notoriously great among many of Peter Altenberg's literary colleagues; many could not contain their patriotic fervor, as Thomas Mann notes with approval, contrasting Austrian writers with their fellow "intellectuals" in the German Reich.[47] There were notable exceptions, however; Schnitzler, most famously Karl Kraus, but also Peter Altenberg. Altenberg did not have it in him to castigate is world in the manner of a Karl Kraus, but he never showed publicly the slightest enthusiasm for the carnage. In his own less strident way he made clear enough his distaste for the war, the profiteers, and the Austrian Establishment in a manner which certainly did not alienate him from his champion Kraus.

Altenberg's circumstances, spiritual and material, remained strained, yet the first of his collections to appear during the war years, *Fechsung* ("Harvest") is, perhaps rather surprisingly, characterized often by a delightful humor besides displaying its awareness of the grim events of war. Where other writers composed battle hymns or wrote essays on the metaphysics of the German people, Altenberg went on as before with a collection pondering the depths of the female psyche and assessing the merits of laxatives. In his view both issues would survive the war. Altenberg's sense of humor is never far from the surface of his work, but in *Fechsung* it parades itself openly and in varying guises in such sections as the "Postscript to *Pròdrŏmŏs*" and the aptly-titled "Splitter" ("Splinters"), aphoristic aperçus which alternate with his usual sketches and studies:

> A happy couple: he does what she wishes - - - and she does what she wishes.

> "She has been so nice to me for almost half a year - - - !"
> Well, six weeks before Christmas, six weeks before her birthday, six weeks before her name-day and six weeks before your visit to her at the spa. That makes a whole half year!

> "What will you do when you lose me?!"
> "I'll find me someone better!"
> "In that case I'll stay with you!"

> For want of things to talk about one says the most appallingly tactless and indiscreet things.

Despite two final "grands amours" with Paula Schweitzer and the actress Anni Mewes, Altenberg increasingly succumbed to a feeling of isolation and failure, and as the war ground on, the writer's depressive obsession with himself came to dominate his two final works *Nachfechsung* ("Late Harvest") and *Vita Ipsa*, published in 1916 and 1918 respectively. These are works of an increasingly fragmentary and fragmented nature, as Altenberg noted in *Nachfechsung*: "My thought processes are getting shorter and shorter, and that means better and better because less and less time-consuming. I shall end up by saying nothing whatsoever. That will be the *best* thing of all."

That process of aesthetic reductionism, always a marked feature of Altenberg's work, has now progressed so far that he comes close to doubting the ability and validity of language to convey meaning at all. Yet he never seems to have seriously contemplated giving up writing, and *Vita Ipsa*, dedicated to "Frau Paula Demant Schweitzer," contains a further 284 items linked only by the fact that they are all "extracts of life." It would appear also that Altenberg's relationship with Kraus suffered considerable strain during the war years, as the satirist laconically notes in his letters to Sidonie Nadherny. Plagued as ever by financial cares, Altenberg observed caustically how Kraus's asceticism impelled him to purchase a motorcar while advising his impecunious friend that 300 crowns a month was ample income for a sickly 55-year old poet. As the war progressed Altenberg's situation deteriorated. His privilege of a free supper at the Graben Hotel, where he lodged, had to be withdrawn, while his beloved Paula married a Dr. Demant and went to live in Innsbruck in the summer of 1917.

Horrified by the slaughter of war, the people who ran it, and their motives for doing so, yet lacking the strategy or ability of Karl Kraus to counter the abuses he perceived, Altenberg grew increasingly aware of his own mortality and the imminence of his death. In *Vita Ipsa*, for instance, he pictures his own funeral while also betraying a preoccupation with reaching at least his sixtieth birthday, knowing that his health, long problematic, had reached a point where an inherently robust constitution could no longer cope. It comes as no surprise that the book on which Altenberg was working virtually up to his death should be entitled *Mein Lebensabend* ("The Evening of My Life"). Posthumously published in 1919, its 333 items demonstrate above all else the author's obsessive despair with himself, a failing drug addict and alcoholic, incapacitated by a fall down the hotel steps while in a drunken stupor. At times his spirits revived, but his already strong sense of isolation was only compounded by the deaths in quick succession of his aged father, Gustav Klimt (6 February 1918), and Egon Schiele (7 October 1918), aged only 28 and victim of the Spanish influenza then ravaging the country.

Altenberg's end came not long after the demise of the Dual Monarchy. The country was riven by strife, the writer was reduced to living off vegetable scraps, but he continued to write virtually to the end. On December 21 he wrote: "The night before last, at 1 a.m. on December 19 a full glass of wine spilled onto my linen and I slept on peacefully in the icy wetness with the windows wide open. In the morning the bronchial catarrh of my youth returned. Sunt certi denique fines!" Peter Altenberg died on 8 January 1919, aged 59 years and 3 months. Karl Kraus gave the funeral oration on 11 January before a gathering of some 400 mourners, among them Kraus's archenemy Hermann Bahr, Arnold Schoenberg, and Adolf Loos, who designed the memorial stone for the dead artist. As he had requested in his autobiographical sketch in "Was der Tag mir zuträgt," it bore the inscription "Er liebte und sah" —he loved and saw. Altenberg was allocated a "grave of honor" ("Ehrengrab") by the municipality of Vienna, a distinction reserved for eminent figures from the world of arts and letters. His death unleashed a deluge of words of remembrance in the press and literary journals; for Adolf Loos at least Vienna had buried its greatest literary son since the death of Franz Grillparzer.[48] Moreover, far from dying a pauper, Altenberg bequeathed a sum reputed to be in the vicinity of 100,000 crowns to the Society for the Prevention of Cruelty to Children ("Kinder-Schutz- und Rettungsgesellschaft").[49] Reactions to Altenberg's death showed just how special his standing in the world of Austrian letters was. Certainly his engaging personality and unique approach to life come across clearly in the many tributes to him; and the affection he inspired was widespread and genuine.

Assessments of Altenberg's status as a writer are bound to be subjective and divergent, as I tried to indicate at the beginning of this essay, and I would not feel it proper to make categorical statements here about his literary "worth." There is much in his writing which seems repetitious and flat, much that was written for the moment with no thought of posterity, but there are also times when a very special quality shines through his often elusive prose. As Robert Musil, a stern enough judge, concluded when reading Altenberg: ". . . is he a great poet? Feeling: mostly no, sometimes yes."[50] Franz Kafka responded more warmly to Altenberg's art: "For Altenberg is really a poet. His little anecdotes reflect his entire life. And every step, every gesture he makes guarantees the veracity of his words. Peter Altenberg is a genius of trivialities, a strange idealist who discovered the beauties of the world like cigarette-butts in the ashtrays of cafés."[51] Perhaps, then, as we approach our own fin-de-siècle, we may renew our acquaintanceship with the work of an exquisite miniaturist who in his ability to "love and see" extracted poetry from the most mundane and everyday sources. Not without good reason did he supply as the motto for the *Bilderbögen des kleinen Lebens* the words of Goethe: "Es gibt nichts *Unbedeutendes* in der Welt. Es kommt nur auf die Anschauungsweise an!" ("There is nothing *insignificant* in the world. It only depends on how you *look* at it!"). Or, in a delightful self-assessment in the same collection: "Not all birds are Lammergeiers, Sea-Eagles and Condors . . . There are also valuable, delightful little birds like the Wren, the Kingfisher, the Crested Tit. They are perhaps even more original, more remarkable, more admirable than the gigantic birds!"

26   Andrew W. Barker

Notes

1. *Das Altenbergbuch.* ed. Egon Friedell, Wien: Wiener Graphische Werkstätte, 1921, p. 72.
2. *Handbuch des deutschen Romans*, ed. K. K. Polheim, Düsseldorf, 1981.
3. In: "Selbstbiographie," *Was der Tag mir zuträgt*, Berlin: Fischer, 1901, p. 6.
4. Quoted from Friedell's postscript to the collection *Bilderbögen des kleinen Lebens*, Berlin: Erich Reiß, 1909, p. 211.
5. J. K. Huysmans, *Against Nature*, translated by Robert Baldick, London: 1959, pp. 198-199.
6. See Wilma A. Iggers, *Karl Kraus: A Viennese Critic of the Twentieth Century*, The Hague: Martinus Nijhoff, 1967, p. 55.
7. Adolf Loos, "Abschied von Peter Altenberg", in: *Peter Altenberg: Leben und Werk in Texten und Bildern*, ed. by Hans Christian Kosler, Munich: Matthes and Seitz, 1981, p. 235.
8. In: "So wurde ich", *Semmering 1912*, Berlin: Fischer, 1913, p. 36.
9. K. G. Just, *Von der Gründerzeit bis zur Gegenwart. Geschichte der deutschen Literatur seit 1871.* Bern and Munich: Francke, 1973, p. 215.
10. See: Gotthart Wunberg, *Das Junge Wien: Österreichische Literatur- und Kunstkritik*, Vol 1, Tübingen: Niemeyer, 1976, p. 607.
11. In: "Selbstbiographie," *Was der Tag mir zuträgt*, Berlin: Fischer, 1901, p. 7.
12. Randolph Klawiter, "Peter Altenberg and Das Junge Wien," Modern Austrian Literature 1 (1969), p. 16.
13. Camillo Schaefer, *Peter Altenberg: Ein biographischer Essay*, 2nd Edition, Freibord, 1980, pp. 33-34.
14. In: "Philosophie," *Fechsung*, Berlin: Fischer, 1915, p. 210.
15. Jost Hermand, *Der Schein des schönen Lebens. Studien zur Jahrhundertwende*, Frankfurt am Main, Fischer, 1971, p. 181.
16. Egon Friedell, *Bilderbögen des kleinen Lebens*, p. 215.
17. J. K. Huysmans, p. 199.
18. Ibid., pp. 198-199
19. Ibid., p. 199
20. Ibid., p. 199

21. Ibid., p. 199
22. Egon Friedell, *Das Altenbergbuch*, p. 14.
23. Hugo von Hofmannsthal, "Ein neues Wiener Buch," *Die prosaischen Schriften gesammelt,* Vol. II, Berlin: Fischer, 1919, p. 81.
24. In: *Wie ich es sehe*, 5th edition, Berlin: S. Fischer, p. 44.
25. In: "Selbstbiographie," *Was der Tag mir zuträgt*, p. 7.
26. In: *Bilderbögen des kleinen Lebens*, Berlin: 1909, p. 212.
27. In: "At Home," *Wie ich es sehe*, p. 44.
28. Camillo Schaefer, p. 104.
29. Arthur Schnitzler, *Tagebuch, 1909-1912*, Vienna: Österreichische Akademie der Wissenschaften, 1981.
30. Helga Malmberg, *Widerhall des Herzens. Ein Peter Altenberg Buch,* Langen and Müller, 1961.
31. Quoted from H. C. Kosler, p. 235.
32. Camillo Schaefer, p. 168.
33. "Gamelang-Musik," *Märchen des Lebens*, Berlin: 1908, p. 107.
34. In: "Das Flügerl," *Märchen des Lebens*, p. 46.
35. This collection was not published as anticipated by Fischer, but rather by the Viennese Society for the Prevention of Cruelty to Children (1932).
36. Egon Friedell, postscript to *Bilderbögen*, p. 207.
37. Ibid., p. 210.
38. Ibid., p. 207.
39. Arthur Schnitzler, *Tagebuch, 1913-1916*, Vienna: Österreichische Akadamie der Wissenschaften, 1983, 31.3.1913.
40. Quoted from H. C. Kosler, pp. 248-249.
41. A translation of this poem appears in Karin Monson: *Alban Berg*, London: MacDonald and Jane, 1983, p. 45.
42. Mosco Carner, *Alban Berg*, Revised Edition, London: Duckworth, 1983, p. 39.
43. Ibid., p. 39.
44. Ibid., p. 39.
45. Quoted from C. Schaefer, p. 149.
46. Arthur Schnitzler, *Tagebuch, 1913-1916*, 1.8.1914.
47. Thomas Mann, *Reden und Aufsätze*, Gesammelte Werke in 12 Bänden, vol. 2, Oldenburg: Fischer, 1960, p. 424.
48. Quoted from H. C. Kosler, op.cit., p. 235.
49. According to H. C. Kosler (pers. comm.) the financial records of the society for 1919 are not available so that the exact details of Altenberg's legacy must remain in some doubt.

28   Andrew W. Barker

28   Andrew W. Barker

50. Robert Musil, *Gesammelte Werke*, edited by Adolf Frisé, vol. 7, Reinbek bei Hamburg: Rowohlt, 1978, p. 842.
51. Gustav Janouch, *Conversations with Kafka*, 2nd edition, London: André Deutsch, 1971, pp. 79-81.

I.   Works by Peter Altenberg in German

Wie ich es sehe. Berlin: Fischer, 1896.
Ashantee. Berlin: Fischer, 1897.
Was der Tag mir zuträgt. Berlin: Fischer, 1901.
Pròdròmòs . Berlin: Fischer, 1906.
Die Auswahl aus meinen Büchern. Berlin: Fischer, 1908.
Märchen des Lebens. Berlin: Fischer, 1908.
Bilderbögen des kleinen Lebens. Berlin: Riss, 1909.
Neues Altes. Berlin: Fischer, 1911.
Semmering 1912. Berlin: Fischer, 1913.
Fechsung. Berlin: Fischer, 1915.
Nachfechsung. Berlin: Fischer, 1916.
Vita Ipsa. Berlin: Fischer, 1918.
Mein Lebensabend. Berlin: Fischer, 1919.
Das Altenbergbuch. Leipzig, Wien, Zürich: Wiener Graphische Werkstätte, 1921.
Der Nachlaß. ed. Alfred Polgar, Berlin: Fischer, 1925.
Die Nachlese. Wien: Lanyi, 1930.
Gesammelte Werke in fünf Bänden. Ed. Werner J. Schweiger. Wien und Berlin: Löcker/Fischer, 1987.

II.   Works in English

King, Alexander. *Alexander King Presents Peter Altenberg's Evocations of Love.* New York: Simon & Shuster, 1960.

III.   Secondary Works in English

Barker, Andrew W. "'Die weiseste Ökonomie bei tiefster Fülle". Peter Altenberg's *Wie ich es sehe*', *Studies in 19th Century Austrian*

Literature, ed. B. O. Murdoch & M. G. Ward. Glasgow: Scottish Papers in Germanic Studies, 3, 1983, pp. 77-101.

'Peter Altenberg's Literary Catalysis', *From Vormärz to Fin de Siècle.* Ed. M. G. Ward. Blairgowrie: Lochee Press, 1986, pp. 91-106.

Broad, Geoffrey. 'The Didactic Element in the Works of Peter Altenberg,' University of Otago, Dunedin: Ph.D., 1980.

Johnston, William M. 'Martin Buber's Literary Debut: "On Viennese Literature"', *The German Quarterly,* 47 (1974), 563f.

Klawiter, Randolph J. 'Peter Altenberg and "Das Junge Wien"' *Modern Austrian Literature,* 1 (1968), pp. 1-55.

Schoenberg, Barbara. 'The Art of Peter Altenberg: Bedside Chronicles of a Dying World.' Diss. University of California in Los Angeles, 1984.

Schoenberg, Barbara. '"Woman-Defender" & "Woman-Offender," Peter Altenberg and Otto Weininger: Two Literary Stances vis-à-vis Bourgeois Culture in the Viennese "Belle-Epoque,"' *Modern Austrian Literature,* 20, (1987), pp. 51-69.

Simpson, Josephine M. N., *Peter Altenberg: a Neglected Writer of the Viennese Jahrhundertwende.* Frankfurt: Peter Lang, 1987.

Timms, Edward. "Peter Altenberg. Authenticity or Pose?" *Fin de Siècle Vienna.* G. J. Carr and Eda Sagarra. Dublin: Trinity College, 1985, pp. 126-142.

IV.   Major Studies in German

Bisanz, Hans. Peter Altenberg: *Mein äußerstes Ideal.* Vienna: Christian Brandstätter, 1987.

Fischer, Jens Malte. 'Peter Altenberg: *Wie ich es sehe* (1896),' *Fin de Siècle. Kommentar zu einer Epoche.* München: Winkler Verlag, 1987, pp. 157-168.

Friedell, Egon. *Ecce Poeta.* Berlin: Fischer, 1912.

Kosler, Hans Christian. *Peter Altenberg: Leben und Werk in Text und Bildern.* München: Mattes und Seitz, 1981.

Köwer, Irene. *Peter Altenberg als Autor der literarischen Kleinform.* Frankfurt: Peter Lang, 1987.

Nienhaus, Stefan. *Das deutsche Prosagedicht.* Berlin: de Gruyter, 1986.

Prohaska, Hedwig. 'Versuch einer Monographie'. Vienna University, Diss., 1948.

Schaefer, Camillo. *Peter Altenberg: Ein biographischer Essay*. Vienna: Freibord, 1980.

Spinnen, W. Burkhard. 'Die Seele in der Kritik. Zur zeitgenössischen Rezeption Peter Altenbergs.' Münster University, Magister-Arbeit, 1983.

Wagner, Peter. "Peter Altenbergs Prosadichtung. Untersuchung zur Thematik und Struktur des Frühwerks," Münster University, Diss., 1965.

Wysocki, Gisela von. *Peter Altenberg. Bilder und Geschichten des befreiten Lebens*. München und Wien: Hanser, 1979.

Leopold von Andrian

Jens Rieckmann

In 1895, shortly after the publication of Andrian's short novel *Der Garten der Erkenntnis* (The Garden of Knowledge) Hermann Bahr, at that time considered by the general public the spokesman of a group of writers known since 1891 as "Young Vienna," proclaimed that there was no name more famous in Europe than that of Andrian. Even before the publication of the novel he had predicted: "If two lines of any of the modern writers should survive, then they will be lines by Andrian."[1] Today most readers, unless they are specialists in Austrian or fin-de-siècle literature, are no longer familiar with the name. Should they come across Bahr's statements, and thereupon consult such standard reference works as the *Encyclopaedia Britannica* or *The Penguin Companion to European Literature*, they would certainly question Bahr's judgement, for they will find no reference whatsoever to Andrian in these and other generally accessible works of reference. They may therefore ask why an essay on Andrian was included in this volume, yet, as I hope will become clear, there are compelling reasons for considering Andrian among the ranks of major figures of modern Austrian literature.

Leopold von Andrian (1875-1951) was born on May 9 in Berlin, a fact that he, an ardent Austrian patriot, tried to suppress all his life. His father, Ferdinand von Andrian, like many of his ancestors in the noble family of von Andrian-Werburg, played a prominent part in Viennese life. In 1870 he founded the Viennese Anthropological Society, and he also became known as one of the co-authors of the so-called "Kronprinzenwerk," a series of essays, published in collaboration with Crown Prince Rudolph, which were critical of the internal situation in the Austro-Hungarian Empire. In 1869 he married Cäcilie Meyerbeer, daughter of the famous Jewish composer Giacomo Meyerbeer. This German-Jewish, Austrian-Catholic heritage, "the hasty amalgamation of two highly developed races," as Andrian termed it in 1895 in a letter to Hofmannsthal,[2] predestined him, as he saw it, to the outsider's existence of an artist and a homosexual that he was to lead most of his life, while apparently being very much of an insider in the high society of turn-of-the-century Vienna. This double existence he saw concretely symbolized in his name Poldi Andrian, as he was known to his friends. In 1894 he noted in his diary: "Feudal Lord and vasall - Andrian/cavalier and stritzi [flaneur and pimp]-Poldi" (TuA 46, 135).

At the age of ten Andrian was admitted to the exclusive Jesuit boarding school at Kalksburg, near Vienna, and it was there that, sometime before the age of twelve, he had the first presentiments of his sexual orientation. Leaving Kalksburg in 1887 because of his delicate health, he continued his education in Italy, accompanied by his private tutor Oskar Walzel. In 1890 he returned to Vienna to attend the prestigious Schottengymnasium, from which he graduated in 1893. As a boy Andrian was precocious and felt lonely and misunderstood. He read voraciously, and at the age of ten started writing poetry. Already he was driven by the ambition to become a great poet and convinced that his fame would raise his family to the most illustrious moment of its history. In 1888 he made his literary debut with a cycle of romances entitled *Hannibal*, which he published at his own cost. This epigonic cycle gave no indication that within a few years Andrian would emerge as one of the most prominent and talented modernist poets of the Young Vienna movement.

Andrian himself notes in his diary that the transition from epigone to modernist poet occurred shortly after he had graduated from the Schottengymnasium and before he enrolled as a law student at the University of Vienna. By this time he had read such "modern" authors as Ebner-Eschenbach, Disraeli, and Maupassant. But it was Bourget, whose *Mensonges* he secretly read during his Greek and Latin lessons, who influenced him profoundly and changed his literary direction. From then on he read such prototypical modern writers as Baudelaire, Loti, Mallarmé, Verlaine, Jens Peter Jacobsen, Maeterlinck, and Wilde. Perhaps even more significant for his development as a writer was his meeting in the late fall of 1893 with Hofmannsthal, who had already emerged as the most promising of the Young Vienna poets.

Even before he made the acquaintance of the nineteen-year-old Hofmannsthal, Andrian had sent one of his poems, "Sie schwieg und sah mit einem Blick mich an" (She Was Silent and Looked at Me with a Glance) to C.A. Klein, the editor of the *Blätter für die Kunst* (Pages for Art). This esoteric literary journal, founded in 1892 by the German symbolist poet Stefan George, appealed to Andrian because, as he put it in his first letter to C.A. Klein, it was "one of the few journals which paints a faithful picture of truly modern art, truly modern endeavors."[3] This poem, like three others which Andrian submitted to the *Blätter für die Kunst* at the end of 1893, depicts in veiled and symbolic terms his love for Erwin Slamecka, a middle class boy whom he had met while still at the Schottengymnasium; Slamecka also figures prominently as Clemens in a key episode in *Garten der Erkenntnis*.

"Sie schwieg und sah mit einem Blick mich an," the best of Andrian's poems to this point in his life, is already characterized by what Hofmannsthal admired most in Andrian's poetry: "these comparisons between two totally different things. . . these remarkable, true, and enigmatic analogies" (TuA 51, p. 170). George, who published this and eight other poems by Andrian in the *Blätter für die Kunst* between 1894 and 1900, said later that Andrian's poetry "was after Hofmannsthal's the best there was at that time;"[4] he dedicated his poem "Den Brüdern" (To the Brothers) to Andrian. In his best poems such as "Ich bin ein Königskind" (I am a Royal Child), "Der Feste Süßigkeit wenn sie zu Ende gehn" (The Sweetness of Feasts When They Near Their End), "Dann sieht die Seele" (Then the Soul Sees) Andrian succeeded in transforming moods into metaphors and symbols. That he was consciously aware of this the following diary entry reveals: "One *sees* a poem. . . first as a color, a basic color and myriad nuances,--then words, phrases, situations occur to one which must be part of it, even before one has made any further plan" (TuA 45, pp. 75-76). Poems, he further noted in his diary, should be "hyper-stylized, everything accidental [must] vanish," for only then can the poem become a symbol "of great and mysterious processes, of states of the soul" (TuA 53, p. 67). Both such poetological statements and the poems he wrote between 1893 and 1895 show Andrian's affinities with the symbolist school of poetry.

In the spring of 1894 Andrian began work on the short novel that was to make him famous, *Der Garten der Erkenntnis*. He had first mentioned it in November, 1893 as *Das Fest der Jugend* (The Feast of Youth) under the rubric: "plans for future works." It was not his first attempt in this genre, nor, as we shall see, was it to be his last. In 1889 he had started a novel entitled *Ad majorem Dei gloriam,* in the manner of Ossip Schubin, a nineteenth-century writer of popular fiction, but he soon abandoned it. Four years later, in October 1893, he had jotted down the idea for a novel "with the background of Vienna, of the Schottengymnasium. . . and the entire school milieu, the Vienna of the inner city, and in addition the affair with E. [Erwin Slamecka] transformed into the feminine" (TuA 42, p. 45). The novel was to be called *Und die Philister banden ihn* (And the Philistines Tied Him Up). The title is indicative of the concept Andrian had in mind. He wanted to tell the story of an artist, conceived as a Christ-like figure, who would be the Messiah and martyr of a new culture based on homoeroticism, which Andrian perceived as a sign of the time. In late April 1894, he noted in his diary: "In a thousand years cultural historians will consider as one of the most remarkable phenomena of our time how our culture suddenly tired of woman and arrogantly desired beauty without purpose" (TuA 53, p. 44). It is not clear why Andrian abandoned this novel in favor of *Garten der Erkenntnis*, but a possible explanation may be found in his programmatic statement of April, 1894: "One ought to extend symbolism to the novel as well" (TuA 52, p. 136). It may have occurred to Andrian that it would be impossible to realize this program in a novel of such confessional and accusatory character as *Und die Philister banden ihn.*

Andrian wrote *Garten der Erkenntnis* between August 1894 and January 1895, and the novel was published by S. Fischer in March 1895 after the Viennese weekly journal *Die Zeit* had rejected it as "dangerous for [the magazine's] continued existence" (TuA 48, p. 57). The sixty-page novel caused a sensation; it was widely and for the most part favorably reviewed in all the leading literary journals of the time. A parody of the novel, entitled "The Story of the Tired Prince and His One Hundred Chambermaids," appeared in Vienna as early as 1897, as sure a sign of its fame as Karl Kraus' satiric mention of the "Kindergarten of Ignorance" in his polemical pamphlet *Die demolirte Literatur* (1896, Demolished Literature).

Bahr, who was instrumental in getting the novel published, admired it enormously. He considered it "the best work. . . produced by European modernism"[5] and compared its author to the mature Goethe. These were of course exaggerations, but Bahr was not alone among contemporary writers in his appreciation of the novel. George knew passages from it by heart, and alluded to it in his poem "Bozen. Erwins Schatten." Hofmannsthal wrote his *Märchen der 672. Nacht* (1895, *Tale of the Merchant Son and His Four Servants*) in response to Andrian's novel, reread it almost every year, and expressed his admiration for it repeatedly in his correspondence with Andrian. Nor was the fame of the novel short-lived; by 1919 four more printings of the novel had appeared.[6] In 1900

Maeterlinck asked Andrian for a copy of the book, in 1904 the poet Albert Verwey translated it into Dutch; and in 1909 Hofmannsthal wrote to Andrian: "By the way, I hardly meet a younger artist or person interested in the arts - who does not start to talk to me about the book."[7] The novel was read and admired by such diverse writers as André Gide, Gerhart Hauptmann, and Thornton Wilder. Symptomatic of the enduring resonance that the novel found is the fact that Klaus Mann in his first autobiography, *Kind dieser Zeit* (1932, Child of These Times), quotes long passages from it.

The wide appeal of the novel can in part be attributed to the sympathy a whole generation felt with the Weltanschauung expressed in it, just as a hundred and twenty years earlier a whole generation had identified with Goethe's *Werther*; by 1902 the novel was referred to as the "Viennese Werther-book."[8] This sympathy found its most eloquent expression in Hofmannsthal's diary. Referring to Andrian's novel he wrote:

> The German Narcissus-book. These are wonderful moments when a whole generation in different countries recognizes itself in the same symbol. This expresses a transitory situation: all of a sudden the dreamlike character of the world was recognized; . . . one was able to explain to oneself what one had searched for continually in outer life. For a moment one was not capable of falling mystically in love with a thing, the poets laid down their crowns and remembered only that they were youths. In conversations there are such moments: everyone looks at the others with intoxicated agreement, they know in common something great beyond all words. There are such moments in large groups of intoxicated people. Why not in the whole generation?[9]

"Ego Narcissus" is one of the mottos with which Andrian prefaced his novel; it foreshadows the major theme of the novel and is a reflection of one of the earliest notes for the *Garten der Erkenntnis* found in Andrian's notebooks: "Narcissus: the mirror of being" (TuA 46, p. 67). The *Weltanschauung* which forms the basis of the novel was simultaneously developed by Andrian on a more abstract, philosophical level in the *Buch der Weltanschauung* (unpublished), which he started to write in November 1894. The central thought in this cosmology is that of the "perversion of the universe." This perversion can be traced to the narcissistic origin of the cosmos, for according to Andrian's cosmology, it was the desire of original matter (known in Greek mythology as "chaos," as "God" in the Judaeo-Christian tradition) to see its own beauty, to objectify itself in order to know itself. For this purpose alone it created the universe. The purpose of the universe is, therefore, a purely aesthetic one; its sole justification is "its incredible beauty" (TuA 47, p. 74). Truth, then, can be found only in beauty, and the artist is a savior, for he alone can redeem beauty, which without him, would not be seen and known. Since, in Andrian's questionable logic, in each successive creation (original matter begets the cosmos, the cosmos the universe, the universe the earth, the earth animals, plants, and man) something is lost, "the universe must be contained in man" (TuA 47, p. 97). Self-knowledge would then be identical with knowledge of the universe, and one of the questions Andrian repeatedly poses at this time is how best to attain this self-knowledge. This quest for knowledge is also the fundamental theme of the *Garten der Erkenntnis*.

Erwin, the protagonist of this miniature *Bildungsroman* (educational novel), is a quester figure, a typically modern variant of this type; at the end of his quest for "the solution to the secret of life" [10] he dies "without having gained knowledge."[11] Although the novel is characterized by the absence of plot in the conventional sense, the protagonist's failure can be traced through a number of stages. After a brief account of the unhappy marriage of Erwin's parents and his father's death, the narrator introduces Erwin at the age of twelve at the Jesuit boarding school at Kalksburg. This initial stage of Erwin's development is marked by a pronounced tendency towards escapism. The boarding-school life is experienced as alien to his soul; his fellow students are feared by him as "spiteful enemies."[12] Instead of participating in their lives he retreats into himself. He finds meaning only in the aesthetically perceived rituals of the church, and vows to become a priest. He imagines his future life as waging a sublime battle on behalf of the church against the world.

At the age of fourteen he becomes sick and is taken by one of the priests to Bozen, where he continues his schooling for the next three years. Now he feels challenged by the worldly life which he had despised; his longing for a life in the church is replaced by a fascination with the "other," a realm in which everything is "forbidden and secretive."[13] He hopes to find this sexual realm revealed in Vienna, to which he moves at the age of seventeen. He comes close to realizing this hope in his friendship with Clemens, a former fellow student, but at their parting "they stood facing each other in their sterile beauty, and could not give each other any of it."[14] Next the poetry of Bourget captures his imagination, and fills him with yearning for a life in which "pain and exultation, sublimity and baseness" are inseparably connected.[15] He hopes to find this life through his relationship with a woman, but the attempt to "fathom a supernatural secret in a natural way" is doomed to failure.[16]

At this point, halfway through the narrative, when all of Erwin's efforts to know the meaning of life have failed, Andrian introduces the most enigmatic character of the novel, the "Stranger." Erwin first meets him in a wine restaurant, follows him, "longing for knowledge,"[17] and leaves him out of fear. He is to meet him twice more, and to think of him as his "enemy" at their last meeting shortly before his death.[18] That Andrian consciously conceived this character as a symbolic figure is clear from the description of the Stranger in the novel and also from one of his notes for the *Garten der Erkenntnis*: "adv. [ersarius] asks him [Erwin] for a light, everything about the adv. meaningful; adv. not Austrian" (TuA 46, p. 3). Erwin's failure to gain knowledge and his rejection of the Stranger's advances are intimately connected. Our interpretation of the novel and our understanding of Erwin's failure depend to a large extent on our interpretation of the "stranger's" symbolic function in the novel.

The Stranger has been interpreted as a personification of Erwin's "unlived life." As such he passes judgement on the withdrawn aesthete.[19] In a psychoanalytical reading one critic has suggested that the stranger manifests the guilt feelings which accompany Erwin's incestuous desire for his mother. According to this reading, Erwin's death is a metaphor for his unresolved identity crisis.[20] As I have suggested elsewhere,[21] there are compelling reasons for understanding the Stranger as a Dionysus figure. Erwin fails in his quest to know the "secret of life" because the narcissistic individual cannot accept the Dionysian wisdom that true knowledge can be attained only in death. A note of Andrian's for the *Garten der Erkenntnis* similarly associates knowledge with death: "From the first moment of our lives we steer towards our death, i.e. knowledge" (TuA 46, p. 79). Seen in this light, Thomas Mann's formula "myth plus psychology," which he coined to characterize the basic quality of his writings,[22] is also applicable to Andrian's novel.

Andrian's striving to apply symbolist poetic techniques to novel writing largely succeeded in the *Garten der Erkenntnis*. The novel is lyrical in character, the language precious and highly stylized. Andrian successfully employed the evocation of objects in order to convey to the reader the dreamlike *états d'âme* of his protagonist. Particularly striking are the mysterious, continued metaphors, which derive their effectiveness from the associative pattern they form in the reader's mind. But the reception of the novel shows that its success was not based solely on its aesthetic qualities. The *Weltanschauung* expressed in it, with its key elements of narcissism, aestheticism, solipsism, the duality of life, and crisis of knowledge, struck a responsive chord in a whole generation. The ideas, themes, and motives of Andrian's novel were further developed and explored in much seminal works as Hofmannsthal's *Das Märchen der 672. Nacht* (1895) and *Reitergeschichte* (1899, *Tale of the Cavalry*), Beer-Hofmann's *Der Tod Georgs* (1902, *Georg's Death*), and Musil's *Die Verwirrungen des Zöglings Törleß* (1906, *Young Törless*).

After a renewed reading of the *Garten der Erkenntnis*, Hofmannsthal wrote to Andrian in April 1900: "As always I cannot believe that the [artistic] powers which produced it [the novel] should turn completely to dust."[23] With the exception of the sonnett "Dem Dichter Österreichs" (To Austria's Poet), written on the occasion of Hofmannsthal's fiftieth birthday in 1924, Andrian did not publish a single poem or narrative after 1895. Yet he did not abandon the hope to be a creative writer, and from 1918 on, as his letters to Hofmannsthal, his diaries and notebooks make abundantly clear, he intended a "retour à l'art" (TuA 176, p. 148). Evidence that he partly realized this goal is a lengthy, unpublished manuscript entitled *Der Lauf zum Ideal. Des Gartens der Erkenntnis zweiter Teil* (The Path To the Ideal. The Second Part of the Garden of Knowledge). He began to write this autobiographical novel, which was to remain a fragment, in 1933, and was quite confident at the time that he would finish it.

Much speculation has surrounded Andrian's falling silent as a poet and novelist. The most commonly held view is that Andrian passed through a language crisis and that this experience served Hofmannsthal as a model for his analysis of a language crisis in his *Ein Brief* (1902), commonly referred to as the *Lord Chandos Letter*. In this fictional letter addressed to his patron Francis Bacon, Lord Chandos explains his lapse into artistic sterility as a consequence of having totally lost "the ability to think or to speak of anything coherently."[24] The theory that Hofmannsthal had Andrian in mind when he wrote *Ein Brief*, was first advanced by Walter Perl in 1958,[25] and has been accepted unquestioningly and widely ever since; as recently as 1985 it was again repeated in an essay on Hofmannsthal and Andrian.[26] For a number of reasons this theory is questionable. It is, for example, curious that in the many attempts Andrian later made to understand the crisis he experienced in the two years following the publication of the *Garten der Erkenntnis* he does not once allude to a language crisis, nor does he ever consider it a reason to explain why, once he had decided to resume writing fiction, it still took him fifteen years, from 1918 to 1933, to get started. Andrian's reflections on language in his notebooks and diaries show an awareness of the limitations of language, and he believed that Austrian writers typically felt a "modesty about words" which resulted from an awareness of the discrepancy between "language which originates in the soul" and everyday language (TuA 46, p. 129). But this language skepticism, which Andrian shared with his fellow Austrian writers at the turn-of-the-century, resulted in a heightened awareness of language rather than in a language crisis.

Andrian was convinced that language was a raw material for the writer like stone for the sculptor, and that he could shape it in any way he wanted. In 1893 he wrote in his notebook: "Everybody, even the so-called educated layman, has the eternal question about the 'what' instead of the 'why', perhaps the raw interest in the subject matter, the psychological [interest]- but people are not aware of which characterizes the artist, the joy in the word, in language, the joy of giving form to language - the terrific difficulty in doing so" (TuA 42, pp. 32-33). Again in 1923, when he was engaged in outlining the sequel to the *Garten der Erkenntnis*, he noted that the writer-artist had a primary relation to language which resulted in "the words becoming new and precious in his mouth" (TuA 99,p. 52).

Andrian's sexual orientation has also been used to explain his falling silent as a poet and the accompanying psychological crisis.[27] This theory deserves careful consideration, for it is true that Andrian's attitudes toward his sexuality were ambivalent and spanned the extremes between exultation and depression. In the early nineties Andrian saw a significant connection between his mission as an artist and his sexual orientation. Recording in 1894 in his diary the impression a statue of Antinous had made upon him, he commented: "Triumphant feeling of the martyr. . . so much have I already suffered, so much shall I still suffer for this cause: but now it has become clear to me that therein lies the future of the. . . world, and that I am an apostle of this religion and therefore a great artist" (TuA 55, p. 35). This new religion, as Andrian conceived it, was characterized by a cessation of the antagonism between the sexes and an increase in homosexuality. He saw the role of the artist in this cultural revolution as that of a trailblazer. In March 1894 he expressed his hope that the "revolution in feeling, in art would create a culture in which woman no longer stands on a pedestal, a quasi antique culture" (TuA 52, p. 52). Of course these speculations were partly motivated self-defensively, as were Andrian's attempts to justify his sexual orientation to himself on the basis of cultural-historical and philosophical grounds. At the end of 1894, for example, he noted in his diary: "The third degree [of hubris] the Greeks did not consider to be a sacrilege: the love for one's own sex" (TuA 48, p. 31). On the one hand, then, Andrian saw in his sexual orientation a sign that he was one of the "chosen ones," as were, according to a note he wrote in the spring of 1894, "Verlaine, Oscar Wilde, Pierre Loti - And many others" (TuA 52, p. 52).

On the other hand, Andrian's sexual orientation collided with his Catholic upbringing. At the beginning of 1896, when his psychological crisis dominated his thinking, he admitted to himself that his sexuality conflicted with every other aspect of his life. In an age and in a social order which repressed sexuality generally and strongly tabooed any deviation from the established norms of sexual behavior, Andrian lived in a constant tension between physis and nomos. The tension grew in his later years as he became a devout Catholic and strove in vain to transform his eros into charitas. It prevented him from achieving that ideal which he first formulated in 1895 and which he tried to realize all his life: "As far as my person is concerned, I wish to transform its multiplicity into unity; in my soul there shall be no opposition between emotions which I love and emotions which I am ashamed of, between outer and inner life, between that which I want and that which I am capable of; finally, there shall be no opposition between by body and my soul, I want to live physically as consciously as I do psychically; I want to possess absolute unity in my entire being, as I believe the Greeks possessed it" (TuA 184, p. 3).

Despite these conflicts it would be an oversimplification to establish a direct relationship between Andrian's sexuality and his falling silent as a poet. In his final summing up of the crisis years, written three years before his death, Andrian himself explicitly rules out such a connection: "But the disgust which overcame me after the hortus [*Der Garten der Erkenntnis*], and paralyzed all activity, was not due to α, Andrian's code for homosexuality, which on the contrary seemed beautiful and interesting to [me]" (TuA 189, p. 52), interesting because, as he noted in the 1930s when he had become a devout Catholic, when he was young "[β, Andrian's code for heterosexuality] [was] not sin enough, c'est le péché de toutlemonde, soyons pervers, le monde est p.[ervers]" (TuA 132, p. 106). There is evidence in Andrian's notebooks, however, that his failure to the planned sequel to the *Garten der Erkenntnis* was in part due to his sexual orientation.

Gabriel, the protagonist of this novel, was to be a self-portrait of Andrian; an indication of the autobiographical, confessional nature of the novel is the constant fluctuation between third person and first person singular in the notes for the novel. A problem Andrian addresses repeatedly in these notes is how to deal with his sexuality. "How," he asks, "could one create the character of G., without taking into account that which in retrospect seems to be essential to him" (TuA 183, p. 174), and he answers his own question by saying: "Undoubtedly one must behold the whole character. . . and how could one achieve this without α" (TuA 183, p. 175). Although he knew that this aspect could not be ignored, he nevertheless could not bring himself to deal with it openly. The dilemma arose because his superego functioned as a censor, as the following note reveals: "Thus he [Gabriel] begins to write. . . Writing shall make it clear to me, and grace. . . here I have the necessary subject matter. . . a writer liberates himself through writing. . . and that would be fine, if α would not rumble deep down within him, and if there were not the break between unconsciousness and consciousness. Because it exists, he cannot put the α into words" (TuA 174, p. 68). For the same reason Andrian later abandoned the idea of writing his autobiography. In 1948 he noted: "Everything, more of less, is a subject for literature, c'est entendu. The whole, outright monstrous nature of V. [Andrian] could also be represented. But never as an autobiography; for that it is too horrendum and pudendum" (TuA 189, p. 50).

But the crisis of 1895 was not caused primarily by Andrian's sexual orientation or by a language crisis; it had its roots in the narcissistic Weltanschauung of the twenty-one-year old. Recalling the crisis in 1948, Andrian declared: "Artistic production was always his goal, but after the hortus came the disenchantment, the disgust, when the stench of the I rose up to him" (TuA 189, p. 51). The crisis was triggered by an "ethical awakening" (TuA 183, p. 234), which caused Andrian to reevaluate his former Weltanschauung centered "exclusively around love for the self" (TuA 183, p. 188), the Weltanschauung expressed in the *Garten der Erkenntnis*. From then on Andrian's motto was "away from the self" (TuA 183, p. 188), and he hoped to achieve this distancing from the self by a "will to objectivity" (TuA 176, p. 24). True knowledge, he was now convinced, could be gained only if one perceived the universe within the self and the universe surrounding the self as separate entities, not as mirror images of each other.

The "ethical awakening" also meant, however, that Andrian found it impossible to continue writing. The imagination, which he considered to be an indispensable faculty for any artist, had become suspect. Since the imagination had been "used in the service of the self,— it is drawn into the crisis," and Andrian felt he had to renounce it. To renounce imagination, however, "involves the renunciation of artistic production" (TuA 174, p. 70). The most extensive and the most moving account of the crisis (which manifested itself in pathological symptoms and undermined Andrian's life for five years from 1895 to 1900, and intermittently thereafter until 1914) is given in the fragmentary novel, *Der Lauf zum Ideal*:

> What collapsed here was an entire system of inner architecture, whose structure had been built on ideas of the self, or had at least been supported by them. . . Overnight it [the catastrophe] had occurred and had destroyed the whole magnificence of the bloom of youth which had sprung from the buds of childhood. He could only think with horror of himself, and with bitter scorn of his dream to be a chosen one among thousands, to be a poet. This dream had arisen from a precocious knowledge, the result of an extraordinary psychic development, favored by an impressionable aesthetic imagination. The dream had brought forth his first poetic sketches, and together with the dream they vanished like figures in a dream. For only on the basis of looking outward, forgetful of the self, can the poet give the blood of life to beings which live in the medium of art. True he possessed that quality which signifies the poet, the quality which is nourished from the depths of the aesthetic faculty, imagination, which formally must be in the use of language, and in content must be an imagination of life. And therefore he was a poet in temperament and attitude toward life, much more so than many who were regarded as poets by their contemporaries, if not by posterity. . . Between him and great poetic achievement stood his self (TuA 17, pp. 31-32).

In the years following the publication of *Garten der Erkenntnis*, Andrian continued his studies as a law student despite his severe psychopathic problems. He passed his final examinations in the summer of 1898 and started his term of "voluntary service" in the Austrian army, but he did not serve the whole year because of his illness. In 1899 he received the Doctor of Law degree from the University of Vienna and entered the Austrian diplomatic service, in which he served with distinction until 1918, when he was appointed general director of the *Burgtheater* in Vienna and also of the Vienna opera. When the Habsburg monarchy collapsed in the same year, he resigned, but despite his short term in office he achieved significant results. He initiated the appointment of Richard Strauss as director of the Vienna opera, and in his discussions with Hofmannsthal, Richard Beer-Hofmann, and Max Reinhardt the idea for the Salzburg Festival evolved. After his resignation from public office Andrian became a private citizen of Liechtenstein, the last principality in central Europe ruled by a descendant of the Habsburgs, and in 1923 he married Andrée Bourée de Poncay-Wimpffen. The motivations for the marriage were in part financial and in part to conceal his sexual orientation.

"Retour à l'art" was Andrian's immediate goal in the years after the First World War, but he had never abandoned his dream to become a major writer. Even at the height of his psychological crisis in 1895 he noted in his diary: "Even if I see Hugo [von Hofmannsthal] as now more accomplished, much more an *'artist'* than myself, the gift of the truly great consists in becoming it gradually, late enough; by anticipating maturity the apes became apes; this image of the beauty of the world will . . . be through knowledge much more beautiful than the earlier, more youthful beauty. And I can— after much disgust, aridness, and even ridiculousness— be much greater than Hugo" (TuA 184, p. 141). After the turn of the century Andrian had taken up drawing, not only as a substitute for his literary ambitions, but also as a means to educate himself in viewing the world outside him objectively. His extensive historical and philosophical studies during his diplomatic service served the same purpose.

In 1919, after a silence of almost twenty-five years, Andrian made the first "attempts to walk" again as a writer by composing a few articles dealing with the origins of the First World War. These, like other essays which he published between 1919 and 1921, were written in the hope that he would gain a reputation as a political writer. He embarked on his return to creative writing in 1923, when he began preliminary work for a first person novel with the title *Eros und Gnade* (Eros and Grace), first mentioned in his diary of 1920 under the title *Der Bastard*. Although he never got beyond the preliminary work, his notes for the novel contain many of the ideas which he was to incorporate ten years later in the fragmentary novel *Der Lauf zum Ideal*. Preoccupied as he was with religious and ethical questions, Andrian abandoned this novel, because he found it impossible to conceive the protagonist's character without having first thought through his new found Weltanschauung theoretically and systematically.

For the next eight years, from 1924 to 1932, Andrian engaged in theological, philosophical, and psychological studies. These resulted in two works: the "philosophical summing up" of his Weltanschauung[28] in the cosmology *Die Ständeordnung des Alls. Rationales Weltbild eines katholischen Dichters* (1930, The Rank Order of the Universe. Rational World View of a Catholic Poet), an attempt to view the world as an hierarchical order with the Catholic church and the aristocracy at the top of the social pyramid, and the summing up of his psychological insights in *De anima et vita Cypriani Morandini,* a conglomeration of twenty-eight notebooks consisting of aphorisms, psychological observations, and self-analysis. The latter work was never published and was never intended for publication. Andrian wrote it, as he explained in a letter to Hofmannsthal, "only for myself."[29] He thought of both works as transitional to a resumption of writing fiction; in 1929 he defended this "detour" in a letter to Hofmannsthal by saying: "Why do I have to occupy myself with all this and know all these interrelations? When I say to know, I mean to relate them myself, to create them, I can only learn through being creative, it is no different with psychology than with metaphysics and theology. - The ultimate reason is that I need this whole enormous apparatus in order *to be poet* without having to lie, and I cannot lie. Poet I must be, because otherwise I am too unhappy, because otherwise I cannot bear to live."[30]

By 1933 Andrian felt sufficiently prepared to resume work on the novel, now entitled *Der Lauf zum Ideal. Des Gartens der Erkenntnis zweiter Teil.* As the title implies, Andrian thought of the novel as a sequel to the *Garten der Erkenntnis.* The major motifs of the earlier novel— Austria, homosexuality, aristocracy, religion, and the self in its totality— were to be revived, although with the significant difference that "ethical questions and the most general sphere of knowledge, God's reality" were to be given center stage (TuA 176, p. 10). The outline which Andrian wrote for the novel indicates its scope. The novel was to be autobiographical, and the entire life of Gabriel, the protagonist, was to be told. The narrated time was to span the period from approximately 1870 to 1932, and the account of Gabriel's life was to be interwoven with the socio-political changes in Austria during this period. The central theme of the novel was to be the problem of how a sinner can be saved by the grace of God: "'Alors ta belle âme est sauvée?/ Mais de quels désirs éprouvée!'"; this quotation, which Andrian noted down in his outline (TuA 176, p. 98), sums up the novel. In the first part of the novel Gabriel's life before his conversion was to be shown. Gabriel shares not only Andrian's dream of becoming a great poet, but also his narcissism: "For Gabriel the world existed for his self and for the enjoyment of his self" (TuA 6466, p. 38). Like Andrian, he undergoes a crisis and tries to overcome it by basing his life on the teachings of the Catholic church. The second part was to depict Gabriel's striving for perfection and his vain attempt to save his soul by means of his own strength. Since such an attempt is necessarily based on hubris, and since he cannot renounce his sensuality, he fails and despairs. The third part was to tell of his being saved through humility and trust in God's love.

Andrian wrote a large part of the novel but he never completed it. In addition to the reasons for his failing to do so mentioned above, he probably also felt compelled by the political events of the thirties to abandon the novel. Increasingly alarmed about the rising sentiment among the Austrian German nationalists for a political union with Nazi Germany, Andrian devoted all his energy to fighting the Anschluss movement in Austria. In essays such as "Hofmannsthal und die österreichische Jugend," (1934, Hofmannsthal and Austrian Youth), he appealed to a younger generation to preserve Austria's independence and not to betray Austria's special ethnographic mission, which he defined as "unitas ex variis."[31] In an essay of 1938, entitled "Die sprachliche Berufung des Österreichers" (unpublished, The Austrian's Linguistic Mission), he condemned the Austrian German nationalists' demand for a "racially pure [German] language" as just as insane as the mania for a "racially pure people" (TuA 6422, p. 18). His campaign against the sentiment for *Anschluss* culminated in *Österreich im Prisma der Idee. Katechismus der Führenden* (1937, Austria in the Prism of the Idea. A Catechism For Leaders), a work which can be characterized as Andrian's political and cultural testament. When Austria became part of the German Reich in 1938, the book was pulped, Andrian's name was blacklisted by the Gestapo, and he spent the next seven years of his life (1939-1946) in lonely exile in Brazil.

Österreich im Prisma der Idee, which Andrian dedicated to Hofmannsthal, is in some respects a summing up of his lifelong preoccupation with Austria's cultural and political situation. Reflections on

Austria's special mission in Europe, and attempts to distinguish Austrian culture from German culture already figure prominently in the diaries of the 1890's. At that time Andrian both shared and rejected the widespread idea that Austria was in decline. In 1894 he noted in his diary: "Our society of today resembles a large city in which a secret disease rages. - Nobody knows for sure whether or not he has it, everyone looks his neighbor furtively in the eyes in order to find out, but there is a tacit agreement - one does not talk about it and glides on"(TuA 52, p. 140). Andrian, like many of his contemporaries, saw the cause of this "secret disease" in the multi-racial composition of the Austro-Hungarian Empire and the decline of Vienna's leading role: "formerly," he wrote in 1894, "Vienna made Austria, just as Paris made France. Something in Vienna is no longer strong enough to exercise power of assimilation, the city is being flooded, Vienna is being Bohemianized, formerly the Bohemians were Viennaized — it is Rome and Byzantium all over again" (TuA 52, p. 177).

This notion of decline led Andrian to see himself as one of the last representatives of Austrian culture before the night of barbarism descended: "It is beautiful," he wrote in 1894, "this role as the last Austrian poets, - we who are at the same time the last echo of the dying Austrian culture" (TUA 53, p. 29). The young Andrian, however, also voiced the conviction that his generation was called upon to regenerate Austrian culture and thus to make its contribution to the general European cultural rejuvenation of the late nineteenth century. In 1895, for example, he noted in his diary: "we do not think of ourselves as lonely innovators, but rather as the Viennese advance post of that great league which Nietzsche called the 'good Europeans'" (TuA 57, p. 112). And despite his misgivings concerning the increasing tensions caused by the nationalist movements within the Austro-Hungarian Empire, he repeatedly expressed his hope that the Austro-Hungarian state, composed of many different peoples, would someday serve as a model for a united Europe.

After the First World War and subsequent developments had shattered these hopes, Andrian observed the socio-political and cultural development in Austria and Europe with increasing disapproval. In *Österreich im Prisma der Idee* he made a last attempt to stem the tide of the time. At the center of the book, and in this respect it echoes Thomas Mann's *Betrachtungen eines Unpolitischen* (1918, *Reflections of a Non-Political Man*), is an attempt to define culture and to differentiate culture from civilization. The book is written as a series of dialogues among

Heinrich Philipp, a representative of the Austrian aristocracy, Gabriel, a Jesuit priest and philosopher, Erwin, a poet, and Franz, an officer in the national guard and a representative of the younger generation. The central question they address in three evenings of philosophical, historical, and political talk concerns the epoch in which they live, whether it is one of cultural decline or cultural ascendancy, and whether there is a specific Austrian culture, distinct from German culture.

They agree that among the symptoms of cultural decline are the demise of intellectual life in the twentieth century, an increase in irrational thought among those who would ordinarily be expected to defend rationality, the lack of a consensus in matters of taste, the corruption of language, the rise of democracy, and, above all, the encroachment of the German upon the Austrian. The nineteenth century is seen as the end of a cultural epoch which had its beginnings in the middle ages. The century did not contribute to the further development of traditional values, but still shared them, at least in the sense that it discussed them while they were slowly sinking and were finally lost in the dark barbaric age which began with the First World War. According to Andrian, what typifies the twentieth century is the rise of mass civilization, politics, and technology, and the decline of culture. In it the ideal of equality triumphs over justice and freedom, and autocratically ruled empires arise whose rulers relentlessly suppress truth, justice, and the happiness of the individual. For Andrian the hope of a cultural rebirth of Austria rests on the restoration of a hierarchical social order, for, as he argues, the source of Austrian culture through the centuries was the house of Habsburg and the Austrian aristocracy. The thrust of Andrian's argument is a deeply conservative one, yet he foresaw more clearly than many of his contemporaries the destructive forces inherent in ideologies based on irrationality.

After his years in exile, Andrian returned to Europe in 1946. In 1949 he married again but died a lonely man in 1951 in Fribourg, Switzerland. He was buried in Alt-Aussee, Austria, not far from the villa where he had spent much of his childhood and adult life. His contributions to Austrian literature and his indefatigable fight for the preservation of Austria's cultural and political independence assure him a permanent place in Austrian cultural history. His life as a whole, is the moving spectacle of a man striving to overcome his weaknesses while aware that he was doomed to fail in his quest for perfection. In the 1930s he summed up his life in words which may serve as his epitaph: "Suffering was a part of everything, . . . on the whole much more than most human beings experience. . . the suffering of a delicate, sensitive being, ceaselessly striving for the good and unable to forsake evil, and yet doomed to fail, aware of his tragedy" (TuA 176, p. 52).

Notes

1. Quoted from Leopold von Andrian's unpublished diaries and workbooks, No.192, p. 87. These are referred to in the text as TuA (Tagebücher und Arbeitshefte), followed by the volume and page number. All translations, unless otherwise noted, are mine. I would like to thank Robert Weiss and the Deutsches Literaturarchiv in Marbach, West Germany, for permission to quote from these unpublished materials. I also thank the Graduate School Research Fund of the University of Washington for a grant which made it possible for me to do research at the Deutsches Literaturchiv.

2. Hugo von Hofmannsthal/ Leopold von Andrian, *Briefwechsel,* ed. Walter H. Perl (Frankfurt Am Main: Fischer, 1968), p. 45.

3. Quoted in: Walter H. Perl, ed., *Leopold von Andrian und die Blätter für die Kunst* (Hamburg: Hauswedell & Co., 1960), p. 22.

4. Quoted in: Leopold von Andrian, *Der Garten der Erkenntnis,* ed. Walter H. Perl (Frankfurt Am Main: Fischer, 1970), p.76.

5. Quoted in: Peter de Mendelssohn, *S. Fischer und sein Verlag* (Frankfurt: Fischer, 1970), p. 210.

6. The novel has been reprinted three times since: in 1948, 1964, and 1970.

7. Hofmannsthal/Andrian, *Briefwechsel,* p. 179.

8. Arthur Moeller van den Bruck, "Das junge Wien," in: A.M.B., *Die moderne Literatur,* vol. 10 (Berlin/Leipzig: Schuster & Loeffler, 1902), p. 24.

9. Hugo von Hofmannsthal, *Reden und Aufsätze III,* ed. Bernd Schoeller and Ingeborg Beyer-Ahlert (Frankfurt: Fischer, 1980), pp. 398-399.

10. Leopold von Andrian, *Der Garten der Erkenntnis,* p. 36.

11. Ibid., p. 58.

12. Ibid., p. 5.

13. Ibid., p. 20.

14. Ibid., p. 25.

15. Ibid., p. 26.

16. Ibid., p. 31.

17. Ibid., p. 43.

18. Ibid., p. 55.

19. Gerhart Baumann, "Leopold von Andrian. Das Fest der Jugend," *Germanisch-Romanische Monatsschrift,* 6 (1956), pp. 145-162.

20. Ursula Renner, *Leopold von Andrians 'Der Garten der Erkenntnis'. Literarisches Paradigma einer Identitätskrise in Wien um 1900* (Frankfurt: Peter Lang, 1981) pp. 202-216.

21. Jens Rieckman, "Narziss und Dionysos. Leopold von Andrians *Der Garten der Erkenntnis*," *Modern Austrian Literature*, 16/1 (1983), pp. 65-81.

22. Quoted in: Karl Kerényi, *Romandichtung und Mythologie. Ein Briefwechsel mit Thomas Mann* (Zürich: Rhein Verlag, 1945), p. 82.

23. Hofmannsthal/Andrian, *Briefwechsel*, p. 144.

24. Hugo von Hofmannsthal, *Selected Prose,* tr. Mary Hottinger, Tania and James Stern (New York: Pantheon, 1952), p. 133.

25. Walter H. Perl, "Leopold von Andrian, ein vergessener Dichter des Symbolismus, Freund Georges und Hofmannsthals," *Philobiblion*, 2 (1958), pp. 303-309.

26. See: H. R. Klieneberger, "Hofmannsthal and Andrian," *Modern Language Review*, 80 (1985), pp. 619-636.

27. See: Walter H. Perl, "Der Dichter Leopold Andrian: Frühvollendung und Verstummen," *Philobiblion*, 14 (1970), pp. 49-56.

28. Hofmannsthal/Andrian, *Briefwechsel* , p. 383.

29. Ibid., p. 430.

30. Ibid., p. 431.

31. Ibid., p. 134.

Bibliography

I.   Works by Andrian:

Hannibal: Romanzen-Cyclus. Venedig: Kirchmeyer & Scozzi, 1888.

Der Garten der Erkenntnis, Berlin: S. Fischer, 1895.

Der Garten der Erkenntnis und die Jugendgedichte. Haag: De Zilverdistel, 1913.

Das Fest der Jugend: Des Gartens der Erkenntnis erster Teil und die Jugendgedichte, with a preface by the author Berlin: S. Fischer, 1919.

"Die Wurzeln des Weltkrieges," *Berliner Tagesblatt* 470 (5 October, 1919), *Berliner Tagesblatt* 507 (26 October, 1919).

"Das erniedrigte und erhöhte Polen," *Österreichische Rundschau* 17 (1921), 892-910; 981-994.

"Das große Salzburger Welttheater," *Hochland* 20 (1922), 177-180.

"Die metaphysische Ständeordnung des Alls: Rationale Grundlagen eines christlichen Weltbildes," *Neue deutsche Beiträge*, 2. Folge, 3 (1927), 55-88.

"Meine Tätigkeit als Intendant der Wiener Hoftheater," *Neue Freie Presse*, 28 October 1928, 29-30; 4 November 1928, 33-34; 8 November 1928, 12-13.

Die Ständeordnung des Alls: Rationales Weltbild eines katholischen Dichters. München: Kosel & Pustet, 1930.

"Hofmannsthal und die österreichische Jugend," *Vaterland* 8 (1934), 130-136.

"Über den Humanismus: Aus den 'Gesprächen dreier Abende'," *Corona* 6 (1935/36), 552-567.

Österreich im Prisma der Idee: Ein Katechismus für Führende, Graz: Schmidt-Dengler, 1937.

"Vaterland und Vaterlandsvolk," *Neues Wiener Tagblatt* 6 (7 January, 1938).

"Polen, Rußland und die Ukrainer," *Die Ostschweiz: Schweizerisches Tagblatt* 514 (6 November, 1939); *Die Ostschweiz: Schweizerisches Tagblatt* 516 (7 November, 1939).

"Deutsche und Russen im polnischen Empfinden," *Die Ostschweiz: Schweizerisches Tagblatt* 522 (10 November, 1939); *Die Ostschweiz: Schweizerisches Tagblatt* 524 (11 November, 1939).

Das Fest der Jugend: Des Gartens der Erkenntnis erster Teil, die Jugendgedichte und ein Sonett, Graz: Schmidt-Dengler, 1948.

"Erinnerungen an meinen Freund," *Hugo von Hofmannsthal: Die Gestalt des Dichters im Spiegel der Freunde*, ed. Helmut A. Fiechtner, Wien: Humboldt, 1949, pp. 52-64.

Hugo von Hofmannsthal- Leopold von Andrian, Briefwechsel, ed. Walter H. Perl, Frankfurt: S. Fischer, 1968.

Der Garten der Erkenntnis: Mit Dokumenten und zeitgenössischen Stimmen, ed. Walter H. Perl, Frankfurt: S. Fischer, 1970.

Frühe Gedichte, ed. Walter H. Perl, Hamburg: Hauswedell & Co., 1972.

II.   Secondary Works on Andrian in English:

Walter H. Perl, "Leopold von Andrian, Writer, Statesman, Philosopher," *Books Abroad*, 27 (1953), 37-38.

Carl E. Schorske, "The Transformation of the Garden," in: Schorske, *Fin-de-Siècle Vienna: Politics and Culture*, New York: Alfred A. Knopf, 1980, pp. 279-321.

Hans Rudolf Klieneberger, "Hofmannsthal and Leopold Andrian," *Modern Language Review*, 80 (1985), 619-636.

III.   Major Studies in German:

Walter H. Perl, *Leopold von Andrian und die Blätter für die Kunst*, Hamburg: Hauswedell & Co., 1960.
Horst Schumacher, *Leopold von Andrian. Werk und Weltbild eines österreichischen Dichters*, Wien: Bergland Verlag, 1967.
Walter H. Perl, "Der Dichter Leopold von Andrian. Frühvollendung und Vestummen," *Modern Austrian Literature*, 2 (1969), 23-29.
Ursula Renner, *Leopold Andrians 'Garten der Erkenntnis.' Literarisches Paradigma einer Identitätskrise in Wien um 1900*, Frankfurt/Main: Peter Lang, 1981.
Jens Rieckmann, "Narziss und Dionysos: Leopold von Andrians 'Der Garten der Erkenntnis," *Modern Austrian Literature*, 16/1 (1983), 65-81.
Hartmut Scheible, "Metaphysik des Fiakers," in: H.S., *Literarischer Jugendstil in Wien*, Müchen: Artemis, 1984, pp. 32-49.

Hermann Bahr

Donald G. Daviau

Hermann Bahr (1863-1934) loomed as a dominating presence within a generation notable for outstanding writers. He considered himself a "Herr von Adabei" (Johnny on the spot), and for over forty years he knew the leading writers, directors, critics, and artists, and participated in every major artistic trend.[1] Through public readings and lectures, through performances of his plays in theaters throughout Austria and Germany, and through his prolific outpouring of writings in all forms except lyric poetry, he remained omnipresent on the cultural scene. The totality of his output—approximately one hundred and thirty books, an uncounted number of published essays, more than 50,000 letters—constitutes in effect a subjective cultural history of Austria from 1890 to 1933. Certainly no other author of his time, neither Arthur Schnitzler, Hugo von Hofmannsthal, nor even Karl Kraus, devoted more attention and energy to Austrian concerns and particularly to the task of revitalizing Austria at the turn of the century. The caricature of Bahr in his own day as "Die Hebamme der neuen Kunst" (The midwife of the new art), actually portrayed him accurately; Bahr did help propel Austria out of its stagnation of the late nineteenth century to a more progressive twentieth-century attitude on the model of the other western European countries. His experiences living and studying in Berlin and Paris along with traveling extensively in Germany, France, and Spain gave him the perspective he required to promote the need for change. He had intended to remain involved in the larger European scene, but when he returned to Vienna in 1891 for a temporary visit before returning to Europe, he became enthused over the number of talented young writers, artists, architects, and musicians he met and decided to stay and help develop a new literature and a new cultural era in Austria.[2] As his goal he wanted to achieve a closer rapprochement of Austria with the rest of Europe and to see Austrian literature and culture modernized and raised to the same level achieved by the other more progressive European countries. Indefatigably he worked at promoting his cultural program of modernity, which for the next fifteen years dominated his thinking and activity. He served as the organizer,[3] the catalyst of his generation in Vienna and accomplished his goal of revitalizing the cultural scene by the time he changed direction in 1906.

As an Impressionist, whose personal motto was "Never and always the same"("Niemals und immer derselbe"),[4] Bahr was shaped as few others by the cultural forces and currents of his day. His writings reflect his attempts to understand and mediate to the public the latest cultural, social, and political manifestations from all over Europe. New intellectual trends and literary fashions were being spawned at a rapid rate, and Bahr embraced many of them in order to explain them to his readers. In literature he began as a Naturalist, quickly embraced Impressionism which best suited his character and personality, brought the Decadent movement from France to Germany and Austria,[5] experimented briefly with Expressionism without ever succeeding in making the transition completely, and finally returned to a traditional Classical outlook, stressing absolute rather than relative values.[6] In politics he belonged briefly to the German National Party headed by Georg Ritter von Schönerer, shifted to a position opposing anti-Semitism, became a dedicated supporter of the Monarchy and the Austrian tradition. In religion he was born a Catholic, turned atheist under the influence of Schönerer, proclaimed himself without church affiliation when he married the minor Jewish actress Rosa Jokl in 1895, and returned to Catholicism in 1914, attending church faithfully every day for the rest of his life.

Because of his frequent changes of direction in his early years, Bahr was satirized as a chameleon (*Verwandlungskünstler*), but his first-hand knowledge of literary trends was necessary to furnish the expertise he required to fulfill the mediating role that he chose to play in educating the public to the newest cultural ideas. Bahr served as the guiding force for several major changes, ranging from the establishment of a new acting style and a modern European repertoire in the Burgtheater, new forms in literature, such as the"Vienna novel" ("Wiener Roman") new directions in art (Secession) and music, to a renewed pride in the Austrian heritage, including the restoration of the baroque tradition, and a serious regard for Austria's role in Europe.

Nothing in Bahr's small-town, middle-class family background would have suggested his future career as a writer and cultural critic. He was born to Alois and Wilhelmine Bahr on 19 July 1863 in the then sleepy provincial town of Linz in Upper Austria, where Adalbert Stifter, the outstanding Austrian prose writer of the nineteenth century, had lived. In sending Bahr to be educated in the Benedictine schools in Linz and Salzburg and in 1881 to the University of Vienna to study classical philology and law, it was expected that he would follow his father with a career in law and bureaucratic service. However, young Bahr was soon attracted to the new discipline of political science, joined Schönerer's rabid pan-German political movement, initially accepting its program of anti-Semitism and its goal of overthrowing the Monarchy to achieve annexation with Germany. In 1883 he was dismissed for life from the university for a political speech which was interpreted as treasonous. Bahr then studied in Graz, Czernowitz, and Berlin (1884-1887). His dissertation was rejected, and he never completed his degree.

He had broken with Schönerer and joined Viktor Adler's Socialist movement in 1886 but grew disenchanted with politics because of its petty economic concerns. After fulfilling his compulsory year of military service, he spent a year in Paris, where he completed the shift from politics to literature, disappointing Adler, who felt that Bahr had great potential for a political career. During his subsequent stay in Berlin (1889-1890) Bahr witnessed the inauguration of Naturalism in the theater and the founding of the "Free stage" ("Freie Bühne"). He became acquainted with the leading Naturalist writers such as Gerhart Hauptmann, Arno Holz, and the director Otto Brahm, whom he tried to challenge for the editorship of the journal *Freie Bühne*. When his attempt failed, Bahr decided to leave Berlin. After a trip to Russia, where he "discovered" Eleonora Duse,[7] Bahr returned to Vienna, where the proper circumstances and abundant talent launched him on a career as a leading spokesman for modernity as the central figure of the so-called Young Vienna group: Hugo von Hofmannsthal, Arthur Schnitzler, Richard Beer-Hofmann, and Leopold von Andrian, with such friends as Felix Salten, Raoul Auernheimer, and the German writer Jakob Wassermann closely affiliated.

In his early years Bahr was a larger than life presence, a charismatic figure who was influential largely through the power of his unquenchable personality. He was prone to exaggeration and always attempted to dazzle, stimulate, and provoke his audiences, particularly in his early career when, strongly influenced by Nietzsche, he lived by the motto "épater les bourgeois." He experimented with all of the literary fashions of his day, not out of lack of character, as detractors alleged, and not to advocate any particular technique, movement, or program.[8] Rather, like Nietzsche, Bahr considered it an essential aspect of modernity to remain receptive to new ideas and trends. Furthermore, his purpose was to mediate new and significant tendencies. He not only stayed abreast of his time, but also prided himself on being ahead of it, causing critics to dub him "The man from the day after tomorrow" ("Der Mann von Übermorgen"). This openness to change and ability to predict trends continued all of his life, as did his mediating role. However, his work in Vienna ended in 1906, when Bahr, resenting the antagonism of the Viennese after the fifteen years of his cultural campaign, departed for Berlin, where he worked for two years as a dramaturge ("Dramaturg") and director with Max Reinhardt. He tried returning to Vienna in 1908 but, finding the atmosphere still inhospitable, moved permanently to Salzburg in 1908 with his second wife, the opera singer Anna Mildenburg, whom he married in 1909, after ending his first marriage (1895) with the minor Jewish actress Rosa Jokl, who had brought him little happiness. In 1922, to allow Mildenburg to teach at the Academy of Performing Arts, Bahr moved to Munich, where he died from arteriosclerosis on 15 January 1934.

Throughout his life Bahr was always a controversial, misunderstood, and underrated thinker and writer, and he remains so today. He wrote quickly, dictating his writings, which he then failed to rework and polish. Hence his best ideas, and he had many of them, often sacrifice their effectiveness because they are scattered in works that are wordy and repetitious or buried in his essays and reviews. Moreover, Bahr could never resist the temptation to overstate for emphasis, causing critics to doubt everything he wrote. As a result of his early image, critics today, influenced largely by the negative views of Karl Kraus, have yet to read his works in order to form a fresh judgment about Bahr's significance on the basis of first-hand knowledge. Part of the current problem with Bahr's reputation results from the lack of his books in print because of the legal complications surrounding Bahr's literary estate.[9] A major breakthrough has taken place in the publication of Bahr's diaries, which rival those of Schnitzler in importance.[10] Those who have read Bahr's works with an open mind recognize them as a valuable and insightful guide through the complex maze of the conflicting currents of Austrian literature from 1890 to1930. Eventually Bahr's vital role will have to be recognized, for until his contribution is acknowledged and he is properly placed at the center of his generation, it is impossible to understand fin-de-siècle Vienna correctly.

For his part Bahr remained oblivious to the opinions of others and followed his own course, unaffected by praise and undeterred by criticism. For example, he withstood the bitter polemic that Karl Kraus waged against him for over forty years, beginning in 1893 and culminating only in 1935 a year after Bahr's death. Kraus had two major reasons for his tenacious and virulent attack: on the personal level Bahr won a lawsuit against Kraus in 1901, and Kraus could never get over the defeat; on the professional level Kraus considered Bahr the most significant and hence the most dangerous exponent of the corrupt journalist practice of mutual reviewing current among theater critics of the day.[11] While Kraus's campaign had little effect on Bahr in his lifetime, without question it has severely diminished Bahr's reputation today, for younger scholars, if they know Bahr at all, do so only on the basis of reading Kraus. Bahr was unconcerned about his reputation in posterity; his ambition was to feel fulfilled as an individual and to become a "real person" ("ein wirklicher Mensch"). The value of his literary and cultural contribution must be judged on the totality of his many varied activities, all of which were devoted to improving the status of culture in Austria and to developing the country into a modern Western nation. In these terms his program was a complete success.

Bahr contributed to revitalizing the cultural scene in a major way during the 1890s with an important series of essays, defining modernity as a way of life. He was strongly influenced by Ibsen, Nietzsche, Maurice Barrés, and Karl Joris Huysmans. A decade before Bahr discovered in Ernst Mach the confirmation of his view that human beings were connected to the real world through their senses,[12] he advocated the necessity of the individual's remaining in a state of constant flux to stay abreast of the changing world. In this way one becomes and remains modern. The result for him and his circle of like-minded friends was to adopt Impressionism as their Weltanschauung. The idea of a fixed ego proved to be a fiction, and only the moment was true. Consequently there was a major shift in the thinking of this generation from absolute to relative values.

Bahr's preoccupation with the theory of perception ("Erkenntnistheorie"),[13] found expression in the sequential volumes *Zur Kritik der Moderne* (1890, On the Criticism of Modernity), *Die Überwindung des Naturalismus* (1891, The Overthrow of Naturalism), *Studien zur Kritik der Moderne* (1894, Studies on the Criticism of Modernity), *Renaissance* (1896, Renaissance), *Bildung* (1900, Education), and *Secession* (1900,

Secession). Since all of Bahr's works in a given year or period concern the same topics, his early novels *Die gute Schule* (1891, The Good School), and *Neben der Liebe* (1892, Alongside of Love), as well as the collections of shorter prose, *Fin de siècle* (1891, Fin de siècle), *Dora* (1893, Dora), and *Caph* (1894, Caph) are all written in an Impressionistic style and feature Decadence and a life of the senses as the best means of staying abreast of the changing outside world, as mandated by his concept of modernity. However, the precepts of Decadence, which preach a reversal of all normal values, i.e. glorification of night over day and of death over life as well as emphasizing perversity, caused Bahr to break with Decadence in 1896. The theoretical background for his artistic views, including Decadence, are found scattered throughout his essays and diaries but never presented in an organized way.

To assist his campaign of culture, Bahr in 1894, together with Dr. Isidor Singer and Dr. Heinrich Kanner, founded the newspaper *Die Zeit*, through which he mediated the new literature and art to the public. Bahr, a friend of Gustav Klimt and Joseph Olbrich, also played a major role in the establishment of the Secessionist art movement founded in Vienna on 1 April 1897. When Klimt was attacked in 1901 for his controversial ceiling murals for the University, Bahr rallied to the aid of his beleaguered friend by hiring the Bösendorfer Hall and delivered a fiery attack on Klimt's detractors in *Rede über Klimt* (1901, Speech about Klimt). He also published *Gegen Klimt* (1903, Against Klimt), a collection of slanderous attacks to serve as a historical record.

By the turn of the century Bahr repudiated Decadence along with Vienna and turned to the provinces as the real strength of Austria, a view which henceforth remained consistent. His thinking underwent a change from considering art the paramount accomplishment of life to stressing the importance of life over art. In terms of the "Geist/Natur or Leben/Kunst" (spirit/nature or life/art) conflict of that era, which dominated German literature, Bahr now came down solidly on the side of life. This view found expression in the prose collection *Wirkung in die Ferne* (1902, *Remote Effect*), in the dramas *Der Athlet* (1899, *The Athlete*) and *Der Meister* (1904, *The Master*), and in the two dialogues, one of Bahr's most successful forms, *Dialog von Tragischen* (1904, Dialogue of the Tragic) and *Dialog von Marsyas* (1905, Dialogue of Marsyas).

Bahr almost died in 1903, and the *Dialog von Marsyas* represents a major turning point in his life and thinking. In 1906, dejected by the lack of response to his campaign of modernity, weary of Kraus's constant attacks, and dismayed by the general climate of hostility, Bahr moved to Berlinn to work for Max Reinhardt. He continued to stay abreast of the latest developments, as can be seen in his volume *Expressionismus* (1915, *Expressionism*, 1925), in which he acknowledged this new movement as more significant than Impressionism. He continued to produce volumes of essays with the topics becoming increasingly oriented toward the Austrian, the classical German, and the ancient classical traditions. He devoted himself to the study of Goethe and developed into a knowledge-able commentator, as seen in the volume of essays *Um Goethe* (1915, On Goethe), in his reviews, and in the insightful comments in his diaries. Other important essay collections include *Inventur* (1912, Inventory), in which Bahr assesses his life and time upon reaching fifty, *Summula* (1921), *Sendung des Künstlers* (1923, Mission of the Artist), and *Labyrinth der Gegenwart* (1929, The Contemporary Labyrinth).

Regardless of his variety of social and political concerns, the theater remained a central interest of Bahr throughout his life, and he became one of the most versatile and knowledgeable theater people of his time. In addition to writing thirty-four dramas, he was also active as a theoretician, historian, and reviewer: *Wiener Theater* (1893, *Viennese Theater*), Premiéren (1902, *Premieres*), *Rezensionen* (1903, *Reviews*), and *Glossen zum Wiener Theater* (1907, *Glosses on the Viennese Theater*). His practi-cal experience included advising Max Burckhardt, the director of the Burgtheater in the 1890s, assisting in the Vienna Volkstheater of Bukovics around 1900, working with Max Reinhardt from 1906-1908, and finally serving as director of the Burgtheater for six months in 1918, just at the end of the war when conditions were particularly difficult. He considered the highpoint of his contribution the scheduling of Goethe's *Die natür-liche Tochter* (The Natural Daughter), on 16 November 1918, right after Austria had been proclaimed a republic, as a warning against anarchy and a plea for unity. Bahr's final major contribution consisted of the two his-torical accounts: *Burgtheater* (1920, Burgtheater), in which he stressed the importance of the Austrian baroque tradition, and *Schauspielkunst* (1923, *The Art of Acting*), in which he repeated his oft-stated view that the actor was the most important element in the theater.

To present his view of Austrian life in its various facets and aspects, Bahr embarked on an ambitious series of twelve novels to present his per-sonal view of Austria, or as he phrased it, to recite his "inner alphabet." The material had been gestating within him, and he wrote in rapid sequence *Die Rahl* (1908, Rahl), *Drut* (1909, Drut), and *O Mensch* (1901,

Oh Man). He continued the series after he left Vienna for Salzburg with *Himmelfahrt* (1916, Ascension) and *Die Rotte Korahs* (1919, The Band of Korah). The last two novels, *Der inwendige Garten* (1927, The Inner Garden) and *Österreich in Ewigkeit* (1928, Austria in Eternity), which were written in Munich, reveal the increasing difficulty Bahr was experiencing in shaping his ideas as his creative powers faded. Of the twelve projected novels, only seven were completed.

All of Bahr's writings are subjective, and these novels were intended as his personal analysis of conditions in Austria, as he has perceived and experienced them. He had presented all of these ideas in other forms, for typically the works of a given time period all concern the same topics. While he disclaimed any attempt to emulate Balzac's "comedie humaine," the intent is similar. Bahr used the novel form as a "creative mirror" ("schaffender Spiegel") that was not intended to reflect precise reality but to refract reality so that its hidden dimensions and significance were rendered visible and meaningful.[14] While none of these novels stands out as a great work of literature, as Bahr himself readily admitted, they remain relevant, eminently readable works even today; above all they serve as informative documents of their time and as essential sources for understanding Bahr and his thinking about major problems of his day.

Even before he began the Austrian cycle Bahr had written three novels: *Die gute Schule*, *Neben der Liebe*, and *Das Theater*. *Die gute Schule*, one of his most significant works, based on his experiences in Paris and his discovery of Decadence, represents an attempt to write a German counterpart to the breviary of Decadence, Karl Joris Huysman's novel *A Rebours* (1887, *Against the Grain*). The subtitle "Seelenzustände" (states of mind) indicates the emphasis on the senses, a focus new to Austria and Germany. *Die gute Schule* caused a minor sensation in Berlin when the work was serialized from April to June 1890 in the Berlin journal *Freie Bühne für modernes Leben*. Bahr made early use of inner monologue to present the struggle of a poor but idealistic painter living in Paris to capture on canvas the perfect colors that he envisions in his mind's eye, his means of overcoming the dichotomy of spirit and nature and achieving a breakthrough to rendering pure truth.

When his efforts fail, the painter attempts to heighten his sense perception through an erotic encounter which degenerates into masochistic brutality. When even these orgies of lust and cruelty fail to bring the desired artistic breakthrough, the artist finally capitulates and becomes "respectable" by selling out to materialistic bourgeois values: if he cannot be a pure artist, he will at least be a financially successful hack. "The Good School" is revealed to have an ironic twist: instead of elevating him, as Gretchen inspired Faust to a higher life, love has caused the painter to descend from the heights of idealism to a bourgeois existence concerned only with material security and personal comfort.

Die gute Schule shows how well Bahr had learned the literary formula of Decadence, and how cleverly he made use of all of its features. At the same time the cynicism of the abrupt ending shows that, in spite of his mastery of the techniques, Bahr lacked any genuine commitment in the principles of Decadence. It is but one example of how he attempted to gain a basic understanding of all movements by practicing them, only to abandon them after he felt he had mastered them. The novel illustrates the decadent aesthetic principle that plot was subordinate to style and form. As is true of *A Rebours*, the language is particularly rich in verbs of action and descriptive adjectives. In 1898 Bahr claimed that in his new style the novel would be only a third as long.[15]

As an offshoot of *Die gute Schule* Bahr wrote *Fin de siècle* (1891), a collection of short prose works intended as finger exercises to practice further the techniques and themes of Decadence. The individual texts are short sketches and prose vignettes, featuring the senses and dealing with psychological states of mind, aestheticism as a way of life, and often perverse sexuality. The volume was clearly aimed at shocking the bourgeoisie, and Bahr was elated when it was banned by the police and confiscated, gaining the book more publicity than it would have received otherwise.

Other works written in Bahr's decadent period were *Russische Reise* (1893, Russian Trip), a stylized diary of his trip to St. Petersburg in late 1890 with the actor Emanuel Reicher and the actress Lotte Witt, *Dora* (1893, a collection of three prose tales, "Dora," "Die Schneiderin," and "Jeanette"), and *Caph* (1894). All of these works display Decadent themes and techniques, emphasizing states of mind described in elegant style rather than plot. *Caph* is the most extreme example of this tendency, as declared in the motto chosen from Bahr's alter-ego Maurice Barrés: "Nothing matters but stylistic form." Unfortunately Bahr's attempt in *Caph* to transform mundane subject matter into the pure gold of literature through elevated language is a failure. His linguistic capability is not brilliant enough to overcome the absence of a substantive plot. Ultimately *Caph* represents Bahr's attempt to push the Decadent formula to its extreme degree before finally recognizing its limitations and turning away from this tendency completely, as he did in 1896.

In his second novel, *Neben der Liebe*, Bahr used the same technique as found in *Die gute Schule* except that the former overheated lavishly-descriptive style has been replaced here with a cooler narrative technique. The contrast resembles a shift from oils to pastels. Where *Die gute Schule* emphasized the bright colors red and green, in *Neben der Liebe* gray tones predominate to reinforce the monotonous lives of the characters. In this short novel, which he always regarded highly, Bahr treats a group of Viennese aesthetes and men about town who lead a shallow passive life without deeper feelings or commitments to any values. The plot concerns an unusual and tragic love story, played out against a richly ornamented background, reflecting the Japanese fad of the time. This psychological novel, which is presented in the form of interior monologue to a large extent in order to represent the complex subtle psychological feelings and thoughts of the protagonist, attempts to illustrate Bahr's views that love and erotic desire only seldom coincide, a circumstance that causes people to live their lives *Neben der Liebe* rather than finding fulfillment in a love which at the same time satisfies erotic desires. The novel conveys another predominating idea of Bahr in the 1890s, namely, the fatalistic view that human destiny is determined not by free will but by external powers over which the individual has no control.

Bahr's early novels do not belong to the Austrian cycle, but his third novel *Theater* moves closer in that direction as a precursor of *Die Rahl*. *Theater* is a frame novel with the outer narrative presented in the first person. Bahr introduces details from his own experiences in this insider's view of the theater life of that time. His narrative strength lay in creating rounded believable characters and in his ability to create brilliant set pieces within the novels. His greatest deficiency, as he recognized himself, was his inability to interweave plot and the characters into a unified whole that is ultimately greater than the sum of its parts. His novels tend to be unilinear and two-dimensional rather than developing multiple levels. Thus they never achieve the complexity and interpretative ambiguity of great novels but invariably end with a clear-cut resolution. Partly this limitation results from the tendentious nature of the novels, for Bahr utilizes each of them to convey his subjective views of a specific area of Austrian life. He is always clearly the recognizable author, and the fictional world of the novel never assumes an autonomous life of its own. An essayistic quality dominates the novels, and at times there is little difference, even in wording, between Bahr's novels and his essays.

In *Theater*, one of Bahr's most successful novels, Bahr sought to explore and expose the make-believe world of the theater, with which he had become somewhat disenchanted on the basis of his close involvement both with actors and theater life. The novel is also intended as another demonstration of the power of fate against which the human being is helpless. All of life is simply a lottery, and one cannot do anything about it. He illustrates that the emphasis on rationality and education (*Bildung*), so prized by the nineteenth-century liberals, was a false approach to life. The protagonist Mohr also echoes one of Bahr's major ideas that he worked so hard to put into practice, namely, that poetry and life were kept separated when in reality they should be more closely united, so that each would benefit from the other.

Because of the importance of the theater in his life it was a natural choice for Bahr to make this world that he knew so well and that continually attracted him the subject of the first novel of the Austrian cycle, *Die Rahl*. One of the subthemes of *Theater* had been the ability of performers to transform into the characters they were playing. This phenomenon of psychological transformation intrigued Bahr, and he wrote about it extensively in his various reviews, contrasting two main approaches to performing: those who transformed into the part they were playing, like Eleonora Duse, and those who always played only themselves in every role, like Sarah Bernhardt. In *Die Rahl* Bahr specifically concentrates on portraying an actress, Rahl, who is possible modeled on Charlotte Wolter, to demonstrate the mystery of the transformation of an actress into her role and her elevated life on stage contrasted with her empty life in the periods between performances.

This view of Rahl's existence corresponds to Bahr's theory that actors may serve as a model to show people how to live and how to elevate their existence to a higher level of intensity and meaning. From his visits to Greece and his study of Greek life and literature Bahr deduced the importance of reaching beyond oneself, of living at times in states of heightened intensity even at the cost of subsequent low points. During these lows individuals collect their resources and energies for another period of heightened productivity. Only in this way can one accumulate the powers needed in order to accomplish a higher purpose. It is necessary to lie fallow at periods in order to collect one's inner strength to rise to greatness beyond oneself. One can recognize in this ideal not only its Greek origins, but also the influence of Nietzsche with his attack on mediocrity and the attitude of playing it safe in life. Bahr gave this theme its finest treatment in the one-act play *Der arme Narr* (1906, The Poor Fool), based loosely on the life of his former student friend, Hugo Wolf.

Die Rahl also contains another of Bahr's favorite themes at this time: the conflict between spirit and nature (Geist und Natur), the major conflict reflected in Austrian and German literature from 1890 up to World War I. Here the contrast is shown between Professor Samon, who would like to marry Franz Heitlinger's widowed mother, and Franz's father, who was diametrically opposed to Samon in character and nature. Franz's father and Samon represent the opposing qualities of individualism and submissiveness, imagination and passivity, originality and sterility, progress and convention, feeling and reason, change and tradition. Bahr repeatedly stressed these contrasts in his subsequent works, as he tried to break down the attitude of clinging to the status quo and fearing the new.

The novel also touches on the theme of anti-Semitism, and shows how far Bahr has distanced himself from his early radical days as a follower of Schönerer. The young Jew Beer, who is determined to improve social conditions in Austria, is a totally positive character with an optimistic view of the future and the new humanity that it will bring. In the friendship of the two boys Bahr portrays the unity that is needed for progress, introducing another of his major themes: the isolation of individuals in Austria as a handicap to progress. Bahr leaves no doubt about his great faith in the energy and resolve of the young generation. He fully expects that they will succeed in producing the changes needed to enhance life in Austria.

The optimism that characterized the ending of *Die Rahl* turned to pessimism in *Drut* (1909) with its critical examination of bureaucracy in Austria. The two works form a sequential pattern, and several of the characters from *Die Rahl* reappear in *Drut*. Criticism of the bureaucratic system in Austria was a major topic of Bahr's essays during these years, as found in *Wien* (1907, Vienna), *Buch der Jugend* (1908, Book of Youth), *Dalmatinische Reise* (1909, Journey to Dalmatia), *Tagebuch* (1909, Diary), and *Austriaca* (1911, Austrian Matters). *Drut* represents Bahr's fictionalization of the ideas in the essays, above all, his view that Austria was controlled by a tightly knit bureaucracy whose main purpose was to perpetuate itself in power and to serve itself rather than the country.

An integral part of this autonomous bureaucracy was the institution of the *Hofrat* (Privy Councilor), a titular figure whom Bahr constantly satirized as a menace to the country until he changed his attitude in the 1920s. Bahr approaches the Hofrat not as an individual but as a type. His view of this group's oppressive hold on the country is reflected in the title *Drut*, which refers to the upper Austrian superstition of the *Drut* or *Trud*, a malicious witch who appears during the night to sit on a victim's heart, causing a painful lingering death by suffocation. To Bahr this figure was the perfect symbol of Austrian bureaucracy. Just as in the dramas *Der Krampus* (1902) and *Sanna* (1905), in which he had shown the *Hofrat* sitting like a *Trud* on his own family, suppressing all freedom of spirit and emotion, in *Drut* he portrays bureaucracy as a *Trud* oppressing and stifling the whole country. Bahr's view of bureaucracy as the enemy was shared by his Upper Austrian countrymen, who were suspicious of all officials and in fact of anything that emanated from Vienna.

The novel illustrates the controlling coalition of government and church and also that behavior tolerated in Vienna is not permissible in the provinces. The quixotic nature of justice, the system of protection and connections, and the ruthless competition forced on young administrators trying to curry favor with superiors are all represented. Klemens is trapped between the ambition of his father and the equally relentless system headed by Minister Doltsch, whose one ambition is to survive regardless of any other consideration. Thus to keep peace with the church, his major rival for power, he sacrifices the Baron without a qualm, just as he would anyone or anything else. Survival in the system depends solely on following the prescribed conservative practices. If through chance one is deflected from this traditional course and attempts to become a real person by attempting to break through the fetters of rational life to find individual freedom, there is no possibility of success in this system. Although at the end of *Die Rahl* the two young schoolboys had optimistically believed that they would be able to change the system, the Baron's fate demonstrates the hopelessness of this view.

After 1900 Bahr became a major advocate of the Nietzschean "Lebensphilosophie" (philosophy of life) and the Bergsonian "élan vital." How to become a real or genuine human being formed one of Bahr's most basic themes, as he repeatedly attacked the artificiality of Austrian life, the concept of façade and role-playing, resulting in lonely, isolated, unfulfilled lives and making it impossible for Austrians to work together as was necessary to create a true sense of nation. In his novel *O Mensch* (1910), which, in Bahr's usual manner of describing trends, utilizes as a title the topical Expressionist cry for the human being. Bahr shifts his emphasis from politics to religion, although not to the religion of the church, to which Bahr is still hostile at this time, but, like the Expressionists, to a vision of a free, open, all-embracing natural religiosity that proclaims the essential goodness of all human beings. Like many Expressionist works, this novel with its message of the world's need for more love and humaneness has no plot but consists of a series of encounters between various Austrian types. Bahr was so concerned here with expressing his idealistic precepts of life that he lavished all of his attention on the message and little on the form. The characters for the most part engage in monologues, and enunciate their views on such issues as life, happiness, and religiosity with a minimum of interaction and development.

While the novel features a need for a secular religious renaissance, Bahr does not ignore the continued discussion of the social situation in Austria. The customary themes of the isolation of Austrians from one another, indeed, the outright hostility of Austrians to each other, particularly to anyone striving for accomplishment in any area of life, are strongly in evidence here. Bahr, like other writers, constantly criticized Austrian treatment of even their greatest creative talents from Grillparzer to Mahler. To be appreciated *O Mensch* must be read with the heart, that is, felt more than perceived rationally, in the manner of most Expressionist works. Not until 1916 did Bahr resume his chronicle of Austria with another autobiographical novel, *Himmelfahrt,* describing his return to the Catholic Church in 1914. This novel, which specifically treats the intellectual's path to religion, was widely discussed at the time and was generally either praised or attacked, depending on the critic's attitude toward Bahr in general. More attention was focused on the work as exemplifying Bahr's latest phase than on the merits of the novel itself. The decline of religiosity in the twentieth century under the impact of science and materialism was, in Bahr's view, a major problem of his time. The novel describes the dilemma of intellectuals caught in the conflict between science and religion, a topic that Bahr treated again in a lengthy philosophical essay *Wissenschaft und Glaube* (1917, Science and Faith).

Bahr, who knew whereof he spoke from personal experience, enjoined twentieth-century man to end his frantic pursuit of trendy "isms" and instead to find a solid anchor within himself through religion. Significantly in *Himmelfahrt* it is not simply religion but organized religion that has become important, as reflected in Bahr's own return to the Church. Through his association with clergymen Bahr had learned that the universal natural religion he had espoused in *O Mensch* is not an adequate substitute for the Church; as a result Bahr no longer advocates that people try to seek God directly, but he insists they must use the mediation of the Church. Although he himself chose Catholicism and became an active spokesman for the Catholic Church on many issues, and although he believed that the Catholic Church was the proper choice for everyone, ultimately his main concern was that everyone have a religious affiliation. As usual Bahr points the general direction to follow, but he leaves the final choice of the specific path to the individual.

Following the war Bahr addressed the major questions of anti-Semitism, Zionism, and the Jewish question, some of the most fundamental human and social problems of his day, in *Die Rotte Korahs* (1919, The Band of Korah), his longest, most ambitious, and most successful novel. Here Bahr addressed complex, difficult problems of race, the nature of Austrian character, and the future mission of Austria after the country had been reduced following World War I from the approximately fifty million of the Austro-Hungarian Monarchy to a torso (*Rumpfstaat*) of approximately seven million people. *Die Rotte Korahs* is Bahr's strongest statement against the unfairness and the unjustifiability of anti-Semitism, continuing his opposition to such prejudice, begun in *Antisemitismus* (1894) and continuing to the end of his life.

As a new theme in his writings Bahr introduces his latest discovery that Austria's strength resides in its ordinary people, who will enable Austria to fulfill its mission of serving as a cultural and political mediator within the framework of the European community. He felt that Europe needed Austria because of its particular talents and characteristics and that Austria because of its geographical location and its baroque heritage would play a central mediating role in Europe. In this sense, the novel represents Bahr's attempt to unite his countrymen, to reawaken national pride, and to instill confidence in the future in the aftermath of war.

After another lengthy interlude, this time of eight years, Bahr resumed his novel series with *Der inwendige Garten* (1927, The Inward Garden) and *Österreich in Ewigkeit* (1929, Austria in Eternity). In the interim he had continued to turn out dramas, essays, and his weekly diary installments at a prolific rate. Most of his writings in the 1920s and into the 1930s deal with political and social events caused by the reduction of Austria to a small nation and the shift of government from monarchy to republic, changes that he accepted only begrudgingly. Nevertheless, he continued to emphasize his optimism for the future of Austria, while retreating increasingly into an idealized Upper Austrian world of Stifter in his writings to create a portrait of society as he believed it should be: progressive, with social stability, in harmony with nature, and populated with baroque figures who achieve a meaningful life anchored in Catholicism. The primary theme of both novels concerns the idea of the importance of social stability in the country. The first of these extremely weak novels attacks the numerous factions and para-military groups that were formed in the 1920s, creating an atmosphere of political turbulence, while the second denounces the Nazi movement in Austria.

Given his great native ability as a conversationalist, his love of argument, and his gift for dialogue and mimicry, the dramatic form was an ideal medium for Bahr. His extensive background as a theater critic and his considerable experience as *Regisseur* and *Intendant* gave him a working knowledge of the craft of playwriting shared by few dramatists. Yet with all his expertise Bahr never wrote a play of sufficient substance to endure. His thirty-four dramas are all commentaries on issues of his day and involve the same social criticism found in his essays and novels. His light comedies, including his most popular and appealing play, *Das Konzert* (1909, *The Concert*), while still appealing today, never aspired to the higher levels of comedy. Bahr relegated his dramatic works to the level of Eduard von Bauernfeld.

Throughout his career as a dramatist Bahr used the criterion of theatrical effectiveness to determine whether a play was good or bad. His standard for a good drama was simple: a play that could produce in the audience the mood desired by the dramatist was a success;[16] otherwise it was a failure. The audience had to be swept into the action immediately and then had to be sustained by it. The primary aim of his plays was to entertain. If they also achieved the status of literature, that must come in addition to their theatrical merits, not in their place. Secondarily they were to educate, to uplift, and ultimately to help unify the public. His plots often reveal clever twists and amuse by turning accepted notions inside out. At times he had to resort to such stock devices as the *deus ex machina* or the services of a *raisonneur* to resolve the action. As in his novels Bahr's creative ability frequently failed to equal the level of his conceptions. Yet because he was so thoroughly at home in the theater, knew the capabilities of performers, and possessed a gift for witty dialogue and realistic characterization, he managed to conceal the weaknesses of plot, at least during performances. He utilized every theatrical device, including the interjection of songs and dances in the manner of the Viennese folk-play tradition, and he often tailored roles to specific performers.

Bahr began his career as a dramatist with the tendentious political plays *Die neuen Menschen* (1887, The New Human Beings) and *Die grosse Sünde* (1888, The Great Sin), which illustrate his attraction to topical subjects. They also reflect Bahr's tendency to "direct" the production by means of lengthy stage directions. Following the farce *La Marquesa d'Amaëguie* (1888), which displays his fondness for antithesis, and *Die Mutter* (1891, The Mother), his one experiment in using Decadent themes in drama, Bahr wrote *Die häusliche Frau* (1893, The Domestic Woman), a comedy in four acts that offers all the features of technique, style, and dialogue that characterize his subsequent comedies. The plot, which is set in Berlin, concerns an averted seduction; a wife who is taken for granted by her philistine husband becomes vulnerable to the advances of a sculptor friend, a typical aesthete. The danger is avoided after numerous complications, and the action is happily resolved.

After these early experiments Bahr attempted to put into practice his theories of the actor's preeminence in the theater. The texts were loosely written to allow the actors the latitude to improvise: "My idea was to share the theme with the performer. He has the violin, I merely want to accompany him on the piano."[17] Bahr began the major line of his dramas with *Das Tschaperl* (1898, The Fool), "ein Wiener Stück," which deals with the topical themes of women's emancipation and the elimination of the double standard. This bourgeois melodrama, with its overtones of Ibsen's *The Doll House*, may serve as a representative example of Bahr's formula for producing successful theater: a blend of comic and tragic elements, a mixture of wit and irony, a surprising twist of plot, spritely dialogue, theatrical effects, pathos, the use of Viennese dialect, and well-drawn main characters. Bahr vainly tries to present basic problems in such a way that the audience is forced to confront them from a new perspective.

More successful in combining theatrical and literary values is the comedy *Josephine* (1899), which retains its comic vitality with its good-naturedly humorous demythologizing of Napoleon. *Josephine* is an important work reflecting Bahr's belief in the power of fate as the controlling force in life, a theme that recurs in the dramas *Der Athlet* (1899, The Athlete) and *Der Meister* (1904, *The Master*, 1918), as well as in the novels *Das Theater*, *Die Rahl*, *Drut*, and *O Mensch*. Man as a pawn of fate was a popular theme among all of the *Young Vienna* writers. For Bahr fate became a substitute for the God he was trying to avoid until he finally regained his religiosity in 1914. He employs the metaphor of the world as a theater with fate as the director, who ensures that people play their allotted role in life whether they like it or not. Originally he had intended to write a trilogy portraying the three basic stages of existence: "How man presumes to live for himself but then is ordained by fate to carry out his destiny until he has done his duty, performed his task, played his role to the end, and can be released again by fate."[18] The idea of fate controlling life is demonstrated again in *Der Star* (1899), another "Wiener Stück" that presents essentially a less successful version of the novel *Das Theater*, and *Der Athlet* (1900), a thesis play in which the protagonist learns that there are forces in the world stronger than his will.

Bahr's turn to the provinces and his reaction against Vienna is reflected in the dialect play *Der Franzl* (1900), a tribute to his fellow Austrian poet Franz Stelzhamer, and in *Die Wienerinnen* (1900, Viennese Women), one of his more successful and enduring comedies. In the vacuous rich young Viennese socialites, Daisy and Marie, Bahr portrays his growing negative view of the Viennese upper class as devoid of substance and giddily pursuing every superficial trend in order to be considered fashionably modern. *Die Wienerinnen* treats the conflict between genuineness and artificiality in life as well as in art. The world of integrity and wholesomeness is represented by Josef Ulrich (modeled on Joseph Olbrich), an architect and strong-willed individualist from the provinces who marries a Viennese socialite. Bahr shows how serious ideas such as modernity, the equality of women, and the Secession were perverted into ridiculous fads. He also repeats several of his standard themes: the obstructionist bureaucracy, the resistance to progress, and the indifference of the Viennese to Austrian artists. The play represents Bahr's defense of Olbrich, who left Vienna to work in Darmstadt, where he felt more appreciated.

Bahr's hostility toward politicians and bureaucracy is repeated in *Der Apostel* (1901) which uses the theater as a tribune to expose the corruption and incompetence of politicians, who are incapable of regenerating society because they spend most of their time working for their own advantage rather than for the benefit of the people and the country. Bahr's favorite ideas of this period are all represented in the play, whose major weakness results from Bahr's enchantment with the saintliness of his protagonist to the point that he ignored his own plot. All the complications are left unresolved, as the play concludes with an idealistic sermon of the Apostle. Again Bahr sacrificed dramatic unity for a theatrical ending, a utopian alternative to party politics. The intended satire of politicians dissolves into a euphoria of love and benevolence. Had Bahr written this play a decade later it would have fitted into the context of Expressionist drama with its antirational stance and its fervent plea for the universal brotherhood of man. As it was, *Der Apostel* left most of Bahr's contemporaries bewildered and dissatisfied. The politics of Austria also serve as the theme of *Der Krampus* (1902), one of Bahr's most popular comedies that is still revived today.

In *Der Meister*, which was awarded the Bauernfeld Prize, Bahr again presented a domineering title figure surrounded by subordinate characters who represent viewpoints rather than being fully realized individuals. The play resembles *Der Athlet* in its technique of antithesis, in its attack on rationality as the guiding force in life, and in its focus on the double standard, the rights of women, and the subservience of all people to the laws of nature. The influence of Ibsen and Dumas is seen in the tendentiousness of the play and that of Nietzsche in the Master's philosophy of supremacy. The Master feels sovereign in the world because of his powerful will which has led to his success as a self-made man. Like *Der Athlet*, he must learn that he does not control life but plays only a subordinate role. Human happiness lies solely in the feeling that a higher power propels us in any direction it wishes and that we have to obey: "We are innocent: it is stronger. How stupid of us now to become so emboldened as to be cleverer than fate, which exerts its control through our passions—if we cut them off with the scissors of reason, then dear Master—Oh!"[19]

Bahr rested some of his hopes for lasting fame on the drama *Sanna* (1905), a variation of *Der Krampus* in a tragic key. It treats the same conflict between individual feeling and social convention set two generations later in 1847, the Biedermeier or *Vormärz* period when resignation was the prevailing spirit. The play illustrates Bahr's belief at this time that the principal goal of life was personal fulfillment. He was opposed to the suppression of instincts and inclinations, which, as seen in *Die Rahl*, he saw as the aim of both school and family in his own day. When one of his daughters reproves her father for having taught them wrongly, he replies: "And the law? And duty? And the state? Eh, the state? That is the main point!" Her response is emphatic: "No, old man. The point is that one lives, lives, lives!"[20] The importance to Bahr of self-fulfillment, independence of spirit, and following one's instincts in life can also be seen in *Wien* (1907), and *Buch der Jugend* (1908). For Bahr the individual was more important than the state or any other institution, and he lashed out violently at the system that robbed its citizens of their individuality, initiative, and personal happiness.

Bahr's interest in the psychology of repression and in the idea of the fluid ego acquired from Ribot's *Maladies de la personalité* (Illnesses of the personality) and Mach's *Die Analyse der Empfindungen* (1888, *The Analysis of Perceptions*) became the basis of *Die Andere* (1906, The Other), Bahr's most complex psychological drama. In 1904 he had written two essays on Mach: "Der Philosoph des Impressionismus" (The Philosopher of Impressionism), in which he described Mach's ideas as the basis of the impressionist's view of life, and "Das unrettbare Ich" (The Unsalvageable Ego), in which he explained Mach's theory of the fixed ego.[21] Because of this changeable condition of the ego the human being is capable of unlimited transformation of character, an idea that became a basic theme for Bahr as well as for Hofmannsthal. In addition to the psychological basis of *Die Andere*, Bahr also deals with the conflict between civilization and nature (*Geist* and *Natur*), defining *Geist* as the sum of social pressures. In the *Dialog vom Marsyas* (1905) Bahr had affirmed the ascendancy of life over art, and the play reflects again the "Lebensphilosophie" in its orientation toward a natural existence based on instinct as opposed to one dominated by cultural, social, or political forces. Bahr, who had fervently evangelized for the new humanity from his first drama *Die neuen Menschen*, now expressed his disappointment over the lack of progress by lashing out at the institutions that he felt made change impossible. He had come to the same conclusion that Schnitzler later reached, namely, it was impossible for individuals to surmount their environment and therefore the institutions must be changed so that man can develop. Throughout his writings he had repeatedly shown that individuals who tried to bring about social change were defeated by their own deep-seated training and atavistic feelings, which could not be overcome. Nevertheless, *Die Andere* ends on a note of cautious optimism. The outbreak of revolution in Russia symbolizes not only the rebirth that society needs, but also represents in Bahr's view the only way to accomplish social change.

Die Andere, which is dedicated to Anna Mildenburg, has the densest thematic texture of any of Bahr's dramas, as the author attempts to interweave psychological, cultural, and political levels of actions. The play tries to capture dramatically the idea of the changed personality by portraying a human being, Hess, who becomes so estranged from the person he was previously that he can no longer assume responsibility for the actions of the former without completely denying the new person he has become. Bahr felt that he had failed: "The problem is beyond the reach of my creative powers. Ultimately it can be represented only in a mythical figure."[22]

One of Bahr's best and most accomplished works is the one-act drama *Der arme Narr* (1906), which had its premiere in the Burgtheater on 29 November 1906 with Kainz in the title role. The play once again reflects his preoccupation with the conflict between intellect and nature. Bahr repeats his injunction to follow the dictates of feeling and live life to the fullest. As he frequently does, Bahr employs the antithesis of two brothers, Vincenz, who has lived his entire life in anxiety and resignation, and Hugo (possibly modeled on Hugo Wolf), who has dared to venture to the extremes of life even at the risk of his own sanity. The play turns on the central paradox that the sickly protagonist, who has nearly lived himself to death, emerges as the stronger force and is shown to have made the wiser choice.

Das Konzert (1909, *The Concert*, 1921), with its variation on the themes of marriage, role-playing, and the erotic round dance of life, was and has remained Bahr's greatest dramatic success. It is still revived today successfully. Bahr did not regard this comedy as superior to his other plays and attributed its success to the appeal of the Austrian manner to world audiences.[23] This explanation fails to explain the attraction of the play adequately; for when the director Leo Dietrichstein changed the setting from Vienna to New York for the American stage, it was the hit of the New York season. The popularity of *Das Konzert* can more properly be attributed to its captivating plot, ageless theme—the tyranny of sex—and sympathetic characters. Bahr reacted to the outbreak of World War I with the propagandistic essays *Kriegssegen* (1914, Blessings of war) and *Das österreichische Wunder* (1915, The Austrian Miracle), in which he viewed the war as a means of unifying the Germans and Austrians and also as a way for people to relinquish role-playing and reveal their real character. These patriotic themes were incorporated in *Der muntere Seifensieder* (1915, The Cheerful Soapmaker), a trivial topical play subtitled "Ein Schwank aus der deutschen Mobilmachung" (A Jest Based on the German Mobilization). This farcical work gave Bahr an opportunity to satirize the ridiculous excesses at the beginning of the war: arresting people as spies, shooting at stars thinking they are enemy planes, hasty marriages, people trying to hide their physical defects to enlist, and other foolish responses. While his plea for unity and an end to role-playing was sincere, the vehicle was too shallow for the play to make any impact.

Die Stimme (1917, The Voice), the reworking of the theme of *Himmelfahrt*—an intellectual's way to religious faith—was Bahr's last attempt at a major play. It is a literary rather than a theatrical work and is one of three plays (the others being *Der Franzl* and *Sanna*) on which he set his hopes for posterity. The seriousness of Bahr's purpose can be seen in his efforts to rise above superficial stage effects and to portray the inner growth of his protagonist during the course of the play. *Die Stimme* is a purely psychological drama portraying the intellectual fencing of the protagonist and his introspective soul-searching. One can only empathize with his spiritual transformation and in a sense accept it, as he does, on faith, since it cannot be proved or demonstrated factually.

Bahr's subsequent plays show a marked decline in substance and quality and add nothing to his reputation as a dramatist. In *Der Augenblick* (1917, The Moment), written the same year as the volume of essays entitled Um Goethe (On Goethe), Bahr reworked the plot of Goethe's *Der Mann von fünfzig Jahren* (The Man of Fifty) into a psychological comedy of fidelity with the message that virtue cannot be imposed from the outside but must come from inner conviction. In *Der Unmensch* (1919, The Inhuman Man), which is set in the immediate post World War I period in Vienna, Bahr was possibly following Lessing's injunction to write comedies after a war. The central theme is reminiscent of Schnitzler's *Das weite Land* (The Far Country), a man encourages his wife to be unfaithful because in this way she can perhaps save the life of another man. At the same time Bahr was satirizing postwar conditions to show that nothing essential had really changed in the transition of Austria from monarchy to republic. As he repeatedly stated, the strength of Austria lay in its ordinary citizens, and the form of government was of little consequence.

The importance of the plays today is their reflection of Bahr's world, for they supplement his novels and essays as an important aspect of his literary and cultural contribution. They provide a survey of the theater in Austria over a forty-year period, reflecting changing dramatic styles and attitudes and serving as an historical reflection of the era in which they were written.

Bahr's dramatic oeuvre contains several plays of genuine merit—*Josephine, Der Franzl, Sanna, Der Meister, Der arme Narr, Der Faun, Das Konzert*, and *Die Andere*— and many of theatrical effectiveness. *Das Konzert* has proved to be his most durable play rather than *Der Franzl, Sanna*, or *Die Stimme*, on which he had predicted his future reputation would rest. If one excludes the plays of Hofmannsthal and Schnitzler, one can agree with Castle's final assessment: "If one looks back over the total production of the last thirty years of German comedy, one will have to say that Bahr did not raise himself above his time, but he also did not sink below it."[24]

Notes

1. Herman Bahr, *Selbstbildnis* (Berlin: S. Fischer, 1932), p. 2.
2. Ibid, p. 228-229.
3. Peter de Mendelssohn, *S. Fischer und sein Verlag* (Frankfurt am Main: S. Fischer, 1970), p. 191-192).
4. Hermann Bahr, "Selbstbildnis," in *Inventur* (Berlin: S. Fischer, 1912).
5. Cf. Donald G. Daviau, "Hermann Bahr and Decadence," *Modern Austrian Literature*, Vol. 10, No. 2 (June 1977), 53-100.
6. Cf. Donald G. Daviau, "Hermann Bahr und die Tradition" in Margret Dietrich, ed., *Hermann Bahr Symposion. "Der Herr aus Linz"* (Linz: Bruckner Haus, 1987), pp. 33-50.
7. Hermann Bahr, "Eleonor Duse," *Der Thespiskarren* (Wien: Andermann, 1943), pp. 315-321.
8. Hermann Bahr, "Das junge Österreich," in *Studien zur Kritik der Moderne* (Frankfurt am Main: Literarische Anstalt, 1894), pp. 93-94.
9. Cf. Donald G. Daviau, "Hermann Bahr's *Nachlaß*," in *Journal of the International Arthur Schnitzler Research Association* 2 (Autumn 1963), 4-27.
10. Reinhard Farkas, *Hermann Bahr. Prophet der Moderne. Tagebücher 1888-1904* (Wien: Böhlau, 1987). Additional volumes will follow.
11. Karl Kraus, *Die Fackel* 69 (1901), 6-7.
12. Claudia Monti, "Die Mach-Rezeption bei Hermann Bahr und Robert Musil," *Musil Forum*, 10. Jg., 1. und 2. Heft (1984), 201-213.
13. Cf. Manfred Diersch, "Hermann Bahr: Der Empiriokritizismus als Philosophie des Impressionismus," *Empiriokritizismus und Impressionismus* (Berlin: Rutten and Loening, 1973), pp. 46-82.
14. "We need a mirror that does not simply reflect, but also conveys the meaning of life." Hermann Bahr, *Der inwendige Garten*. (Hildesheim: Borgmeyer, 1927), P. 122.
15. Hermann Bahr, *Die gute Schule* (Berlin: S. Fischer, 1898), p. II.
16. Hermann Bahr, "Ein unbeschriebenes Blatt," *Wiener Threater* (Berlin, S. Fischer, 1898), p. 336.
17. Hermann Bahr, "Verisimo," *Wiener Theater*, pp. 481-482.
18. Hermann Bahr, *Josephine* (Berlin: S. Fischer, 1898), pp. vii-viii.
19. Hermann Bahr, *Der Meister* (Berlin: S. Fischer, 1904), pp. 107-108.
20. Hermann Bahr, *Sanna* (Berlin: S. Fischer, 1905), pp. 121-122.

21. Hermann Bahr, *Dialog vom Tragischen* (Berlin: S. Fischer, 1904), pp. 70-101 and 102-115.
22. Hermann Bahr, *Inventur* (Berlin: S. Fischer, 1912), p. 47.
23. Hermann Bahr, *Selbstbildnis*, p. 288.
24. Eduard Castle, "Die neue Generation um Hermann Bahr," in *Deutsch-Österreichische Literaturgeschichte*, ed. J. Nagl, J. Zeidler, and E. Castle, Vol. 4, Wien: Carl Fromm, 1937), pp. 1697-1698.

Bibliography

I. Works by Hermann Bahr in German

Die Einsichtslosigkeit des Herrn Schäffle: Drei Briefe an einen Volksmann. Zürich: Schäbelitz, 1887.
Die neuen Menschen. Drama. Zürich: Schäbelitz, 1887.
La Marquesa d'Amaëgui: Eine Plauderei. Zürich: Schäbelitz, 1888.
Die grosse Sünde: Ein bürgerliches Trauerspiel. Zürich: Schäbelitz, 1889.
Zur Kritik der Moderne. Essays. Zürich: Schäbelitz, 1890.
Die gute Schule. Novel. Berlin: S. Fischer, 1890.
Fin de Siècle. Prose tales. Berlin: Ad. Zoberbier, 1891.
Die Mutter: Drama. Berlin: Sallischer Verlag, 1891.
Die Überwindung des Naturalismus: Zweite Folge von "Zur Kritik der Moderne." Essays. Dresden: Pierson, 1891.
Russische Reise. Prose tale. Dresden: Pierson, 1893.
Die häusliche Frau. Comedy. Berlin: S. Fischer, 1893.
Dora. Drei Novellen. Berlin: S. Fischer, 1893.
Neben der Liebe. Novel. Berlin: S. Fischer, 1893.
Der Antisemitismus. Interviews. Berlin: S. Fischer, 1893.
Aus der Vorstadt. Volksstück. Wien: Konegen, 1893.
Caph. Skizzen. Sketches. Berlin: S. Fischer, 1894.
Studien zur Kritik der Moderne. Essays. Frankfurt am Main: Rütten & Loening, 1894.
Die Nixe. Drama. München: Rubinverlag, 1896.
Juana. Drama. München: Rubinverlag, 1896.
Renaissance: Neue Studien zur Kritik der Moderne. Essays. Berlin: S. Fischer, 1897.
Tschaperl: Ein Wiener Stück. Berlin: S. Fischer. 1897.
Theater. Novel. Berlin: S. Fischer, 1897.
Josephine. Play. Berlin: S. Fischer, 1898.

Der Star: Ein Wiener Stück. Berlin: S. Fischer, 1898.

Wiener Theater (1892-1898). Theater Reviews. Berlin: S. Fischer, 1899.

Die schöne Frau. Novellas. Berlin: S. Fischer, 1899.

Der Athlet. Play. Bonn: Albert Ahn, 1899.

Wienerinnen. Comedy. Bonn: Albert Ahn, 1900.

Secession. Essays. Wien: Wiener Verlag, 1900.

Der Franzl: Fünf Bilder eines guten Mannes. Play. Vienna: Wiener Verlag, 1900.

Bildung. Essays. Berlin: Schuster & Loeffler, 1900.

Der Apostel. Play. München: Albert Langen, 1901.

Rede über Klimt. Speech. Wien: Wiener Verlag, 1901.

Der Krampus. Comedy. München: Albert Langen, 1902.

Wirkung in die Ferne. Novellas. Wien: Wiener Verlag, 1902.

Premiéren. Theater reviews. München: Albert Langen, 1902.

Rezensionen (Wiener Theater 1901-1903). Theater reviews. Berlin: S. Fischer, 1903.

Dialog vom Tragischen. Essay. Berlin: S. Fischer, 1904.

Der Meister. Comedy. Berlin: S. Fischer, 1904.

Unter Sich: Ein Arme-Leut'-Stück. Wien: Wiener Verlag, 1904.

Sanna. Play. Berlin: S. Fischer, 1905.

Dialog vom Marsyas. Essays. Berlin: Bard, Marquardt & Co., 1905.

Die Andere. Play. Berlin: S. Fischer, 1905.

Der arme Narr. Play. Wien: Konegen, 1906.

Josef Kainz. Monograph. Wien: Wiener Verlag, 1906.

Glossen zum Wiener Theater (1903-1906). Theater reviews. Berlin: S. Fischer, 1907.

Ringelspiel. Comedy. Berlin: S. Fischer, 1907.

Grotesken (Der Klub der Erlöser. Der Faun: Die tiefe Natur). Plays. Wien: Konegen, 1907.

Wien. Essays. Stuttgart: Carl Krabbe, 1907.

Die gelbe Nachtigall. Comedy. Berlin: S. Fischer, 1907.

Die Rahl. Novel. Berlin: S. Fischer, 1908.

Stimmen des Bluts. Novellas. Berlin: S. Fischer, 1908.

Tagebuch. Diary. Berlin: Paul Cassirer, 1909.

Buch der Jugend. Essays. Wien: Heller, 1908.

Drut. Novel. Berlin: S. Fischer, 1909.

Dalmatinische Reise. Essays. Berlin: S. Fischer, 1909.

Das Konzert. Comedy. Berlin: S. Fischer, 1909.

O Mensch. Novel. Berlin: S. Fischer, 1910.

Die Kinder. Comedy. Berlin: S. Fischer, 1911.

Das Tänzchen. Comedy. Berlin: S. Fischer, 1911.

Austriaca. Essays. Berlin: S. Fischer, 1911.

Das Prinzip. Comedy. Berlin: S. Fischer, 1912.

Inventur. Essays. Berlin: S. Fischer, 1912.

Essays. Leipzig: Insel, 1912.

Parsifalschütz ohne Ausnahmegesetz. Essay. Berlin: Schuster & Loeffler, 1912.

Bayreuth (von Anna Mildenburg und Hermann Bahr). Essays. Leipzig: Rowohlt, 1912.

Das Phantom. Comedy. Berlin: S. Fischer, 1913.

Das Hermann-Bahr-Buch. Berlin: S. Fischer, 1913.

Dostojewski. Essays. München: Piper, 1914.

Der Querulant. Comedy. München: Delphin, 1914.

Erinnerung an Burckhard. Essay. Berlin: S. Fischer, 1914.

Kriegssegen. Essays. München: Delphin. 1914.

Salzburg. Essay. Berlin: Bard, 1914.

Das österreichische Wunder. Essays. Stuttgart: "Die Lese," 1915.

Rudigier. Essay. Kempten: Kösel, 1915.

Der lustige Seifensieder. Comedy. Berlin: S. Fischer, 1915.

Expressionismus. Essay. München: Delphin, 1916.

Himmelfahrt. Novel. Berlin: S. Fischer, 1916.

Die Stimme. Play. Berlin: S. Fischer, 1916.

Um Goethe. Essays, Wien: Urania, 1917.

Schwarz-Gelb. Essays. Berlin: S. Fischer, 1917.

Vernunft und Wissenschaft. Essay. Innsbruck: Tyrolia, 1917.

Der Augenblick (nach Goethe). Comedy. Berlin: Ahn & Simrock, 1917.

1917. Diary. Innsbruck: Tyrolia, 1918

Adalbert Stifter: Eine Entdeckung. Essays. Wien: Amalthea, 1918.

1918. Diary. Innsbruck: Tyrolia, 1919.

Die Rotte Korahs. Novel. Berlin: S. Fischer, 1919.

1919. Diary. Leipzig: Tal, 1920.

Ehelei. Play. Berlin: Ahn & Simrock, 1920.

Der Unmensch. Comedy. Berlin: Erich Reiss, 1920.

Spielerei. Play. Berlin: Ahn & Simrock, 1920.

Burgtheater. Essay. Wien: Wiener literarische Anstalt, 1920.

Summula. Essays. Leipzig: Insel, 1921.

Bilderbuch. Essays. Wien: Wiener literarische Anstalt, 1921.

Liebe der Lebenden. Diaries. 3 vols., Hildesheim: Borgmeyer, 1921-23.

Kritik der Gegenwart. Diary. Augsburg: Haas & Grabherr, 1922.

Sendung des Künstlers. Essays. Leipzig: Zellenbücherei, Dürr & Weber, 1923.
Selbstbildnis. Autobiography. Berlin: S. Fischer, 1923.
Schauspielkunst. Essay. Leipzig: Zellenbücherei, Dürr & Weber, 1923.
Notizen zur neueren spanischen Literatur. Essays. Berlin: Stilke, 1926.
Der Zauberstab: Tagebücher von 1924 bis 1926. Diaries. Hildesheim: Borgmeyer, 1926.
Der inwendige Garten. Novel. Hildesheim: Borgmeyer, 1927.
Himmel auf Erden. Essays. München: Verlag Ars Sacra, Josef Müller, 1928.
Das Labyrinth der Gegenwart. Essays. Hildesheim: Borgmeyer, 1929.
Österreich in Ewigkeit. Novel. Hildesheim: Borgmeyer, 1929.
Die Hexe Drut. Novel. New ed. München: Siebenstäbeverlag, 1929.

Bibliographies

Nimmervoll, Hermann. "Materialien zu einer Bibliographie der Zeitschriftenartikel von Hermann Bahr (1883-1910)," *Modern Austrian Literature* 13, no. 2 (1980) 27-110.
Thomasberger, Kurt. "Bibliographie der Werke von Hermann Bahr," in *Ein Leben für das europäische Theater*, edited by Heinz Kindermann, 347-368. Graz-Köln: Böhlau, 1954.

Collections

Mensch, werde wesentlich. Ed. Anna Bahr-Mildenburg. Graz: Styria, 1934.
Essays. Ed. Heinz Kindermann. Wien: H. Bauer, 1962.
Kritiken. Ed. Heinz Kindermann. Wien: H. Bauer, 1963.
Sinn hinter der Komödie. Ed. Rudolf Holzer. Graz: Stiasny, 1965.
Zur Überwindung des Naturalismus. Ed. Gotthart Wunberg. Stuttgart: Kohlhammer, 1968.
Das junge Wien: Österreichische Literatur- und Kunstkritik. Ed. Gotthart Wunberg. 2 vols. Tübingen: Niemeyer, 1976. Includes 134 essays of Bahr, 1887-1902.

Correspondence

Daviau, Donald G., ed. *The Letters of Arthur Schnitzler to Hermann Bahr*. Chapel Hill: University of North Carolina Press, 1978.

Fellner, Fritz, ed. *Dichter und Gelehrter: Hermann Bahr und Josef Redlich in ihren Briefen, 1896-1934*. Salzburg: Neugebauer, 1980.

Gregor, Joseph, ed. *Meister und Meisterbriefe um Hermann Bahr*. Wien: H. Bauer, 1947.

Hirsch, Rudolf, ed. "Hugo von Hofmannsthal und Hermann Bahr: Zwei Briefe," in *Phaidros* 1 (1947) 85-88.

Schmidt, Adalbert, ed. *Hermann Bahr: Briefwechsel mit seinem Vater*. Wien: H. Bauer, 1971.

Diaries

Hermann Bahr, *Prohet der Moderne, Tagebücher 1888-1904*. Ed. Reinhard Farkas. Wien: Böhlau, 1987.

II.   Works in English

The Concert, adaptation by Leo Dietrichstein, in *Chief Contemporary Dramatists*. Ed., A.T. Dickinson. Boston, New York: Houghton Mifflin, 1921.

The Master, adaptation by R.T. Gribble. New Tork: Brown, 1918.

Expressionism, translated by R.T. Gribble. London: Henderson, 1925.

"His Beautiful Wife," in *Austrian Short Stories*. Ed. Marie Busch. London: Oxford, 1929.

"The Spook," in *Great Stories From Austria*. Ed. Curt Strachwitz. London: Pallas, 1938.

Salzburg. Wien: Agathonverlag, 1947.

III.   Secondary Works in English

Brecker, Egon W. "Hermann Bahr and the Quest for Culture: A Critique of his Essays." Ph.D. dissertation, University of Wisconsin, Madison, 1978.

Chandler, Frank W. "The Austrian Contribution: Schnitzler, Bahr, Schönherr, von Hofmannsthal." *Modern Continental Playrights*. New York: Harper & Row, 1931, pp. 345-65.

Daviau, Donald G. "Hermann Bahr: The Catalyst of Modernity in the Arts in Austria." *Arthur Schnitzler and His Age*, ed. P.O. Tax and Richard Lawson. Bonn: Bouvier, 1984, pp. 30-68.

——. "Hermann Bahr and the Viennese Secession." *FMR*, Vol. I, No. 3 (1984), 42-47.

——. "Hermann Bahr and the Radical Politics of Austria in the 1880s." *German Studies Review* 5, no. 2 (May 1982), 163-85.

——. "Experiments in Pantomime by the Major Writers of *Jung-Wien*." In *Österreich in amerikanischer Sicht*. New York: Austrian Institute, 1981, 19-26.

——. "Hermann Bahr and the Secessionist Art Movement in Vienna." In *The Turn of the Century German Literature and Art, 1890-1915*, edited by Gerald Chapple and Hans H. Schulte. Bonn: Bouvier, 1981, pp. 433-62.

——. "Hermann Bahr and Gustav Klimt." *German Studies Review* 3, no. 1 (February 1980), 27-49.

——. "Herman Bahr's *Josephine*: A Revisionist View of Napoleon." *Modern Austrian Literature* 12, no. 2 (June 1979), 93-111.

——. "Hermann Bahr and Decadence." *Modern Austrian Literature* 10, no. 2 (June 1977), 53-100.

——. "Hermann Bahr's Cultural Relations with America." *Österreich und die Angelsächsische Welt*, ed. Otto Hirsch. Wien, Stuttgart: Braumüller, 1968, pp. 482-522.

——. "The Friendship of Hermann Bahr and Arthur Schnitzler." *Journal of the International Arthur Schnitzler Research Association* 5 (Spring, 1966), 4-37.

——. "Hermann Bahr's Nachlaß." *Journal of the International Arthur Schnitzler Research Association* 2 (Autumn 1963), 4-27.

——. "Hermann Bahr as Director of the Burgtheater." *The German Quarterly* 32 (January 1959), 11-21.

——. "*Dialog vom Marsyas*: Hermann Bahr's Affirmation of Life over Art." *Modern Language Quarterly* 20 (December 1959), 360-70.

——. "The Misconception of Hermann Bahr as a Verwandlungskünstler." *German Life and Letters* 11 (April 1958), 182-92.

Drake, William A. "Hermann Bahr." *In Contemporary European Writers*. New York: John Day, 1928, 184-91.

Ende, Amelia von. "Literary Vienna." *Bookman* 38 (September 1913-February 1914), 141-55.

Grünzweig, Walter. "'Mit dem Phallus philosophieren? Hermann Bahr's Vision of Walt Whitman's 'Erotokratie,'" in *Modern Austrian Literature*, Vol. 21, No. 2 (June 1988), pp. 1-12.

Hofmannsthal, Hugo von. "Die Mutter." In *Prosa 1*. Frankfurt am Main: S. Fischer, 1950, 16-23.

Lehner, Friedrich. "Hermann Bahr." *Monatshefte* 39, no. 1 (1947), 54-62.

Macken, Mary M. "Chronicle: Hermann Bahr, 1863-1934." *Studies: An Irish Quarterly Review* 23 (March 1934), 144-46.

_____. "Hermann Bahr: His Personality and his Works." *Studies: An Irish Quarterly Review* 15, no. 67 (March 1926), 34-46.

Oswald, Victor A. "The Old Age of Young Vienna." *Germanic Review* 27, no. 3 (October 1952), 188-99.

Pollard, Percival. "Bahr and Finis." *Masks and Minstrels of New Germany*. Boston: John W. Luce, 1911, 290-99.

Simmons, Robert Edward. "Hermann Bahr as a Literary Critic: An Analysis and Exposition of his Thought." Ph.D. dissertation, Stanford University, 1956.

IV.   Major Studies in German

Burdach, Konrad. "Wissenschaft und Journalismus (Betrachtungen über und für Hermann Bahr)," in *Preussische Jahrbücher* 193 (1923), 17-31.

Cysarz, Herbert. "Alt-Österreichs letzte Dichtung, 1890-1914." *Preussische Jahrbücher* 211 (1928), 32-51.

Daviau, Donald G. *Der Mann von Übermorgen. Hermann Bahr (1863-1934)*. Wien: Österreichischer Bundesverlag, 1984.

_____. "Hermann Bahr in seinen Tagebücher," *Literatur und Kritik*, Heft 199/200 (1985) 485-494.

_____. "Hermann Bahr, Josef Nadler, und das Barock," in *Vierteljahrsschrift des Adalbert-Stifter Institut*, Jg. 35, Folge 3/4 (1986), 171-190.

_____. "Hermann Bahr und die Tradition." *Hermann Bahr Symposion. "Der Herr aus Linz,"* ed. Margret Dietrich. Linz: Bruckner Haus, 1987, pp. 33-50.

_____. "Hermann Bahr und Antisemitismus, Zionismus und die Judenfrage," *Literatur und Kritik*, No. 221-222 (1988), 21-41.

Diersch, Manfred. "Hermann Bahr: Der Empiriokritizismus als Philosophie des Impressionismus." *Empiriokritizismus und Impressionismus*. Berlin: Rütten & Loening, 1973, 46-82.

Dietrich, Margret, ed. *Hermann Bahr Symposion.* "Der Herr aus Linz." Linz: Bruckner Haus, 1987.

Farkas, Reinhard, *Hermann Bahr. Dynamik und Dilemma der Moderne.* Wien: Böhlau, 1989.

Hirsch, Otto Michel, "Hermann Bahr, der Novellist und Dramatiker." *Xenien* 2, no. 11 (1909), 279-289.

Hofmannsthal, Hugo von. "Zum Direktionswechsel im Burgtheater." *Neue Freie Presse,* 5 July 1918, 1-2.

Kindermann, Heinz. *Hermann Bahr: Ein Leben für das europäische Theater.* Graz: Böhlau, 1954.

Jahnichen, Manfred. "Hermann Bahr und die Tschechen." *Slavische-Deutsche Wechselbeziehungen in Sprache, Literatur und Kultur,* edited by W. Kraus, J. Belic, and V.I. Borkovskij. Berlin: Akademie Verlag, 1969, 363-77.

Meridies, Wilhelm. *Hermann Bahr als epischer Gestalter und Kritiker der Gegenwart.* Hildesheim: Borgmeyer, 1927.

_____. "Hermann Bahrs religiöser Entwicklungsgang." *Das heilige Feuer* 15 (March 1928), 270-78.

Nadler, Josef. "Vom alten zum neuen Europa." *Preussische Jahrbücher* 193 (1923), 32-51.

_____. "Hermann Bahr und das katholische Österreich." *Die neue Rundschau* 34 (1923), 490-502.

_____. *Literaturgeschichte Österreichs.* Salzburg: Müller, 1951, 397-406, pp. 414-416.

Nagl, J., Zeidler, J., and Castle, E. *Deutsch-Österreische Literatur-Geschichte,* vol. 4. Vienna: Fromm, 1937.

Nirschl, Karl. *In seinen Menschen ist Österreich: Hermann Bahrs innerer Weg.* Linz: Oberösterreichischer Landesverlag, 1964.

Rieckmann, Jens. *Aufbruch in die Moderne.* Königstein/Ts.: Athenäum, 1985.

Romero, Christine Zehl. "Die konservative Revolution: Hermann Bahr und Adalbert Stifter." *Germanisch-Romanische Monatsschrift* 56 (1975), 439-454.

Salten, Felix. "Aus den Anfängen. Erinnerungskizzen." *Jahrbuch deutscher Bibliophilen* 18-19 (1932-33), 31-46.

Sprengler, Joseph. "Hermann Bahr—Der Weg in seinen Dramen." *Hochland* 2 (1928), 352-366.

_____. "Hermann Bahrs Tagebücher." *Das literarischer Echo* 22 (1919-20), 262-265.

Wagner, Peter. *Der junge Hermann Bahr*. Giessen: Druck: der Limburger
    Vereinsdruckerei, 1937.
Widder, Erich. *Hermann Bahr: Sein Weg zum Glauben*. Linz:
    Oberösterreichischer Landesverlag, 1963.

Richard Beer-Hofmann

Esther N. Elstun

As an arbiter of taste whose aesthetic judgment was widely respected and as a friend, confidant, and adviser to others, Richard Beer-Hofmann was undoubtedly the most influential member of the turn-of-the-century literary circle, Young Vienna.[1] Though his own production was sparse, several factors combine to explain his profound influence on his contemporaries: in both content and style Beer-Hofmann's early novel, *Der Tod Georgs*, is probably the most representative example of literary *Jugendstil* in the German language, and its stream-of-consciousness technique, though long since familiar to subsequent generations of readers, was still strikingly innovative at the turn of the century. His influence also stemmed from his work in the theater, much of it in collaboration with Max Reinhardt; as both a dramatist and a director Beer-Hofmann was extensively involved in efforts to revitalize the theater and free it from what he and others regarded as the cul-de-sac of Naturalism. To some extent, finally, his influence can be attributed to his personal charm, his persuasive advocacy of his literary theories, and his reputation for uncompromising artistic integrity.[2]

The son of Hermann Beer, a Viennese attorney, and his wife Rosa (née Steckerl), Beer-Hofmann was born in Vienna on 11 July 1866. His mother died within days of his birth, and he was adopted and reared by an aunt and uncle, Berta and Alois Hofmann. By his own account (in *Paula, ein Fragment*) he enjoyed a remarkably secure and happy childhood. Anti-Semitism had by no means disappeared, but by the mid-1860s the Jews of imperial Austria had been granted most citizens' rights and were assimilated to a degree that enabled families like Beer-Hofmann's to enter the prosperous upper-middle class. The scene of his early childhood was Brünn (now Brno), where Alois Hofmann owned a textile factory. In 1880 the family moved to Vienna. There Beer-Hofmann completed his schooling at the prestigious Akademisches Gymnasium, and in 1883 entered the University of Vienna. When he earned his doctorate in law (1890), the family expected him to join Hermann Beer's law firm, but to their consternation and dismay he was unwilling to do so. Like many Jewish sons of similar background Beer-Hofmann felt far more powerfully drawn to the arts than to the "respectable" profession for which he had been trained.

In 1890 he also met Arthur Schnitzler. Their acquaintance quickly developed into what was to be a lifelong friendship, probably the firmest and most gratifying in both men's lives.[3] Schnitzler soon introduced Beer-Hofmann to the other members of Young Vienna, who met regularly at the Café Griensteidl for animated discussions of artistic topics: Hugo von Hofmannsthal, Jakob Wassermann, Felix Salten, Peter Altenberg, Paul Goldmann, and Alfred Kerr. They were often joined by Hermann Bahr, who tended to exaggerate the extent of his influence on them, but who undoubtedly did much to help publicize their work and establish their literary reputations.[4]

By December 1891 Beer-Hofmann had completed *Camelias*, the story of a decadent middle-aged dandy named Freddy. Its use of interior monologue, lack of external action, almost total absence of description and exposition, and the characterization of Freddy—all mark it as a *fin-de-siècle* work that is not very original but characteristic of the themes that preoccupied the writers of Young Vienna and indicative of the changes that narrative prose began to undergo around the turn of the century.[5]

Beer-Hofmann's next venture was the four-act pantomime, *Pierrot Hypnotiseur*, written in 1892. Though never published in his lifetime, it documents his passion for the theater from this early period.[6] The work is also a testimonial to his friendship with Hofmannsthal.[7]

By July 1893 Beer-Hofmann had completed a second, longer tale, *Das Kind*.[8] Stylistically it reflects an artistic independence largely lacking in *Camelias* and suggests that Beer-Hofmann had acquired greater confidence in his own craftsmanship and instincts as a writer in the meantime. The plot is still the familiar fare of "Viennese decadence" but with some important differences. Paul, a young dandy whose affair with the servant girl, Juli, has produced an unwanted child, learns that the infant has died. Driven by guilt, remorse, and pity for the helpless child, he tries unsuccessfully to find the peasant couple to whom July had given it, and to find the child's unmarked grave in the village cemetery. The experience leads Paul to an awareness of his own past selfishness and to some tentative conclusions about the nature of life. Death and the transitoriness of human existence comprise the central themes of the story, but they are linked to other themes that also preoccupied the young Beer-Hofmann: the desire to believe in a universal order that has meaning and purpose despite the unremitting awareness of suffering and evil in the world, and the possibility of doubt as a way to faith. These were to become recurring motifs in Beer-Hofmann's work, developed most fully in the cycle of Biblical dramas, *Die Historie von König David.*

Five years after the conferral of Beer-Hofmann's law degree his family was still deeply troubled by his refusal to practice law and his apparent indifference to such middle-class values as thrift, industry, and orderly habits. They were also very skeptical about his prospects as a writer.[9] By December 1895 Beer-Hofmann had resolved "to leave home for a year or two, travel about the world . . . and when I return . . . if there is still in me a strong, irrepressible urge to do so, only then try again to write."[10] As these lines suggest, he had doubts of his own about his future as a writer, and letters of Schnitzler and Hofmannsthal confirm that his writing was not progressing well.[11] Both friends believed that Beer-Hofmann's difficulties were caused by a lack of self-discipline, a failure to apply himself steadily to his writing.[12] These may indeed have been contributing factors, but the problem was much more complex.

As a writer Beer-Hofmann had a profound sense of calling (*Auserwähltsein*), but he sometimes experienced it as an excruciating burden.[13] Another aspect of the problem was his uncompromising view of language; the inevitable concomitant was an at times agonizing dissatisfaction with what he had produced.[14] He also felt intense ambivalence about writers and their craft, regarding them on the one hand as uniquely favored and on the other as deceivers, almost in the criminal sense. In 1895 these feelings had clearly caused a crisis (like that of Hofmannsthal's Lord Chandos); all his life Beer-Hofmann remained convinced that the writer's activity could be justified only ". . . because he *must* create and cannot do otherwise . . . and . . . because he helps others by providing them with beauty."[15]

At times this combination of factors caused periods of inner anguish during which Beer-Hofmann found it impossible to write. The last months of 1895 were such a period, but his resolve to leave Vienna was not carried out. The reason was Paula Lissy. They met by chance, a fact Beer-Hofmann always emphasized because it underscored the overwhelming sense of destiny he felt to be at work in his and Paula's marriage.

The Lissys were of Italian and Alsatian Catholic origins. When Beer-Hofmann first saw Paula, she was a girl of sixteen working in a confectioner's shop. Her mother had died shortly before, leaving her in the care of two older brothers. Beer-Hofmann courted her despite their strong opposition and for a time concealed the courtship from his own family as well.[16]

The young couple spend the summer of 1897 in Bad Ischl. Paula was expecting their first child, Mirjam. Two weeks after her birth in September 1897 Beer-Hofmann wrote the "Schlaflied für Mirjam."[17] It is not a lullaby in the traditional mode despite the conventional opening and closing lines of its four stanzas. The intervening lines express somber reflections about life and the human condition: in the first strophe the poet's melancholy awareness of death, in the second his sense of the ultimate loneliness and isolation of the individual, and in the third his awareness of the transitoriness of life and the finality of individual human existence. The fourth strophe affirms life in spite of the conclusions drawn in the preceding verses, advancing the concept of continuity as a source of comfort and an answer to death. Parental love, an equally important theme of the "Schlaflied," is sounded in the opening and closing lines of every strophe. The poem is richly musical and masterfully constructed with flawless symmetry and complete correspondence between content and form: in each stanza the somber reflections framed by the opening and closing lullaby lines produce an alternation of major themes with a final focus on the motif of parental love.

Beer-Hofmann wrote only some twenty lyric poems in the course of his life; the "Schlaflied" is the best of them and richly deserves the fame it enjoys.[18] The poem was cast as a whole from the beginning and did not undergo the painstaking revision that was otherwise so characteristic of Beer-Hofmann's work.

Der Tod Georgs, by contrast, was clearly "a difficult birth." Beer-Hofmann had begun the novel in 1893, but progress was slow; despite the happiness he had found with Paula he still suffered periods of extreme nervousness and depression. Better progress was made in 1898, perhaps because of the resolution of his personal situation. On 14 May he and Paula were married in a Jewish ceremony in Vienna with Arthur Schnitzler and Leo Van Jung serving as witnesses.[19] The Beer-Hofmann's second child, Naemah, was born in December of that year.

Der Tod Georgs was published in 1900. In its language, motifs and imagery it is a *Jugendstil* novel.[20] The antithesis of tight, terse prose, its language is fraught with symbolism and "splendor-laden images," in which the word itself sometimes seem like an ornament.[21] Beer-Hofmann consciously avoids "Allerweltsworte" (GW 585), language distorted or stripped of its power through constant—and careless—use in everyday discourse. This intense effort to revitalize literary language and cleanse it of worn-out effects is one of the notable characteristics of *Jugendstil* writers.[22] Other *art nouveau* aspects of the novel are its image of woman, "an ideal of delicate slenderness . . . of thin, pale, still undeveloped girls' bodies;"[23] its protagonist, a sensitive, high-strung aesthete: its representation of the fantastic, the opulent, and the exotic; and its floral and avian imagery and pronounced water symbolism.[24]

Der Tod Georgs is also one of the earliest literary works in German to employ the stream-of-consciousness technique. Its interior monologues are narrated rather than quoted ("erlebte Rede"), but the third-person narrator functions entirely anonymously, neither providing any information about himself nor interrupting the story to comment on its developments. This lack of narrative intrusion and Beer-Hofmann's liberal use of adverbs, particles, and dashes—which suggest the associative nature of thoughts and strengthen the illusion that they are being directly transmitted as they occur—give the novel virtually the same immediacy and intimacy that first-person interior monologue conveys.

Beer-Hofmann's treatment of dreams and their relation to life is another respect in which *Der Tod Georgs* signals important new trends in prose fiction. Dating back to the Baroque, to Shakespeare and Calderon, dream literature as such was not new when Beer-Hofmann's novel appeared, but his protagonist differs significantly from the heroes of earlier works of this genre (such as Rustan in Grillparzer's *Der Traum ein Leben*). He is far more sophisticated, and his initial characterization—in particular his high-strung nerves, his aesthetic sensibilities, and his inability to cope with life—marks him as a representative of *fin-de-siècle* decadence. Another difference lies in the fact that, upon waking, he analyzes his dream in a thoroughly modern way, attempting to fathom its psychological implications. The dream begins, moreover, *in medias res*; the reader learns eventually that it was a dream but only after it ends. In the use of this technique Beer-Hofmann anticipated the tendency of many later writers to give no clear indication of where the real leaves off and the imagined sets in.

The major themes of *Der Tod Georgs* are woman, death, the relation of the dream to life, and the problem of decadence with its symptoms of narcissism, nervousness, lack of will, and fear of involvement in life. The only external action of any consequence is Georg's death, and even that is important only as the impetus for the wide-ranging recollections and reflections of the protagonist Paul, whose mind is the locus of almost everything that "happens."

In Part I Beer-Hofmann uses comparison and contrast to provide the initial characterization of Paul: he longs to be like his friend, the physician Georg, to have his healthy perceptions, strong will, and firm belief in what he wants (GW 524). Paul emerges from Part I as a young man with fundamentally conflicting desires: he envies Georg his fitness for life and his involvement in it, but he also wants to remain aloof from the turmoil, pain, and ugliness of life in a spiritual limbo where he can enjoy the aesthetic pleasures undisturbed (GW 528).

The woman motif is represented in Part I by two variations of a single type: the girl Paul encounters on his nocturnal walk along the river, and the fantasy figure of the woman he sees in the clouds. Like Paul, they both stand on the periphery of life. This is suggested by the unawakened sexuality of the girl by the river (GW 526), and the woman in the clouds, whose body appears to be wrapped in a shroud, foreshadows the dying wife of Part II.

The dream that comprises nearly all of Part II ranges over a huge span of time from the "present," in which Paul's "wife" is dying, to antiquity, the scene of orgiastic love-death rites in a Syrian temple. As Paul thinks about the dream after waking, the reader sees it in several lights, first as a form of reality whose impressions and experiences are far more vivid and intense than those of the waking state. In the dream Paul had felt a mysterious unity with all things, past as well as present, and everything had been important. He cannot communicate any of this to others, however (GW 551), and here the dream becomes a vehicle for Beer-Hofmann's fictional representation of his own Lord Chandos experience.

The dream also appears as a realm of existence in which human beings enjoy a sovereignty they do not possess in the waking state: "Like a stranger he had been tossed into the world in which he lived his waking hours, never understanding it . . . . But the world in which he dreamed was born of him; he set the boundaries of its heavens and its earth. In it he was omniscient, and all things knew of him (GW 607)."[25] In retrospect Paul recognizes that this omniscience and sense of control are the reason why he had always preferred his dreams to his waking hours, why he had always feared life and tried to remain detached from it.

The dream is represented as the prophetic shaper of life. In it Paul experiences everything of importance that will happen to him in the waking state in Parts III and IV, and the development of his character in these last two parts proceeds along lines established in the dream.

In Part II the woman motif is represented by the dying wife and thus closely linked to the theme of death. Characterized earlier as unawakened to life, the woman is now in the Nietzschean sense unfit for it: she is childless and dying in young adulthood of an incurable disease. Her thoughts reflect an intense awareness of the preciousness of life and a profound sense of her own aloneness: "An incredible injustice was happening to her; mockingly a world went on, and she alone had to die. Nothing helped her to live, no one died with her—and in her eyes was the helpless hatred of the dying toward all that lived" (GW 565).

The preciousness of life also underlies the ancient Syrian love-death rites of the Astarte-worshippers. What drives the ritualists to the temple is the desire to dispel the monotony of their days and "knowing the innate, deep horror of death—to awaken jubilantly the slumbering lust for life" (GW 548). Here as in the attitude of the dying wife the fear of death and the awareness of the preciousness of life appear as the two sides of a single coin.

The novel's themes undergo further development in Part III as Paul accompanies Georg's body to Vienna for burial. His reflections about Georg's compassion and understanding, his power to help people and to ease their suffering, seem to be moving Paul closer to the unity with all life and the sense of a mysterious but purposeful universal order that he had felt in his dream. In wishing that Georg had lived to enjoy a happy old age, however, Paul recognizes that he has never seen old age and happiness together in a human face. The elderly he has encountered pass before his mind's eye: a ghastly procession of feebleness, infirmity, and physical deterioration. Comparing these images to Georg's vitality and youthful appearance at the time of his death, Paul concludes that his friend, like the youths of Argos, should be counted among the fortunate after all.

At the beginning of Part IV Paul is still alone, wrapped in the cocoon of his self-imposed aloofness from life. In this final section of the novel he experiences a surprising transformation. The impetus for it is provided by two women he sees on a solitary walk in the park at Schönbrunn, one of whom bears a striking resemblance to the female figures of Part I and the dying wife of Part II. The sight of them sets in motion Paul's recollection of his dream and the long-forgotten insights to which it had brought him. Reflecting further, he now concludes that the universal order is not only purposeful and unifying but also just in some cosmic sense that transcends human understanding. In these final pages, moreover, Paul's affirmation of life and the universal order acquires a new and unexpected dimension: we learn that he is a Jew and that his newly won belief is linked to the Jewish tradition (GW 616, 621-622).

Der Tod Georgs thus provides the first unequivocal *literary* expression of Beer-Hofmann's affirmation of his Jewishness, but there were earlier indications of its growing importance in his life and thought. At a time when late nineteenth-century Austrian liberalism had given way to reactionary forces that included virulent Anti-Semitism he gave his children Old Testament names and proudly acknowledged his Jewishness in other ways as well.[26] In 1896, after reading *The Jewish State*, he wrote to its author, Theodor Herzl: "What appealed to me more than anything in your book was what stood behind it. At last a person who does not bear his Jewishness resignedly, like a burden or a calamity, but on the contrary is proud to be the legitimate heir of an ancient culture."[27] Though Beer-Hofmann here refers to Judaism as a cultural legacy, it is doubtful that he viewed it only as that, even at this early point in his life. *Das Kind* already hints of the struggle to believe in a just God. Jewish ethics and religion, in particular the covenant with God, are the core of the *David* cycle, for which Beer-Hofmann began to lay plans in 1898 and which he unquestionably regarded as his most important work.

In 1901 Beer-Hofmann moved his family to Rodaun. There he and Hofmannsthal enjoyed a closer association than ever, as neighbors, with frequent opportunities to exchange ideas and share their work-in-progress. Beer-Hofmann was working on a five-act play, *Der Graf von Charolais*. Under the direction of Max Reinhardt (and Beer-Hofmann's personal supervision) it premiered on 23 December 1904 at the Neues Theater in Berlin.[28] In 1905 Beer-Hofmann received the Schiller Prize for the play, sharing the award with Carl and Gerhart Hauptmann. *Charolais* is a profoundly pessimistic work that seems to retract its author's earlier affirmation of life and belief in a just universal order. Within the context of Beer-Hofmann's total oeuvre, however, *Charolais* is the artistic expression of his agonizing struggle to reconcile his concept of God and the universal order with the suffering and injustice he saw in the world. In *Das Kind* he had already expressed the idea of doubt as a way to faith; his development from *Der Tod Georgs* to the *Historie von König David* by way of *Der Graf von Charolais* attests to that process at work in his own life.

The mysterious and unpredictable workings of fate constitute the drama's dominant motif. In acts I-III (GW 323-407) through a series of apparent accidents and coincidences Charolais not only restores his deceased father's honor but achieves a happiness and good fortune he had never dreamed possible: marriage to the beautiful Desirée, whose father, a distinguished judge, also makes him a wealthy man. In acts IV-V (GW 407-466) it is the same unpredictable fate that destroys his happiness irreversibly: Desirée is seduced by her *bon vivant* cousin Philipp, Charolais kills him, and Desirée commits suicide.

Within the framework of the fate motif Beer-Hofmann treats other themes familiar to the reader from his earlier work: death and its concomitant, the joy at being alive; love and the concept of continuity as an answer to death. While the play's message about the capriciousness of fate is bitterly pessimistic, its treatment of love and continuity is not. Indeed, *Charolais*'s positive representation of love makes its irreparable loss seem all the greater catastrophe. Many forms of love are treated with almost as many nuances as there are characters: the love between parent and child; conjugal love; erotic love; the love between friends; and ultimately also the question of love of God.

Red Ike is the play's most moving spokesman for the love between parent and child (GW 357), but the sentiments he expresses are reflected in all of the play's parent-child relationships. Conjugal love and continuity as an answer to death are expressed in terms of sexual union in the final scene of the play when Charolais says:

> In her was refuge and security!
> Her arms about my neck protected me,
> Her breath—peace! Her lips—happiness!
> Her body—promise! To become one with her,
> To flee into her, I embraced her,
> Clung to her, let my life flow into her,
> And held her—my answer to death! (GW 449)[29]

Here and in all its other forms love appears as the only thing that makes life tolerable, alleviates the loneliness of the individual, and gives substance to human life.

Like all of Beer-Hofmann's dramatic works *Charolais* is written in blank verse. In the early years of this century verse drama was already something of an anachronism.[30] The fact that Beer-Hofmann nonetheless achieves powerful effects in the play is a measure of his skill as a dramatist.[31]

Another question is whether *Charolais* is really tragedy. It does share some of that genre's characteristics: the characters are obviously exposed to destructive forces that lie "outside the governance of reason or justice," and the play certainly tells us that "things are as they are, unrelenting and absurd" (Steiner 9). But there are also significant differences between the characters in *Charolais* and those of classical tragedy. Charolais and Desirée are not morally responsible for the catastrophe that befalls them; on the contrary they appear as the helpless victims of irrational and cruelly capricious forces over which they have no control (GW 464-465).[32] Heroic struggle is another element of tragedy missing from the play.[33] And its catastrophe is not irreparable in the classically tragic sense: once done, it cannot be undone, but one feels that it could have been avoided altogether.[34]

As the foregoing suggests, *Charolais* is not without flaws, and Beer-Hofmann's efforts to resuscitate verse drama did not enjoy lasting success. The play is a literary *tour-de-force* nonetheless and a memorable theatrical experience.

The 150th anniversary of Mozart's birth was celebrated in 1906, and Beer-Hofmann agreed to write a commemorative piece for the festival year: the *Gedenkrede auf Wolfgang Amadéus Mozart*.[35] Its opening paragraphs, which provide a rich and colorful description of the Salzburg region, give the first part of the piece a fairy-tale atmosphere.[36] In vivid terms that evoke the glittering splendor of eighteenth-century court life Beer-Hofmann recalls events in the life of Mozart the child that were indeed like those of a fairy-tale: his reception by the King and Queen of England and at the court of the Holy Roman Emperor, the Pope's bestowal of the Order of the Golden Spur. The mood becomes darker as he traces the human passions and the death motif in Mozart's works (GW 651-652).[37] Through a comparison of Mozart and Beethoven as representatives of a waning and an ascending age Beer-Hofmann alludes to the ominous changes the new age will bring. These lines, which suggest that he saw himself, like Mozart, at the end of a glittering age and on the threshold of a painful and turbulent one, give the concluding passages of the *Gedenkrede* a distinctly prophetic tone.

In May 1909 Beer-Hofmann began to write *Jaákobs Traum*, the first play in the Biblical cycle, *Die Historie von König David*. His work on the *Historie* had begun in 1898, and the last dated part, a scenario of *Davids Tod*, was completed in 1937. The *David* cycle thus occupied him for most of his adult life.[38]

Intended as a prologue to provide the ancient mythological background of the David story, *Jaákobs Traum* is nonetheless a complete drama in its own right. The play is structured simply, consisting of two parts. It treats three distinct episodes in the Biblical story: Jacob's theft of the blessing, the reconciliation of Jacob and Esau, and Jacob's vision and fateful decision at Beth-El.

The play is overwhelmingly dominated by the motif of suffering and doubt as the preponderant elements of Israel's calling (*Auserwähltsein*). Jacob has no doubt that God exists (GW 41); the doubts and questions that cause him intense spiritual anguish stem from his bitter struggle to understand the contradictory nature of God. He cannot fathom this deity who promises endless blessing, gives Abraham the son he yearned for, and then directs him to kill the child and offer him up as a sacrifice (GW 40-42). In the vision the outcast angel Samáel cannot reconcile the concept of a just and omnipotent God with the existence of suffering in the world He created (GW 71). Jacob feels a strong sense of kinship with him, for Samáel's questions are the very ones that Jacob himself has struggled with. For him as for Samáel, God is a painful wound; the more they probe it, the more intolerably it hurts, but they cannot leave it alone. The suffering of *Auserwähltsein* is also treated in the reconciliation scene. Here Jacob's lines reflect Beer-Hofmann's conviction that the destiny of the elect is to be the *exculpator dei*, and that this entails so much suffering that one may well ask whether *Auserwähltsein* is not more curse than blessing (GW 58-59).

Jacob's development is from the reluctant object of God's election to a free and independent individual. God has singled him out, but only he can make the decision to accept or reject the covenant God offers (GW 76). In reaching his decision Jacob is not influenced but offended by the archangel's dazzling promises of worldly wealth and power (GW 75). He is equally unmoved by the agony Samáel prophesies for him and his descendants (GW 78-79). Jacob knows, moreover, that his doubts are not forever laid to rest. His suffering and doubt have led him to "that ultimate serenity, which we can bear only when it is born of the last bitterness and deepest anguish,"[39] but he is aware that the battle will be fought many times over. His decision to enter into the covenant is an affirmation of God *despite* His incomprehensible and contradictory ways: "I love Him—as He is! Cruel and merciful, / Pure light— and chasm dark and deep!" (GW 80) The decision is also the outgrowth of Jacob's willingness to be the *exculpator dei* despite his knowledge that that is a far more difficult role than being the *advocatus diaboli*. Through this view of the covenant Beer-Hofmann advances the idea that God needs man as much as man needs God. An interesting aspect of God's need is the status Jacob acquires as a result. Their relationship is not that of master and servant; they are partners, equal in the sense that each is a voluntary party to the covenant, and each is indispensable to the other and knows it.

Other familiar themes undergo further development in *Jaákobs Traum*. The motif of posterity as an answer to death is sounded in the lines in which Jacob envisions the future life of Idnibaál, the slave he has freed (GW 50). In the play as a whole the concept of continued life through one's seed is expanded to encompass an entire people and linked to the motif of fate. Sealed by Jacob's covenant with God, Israel's destiny is to be His advocate. Jacob assumes both the pride and the burden of this destiny, asking only that his descendants not be allowed to forget the purpose of their election (GW 83-84).

The theme of the unity of all life is reflected in Jacob's love of nature, his sense of oneness with all creation—past, present, and future—and in his and Esau's reconciliation: their brotherhood, originally an accident of birth, is voluntarily affirmed and renewed in this scene, which also suggests that each individual is as God needs him to be for the furtherance of a grand design (GW 62).

Jaákobs Traum is the dramatic re-creation of an ancient myth whose motifs, focusing as they do on the God-man relationship, are religious in nature. But the play is also an allegory of the poet and his calling. In Beer-Hofmann's view the poet, like Jacob, is God's elect; the purpose of his election, like Israel's, is to be the *exculpator dei*. Like Jacob, the poet lives in a state of grace: more sensitive than others to every aspect and phenomenon of life, he experiences its joys with particular intensity. But his sensitivity also heightens his awareness of life's pain and ugliness. The poet's *Auserwähltsein* thus also includes so great a measure of suffering that he experiences it as both curse and blessing.[40]

Beer-Hofmann completed *Jaákobs Traum* in 1915. It was not his intention to permit the publication or performance of finished parts of the *Historie* until the entire cycle was completed. An exchange of letters with Gustav Landauer suggests that the rising tide of anti-Semitism caused him to change his mind in the hope that the play would "speak to people" (Landauer 2: 340). *Jaákobs Traum* was published in 1918 and had its premiere at the Burgtheater in 1919.

The renewal of the drama had been one of Beer-Hofmann's major concerns since the turn of the century, and in 1921 he was awarded the Nestroy Prize for his work in the theater. At Reinhardt's urging he also began to write *Das goldene Pferd*, an opulent pantomime that he described as "a tempting effort . . . to give up the word, to invent a course of events . . . in such a way that it would be understandable and captivating through action, gesture, mimicry, the play of beautiful, well-trained bodies, light, color and music" (GW 467).[41]

After 1921 Beer-Hofmann's work on the *David* cycle was frequently interrupted by his increasing involvement as both writer and director in theatrical staging and production at Vienna's Theater in der Josefstadt, the Salzburg *Festspiele*, and the Burgtheater. For the centennial of Goethe's death (1932) he revised both parts of *Faust* and directed a production of it which remained part of the Burgtheater's standard repertory until 1938.

Der junge David, the second play in the Biblical cycle, was completed and published in 1933. The central theme of the play is faithfulness (*Treue*), which is represented as the logically necessary consequence of the decision to affirm the world order despite God's unfathomable and apparently contradictory ways. The young David undergoes the same suffering and doubt as his ancestor Jacob, and, like him, he experiences *Auserwähltsein* as both a state of grace and a painful burden. He also reaches the same conclusions, renewing and perpetuating the covenant in his forebear's spirit.

Closely linked to the theme of faithfulness is the motif of love, which is treated primarily in the relationship of David and Maácha. Paula Beer-Hofmann was undoubtedly the model for Maácha, and this aspect of the play is Beer-Hofmann's fictional representation of his own experience of love. Like *Charolais*, however, *Der junge David* treats many other forms of love as well. Here faithfulness and the willingness to self-sacrifice appear without exception as love's essential characteristics. The play's treatment of this complex of themes is greatly expanded through its association with the history of Israel, but the playwright's message remains the same: for a people as for individuals the sense of life lies in faithful self-sacrificing love and service to God ("as he is") and to the human community.

Structurally *Der junge David* is comprised of seven scenes that Beer-Hofmann called "Bilder." That designation is significant, for it indicates that here too he was concerned with a revitalization of the drama, this time through a fusion of action (*Handlung*), pageantry (*Festspielelemente*), and *tableaux vivants*. The effort to fuse these elements is more successful in some scenes of the play than in others. In Scene 3 and in the first part of Scene 7, for example, the action and the tableau tend to vie with, rather than complement, each other. One of the finest scenes is "Königszelt in Gibea" (Scene 2), in which the elements of pageantry enhance rather than compete with the spoken lines, so that the action and the characterization of Saul and his family proceed at a vigorous pace that forestalls any decline in the audience's interest. The same is true of the brief but excellent Scene 6, in which the news of Saul's death and David's swift departure for Hebron are skillfully complemented by a vignette of the camp life of the soldiers. Beer-Hofmann's application of these techniques is, in general, most successful when his pictures of "life in all its fullness" are not so detailed or extended that they threaten to obscure the central action.

The external action of the "Vorspiel auf dem Theater zu *König David*," completed in 1935, is to bridge the twenty-five-year period between *Der junge David* and *König David*. The David we encounter here is a man who has become a myth in his own lifetime and has lost the lofty dreams and ideals as well as the purity of his youth. Beer-Hofmann's notes on *Davids Tod* suggest that in the last drama of the cycle he intended to show David's re-emergence from "the rigid shell of his own myth," a great human being ennobled by suffering.[42]

The reader soon recognizes, however, that the inner purpose of this prologue is to provide Beer-Hofmann's *apologia* of himself and his artistic convictions. Initially he speaks in the guise of "Der Prolog" but eventually abandons even that transparent disguise. The lines he speaks are intensely earnest and unquestionably express his deepest convictions about the nature and purpose of art, the writer, his task, and his relationship to the word. He avoids pomposity, however, and gives this part of the prologue much charm and humor by having his wife appear (as "Frau des Prologs") and by engaging in a spirited exchange with the audience. The reproachful questions and highly critical comments that members of the audience express make clear that Beer-Hofmann had a very keen understanding of the reader/spectator's viewpoint and expectations. His response to the questions and comments is an emphatic rejection of art as an esoteric self-serving phenomenon but also an unequivocal statement of his unwavering conviction that the writer's true service to others lies in uncompromising service to the word; if he engages in calculated efforts to please, he prostitutes his art and betrays his high calling.

The Hitler regime's first "Black List of Literature" (1933) made Beer-Hofmann a forbidden author in Germany.[43] After the *Anschluß* (1938) he and Paula were in mortal danger. They left their villa in Vienna's Cottage Quarter in the spring of 1938 and lived in hiding while preparations were completed for their journey into exile. The following passage from *Paula, ein Fragment* conveys the extent to which their love sustained them:

> . . . whatever may come for us . . . as long as my hand may rest in hers I am safe—nothing can happen to me . . . my lips glide gently across her fingers, displacing the shining honey-colored bishop's ring that has become a bit too large . . . her glance points to the ring: "When you bought it . . . in Venice it was also a bit too large . . . and you asked me whether I would sometimes wear the ring—and I said: always! And you said: 'don't promise . . . how do you know what might yet come—you're still so young!' Now I'm no longer young—and I did wear it always, and everything that came was beautiful—you do know that—my Richard—don't you?" "Yes." (GW 854-855)

On the evening of 19 August 1939, thirteen days before the Nazi invasion of Poland and the outbreak of World War II, Beer-Hofmann and Paula left Vienna for the last time en route to the United States via Switzerland. Paula, who had suffered a severe heart attack the preceding winter, collapsed in Zurich and died on 30 October. Unable to obtain permission to remain in Switzerland, Beer-Hofmann was forced to continue the journey alone. He lived the rest of his life in New York.

The exile years were devoted to the writing of *Paula, ein Fragment*.[44] Beer-Hofmann insisted that it was a book of memoirs, not a work of fiction, but it is certainly as much "Dichtung" as "Wahrheit," especially in respect to his organization of the material and the narrative techniques he uses. The book's foreword ends with a quotation from Dante's *La Vita Nuova* which suggests how Beer-Hofmann wanted *Paula* to be understood but which might also be viewed as the underlying theme of his entire oeuvre: "Behold a God stronger than I; He comes and will rule over me" (GW 679).

Paula is divided into five main parts of greatly varying length, in which Beer-Hofmann, functioning this time as a first-person narrator, related episodes and experiences from his and Paula's life. The fragments derive their external unity from the fact that he and she are the central figures throughout; as a literary work the fragments also have an internal unity which stems primarily from Beer-Hofmann's use of recurring motifs as an organizing principle, a technique he had also employed in *Der Tod Georgs*.

Paula has two central themes which Beer-Hofmann really fuses into one: love and destiny. The reader has a powerful sense of destiny at work in the lives of this couple: in their meeting each other at all, in their love for each other and their marriage despite great obstacles, in their life together. The fragments provide a vivid picture of Paula, her appearance, personality, and character, but also shed light on the many facets of Beer-Hofmann's love for her and hers for him. How completely this love dominated his life as a man is suggested by this passage: "Sometimes, when I watch the children at play and tenderness surges up in me, I am suddenly alarmed, for it flashes through me that I cannot think of them except as 'her children' . . . and just as I love her cheeks and her hand—so do I love the children, who are a part of her . . . " (GW 857)

Their love had an equally decisive influence on Beer-Hofmann's work as a writer, as the entire *Paula* volume makes clear. Beer-Hofmann also dedicated the 1941 edition of his lyric poetry (*Verse*) to Paula in lines that identify her as his poetic muse (GW 653).[45]

As a literary work *Paula* develops and refines the narrative techniques that Beer-Hofmann had first used in his early prose fiction. But the volume also needs to be seen in two other ways: as a historical work and as a document of exile. The world had undergone devastating changes that had erased nearly every trace of the life and times Beer-Hofmann recreated in *Paula*, and the book tells us much about an era that we would otherwise be hard pressed to understand. As a document of exile *Paula* attests above all to the steadfastness of Beer-Hofmann's convictions about life and the universal order despite the pain and injustice he had suffered at the hands of the National Socialists.

Beer-Hofmann was granted United States citizenship in March 1945. On 18 May of that year the National Institute of the American Academy of Arts and Letters presented him with its "Award for Distinguished Achievements."[46] Beer-Hofmann linked the two events in his acceptance speech:

> When I came to these shores, I could by no stretch of my imagination foresee that I was to receive again what had been taken from me by tyranny: a home, a working place, a country that was to be mine by choice and by right, and now—this proof of human sympathy, of understanding and recognition. To me—this has come as a lesson in democracy. For: respect for the dignity of man, the

basis of democracy, is at the same time the very foundation of any sincere artistic endeavor. A writer's task can never hope to be complete. Yet it was worth trying—if only to learn this lesson.[47]

Four months later, on 26 September 1945, Beer-Hofmann died of pneumonia in New York.

Notes

1. The critic Alfred Gold called Beer-Hofmann "the advisory con-science, the personified measuring-stick" of Young Vienna. "Ästhetik des Sterbens," *Die Zeit* (Vienna) 24 February 1900. This and all other translations are mine. See also Hugo von Hofmannsthal/Richard Beer-Hofmann Briefwechsel, Ed. Eugene Weber (Frankfurt a.M.: S. Fischer, 1972), p. 69.

2. Alfred Kerr called Beer-Hofmann a person "from whom something charmingly joyous emanated." *Die Welt im Drama* (Cologne: Kiepenheuer and Witsch, 1964), p. 102. Hermann Bahr spoke of his warmth and kindness. *Meister und Meisterbriefe um Hermann Bahr*, Ed. Josef Gregor (Vienna: Bauer-Verlag, 1947), p. 184. Erich Kahler recalled him as "handsome and strong" in "Richard Beer-Hofmann," *Neue Rundschau*, 56-57 (1945/46), 237, and noted that "he was surrounded by friends wherever he went . . . " in "Richard Beer-Hofmann," *Commentary* 1 (1946), 45. Beer-Hofmann's integrity was summed up by Hofmannsthal, who called him "the sternest and most incorruptible critic I have." *Briefe 1900-1909* (Vienna: Bermann-Fischer, 1937), pp. 97-98.

3. See Arthur Schnitzler, *Tagebuch 1909-1912* and *Tagebuch 1913-1916* (Vienna: Verlag der Österreichischen Akademie der Wissenschaften, 1981 and 1983); *Georg Brandes und Arthur Schnitzler: ein Briefwechsel*, Ed. Kurt Bergel (Bern: Francke 1956), p. 48; Olga Schnitzler, *Spiegelbild der Freundschaft* (Salzburg: Residenz Verlag, 1962).

4. For a detailed account of Bahr's association with Young Vienna see Donald G. Daviau, *Hermann Bahr* (Boston: Twayne, 1985).

5. Schnitzler called *Camelias* an "absolutely witty, stylistically brilliant sketch" (O. Schnitzler 135).

6. *Pierrot Hypnotiseur* was first published as an appendix to Rainer Hank, *Mortifikation und Beschwörung* (Frankfurt a.M.: Lang, 1984).

7. See the prologue to Hofmannsthal's early drama, "Der Tor und der Tod" (Beer-Hofmann is "Galeotto") in *Nachlese der Gedichte* (Berlin: S. Fischer, 1934), p. 86; and Hank, pp. 254-260.

8. *Das Kind* and *Camelias* were published under the title *Novellen* (Berlin: Freund and Jaeckel, 1893). A second printing appeared in 1894.

9. These concerns are expressed in unpublished letters from Alois Hofmann to Beer-Hofmann, now in the collection of family papers and personal documents in the Leo Baeck Institute, New York.

10. Richard Beer-Hofmann, "Paula, ein Fragment," *Gesammelte Werke* (Frankfurt a.M.: S. Fischer, 1963), p. 748. Unless otherwise noted, all quotations from Beer-Hofmann's works are from this edition, hereafter appearing in the text as GW, and all translations are mine.

11. *Hugo von Hofmannsthal-Arthur Schnitzler Briefwechsel*, eds. Therese Nickel and Heinrich Schnitzler (Frankfurt a. M.: S. Fischer, 1964), pp. 23-24, 58, 88, 93, 135, 199.

12. *Hofmannsthal-Beer-Hofmann Briefwechsel, p.* 35, and *Brandes-Schnitzler Briefwechsel*, p. 72.

13. See O. Schnitzler, pp. 146-147 and Antje Kleinewefers, *Das Problem der Erwählung bei Richard Beer-Hofmann* (Hildesheim: Olms, 1972).

14. Schnitzler called Beer-Hofmann's obsession with refining each work to perfection his "Perfektomanie." Rilke admired this trait, referring to the "wonderful rarity and selectivity of his production." *Briefe aus Muzot*, ed. Ruth Sieber-Rilke and Carl Sieber (Leipzig: Insel Verlag, 1937), p. 145. Karl Kraus spoke of it with biting sarcasm in *Die demolirte Literatur* (Wien, 1897).

15. Werner Vordtriede, "Gespräche mit Beer-Hofmann," *Neue Rundschau* 63 (1952), pp. 131, 139-140. See also Richard M. Sheirich, "*Frevel* and *der erhöhte Augenblick* in Richard Beer-Hofmann," *Modern Austrian Literature* 13, no. 2 (1980), pp. 1-16.

16. This is apparent from an unpublished letter (now in the Leo Baeck Institute) that Beer-Hofmann wrote to his aunt, Agnes Beer, while he and Paula were on a trip to Scandinavia in the summer of 1896.

17. The poem was first published in the *Jugendstil* journal *Pan* in 1898, and widely admired for its extraordinary lyrical beauty. See also GW, p. 654.

18. Beer-Hofmann's lyric poetry was first published in book form by Bermann-Fischer in 1941 under the title, *Verse*. See also GW, pp. 653-674.

19. Leo Van Jung was a Viennese musician whom Beer-Hofmann had met in Pörtschach in 1890. They became lifelong friends.

20. Cf. Jens Malte Fischer, "Richard Beer-Hofmann 'Der Tod Georgs,'" *Sprachkunst* 2 (1971), p. 227; and Jürgen Viering, "Jugendstil und Empfindsamkeit," *Euphorion* 71 (1977), pp. 180-194.

21. Richard Specht, "Literatur der Gegenwart," *Ewiges Österreich*, Ed. Erwin Rieger (Vienna: Manz, 1928), p. 44. See also Viering, pp. 180-183.

22. Walter Lennig, "Der literarische Jugendstil," *Jugendstil*, ed. Jost Hermand (Darmstadt: Wissenschaftliche Buchgesellschaft, 1971), p. 375.

23. Dolf Sternberger, "Sinnlichkeit um die Jahrhundertwende," *Jugendstil*, p. 104.

24. Robert Schmutzler, "Der Sinn des Art Nouveau," *Jugendstil*, pp. 298-300.

25. For Beer-Hofmann dreams were not a form of escapism. Why he attributed a therapeutic value to them is explained in his prose fragment, "Entgeheimnissung," GW, pp. 635-636.

26. In addition to Mirjam and Naemah, the Beer-Hofmanns had a son, born in 1901, whom they named Gabriel.

27. Quoted in Alfred Werner, *Richard Beer-Hofmann. Sinn und Gestalt* (Vienna: Glanz, 1936), p. 8.

28. *Der Graf von Charolais* was published by S. Fischer in 1905.

29. As Theodor Reik noted, sexual union is seen here "not only as an escape from the danger of death, but also as a promise of rescue and immortality." *The Secret Self* (New York: Farrar, Straus & Young, 1952), p. 303.

30. George Steiner, *The Death of Tragedy* (New York: Knopf, 1961), pp. 304-305, 309.

31. Robert Musil noted that the effects are achieved very naturally, and hence do not seem like cheap theatrical tricks. "Der Graf von Charolais," *Theater*, ed. Marie-Luise Roth (Munich: Rororo, 1965), p. 132.

32. See Vordtriede, p. 144 and Steiner, p. 222.

33. Of all critics, Werner Kraft stated this point most strongly: "Precisely fate, against which the tragic hero struggles heroically, is here eroded and reduced to a mechanical, psychoanalytical 'it', which allows room only for marionettes who no longer struggle at all." *Wort und Gedanke* (Bern: Francke, 1959), p. 196.

34. Alfred Kerr suggested this in his review of the play: "Nowadays there is nothing tragic . . . that would not seem ridiculous within a foreseeable period of time . . . . That is exactly why we become uneasy at this ending: when the husband insists on the destruction of the faithless wife; when the just father says everything but this . . .

'don't be heroic, be reasonable!'" "Der Graf von Charolais," *Neue Rundschau* 16 (1905), p. 250.

35. First published in the *Frankfurter Zeitung* in 1906. See also GW, pp. 648-652.

36. When Beer-Hofmann spoke of the *Gedenkrede* as a fairy tale (Vordtriede, p. 126), he was surely thinking of the Oriental genre, in particular his beloved *Thousand and One Nights*. One of the major differences between the European and the Oriental fairy tale is the latter's "love of description." Max Lüthi, *Volksmärchen und Volkssage* (Bern: Francke, 1966), pp. 19-20.

37. This part of the *Gedenkrede* is reminiscent of the somber note Mörike injected into *Mozart auf der Reise nach Prag*, with the *memento mori* theme of the poem that brings the novella to a close.

38. Beer-Hofmann's plans for the *Historie* changed more than once over the years. According to the plan he ultimately adopted, it was to consist of *Jaákobs Traum, Der junge David, König David* and *Davids Tod*. Only *Jaákobs Traum, Der junge David* and the "Vorspiel . . . zu *König David*" exist in finished form. The manuscripts and Beer-Hofmann's voluminous notes on the cycle are in the Houghton Library of Harvard University. See Richard M. Sheirich, "Beer-Hofmann's 'Die Historie von König David': The Unpublished Manuscripts," diss., Harvard University, 1964, and Hans-Gerhard Neumann, *Richard Beer-Hofmann. Studien und Materialien zur "Historie von König David"* (Munich: Fink, 1972).

39. Gustav Landauer to Beer-Hofmann 25 December 1904. *Gustav Landauer: Sein Lebensgang in Briefen.* Ed. Martin Buber (Frankfurt a. M.: Rütten & Loening, 1929), Vol. 1, pp. 129-130.

40. These ideas are also expressed in many of Beer-Hofmann's aphorisms. See especially "Ultra Posse" (GW, p. 626) and "Die Beschenkten" (GW, p. 629).

41. Parts of *Das goldene Pferd* appeared in the *Neue Freie Presse* (Vienna) 12 October 1930. The complete pantomime was first published in the *Neue Rundschau* in 1955. See also GW, pp. 467-519.

42. Sheirich, "Beer-Hofmann's 'Historie'", p. 352.

43. Hermann Kunisch, Ed. *Handbuch der deutschen Gegenwartsliteratur* (Munich: Nymphenburger Verlagshandlung, 1965), p. 678. One cannot help but suspect a connection between the publication of the Black List on 23 April and Beer-Hofmann's prolonged illness soon thereafter. *Daten*, an unpublished personal notebook, includes

under 1933 the terse notation: "Ill. At home. In bed from May to June (heart)."

44. "Herbstmorgen in Österreich," one of the longest *Paula* fragments, was published by the Johannespresse, New York, in 1944. The entire work, edited by Otto Kallir in accordance with Beer-Hofmann's detailed instructions, was published in 1949. See also GW, pp. 677-871.

45. There is strong evidence that Paula was also the model for the female figures in *Der Tod Georgs* and for Maácha and Ruth in *Der junge David*. See Esther N. Elstun, *Richard Beer-Hofmann: His Life and Work* (University Park and London: Pennsylvania State University Press, 1983), pp. 41, 49, 165-168.

46. In a letter written to me on 13 June 1973 Thornton Wilder confirmed that he was among those who nominated Beer-Hofmann for this award: "I first met Dr. Beer-Hofmann and his family in Vienna in about 1933. I already had read his play about Jacob and some of his lyrics and my admiration and esteem was increased on learning to know him personally. I was proud to be among those who recommended him for the award at the Academy . . . . " See also O. Schnitzler, p. 125.

47. I am indebted to the late Mirjam Beer-Hofmann Lens for supplying the text of this speech. See also Eugene Weber, "Richard Beer-Hofmann: Briefe, Reden, Gedichte aus dem Exil," *Literatur und Kritik* 10 (1975), pp. 469-479.

Bibliography

I.   Works by Beer-Hofmann in German

Novellen. Berlin: Freund & Jaeckel, 1893.
Der Tod Georgs. Berlin: S. Fischer, 1900.
Der Graf von Charolais. Berlin: S. Fischer, 1905.
Gedenkrede auf Wolfgang Amadé Mozart. Berlin: S. Fischer, 1906.
Jaákobs Traum. Berlin: S. Fischer, 1918.
Der junge David. Berlin: S. Fischer, 1933.
Vorspiel auf dem Theater zu König David. Wien: Johannespresse, 1936.
Verse. Stockholm, New York: Bermann-Fischer, 1941.
Herbstmorgen in Österreich. New York: Johannespresse, 1944.

Paula, ein Fragment. Ed. Otto Kallir. New York: Johannespresse, 1949.
"Das goldene Pferd. Pantomime in sechs Bildern." *Neue Rundschau* 66 (1955), pp. 679-726.
Gesammelte Werke. Introd. Martin Buber. Frankfurt a.M.: S. Fischer, 1963.
Der Tod Georgs. Afterword Hartmut Scheible. Stuttgart: Reclam, 1980.
"Pierrot Hypnotiseur." Ed. Rainer Hank. *Mortifikation und Beschwörung.* Frankfurt a.M.: Peter Lang, 1984.

II.   Works in English Translation

"Memorial Oration on Wolfgang Amadeus Mozart." Trans. Samuel R. Wachtell. *Heart of Europe.* Ed. Klaus Mann, Hermann Kesten. Introd. Dorothy Canfield Fisher. New York: Bermann-Fischer, 1943. 579-583.
"Lullabye for Miriam." Trans. Sol Liptzin. *Poet Lore* 47 (1941): 290.
Jacob's Dream. Trans. Ida Bension Wynn. Introd. Thornton Wilder. Foreword Sol Liptzin. New York: Johannespresse, 1946.

III.   Secondary Works in English

Elstun, Esther N. *Richard Beer-Hofmann: His Life and Work.* Penn State Series in German Literature. University Park and London: Pennsylvania State University Press, 1983.
_____. "Richard Beer-Hofmann: The Poet as *Exculpator Dei.*" *Protest, Form, Tradition: Essays on German Exile Literature.* Ed. Joseph P. Strelka, Robert Bell, and Eugene Dobson. University, Alabama: University of Alabama Press, 1979.
Harris, Kathleen and Richard M. Sheirich. "Richard Beer-Hofmann: A Bibliography." *Modern Austrian Literature* 15, no. 1 (1982), 1-60.
Liptzin, Sol. *Richard Beer-Hofmann.* New York: Bloch, 1936.
Reik, Theodor. *The Secret Self.* New York: Farrar, Straus & Young, 1952.
Sheirich, Richard M. *"Frevel* and *der erhöhte Augenblick* in Richard Beer-Hofmann: Reflections on a Biographical Problem." *Modern Austrian Literature* 13, no. 2 (1980), 1-16.

IV.   Major Studies in German

Hank, Rainer. *Mortifikation und Beschwörung*. Frankfurt a.M.: Peter Lang, 1984.

Kleinewefers, Antje. *Das Problem der Erwählung bei Richard Beer-Hofmann*. Hildesheim: Georg Olms, 1972.

Neumann, Hans-Gerhard. *Richard Beer-Hofmann. Studien und Materialien zur Historie von König David*. Munich: Wilhelm Fink, 1972.

Oberholzer, Otto. *Richard Beer-Hofmann*. Bern: Francke, 1947.

Werner, Alfred. *Richard Beer-Hofmann. Sinn und Gestalt*. Vienna: H. Glanz, 1936.

Marie von Ebner-Eschenbach

Danuta S. Lloyd

Marie von Ebner-Eschenbach is not only recognized as one of the most prominent writers of Poetic Realism, along with Gottfried Keller, Conrad Ferdinand Meyer, Theodor Storm, Annette von Droste-Hülshoff, and others, but also ranks as one of the most outstanding Austrian women writers. Yet that reputation was not easily won. Her literary career was fraught with disappointments and setbacks, the earliest discouragements coming from her own family, who considered her poetic aspirations an anathema, and not worthy of an aristocrat.[1] These difficulties notwithstanding, Ebner reminisced about her early ambitions in *Aus einem zeitlosen Tagebuch* (*From a Timeless Diary*), written in 1916, shortly before her death: "I was still a young girl, almost a child, my dream-like views, my likes and dislikes changed like April weather, but one thing stood clearly and firmly in my mind: the conviction that I shall not walk this earth without having left behind at least a slight trace of my footprints upon it."[2]

Ebner's childhood wish was realized in more than one way. Not only did she leave a rich literary legacy whose scope and depth are only now beginning to be evaluated properly,[3] but also an indelible mark on all those with whom she associated and with whom she conducted a lively correspondence. In this context one should mention her friendship with Franz Grillparzer, one of Austria's greatest literary figures, whom she immortalized in her *Erinnerungen an Grillparzer* (1915, *Reminiscences of Grillparzer*) as well as her correspondence with Paul Heyse, the prolific novelist and editor of *Neuer deutscher Novellenschatz* (*New Treasury of German Novellas*), where Ebner's short story *Die Freiherren von Gemperlein* (*The Barons von Gemperlein*) first appeared in 1881; Julius Rodenberg, the editor of the *Deutsche Rundschau*, the leading literary periodical of 19th-century

Germany, where most of her significant works were published; Louise von Francois, the author of *Die Letzte Reckenburgerin* (*The Last of the Reckenburgs*, 1871), one of the outstanding novels of the period; Heinrich Laube, a member of Young Germany, Director of the *Hofburgtheater*, and subsequently head of the Vienna *Stadttheater;* Dr. Josef Breuer, her physician and a colleague of Sigmund Freud; the Austrian novelist Ferdinand von Saar and so many others.

Marie von Ebner-Eschenbach (née Countess Dubsky), a member of one of the leading aristocratic families of nineteenth-century Austria, was born in Zdislawitz, her family's Moravian estate. Her birth and death dates (1830-1916) coincide with those of the Austrian Emperor Francis Joseph I. Since childhood imbued with a strong sense of history, to which her diaries and her autobiographical works attest, Ebner followed assiduously the political affairs of the Empire, shaken again and again by revolutions and internal strife. Her father, Count Franz von Dubsky, a retired major and former Chamberlain to Emperor Francis I, was the scion of an old Catholic Czech noble family, while her mother, Marie Vockel-Dubsky, descended from a line of Saxon Protestants whose ancestors had settled in Moravia centuries before.[4] Ebner's long life— she lived to be over eighty-five—spent in the Moravian country-side surrounded by Czech servants and villagers on the one hand, and in the aristocratic and intellectual salons of Vienna on the other, provided her with the unique opportunity to compare and contrast, and make observations about life as it unfolded itself in its ethnic and religious duality. Her works, which reflect the socio-political and cultural problems facing the reign of Francis Joseph I, concentrate mainly on the interrelationship between the two worlds, those of the village and the country palace, the Austrian and the Slav, the master and the servant.[5]

Two collections of her short stories, dealing with these closely linked, yet divergent social and ethnic spheres are appropriately entitled *Dorf- und Schloßgeschichten* (*Tales of the Village and the Palace*) and *Neue Dorf- und Schloßgeschichten* (*New Tales of the Village and the Palace*), which appeared in 1883 and 1886 respectively. While emotionally inextricably bound to the Slavic world represented by the Czech servants and nannies of Zdislawitz, to which she bears witness in her autobiographical essay "Aus meinen Kinder- und Lehrjahren" ("From my Childhood and Apprenticeship Years"), intellectually she was drawn early in life to the German world of letters.[6] In Vienna the attractions of the *Burgtheather* opened for the aspiring young author worlds hitherto unknown to her. In her last autobiographical work *Meine Kinderjahre* (1906, *My Childhood*), written at the age of 76, she acknowledges her indebtedness to it: "Our old Burgtheater! It was for me and must certainly have been for many a source of noble joy, an educational tool without equal. I owe it the basis of my aesthetic education, which had begun then and which today — has by far not come to an end."[7]

The *Burgtheater* with its classical repertory, which included works of Shakespeare, Schiller, and Goethe, was instrumental in Ebner's desire to become a dramatist. According to Moritz Necker, her biographer, Schiller exerted a special influence on the young countess.[8] However, after many unsuccessful attempts at drama, dealing with such historical figures as Mary Stuart, Marie Roland, Richelieu, and others, and climaxing with the social satire *Das Waldfräulein* (*The Forest Nymph*), produced in Vienna in 1873, the author bade a permanent farewell to the theater. Discouraged by bad reviews and censure from her own close family, Ebner turned to the genre of the short tale, at which she became an expert. Her first success came in 1875 with the appearance of *Ein Spätgeborener* (*A Latecomer*), when she had reached the age of forty-five. This story of a struggling artist reflects, according to her own account, the disappointments and tribulations of her career.[9]

As a short story writer Ebner reached into the inexhaustible treasury of country life in and around Zdislawitz to create her heroes and heroines, even though the misery of the urban poor — as depicted in *Die Großmutter* (1875, *The Grandmother*)—and the problems of the middle class did not remain foreign to her.[10] Her tales sing praises of the indomitable spirit of the simple people in the face of the vicissitudes of their socially deprived daily existences. More often than not, she pits the exploited villagers against their privileged aristocratic masters. In this she shows affinity for Ivan Turgenev, who in his *Fathers and Sons* (1852) attacked his own class for its frivolity and lack of social responsibility.[11] Ebner acknowledged that indebtedness to Turgenev in the 27 September 1908 entry of her diary: "The only writer in whose style I immersed myself and still do, in order to learn from him, is Turgenev. His people have a similarity to our people; he has made his country people, as I have done, the object of his love and his solicitude; he associated with them and depicted them as they are. He is my never-attained model."[12]

Endowed with a social consciousness, rare among her class,[13] Ebner explored in many of her works the abuses of the aristocratic overlords of the Habsburg Empire during the period of the so called *Vormärz*; i.e., the period prior to the March Revolution of 1848. In her novel *Unsühnbar* (1879, *Inexpiable*), linked by its theme of marital infidelity to Flaubert's *Madame Bovary*, Maria Dornach, the heroine, expresses shock at hearing of the moral depravity and seeing the social abandonment to which the villagers on her father's estate in Wolfsburg are condemned:

> What abominations, . . . no, you did not have to become what you are, you deplorable ones! You did not have to sink into the morass, in which you are foundering. If there had been only a few judicious and compassionate ones among those who throughout the ages ruled over you absolutely, they would have led you to the knowledge of good. They possessed the power, why not also the justice, the generosity, the loving heart?[14]

She blames this state of affairs on the aristocratic rulers, whose inhumanity and ruthlessness, exercised with impunity, reduced the peasant population to the status of slaves. Maria Dornach, "the child of the new era," sees this enslavement reflected in their faces:

> Whether young or old, . . . whether female or male, in all these faces, which turned toward her, Maria saw the reflection of a mysterious inherited wrong. And in her awoke the thought: "What calls out to you here with silent and instinctive lament, is an eternal servitude struggling for deliverance. We the masters, they the servants. Starving in body and soul, they earn—our bread; they struggle stooped to the earth, year after year, so that our spirit could roam freely, and unhindered to the limits of knowledge...Without their hard work no rest for us, no enjoyment, no art, no knowledge..."[15]

No less condemning is Ebner's depiction of Koloman Zapolya, the Hungarian grandee, in *Der Erstgeborene* (*The Firstborn*, 1905), who ruthlessly claims his feudal prerogative of the *droit du seigneur* by raping his groom's bride Ilona. Ilona's innocence and her violent protestations exacerbate the inhumanity of Koloman's transgression. Similarly, the Countess in *Er lasst die Hand küssen* (1886, *He Bids Farewell*) thoughtlessly sentences her young servant, to death in the name of morality, by invoking the feudal master's right to public flogging.[16] Yet Koloman Zapolya's brutality and the Countess's frivolity seem trivial as compared with the grave sins of Countess Beate in *Ein Edelmann* (1875, *A Nobleman*) a terror-evoking figure captured by the author with stark realism. Imperious and haughty—Countess Beate represents the best and the worst of her family—she stoops to murder to preserve her family's estate for Egon Wolfram, a nephew whom she deems worthy to be heir to the once proud and lofty line of the Tannbergs, only to discover that her heinous crime was in vain. Egon Wolfram, a true "noble man," who relinquished his rights to the entailed estate when he married the daughter of a Protestant minister, refuses to accept it, for he does not want his son Max to become "a martyr to the past." In his advice to him he questions the raison d'être of the aristocratic class in view of the changing times: "The faithful adherence to the lofty and noble concepts of honor, which give his class [i .e. the nobleman's] the right to existence, imposes duties which are no longer accompanied by privileges, and the one who conforms to them is not only a follower, but a victim of tradition."[17]

Ebner was more than aware that the time for the aristocratic classes was rapidly running out. In the words of Dembowski, the Polish aristocrat turned revolutionary (*Der Kreisphysikus* [1883, The District Doctor]), and a historical figure of the Peasant Revolt in Galicia in 1846, Ebner allows the possibility that the exploited masses could one day rise and annihilate those who oppressed them for centuries: "The oppressors are few, the oppressed many. If the oppressed would rise and demand in the name of the All-Just their share of the earth, then the power of the mighty would be like chaff."[18] Ebner's conviction that the aristocratic class has reached its moral nadir also becomes apparent in one of her best short stories, *Die Freiherren von Gemperlein* (1879, *The Barons von Gemperlein*), written in a humorous vein. Ferdinand von Saar, Ebner's devoted friend, called it "the glittering jewel of humoristic narrative art."[19] Here the author, fully aware of the shortcomings of her protagonists, weighs with objectivity the faults against the positive attributes of the two eccentric Barons. Although naive and impractical, the two noblemen possess one overriding quality—a strong attachment to their ancestral estate of Wlastowitz. However, as admirable as this loyalty might be, Ebner does not consider the two contentious brothers, Friedrich and Ludwig, whose antics are carried *ad absurdum*—one of the Barons falls in love with a printer's error in the Gotha Genealogical Almanac!—as viable members of society. Amused by their naive, extreme political views, be they reactionary or radical, she prefers to let them fade quietly into oblivion: "They passed without leaving an heir to their name, and thus the old family of the Gemperleins became extinct, like so many beautiful things on this earth."[20]

Similarly in the two countesses Muschi and Paula (1885, *Comtesse Muschi, Comtesse Paula*), Ebner exposes with wit and humor the superficiality of the education of the young women of her circles. Unaware of the more serious aspects of existence, since their sole goal is to please, the young countesses spend their time dancing and riding, while their education is limited to the knowledge of French and some music. Ebner's light and elegant style does not conceal the gravity with which she viewed the situation, as a passage from *Aus Franzensbad*, one of her earliest prose works, confirms:

> But where would the daughters of our aristocracy have had the opportunity to think and to suffer? Flighty as their feelings, shallow as their judgments are their inclinations and their conversations. Never was seriousness of life revealed to them, never did they stand with inspiration before a truth or a beauty, since after all their mothers taught them that seriousness is nothing but disguised boredom, inspiration a ridiculous fancifulness.[21]

Similar references to the young countesses and for that matter young gentlemen can be found throughout her work.[22] Her criticism of her class is harsh and inexorable since she herself, as a member of one of the oldest families of the Empire, felt partly responsible for its past failures and its present moral impotence to accept the challenges of the new era.

Despite her rather pessimistic view concerning the human race as a whole Ebner showed a special predilection for the idiosyncratic and the extraordinary in the human character. Through this unique insight into the complexities of human nature Ebner succeeds in creating unforgettable eccentric figures whose affinity to the whimsical world of Jean Paul Richter is unmistakable. Her *Käuze*, eccentrics, despite their lack of worldliness, must be considered heroes in their own right, as they assert their beliefs and convictions in environments hostile to them. Among these one should mention Mansuet Weberlein, the gnomish clerk of a wine merchant who fancies for himself a military career, in the novel *Božena* (1876); Habrecht, the idealistic teacher and social reformer in *Das Gemeindekind* (1887, *The Child of the Parish*), and the pedantic cavalry captain Brand in *Rittmeister Brand* (1887, *Captain Brand*) to name only a few. They possess high ideals and a social awareness unmatched by many of the aristocrats, whose ethical code—the preservation of appearances (schöner Schein)—reduced them to virtual relics of another era, such as Count Wolfsberg (*Unsühnbar*), Tante Beate (*Ein Edelmann*), or Prince Seinsburg (*Am Ende*, 1885 [*In the End*]). Furthermore onto the eccentric character of the Privy Councillor (1915, *Der Herr Hofrat*),whom she patterned on Grillparzer, Ebner projected many of her own views concerning the existing state of the arts in Austria. Seeing the classical ideals of Schiller and Goethe abandoned in favor of sensationalism and quick profit, she uses the Privy Councillor, the old curmudgeon whose embittered heart is struck mercilessly by the arrow of Cupid, as her gadfly. Who could be better qualified to speak against the deterioration of good taste and quality in art, than the sensitive art lover and connoisseur himself: "The theater as an artistic pleasure, as an educational institution for the mighty and the lowly, is dead. There are tragedies, but no longer tragedy, there is no drama, only actors."[23] Deploring the lack of divine inspiration in the arts, he lashes out at the hacks of the trade: "Where is the divine force which elevates us to the heights of life, where is the passion which by annihilating and destroying still is capable of inspiring? The clever hands, for whom the heights are unattainable, reach down to the depths of life."[24]

Ebner, who set the highest artistic standards for her own work—art as "the temporal revelation of the eternally beautiful and eternally good"[25] (*A Latecomer*)— demanded the same of her fellow artists. Her aphorisms, which constitute a major part of her artistic *oeuvre* and which place her in the ranks of the top European aphorists such as La Rochefoucauld, Lichtenberg, Nietzsche, and others, testify to that. The first collection of 300 *Aphorismen* (*Aphorisms*), was published in 1880 and brought the author much recognition. They are, in the words of Anton Bettelheim, "the essence of her ethics and aesthetics."[26] At the same time, as the author's most personal pronouncements on life, art, morals, and society, they constitute a true "diary of her soul."[27] Exhibiting an unprecedented insight into the human psyche and the social relationships between men and women, the aphorisms sparkle with humor and ingenuity, and astound with their pithiness. Despite her adherence to the so-called "Old School," she unabashedly proclaims: "Not to participate in the spiritual progress of one's time means to remain morally backward."[28] With an almost childlike directness reinforced by the rationality of a dialectician Ebner expostulates on artistic and moral values. Little escapes her keen sense of observation, as she delineates the fine relationships between the artist and his work, the individual, and his conscience, between men and women:

> A relationship closer than that between the mother and the child is that between the artist and his work.[29]
> I believe that the only writer who has a true and irresistible calling is the one who would write, even if he knew that he would never be read.[30]
> If you have only a choice between an untruth and a crudity, then choose the crudity; if however, the choice must be made between an untruth and a cruelty, then choose the untruth.[31]
> The association with an egotist is so pernicious, because self-defense gradually forces us to slip into his error.[32]
> If the man has the position and the woman the intelligence, then there is a good marriage.[33]
> Women are grateful for selfless love, but selfish love they reciprocate.[34]

Deploring the unworthiness of human beings ("Most people need more love than they deserve[35]) and their intrinsic iniquity ("A human being—he can become a true image of God. Human beings—the devil himself would refuse to be compared with them"[36]), she concedes with considerable irony the necessity for human companionship: "You are nothing, nothing without the others. The most confirmed misanthrope still needs human beings, even if only to scorn them."[37]

The aphorisms also call for a reevaluation of the role of woman in society. No emancipator herself, even though lauded by German feminists,[38] she devoted much of her work to analyzing and reexamining the traditional relationship between men and women. Her most striking aphorisms speak at times jocularly of the cavalier fashion with which women have been treated over the centuries by society:

> Men lead in all aspects of human existence; only on the way to heaven do they give precedence to women.[39]

One should not demand truthfulness from women as long as one brings them up to believe that their foremost aim in life is—to please.[40]

The question of women's rights surfaced when a woman learned to read.[41]

Wise women are quiet when men speak; however, never so quiet as when men speak nonsense.[42]

Finally an aphorism for which Ebner received undue notoriety avers: "An intelligent woman has millions of natural enemies: —all stupid men."[43]

This single example notwithstanding, Ebner's aphorisms lack the condescension and the acrimony toward the opposite sex so typical of the aphorisms of Karl Kraus, Nietzsche, Lichtenberg, and even La Rochefoucauld. In that respect she remained neutral, applying the standards of self-reliance, self-discipline, and personal heroism to all human beings alike. In the manifold structure of moral and ethical values, Ebner sets the highest score on goodness, just as on the opposite side of the spectrum she considers egotism to be the worst evil:

How wise one must be, in order to be always good![44]
The intellect is an intermittent, goodness a permanent spring.[45]
The great create that which is great, the good that which is permanent.[46]
One can be wise out of goodness, and good out of wisdom.[47]

Although not generally cynical, Ebner sometimes resorts to irony:

The world belongs to those who want to have it and is disdained by those to whom it should belong.[48]
The wiser man gives in! A sad truth, which proves the universal supremacy of stupidity.[49]

Ebner's aphorisms are also a testimony to her stoically heroic attitude toward life:

A proudly borne defeat is also a victory.
How much motion is generated in striving toward repose!
Do not call yourself poor because your dreams were not fulfilled; truly poor is the one who never dreamed.[50]

Although the genre of the aphorism seems to have been traditionally a masculine domain, Ebner as a woman asserted her position quite
successfully in that form. This may be attributable in part to her childlike sense of wonder and reverence for God's creatures, large and small,
together with the analytical mind of a rational thinker; as Louise von
Francois, a fellow writer and friend, concisely noted: she combined the
heart of a child with the brain of a man.[51]

Much of the early Ebner scholarship refused to recognize her as a
serious thinker who tackled controversial subjects; consequently, a
rather one-sided picture of her work emerged.[52] However, when one
subjects her work to a thorough analysis, it becomes apparent that she
did not shy away from treating delicate moral and social issues.
According to Gertrud Fussenegger, she even delved into areas of the
subconscious which were not discovered until the advent of modern psychology.[53]

In *Die Reisegefährten* (1901, *The Travel Companions*) Ebner deals
with the moral issues pertaining to euthanasia. The protagonist, an old
doctor and agnostic, admits to his traveling companion, a young
Russian, that he knowingly killed a patient entrusted to his care. Ebner's
sympathies are with the doctor. Far from advocating the general acceptance of euthanasia, Ebner nevertheless finds some justification for it in
the greater good which can result from it: moral relativism at its best!
The doctor, who remains here unnamed, views euthanasia as an act of
mercy rather than a crime and is not moved to repentance: "To prolong
the life of this man meant to prolong his suffering, to make his children
unhappy or to kill them. I stopped him from suffering and torturing. The
man who ruined and embittered the existence of so many had an easy
and painless death..."[54]

Yet, though having usurped the divine power over life and death,
the doctor is not willing to admit the universal applicability of his
action:

> What someone else should do, I do not know. I have never
> lived in the skin of another, I cannot take upon myself the deli-
> cate balance between insight and ability, outer and inner com-
> pulsion and so many things which constitute man's moral obli-
> gations.—I have dared to seize the spokes of the wheel of for-
> tune. If it chooses to crush me because of it—so be it!
> Fortunately I may hope that the retribution will affect me
> alone,...[55]

Thus the moral question as to what constitutes good or evil must ultimately be decided according to individual conscience, not any moral code. According to Ebner's relativistic set of values, any action performed in the name of humanitarianism or the so called "greater good" is justifiable. Motivated by these "higher ideals," Maria Dornach (*Inexpiable*) spares her husband the disgrace of a scandal, just as the doctor condemns a man to death for the sake of others. Neither can be rewarded but must assume the consequences of social ostracism on the one hand, and isolation on the other. Unlike Grillparzer's characters, Ebner's heroes and heroines are fully involved in the affairs of the world, neither renouncing nor escaping moral commitment. For example, Curate Leo Klinger in the novel *Glaubenslos?* (1893, *Without Faith?*), the idealistic priest who upon the assumption of his pastoral duties in a corrupt mountain village, is shaken by despair and loss of faith at his inability to cope with evil, does not abandon his post but continues to serve mankind as a humanitarian. Ironically Curate Leo, who was unable to deal with the harsh truth of reality as a believer, finds himself better equipped to bridge the gap between theory and practice as a doubter who has overcome a religious crisis. In his decision to stay with his corrupt flock he is guided by altruistic motives: "His battle was fought out. Oh well! to comfort, to help, to ameliorate. To live and to die, unknown, unmentioned, in the concealing shadows in which his entire character can unfold. A quiet guardian at one of the innumerable springs, from which good and evil flow into the world."[56]

The subject of evil as an omnipresent destructive force, undermining the harmony of the world, occupied Ebner consistently during the latter part of her life.[57] In a story published in 1894, entitled *Das Schädliche* (*The Varmint*), Ebner poses the problem of man's helplessness when caught in the clutches of the inscrutable laws of heredity. The evil character of Edith, the protagonist, is inherited by her daughter, Lore. The father, who had for years been a sad witness to the misbehavior of both, now stands by, allowing the bullet aimed by an unhappy suitor at Lore, who is on her way to a tryst, to strike and kill her, justifying his behavior with the following rationale: vermin in the biological hierarchy of life have to be eradicated for the survival of the species. Therefore, Lore, the very incarnation of evil, must be eliminated: "She lives for the ruination of everyone who approaches her, she is the varmint: away with the varmint from the world! Let fate prevail! Let it happen!"[58]

The father's acquiescence to the murder of his own child can only be explained in terms of that same moral relativism. Lore's death prevents the inherent evil in her from being perpetuated in her children. The novel ends on a somber note, as the father pleads desperately for a death penalty. Ebner does not present a definite solution to the problem here; however, her empathy for the distressed father is unmistakable. It is quite clear from the above that Ebner was not a "writer of idylls," as one of the early critics naively referred to her.[59] Neither does Ebner consider evil surmountable, as Ernst Alker fallaciously argues;[60] evil can only be eradicated by force. Ebner shows that pedagogy failed in Lore's case, just as it failed in the case of Edinek, the protagonist in *Unverbesserlich* (1910, *Incorrigible*). By the same token Maria Dornach, despite her moral rectitude and her upbringing, succumbs to her inherited sensuality, over which she has no control. The question could be asked here as to what extent Ebner was willing, as deeply rooted as she was in the German classical tradition, to concede the validity of the new theories of naturalism and moral determinism. As much as she wanted to believe in man's ability to shape his own destiny, she also realized his limitations, as another of her aphorisms so poignantly illustrates: "Whoever believes in the freedom of man's will, has never loved and never hated."[61]

However, in extraordinary cases an individual can and will at least to some extent overcome heredity and *milieu* to his best advantage, as is the case in the novel *Das Gemeindekind* (1887, *The Child of the Parish*). Despite the hereditary taint and the prejudice of his fellowmen toward him, Pavel Holub, the village outcast and the son of an alcoholic turned murderer, raises himself to become a useful member of society. By the all too predictable laws of Naturalism Pavel, left to his own devices in the corrupt environment of a backward mountain village, should have followed in the footsteps of his father. However, he is able to defy the hypocrisy of the villagers, including that of the local priest, by virtue of his faith in himself, in accordance with Ebner's dictum: "If there is a faith that can move mountains, it is the faith in one's own strength."[62] His pragmatism and philosophically empirical outlook on life, so unlikely for a village outcast, allow him to create an acceptable *modus vivendi* between the villagers and himself. His mother's hesitation to join him after her release from prison "der Leute wegen" (because of public opinion), he dismisses with his own homespun philosophy: "The worst people frequently become the best, when they need you. Well, dear mother, that would indeed be quite strange, if one did not sometime need two people like us. You will remain with me, dear mother."[63] But despite his success Pavel does not fully trust himself. He consciously refuses to marry, for fear of succumbing to his own evil impulses. His existential outlook on life, devoid of any metaphysical speculations or, for that matter, any faith in Divine Providence, makes him into a courageous, albeit a lonely individual.

Similar pragmatism motivates the hero of Ebner's *Die Spitzin* (1901, *The Pommeranian*), a deeply psychological tale about a dog. Provi Kirchhof, the village foundling and animal tormentor, awakens one day in the goat stall, which he inhabits together with a Pommeranian, to discover that an inner compulsion born out of compassion for a helpless puppy, whose mother he had mortally wounded, arouses in him a social consciousness he had never possessed. By overcoming his pride and obstinacy Provi exercises his free will at the cost of humiliation to himself, when he begs the *Schoberwirtin* for some milk for his new charge. Ebner's insight into this wretched soul reveals her perspicacity and deep knowledge of a child's psyche.

Thus the philosophy of reliance on oneself, expressed so eloquently in her works, succeeds in sustaining Pavel in his existential struggle and in arousing Provi's social awareness; however, it fails to prevent Maria Dornach's moral downfall and the ensuing religious crisis (*Inexpiable*). Here, according to Gertrud Fussenegger, Ebner becomes a "Kierkegaardian pessimist."[64] Her heroine, relying too much on her own strength, fails to find solace and comfort in the forgiveness of her Church. This awareness of the presence of the darker sides of the human psyche brings Ebner's works within the scope of the school of Naturalism; in its familiarity with the complexities of human nature and its subconscious, especially that of the child, it also antedates the scientific work of Freud.

Ebner's artistic skill in the portrayal of children can hardly be matched in German literature. Although attempts had been made in the nineteenth and the beginning of the twentieth century to assign a larger role to the child, the subject had generally been neglected.[65] Ebner's special love and understanding for the child, particularly a motherless child—Ebner's own mother, Marie Vockel-Dubsky died shortly after her birth—equipped her with a unique knowledge of the child's vulnerable soul.[66] Richard M. Meyer recognized this quality as early as 1912, when he wrote "There is no greater master of child psychology."[67]

Ebner's first-hand experience with children can he traced back to her own immediate family—since she was one of Count Dubsky's seven children [68] — as well as to her extended family of nieces and nephews. Ebner herself, married for almost fifty years to her first cousin, Fieldmarshal Moritz von Ebner-Eschenbach, was denied the happiness of children. Yet as a student of the human psyche she was able to create literary monuments to the abandoned, troubled, and mistreated children, regardless of their social or ethnic origin. In the character of little Clary in *Die erste Beichte* (1875, *The First Confession*), Ebner depicts with psychological finesse a seven-year-old's religious crisis precipitated by the inordinately harsh demands of a disciplinarian father. Clary, who bears the features of the young author herself, was left more or less to her own devices after the premature death of the mother, in the care of a governess and a loving but petulant father. During the preparation for her First Communion the precocious Clary takes the commandments of her faith too literally, precipitating a moral crisis. The child's metaphysical broodings, not unlike those of the author herself as depicted in *Meine Kinderjahre* (1906, *My Childhood*), lead to an attempt at suicide, thus compounding the moral problem for her solicitous priest, Father Joseph. Seldom does one find a better and more realistic portrayal of the fragility of the conscience-stricken soul of a seven-year-old as contrasted with the spiritual impotence of the adult world. In her concern for children Ebner pointed to their uniqueness and pleaded for their rights, be it in the village foundling Provi Kirchhof in the *Pommeranian*, Pavel Holub in the *Village Ward*, Georg Pfanner, the exploited pupil in *Der Vorzugsschüler* (1901, *The Honor-Roll Pupil*), Franzko in *Ein Verbot* (1897, *An Interdiction*), or the orphaned Pia in *Der Fink* (1897, *The Finch*). Their suffering, heroism, and courage in a world of insensitive adults, make them into some of the most skillfully and sympathetically created characters in her work. In that respect Ebner stands at the threshold of the twentieth century as a champion of the modern era.

Furthermore Ebner's portraiture of women is especially characteristic of her modernity.[69] Her numerous heroines—independent, emotionally strong, and tenacious—such as the faithful servant Božena (1876, *Božena*), the noble-minded Countess Marie Dornach (*Inexpiable*), the jilted Anna (*Die Totenwacht* [1894, *The Death Watch*]), the introspective Frau Kogler (*Without Faith?*), the washerwoman Josepha Lakomy (*Die Unverstandene auf dem Dorfe* [1886, *The Misunderstood Village Woman*]), Lotti (*Lotti die Uhrmacherin* [1880, *Lotti the Watchmaker*]) and so many others, stand as figures chiseled out of bronze. Faced with the socially insuperable odds against them, these women assert themselves as individuals, whose resolution acquired in adversity frees them from dependence on men and society. Self-reliance and moral strength accord them that added aura of the new femininity.

By contrast, Ebner's most sympathetically drawn male figures are the eccentrics, the unconventional idealists and dreamers, and the countless priests, such as Curate Leo Klinger and Pater Thalberg in *Without Faith*?, Pater Joseph in *Die erste Beichte*, Pater Emmanuel in *Unverbesserlich*,who devote their lives unselfishly and stoically to their flocks and of whom Ebner once wrote: "A noble priest comes closest to perfection."[70]

Finally, it would be amiss not to mention Ebner's samaritan spirit, which extends to the realm of animals and birds. An expert horsewoman, Ebner combatted the mistreatment of horses especially,[71] while her love for dogs is demonstrated in the following aphorism:

> Among a hundred people, I love only one, among a hundred dogs, ninety nine.[72]

The hound Krambambuli (1875, *Krambambuli*), and the Pommeranian (1901, *The Pommeranian*) whose loyalty and trust are matched only by a few of their human counterparts, stand as living moments to her four-legged friends. It is not without cause that the International Society for the Prevention of Cruelty to Animals bestowed its silver medal on her.[73]

Ebner fought long and hard for recognition of her work, and when it did come largely because of her long association with and support from Julius Rodenberg, the able editor of the *Deutsche Rundschau,* she joined the ranks of so many other great nineteenth-century novelists whose works appeared in the pages of this highly respected periodical. Her greatest popularity as a writer fell in the period of the last two decades of the nineteenth-century, when numerous editions of her individual as well as collected works appeared. In 1900 two biographies, one by Anton Bettelheim (*Biographische Blätter*), and another by Moritz Necker (*Marie von Ebner-Eschenbach nach ihren Werken geschildert*) appeared extolling her contributions. The same year the University of Vienna bestowed upon her the first honorary doctorate ever granted a woman. Ebner was honored and feted by young and old.

As an avid reader, she eagerly followed the literary and political events of her times, referring to World War I, as "the greatest and most horrible of all wars."[74] Despite her privileged social position, she chose the salons of the Viennese intellectuals over those of her aristocratic peers. She demanded as much of herself as she did of her fellowmen, but she never failed to see the world from the perspective of a true humorist. Never condescending, always refreshing, her humor is devoid of sarcasm. Her benevolent smile, focused tolerantly on the human race with all its faults and shortcomings, is never dogmatic. By choosing to elevate the simple and the underprivileged of the country and the village to the level of heroes and heroines, Ebner accomplishe what neither legislation nor force would have been able to achieve: she nullified the artificially imposed barriers of class, ethnicity, and religion. In a spirit of humanitarianism and common sense she stressed those values and qualities in men and women which, unhindered by human institutions, she believed could actually prevail.

Notes

1. See Marie von Ebner-Eschenbach's diary entries of January 9 and November 16, 1867; and July 18, 1875, as quoted by Anton Bettelheim, *Marie von Ebner-Eschenbachs Wirken und Vermächtnis* (Leipzig: Quelle und Meyer, 1920), pp. 110, 120, and 108 respectively. Henceforth abbreviated as *W.u.V.* Ebner's earliest censure came from her beloved maternal grandmother as reported in her autobiographical work *Meine Kinderjahre* in Marie von Eschenbach. *Sämtliche Werke* (Berlin: Gebrüder Paetel, n.d.), VI, 633. Henceforth cited as *S.W.*

2. *S.W.*, IV, 633. All translations in this essay are mine.

3. For the first time since the author's death in 1916 a critical edition of her works is finally being undertaken by the Bouvier Verlag in Bonn under the general editorship of Karl Konrad Polheim. So far three volumes have appeared: *Unsühnbar* (1978), edited by Burkhard Bittrich; *Božena* (1980), edited by Kurt Binneberg, and *Das Gemeindekind* (1983), edited by Rainer Baasner. A fourth volume, *Tagebücher I*, 1862-1868, ed. by K. K. Polheim and Rainer Baasner appeared in 1989 in the Niemeyer Verlag in Tübingen. In addition the following volumes have been announced as fourthcoming: vol. 4, *Autobiographische Schriften* I, "Meine Kinderjahre," and vol. 5 *Autobiographische Schriften* II, "Meine Erinnerungen an Grillparzer," edited by Christa Maria Schmidt.

4. For further biographical information see Anton Bettelheim, *Biographische Blätter* (Berlin: Gebrüder Paetel, 1900); and *Marie von Ebner-Eschenbachs Wirken und Vermächtnis* (Leipzig: Quelle und Meyer, 1920), and Moritz Necker, *Marie von Ebner-Eschenbach*. Nach ihren Werken geschildert (Leipzig und Berlin: Georg Heinrich Meyer, 1900). See also Ebner's autobiographical essay "Aus meinen Kinder- und Lehrjahren" in *Letzte Worte. Aus dem Nachlass herausgegeben von Helene Bucher* (Wien, Leipzig, München: Rikola, 1923).

5. See Siegfried Scheibe in his *Nachwort* [Epilog] to Marie von Ebner-Eschenbach. *Geschichten aus Dorf- und Schloss* (Leipzig: Dieterich'sche Verlagshandlung, 1967), p.624f. See also Danuta S. Lloyd, "*Dorf* and *Schloss*: The Socio-Political Image of Austria as Reflected in Marie von Ebner-Eschenbach's Works." *Modern Austrian Literature*, 12, Nos.3/4 (1979), 25-44.

6.   In *Letzte Worte*, pp. 33-59; see note 4.

7.   S.W., VI, 661. The *Burgertheater* had a similar effect on Stefan Zweig as reported in his autobiographical work *The World of Yesterday*.

8.   Moritz Necker in his biography of the author writes: "This predilection for Schiller appears to me to be an expression of her innermost nature, as a result of a type of affinity with the classical writer." (*Marie von Ebner-Eschenbach*, p. 223). Cf. also Ebner's own account of the effect Schiller's works exerted on the young countess in *Meine Kinderjahre, S.W.*, VI, 657f. Further evidence of her enthusiasm for Schiller is a dramatic poem, entitled *Dr. Ritter* (1869) written in his honor.

9.   See Anton Bettelheim, *W. und V.*, p.248.

10.   In a note of September 27, 1908, Ebner writes: "I owe my inspiration to my old Zdislawitz. Božena, Pavel, Anna, the washerwoman (*The Misunderstood Village Woman*), etc. — they all come from there." In *Marie von Ebner-Eschenbach. Weisheit des Herzens* [*Wisdom of the Heart*]. Eingeleitet und ausgewählt von Heinz Rieder. 2. Auflage. (Graz und Wien: Stiansny Verlag, 1964), p. 124. Henceforth abbreviated as *Weisheit des Herzens*.

11 .   In a letter of April 14 (26), 1862 to K. K. Sluchevsky, Turgenev writes the following about his *Fathers and Sons:* "My entire tale is directed against the leading class." (As quoted by Ralph E. Matlaw, ed. and trans. in J. Turgenev, *Fathers and Sons* [New York: Norton, 1966], p. 185.)

12.   *Weisheit des Herzens*, p.124.

13.   See her reaction to the punishment of a pond digger on her father's estate as reported in her "Aus meinen Kinder-und Lehrjahren" in *Letzte Worte*, p. 44.

14.   *Unsühnbar*, S.W., IV, 185.

15.   *Ibid.*, p. 36.

16.   *Er lasst die Hand küssen*, S.W., II, 332-353. See Lore M.Dormer's excellent study "Tribunal der Ironie, Marie von Ebner-Eschenbachs Erzählung 'Er lasst die Hand küssen.'" *Modern Austrian Literature*, 9, No. 2 (1976), 86-97.

17.   *Ein Edelmann*, S.W., 191.

18.   *Der Kreisphysikus*, S.W., II, 59.

19.   See Heinz Kindermann, ed. *Briefwechsel zwischen Ferdinand von Saar und Marie von Ebner-Eschenbach*. (Wien: Wiener Biblio-

philen-Gesellschaft, 1957), p. 9. [Correspondence between Ferdinand von Saar and Marie von Ebner-Eschenbach]

20. *Die Freiherren von Gemperlein*, *S.W.*, I, 490.
21. *Aus Franzensbad. Sechs Episteln* [From Franzensbad, Six Letters] (Leipzig: Walther Fiedler, n.d.), p. 83.
22. Cf. for example *Unsühnbar*, S.W., IV, 72.
23. *Der Herr Hofrat*, S.W., V, 11.
24. *Ibid.*, p. 28f.
25. *S.W.*, I, 36.
26. Anton Bettelheim, *W. und V.*, p. 9.
27. *Ibid.*, p. 37.
28. *Aphorismen*, S.W., I, 584.
29. *Ibid.*, p. 623.
30. *Weisheit des Herzens*, p. 72.
31. *Aphorismen*, S.W., I, 596.
32. *Ibid.*, p. 600.
33. *Ibid.*, p. 614.
34. *Weisheit des Herzens*, p. 73.
35. *Aphorismen*, S.W., I, 584.
36. *Weisheit des Herzens*, p. 75.
37. *Aphorismen*, S.W., I, 624.
38. See Helga H. Harriman, "Marie von Ebner-Eschenbach in Feminine Perspective." *Modern Austrian Literature*, 18, No. 1 (1985), 35.
39. *Aphorismen*, S.W., I, 630.
40. *Ibid.*, p. 588.
41. *Ibid.*, p. 612.
42. *Weisheit des Herzens*, p. 79.
43. *Aphorismen*, S.W., I, 594.
44. *Ibid.*, p. 582.
45. *Ibid.*, p. 587.
46. *Ibid.*, p. 598.
47. *Weisheit des Herzens*, p. 90.
48. *Aphorismen*, S.W., I, 606.
49. *Ibid.*, p.582.
50. *Ibid.*, pp. 629, 602, 626 respectively.
51. As quoted by Anton Bettelheim, *W. und V.*, p. 9.
52. For example, Gabriele Reuter, *Ebner-Eschenbach* (Berlin und Leipzig: Schuster und Loeffler, n.d.), refers to the author as "die Dichterin der Idylle." ["the writer of idylls"], p. 5.

53. See Gertrud Fussenegger, *Marie von Ebner-Eschenbach oder Der gute Mensch von Zdislawitz. Ein Vortag.* (München: Delp, 1967), p. 13.

54. *Die Reisegefährten*, S.W., V, 253.

55. *Ibid.*, p. 260.

56. *Glaubenslos? S.W.*, IV, 359.

57. See Mechtild Alkemade, *Die Lebens- und Weltanschauung der Freifrau Marie von Ebner-Eschenbach. Mit sechs Tafelbeilagen und dem Briefwechsel Heyse und Ebner-Eschenbach. Deutsche Quellen und Studien*, Bd. XV (Graz, 1935), p. 247.

58. *Das Schädliche*, S.W., IV, 430.

59. Gabriele Reuter, p. 59. See fn. 52.

60. Ernst Alder, *Die deutsche Literatur im 19. Jahrhundert. 1832-1914.* (Stuttgart: Kröner, 1961), p. 610.

61. *Aphorismen*, S.W., I, 583.

62. *Ibid.*

63. *Das Gemeindekind*, S.W., II, 610.

64. Gertrud Fussenegger, *Marie von Ebner-Eschenbach oder Der gute Mensch von Zdislawitz*, p. 37.

65. Cf. C.F. Meyer's *Leiden eines Knaben* (1983), G. Hauptmann's *Hanneles Himmelfahrt* (1893), F. Wedekind's *Frühlings Erwachen* (1891), Hesse's *Unterm Rad* (1905), and R. Musil's *Verwirrungen des Zöglins Törless* (1906), which all try to deal with the problems of youth.

66. See Danuta S. Lloyd, "Waifs and Strays: The Youth in Marie von Ebner-Eschenbach's Village Tales." *Views and Reviews of Modern German Literature. Festschrift for Adolf D. Klarmann* ed. by Karl S. Weimer (München: Delp, 1974), pp. 39-60.

67. Richard M. Meyer, *Die deutsche Literatur des 19. Jahrhunderts* (Berlin: Georg Bondi, 1912), p. 428.

68. See Paul Heyse and Ludwig Laistner, eds. *Neuer deutscher Novellenschatz* (Berlin, n.d.), vol. I, p. 193.

69. See Moritz Necker, *Marie von Ebner-Eschenbach. Nach ihren Werken geschildert.* p. 218. See fn. 8.

70. As quoted by A. Bettelheim, *W. und V.*, p. 292.

71. See her diary entry of Febuary 10, 1912, as quoted by A. Bettelheim, *W. und V.*, pp. 291f.

72. *Weisheit des Herzens*, p. 85.

73. See Anton Bettelheim, *W. und V.*, p. 291.

74. See her diary entry of May 23, 1915, as quoted by A. Bettelheim, *W. und V.*, p. 298.

Bibliography

I. Works by Marie von Ebner-Eschenbach in German

Aus Franzensbad: Sechs Episteln von keinem Propheten. Anonymous, Leipzig: Carl B. Lorck, 1858; reprinted with name 1913; reprint of 1858 edition Vienna: Österreichischer Bundesverlag, 1985.

Maria Stuart in Schottland: Trauerspiel. Wien: Mayer, 1860.

Die Veilchen: Lustspiel. Wien: Wallishauser, 1862.

Marie Roland: Trauerspiel. Wien: Wallishauser, 1867.

Doctor Ritter: Dramatisches Gedicht. Wien: Jasper, 1869.

Die Prinzessin von Banalien: Ein Märchen. Wien: Rosner, 1872.

Männertreue: Lustspiel. Wien: Walllishauser, 1874.

Erzählungen. Stuttgart: Cotta, 1875.

Božena : Erzählung. Stuttgart: Cotta, 1876.

Aphorismen. Berlin: Ebhardt, 1880.

Neue Erzählungen. Berlin: Ebhardt, 1881.

Dorf- und Schloßgeschichten. Berlin: Paetel, 1883.

Zwei Comtessen. Berlin: Ebhardt, 1885.

Neue Dorf- und Schloßgeschichten. Berlin: Paetel, 1886.

Die Unverstandene auf dem Dorfe. Berlin: Paetel, 1886.

Das Gemeindekind: Erzählung. 2 volumes, Berlin: Paetel, 1887.

Lotti, die Uhrmacherin: Erzählung. Berlin: Paetel, 1889.

Miterlebtes: Erzählungen. Berlin: Paetel, 1889.

Ein Kleiner Roman: Erzählung. Berlin: Paetel, 1889.

Unsühnbar: Erzählung. Berlin: Paetel, 1890.

Margarete. Stuttgart: Cotta, 1891.

Ohne Liebe: Lustspiel in 1 Akt. Berlin: Bloch, 1891.

Drei Novellen. Berlin: Paetel, 1892.

Parabeln. Märchen und Gedichte. Berlin: Paetel, 1892.

Glaubenslos?: Erzählung. Berlin: Paetel, 1893.

Gesammelte Schriften. 10 volumes, Berlin: Paetel, 1893-1910.

Das Schädliche; Die Totenwacht. Berlin: Paetel, 1894

Rittmeister Brand; Bertram Vogelweid. Berlin: Paetel, 1896.

Am Ende: Scene in einem Aufzug. Berlin: Bloch, 1897.

Alte Schule: Erzählung. Berlin: Paetel, 1897.

Hirzepinzchen: Ein Märchen. Stuttgart: Union, 1900.
Aus Spätherbsttagen: Erzählungen, 2 volumes. Berlin: Paetel, 1901.
Agave. Berlin: Paetel, 1903.
Die arme Kleine: Erzählung. Berlin: Paetel, 1903.
Ein Spätgeborener: Erzählung. Stuttgart: Cotta, 1903.
Uneröffnet zu verbrennen. Berlin: Niemeyer, 1905.
Die unbesiegbare Macht: Zwei Erzählungen. Berlin: Paetel, 1905.
Meine Kinderjahre: Biographische Skizzen. Berlin: Paetel, 1906.
Altweibersommer. Berlin: Paetel, 1909; enlarged, 1910.
Genrebilder: Erzählungen. Berlin: Paetel, 1910.
Stille Welt: Erzählungen. Berlin: Paetel, 1915.
Meine Erinnerungen an Grillparzer: Aus einem zeitlosen Tagebuch.
    Berlin: Paetel, 1916.
Sämtliche Werke. 6 volumes, Berlin: Paetel, 1920.
Letzte Worte. Aus dem Nachlaß. Helene Bucher, Wien: Rikola, 1923.
Der Nachlaß der Marie von Ebner-Eschenbach, ed. Heinz Rieder, 4 vol-
    umes, only one volume appeared, Wien: Agathonverlag, 1974.
Gesammelte Werke in drei Einzelbänden, ed. Johannes Klein, 3 volumes,
    München: Winkler, 1956-1958.
Weisheit des Herzens, ed. Heinz Rieder, Graz & Vienna: Stiasny, 1958.
Gesammelte Werke, ed. Edgar Gross, 9 volumes, München:
    Nymphenburger Verlagshandlung, 1961.
Das Waldfräulein: Lustspiel in drei Aufzügen, ed. Karl Gladt, Wien:
    Belvedere, 1969.
Marie von Ebner-Eschenbach: Kritische Texte und Deutungen, ed. Karl
    Konrad Polheim, 3 volumes published; *Unsühnbar*, ed. Burkhard
    Bittrich, Bonn: Bouvier Verlag Herbert Grundmann, 1980; *Das
    Gemeindekind*, ed. Rainer Baasner, Bonn: Bouvier Verlag Herbert
    Grundmann, 1983; *Tagebücher I, 1892-1869*, ed. Karl Konrad
    Polheim and Rainer Baasner, Tübingen: Max Niemeyer, 1989.

Letters

"Briefe von Franz Grillparzer," ed. Carl Glossy, *Grillparzer-Jahrbuch* 8
    (1898), 256-260.
"Briefe Grillparzers an die Gräfin Dubsky," ed. Moritz Necker, ibid., pp.
    214-215.
"Marie von Ebner-Eschenbach und Gustav Frenssen," ed. Anton
    Bettelheim, *Östereichische Rudschau* 53 (1917), 175-179.

Der Dichterinnen stiller Garten. Marie von Ebner-Eschenbach und Enrica von Handel-Mazetti. Bilder aus ihrem Leben und ihrer Freundschaft, ed., Johannes Numbauer, Freiburg i. B.: Herder, 1918.

"Marie von Ebner-Eschenbach und Gustav Frenssen," *Wiener Biographen-Gänge* (1921), 252-259.

"Briefe der Ebner an Friedrich Pecht," *Der Sammler* (Münchner-Augsburger Abendzeitung) nos. 104, 106 (1925).

"Ferdinand von Saar's und Marie von Ebner-Eschenbach's unbekannte Briefe," ed. Graf O. Seefried, *Neue Freie Presse*, 16 September 1928.

"Briefwechsel von Marie von Ebner-Eschenbach und Paul Heyse," in Mechtild Alkemade, *Die Lebens- und Weltanschauung der Freifrau Marie von Ebner-Eschenbach*, Graz: Stiasny, 1935, pp. 257-398.

"Aus Briefen an einen Freund. Marie von Ebner-Eschenbach an Hieronymus Lorm," *Deutsche Rundschau* 249 (1936), 67-74, 212.

"Aus ungedruckten Briefen an Dichter," ed. Heinz Rieder, *Turm* 2 (1946), 333.

Briefwechsel zwischen Ferdinand von Saar und Marie von Ebner-Eschenbach, ed. Heinz Kindermann, Wien: Wiener Bibiophilen-Gesellschaft, 1957.

"Aus Raabes Briefwechsel," ed. Karl Hoppe, *Jahrbuch der Raabe-Gesellschaft* (1963), 31-63.

Franz Graf Dubsky, "Aus meinem Briefwechsel mit Marie von Ebner-Eschenbach," *Mährisch-Schlesische Heimat* 10 (Steinheim/Main 1965): 249-261.

Marie von Ebner-Eschenbach—Dr. Josef Breuer: Ein Briefwechsel, ed. Robert A. Kann, Vienna: Bergland, 1969.

II.   Works in English Translation

Aphorisms. Translated by Mrs. Annis Lee Wister. Philadelphia: Lippincott, 1883. Reprinted in *The German Classics*. Eds. Kuno Francke and W.G. Howard. New York: 1913-1914. Vol. 13, 429-448.

Beyond Atonement. Translated by Mary A. Robinson. New York: Worthington, 1892.

The Child of the Parish. A Novel. Translated by Mary A. Robinson. New York: R. Bonner's Sons, 1893.

The Two Countesses. Translated by Ellen Waugh. London: T. F. Unwin, 1893. Appeared simultaneously in New York: Cassell, [1893].

"The District Doctor." Translated by Julia Franklin. In *The German Classics.* Eds. Kuno Francke and W.G. Howard. New York: 1913-1914. Vol. 13, 345-416.

"Krambambuli." Translated by A.I.Du P. Colemn. In *The German Classics.* Eds. Kuno Francke and W.G. Howard. New York: 1913-1914. Vol. 13, 417-428.

Aphorisms. Trans. by G.H. Needler. Toronto: Burns and Mac Eachern, 1959.

"Jakob Szela" and "The Finch." Translated by Marie Busch. In *Selected Austrian Short Stories,* edited by Marie Busch, 59-101. Reprint. Freeport, N.Y.: Books for Libraries Press, 1971.

"'Talent is Only Another Word for Power': A Letter from Marie von Ebner-Eschenbach (1830-1916)." Translated by Helga H. Harriman. *Women's Studies International: A Supplement of the Women's Studies Quarterly,* no. 3 (1984): 17-18.

Seven Stories by Marie von Ebner-Eschenbach. Translated and with an introduction by Helga H. Harriman. Columbia, S.C.: Camden House, 1986.

III.   Secondary Works in English.

Bramkamp, Agathe C. *Marie von Ebner-Eschenbach and her Critics.* Ann Arbor, Michigan: University Microfilms, 1986. Ph.D. diss., Cornell University, 1984.

Doyle, M. Rosa. *Catholic Atmosphere in Marie von Ebner-Eschenbach: Its Use as a Literary Device.* 1936. Reprint. New York: AMS Press, 1970.

Edrich, Eva K. *Women in the Novels of George Sand, Emily Bronte, George Eliot and Marie von Ebner-Eschenbach: To Mitigate the Harshness of all Fatalities.* Ann Arbor, Michigan: University Microfilms, 1985. Ph.D. diss., University of Denver, 1984.

Goodman, Katherine Ramsey. *German Women and Autobiography in the 19th Century: Louise Aston, Fanny Lewald, Malwida von Meysenbug and Marie von Ebner-Eschenbach.* Ann Arbor, Michigan: University Microfilms, 1977. Ph.D. diss., University of Wisconsin, 1977.

Harriman, Helga H. "Marie von Ebner-Eschenbach in Feminist Perspective." *Modern Austrian Literature* 18, no. 1 (1985): 27-38.

Lloyd, Danuta Eugenia Swiecicka. *A Woman Looks at Man: The Male Psyche as Depicted in the Works of Marie von Ebner-Eschenbach.* Ann Arbor, Michigan: University Microfilms, 1969. Ph.D. diss., University of Pennsylvania, 1969.

_____. "Waifs and Strays: The Youth in Marie von Ebner-Eschenbach's Village Tales." In *Views and Reviews of Modern German Literature. Festschrift for Adolf D. Klarmann,* edited by Karl S. Weimar, 39-50. Munich: Delp, 1974.

_____. "Dorf and Schloss: The Socio-Political Image of Austria as Reflected in Marie von Ebner-Eschenbach''s Works." *Modern Austrian Literature* 12, no.3/4(1979): 25-44.

Thum, Reinhard. "Parental Authority and Childhood Trauma: An Analysis of Marie von Ebner-Eschenbach's *Die erste Beichte.*" *Modern Austrian Literature* 19, no. 2(1986): 15-31.

IV.   Major Studies in German.

Aichinger, Ingrid. "Harmonisierung oder Skepis? Zum Prosawerk der Marie von Ebner-Eschenbach." *Österreich in Geschichte und Literatur* 16 (1972): 483-95.

Alkemade, Mechtild. *Die Lebens- und Weltanschauung der Freifrau Marie von Ebner-Eschenbach.* Mit sechs Tafelbeilagen und dem Briefwechsel Heyse und Ebner-Eschenbach. In *Deutsche Quellen und Studien*, Hrsg. von W. Kosch, Bd. 15. Graz und Würzburg: Wächter 1935.

Ashliman, Dee L. "Marie von Ebner-Eschenbach und der deutsche Aphorismus." *Österreich in Geschichte und Literatur* 18 (1974): 155-65.

Bettelheim, Anton. *Marie von Ebner-Eschenbach. Biographische Blätter.* Berlin: Gebrüder Paetel, 1900.

_____. *Marie von Ebner-Eschenbach's Wirken und Vermächtnis.* Leipzig: Quelle und Meyer, 1920.

Beutin, Heidi. "Marie von Ebner-Eschenbach, *Božena* (1876), Die wiedergekehrte 'Fürstin Libussa'." In *Romane und Erzählungen des bürgerlichen Realismus*, edited by Horst Denkler, 246-59. Stuttgart: Reclam, 1980.

Dormer, Lore Muerdel. "Tribunal der Ironie. Marie von Ebner-Eschenbach's Erzählung 'Er lasst die Hand küssen'." *Modern Austrian Literature* 9, no. 2 (1976): 86-97.

Ehrentreich, Alfred. "Marie von Ebner-Eschenbach und Schloss Zdislawitz." *Neue Deutsche Hefte* 30 (1983): 553-58.

Fussenegger, Gertrud. *Marie von Ebner-Eschenbach oder Der gute Mensch von Zdislawitz.* München: Delp, 1967.

Necker, Moritz. *Marie von Ebner-Eschenbach.* Nach ihren Werken geschildert. Leipzig und Berlin: G.H. Meyer, 1900.

Rossbacher, Karlheimz. "Marie von Ebner-Eschenbach. Zum Verhältnis von Literatur und Sozialgeschichte am Beispiel von 'Krambambuli'." *Österreich in Geschichte und Literatur* 24 (1980): 87-106.

Veselý, Jiri. "Tagebücher legen Zeugnis ab. Unbekannte Tagebücher der Marie von Ebner-Eschenbach." *Österreich in Geschichte und Literatur* 15 (1971): 211-41.

_____. "Turgenev in den ungedruckten Tagebüchern von Marie von Ebner-Eschenbach. (1863-1909). *Zeitschrift für Slawistik* 31(1986): 273-277.

Theodor Herzl

Richard H. Lawson

Wolf Theodor Herzl, the guiding genius of modern Zionism as well as an often overlooked Austrian writer of modest talent, was born in Pest (in 1873 incorporated into Budapest), Hungary on 2 May 1860. His parents were Jakob and Jeanette Diamant Herzl, who already had a one-year-old daughter Pauline. Both the Herzl and the Diamant families were German-speaking Jews of the middle class, although the enterprising Jakob Herzl had learned Hungarian during youthful employment in Debrecen. In Pest he began a freight-forwarding business, became a bank director, made a fortune, lost it in the crash of 1873, and recouped moderately as a stockbroker.

Jakob's business ventures often kept him away from home. The chief role in raising the children was willingly played by Jeanette, a beautiful, intelligent, and strong-willed woman with a keen wit. The relationship between her and her son Theodor was close and sympathetic; indeed, the family thrived in mutual affection. Theodor grew up adoring his mother (and his sister as well before her death from typhus in 1878). The close maternal relationship continued into his adulthood and marriage.

Besides seeing that Theodor attended school—even when his grades and his interest lagged—his mother early engaged tutors from whom he learned French, English, and piano (also by some accounts Hebrew and Italian, but that was probably a bit later).[1] She and her husband inculcated in the boy a sense of morality and values, of which the foundation was honesty. Her method was not simply to dispense precepts, but also to offer relevant stories and parables from German literature. Jeanette Herzl, not untypically for devout Jews in Austria-Hungary, was steeped in German culture and German literature and she wanted her children to be similarly cultured.

Literary seeds were thus sown early and often in the already literari-ly-inclined mind of Theodor Herzl. A few—a distinct minority—of his earliest literary efforts were in Hungarian. But he seems to have made a conscious decision to favor German, the language of his home and his education, whereas many of his fellows reacted to the growing influence of Magyarization by adopting Hungarian.

He completed *Realschule* (grade school) in February 1875 after a period of precocious disillusionment and mediocre grades that hardly reflected his voracious self-directed reading of German literature. His favorites were Heine and Lenau. But wishing to enter a classical Gymnasium and still lacking a basic knowledge of Latin and Greek, he was obliged to resort to private tutoring for a year, whereupon he was admitted to the Protestant gymnasium in February 1876. The student-body of the presumably Protestant gymnasium was in fact predominantly Jewish, so that besides finding himself in a congenial academic environ-ment for a change he was also spared the Jew-baiting atmosphere that had increasingly prevailed in his grade school after the economic collapse of 1873.

As a gymnasium student he soon developed a reputation as a genial nihilist, rationalistic, ironic, mocking, whose barbs could as well be direct-ed at Moses as at Jesus. This impudence constituted his first serious turn from Judaism to the secular assimilationism all about him. At the same time he remained highly sensitive to his parents' religious feelings and to their grief—not to speak of his own—at the death of Pauline Herzl. The surviving family members came even closer together. Four months after Pauline's death Herzl passed, with middling approval, his final compre-hensive examination. He was ready for university and he was more than ready to leave Budapest, a city still somewhat provincial despite growth and ever more Magyarized. He had already decided to become a writer.

Writing, however, was recognized by his parents, who were and continued to be extremely generous in support of their son's education, as unlikely to assure a financially stable livelihood. Herzl did not need a lot of persuasion to see the wisdom of enrolling in law, which he did in fall 1878, although not in Budapest, but in Vienna. His parents, probably associating Budapest with the death of their daughter, also found the time propitious to sever their connection with the Hungarian city and to move to the imperial capital. New and different though it was, Herzl adapted enthusiastically to Vienna. His enthusiasm for his six-year legal curricu-lum, once he started it, was less marked, as was that for Judaism, at least in its official form. He rarely went to synagogue.

He continued to write—comedies and novellas—and he entered with gusto into the social life centered about the university, including the visiting of prostitutes, quite in conformity with the double standard then notoriously prevalent in Vienna. He was attracted to the idea of joining a fraternity. This was Albia, which if perhaps uncertain of its direction in 1881, could hardly avoid being swept up shortly in the pan-German, anti-Semitic movement ignited and fanned among the students and the petite bourgeoisie by Georg Schönerer. Members of Albia took dueling very seriously, and Herzl was obliged to spend many hours taking instruction. But because he lent the Albians the polish of his literary writing, he stayed in their good graces with only one duel to his credit. By early 1883 he denoted himself as an inactive member.

Herzl fell out with Albia and vice versa as a consequence of a *Trauerkommers* (mourning festivity) for Richard Wagner celebrated by some four thousand students belonging to the fraternities comprised in the Union of German Students. Egged on by drink, by an emotional speech by Hermann Bahr, and by Georg Schönerer's inflammatory "Hoch unser Bismarck!" ("Long live our Bismarck!"), the assemblage turned into an ugly anti-Semitic demonstration. On Herzl's reading about the affair in the newspaper the next day he sent an elaborately indignant letter of protest and resignation to the appropriate officer of Albia, who responded with insults.

Nearing the completion of his legal studies, Herzl had a number of literary pieces to his credit. If acceptance for publication was infrequent, it was still a rather auspicious start for an aspiring author soon to receive his doctorate in law. A one-act comedy, *Compagniearbeit* (Company Work), was published in 1880, when Herzl was halfway through his legal studies. A more significant piece, reflecting his legal studies, was the one-act comedy, *Die causa Hirschkorn* (The Hirschkorn Case), which he published himself in 1882. On 18 December of that year he sent a copy to Ernst Hartmann, celebrated actor and director at the Burgtheater, together with a whimsical and flattering (to Hartmann) letter in which he characterizes the play as "the daughter of juridical boredom and a passing journeyman who presumptuously enough calls himself 'a good inspiration.'"[2] It was not, however, good enough for the Burgtheater. Hartmann replied in a friendly vein and sent the comedy on to the Burgtheater, which rejected it. It received an amateur production in Vienna in 1885.

In 1882 Herzl was unable to find a publisher for his novella, *Hagenau.* As in *Compagniearbeit* the hero is a nobleman, a Count von Hagenau, who is also a shy artist. The Count, trying to emulate his friend, a middle-class Doctor of Jurisprudence, in the exercise of the noble virtues, comes up against the intolerance of a physician who is a doctrinaire democrat. The Count wonders: have not class- and race-distinctions been leveled out? Not really. The dividing line between classes has just been established a little lower on the scale, but the distinctions remain as distinct as before. Presumably the idealistic Count, the middle-class J.U.D., and the egalitarian physician are all personae of the young, idealistic, legally-trained author. Eighteen years later, in 1900, the novella was published under a pseudonym in the Vienna *Neue Freie Presse*, the newspaper for which Herzl had by that time served as a star Paris correspondent.

During the latter years of his law studies Herzl also deluged editorial offices with feuilletons. Now and then one was accepted but most suffered the same fate as the longer works. His first real literary success was reserved for slightly later, after he had received his law degree and after he had been a year in the civil service.

Herzl's best friend and companion in failed literary endeavors was Heinrich Kana, an otherwise lonely and idiosyncratic young man. Kana had a gift for critical insight, a gift which he believed was identical with creative talent. Even his critical talent, much esteemed by Herzl, was fallible. Kana had roundly condemned a feuilleton by Herzl entitled "Das Alltägliche" (1885, The Quotidian). Much to Herzl's astonishment it was then accepted by the *Wiener Allgemeine Zeitung*. Herzl's letter of 28 May 1885 to Kana is a touching blend of restrained joyfulness and friendly considerateness. Herzl's friendship with the brilliant yet marginal Kana continued into the former's period of successful authorship and indeed until the latter's suicide on 6 February 1891, by which Herzl was deeply affected.

Toward the beginning of July 1883 Herzl passed his final law examination. He received the approval of a majority of the examiners. Kana spread the word that his friend had received unanimous approval, a puff for which Herzl reproached him. Jakob Herzl, like Theodor pleased that he had passed at all, underwrote a trip for the latter to Germany and Switzerland to recover from the exhaustion of study. But Herzl's travel-buoyed spirits were depressed in September by the news that he had not won first prize in the feuilleton contest of the *Wiener Allgemeine Zeitung*; in fact his name was not even mentioned.

In a year of recuperation, writing, and parentally-supported travel it became clear that he was not yet in a position to support himself through literary endeavor. On 30 July 1884, however, he received official permission to become a legal clerk before the district court in Vienna; five days later he entered the state service. Subsequently he arranged a transfer to Salzburg. While his performance reviews in both Vienna and Salzburg were highly commendatory, he found that his heart was not in the law. Despite his affection for Salzburg, when his appointment there expired on 5 August 1885, he resigned from the civil service to pursue the career of a free-lance writer. Looking back thirteen years later he noted that he would have liked to remain in Salzburg if he could have foreseen eventual promotion to judge; such promotions, however, were not open to Jews. Somewhat paradoxically, Herzl was so detached from Judaism in 1885 that were it not for personal pride—as well as consideration for his parents—he would have converted to Christianity.

His decision to commit himself to writing was probably helped by a meeting during the preceding January with the celebrated actor Friedrich Mitterwurzer.. Whereas the actor was bored beyond endurance by Herzl's reading from his full-length drama, *Die Enttäuschten* (The Disappointed), Mitterwurzer accepted for production the one-acter *Tabarin*, a loose adaptation of a sketch by the French Jewish playwright Catulle Mendes. *Tabarin* would be Herzl's dramatic breakthrough.

Herzl departed for Berlin on 20 November 1885, armed with letters of recommendation and three plays: *Die causa Hirschkorn, Tabarin,* and *Muttersöhnchen* (Mother's Little Boy), a four-act comedy that he self-published that same year. As he made the theater rounds in Berlin, he wrote reports for the Vienna humorous weekly, *Der Floh* (The Flea) as well as the *Wiener Allgemeine Zeitung. Die causa Hirschkorn* found tentative acceptance, but the major work, *Muttersöhnchen*, found only rejections, much to Herzl's discouragement. Then came the surprise announcement from New York that the Mitterwurzer staging of *Tabarin* in that city was a sensational success. Herzl took heart.

Tabarin is a Parisian clown of 1620. In his most popular comic sketch he returns from a trip and finds his wife and her lover in a compromising situation. Catulle Mendes had added tragedy and pathos to the ribald encounter: Before a laughing crowd Tabarin plays his favorite role of the cuckolded husband. As the lover embraces Tabarin's unfaithful wife, Tabarin lifts from the stage a curtain that exposes his living room, where he perceives in reality the scene that he has just played. As though in jest he accepts a dagger from a spectator, rushes back into his house, and stabs his faithless wife. While he drags her across the stage, she whispers "Canaille!" ("Scum!") and expires. Her husband shouts for lawmen, confesses his guilt, and demands to be slain. It was Herzl's merit to have invested Mendes's schematic buffoonery and pathos with verisimilitude. Mitterwurzer's playing of Tabarin in New York was an explosive triumph of acting—or rather overacting. After its singular New York success under the aegis of Mitterwurzer *Tabarin* was not staged again until 1895-96.

While still a law student Herzl had been introduced into the house of a wealthy merchant, Jacob Naschauer. He seems to have been attracted early to Julie, the fourth of the five Naschauer children. And Julie *was* a child at that point, fifteen or sixteen, a decade younger than her admirer and by no means the first mid-teen girl to whom he had been attracted. But Julie came from the right social class, and he now had a literary success from which he might be entitled to project an ample income. Indeed, while Julie felt drawn to him, she was from a socioeconomic level that was almost too right: the Naschauers were very wealthy in comparison with the Herzls. Because, moreover, Julie was so young—also spoiled and extremely emotional—Herzl was obliged to endure several separations. Given to depression in any case, he was helped to restorative trips by his parents, who knew that travel was a reliable palliative.

In this uncertain atmosphere Herzl wrote in the space of about four years three comedies, two of which seem to contain predominantly autobiographical themes. Comedies were his forte, however unconvincing his characterizations. If his characters were stereotypes, Herzl did seem to be declaring independence of a sort from the prevailing popular comedies that were heavily dependent on double-entendres. He rarely resorted to this time-honored comedic staple although, as can be seen in *Tabarin* and in *Der Flüchtling* (The Fugitive), discussed below, he had no inhibitions against bedroom plots.

In 1885 he wrote the three-act comedy, *Seine Hoheit* (His Highness). It waited until 1888 for production in Prague, Berlin, Vienna, and Breslau. His Highness is not a person but rather money, money as in the Latin phrase, *consortium omnis vitae*. Only in this case, as the lawyer Dr. Ahsdorf phrases it, not just a partnership for the whole of life but a partnership with which to speculate. Events of the labored plot prove him right, with the notable exception of the actions of the heroine Lucy. Determined to get a job, she is moved to break off the courtship of the wealthy Franz Hellweg, who has been deceived and humiliated by Lucy's mother's pretentiousness. It seems unlikely that this play could have done much to consolidate Herzl's esteem in the eyes of Berlin producers and editors.

In one creative week in January 1887 Herzl wrote the one-act bedroom comedy, *Der Flüchtling*, which he forwarded to Ernst Hartmann. It revolves about the amorous pursuits of Margarethe von Gerditz and her estranged husband Hans, her companion Adele, and Adele's lover Rödiger. These characters are pure types, a fact that Hartmann seems to have quickly spotted. Within less than a week of his receipt of the play he wrote a friendly letter to Herzl encouraging him to draw his characters "more from life than in the world as you imagine it," to form his characters "after living models rather than plaster-of-Paris models in a theatrical museum."[3] *Der Flüchtling* was eventually produced at the Burgtheater on 4 May 1890, but Herzl's anger at its long delay in limbo was still alive when it was produced in June 1893 in Berlin, as is evident in a letter that he wrote to Schnitzler on 15 June.[4]

The case with the four-act comedy, *Die Wilddiebe* (The Poachers), was quite different, at least as to its production, its popularity, and its rewards. But its genesis was different too. Herzl enlisted as a collaborator one Hugo Wittmann, whose only stipulation was that the collaboration be anonymous because he had already engaged in too many collaborative efforts for the critics to stomach. *Wilddiebe* was premiered—both of its playwrights unnamed—in Vienna at the Hofburgtheater in March 1889. Receiving critical acclaim there and elsewhere in Austria and Germany, it made money for Herzl and Wittmann. Herzl's engagement to Julie Naschauer early in 1889 had made him keenly perceptive of his need for money. His perceptions proved all too accurate after the wedding ceremony, which took place on 25 June in Reichenau, a mountain village some forty-three miles southeast of Vienna.

Nowadays the characterizations and plot of *Wilddiebe*—mistaken identities, piquant situations in a resort hotel in Ostende—do not seem so different from those in *Der Flüchtling* (the *Wild* in *Wilddiebe*, the game, are attractive women and girls, the *Diebe* are their pursuers). After the success of *Die Wilddiebe* became impossible to ignore, *Der Flüchtling* was after all deemed suitable for the Burgtheater, where it too enjoyed success—but Herzl abstained from rejoicing.

The four-act comedy that ultimately bore the title *Was wird man sagen?* (What Will People Say?), which dealt with the counterproductive rigidity of class consciousness, first emerged from Herzl's workroom in late 1889 under the title *Der Bernhardiner* (The Bernardine). Rejected by the Burgtheater, it was produced in Prague and Berlin in 1890, in the first case to apathetic response, in the second as—Herzl's words—"one of the most shameful failures."[5]   The failure Herzl attributed to the star's, Ludwig Barnay's, insistence on playing seriously what was written to be played as comedy.   The antipathy of the powerful critic Paul Schlenther also played a key role in the failure of the play and in Herzl's disgust at its reception.   The possibility of recoupment with the artist-comedy *Prinzen aus Genieland* (Princes from the Land of Genies) was thwarted, in Herzl's exasperated view, by the refusal or Barnay to appear in the play.   It waited from 1889 to 1891 for a critically successful production at the Carl Theater in Vienna.

Amid the travails of trying to establish himself as a consistently successful and seriously recognized playwright Herzl became a father twice within fifteen months.   Julie Naschauer Herzl gave birth to a daughter Pauline on 29 March 1890 and to a son Hans on 10 June 1891.   The Herzls' third child, Margarete, called Trude, was born on 20 May 1893 in Paris during Herzl's term as Paris correspondent for the Vienna *Neue Freie Presse*.   Fatherhood undoubtedly helped Herzl adopt a less aloof stance toward the world, conceivably then to adopt Ernst Hartmann's counsel to characterize more from life, less from abstract notions of life. If that altered point of view was in the making it failed to prevail—as far as drama was concerned—until 1894, when he wrote *Das neue Ghetto* (1895; *The New Ghetto*, 1955).   In the meantime, despite the births of Pauline and Hans the Herzl marriage was on a rocky road.   Theodor and Julie were of basically incompatible character.   To simplify grossly, he was primarily an intellectual, she a social creature.   He was used to financial responsibility, she was not.   He was still excessively close to his mother.   Seeking amelioration in travel, as was his wont, he traveled now to escape the stress at home.   Yet divorce, if considered, was not sought out of deference to family sensitivity and the aroma of social disgrace.

Against this background of parenthood and marital stress Herzl again entered into a collaboration with the redoubtable Hugo Wittmann. Their jointly-written four-act comedy, *Die Dame in Schwarz* (The Lady in Black), was premiered at the Burgtheater on 6 February 1891 (or more likely 1890—sources differ).   But its reception was strikingly less enthusiastic than that accorded the previous collaboration, *Wilddiebe*.   Shortly after February 1890 Herzl received a commission from Alexandrine von Schönerer, director of the Theater an der Wien, to write a libretto for an operetta.   Adolf Müller composed the music, Herzl wrote in the summer of 1890 in Reichenau the text for *Des Teufels-Weib* (The Devil's Wife), a potboiler adapted from the hardly more distinguished fantasy, *Madame le diable*, by the popular and prolific Henri Meilhac in collaboration with A. Mortier. Despite its popularity—sixty consecutive performances at the Theater an der Wien—the Herzl-Müller collaboration added little to Herzl's reputation as a playwright. Again he proved unable to breathe life into his characters. Both the title and the fantastic plot inherited from the French original fail to reflect the state of Herzl's marriage. But some cynics thought that the picture of a devilish woman on the musical score looked like Julie Herzl!

While on a vacation trip that included France and Spain, Herzl was appointed on 2 October 1891 Paris correspondent for the famed liberal newspaper, the *Neue Freie Presse*, Austria's most esteemed. He had departed from Vienna in June, leaving a letter for Julie that suggested a peaceful separation and a child-custody agreement. He accepted the coveted Paris post without returning to Vienna. (Later Julie and the children would join him in Paris.) The invitation from the *Neue Freie Presse* was not exactly out of the blue—Herzl had had feuilleton essays accepted by the paper and most recently had attracted a warm reception for his penetrating essay on an out-of-the-way Pyrenees village, "Luz, das Dorf" (The Village of Luz).

Herzl's feuilletons, grouped under such headings as "Reisen," "Aus den Pariser Tagen," "Von Kindern," "Wiener Stimmungen," and "Philosophische Erzählungen" (Travels, From My Paris Days, Of Children, Vienna Moods, and Philosophical Stories), are typically lively, perceptive, and urbane. And the characters, drawn from life, are genuine.

Philosophische Erzählungen—a much larger number of items are included in a collection by that same title in 1900—are fictional sketches and fables averaging about twenty pages in length. If they are not literarily demanding, they are nonetheless gems of their genre. They date back to the 1880s and extend forward to include the first years of Herzl's Zionist conversion. By and large they are cerebral pieces, short on action, long on urbane reflection. For example, in "Eine gute Tat" (1888, A Good Deed) an aging actor, to spite his mean-spirited critics and to show how magnanimous he is, sets up as his protegé a proletarian neophyte of presumably modest talents. The only trouble is, the over-the-hill actor's phony magnanimity backfires when the neophyte suddenly blossoms into a formidable talent—and rival.

A frequent fictional hero in the *Erzählungen* is the impresario Spangelberg, a bon vivant, trickster, and manipulator—of individual artists as well as the masses. In "Pygmalion" (1887) Spangelberg has created the female celebrity Geraldini out of a shoemaker's daughter and has fallen in love with her—a development that gives la Geraldini the upper hand and enables her to search out a young nobleman for herself. Here Spangelberg is duped; usually, as in "Der Aufruhr von Amalfi" (1888, The Riot at Amalfi), he prevails. It takes a riot and risk of life and limb to convince the doubters of his wisdom: when you have tossed your last coin to the multitude, even if the total amounts to but ten francs, you will have incited a riot from which you will be lucky to escape with your life.

In the fable "Das Wirtshaus zum Anilin" (1896, The Aniline Inn) the central character is a professor of philosophy cursed with a shrewish wife. Intending to commit suicide in the river, the professor is dissuaded by the innkeeper, who dispenses surprisingly erudite but not inappropriate counsel: it is better to put up with your Xanthippe; as aniline dyes are derived from tar, so happiness may be reclaimed from life. By now Herzl's philosophical stories have become ever more serious and autobiographical.

Related to the earlier "Aufruhr in Amalfi" but more complex is "Solon in Lydien" (1900, Solon in Lydia). The lawgiver Solon, absenting himself from Athens for ten years to avoid the temptation to ease the stern new laws put into effect there, finds himself a guest of Croesus, King of Lydia. One of the latter's subjects, the young Eukosmos, comes forward with a method of producing grain chemically—an epochal labor-saving device. Eukosmos will reveal his process in return for the hand of Croesus's daughter in marriage. When Croesus turns to Solon for advice, the lawgiver, though personally well disposed toward Eukosmos, declares that the inventor must be slain, or his invention would subvert the world order and deprive people of hunger with unwelcome social results. Croesus, hesitant, orders a test: free grain is distributed to the people, who, sure enough, become lazy, self-indulgent, and rebellious. Solon tries to induce Eukosmos not to publicize his invention, but the latter, blinded by his idealism, misunderstands the reality. At that, Solon hands him the fatally poisoned wine. From tales like this and "Der Aufruhr in Amalfi" it is fair to infer that Herzl has no very high opinion of the masses or of egalitarianism.

Herzl's playwriting was at first abandoned during his reportorial tenure in Paris and resurfaced in 1894 under most unusual circumstances. In Toulon in fall 1883 to report on the visit of the Russian fleet to that port, he caught malaria. Treatment with quinine injections raised an abscess on his thigh that had to be repeatedly lanced. By spring 1894 he was immobilized, a virtual cripple. As he wrote a Prague friend, Heinrich Teweles on 19 May 1895, "then literature touched me again."[6] In one week he wrote a one-act comedy in verse, *Die Glosse* (The Marginal Note). Turned down by the Burgtheater in May 1894, it remained unproduced although it was published in the following year. At once painfully didactic, operalike, and autobiographical, it takes place in the Bologna of the thirteenth century. The lawyer Philippus, dissatisfied with his frivolous wife, devotes himself to an exhaustive glossing of Roman law for contemporaneous relevance. Along comes Aimeric (cf. *aimer* "to love"), the adventurer, the free spirit, the Spangelberg type that had been Herzl's ideal, and seeks to seduce Philippus's wife. But when the cuckolded husband challenges Aimeric to a duel, it emerges that the adventurer has gout and cannot fight. His forced renunciation may suggest that Herzl is renouncing his long-cultivated Spangelberg ideal.

If this suggestion is correct, then a liberated and dedicated Herzl is ready to turn to his real metier, what he called "die Judensache" (the Jewish matter). *Das neue Ghetto* (originally just *Das Ghetto*) is Herzl's most accomplished and significant play. Although rarely produced nowadays, it does turn up in anthologies. From the literary-historical point of view it is an epigonous bourgeois tragedy about a decade late; Gerhart Hauptmann and Naturalism were the new literary fashion. Its importance lies rather in its marking the beginning of Herzl's definitive turn to the Jewish matter. Although he professed to be maintaining his calm while writing the play, he probably was protesting too much: writing it in the space of seventeen days presumes emotional commitment. In addition to commitment there is another reason that *Das neue Ghetto* is his best play. Some of its characters begin to breathe and to come alive to a degree unapproached in his earlier plays.

As a veteran of stage successes as well as stage failures Herzl knew he was going to have a prickly problem in getting *Das neue Ghetto* onto stage at all. For its subject would, in his opinion, embarrass Jewish producers and, if produced, it would annoy Jewish theatergoers. In any case he wanted it to stand or fall on its merits, not on either his repute or, as he feared, his disrepute as a playwright. So he put it forward under a pseudonym, Albert Schnabel, and enlisted his friend Arthur Schnitzler to be his agent and take it around to producers in Vienna. Under no circumstances was Schnitzler to reveal the secret shared by Herzl and Schnitzler only: that the ostensible Albert Schnabel was Herzl.

In a letter to Schnitzler from his Paris address on 17 December 1894 Herzl declared that the play embodied no intention of saving or rescuing

Jews; he wanted only to present "die Frage" (the question) for discussion. Nor was he motivated by any wish for money or fame. He simply wanted to speak out by means of the play: "What happens beyond that, I couldn't care less."[7] In a letter to Schnitzler of 9 January 1895 Herzl confessed that he had been at the point of blurting out the authorial secret to the sculptor Samuel Friedrich Beer, for whom Herzl had been sitting for a bust. Fortunately he had resisted the revelatory impulse then and also with his old friend, Max Nordau, whose reading of *his* latest work to Herzl had left the latter feeling demolished.[8] But Herzl held his tongue before Nordau too, to whom he then dedicated *Das neue Ghetto* "in cordial friendship."

Schnitzler's entrée in Viennese theatrical circles still failed to secure an acceptance of the play of the putative Albert Schnabel. Herzl, now determined on a Prague premiere, turned to his friend from that city, Heinrich Teweles. From Paris he emphasized to Teweles in a brief letter of 14 May 1895 that the secrecy about the true authorship of the play was to prevail until he, Herzl, gave the word.[9]

In a several-page letter of 19 May Herzl waxes expansive about the origin and history of *Das neue Ghetto*. When on his travels in Spain he had contemplated writing a novel about the modern Jew vis-à-vis the restrictions to which the Jew is subject, a problem that he had discussed with Samuel Beer. The very next day he had started writing the play in an exuberant frame of mind.

Still addressing Teweles, Herzl gives a synopsis—doubtless from Schnitzler—of its rejections in Vienna. At the Raimund Theater it had been given to two readers, one a Christian, one a Jew. "The Christian said, 'This is dynamite!' The Jew said, 'This is an affront to the Jews!'"[10] The play is really to be regarded, says Herzl—in whom we note no small ambivalency about just what it really is—as a rabbinical sermon, given not in the synagogue but in the freedom of the theater. For some while he had had the idea that his life should know no higher purpose than that of taking up the cudgels for the Jewish matter, but in a freer, higher, and more special way than anyone had done so far. His description of his resolve to his friend, the anti-Semitic French author Alphonse Daudet, had elicited the reply, "That's great! That's great!"[11] We infer that *Das neue Ghetto* is the first step of this larger resolve.

It would be followed, Herzl continued in his long and expressive letter to Teweles, by many other works. Vanity played no role in this ambition—hence his desire that *Das neue Ghetto* be judged apart from the reputation of its author. The play, he believed, had the "tone" required to solve the Jewish question and to lead the Jews out of the ghetto (he was referring to the new, nonphysical, unwalled ghetto). Perhaps Teweles's reply touched on Herzl's evangelistic assessment of the play. In the event, Herzl remarked on 6 June that if Teweles is not consumed by the Jewish question, he, Herzl, is, and totally.[12] Clearly his goal now is much more evangelistic than he had told Schnitzler on 17 December of the previous year.

Teweles had no better luck in finding acceptance of the play in Prague than Schnitzler had enjoyed in Vienna. The administrator of cultural affairs, a Dr. Rosenbacher, feared that a production would result in unfortunate consequences for the Jews.[13] *Das neue Ghetto* was finally premiered, to loud acclaim, at the Carl Theater in Vienna on 5 January 1898; it was performed in Berlin the next month. The critics were less enthusiastic than the audiences. And the Vienna audience at least, once outside the theater, quite possibly had little sympathy with Herzl's by then more fully developed Zionist position.

The ultimately successful productions, keenly desired as they were by Herzl, were perhaps not the most important thing about *Das neue Ghetto*, not even to Herzl. For even while his still pseudonymous play was being futilely shopped around in Prague in the spring of 1895, Herzl was in a fervor of insight and resolution—of which the play was a single "eruption." This is the term he used in a letter to Schnitzler on 23 June.[14] He credited Schnitzler, who had a keen and realistic insight into human nature, with having foreseen that he, Herzl, would not really be unburdened by the "eruption" that was *Das neue Ghetto*.

Indeed, Herzl in a "fervor of production" had already started something new, different, and greater, something, he declared, of the most profound significance to him and to his future life. Admonishing Schnitzler not to think him overexcited—despite his use of the term "fervor"—he went on to assert that he is not thinking of dying (*that* must have brought the psychologist Schnitzler up short) but of a life full of many deeds that would extinguish, exalt, and reconcile all the baseness and confusion that had ever been in him.[15] Thence *Der Judenstaat*. But it behooves us now to examine *Das neue Ghetto* in some detail, for in addition to being Herzl's best play it stands in close relationship to the emergence of *Der Judenstaat*.

The publication history of *Das neue Ghetto* includes no triumph to parallel its belated triumph on stage. The published version, different in numerous details, benefited in at least one singular detail from the play-writing acumen of Schnitzler. The hero Jacob Samuel's last speech had contained the admonition: "Jews, my brothers, they will let you live only if you know how to die." When Schnitzler pointed out that Jews have always known only too well how to die, Herzl simply substituted the more eloquent two-word elision of the final clause: "if you. . ."[16] It was 1897 before the revised play was published under the auspices of the Zionist weekly, *Die Welt*, which Herzl had founded earlier that year. In 1903 two new printings were published by Herzl himself. A new edition was finally brought out in 1920 by R. Löwit of Vienna and Berlin.

Some of the characters in *Das neue Ghetto* are to a degree derived from flesh-and-blood prototypes. The parents of the young lawyer, Dr. Jacob Samuel—the father a watchmaker, the mother a housewife—resemble Herzl's parents in their petit-bourgeois uprightness. Similarly, or even more so, Jacob Samuel's bride, Hermine Hellmann, daughter of a well-to-do merchant family, resembles the Julie Naschauer whom Herzl married: charming but spoiled, vain, and very haut-bourgeoise. Jacob Samuel is an obvious projection of the playwright, an ambitious and idealistic young lawyer, in a professional milieu that permits a greater indulgence of ideal-ism that was accorded the real-life state's attorney's clerk in Salzburg in 1885, namely, private, if less than prosperous, practice in Vienna in 1893.

Before his marriage to Hermine Hellmann, Jacob Samuel has asso-ciated mostly with non-Jews or with Christianized Jews. His marital alliance with the Hellmann family, however, puts him in regular contact with mercantile Jews and their associates, with Jews who play the stock market and contrive financial deals, who, in short, regard money-making as the chief business of life. If this orientation runs counter to Jacob Samuel's grain, it alienates intolerably Samuel's closest friend and col-league, Franz Wurzlechner, a Christian. Because Wurzlechner essays a political career, to which any connection with Jewish stock-market specu-lators would be anathema, he finds it expedient to renounce formally his friendship with Samuel. We are thereby allowed to dwell on the irony that the Jewish preoccupation with money, which so disgusts Wurzlechner, is precisely that sphere of activity that Christians had relegated to Jews dur-ing the ghetto era. Not surprisingly, what was foisted on the inhabitants of the "old" ghetto does not magically disappear from among the pursuits of the inhabitants of the "new" ghetto.

Samuel's parvenu brother-in-law Rheinberg and the latter's associ-ate Wasserstein, a professional stock-market speculator—and a very well-drawn, not entirely unsympathetic character—launch a heavily-leveraged buy-out scheme to obtain a coal mine in Dubnitz that has been allowed to deteriorate into little more than a cash-cow supporting the self-indulgent lifestyle—centered on racing—of its owner, retired cavalry Captain von Schramm. The latter, we will have already guessed, is a Christian. The physical deterioration of the mine long held by his family has proceeded to the danger point; he ruthlessly exploits and endangers the lives of the Slovenian miners who comprise his work force.

Reluctantly Samuel has agreed with his brother-in-law Rheinberg to draw up by-laws for the closely held stock company that would buy Schramm's mine. Jacob Samuel is a lawyer who is happier doing pro bono work for socialists, but he feels that he has to respond to his new family connections and to his wife's desire to be fashionably dressed. To his office next comes the representative of the endangered and starving miners, Peter Vednik, the only one of their number who can speak at least half-passable German. It comes to light that a mine disaster is likely at any moment. Samuel takes the train to Dubnitz and organizes the workers in a strike, which is, however, shortly broken to the extreme disadvantage of the miners.

Their additionally straitened circumstances are as nothing, however, compared with the disaster that follows. Water has gathered in the unsafely maintained mine; Schramm orders blasting in another part of the mine; the combined result is catastrophe for both mine and miners. The stock of the crippled mine falls precipitously. Schramm, having mortgaged his stock, is financially ruined. Blaming Rheinberg, the principal of the buy-out scheme, he seeks restitution. But Rheinberg refuses even to see him. It is not he and Wasserstein who have ruined Schramm, Rheinberg asserts, but the latter's imprudent management of his property plus the natural fluctuation of the stock market.

Samuel, on the other hand, does receive Schramm. Rejecting complicity in the financial maneuverings, Samuel emphasizes Schramm's inhumane exploitation of his work force and his incompetent management as the true cause of the stock depreciation and thus of Schramm's insolvency. At this cool assessment Schramm hurls the epithet "pack of Jews." Given the opportunity to retract it, Schramm only reiterates it. Samuel rushes at Schramm and boxes his ears before others break up the melée. In the duel that follows Jacob Samuel is shot by Captain von Schramm and shortly dies. This is the tragic and ironic sequel to an encounter five years earlier between Schramm and Samuel, when Samuel, to avert imposing stress on his mortally ill father, had opted out of a duel with Schramm by offering an apology.

Throughout Herzl emphasizes the reality that in the new ghetto Jews are not permitted to behave in the same ways as Christians. Jews must ever be on guard against lapses that are taken for granted when committed by Christians. Jews are obliged to act in a more Catholic way than the Pope as the price for being permitted to reside in that unsatisfactory fringe territory called the new ghetto. But—to pursue Herzl's implication, both textual and nontextual—it avails nothing for Jews to declare that they are not going to take discriminatory abuse anymore. As long as they are inter-mixed with Christian society, indulgence is fragile and temporary, subject to abrupt revocation. The answer, extratextual and compellingly personal, is Zionism.

Herzl's conversion to Zionism, as recorded in the diary that he began about Whitsunday 1895 and continued to 16 May 1904—within two months of his death— started in fall 1894 and was complete by May 1895. There is no warrant for imagining that *Das neue Ghetto* was the launching pad for his new Zionist life except to the extent that what in the play is implicit to the reader can hardly have been less so to the play-wright. Actually the play seems more correctly regarded as pertaining to his past existence rather than to his future Zionist existence. It marks the apogee of his playwriting, his closest brush with a first-rate drama—in a mold, however, that was already out of date. And yet it was far from an unqualified success. Having to shop it around anonymously to producers through the good offices of his friends Schnitzler and Teweles cannot have left Herzl's sensitive pride untouched. A quasi-failure then on top of fail-ures? Having five of your ten or eleven—so far—produced plays put on at the Burgtheater hardly seems to equate with the kind of failure that some critics like to see in Herzl as a kind of prerequisite for his change of direction.

Perhaps conversions do not require external reasons. As with Herzl's less than wholly rewarding dramatic career—whereas his reportage and feuilletons are on the whole excellent—so with the Dreyfus affair that unrolled before his correspondent's eyes in France. It is easy but risky to accord it too much importance in Herzl's Zionist conversion. Herzl was fully aware that Captain Alfred Dreyfus was a flawed martyr. Still, the spectacle of that—in his view—most rational of countries, France, giving vent to long-suppressed therefore particularly virulent anti-Semitism can only have complemented the unease so convincingly reflected in *Das neue Ghetto*. The problem is that the Dreyfus case had not yet assumed the character of outright anti-Semitism in fall 1894 when Herzl's conversion began. Its causality can at most be only secondary. On 17 November 1895, for instance, Herzl's diary records that he was moved by the Dreyfus affair—but Herzl was already a Zionist by then.

Herzl did not invent the term Zionism, much less the concept. The former was the merit of Nathan Birnbaum a few years earlier, and in the latter Herzl had several predecessors, among them Birnbaum. Herzl had, however, the special merit of excluding all utopianism from his Zionist projections as they were refined and as they matured in 1894-95. With his Zionist novel, *Altneuland* (1902; *Old New Land*, 1902-3), Herzl does turn later to utopianism in fiction.

On about 2 May 1895 Herzl composed a letter, sent some two weeks later, to Baron Maurice de Hirsch (Moritz Hirsch, Freiherr von Gereuth), a free-thinking Jew and quite likely Europe's wealthiest man, born in Munich, then of Brussels. Herzl requested a meeting with Hirsch, a well-known philanthropist, to discuss the Jewish question. Hirsch, suspicious, requested in turn that Herzl send him his proposals in writing. Herzl astutely suggested that Hirsch had the opportunity to become much more than a conventional philanthropist such as George Peabody (1785-1869). With that appeal to his pride and possibly his vanity as well Hirsch agreed to a meeting.

Hirsch's philanthropy had consisted in rescuing ghettoized Jews and enabling them to live as farm laborers and as tradesmen in, for example, the United States or Argentina. His proposal to establish agricultural and craft schools for the severely persecuted Jews of the Russian Pale had been denied by the Tsar. Herzl on the other hand thought that philanthropic resettlement produced *shnorrers* (beggars)—his use of Yiddish is doubly pejorative—that first the Jews must be made strong as a race and then they could, if necessary, emigrate. In Herzl's mind Hirsch would be the Maecenas and Herzl would supply the ideas and the inspiration. But Hirsch had no sympathy with the idea of making Jews strong and conceivably warlike.

By 2 June Herzl had come to the conclusion that the Jews must have a self-governing nation-state of their own. Until 16 June he pondered the questions: what kind of state (nondemocratic republic); where? (Palestine or Latin America); and by what means? (British style: a Society of Jews and a Chartered Company). This outline failing to enlist Hirsch's support, Herzl turned to Moritz Güdemann, Chief Rabbi of Vienna, in three letters of 11, 16, and 17 June, whose responses blew hot and cold. Then, after discussion with his friend Friedrich Schiff, Herzl himself blew cold and told Hirsch by letter on 18 June that he had given up the idea. He quickly reconvinced himself, however.

This is the background for Herzl's theoretical work, *Der Judenstaat* (1896, *The Jewish State*), which was conceived in Paris in June (Herzl was still on duty with the *Neue Freie Presse*), written in Vienna in November, and first mentioned in his diary on 10 January 1896. The German title really means The State of, or for, the Jews, not quite the same as The Jewish State. But by 1899 Herzl was using the latter English version in his diary with its implication of a religious, Torah-ruled state, toward which political necessity was impelling him—or at least forcing him to be more encompassing in his considerations.

In an author's preface and a lengthy introduction Herzl establishes his premises. Utopianism is out of the question; it cannot be afforded, given the misery of the Jews, which is the propelling force of Zionism. If only the Jews could be left in peace—but he does not believe that likely. The enmity of others has consolidated the Jews into a nationality. Hence the Jewish question is neither a social nor a religious one; it is a national question.

The Jewish question is precisely the focus of Herzl's second chapter. Previous philanthropic diversion of poor Jews has been on a pitifully small scale and moreover a failure; even if they prosper, that merely creates anti-Semitism. But what has been a failure on a small scale need not be a failure on a large scale. With the friendly cooperation of interested governments there would be created first a Society of Jews and thereafter, as its financial arm, an economically productive Jewish Company. What is needed is sovereignty over a nation-sized portion of the world as a goal of immigration, which would begin with the poorest Jews first. With the approval of the European powers the Society would commence negotiations looking toward the acquisition of such a piece of earth. There are two leading possibilities, both of which have experienced infiltrating—thus in Herzl's view doomed—Jewish colonizations: Palestine and Argentina.

In Chapter Two Herzl draws his oft-cited distinction between modern anti-Semitism and that of earlier times. The former is a general result of emancipation. Its remoter specific cause is the Jews' medieval loss of the ability to assimilate. Its nearer specific cause, to which Herzl frequently harks, is the excessive production of mediocre Jewish intellects who can find neither upward nor downward social mobility.

Herzl devotes Chapter Three to details of his proposed Jewish Company: its method of raising money and its operation. He repeatedly advocates a seven-hour workday. In Chapter Four, refuting in advance the charges that he is a visionary, he offers practical suggestions on emigration and on settlement in groups.

Chapter Five concerns the relationship between the Society of Jews and the Jewish state. Drawing from the model of the *negotiorum gestio* of Roman law he declares that the operating manager or *gestor* of the Jews in the new state must be the Society of Jews, which will further appoint a council of jurists to draw up a constitution. Having for four years reported on parliamentary government and debates in Paris, Herzl was dubious, to say the least, about unlimited government and professional politicians—but also about popular referenda and the masses as a political entity. He advocated what we would today call trickle-down democracy. His ideal forms of government were the democratic monarchy or the aristocratic republic, because in either case the form and the principle of government tend to restrict one another. Perhaps no opprobrium should attach to these somewhat Jeffersonian advocacies. In addition to reporting on the French Parliament, Herzl was after all a citizen of Habsburg Austria with its carefully franchised electorate. Even Great Britain, his model in so many details, offered a severely restricted franchise.

Herzl envisioned a legal code that unifies the laws of the former countries of the Jewish immigrants. As to the language of the new state Herzl issued a permissive recommendation guaranteed to create chaos. He know German, Hungarian, and French perfectly, but he rarely spoke Hungarian. He did not know enough Hebrew to—in his own formulation—buy a tram ticket;[17] when he quoted Hebrew he had to resort to prepared transliterations in Roman letters. Of Yiddish he had the lowest opinion. He worked diligently to improve his accented English. This linguistically sophisticated citizen of Habsburgia makes a naive but Darwinian suggestion about the language of the new Jewish state. Let each immigrant use his own language, and the one of greatest general utility will be adopted—still without compulsion. No Yiddish though. Religious freedom will be tolerated, certainly not a theocracy. As the professional army—whose purpose is to preserve neutrality—is kept to its barracks, so the priests are to be kept in their temples.

The brief conclusion of *Der Judenstaat* is more inspirational than explicatory. Again Herzl insists on his nonutopian point of view. He contemplates no universal brotherhood. His concept is *not* a beautiful dream.

For antagonism—we might today call it creative tension—is prerequisite to man's highest liberational efforts. Those efforts are, in his view, mostly technical and scientific; literature he does not often mention. Finally, as soon as his plan is initiated, anti-Semitism will end.

The publication of *Der Judenstaat* catapulted Herzl as the leader of Zionism into the arena of international diplomacy, intrigue, and finance. Further, as such a leader he was obliged to organize the masses of Jews in support of his project. Especially was the latter true after his attempt to enlist the backing of Baron Edmond de Rothschild proved no more successful than his appeal to Baron de Hirsch. Nor was opposition to Herzl's brand of Zionism confined to the levels of the extremely rich as represented by Rothschild and Hirsch. It existed at all levels among Jews and non-Jews alike and for a variety of reasons, of which the most prominent was political. (Herzl's in-laws, the Naschauers, were anti-Zionist.) Having declared a nation-to-be, Herzl naturally had to contend with adherents of existent nationalisms as well as with those to whom nationalism was anathema. In the first group were the major European powers plus—and hardly least—the Ottoman Empire, on whose Palestinian territory the Jewish state was to arise.[18]

As a celebrity Herzl enjoyed access to exalted levels of politics, statecraft, and intrigue. This he exploited with inconsistent success to gain entry to the very highest levels: Joseph Chamberlain, Kaiser Wilhelm II, Sultan Abdul Hamid II, and Vyacheslav Plehve. Within his lifetime, however, which ended prematurely at age forty-four in 1904, his international negotiations bore no fruit.

His efforts to marshal a Jewish force behind him and thereby to strengthen his hand at the diplomatic table found spectacular public form—he wanted it to be spectacular and thus effective—in a series of international Zionist Congresses. The first was at Basel in 1897; subsequent Congresses met in that city almost annually except for 1900 when the meeting was held in London. In addition to the Congresses there was the Zionist organization itself to nurture and defend.

In the personal and family realm, which was virtually subsumed in Herzl's Zionist activity, he suffered on every front. He was alienated from Julie, with whom, however, he continued to live when in Vienna. He felt guilty about neglecting his children, for whose frail health he blamed Julie. His worry about personal finances—he was dependent on his modest *Neue Freie Presse* income and drew on Julie's dowry for Zionist purposes—was continuing and genuine. *Die Welt*, the weekly Zionist newspaper that he had founded in 1897, was a constant drain on his personal finances. He feared that at his death his children would be inadequately provided for. Finally, his health was deteriorating. Barely into his forties, he felt like an old man, and indeed his years were numbered.

Herzl's literary contribution to the movement that was now his life was *Altneuland*, a visionary and futuristic novel anticipating the Jewish state. He began drafting it in 1899, but the demands of the Zionist movement forced him to abandon it for a year. Despite Herzl's nonutopian arguments in *Der Judenstaat* he gravitated toward utopianism in *Altneuland*, which thereupon achieved the distinction of being the only utopian novel written by an author whose ideas led to the actual founding of a state.

The hero of *Altneuland* is Friedrich Loewenberg, a dashing young Viennese Jew, a lawyer, unhappy and poor. His fiancée Ernestine Loeffler, a member of the Jewish haute bourgeoisie so tellingly portrayed in *Das neue Ghetto*, rejects him in favor of the well-connected broker, Leopold Weinberger, whose future is guaranteed by the family firm, Samuel Weinberger and Sons. Friedrich, dejected, responds to an ad seeking an educated and desperate young man prepared to make a final experiment with his life.

Who placed such a problematic advertisement? A Mr. Kingscourt, whose name was Königshoff when he was a Prussian officer, more recently an American millionaire, cuckold, misanthrope, and misogynist. Having bought a Pacific island and a yacht in which to sail there, he seeks a male companion for the trip and for lifelong residency with him on his island refuge. Friedrich, wanting only to take leave of life, is game. Before the travelers depart there is a vignette of a Jewish beggar boy, David Littwak (the surname means "Lithuanian Jew"), whose family Friedrich enables to migrate with their son to Palestine.

En route to their Pacific refuge the travelers visit the Palestine of 1902: poor, dirty, and undeveloped. Thereafter they sail off via the Suez Canal and the Red Sea. In 1923—some twenty-two years into the future from the time the novel was written—after living for two decades on Kingscourt's island they find themselves once more on the Red Sea, nearing Palestine. Touching at Port Said they discover that it has deteriorated into a provincial backwater. Whereas Haifa, where they finally dock, is now a great and prosperous port. There they meet up with the now-adult David Littwak, soon-to-be President of the new Palestine, who guides the astonished strangers around the highly advanced, technologically developed country.

Altneuland is an unabashed *Schlüsselroman* as well as a utopian novel. Friedrich Loewenberg is Theodor Herzl, Kingscourt is Philipp zu Eulenburg, German Ambassador to Austria from 1894 to 1902 and Herzl's avenue to Kaiser Wilhelm. (Eulenburg's homoerotic proclivity emerges only palely and nonspecifically in Kingscourt.) Ernestine Loeffler is Julie Naschauer Herzl. Miriam, a schoolteacher whom Friedrich Loewenberg marries, is Herzl's daughter Pauline, to whom he dedicated the book. David Littwak is David Wolffsohn—in fact a Lithuanian Jew—who was to succeed Herzl as President of the international Zionist organization.

As its utopian tendency is plain, as its characters are plain, so is the purpose of *Altneuland* plain: to paint an attractive picture of what a Jewish Palestine could be expected to become in a mere two decades after Zionist settlement. Herzl had met no Arabs when he visited Palestine in 1898; he seems not to have imagined a difficulty in that quarter. His Arab spokesman in *Altneuland*, Reschid Bey, like the Jews, speaks German, lives well, and asserts that his coreligionists are enriched by the Jewish presence.

Herzl's output of plays did not cease abruptly with his 1895 conversion to Zionism and his subsequent immersion in a vastly different and vastly more committed and exhausting lifestyle. Nor indeed did his plays come to a total halt after his emergence on the world stage of international politics at the first Zionist Congress in 1897. Works in progress were lying in his desk drawer at one and perhaps at both of these turning points. In two other instances he turned to dramatizing previously published prose sketches. He produced just four plays in the nine years remaining between 1895 and his death in 1904, but that number reflects the change in the direction of his life.

Herzl had begun *Unser Kätchen* (Our Katie), a four-act comedy, in June 1891 under the title *Die Fleischtöpfe Ägyptens* (The Fleshpots of Egypt). He had worked on it intermittently but dropped it in 1894. He finally completed it with a burst of activity in 1898, wanting to clear his desk before his Palestine trip in the fall of that year. To obtain a sense of accomplishment he even read it to a group of Burgtheater actors shortly before his departure. But it was not destined for Burgtheater performance, for it was prohibited by the censor in January 1899 on the grounds that it traded in free-thinking immorality. Actually it was a somewhat bitter marital comedy not without apparent references to his own unhappy marriage. It was premiered in February at the Deutsches Volkstheater in Vienna, where it was well received.

In October 1900 Herzl completed a four-act play called *Gretel*, which he had worked on before 1897 under the title *Die sündige Mutter* (The Sinful Mother). It too, as the original title suggests, seems rooted in his disaffection with Julie Herzl. The mother, the sensual and hysterical Marianne Winter in the play, enters into an adulterous relationship with a young sophisticate named Edgar Böheim (cf. "Bohemian"). In punishment for her mother's sin the child Gretel falls ill. That brings Marianne to repentance and, in an ecstasy of guilt, to confession to her husband. Gretel recovers. Marianne, feeling that her husband wants to take Gretel from her to punish her, commits suicide.

One could hardly call *Gretel* immoral in the fashion of *Unser Kätchen*—it is *too* moral to escape the burden of sentimentalism, yet it is also gripping, not least owing to the characterization of Gretel, who for all her childish innocence reveals more profound, possibly adult, possibilities. On the other hand, imputing adult possibilities to children is a sign by which authors reveal their lack of sufficient acquaintance with real children—and Herzl's life now left him all too little time for his children.

Gretel was in rehearsal in March 1900 at the Raimund Theater in Vienna. There was a laudatory review by F. Sch. (Friedrich Schutz) on 5 April in the *Neue Freie Presse*. As was its custom the great liberal newspaper reported on the literary-dramatic accomplishments of its celebrated correspondent, who called the journal his "slave-owners,"[19] while it remained utterly silent about his Zionist-political-diplomatic activities. (Herzl lived in fear of losing his job—and income—at the *Neue Freie Presse* while he simultaneously feared to resign and go onto the payroll of the international Zionist organization, whose not always sympathetic upper echelon could cut him off at any time.)

I Love You—the English title was Herzl's—was an unprepossessing failure, a one-act comedy of confusion, based on an earlier feuilleton. Not for the first time was Herzl driven in 1900 to the expedient of self-publication. *Solon in Lydien* (1904, Solon in Lydia) was three-act play based on the *Philosophische Erzählung* of the same name, in which the idealistic youth invents a method of manufacturing grain without labor and fails to perceive Solon's life-and-death reason for extirpating such an invention—as well as its imperceptive inventor. The story Herzl had written in 1900; the play came in the following year, although it had to wait until Herzl's last year of life, 1904, to be published.

Herzl was worn down by the stress of his unremitting labors for Zionism, by the stress with Julie, the ill health of his children, especially of Pauline, by his personal financial situation, and finally by heart problems of long standing. In the spring of 1904 his physical appearance gave his friends cause for worry. After 16 May his diary entries ceased. Cure regimens at Franzensbad and Edlach did not avail him. On 3 July he died at Edlach near Reichenau, where he had married Julie.

Herzl's importance for Zionism during the nine years between his conversion and his death is literally epochal. His importance in the annals of Austrian—not to speak of German—literature is markedly less. One could make a case that his literary work has been cast into an unwarrantable depth of shadow by his Zionist accomplishments. True, his dramas lacked originality and—at least until *Das neue Ghetto*—credible characterizations. His drawing-room comedies were both fragile and epigonal. Only by wedding the anachronistic genre to the Jewish upper middle class in *Das neue Ghetto* did Herzl make an approach to creating significant literature, and for that melding he was reviled, chiefly by Jews. In the field of the sketch, the feuilleton, Herzl excelled. Here his considerable powers of observation and his precision, even elegance of language were in a suitable frame. It was not a frame, however, that carried much weight, critically speaking. Putting his feuilletons and brief narratives between hard covers was fine, but Herzl was not blind to their journalistic origin and ephemeral destiny. It is sometimes said that his one novel, *Altneuland* would be an excellent novel of its utopian kind, were its characters more convincingly nuanced. Drawn from real life as they were, they yet lack the spark of verisimilitude. But this is among other things a *Tendenzroman,*, a novel with a propagandistic purpose, in which the absence of finely delineated characters does not amount to a serious flaw. As a novel of persuasive intention *Altneuland* works.

Notes

1. If any Hebrew was learned by the child it must have been forgotten by the adult, who made light of his inablility to phrase mundane questions in Hebrew. See Alex Bein, *Theodor Herzl. Biographie* (Frankfurt am Main: Ullstein, 1983), p. 131.
2. Ibid., p. 36.
3. Reproduced in Leon Kellner, *Theodor Herzls Lehrjahre 1860-1895)* (Wien: R. Löwit, 1920), p. 69.
4. Ibid., p. 115.
5. Letter to Schnitzler, 15 June 1893. Reproduced in Kellner, pp. 114-116; quote is from p. 115.
6. The letter is reproduced in Kellner, pp.151-155. The quoted passage is on p. 152.
7. "Was weiter geschieht, ist mir Wurscht." Letter reproduced in Kellner, p. 148.
8. Reproduced in Kellner, pp. 148-149.
9. Reproduced in Kellner, pp. 149-150.
10. The letter is reproduced in Kellner, pp. 151-155. The quoted passage is on p. 154.
11. Reproduced in Kellner, p. 155, where Herzl gives Daudet's French as "C'est beau! C'est beau!" A slightly different version appears in Desmond Stewart, *Theodor Herzl* (Garden City, N.Y.: Doubleday, 1974), p. 173: "Comme c'est beau! comme c'est beau!"
12. Reproduced in Kellner, pp. 156-157.
13. Kellner, p. 157.
14. He uses *Eruption* in German. The letter is reproduced in Kellner, pp.157-159. Herzl's discussion of his *Eruption* is on p. 157.
15. This part of the letter is in Kellner, p. 159.
16. As Stewart tells it, p. 152, the elision is unique to the English translation. It is also in the German R. Löwit edition of 1920, and I suspect before that.
17. Bein, p. 131.
18. Other venues that at one time or another received serious consideration were Cyprus, Sinai, and a region in former British East Africa (called Uganda in the discussions but not identical with the present Uganda).
19. Quoted in Bein, p. 233.

Bibliography

I.   Works by Theodor Herzl in German

Plays

Compagniearbeit. Lustspiel in einem Act. Wien: Wallishausersche Buchhandlung, 1880.

Die causa Hirschkorn. Lustspiel in einem Act. Wien: privately printed, 1882.

Tabarin. Schauspiel in einem Act. Stage manuscript, [1884].

Muttersöhnchen. Lustspiel in vier Acten. Wien: privately printed, 1885.

Seine Hoheit. Lustspiel in drei Acten. [1885].

Der Flüchtling. Lustspiel in einem Aufzug. Universalbibliothek, no. 2387. Leipzig: Philipp Reclam jun., [1887].

Der Schwanenhals. Lustspiel in vier Acten. Wien: hectographed, 1888.

Was wird man sagen?: Lustspiel in vier Acten. Wien: Gabor Steiner, 1890.

Die Dame in Schwarz. Lustspiel in vier Acten. In collaboration with Hugo Wittmann. Anonymously printed, 1890.

Prinzen aus Genieland. Lustspiel in vier Acten. Wien: A. Entsch, 1892.

Die Glosse. Lustspiel in einem Act. Dresden-Leipzig-Wien: E. Piersons Verlag, 1895.

Das neue Ghetto. Schauspiel in vier Acten. Wien: Verlag der "Welt," 1898. 2nd and 3rd eds., Wien: privately printed, 1903. New ed., Wien: R. Löwit, 1920.

Unser Kåtchen. Lustspiel in vier Acten. Wien; privately printed, [1899].

Gretel. Schauspiel in vier Acten. Wien, 1899.

I Love You. Lustspiel in einem Act. Wien: privately printed, 1900.

Im Speisewagen. Ein elegischer Schwank. Wien: Neue Freie Presse, 1900.

Solon in Lydien. Ein Schauspiel in drei Acten. Wien-Leipzig: Wiener Verlag, 1904.

Operetta

Des Teufels-Weib. Music by Adolf Müller. Hamburg: August Cranz, 1889 [or more likely 1890].

Literary Prose

Neues von der Venus. Plaudereien und Geschichten. Leipzig: F. Freund, 1887.

Buch der Narrheit. Leipzig: F. Freund, 1888.

Das Palais Bourbon. Bilder aus dem französischen Parlamentsleben. Leipzig: Duncker und Humblot, 1895.

Philosophische Erzählungen. Berlin: Gebrüder Paetel, 1900. 2nd ed., Berlin-Wien: Benjamin Harz, 1919.

Feuilletons. 2 vols. Wien-Leipzig: Wiener Verlag, 1903. 2nd ed., Berlin: I. Singer, 1911. 3rd ed., Wien: Benjamin Harz, [1921].

Zionist Writings

Der Judenstaat. Versuch einer modernen Lösung der Judenfrage. Leipzig-Wien: M. Breitensteins Verlagsbuchhandlung, 1896. Many subsequent editions.

Der Baseler Congress. Wien: Verlag der "Welt," 1897.

Altneuland. Roman. Leipzig: Hermann Seemanns Nachfolger, [1902]. Many subsequent editions.

Theodor Herzls Tagebücher. 3 vols. Berlin: Jüdischer Verlag, 1922-23.

Gesammelte Zionistische Werke. 5 vols. Tel-Aviv: Hozaah Inrith, 1934-35.

Briefe und Tagebucher. Ed. Alex Bein, Hermann Greive, Moshe Schärf, and Julius H. Schoeps. 7 vols. Berlin: Propylaen, in progress.

II.   Works in English Translation

The Congress Addresses, trans. Nelly Straus. New York: Federation of American Zionists, 1917.

The Tragedy of Jewish Immigration. New York: Zionist Organization of America, 1920.

The Jewish State: An Attempt at a Modern Solution of the Jewish Problem, trans. Sylvie d'Avigdor. 2nd ed., London: Central Office of the Zionist Organization, 1934.

The New Ghetto, trans. Heinz Norden. New York: The Theodor Herzl Foundation, 1955.

The Complete Diaries of Theodor Herzl, ed. Raphael Patai, trans. Harry
    Zohn. 5 vols. New York-London: Herzl Press and Thomas
    Yoseloff, 1960.
Altneuland, Old-New Land, trans. Paula Arnold. Haifa: Haifa Publishing
    Co., 1960. *Old-New Land*, trans. Lotta Levensohn. New York:
    Bloch Publishing Co. & Herzl Press, 1960.

III.   Secondary Works in English

Adler, Joseph. *The Herzl Paradox: Political, Social, and Economic
    Theories of a Realist*. New York: Hadrian, 1962.
Bein, Alex. *Theodor Herzl: A Biography*, trans. Maurice Samuel.
    Philadelphia: Jewish Publication Society, 1940, 1942, 1943, 1945,
    1948; 6th rev. ed. 1956. European ed., London: Horovitz, 1957.
    paperback eds., New York: Meridian, 1962; New York: Atheneum,
    1970.
Chouraqui, André. *A Man Alone: The Life of Theodor Herzl*, trans. Yael
    Guiladi. Jerusalem: Keter, 1960.
Cohen, Israel. *Theodor Herzl: Founder of Political Zionism*. New York:
    Thomas Yoseloff, 1959.
———-. *Theodor Herzl: His Life and Times*. London: Jewish Religious
    Educational Publications, 1953.
Ellern, Hermann and Bess. *Herzl, Hechler, the Grand Duke of Baden
    and the German Emperor: 1896-1904*. Documents found by, and
    reproduced in facsimile. Tel-Aviv: Ellern's Bank Ltd., 1961.
Elon, Amos. *Herzl*. New York: Holt, Rinehart & Winston, 1975.
Falk, Avner, "Freud and Herzl," in *Contemporary Psychoanalysis* 40
    (1978), 357-387.
Finkelstein, Norman R. *Theodor Herzl*, New York: Franklin Watts,
    1987.
Fränkel, Josef. *Lucien Wolf and Theodor Herzl*. London: Jewish
    Historical Society of England, 1960.
———-. "Moritz Güdemann and Theodor Herzl," in *Year Book of the Leo
    Baeck Institute, London* 11 (1966), 67-82.
———-. *Theodor Herzl: A Biography*. London: Ararat, 1946.
Goldmann, Nachum *The Genius of Herzl and Zionism Today*. Jerusalem:
    Organization Deparment of the Zionist Executive, 1955.
Haas, Jacob de. *Theodor Herzl: A Biographical Study*. 2 vols. New
    York: Leonard, 1927.

Handler, Andrew. *Dori: The Life and Times of Theodor Herzl in Budapest.* University, Ala.: University of Alabama Press, 1983.

Herzl Year Book, ed. Raphael Patai. New York: Herzl Press. Vol. 1, 1958; vol. 2, 1959; vol. 3, Herzl Centennial Volume, 1960; vol. 4, 1961-62; vol. 5, Studies in the History of Zionism in America: 1894-1919, 1963; vol. 6, 1965; vol. 7, 1971.

Heymann, Michael. "Herzl and the Russian Zionists: Dissension and Agreement," in *Zionism: Studies in the History of the Zionist Movement and the Jews in Palestine, III.* Tel-Aviv, 1973. Pp. 56-99, 613-614. [In Hebrew, with a summary in English.]

Kotker, Norman. *Herzl, the King.* New York: Scribner, 1972.

Lewisohn, Ludwig, ed. *Theodor Herzl: A Portrait for This Age.* Cleveland-New York: World, 1955.

Loewenberg, Peter. "Theodor Herzl: A Psychoanalytic Study in Charismatic Political Leadership," in Benjamin B. Wolman, ed., *The Psychoanalytical Interpretation of History.* New York: Basic Books, 1971. Pp. 150-191.

Neumann, Emanuel. *The Birth of Jewish Statesmanship: The Story of Theodor Herzl's Life.* New York: Zionist Organization of America, 1940, 1949, 1960.

Patai, Josef. *Starr over Jordan: The Life of Theodor Herzl*, trans. Francis Magyar. New York: Philosophical Library, 1946.

Rabinowicz, Oskar K. "Herzl and England," in *Jewish Social Studies* 13 (1951), 25-46.

———. *Herzl: Architect of the Balfour Declaration.* New York: herzl Press, 1948.

———. "Herzl the Playwright," in *Jewish Book Annual* 18 (1960-61), 100-115.

Schnitzler, Arthur. "Excerpts from the Correspondence between Theodor Herzl and Arthur Schnitzler (1892-1895)," in *Midstream: A Quarterly Jewish Review* 6 (Winter 1960), 46-64.

Stern, Arthur. "The Genetic Tragedy of the Family of Theodor Herzl," in *Israel Annals of Psychiatry and Related Disciplines* (April 1965).

Stewart, Desmond. *Theodor Herzl.* Garden City, N.Y.: Doubleday, 1974.

Vital, David. *The Origins of Zionism.* Oxford: Clarendon, 1975.

Weisgal, Meyer W., ed. *Theodor Herzl: A Memorial.* New York: The New Palestine, 1929.

IV.   Major Studies in German

Bein, Alex. *Theodor Herzl: Biographie.* Wien: Fiba, 1934. Paperback ed., Frankfurt am Main: Ullstein, 1983.

Blumenthal, E.P. *Diener am Licht: Eine Biographie Theodor Herzls.* Frankfurt am Main, 1977.

Bodenheimer, Henriette Hannah. *Im Anfang der Zionistischen Bewegung* Frankfurt am Main: Europäische Verlagsanstalt, 1965.

Bodenheimer, Max and Henriette. *Die Zionisten und das kaiserliche Deutschland.* Bamberg: Schäuble, 1972.

Diamant, Paul. *Theodor Herzls väterliche und mütterliche Vorfahren.* Jerusalem: Bamberger & Wahrmann, 1934.

Elon, Amos. *Theodor Herzl: Eine Biographie.* Wien, 1974, 1979.

Fränkel, Josef. *Theodor Herzl: Des Schöpfers erstes Wollen.* Wien: Fiba, 1934.

Friedemann, Adolf. *Das Leben Theodor Herzls.* Berlin: Jüdischer Verlag, 1914.

Georg, Manfred. *Theodor Herzl: Sein Leben und sein Vermächtnis.* Berlin: R.A. Höger, 1932.

Kallner, Rudolf. *Herzl und Rathenau.* Stuttgart: Klett, 1976.

Kastein, Joseph [Julius Katzenstein]. *Theodor Herzl: Das Erlebnis des jüdischen Menschen.* Wien: R. Löwit, 1935.

Kellner, Leon. *Theodor Herzls Lehrjahre 1860-1895.* Wien: R. Löwit, 1920.

Kohn, Hans. *Die politische Idee des Judentums.* München: Meyer & Jessen, 1924.

Leser, Norbert, ed. *Theodor Herzl und das Wien des Fin de Siècle.* Wien: Böhlau, 1987.

Nussenblatt, Tulo, ed. *Theodor Herzl Jahrbuch.* Wien: Dr. Heinrich Glanz Verlag, 1937.

Schoeps, Julius H. *Theodor Herzl: Wegbereiter des politischen Zionismus.* Frankfurt am Main, 1975.

Hugo von Hofmannsthal

Lowell A. Bangerter

Hugo von Hofmannsthal's initial impact upon his contemporaries was that of an enigma. One of his close friends later pointed to a "complete uniqueness and strangeness" that was encountered by all who became acquainted with the fledgling poet.[1] This apartness was not so much a product of his rich and diverse heritage as it was a result of his personal response to the forces that shaped his life.

Born in Vienna in 1874, Hofmannsthal was the only son of a bank director. In 1884 he entered the Wiener Akademisches Gymnasium, where he became an avid reader whose precocious intellectual accomplishments set him apart from other pupils his age. While still in school he published his first literary efforts and met several of the young modernist writers who gathered frequently at the Café Griensteidl. Among these early contacts were Hermann Bahr, Arthur Schnitzler, and Felix Salten.

A stormy fifteen-year friendship with the German symbolist poet Stefan George began in 1891. Impressed by the artistic maturity of Hofmannsthal's first poems, George went to Vienna specifically to meet the young lyricist. During the years that followed much of Hofmannsthal's work appeared in George's journal *Blätter für die Kunst*.

After law school at the University of Vienna Hofmannsthal spent a year in military service. He returned to the university in 1895, where he eventually received a doctorate in Romance philology. He then married Gertrud Schlesinger in 1901 and settled in Rodaun near Vienna. Although Rodaun remained his home until his death, he frequently traveled abroad. Many of his important early works were written in Italy, which became his second home.

Besides the friendship with Stefan George two other relationships were important for Hofmannsthal's creative development. In 1903 he met Max Reinhardt, who involved him actively in the theater. Reinhardt produced Hofmannsthal's *Elektra* (1904, Electra), a free rendering of Sophocles's drama, which gave Hofmannsthal his first theatrical success and broke ground for the collaboration with Richard Strauss that began in 1906. A modified version of *Elektra* was the first of six opera libretti that Hofmannsthal wrote for Strauss.

During World War I Hofmannsthal served in both the Austrian army and the Austrian War Ministry. After the collapse of the monarchy his deep feelings of loss caused him to work toward preserving and restoring Austrian and German culture. He helped found the Salzburg Festival in 1917, and during the following decade he published anthologies of writings by earlier German-language authors in an effort to revive interest in the literary heritage. For the rest of his life he was totally committed to promoting the cultural tradition that meant so much to him.

When poems such as "Frage" (1890, "Question") and "Vorfrühling" (1892, "Early Spring") appeared, they received wide acclaim as reflections of superb mastery of creative technique. They were also praised for their freshness and vitality. During his "lyric decade" (1890-1900), Hofmannsthal produced many works of enduring beauty, creations that capture in verse the important elements of his approach to life and its phenomena.

Hofmannsthal's poetry is firmly rooted in European tradition. His ideas and prosody were drawn from various models. A good illustration of this fact is the third of his "Terzinen" (1895, "Stanzas in Terza Rima"). The entire piece centers on the first line, which is little more than a translation of Prospero's famous words from William Shakespeare's *The Tempest* (c. 1611): "We are such stuff as dreams are made of."

Although tradition was important in Hofmannsthal's approach to art, he did not separate himself from the literary movements of his own time. His most important poems are excellent examples of impressionism. Like other impressionists, he documented in verse an acute consciousness of incidentals, transitory things, and the unique spiritual condition in all its most subtle variations, distinctions, tints, and shades. He also adhered to the impressionist demand for the greatest possible perfection and purification of language and form.

Hofmannsthal was especially effective in the poetic presentation of visual elements. One of his contemporaries attributed to him "the ability to observe nature and life through the eyes of a great painter and to create in that style,"[2] while another critic has called him "a combiner of spiritual with sensual sight, an impressionist of seeing."[3] The power of his visual imagery is illustrated effectively in the second of his "Terzinen," a particularly compelling treatment of the theme of death:

> The hours! When we gaze out into the blue
> Of ocean waves and grasp death's meaning there,
> All horror gone, a light yet solemn view,
>
> Like little girls who look so pale and fair
> With their enormous eyes, who always freeze,
> And in the evening mutely stand and stare,
>
> And recognize that life now softly flees
> From sleepy limbs to trees and grassy bed,
> And smile affected smiles with weary ease
>
> Like persecuted saints whose blood is shed.[4]

Examination of death as an important dimension of human experience is one typical aspect of Hofmannsthal's lyric interpretation of existence. In his poems death has the power to bring together present, past, and future into an eternal "now." This view plays a major role in the development of his concept of "preexistence."

Preexistence is the condition of man apart from mortality. It is where (and when) the human being resides before this life, after dying, or when temporarily removed from the tangible world in dreams. Within the context of absolute existence life on earth is a transitory state. Hofmannsthal sees man following a course back and forth between mortality and preexistence, moving through a series of life forms in an infinite purification process. In lines from "Ghaselen II" (Ghazel II), a poem written in 1891, he likens the development of the poet to that of the individual soul:

> Every living spirit wanders through the hierarchy of beings,
> Changing, purifying forms, becoming happy, greater, brighter, On it
> lives in worm, in frog, in vampire bat, in lowly slave, Then in dancer,
> in poet, vagabond, and noble fighter. (*GLD*, p. 488)

The transformation process, although clearly one of refinement, does not always move upward. The transition may be from bat to slave, or from poet to vagabond.

In his poetry Hofmannsthal used three special metaphors for life: the drama, the dream, and the game. The drama metaphor is most clearly developed in poems such as the elegy "Zum Gedächtnis des Schauspielers Mitterwurzer" (1898, In Memory of the Actor Mitterwurzer), which presents the actor as a symbol for man, and "Prolog zu dem Buch Anatol" (1893, "Prologue to the Book 'Anatol'"). The latter poem places both poet and reader inside the framework of a theater of life, performing "plays that we have fashioned" and "comedies of our own spirit" (*GLD*, p. 44). In his dream imagery, Hofmannsthal depicted life as an internal process of creation. "Terzinen III" suggests that dreams assist in the forming of personal identity. Because "the stuff of which we're made has properties / like that of dreams . . ." (*GLD*, p. 18), we merge with our dreams and become one with them. Life viewed as a game is less well developed in the poetry than in Hofmannsthal's other writings, where he emphasizes adult games and the gambler as a symbol for man. In the lyrics it is primarily the child's game that becomes an aspect of a privately created universe. "Der Jüngling und die Spinne" (1899, The Youth and the Spider), for example, presents a situation in which, while forming a world within himself, the young protagonist "teaches" its inhabitants games.

Hofmannsthal's three metaphors are especially significant for his conception of his own identity as a poet. He saw the poet as a productive mixture of the actor, the dreamer, and the player-of-games. Such a synthesis, he felt, would yield the ultimate creator who could assist others to create through finding things that lie within themselves.

One of Hofmannsthal's most important purposes in writing was the clarification and education of the self. That fact is especially evident in his essays. He wrote nonfiction throughout his life, eventually composing more than two hundred different pieces. The topics covered are extremely diverse, ranging from geography to drama, from music to classical philosophy. Each subject received careful attention and is presented in a manner that places emphasis on the author's key concerns.

The essays are remarkable for their diversity of form. In addition to traditional expository approaches Hofmannsthal used created dialogues or fictional letters to present his ideas. For each essay he selected a style and form specifically suited to the content. Most of these writings are more creative than analytical. They typically feature poetic imagery and language that is rhythmic and rich in color and nuance.

Especially characteristic of Hofmannsthal's early essays in both tone and direction is "Poesie und Leben" (1896, Poesy and Life). In this particular work he openly challenged the validity of contemporary literary criticism, arguing that it was too superficial. By insisting that both reviewers and public penetrate beyond incidentals in their evaluations Hofmannsthal hoped to motivate a change in common perceptions of art.

The young essayist was especially disturbed by modern criticism's tendency to dissect literature. He felt that critics who dwelt on individual aspects of a work, were losing sight of the meaning of the whole. Accordingly, he contrasted his own approach with that of other commentators in these words: "Their praise is directed toward fragments and parts, mine toward the whole; their appreciation toward the relative, mine toward the absolute." (*P I*, p. 262)

This passage offers important insight into Hofmannsthal's critical approach to literature and to life. Each essay, regardless of topic, reveals his concern for the composite, the synthesis. In her detailed treatment of the essays Elsbeth Pulver concluded that they demonstrate "the writer's unceasing effort to grasp the phenomena to which he addresses himself—individual works, literary figures, complete eras, even national literatures—in their living entirety."[5]

"Poesie und Leben'" places special emphasis on the concept of wholeness with respect to the relationships between literature and the real world. Unlike the German realists and naturalists, Hofmannsthal argued that reality is not a necessary part of literature because a literary work is a valid, unique, independent whole. He defined the distinction between literature and life in these words: "No direct path leads from poesy to life, nor does any lead from life to poesy." (*P I*, p. 263)

According to Hofmannsthal, the strength of literature should be its capacity to symbolize rather than to imitate life. He concluded that both literature and literary criticism were failing because neither the writer nor the critic understood that fact. The poet had apparently lost the ability to use language to create a symbolic whole, and the critic had completely lost sight of the concept of wholeness.

In spite of a strong element of subjectivity in this early essay Hofmannsthal remained almost casual in presenting his ideas. The form is that of a lecture, but the style is chatty. Occasional witty comments make the essay less intimidating, and the arguments are framed in gently persuasive language. The result is very readable.

Hofmannsthal's most famous essay, "Ein Brief" (1902, "The Letter of Lord Chandos"), is a fictional letter from Phillip Lord Chandos, an invented figure, to Sir Francis Bacon, the famous seventeenth-century

English scientist and philosopher. In the letter Chandos explains his abandonment of all literary activity. His discourse examines the situation of the writer who has lost the ability to express himself meaningfully because he can no longer wrestle at all with language. In comparing his current condition with his earlier life, when his literary activities were based on a view of existence as a great unity, Chandos says: "My situation, in short, is this: I have completely lost the ability to think or speak about anything at all with continuity." (*P II*, p. 11)

Chandos views his present state as the product of a gradual psychological fragmentation caused by the collapse of his rapport with language. The breakdown progressed from inability to discuss general topics because of a loathing for abstract terms such as "spirit" and "soul" to a complete disintegration of linguistic coherency. In the latter circumstances he could describe nothing at all for lack of understandable concepts. Even the words themselves became meaningless.

The loss of effective language usage isolated Chandos from the world and placed him out of touch with his own identity. Interpreting Chandos's condition, the famous Austrian author Hermann Broch wrote: "The mystic intuitive unity of self, expression, and thing has been lost to him in a single blow, so that his ego is brought to the most hermetic isolation, isolated from a rich world to which he no longer has access, a world where the things will no longer communicate to him, not even their names."[6]

Although Chandos has not yet recovered from the breakdown, there are signs that a change is beginning to take place; he appears to be moving toward a new view of the world. Instead of seeing himself as part of a great whole, he approaches a perception in which all external things are a part of himself and he becomes the unifying principle.

Based on statements in his correspondence and other evidence, a common interpretation of the essay styles it as Hofmannsthal's attempt to cope with a personal creative crisis. Donald G. Daviau has repudiated the specifics of the perceived relationship between the Chandos letter and Hofmannsthal's life in these words: "It is important to correct this false interpretation, not only because it is wrong, but also because it distorts the 'formidable unity of the work' by falsely dividing Hofmannsthal's oeuvre into two parts, while in actuality it progresses from the beginning to end in one straight line of unbroken development."[7]

Two things make the common "crisis theory" at least questionable. Hofmannsthal himself insisted that the direct stimulus for "Ein Brief" came from an encounter with Bacon's essays which motivated a desire to create something in that literary tone.[8] More importantly, the essay suggests that Hofmannsthal was not experiencing the problems of the fictitious Chandos. The letter is a masterpiece of literary artistry, with images that are vibrant, bright, and colorful. The selection of words and the organization and presentation of ideas are flawless. The result is not the work of a spiritually disturbed artist but that of a virtuoso.

Among Hofmannsthal's most fascinating works are some masterfully executed prose narratives. These stories offer intense psychological illumination of the human condition by focusing on problems related to the search for personal identity and the encounter with self.

For Anton Lerch, the central character in Hofmannsthal's famous story *Reitergeschichte* (1908, *Cavalry Patrol*), the rejection of personal identity is a blatant act of self-destruction. On the surface Sergeant Major Lerch is executed for insubordination. In reality his crime is an external manifestation of refusal to accept his own higher nature.

Reitergeschichte is framed in historically identifiable circumstances. The year is 1848, the context the war conducted by the Austrians against the Italian Liberation Army. Projected against that background are the events leading to Lerch's refusal to obey an order to release a captured horse, an act that causes his commanding officer to shoot him.

Lerch's problem arises out of inclinations that lead him away from his basic responsibilities to himself. Memories initially distract him from his orderly military duties. Riding through Milan after a series of battles, he is attracted to a woman whom he knew in the past. He slips away from his squadron, thereby symbolically forsaking the identity of an honorable noncommissioned officer. Although he returns almost immediately, an internal change has begun to occur. He has mentally entered the atmosphere of civilian life. A dormant baser self has begun to stir.

The critical phase of Lerch's self-betrayal begins with his entry into a dream state where he is even more vulnerable to aroused internal drives. A sudden thirst for money pushes him into a nearby squalid village in search of something that can bring him a handsome bonus. His progress through the repelling wayside town is figuratively an excursion into his own inner world. As one critic says, the village is "the projection of his chaotic insides."[9]

His movement through the village, which has all the qualities of a nightmare ordeal, leads Lerch to an important confrontation on a bridge at its outskirts. There he meets his double riding toward him from the other side. He rejects the specter, warding it off with an uplifted hand. For critics, the bridge scene is extremely controversial. It has been given various interpretations. One scholar views the hand stretched against the apparition as Lerch's refusal to let knowledge of the self become a working force within him.[10] Another writer interprets the double as a traditional messenger of death.[11] Such interpretations present the double as some manifestation of Lerch's self with which he cannot cope, and to that extent they are equally valid.

Because Lerch's double comes from across the bridge, where his squadron is, it can also be argued that the figure represents Lerch's old, honorable, military self, the identity that he must assume once more in order to survive when he rejoins his unit. By rejecting this other self, he confirms the new dominance of his baser nature. When he is later ordered to release a captured horse, he becomes angry and refuses to obey, thereby inviting his own execution.

Unlike other stories, Hofmannsthal's unfinished novel, *Andreas oder Die Vereinigten* (1932, *Andreas; or, The United*), presents coming to grips with one's self as a constructive process. It equates the search for identity with the natural progress of maturation. *Andreas* describes an educational journey from Vienna to Venice in 1778. During his travels young Andreas von Ferschengelder must cope with love and its consequences, negative dimensions of life, and the impact of art upon him. He experiences life as a series of fragments. Among the more important of these are a love affair that is interrupted because of the treachery of a villainous hired servant, involvement with the family of an impoverished nobleman who earns a living by snuffing out theater lamps, participation in a virginity lottery conducted by the nobleman's daughter Zustina, and contacts with various enigmatic figures including another daughter of the nobleman who lives by herself as a coquette, the artist Zorzi, the Maltese Knight Sacramozo, and some mysterious women encountered during a chance visit to a small church.

The protagonist's primary educational task is to integrate into a coherent whole the diverse elements of his experience. He gains understanding of himself and others by willingly playing roles that are related to Hofmannsthal's major poetic metaphors for life.

One facet of Andreas's identity surfaces during his experience with the hired servant. Gotthilff awakens the dreamer in Andreas by taking advantage of aspects of his employer's nature of which the latter is not even aware. As Richard Alewyn has pointed out, Gotthilff can maneuver the unsuspecting young man because he understands "with infamous sureness how to detect Andreas's most secret weaknesses and vulnerabilities and how to ally himself with the dreams and drives that slumber unknown and untamed deep within him."[12] Thus, when Gotthilff boasts of his exploits with women, Andreas dreams of playing the lover, and when the servant steals his horse, saddle, and half his money, Andreas internalizes the situation and envisions himself as a criminal like Gotthilff.

In Venice other aspects of Andreas's identity emerge as he plays other roles. By participating in Zustina's virginity lottery he becomes a game player. While living with the nobleman Prampero and his family, all of whom are employed in the theater, he participates in Hofmannsthal's theater of life, experiencing Venice as "an intellectual masquerade, full of erotic depths and superficialities."[13]

Because *Andreas* remained a fragment, it is not completely clear how Hofmannsthal intended to finalize the identity of his protagonist. Nevertheless, there is significant evidence to suggest that his vision of the mature Andreas focused heavily on the unfolding of his nature as a consummate actor. In his notes to the novel Hofmannsthal indicated that Andreas would model himself after the Maltese Knight Sacramozo. He wrote: "In the company of the Maltese Knight, indeed only through a relationship with him, Andreas's existence purifies and collects itself." (*E*, p. 203). In another note the author pointed to the fact that Andreas would eventually recognize in Sacramozo "a master of the playing of his own role." (*E*, p. 204). These two references would seem to indicate that Hofmannsthal intended to have Andreas achieve that same mastery.

It is consistent with Hofmannsthal's perception of the relationship between life and art that theater should become his strongest metaphor for human existence. To Hofmannsthal theater was life as he personally experienced it. For that reason it is not surprising that dramas are his best-remembered contribution to Austrian literature nor that some of his most famous plays are built around his stage metaphor for life.

Among the works that emphasize the symbolic representation of life as theater are *Der Tor und der Tod* (1984, *Death and the Fool*), *Das kleine Welttheater* (1897, *The Little Theater of the World*), *Jedermann* (1911, *The Play of Everyman*), and *Das Salzburger große Welttheater* (1922, *The Salzburg Great Theater of the World*). The most representative creations in this series are perhaps *Der Tor und der Tod*, Hofmannsthal's best-known and best-loved short lyric play, and *Das Salzburger große Welttheater*, which borrowed its central metaphor from Pedro Calderon de la Barca's *El gran teatro del mundo* (c. 1635, *The Great Theater of the World*).

In *Der Tor und der Tod* the tragedy of Claudio, the fool, is that of an individual who has neither appreciated nor properly performed his assigned part in life's drama. For that reason he is unprepared to die when the time comes. Claudio's problem is that he has rejected the role of actor, preferring that of spectator. He has therefore never really partaken of life in its fullness. The growing awareness that he has somehow missed important dimensions of experience causes Claudio to resist Death's summons, arguing that he has not lived. Death rejects his plea for mercy but grants him a brief respite in order to teach him a proper respect for life.

One by one three accusers return from the dead to confront Claudio with his guilt: his mother, a young girl whom he mistreated, and a friend who loved the girl. Their reproaches are summarized by the friend, who says that he is happier dead than is Claudio alive, because Claudio enjoys no meaningful relationships with anyone. Finally, as Claudio confesses that his life has been a miserable failure, his lines contain the essence of Hofmannsthal's indictment against the person who ignores the opportunity to master the role that is given him: "As on the stage a bad comedian passes, / . . . / So too across this greater stage of life / I've moved without conviction, strength, or worth." (*GLD*, p. 219)

Das Salzburger große Welttheater is Hofmannsthal's strongest portrayal of life as a drama. It benefited from the earlier exploration of several problems in *Jedermann*. Among them are the question of free agency, the need for positive action, man's social role, and the appropriate attitude toward death. In the later play Hofmannsthal expanded and perfected his treatment of these issues while integrating them into a clear theatrical illustration of his personal view of absolute existence.

The central idea of Calderon's *El gran teatro del mundo* was especially attractive to Hofmannsthal because it provided a suitable framework for the explicit development of his concept of "preexistence." In the Spanish model the world builds a stage upon which individuals perform the play of life in the roles given them by God. Hofmannsthal's treatment of this metaphor gives special attention to the premortal realm and the unborn actor-souls. In particular, the Austrian dramatist endows the unborn spirits with individuality and the ability to make free-will decisions.

The notions of free agency and responsibility for its exercise are crucial to Hofmannsthal's play. When the Master instructs the World concerning his expectations, he insists upon a drama of life that is "a living, secret, free operation." (*D III*, p. 257). Accordingly, an angel then emphasizes to the actor-souls the importance of how they play their roles as opposed to that of the nature of the roles themselves.

Hofmannsthal's ideas concerning individual freedom are offered in their clearest form in his treatment of the Beggar's role. In the premortal domain the soul who is assigned to be the Beggar rejects his part until he is convinced that it will afford him the freedom to act for himself. When he later appears on the World's stage, he takes full responsibility for his words and actions. The play reaches its high point when the Beggar picks up an axe, turns on the other characters, and threatens to destroy them and take power for himself, insisting in very modern fashion that all of their privileges are stolen. Just as he raises the axe, however, he sees a vision that moves him to exercise his will against his earlier inclination. By staying his hand he carries out the positive action for which he had longed in the realm of preexistence. As Hanns Hammelmann has pointed out, Hofmannsthal could rightfully call the play his own, despite the pattern provided by Calderon, "because the powerful active figure of the beggar here gives the play an entirely new dramatic meaning and climax."[14]

For the Beggar the primary effect of his free-will deed is that while still alive he regains awareness of his identity as an actor on the stage of life. This perception then enables him to face death happily, knowing that he has played his role well. The Beggar's act of conversion is more than a simple assertion of free will. It represents an inner change that Hofmannsthal deemed necessary for his contemporaries. After World War I, he was appalled by the selfishness and cynicism that he encountered. He regarded *Das Salzburger große Welttheater* as a prescription for the healing of society's ills.

Social criticism is an important element in all of Hofmannsthal's life dramas. It is especially visible in his comedies. Works such as *Der Schwierige* (1921, *The Difficult Man*) and the opera *Arabella* (1933, *Arabella*) offer strong criticism of Viennese society while illuminating the idea that man as an actor plays his best role when playing himself.

Der Schwierige, which one renowned critic has called "the most perfect comedy of the twentieth century,"[15] elaborates problems that arise out of the central character's handling of his own role and his reactions to the conscious roles played by others. At first, Hans Karl Bühl declines to let his true identity show through his mask. As a result others perceive him inaccurately. When he is drawn into the social context, however, circumstances force his inner nature into the open with tragicomic repercussions. Of all Hofmannsthal's characters, Bühl is among the most human and therefore the most complex. More than anything else he illustrates that "the difficult man" is an appropriate designation for man, the actor.

The idea that life is a game is developed in several of Hofmannsthal's dramas. Included among them are *Gestern* (1891, Yesterday), *Der Abenteurer und die Sängerin* (1909, The Adventurer and the Singer), *Cristinas Heimreise* (1910, *Cristina's Journey Home*), and *Der Unbestechliche* (first act only, 1923: complete play, 1933, The Incorruptible Man). These works present two kinds of players at the game of life. For one type, the adventurer, life is a game of chance. For the other, whose approach to human experience is based upon complete understanding of life's rules and possibilities, it is a game of skill. The male protagonist in *Der Abenteurer und die Sängerin* provides an excellent example of the first alternative, while the title figure of *Der Unbestechliche* is Hofmannsthal's most successful rendering of the second one.

Hofmannsthal's adventurer figures, including Baron Weidenstamm in *Der Abenteurer und die Sängerin,* are patterned after the archetype of the life-game player, Casanova. Weidenstamm's role, like that of Florindo, the young libertine in *Cristinas Heimreise* was based specifically on material from Casanova's memoirs.

Because it was written while Hofmannsthal was still struggling with important details of dramatic technique, *Der Abenteurer und die Sängerin* lacks flair and polish. Nevertheless, it is an important work for at least two reasons. It offers an excellent representation of the adventurer as a basic human type, and it is Hofmannsthal's first major expansion of the game metaphor as an analogy for life.

The drama focuses on an encounter between the middle-aged adventurer, Weidenstamm, and a former mistress, Vittoria. Now married to Lorenzo Venier, Vittoria revives her earlier relationship with Weidenstamm by introducing him to a son he has never known. Until now she has passed the young man off as her brother. When her husband notes the similarity between Cesarino and a picture of the young Weidenstamm, Vittoria admits that Cesarino is Weidenstamm's son but insists that he is nonetheless her brother. She simply says that they had two different fathers. Venier accepts her explanation, and further complications are averted when Weidenstamm is forced to leave the city because another former mistress has recognized him and threatened to expose him to the authorities.

The game metaphor is embedded in both the background and the action of the play. Even time and place add to the overall game atmosphere. With reference to this work Günther Erken has characterized eighteenth-century Venice in these words: "Gaming is an ingredient, almost the essence of this world."[16] The drama begins accordingly at an evening gambling party. During the first half of the piece the other characters circulate between the gaming table and Weidenstamm, the embodiment of game playing.   In characterizing his own approach to life Weidenstamm says: "we commit the greatest inanities for the sake of a woman whom we have seen in passing; and in order to open the laces of a bodice, we stake our lives without hesitating a moment, even before we know what the bodice hides.". (*D I*, p. 163). In other words, the man who views life as a game of chance typically wagers himself against a greater portion of life, whatever that portion might be. For all of Hofmannsthal's gamblers such action fails to bring lasting happiness.

From Hofmannsthal's point of view the only possibility for success in the game of life is to remove the element of chance and play life as a game of skill. His one major successful illustration of a player who understands that fact is Theodor, "'the incorruptible man." Unlike the adventurer figures who gamble their lives away, the title figure of *Der Unbestechliche* views life as a game of billiards. He sees himself as a player at the billiard table. The people around him are the balls, whose interactions he determines with carefully controlled strokes of the cue. Theodor's mastery of the game is based upon a thorough knowledge of his opponent, the "balls" and their potential, and effective playing strategy.

The other player in this game is Jaromir, an adventurer who is no match for Theodor in the game of life. Theodor was formerly Jaromir's valet. Unable to tolerate Jaromir's life style, he resigned and was hired by Jaromir's mother as her major-domo. Now Jaromir has married and brought his young wife Anna to live at his mother's estate. In an attempt to maintain the ties with his former existence he has invited two of his mistresses for a visit. When the baroness refuses to allow Theodor to respond to the situation, Theodor resigns, leaving the household in confusion. To restore order the baroness must give Theodor a free hand. Gleefully he upsets Jaromir's plans and sends the two young women packing.

Theodor's knowledge of Marie and Melanie enables him to deal with them effectively. He compares the anticipated action to two billiard shots. One shot he plays directly, the other off the cushion. In the "direct" shot he appeals to Marie's sense of guilt at having left her father alone, and she quickly leaves. The off-the cushion play is more subtle. In this case, Theodor reveals to Melanie that she has become a character in an autobiographical novel that Jaromir is writing. By focusing her attention on what will happen if her cousins see Jaromir's book he easily persuades her to flee with the manuscript. Meanwhile Anna has confessed to Jaromir that she is jealous of the two women. He has come to his senses and promised to reform, thereby bringing Theodor's game to a happy conclusion.

In Hofmannsthal's works for the stage the theater and game metaphors offer different ways to interpret experienced reality. On the other hand, plays that focus attention on the dream metaphor explore the idea that the dreamer creates an alternate reality. The most important of these works are *Das Bergwerk zu Falun* (written, 1899 published, 1933; *The Mine at Falun*), Hofmannsthal's first five-act drama, and *Der Turm* (1925, second version, 1927; *The Tower*), his final major tragedy. Hofmannsthal's thinking with respect to dream phenomena was stimulated by Freud's studies concerning the psychology of dreams. In 1924 Hofmannsthal predicted that during the course of the century Freud's influence would be far greater than that of the ideas which dominated perceptions of man's inner nature during his own childhood.[17]

Das Bergwerk zu Falun is in part a product of Hofmannsthal's preoccupation with the European cultural heritage. It is based on a story written by E. T. A. Hoffmann in 1819. Hoffmann, however, was only one of several authors who created literary works dealing with the events surrounding the recovery of a body from a mine at Falun, Sweden.

In the incident the body of a miner who died in 1670 was discovered fifty years later, perfectly preserved in vitriolated water. Nobody recognized the man until an old woman identified him as her fiancé, who had perished shortly before their wedding day. This situation provided the basis for E. T. A. Hoffmann's story of Elis Fröbom, an unhappy seaman turned miner, whose encounters with the ghost-miner Torbern, dreams of a magical underground realm, love affair with his employer's daughter, and mental deterioration set the stage for his death in a cave-in and the peculiar delayed reunion of the lovers.

Hofmannsthal's dramatization of the story maintains much of the external pattern of events but excludes the reunion at the end and changes Elis's nature. Instead of emphasizing the young man's insanity as Hoffmann does, Hofmannsthal makes his central character a dreamer. Thus, dream as a creative force determines Elis's actions and shapes the play's situation.

Elis has inherited his father's ability to create an alternate dream reality. Recognition that dreams are the key to his very identity eventually makes him aware that he belongs to another world. From that point on his longing for the other existence grows into a death wish. The stages along his path then include the visionary encounter with Torbern, who points the way into the subterranean realm, a dream experience in the domain of the queen of the mine, a preparatory period as a successful miner, during which he falls in love with the mine owner's daughter Anna, and the final free-will renunciation of all connections to mortality. The most important aspect of Elis's decision to forsake mortal reality is that it brings him fulfillment. Once he has made up his mind, he is at peace with himself. As he bids Anna farewell, he can honestly tell her that he is happy.

Like *Das Bergwerk zu Falun*, *Der Turm* is based on material developed in an earlier literary work by another writer. In this instance the model was another play by Calderon, *La vida es sueño* (1635, *Life Is a Dream*). What interested Hofmannsthal most about the Spanish comedy was the idea of "descending into the uttermost depths of the uncertain labyrinthine kingdom 'self' and finding there the non-self or the world."[18]

When he began to work with Calderon's material in 1902, Hofmannsthal limited himself to preparing a German version of *La vida es sueño*. That play presents the story of Sigismund, son of Basilius, King of Poland. Basilius has kept Sigismund locked in a tower because of a prophecy that Sigismund would become a terrible despot. Before turning the kingdom over to a nephew Basilius decides to test Sigismund. The latter is given a sleeping potion, brought to the palace, and installed as ruler. During the test Sigismund fulfills the prophecy and is returned to the tower. When he awakens there, he concludes that everything has been a dream, but he resolves that if his "dreams" put him on the throne again, he will act differently. Circumstances give him a second chance and he redeems himself, thereby finding fulfillment when his dream life becomes reality.

World War I made Hofmannsthal skeptical about the possibility of a positive resolution of Sigismund problem. The dream metaphor still seemed appropriate, but life had become a nightmare. When he took up the same material again in 1916, he approached it from the point of view that Sigismund would be destroyed in a world of chaos. For that reason *Der Turm* retained little of the original plot aside from the basic situation of Sigismund's imprisonment, test, and return to captivity. The new Sigismund becomes a victim, unable to reconcile his inner world with the forces around him.

The ultimate goal of Hofmannsthal's writings was twofold. On one level he saw his task as that of providing the reader with access to the broad spectrum of human experience. On another he hoped to supply the tools, motivation, and raw materials that might enable an individual to achieve a personal artistic synthesis. Through his poems, essays, plays, stories, and his many other literary and cultural endeavors he accomplished much toward the realization of those purposes. In so doing he became one of the most important figures in Austrian literary history.

Notes

1. Rudolf Borchardt, "Erinnerungen," in *Hugo von Hofmannsthal,* ed. Helmut A. Fiechtner (Bern and Munich: Francke, 1963), p.83. All translations are mine.

2. Hermann Ubell, "Die Blätter für die Kunst," in *Hofmannsthal im Urteil seiner Kritiker,* ed. Gotthart Wunberg (Frankfurt am Main: Athenäm, 1972), p.65.

3. Albrecht Schaeffer, "Hugo von Hofmannsthal," in Wunberg, pp. 306-307.

4. Hugo von Hofmannsthal, "Terzinen II," in *Gesammelte Werke in Einzelausgaben: Gedichte und Lyrische Dramen,* ed. Herbert Steiner (Frankfurt am Main: Fischer, 1963), pp. 17-18. Unless otherwise noted, subsequent quotations from Hofmannsthal's writings will be cited by page in the text, with reference to the appropriate volume of this edition of the collected works, according to the following notation: *Erzählungen: E; Gedichte und Lyrische Dramen: GLD; Dramen I-IV: D I-IV; Lustspiele I-IV: L I-IV; Prosa I-IV: P I-IV; Aufzeichnungen: A.*

5. Elsbeth Pulver, *Hofmannsthals Schriften zur Literatur* (Bern: Haupt, 1956), p.22.

6. Hermann Broch, *Hofmannsthal und seine Zeit* (Frankfurt am Main: Suhrkamp, 1974), p.92.

7. Donald G. Daviau, "Hugo von Hofmannsthal, Stefan George und der Chandos Brief: Eine neue Perspektive auf Hofmannsthals sogenannte Sprachkrise," in Karl Konrad Phlheim, Hrsg., Simm und Symbol, Festschurift für Joseph P. Strelka (Bern, Frankfurt am Main: Peter Lang, 1987), p.229.

8. Hugo von Hofmannsthal and Leopold von Andrian, Briefwechsel, ed. Walter Perl (Frankfurt am Main: Fischer, 1968), p.160.

9. Volker O. Durr, "Der Tod des Wachtmeisters Anton Lerch und die Revolution von 1848: Zu Hofmannsthals *Reitergeschichte,*" *German Quarterly* 45 (1972), 42.

10. Ulrich Heimrath, "Hugo von Hofmannsthals 'Reitergeschichte,'" *Wirkendes Wort* 21 (1971), 315.

11. Richard Alewyn, *Über Hugo von Hofmannsthal* (Göttingen: Vandenhoeck und Ruprecht, 1967), p. 84.

12. Alewyn, p.129.

13. Hermnn Broch, "Die Prosaschriften," in *Hugo von Hofmannsthal,* ed. Sibylle Bauer (Darmstadt: Wissenschaftliche Buchgesellschaft, 1968), p.103.

14. Hans A. Hammelmann, *Hugo von Hofmannsthal* (London: Bowes and Bowes, 1957), pp.36-37.

15. Wilhelm Emrich, "Hofmannsthals Lustspiel 'Der Schwierige,'" in Bauer, p. 437.

16. Günther Emrich, *Hofmannsthals dramatischer Stil* (Tübingen: Niemeyer, 1967), p.21.

17. Hugo von Hofmannsthal and Carl J. Burckhardt, *Briefwechsel,* ed. Carl J. Burckhardt (Frankfurt am Main: Fischer, 1956), p. 161.

18. Hugo von Hofmannsthal and Harry Graf Kessler, *Briefwechsel 1898-1929,* ed. Hilde Burger (Frankfurt am Main: Insel, 1968), p. 280.

Bibliography

I. Works by Hofmannsthal in German

Gestern. Wien: Verlag der Modernen Rundschau, 1891.

Der Tor und der Tod. Munchen: Knorr und Hirth, 1899.

Die Hochzeit der Sobeide. Berlin: Entsch, 1899.

Theater in Versen. Berlin: Fischer, 1899.

Der Kaiser und die Hexe. Leipzig: Insel, 1900.

Der Schüler. Berlin: Fischer, 1902.

Ausgewählte Gedichte. Berlin: Verlag der Blätter für die Kunst, 1903.

Das kleine Welttheater. Leipzig: Insel, 1903.

Elektra. Berlin: Fischer, 1904.

Unterhaltungen über literarische Gegenstände. Berlin: Bard und Marquardt, 1904.

Das gerettete Venedig. Berlin: Fischer, 1905.

Das Märchen der 672. Nacht und andere Erzählungen. Wien and Leipzig: Wiener Verlag, 1905.

Kleine Dramen. Leipzig: Insel, 1906.

Oedipus und die Sphinx. Berlin: Fischer, 1906.

Der weiße Fächer. Leipzig: Insel, 1907.

Die gesammelten Gedichte. Leipzig: Insel, 1907.

Die prosaischen Schriften 3 vols. Berlin: Fischer, 1907, 1917.

Vorspiele. Leipzig: Insel, 1908.

Der Abenteurer und die Sängerin. Berlin: Fischer, 1909.

Die Frau im Fenster. Berlin: Fischer, 1909.

Cristinas Heimreise. Berlin: Fischer, 1910.

König Oedipus. Berlin: Fischer, 1910.

Alkestis. Leipzig: Insel, 1911.

Der Rosenkavalier. Berlin: Fischer, 1911.

Jedermann. Berlin: Fischer, 1911.

Ariadne auf Naxos. Berlin and Paris: Fürstner, 1912.

Der Bürger als Edelmann. Berlin: Fürstner, 1916. (Libretto)

Dame Kobold. Berlin: Fischer, 1920.

Die Frau ohne Schatten. Berlin: Fischer, 1920. (prose fiction)

Reitergeschichte. Wien: Trache, 1921.

Der Schwierige. Berlin: Fischer, 1921.

Reden und Aufsätze. Leipzig: Insel, 1921.

Das Salzburger große Welttheater. Leipzig: Insel, 1922.

Die grüne Flöte. Wien und Leipzig: Universal-Edition, 1923.

Florindo. Wien and Hellerau: Avalun, 1923.

Prima Ballerina. Wien and Leipzig: Universal-Edition, 1923.

Augenblicke in Griechenland. Regensburg and Leipzig: Habbel und Naumann, 1924.

Achilles auf Skyros. Wien and new York: Universal-Edition, 1925.

Der Turm. München: Verlag der Bremer Presse, 1925. (Second Version: Berlin: Fischer, 1927.)

Die Ruinen von Athen. Berlin: Fürstner, 1925.

Früheste Prosastücke. Leipzig: Gesellschaft der Freunde der deutschen Bücherei, 1926.

Drei Erzählungen. Leipzig: Insel, 1927.

Der Tod des Tizian. Leipzig: Insel, 1928.

Die ägyptische Helene. Leipzig: Insel, 1928.

Loris. Berlin: Fischer, 1930.

Die Berührung der Sphären. Berlin: Fischer, 1932.

Wege und Begegnungen. Leipzig: Reclam, 1931.

Andreas oder Die Vereinigten. Berlin: Fischer, 1932.

Das Bergwerk zu Falun. Wien: Wiener Bibliophilen-Gesellschaft, 1933.

Arabella. Berlin: Fürstner, 1933.

Der Unbestechliche. Berlin: Fischer, 1933.

Nachlese der Gedichte. Berlin: Fischer, 1934.

Dramatische Entwürfe. Wien: Verlag der Johannes-Presse, 1936.

Festspiele in Salzburg. Wien: Bermann-Fischer, 1938.

Gesammelte Werke in Einzelausgaben, ed. Herbert Steiner, 15 vols. Stockholm: Bermann-Fischer, 1945ff.; Frankfurt am Main: Fischer, 1950ff.

Sylvia im "Stern," ed. Marten Stern. Bern and Stuttgart: Paul Haupt, 1959.

Das erzählerische Werk. Frankfurt am Main: Fischer, 1969.

Sämtliche Werke, eds. Rudolf Hirsch, Clemens Köttelwesch, Heinz Rölleke, and Ernst Zinn, 38 vols. Frankfurt am Main: Fischer, 1974ff.

Gesammelte Werke, ed. Bernd Schoeller, 10 vols. Frankfurt am Main: Fischer Taschenbuch Verlag, 1979.

Correspondence and Diaries

Buch der Freunde. Leipzig: Insel, 1922.

Briefe 1890-1901. Berlin: Fischer, 1935.

Der Briefwechsel Hofmannsthal-Wildgans, ed. Joseph A. von Bradisch. Zurich, Munich, Paris: Franklin Presse, 1935.

Briefe 1900-1909. Wien: Bermann-Fischer, 1937.

Briefewechsel zwischen George und Hofmannsthal, ed. Robert Boehringer. Berlin: Bondi, 1938.

Strauss, Richard and Hugo von Hofmannsthal. *Briefwechsel,* eds. Franz and Alice Strauss. Zürich: Atlantis, 1952.

Hofmannsthal, Hugo von and Eberhard von Bodenhausen. *Briefe der Freundschaft,* ed. Dora von Bodenhausen. Berlin: Eugen Diederichs, 1953.

Hofmannsthal, Hugo von and Rudolf Borchardt. *Briefwechsel,* eds. Marie Luise Borchardt and Herbert Steiner. Frankfurt am Main: Fischer, 1954.

Hofmannsthal, Hugo von and Carl J. Burckhart. *Briefwechsel,* ed. Carl J. Burckhart. Frankfurt am Main: Fischer, 1956.

Hofmannsthal, Hugo von and Arthur Schnitzler. *Briefwechsel,* eds. Therese Nickl and Heinrich Schnitzler. Frankfurt am Main: Fischer, 1964.

Hofmannsthal, Hugo von and Helene von Nostitz-Wallwitz. *Briefwechsel,* ed. Oswalt von Nostitz. Frankfurt am Main: Fischer, 1965.

Hofmannsthal, Hugo von and Edgar Karg von Bebenburg. *Briefwechsel,* ed. Mary E. Gilbert. Frankfurt am Main: Fischer, 1966.

Briefe an Marie Herzfeld, ed. Horst Weber. Heidelberg: Stiehm, 1967.

Hofmannsthal, Hugo von and Leopold von Andrian. *Briefwechsel*, ed. Walter Perl. Frankfurt am Main: Fischer, 1968.

Hofmannsthal, Hugo von and Willy Haas. *Ein Briefwechsel*, ed. Willy Haas. Berlin: Propyläen, 1968.

Hofmannsthal, Hugo and Harry Graf Kessler. *Briefwechsel 1898-1929*, ed. Hilde Burger. Frankfurt am Main: Insel, 1968.

Hofmannsthal, Hugo von and Josef Redlich. *Briefwechsel*, ed. Helga Fussgänger. Frankfurt am Main: Fischer, 1971.

Hofmannsthal, Hugo von and Richard Beer-Hoffmann. *Briefwechsel*, ed. Eugene Weber. Frankfurt am Main: Fischer, 1972.

Hofmannsthal, Hugo von and Ottonie von Degenfeld. *Briefwechsel*, ed. Marie Therese Miller-Degenfeld. Frankfurt am Main: 1974.

Hofmannsthal, Hugo von and Raoul Auernheimer. Correspondance, ed. Donald G. Daviau, *Modern Austrian Literature*, Vol. 7, Nos 3/4 (1974), 209-307.

Hofmannsthal, Hugo von and Rainer Maria Rilke. *Briefwechsel 1899-1925*, eds. Rudolf Hirsch and Ingeborg Schnack. Frankfurt am Main: Insel, 1978.

Hofmannsthal, Hugo von and Max Mell. *Briefwechsel*, eds. Margret Dietrich and Heinz Kindermann. Heidelberg: L. Schneider, 1982.

Schmujlow-Claassen, Ria and Hugo von Hofmannsthal. *Briefe. Aufsätze. Dokumente*, ed. Claudia Abrecht. Marbach am Neckar: J.G. Cotta, 1982.

Briefwechsel mit Ottonie Gräfin Degenfeld und Julie Freifrau von Wendelstadt, eds. Marie Therese Miller-Degenfeld and Eugene M. Weber. Frankfurt am Main: Fischer, 1986.

II.   Works in English

Electra. Trans. Arthur Symons New York: Brentano's, 1908.

The Rose-Bearer. Trans. Alfred Kalisch. Berlin: Fürstner, 1912.

Death and the Fool. Trans. Max Batt. Boston:Badger, 1913.

The Death of Titian. Trans. John Heard, Jr. Boston: Four Seas, 1914.

The Legend of Joseph. Trans. Alfred Kalisch. Berlin: Fürstner, 1914.

Venice Preserved. Trans. Elisabeth Walter. Boston: Badger, 1915.

Cristina's Journey Home. Trans. Roy Temple House. Boston: Badger, 1916.

The Play of Everyman. Trans. George Sterling and Richard Ordynski. San Francisco: A.M. Robertson, 1917.

The Lyrical Poems of Hugo von Hofmannsthal. Trans. Charles Wharton Stork. New Haven: Yale University Press, 1918.

Ariadne on Naxos. Trans. Alfred Kalisch. Berlin: Fürstner, 1922.

Helen in Egypt. Trans. Alfred Kalisch. Berlin: Fürstner, 1928.

Andreas, or the United. Trans. Marie D. Hottinger. London: Dent, 1936.

Selected Prose. Trans. Marie Hottinger and Tania and James Stern, New York: Pantheon, 1952. (Contains *Andreas, Moments in Greece, A Tale of the Cavalry,* "The Letter of Lord Chandos," and several other essays and short pieces of fiction.)

The Woman without a Shadow. Trans. Publicity Dept. Decca Record Co. London: Decca Record Co., 1957.

Poems and Verse Plays, ed. Michael Hamburger. New York: Pantheon, 1961. (Contains, in addition to the poems, *The Marriage of Zobeide.* Trans. Christopher Middleton, *The Emperor and the Witch.* Trans. Christopher Middleton, *The Little Theater of the World or the Fortunate Ones.* Trans. Michael Hamburger, *The Mine at Falun.* Trans. Michael Hamburger, *Death and the Fool.* Trans. Michael Hamburger.)

Selected Plays and Libretti, ed. Michael Hamburger. New York: Pantheon, 1963. (Contains *Electra.* Trans. Alfred Schwarz, *The Cavalier of the Rose.* Trans. Christoper Holme, *The Difficult Man.* Trans. Willa Muir, *The Salzburg Great Theater of the World.* Trans. Vernon Watkins, *The Tower.* Trans. Michael Hamburger, *Arabella.* Trans. Nora Wydenbruck and Christopher Middleton.)

Three Plays. Trans. Alfred Schwarz. Detroit: Wayne State Univ. Press, 1966. (Contians *Electra, Death and the Fool, The Tower.)*

Oedipus and the Sphinx. Trans. Gertrude Schoenbohm. In *Oedipus: Myth and Drama,* ed. Martin Kalisch. New York: Odyssey, 1968.

Correspondence

Strauss, Richard and Hugo von Hofmannsthal. A *Working Friendship.* Trans. Hanns Hammelmann and Ewald Osers. New York: Random House; London: Collins, 1961.

III.   Secondary Works in English

Bangerter, Lowell A. *Hugo von Hofmannsthal.* New York: Ungar, 1977.

Broch, Hermann. *Hugo von Hofmannsthal and His Time,* ed. Michael P.

Sternberg. Chicago: University Press, 1984.

Coghlan, Brian L. *Hofmannsthal's Festival Dramas.* Cambridge: Cambridge University Press, 1964.

Daviau, Donald G. and George J. Buelow. *The "Ariadne auf Naxos" of Hugo von Hofmannsthal and Richard Strauss.* Chapel Hill: University of North Carolina Press, 1975.

Evans, Arthur R., Jr., ed. *On Four Modern Humanists.* Princeton: Princeton University Press, 1970.

Gray, Ronald D. *German Tradition in Literature.* Cambridge: Cambridge University Press, 1966.

Hammelmann, Hanns A. *Hugo von Hofmannsthal.* London: Bowes and Bowes, 1957.

Kovach, Thomas. *Hofmannsthal and Symbolism.* New York, Bern, Frankfurt am Main: P. Lang, 1985.

Miles, David. *Hofmannsthal's Novel Andreas.* Princeton: Princeton University Press, 1972.

Norman, F., ed. *Hofmannsthal.* London: London Institute of Germanic Studies, 1963.

Segal, N. *The Banal Object: Theme and Thematics in Proust, Rilke, Hofmannsthal, and Sartre.* London: London Institute of Germanic Studies, 1981.

Sondrup, Steven P. *Hofmannsthal and the French Symbolist Tradition.* Bern, Frankfurt am Main: P. Lang, 1976.

IV.   Major Studies in German

Alewyn, Richard. *Uber Hugo von Hofmannsthal.* Göttingen: Vandenhoeck und Ruprecht, 1967.

Bauer, Sibylle, ed. *Hugo von Hofmannsthal.* Darmstadt: Wissenschaftliche Buchgesellschaft, 1968.

Erken, Günther. *Hofmannsthals dramatischer Stil.* Tübingen: Niemeyer, 1967.

Koch, Hans Albrecht. *Hugo von Hofmannsthal: Bibliographie 1964-1976.* Freiburg in Breisgau: Deutsches Seminar, 1976.

Weber, Horst. *Hugo von Hofmannsthal: Bibliographie des Schrifttums 1892-1963.* Berlin: DeGruyter, 1966.

Weber, Horst. *Hugo von Hofmannsthal Bibliographie: Werke, Briefe, Gespräche, Übersetzungen, Vertonungen.* Berlin and New York: DeGruyter, 1972.

Karl Kraus

Harry Zohn

The essential untranslatability of the Austrian satirist Karl Kraus has been axiomatic for a long time. This is why only a small fraction of his voluminous literary output has appeared in translation and Kraus is relatively unknown beyond the confines of the German-speaking world. There is much truth in Kraus's observation that "a linguistic work translated into another language is like someone going across the border without his skin and putting on the local garb on the other side."[1] The vitriolic Viennese, a man who hauled the powerful and the pitiful alike before a tribunal of total satire, was a legend in his lifetime (1874-1936), a person adored or vilified by many of his contemporaries. After a decade of desuetude his work was rediscovered and republished in Germany and Austria after the Second World War, and a number of books on Kraus in English as well as translations from his writings are available. Yet the problem of limited access to him remains. As Erich Heller put it, "Karl Kraus did not write 'in a language,' but through him the beauty, profundity, and accumulated moral experience of the German language assumed personal shape and became the crucial witness in the case this inspired prosecutor brought against his time."[2] Kraus's timelessness (and at long last his *relative* exportability and translatability) derive at least in part from certain parallels between his age and ours, and from the need of our age for his vibrant pacifism, his defense of the spirit against dehumanizing tendencies, and his "linguistic-moral imperative," which equates purity of language with purity of thought, a return to the sources of spiritual strength, and steadfastness of moral purpose.

Karl Kraus lived a life that oscillated between love and hate. ("Hate must make a person productive," he once wrote; "otherwise one might as well love.")³ He was born on 28 April 1874 at Jičín, a small Bohemian town northeast of Prague, the son of a prosperous manufacturer of paper bags. In 1877 the family moved to Vienna, and Kraus spent the rest of his life in that city, with which he—like Sigmund Freud, another Czech-born Jew—had a love-hate relationship. His was a family constellation that was typical at the turn of the century: the sons of Central European Jewish businessmen—often self-made men and heads of patriarchally organized families—rejected the family business in favor of a literary career. Franz Kafka, Stefan Zweig, Franz Werfel, and others joined Kraus in following this path.

Having attended the University of Vienna without taking a degree, Kraus attempted a career on the stage. His failure as an actor turned him irrevocably to journalism and literature, though his talent for mimicry and parody found ample expression in his later public readings. He once said of himself that he was perhaps the first writer to experience his writing as an actor: "When I give a reading, it is not acted literature, but what l write is written acting."⁴ In 1892 Kraus began to contribute book reviews, theater criticism, and other kinds of prose to various newspapers and periodicals. In his twenties, however, the satirical impulse became too strong for any sort of accommodation, and Kraus rejected the prospect of becoming a sort of "culture clown" absorbed by a deceptively slack and effete environment. Because work within the Establishment seemed to be hedged in with multifarious taboos and considerations of a personal and commercial nature, Kraus turned down a job offer from Vienna's most prestigious daily, the *Neue Freie Presse*, and founded his own journal. The first issue of *Die Fackel* (The Torch) appeared on April 1, 1899 and turned out to be anything but an April Fool's joke. Kraus at first enlisted the services of other writers, though these never contributed more than about one-third of this aggressive journal's contents. From 1911 to 1936 *Die Fackel* carried Kraus's writings exclusively: "I no longer have any collaborators. I used to be envious of them. They repel those readers whom I want to lose myself."⁵ This statement indicates the uncompromising nature of this unique satirical journal in which Kraus effectively clipped his era and put it between quotation marks. Quotation is the hallmark of his satire, and in its use he was guided by the conviction that what was most unspeakable about his age could be spoken only by the age itself.

The thirty-seven volumes of *Die Fackel* represent a gigantic effort to fashion the imperishable profile of an age from such highly perishable materials as newspaper reports. They contain the major part of Kraus's literary output; most of the satirist's publications in book form represent distillations from the pages of *Die Fackel*. The journal is a history of the times, a running autobiography, a world stage on which Kraus dramatized himself and his mission, and above all an enormous pillory. The small-format red *Fackel* had a remarkable satiric *genius loci*; material that might have attracted scant attention elsewhere received heightened relevance in its pages, and "little" people became "great" there. Thus Kraus's periodical continued to have numerous "contributors," albeit unwilling and unwitting ones. J. P. Stern has attempted to assess the uniqueness and significance of the *Fackel* in these words: "To delimit the intellectual region in which to place this journal, one would have to think of Péguy minus his Catholicism and patriotism; of F. R. Leavis uninvolved in any education 'establishment,' plus genius; of the satirist in George Bernard Shaw as milk-and-water to Kraus's vitriol; of the early Wittgenstein's equation of 'language' and 'world'; of H. L. Mencken's criticism of the leisure class; of the poet Siegfried Sassoon's 'scarlet major at the base'; of the early Evelyn Waugh's satirical type-casting—and all this would have to be translated into the peculiar medium of Vienna."[6].

Kraus began to write when a century top-heavy with historical and cultural events and innovations was approaching its end. In the specific case of his homeland, which was both the source and the target of his satire, the Habsburg dynasty, worn out after a reign of some six hundred years, was coming to an end, and so was Austria-Hungary, the political constellation of its last half-century. The reign of Emperor Franz Joseph, a prime target of Kraus's satire, spanned almost seven decades and witnessed the slow, inevitable dismantling of an old political, social, and cultural structure. It was a time of overrefinement and overripeness to the point of decay and death, and Kraus's marked apocalyptic stance as a "late" warner and prophet of doom derived from his epoch's *Zeitgeist*: transitoriness, disintegration, and inner insecurity. Ironically, Karl Kraus shared his initials with Imperial-Royal Austria, the *kaiserlich-königlich* empire, designated by K. K.—a country which Robert Musil in his novel *Der Mann ohne Eigenschaften* (The Man Without Qualities) called "Kakania." Kraus came to regard this centrally located empire as a proving ground for world destruction.

Kraus's first major satirical work was a literary satire entitled *Die demolirte Literatur*, a witty diatribe about the razing of a Vienna café frequented by the literati. His pamphlet *Eine Krone für Zion* is a lampoon of political Zionism, the creation of Theodor Herzl, an editor of the *Neue*

Freie Presse, written from the standpoint of an assimilated European Jew and sympathizer with Socialism. Kraus has been called everything from "a shining example of Jewish self-hatred" (Theodor Lessing) to "an arch-Jew" (Berthold Viertel).[7] His writings lend support to all of these judgments, but it must be borne in mind that the man who once noted that according to the latest census Vienna had 2,030,834 inhabitants—"that is, 2,030,833 souls and myself"[8]— refused to be part of *any* ethnic, political, or social group. In 1899 he left the Jewish fold, and after remaining *konfessionslos* (religiously unaffiliated) for some years he secretly converted to Catholicism in 1911. Eleven years later he left the Catholic church again to protest publicly what he regarded as its unwholesome participation in pseudo-artistic and commercial aspects of the Salzburg Festival, the creation of two men he disliked, the poet Hugo von Hofmannsthal and the theatrical director Max Reinhardt. Frank Field's view that Kraus's Jewishness is "of vital importance in understanding the particular extremism and sense of the apocalyptic which pervades his work" and that Kraus "attacked his own people in the same way that the prophets of the Old Testament castigated the unworthiness of the Israelites fur the trust which God had placed in them"[9] is supported by Kraus's statement of 1913: "l believe I can say about myself that l go along with the development of Judaism up to the Exodus, but that I don't participate in the dance around the Golden Calf and, from that point on, share only in those characteristics which were also found in the defenders of God and in the avengers of a people gone astray."[10]

If Kraus's early satiric writings were directed largely against standard aspects of corruption, the second period of his creativity may be dated from the appearance of his essay "Sittlichkeit und Kriminalität" (Morality and Criminal Justice) in 1902, which became the title essay of a book-length collection issued six years later. On the basis of contemporary court cases Kraus concerned himself with the glaring contrast between private und public morality and with the hypocrisy inherent in the administration of justice in Austria. In turning a powerful spotlight on a male-dominated society with its double standards, its shameless encroachment on privacy, and its sensation-mongering press, Kraus expressed many ideas and attitudes that are germane to present-day concerns: women's rights, child abuse, sexual mores, education, "gay liberation." The gloomy, bitter wit of this collection gave way to lighter humor in Kraus's next book, *Die chinesische Mauer* (The Great Wall of China (1910)). Writing about Peary's contested discovery of the North Pole in

1909, Kraus remarked with awful prescience that "progress celebrates Pyrrhic victories over nature, making purses out of human skin."[11]

Kraus's unremitting satirical warfare against the press was motivated by his view of journalism as a vast switchboard that concentrated and activated the forces of corruption and dissolution. Recognizing a disturbing identity between *Zeit* and *Zeitung*, his age and the newspapers it spawned, with *Worte* (words) usurping and destroying *Werte* (values) and news reports *causing* as well as *describing* actions, he had apocalyptic visions of the destruction of the world by the black magic of printer's ink. One of Kraus's aphorisms belongs in this context: "One ought to acknowledge the significance of the fact that gunpowder and printer's ink were invented simultaneously."[12] Kraus was convinced that the moving forces of his time were not entrenched in parliaments but in editorial offices controlling capital and the government, influencing public opinion as well as the arts and sciences, and destroying thought, taste, receptivity, and imagination. Decades before Hermann Hesse coined the phrase "das feuilletonistische Zeitalter" in his utopian novel *Das Glasperlenspiel (The Glass-Bead Game)* Kraus recognized his age as "the age of the feuilleton" in which newspaper reports took precedence over events, form eclipsed substance, and the style, the atmosphere, the "package" were all-important. The press was seen as the polluter of language and poisoner of the human spirit. In his polemic essay "Heine and the Consequences" (1910) Kraus excoriated the nineteenth-century German-Jewish poet and essayist for introducing the feuilleton in Germany and providing an inheritance on which journalism has drawn ever since: its function as an intermediary between art and life and as a parasite on both, creating a deleterious, linguistically deceitful mixture of intellect and information, reportage and literature. "To write a feuilleton," wrote Kraus, "is to curl locks on a bald pate; but the public likes these curls better than a lion's mane of thought."[13]

"My language is the common prostitute that I turn into a virgin."[14] This aphorism illuminates both Kraus's mission and his method. While many poets have striven to restore pristine purity to language and to make it once more a serviceable vehicle for poetic expression, Kraus's obsession with language went considerably beyond such a pursuit. He saw an absolute congruity between word and world, language and life; the unworthiness of his "language-forsaken" age was for him defined by its treatment of language. For him language was the moral criterion and accreditation for a writer or speaker. J. P. Stern, to be sure, suspects that what he has called Kraus's "moral-linguistic imperative" may be an indication that the satirist was "succumbing to the curse of Vienna—the city in which the experiment of replacing morality and politics by the life of the imagination was carried to the point of moral paralysis and political disintegration."15 To Kraus language was the mother of thought, not its handmaiden, the divining rod capable of finding hidden sources of thought. Despite the fact, however, that Kraus raised language to an almost apocalyptic significance, he never developed a theory or philosophy of language, being essentially an unsystematic and anti-philosophical thinker. Yet the Vienna Circle of logical positivists was greatly interested in Kraus's relationship to language, and there are certain parallels between Kraus's thought and the ideas of Ludwig Wittgenstein, the foremost figure of that circle— for example, their insight into the fundamental connection between, or even identification of, aesthetics and ethics. Wittgenstein learned from Kraus how to think in and through language, yet he thought *against* language, which was for him an obstacle to thought that had to be painstakingly surmounted, whereas Kraus fought *for* language, mystically uncovering thought through it. What Kraus and Wittgenstein really had in common was their endeavor to fashion a fortress capable of standing inviolate against the corruption of language and morals they saw all around them.

It is all but impossible to convey in English an idea of Karl Kraus's style. Its allusiveness, its attention to verbal associations, and its artful plays upon words make reading Kraus in the original a rare intellectual delight. Kraus was not only a master of the art of punning, with a deep seriousness underlying his verbal wit, but also a skillful practitioner of various subtle stylistic devices based upon the spirit of German grammar and Kraus's enjoyment of what he termed *Sprachlehre*. Punning often constitutes a *reductio ad absurdum* of language and serves to test the truthfulness or mendaciousness of a statement or a mentality. The aphorism was a literary form which Kraus, an admirer of his forerunners J. C. Lichtenberg and Johann Nestroy, used extensively. Some aphorisms were distilled from a longer text in prose or poetry; in other instances an aphorism was lyrically expanded into an epigram or served as the nucleus of a prose piece.

Kraus's poetry was not fully appreciated in his lifetime, being decried as unoriginal, too cerebral, and not elemental enough. But this poetry has increasingly come to be regarded as an integral and important part of his *oeuvre*, and critics like Werner Kraft, Leopold Liegler, and Caroline Kohn have written perceptively about this aspect of Kraus's creativity. When one perceives that much of Kraus's prose is lyrical or poetic, it is easy to see his poetry as only a special coinage from the same mint.

Kraus began to write poetry relatively late in life; his first poems did not appear in the *Fackel* until 1912 and 1913. But then nine volumes of poetry and rhymed epigrams were published between 1916 and 1930 under the modest collective title *Worte in Versen*. In his verse Kraus admittedly was an epigone rather than an innovator, indebted to the Goethean and Shakespearean traditions. He was "unoriginal" in that he usually needed some occasion to trigger his art, as an oyster needs the irritation of a grain of sand to produce a pearl. The poems are seldom "romantic" in the sense of being products of rapture or intoxication; they spring, rather, from the rapture of language and logic.

Some of Kraus's poems are versified glosses and polemics, lyrical versions of Fackel texts, or satiric ideas given purified and aesthetically appealing form; others represent autobiographical excursions. Their abstraction and concision often presuppose familiarity with Kraus's other works, his life, and his personality; in this sense the poems add up to a lyrical *roman à clef*. "I do not write poetry and then work with dross," Kraus once wrote; "I turn the dross into poetry and organize rallies in support of poetry."[16] To a certain extent Kraus's poetry is *Gedankenlyrik* in Friedrich Schiller's sense — poetry with a cargo of thought, reflecting a tradition coming to an end and an effort to preserve that tradition. The satirical poems are really *Gebrauchslyrik*, functional verse, pithy poetry with a purpose. Yet Kraus's poetry also represents a kind of satirist's holiday in that the poet, so widely regarded as a hater, is here free to reveal himself fully and unabashedly in his love of mankind, the human spirit, nature, and animals. In this sense it represents the "yea" of a great naysayer. Poetry to Kraus was like a freer, purer world, one harking back to the German classical tradition, in which the poet, freed from the goads of the satiric occasion and the burden of an ever-wakeful moral conscience, was able to reflect at leisure on love, nature, dreams, and wonderment.

The word *Ursprung* (origin, or source) figures prominently in Kraus's thought and poetry. In his orphic epigram "Zwei Läufer" (Two Runners, 1910) Kraus depicts two antithetical forces alive in the human spirit, one that he loves and one that he hates. The world is perceived as a circuitous route back to the *Ursprung*. Intellectuality may be the wrong road, but it does lead back to immediacy; satire is a roundabout way to poetry; and poetry is to Kraus a philosophical or linguistic detour on the way to a lost paradise. Kraus saw himself as being midway between

Ursprung and *Untergang*, the origin or source of all things and the end of the world (or of the human spirit) as conjured up by his satiric vision, and he viewed language as the only means of going back to the origin: the origin that was forever the goal. This *Ursprung* represents a kind of naive realism, a secular idea of Creation that is diametrically opposed to the tendency of speculative philosophy to make *homo cogitans*, cerebral man, the center of reality. In contrast to this Kraus posits the unity of feeling and form from which all art, morality, and truth spring. This world of purity constitutes a timeless counterpoise to the world against which Kraus the satirist struggled, and such an inviolate nature stands in mute yet eloquent contrast to a contemporary world and society which Kraus, in a sardonic pun fully comprehensible only to those familiar with German synonymous prefixes, perceived not as a *Gegenwart* (present time) but as a *Widerwart* (repulsive age).

In his poetry Kraus was guided by his conviction that the quality of a poem depended on the moral stature and ethical mission of the poet. In his view a satirist was only a deeply hurt lyricist, the artist wounded by the ugliness of the world. In *Worte in Versen* rhyme and meaning are inseparably fused. Kraus's conception of rhyme is similar to that of the German Romantic critic Friedrich Schlegel who described it as the surprising reunion of friendly ideas after a long separation. To express an idea from Kraus's poem "Der Reim" (The Rhyme) in a bit of macaronic verse, "Rhyme is the landing shore/ for two thoughts *en rapport*." Caroline Kohn has classified Kraus's poetic output under these rubrics: Women, Desire, Love; Nature; Personal, Philosophical; Artist, Language; Dream; Society; Justice; Clichés, Ink, Press; Technology, War; Vienna, Austria; Berlin, Germany.[17]

Two of Kraus's best-known poems refer to his nocturnal working habits. "Nächtliche Stunde" (Nocturnal Hour), set to music by Eugen Auerbach in 1929, is a profound and poignant expression of Kraus's situation written with great visionary power and economy of syntax and symbolism. It is structurally notable for the recurring unrhymed first and last line of each of its three stanzas and the reiteration of transitoriness in the opening line of each. There is an increase in inwardness and depth until the final synthesis of night, winter, life, spring, and death. As Kraus once pointed out, three times the unrhymed last line belongs to the bird's voice, which accompanies the experience of work through the stages of night, winter, and life. What the poet considers, weighs, and grades as he works is presumably the possibility of changing this "language-forsaken" world through his efforts; a hero of creative work in Thomas Mann's sense, he continues to do his duty even as death approaches. The no less beautiful poem "Der Tag" (The Day), set to music by Kraus's longtime piano accompanist Franz Mittler, is also based on the theme night-day-death. As the day breaks through the window, daring to disturb the claustrophobic intensity of the satirist's nocturnal labors, the bleary-eyed writer expresses surprise at the fact that the impure, desecrated day can have the audacity to dawn after an apocalyptic night of struggle with the affairs of an ungodly, corrupt world—matters which the *Zeitgeist* keeps presenting in violation of an ideal, undefiled realm of pure humanity. The satirist has borne witness to the possibility of such humanity and has in mute, joyless toil erected an edifice of words in its support. The *memento mori* provided by a hearse outside carrying some poor wretch to his or her final resting place gives the satirist an awareness of earthly evanescence and fills him with boundless sympathy with human suffering. Yet his self-effacing fanatical work in the service of the word, his ceaseless defense of language, and his search for eternal truths as a bulwark against the encroachments of the age is a necessary humanizing function with distinct religious overtones. His prayer is for the poor soul outside as well as for himself, but especially for a mankind gone astray and bound for perdition. Yet it is properly understood only in a larger context. Franz Kafka once described his obsessive writing as a form of prayer, and this was also Kraus's conception of his own work. One of his aphorisms is pertinent here: "When I take up my pen, nothing can happen to me. Fate, remember that!"[18]

Ernst Krenek, who came under Kraus's spell at an early age, has included settings of both "Nächtliche Stunde" and "Der Tag" in his song cycle *Durch die Nacht* (Through the Night), composed in 1930-1931, which also contains five other Kraus poems. "Schnellzug" (Fast Train), written in 1920 and set by Eugen Auerbach, has the evanescence and perceived meaninglessness of life as its theme and the dichotomy between inside and outside as its focus. The poet's staleness on a dirty crowded train is contrasted with the lucid yet unspecific and non-concrete landscape outside which tends to blur and blunt his perceptions. Though he is forced to stay aboard with the aimless multitude of his traveling companions, his disgust at his situation is a kind of rebellion. Being locked into his life of dedication and self-abnegation, he is fated to yearn for integration into the vanishing scenery.

A number of Kraus's poems are tributes to friends and other people he admired. Cases in point are "An einen alten Lehrer" (To an Old

Teacher), a celebration of Heinrich Sedlmayer, his German and Latin
teacher; "Die Schauspielerin" (The Actress) and "Annie Kalmar", both in
memory of the first of several women of uncommon physical and spiritual
beauty in Kraus's life, a talented actress who died in 1901 at a tragically
early age; "Peter Altenberg" (1919), a poetic obituary of one of the few
contemporary writers whom Kraus befriended; and "An meinen Drucker"
(To my printer), a birthday tribute to Kraus's faithful printer Georg
Jahoda. A number of satirical poems and songs form parts of Kraus's
plays. "Gebet" (prayer) is spoken by the Grumbler, the Kraus figure in
The Last Days of Mankind, as is "Mit der Uhr in der Hand" (With
Stopwatch in Hand), based on a 1916 news item about a submarine sinking a fully loaded troop transport in the Mediterranean in forty-three sec-
onds. Also from that play is the trenchantly funny self-exculpatory ditty
sung by Emperor Franz Joseph in his sleep. "Das Schoberlied"
(Schober's Song) from *Die Unüberwindlichen* (The Unconquerable) is a
mordant self-portrait of Vienna's police chief and Austria's sometime
chancellor, and "Das Lied von der Presse" (The Song of the Press), from
the literary satire *Literatur oder Man wird doch da sehn* (Literature, or
We'll See About That, 1921) sums up Kraus's feelings about the press
("At first, in the beginning/ there only was the press/ and then the world
came spinning/ to join our great success" in the translation by L. Golden
and H. Zohn). Among Kraus's autobiographical poems are "Bunte
Begebenheiten" (Colorful Goings-On) about the Salzburg Festival and its
commercialization and vulgarization, for which Kraus blamed its prime
movers, Hugo von Hofmannsthal and Max Reinhardt as well as the
Catholic church; and "Nach dreißig Jahren" (After Thirty Years), subtitled
"Retrospect of Vanity", which finds the satirist looking back on three
decades of *Die Fackel* and taking stock of his achievements.

Kraus evidently needed an idealized private sphere of wholeness,
purity, and love to provide a counterpoint (and counterpoise) to the
cacophony of corruption that he perceived all around him. Such a sphere
was provided for him from 1913 to the end of his life by a Czech aristocrat, Baroness Sidonie Nádhérny von Borutin. Her family estate at
Janowitz (Janovice, near Prague) became Kraus's *buen retiro*, a Garden
of Eden six and a half hours from Vienna. A modern mythology about a
Tristan and Isolde living through the last days of mankind is multifariously
expressed in Kraus's letters to "Sidi" (long believed lost, but rediscovered
in 1969 and published five years later), in many of Kraus's poems
addressed to her or inspired by shared experiences, and in the dedication

of several volumes to the woman who, as Kraus once put it, had a true appreciation of only two books, "the railroad time-table and *Worte in Versen*." Kraus proposed marriage to Sidonie on several occasions, but he was rejected and remained unmarried. Their relationship, however, survived Sidonie's engagement to one man and marriage to another. Among the approximately fifty "Sidi poems" are "Fernes Licht mit nahem Schein" (Distant Light with Glow So Near) and "Wiese im Park" (Lawn in the Park), a poem with tragic undertones written on a sad Sunday in November 1915. The poet wants to relieve the darkness of the times by recapturing the timeless past, in particular his childhood. But his firm footing and reposeful communion with nature vanish, the spell is broken, and the present bleakly reasserts itself in the form of a "dead day."

Finally, mention must be made of Kraus's translations from Shakespeare. Kraus, who knew little or no English (or any foreign language, for that matter), used existing translations of Shakespeare as a basis for versions (*Nachdichtungen*, free re-creations in the spirit of the original rather than accurate translations) which, he felt, would capture Shakespeare's spirit more fully and would add it to the treasure house of German letters more enduringly than other translators had done. In this effort he was guided by his superior poetic sense and his unerring linguistic instinct. Commenting on Kraus's edition of the *Sonnets*, Albert Bloch (Kraus's first translator into English) remarked that if Kraus had known English, his versions would not have been so beautiful. "Perhaps the result is not always immediately identifiable as Shakespeare," the reviewer admits; "certainly it is always undeniably Karl Kraus...."[19]

The life and work of Karl Kraus were eminently theatrical, and he served the theater in a variety of capacities: as a critic, translator, adapter, playwright, reciter, and—last and definitely least—a sometime actor. Kraus's mode of thinking and writing was essentially theatrical, and *Die Fackel* may be regarded as a theater in itself, an enormous world stage on which Kraus dramatized himself and his ethical, didactic, aesthetic, and, above all, satiric mission. His celebrated prose style and his poetry are replete with expressive, rhetorical, and theatrical elements. In his life and work, his criticism and showmanship, ethics and aesthetics were invariably linked.

Many of Kraus's feuds were carried on with theater people (Bahr, Bauer, Buchbinder, Bukovics), and he came to take a highly personal and polemical view of such celebrated actors as Tressler, Kainz, Odilon, Moissi (all negative), Girardi, Sonnenthal, Wolters (all positive). All his life he championed and yearned for the old Burgtheater with its perceived dignity, integrity, artistry, and congruence of ethical and aesthetic purpose. Later in life he evoked that theater's traditional style in programmatic opposition to what he regarded as the corruption, commercialism, politicization, charlatanry, sensationalism, and "feuilletonism" of the superproductions of directors like Leopold Jessner, Erwin Piscator, and Max Reinhardt. Kraus drew a distinction between *Buchdrama* (literary drama and *Bühnendrama* (stage drama), and he increasingly came to take a reader-centered view, regarding drama as literature in which language and ideas were paramount and the reader's imagination was enlisted. (His all but unperformable play *Die letzten Tage der Menschheit* may be viewed as an extreme form of *Buchdrama*.) Between 1916 and 1925 three out of four of Kraus's readings were devoted to plays by other authors, and these included *Bühnendramen*, or actors' vehicles, though Kraus was aware that he could not have acted the roles he read in such austere fashion.

The outbreak of the war in 1914 marked a turning point in Kraus's life and creativity, and the outraged convictions of the pacifist and moralist inspired him to produce his most powerful and most characteristic work. Following several months of silence at a time when other writers were rushing to the ramparts of rhyme and boarding the bandwagon of banality, Kraus delivered a sardonic public lecture on November 19, "In These Great Times...," which may be regarded as the germ cell of his extensive wartime output. He viewed the war as the tragedy of mankind enacted by figures with all the stature, substance, and truthfulness of characters in an operetta. Without waiting for the detachment that time might have brought he set to work on his magnum opus as a dramatist (and satirist), the powerful pacifistic play *Die letzten Tage der Menschheit*, a monumental dramatic repository of most of his satiric themes and techniques. Most of the 209 scenes of its five acts were first sketched during the summers of 1915, 1916, and 1917; the rhymed prologue dates from July 1915 and the Epilogue from July 1917. In his preface to this early example of a documentary drama Kraus wrote: "The performance of this drama, which would, in earthly terms, require about ten evenings, is intended for a theater on Mars. Theatergoers of this world would not be able to bear it. For it is blood of their blood, and its contents are those real, unthinkable years, out of reach for the wakefulness of the mind, inaccessible to any memory and preserved only in gory dreams, when characters from an operetta enacted the tragedy of mankind...."[20] Having refused offers by Reinhardt and Piscator to stage this play, which covers more than 800 printed pages, Kraus permitted only performances of the Epilogue in Vienna (1923, 1924) and Berlin (1930) in addition to reading his own "stage version" in 1930. After World War ll, however, an abridgment for the stage and television by Heinrich Fischer and Leopold Lindtberg paved the way for fully staged performances of the complete work in Basel and Vienna (directed by Hans Hollmann) as well as Dublin (Robert David MacDonald).

Die letzten Tage der Menschheit, originally subtitled "Ein Angsttraum" (A Nightmare), begins with the voice of a newspaper vendor and ends with the voice of God. lt is set in public rather than private places— in the streets of Vienna and Berlin, in offices and barracks, churches and cafés, amusement places and military hospitals, railroad stations and army posts, "in a hundred scenes and hells."[21] The play's 500 characters include pastors and prostitutes, chauvinists and showmen, professors and politicians, teachers and tradesmen, soldiers and sycophants, children and churchmen, inspectors and innkeepers, journalists and jesters, profiteers and policemen, editors and emperors. There are actual persons as well as fictitious ones, and all of them reveal (and often judge) themselves by their authentic speech patterns. The play is a striking amalgam of naturalistic and symbolic elements. The scenes are by turns lyrical and prosaic, comic and tragic; but even what seems to be purely humorous acquires a certain grimness from the context and usually appears as gallows humor. The play has no hero or plot in the conventional Aristotelian sense; it is episodic, with scenes recurring in cyclical patterns and inexorably grinding on to a cataclysmic conclusion. The scenes range in length from one-line "black-outs" in the tradition of the cabaret (more often than not, what is blacked out is the human spirit) to lengthy dialogues, monologues, dramatized editorials, and phantasmagoric tableaux. About one-half of this dramatic typology of man's inhumanity to man consists of authentic (though artistically presented) newspaper articles, war communiqués, court judgments, advertisements, letters, and other documents. Even the scenes and events invented by Kraus reproduce with uncanny accuracy the language of the "great times," which becomes the index of the Nietzschean vision of the disintegration of European culture and of a dying way of life.

"A sorcerer's apprentice seems to have utilized the absence of his master," wrote Kraus in reference to Goethe's poem; 'but now there is blood instead of water."[22] Kraus's wartime waxworks of "Goethe's people" and his fellow Austrians includes such characters as the two fatuous privy councillors who vie with each other in mangling one of the glories of German poetry, Goethe's "Wanderer's Night Song"; the Bavarian story-teller Ludwig Ganghofer, who yodels his way along the front, writes war reports for the *Neue Freie Presse*, and swaps jokes with an appreciative Kaiser; the "patriotic" pastors of the "praise-the-Lord-and-pass-the-ammu-nition" variety, to whom Kraus gives the names of birds of prey; a judge who celebrates his hundredth death sentence; the two fat Berlin profiteers who disport themselves in the snows of the Swiss Alps; Alice Schalek, the first woman accredited to the Austrian army as a correspondent, whose gushy effusions in a denatured language about the emotions of the com-mon man, "liberated humanity," and "the fever of the adventure" and whose search for "human-interest" material amidst destruction, degrada-tion, and death made her a macabre joke and a frequent Krausian target; the grocer Chramosta, whom followers of the contemporary Austrian cul-tural scene will recognize as an ancestor of the cabaret character "Herr Karl"; and the "happy hangman," another all-too-familiar type, who appears on a picture postcard (used by Kraus as an illustration) holding his paws over the head of an executed man while the grinning or smug-look-ing bystanders gather around the lifeless dangling body. Another prime target of Kraus's satire was Moriz Benedikt ("Maledikt"), the editor of the *Neue Freie Presse*, whom Kraus depicted as the "Lord of the Hyenas" and the "Antichrist." Old Man Biach, one of Kraus's fictitious characters and an assiduous mouther of Benedikt's editorials, dies, as it were, of linguis-tic convolution and spiritual poisoning when even he can no longer recon-cile the harsh reality with all the journalistic double-talk and governmental double-think. The twenty-three conversations between the Grumbler, a Kraus figure, and the Optimist function as the choruses of a tragedy; they represent oases of relative repose and reflection. In his running commen-tary the Grumbler constitutes the ever-present anguished conscience of the times and the voice of reason, presenting eschatological views rather than espousing *Realpolitik*, and displaying the kind of conscience, compassion, and consistency that might have saved European civilization.

While the Prologue, ranging from June 28, 1914, the day on which the successor to the Austrian throne, Archduke Franz Ferdinand, and his wife were assassinated, to their third-class funeral, shows with grim real-ism what lies underneath the veneer of the vaunted Austrian *Gemüt-lichkeit*, or easy-going geniality, surrealistic touches are introduced as the tragedy (and the war) rush toward their cataclysmic conclusion. "Corybants and Maenads" spew forth word fragments, and there are choruses of Gas Masks, Frozen Soldiers, 1200 Drowned Horses, and the Dead Children of the Lusitania. The rhymed Epilogue is a harrowing poetic satire raised to a supernatural plane in which many motifs of the play are recapitulated in cinematographic or operatic form. After the silence that follows utter destruction God's voice is heard speaking the words of Kaiser Wilhelm II at the beginning of the war: "Ich habe es nicht gewollt" (I did not will it so)[23]—possibly a final glimmer of hope that man can yet redeem himself and work toward a better destiny.

In 1921 Kraus published *Literatur oder Man wird doch da sehn,* a "magical operetta" satirizing a literary movement in general and Franz Werfel, a Kraus apostle turned apostate, in particular. For the second time Kraus has occasion to demolish a literature (Expressionism rather than Young Vienna), this time not with witty glosses and *aperçus* but by letting it manifest its unworth and speak its death warrant directly. Again the scene is a Vienna café, not the Griensteidl but the Central, a place which Kraus peoples with bourgeois bacchantes and meandering maenads. The Werfel figure is named Johann Wolfgang, and the pretentious, pompous son rebels against his business-minded father in true Expressionistic fashion. Kraus satirizes among other things the effect which Expressionist poets and playwrights, fashionable pseudo-philosophical essayists, psychoanalysts, and other "redeemers" have had on the impressionable *hoi polloi.* The parodistic play includes one of Kraus's best-remembered *chansons,* the "Song of the Press," a concentrated account of Creation sung by a character named Schwarz-Drucker (Ink-Printer), an operetta version of Moriz Benedikt.

In *Traumstück* (Dream Play), a one-act verse drama written at Christmastime 1922, lyrical and grotesque elements intermingle. Kraus himself described this surrealistic fantasy as "a series of visions of dozing and dreaming, born of the experiences of the war, the horrors of the postwar period, bad life and bad knowledge, newspapers, psychoanalysis, love, language, and dreams themselves."[24] A pessimistic monologue of the poet is succeeded by the dream world in which "The Psychoanals" identify themselves as killers of dreams, blackeners of beauty, compilers of complexes, purveyors of neuroses, and exhibitors of inhibitions— people to whom even Goethe's poems are nothing but badly repressed material. After several other visions and encounters the Poet awakens to the insight that the dream has really clarified for him his mission in life: to serve the Word and thus give permanence to his life.

The legacy of Annie Kalmar, an actress whom Kraus admired and loved at the turn of the century and who died tragically young, also shaped

202   Harry Zohn

the one-act play *Traumtheater* (Dream Theater), dedicated to her memory and published in 1924. Here Kraus has the beloved actress "play love" for him so that his love might be purged of jealousy. This improvisatory philosophical-dramatic vignette consists of very brief scenes in both prose and verse which in reality and in dreams explore and illuminate the interpersonal relationships among the Actress, the Poet, the Director, the Old Ass (a member of the audience and a father symbol), and Walter, a high-school student.

Kraus regarded his reading of *Wolkenkuckucksheim* (Cloud-cuckooland), a "Fantastic Verse Play in Three Acts," before an audience of workers as a most beautiful and most fitting celebration of the Austrian Republic. Based on a German translation of Aristophanes' *Ornithes (The Birds)*, this "apotheosis of the Republican idea"[25] (which has never been performed on the stage) reflects an old tradition of the Viennese popular theater, the travesty of classical motifs. Two Athenians who find conditions in their native city (a barely disguised Vienna) unbearable emigrate and become birds in a Bird City. But soon enough the coffeehouse culture, complete with prying journalists, avant-garde poets, psychoanalysts, and warmongers, catches up with them and sets the stage for The Last Days of Birdkind. The play does have a happy ending, however, and the Lark ends it with a Shakespearean solo: All have been dreaming; the confusion of purpose and function is now ended; the birds do not wish to be worshiped by men as gods; no more violence or wars. "We dreamt of power, we live as republicans....*Nie wieder Krieg!*"[26]

With his last play, *Die Unüberwindlichen*, printed in 1928, Kraus returned to the form of the documentary drama. This "Postwar Play in Four Acts" memorializes two of the satirist's feuds: with Imre Békessy, a corrupt Hungarian-born press czar, and Johannes Schober, Vienna's chief of police and Austria's sometime chancellor. Kraus not only accused Schober of collusion with Békessy but also held him responsible for the police riot of July 1927 following the burning of the Ministry of Justice by people enraged by the recent acquittal of killers. "Once again, as in the last days of a mankind whose mysterious continued existence has now given us these scenes," wrote Kraus in his preface, "documents have become figures, reports have materialized as forms, and clichés stand on two legs."[27] In this *pièce à clef*, which combines a Békessiad with a Schoberiad, Kraus appears as Arkus and Békessy as Barkassy (*Barkasse* means "cash money"). Schober is made to sing the mordantly self-revealing "Schoberlied" to a tune of the satirist's own devising. By the time this play was written, Kraus, prevailing over a clique and a claque, had managed almost single-handedly to kick the crook out of Vienna ("Hinaus aus Wien mit dem Schuft" was the slogan of his campaign against Békessy.) Yet despite the fact that such eminent actors as Peter Lorre, Ernst Ginsberg, Leonhard Steckel, and Kurt Gerron starred in the Berlin premiere of Kraus's witty and hard-hitting documentary play in October of 1929, it was evident that plays of standard length were not Kraus's forte. Further performances were cancelled at the behest of the Austrian Embassy, but there was a revival in Leipzig two years later. Kraus remained painfully aware that his admirers turned detractors and the combined forces of the press, the financiers, and the police in the first Austrian Republic were truly unconquerable.

Shakespeare was a living force throughout Kraus's life. Between 1916 and 1936 Kraus recited his adaptations of thirteen plays of the Bard; seven of these as well as Kraus's versions of the *Sonnets* were published in book form between 1930 and 1935. Since Kraus knew little or no English, he was dependent on existing translations; he used these as a basis for renditions that reflect his unerring dramatic, poetic, and, above all, linguistic sense. 123 of his recitals were devoted to Jacques Offenbach. Having attended performances of Offenbach operettas at a summer theater as a child, Kraus developed a lifelong affinity with the man he regarded as the greatest musical dramatist of all times and championed him in programmatic opposition to the Austrian operetta in its "silver age," which he regarded as inane and deleterious. Kraus presented fourteen of Offenbach's operettas, several in his adaptation, with only a piano accompanist; although he could not read music, he sang all the roles. The *couplets* he sang in Offenbach's and Nestroy's works often included Kraus's own *Zusatzstrophen*, or topical stanzas. Kraus regularly performed dramas of Gerhart Hauptmann, Bert Brecht, Goethe, Gogol, Raimund, and Frank Wedekind. In 1905 Kraus arranged the first Viennese performances of Wedekind's controversial Lulu play *Die Büchse der Pandora* (Pandora's Box).

The story of Kraus's postwar writings and polemics is basically the history of his disillusionment. The best that he could say about the Austrian Republic was that it had replaced the monarchy and rid Karl Kraus of that troublesome companion, the other K. K. The satirist engaged in extended polemics with the German-Jewish journalist Maximilian Harden (once an admired model), the German-Jewish critic Alfred Kerr, and the Prague-born poet Franz Werfel (formerly an admirer). One of several apostles turned apostates was the psychoanalyst Fritz Wittels, who presented an anti-Kraus paper at a 1910 meeting of the Vienna Psychoanalytic Society. Kraus's running fight with the "psychoanals," as he called that fraternity, produced such celebrated aphorisms as "Psychoanalysis is that mental illness fur which it regards itself as therapy."[28]

Karl Kraus can perhaps best be described as a basically apolitical man with an *ad hoc* attitude toward politics based on personalities rather than parties or issues. Though he supported the Social Democrats at various times in his life, that party, which held a majority position in postwar Austria, was increasingly at odds with what it regarded as Kraus's carping criticism, his deficient understanding of economics, and his blindness to the achievements and promises of modern technology.

"*Mir fällt zu Hitler nichts ein*"[29] (l cannot think of anything to say about Hitler). This is the striking first sentence of Kraus's work *Die Dritte Walpurgisnatht* (The Third Walpurgis Night; the title refers to both parts of Goethe's *Faust* as well as to the Third Reich), written in the late spring and summer of 1933 but not published in its entirety during Kraus's lifetime. That sentence, the germ cell of the misunderstandings and conflicts that marked and marred Kraus's last years, may be indicative of resignation, though Kraus *could* think of many things to say about Hitler and did indeed say them, but it is primarily a hyperbolic, heuristic device for depicting the witches' sabbath of the time. There had been no *Fackel* for ten months when No. 888 appeared In October 1933. lts four pages contained only Kraus's funeral oration on his friend, the architect Adolf Loos, and what was to be his last poem, with a particularly poignant last line: "*Das Wort entschlief, als jene Welt erwachte*"[30] (The word expired when that world awoke). Kraus sadly contemplated the incommensurability of the human spirit with the unspeakably brutal and mindless power structure across the German border. Once again language was in mortal danger (Kraus's remarks on the subject anticipate and confirm the dictionaries of the language of inhumanity and the murderers' lexica that appeared after the end of the "Thousand-Year Reich"), and the perpetrators of the new horrors obviously were *not* characters from an operetta. As Kraus attempted to deal with the early excesses of the Nazi regime, which made him foresee much of the full fury to come, he seemed engaged in a desperate rearguard action; his writing was like the rambling monologue of a worried man who talks incessantly in an effort to keep the demons at bay. In voicing genuine concern over Germany's pressure on his homeland Kraus for once found himself in Austria's corner. Paradoxically and sadly, this led him to side with what has been widely recognized as the clerico-fascist regime of Chancellor Engelbert Dollfuss, whose assassination in 1934 came as a severe shock and blow to Kraus. Many of the satirist's erstwhile leftist adherents, some of them now Communists and/or emigrants, expected Kraus to join them in their struggle and perhaps to stop Hitlerism with a special issue of *Die Fackel*, but they were disappointed at what they regarded as his equivocation. For his part, Kraus seemed content to reduce his readership to people who in those perilous times did not abandon their interest in Shakespeare, Nestroy, Offenbach, and German style, including Kraus's unique "comma problems." His death of heart failure on 12 June 1936 at the end of a long period of physical and spiritual exhaustion, during which he had pathetically and futilely tried to pit the word against the sword, mercifully saved him from witnessing the Nazi take-over of Austria to the cheers of most of its population, the destruction of his belongings, the death of close friends in concentration camps, and untold other horrors. "In the twelve years that followed the accession of Hitler to power in Germany," writes Frank Field, "things were to happen that surpassed the most pessimistic insights of the satirist: the building of the concentration camp at Buchenwald around Goethe's beech tree, and the processions that took place into the extermination chambers of Auschwitz while elsewhere in the camp the orchestra played selections from Viennese light music—all this only becomes a little more explicable after reading the works of Kraus."[31]

To draw parallels between Kraus's time and *his* language and *our* time and language is a risky undertaking, but apart from the importance of the timeless humanitarian ideals that Kraus espoused, the relevance of his satire to our age is readily apparent. It is not difficult to image what Kraus would have said about the "Newspeak" of our day, about the "Doublethink" described in George Orwell's novel *1984*, or about the denatured language of Watergate, a language that conceals rather than revealing human thought and feeling. Certainly our linguistically permissive and heedless age is as "language-forsaken" as Kraus's time was. Surely a parallel may be discerned between Alice Schalek's use of the word *ausputzen* (clean out) in connection with enemy trenches or the Viennese vulgarism *obidraht* for a similar act and our present-day military's use of terms like "waste" or "off" as euphemisms for "kill." Hardly a day goes by on which the biased reporting of the press and the shameless invasions of privacy committed by journalists and radio and television reporters fail to confirm the satirist's bleak vision. The fact that there is no Karl Kraus today to do battle with the polluters of language and the defilers of the human spirit is one of the minor tragedies of our time.

Notes

1. Karl Kraus, *Beim Wort genommen*, (Munich: Kösel 1955), p. 245. All the aphorisms quoted in this article may be found in English translation in *Half-Truths and One-and-a-Half Truths: Selected Aphorisms of Karl Kraus*, ed. and trans. by Harry Zohn (Montreal: Engendra, 1976; Manchester: Carcanet, 1986).

2. Erich Heller, "Karl Kraus," in *The Disinherited Mind* (New York: Farrar, Straus & Cudahy, 1957, p. 239.

3. Karl Kraus, *Beim Wort genommen*, p. 270.

4. *Ibid.*, p. 284.

5. *Ibid.*

6. J.P. Stern, "Karl Kraus's Vision of Language," *Modern Language Review* 61 (1966), p. 73.

7. Theodor Lessing, *Der jüdische Selbsthass*, (Berlin: Jüdischer Verlag, 1930), p. 43; Berthold Viertel, "Karl Kraus. Ein Charakter und die Zeit," in *Dichtungen und Dokumente*. Munich: Kösel, 1956, p. 259.

8. Quoted in Berthold Viertel, *ibid.*, p. 212.

9. Frank Field, *The Last Days of Mankind: Karl Kraus and His Vienna* (New York: St. Martin's Press, 1967), p. 68.

10. Karl Kraus, "Er ist doch e Jud," in *Untergang der Welt durch schwarze Magie* (Munich: Kösel, 1960), p. 333.

11. Karl Kraus, "Die Entdeckung des Nordpols," in *Die chinesische Mauer* (Munich: Kösel, 1964), p. 272 (in English translation in *In These Great Times: A Karl Kraus Reader*, ed. by H. Zohn, Montreal: Engendra, 1976; Manchester: Carcanet, 1984, p. 56.

12. Karl Kraus, *Beim Wort genommen*, p. 380.

13. *Ibid.*, p. 191.

14. *Ibid.*, p. 293.

15. J.P. Stern, (note 6), p. 83.

16. Karl Kraus, *Literatur und Lüge*, Munich: Kösel, 1958, pp. 205-6.

17. Caroline Kohn, *Karl Kraus als Lyriker (Paris: Didier*, 1968), pp. 68-9.

18. Karl Kraus, *Beim Wort genommen*, p. 294.

19. Bloch, "Karl Kraus's Shakespeare," *Books Abroad* IX (1937), pp. 23-4.

20. Karl Kraus, *Die letzten Tage der Menschheit*, Munich: Kösel, 1957, p. 9.

21. *Ibid.*

22. Karl Kraus, *Beim Wort genommen*, p. 371.
23. Karl Kraus, *Die letzten Tage der Menschheit*, p. 770.
24. Karl Kraus, *Die Fackel* No. 686-90, May 1925, p. 37.
25. C. Kohn, *Karl Kraus* (Stuttgart: Metzler, 1966), p. 145.
26. Karl Kraus, *Dramen* (München: Langen-Müller, 1967), p. 366.
27. *Ibid.*, p. 115.
28. Karl Kraus, *Beim Wort genommen*, p. 351.
29. Karl Kraus, *Die Dritte Walpurgisnacht*, Munich: Kösel, 1952, p. 9.
30. Written on 13 September 1933. English translation in *In These Great Times*, p. 259.
31. Frank Field, op. cit., p. 212.

Selected Bibliography

The standard reference work is the *Karl Kraus-Bibliographie* by Otto Kerry, published by Kösel Verlag, Munich, in 1970. (An earlier version appeared in Vienna in 1954.) Extensive bibliographies are contained in the books by Caroline Kohn and Wilma Iggers (see below). Valuable bibliographical information may be found in the special Karl Kraus issue of *Nachrichten aus dem Kösel Verlag*, Spring, 1964, and in S.P. Scheichl, "Kommentierte Auswahlbibliographie," *Text und Kritik. Sonderband Karl Kraus*, H.L. Arnold, ed., Munich 1975. Scheichl is continuing his bibliographic commentary in the *Kraus-Hefte*, a quarterly appearing in Munich.

Primary Sources

1.   Works by Karl Kraus in German

Die demolirte Literaur. Wien: A. Bauer, 1897.
Eine Krone für Zion. Wien: Moriz Frisch, 1898.
Sittlichkeit und Kriminalität. Wien: Leopold Rosner, 1908.
Sprüche und Widersprüche. München: Albert Langen, 1909.
Heine und die Folgen. München: Albert Langen, 1910.
Die chinesische Mauer. München: Albert Langen, 1910.
Pro domo et mundo. München: Albert Langen, 1912.
Nachts. Leipzig: Verlag der Schriften von Karl Kraus, 1918.

Worte in Versen. Leipzig: Verlag der Schriften von Karl Kraus (vol. I, 1916; II, 1917; III, 1918; IV, 1919; V, 1920).

Worte in Versen. Wien-Leipzig: Verlag "Die Fackel" (vol. VI, 1922; VII, 1923; VIII, 1925; IX, 1930).

Weltgericht, vol. I, II. Leipzig: Verlag der Schriften von Karl Kraus, 1919.

Ausgewählte Gedichte. Leipzig: Verlag der Schriften von Karl Kraus, 1920.

Literatur oder Man wird doch da sehn. Wien-Leipzig: Verlag "Die Fackel," 1921.

Die letzten Tage der Menschheit. Wien-Leipzig: Verlag "Die Fackel," 1922.

Untergang der Welt durch schwarze Magie. Wien-Leipzig: Verlag "Die Fackel," 1922.

Traumstück. Wien-Leipzig: Verlag "Die Fackel," 1923.

Wolkenkuckucksheim. Wien-Leipzig: Verlag "Die Fackel," 1923.

Traumtheater. Wien-Leipzig: Verlag "Die Fackel," 1924.

Epigramme (compiled by Viktor Stadler) . Wien-Leipzig: Verlag "Die Fackel," 1927.

Die Unüberwindlichen. Wien-Leipzig: Verlag "Die Fackel," 1928.

Literatur und Lüge. Wien-Leipzig: Verlag "Die Fackel," 1929.

Zeitstrophen. Wien-Leipzig: Verlag "Die Fackel," 1931.

Die Sprache (edited by Philipp Berger). Wien-Leipzig: Verlag "Die Fackel," 1937.

2.   Postwar Collections (edited by Heinrich Fischer)

(Volumes I to X were issued by the Kösel Verlag, München; Volumes XI to XIV bear the imprint of Albert Langen-Georg Müller, München

I.   *Die Dritte Walpurgisnacht*, 1952.
II.   *Die Sprache*, 1954.
III.   *Beim Wort genommen*, 1955.
IV.   *Widerschein der Fackel*, 1956.
V.   *Die letzten Tage der Menschheit*, 1957.
VI.   *Literatur und Lüge*, 1958.
VII.   *Worte in Versen*, 1959.
VIII.   *Untergang der Welt durch schwarze Magie*, 1960.
IX.   *Unsterblicher Witz*, 1961.
X.   *Mit vorzüglicher Hochachtung*, 1962.
XI.   *Sittlichkeit und Kriminalität*, 1963.

XII. *Die chinesische Mauer*, 1964.
XIII. *Weltgericht*, 1965.
XIV. *Dramen*, 1967.

3.   Additional Collections

Karl Kraus, *Briefe an Sidonie Nádhérny von Borutin*, ed. by H. Fischer
    and M. Lazarus, 2 vols. München: Kösel, 1974.
Karl Kraus, *Frühe Schriften 1892-1900*, ed. J. J. Braakenburg. 2 vols.
    (München: Kösel, 1979).

II.   Works in English Translation

Karl Kraus, *Poems*. Trans. by Albert Bloch. Boston: Four Seas, 1930.
Karl Kraus, *The Last Days of Mankind*. Abridged and edited by Frederick
    Ungar, trans. by Alexander Gode and Sue Ellen Wright. New York:
    Frederick Ungar, 1974.
Karl Kraus, *Half-Truths and One-and-a-Half Truths: Selected Aphorisms*.
    Ed. and trans. by Harry Zohn. Montreal: Engendra, 1976;
    Manchester: Carcanet, 1986.
In These Great Times: A Karl Kraus Reader. Ed. by Harry Zohn. Montreal:
    Engendra, 1976; Manchester: Carcanet, 1984.
No Compromise: Selected Writings of Karl Kraus. Ed. by Frederick Ungar.
    New York: Frederick Ungar, 1977.

III. Secondary Works in English

Benjamin, Walter. "Karl Kraus." In *Reflections*, New York: Harcourt
    Brace Jovanovich, 1978.
Daviau, Donald G. "The Heritage of Karl Kraus." *Books Abroad* 38
    (1964).
Field, Frank. *The Last Days of Mankind: Karl Kraus and his Vienna*. New
    York: St. Martin's Press, 1967.
Grimstad, Kari. *Masks of the Prophet: The Theatrical World of Karl
    Kraus*. Toronto: University of Toronto Press, 1982.
Heller, Erich. "Karl Kraus: The Last Days of Mankind." In *The
    Disinherited Mind*, Cambridge: Bowes and Bowes, 1952.

210   Harry Zohn

Iggers, Wilma Abeles. *Karl Kraus: A Viennese Critic of the Twentieth Century.* The Hague: Martinus Nijhoff, 1967.

Janik, Allan, und Toulmin, Stephen. *Wittgenstein's Vienna.* New York: Simon and Schuster, 1973.

Menczer, Bela. "Karl Kraus and the Struggle Against the Modern Gnostics," *Dublin Review* 450 (1950).

Rosenfeld, Sidney. "Karl Kraus: The Future of a Legacy." *Midstream,* April 1974.

Simons, Thomas W. Jr. "After Karl Kraus." In *The Legacy of the German Refugee Intellectuals,* ed. by Robert Boyers. New York: Schocken, 1972.

Spalter, Max. *Brecht's Tradition.* Baltimore: Johns Hopkins University Press, 1967.

Stern, J. P. "Karl Kraus and the Idea of Literature." *Encounter,* August 1975.

Timms, Edward. *Karl Kraus: Apocalyptic* Satirist. New Haven: Yale University Press, 1986.

Williams, C. E. "Karl Kraus: The Absolute Satirist." In *The Broken Eagle: The Politics of Austrian Literature from Empire to Anschluss.* New York: Barnes & Noble, 1974.

Zohn, Harry. *Karl Kraus.* New York: Twayne, 1971; Ungar, 1979.

IV.   Major Studies in German

Bilke, Martina. *Zeitgenossen der Fackel.* Wien-München: Löcker, 1971.

Jenaczek, Friedrich. *Zeittafeln zur "Fackel": Themen, Ziele, Probleme.* Gräfelfing: Edmund Gans, 1965.

Knepler, Georg. *Karl Kraus liest Offenbach.* Berlin: Henschelverlag Kunst und Gesellschaft, 1984.

Kohn, Caroline. *Karl Kraus.* Stuttgart: Metzler, 1966.

Kraft, Werner. *Karl Kraus.* Salzburg: Otto Müller, 1956.

Liegler, Leopold. *Karl Kraus und sein Werk.* Wien: Richard Lanyi, 1920.

Mautner, Franz H. "Kraus' *Die letzten Tage der Menschheit.*" In *Das deutsche Drama,* vol. 2, ed. by B. von Wiese, Düsseldorf: Bagel, 1958.

Scheu, Robert. *Karl Kraus.* Wien: Jahoda & Siegel, 1909.

Schick, Paul. *Karl Kraus in Selbstzeugnissen und Bilddokumenten.* Reinbek bei Hamburg: Rowohlt, 1965.

Wagner, Nike. *Geist und Geschlecht: Karl Kraus und die Erotik der Wiener Moderne.* Frankfurt: Suhrkamp, 1982.

Ernst Mach

Judith Ryan

Since the invention of supersonic aircraft, concepts such as Mach numbers, Mach reflections, Mach shock lines, and other similar expressions have become key terms in aerodynamics. Yet few enthusiasts who speak knowledgeably about Mach 1 and Mach 2 are aware that Ernst Mach was important not only in the history of modern physics, but also in the development of modern philosophy and psychology. His impact on turn of the century thought was considerable. His ideas were among the most hotly debated of his time, and it was in response to his theories that some of the most revolutionary concepts of our century came into being.

In 1904 the Austrian writer Hermann Bahr published an essay with the provocative title, "Das unrettbare Ich" (The Unsalvageable Self).[1] A quotation from Mach's first psychological study, *Beiträge zur Analyse der Empfindungen* (1886, Contributions to an Analysis of Sensations), the phrase soon became the watchword of an entire cultural epoch, a shorthand way of referring to a whole spectrum of symptoms characteristic of the turn of the century. Although opinion was divided on exactly what it meant to describe the self as "unsalvageable," and more particularly on what consequences were to be drawn from this disquieting notion, there can be no doubt that Bahr had put his finger on the pulse of contemporary culture and given a convincing diagnosis of what ailed it. Were Mach's theories somehow to blame, or was he merely a predecessor in the art of cultural diagnosis? Mach saw himself as neither, but in order to understand his position we shall have to look back to the eighteen-seventies and the intellectual situation from which Mach's thought emerged.

Born in 1838 not far from Vienna, Mach had had a somewhat unusual upbringing. His early education had taken place at home under the tutelage of his father, Johann Mach, who encouraged the boy to share his interests in nature, science, and agriculture. Though he had studied philosophy at the University of Prague, Johann Mach was dedicated to the simple life, and supported his family partly by small-scale farming, partly as a private tutor. Ernst's mother, Josephine, shared her husband's idealism, but was herself more creatively gifted. If we are to judge from the illustrations to Mach's early studies, especially from his famous self-portrait in a chaise longue, young Ernst must have profited from her skill at drawing, though he later reported that he had been extremely puzzled as a child by such techniques as shading, which did not correspond to reality as we see it. But clearly his most important debt was to his father, who spared no pains in demonstrating the elementary laws of physics with the help of everyday objects. Mach commented later that we might learn much about primitive man by observing the behavior of children when they attempt to repair their toys; and indeed, he seems to have learned a certain amount of basic mechanics during his early years by observing the functioning of cords and levers in his playthings. This practical bent must have still been evident when he was dismissed from his first school, a Benedictine Gymnasium at Seitenstetten, on the grounds that he was more suited to learning a trade than to prepare for academic studies. Later on Ernst Mach, at his own request, did spend two years as an apprentice cabinet maker, but not before his father, disappointed with his performance at school but by no means despairing over the boy's abilities, had given him a private education that could certainly vie with that of any Gymnasium (classical high school) in Austria at the time. Though bored by the Latin and Greek authors, young Ernst attained considerable mastery in these two languages, as well as in the subjects that naturally fascinated him more: algebra, geometry, and the sciences. With this grounding, Mach was now able to hold his own at the second Gymnasium to which he was sent at the age of fifteen, where he was particularly inspired by his teachers of biology and physics. At seventeen he entered the University of Vienna, where he soon concentrated on physics and mathematics, receiving his doctorate in 1860 at the age of twenty-two.[2]

Mach's early life, with its combination of practical and academic interests, the relative isolation of his family, and his only sporadic exposure to the traditional school system, equipped him well for his later career. His longstanding resistance to rote learning in favor of what can be observed with one's own eyes suited him well to a life of scientific experimentation, and his skills in drawing and cabinet making meant that he could draw his own diagrams and design his own equipment. Even more important, perhaps, was the combination of philosophical and scientific inquiry to which his father had accustomed him from early childhood.

The notion that philosophy and science should go hand in hand became a recurrent theme in his work throughout his life.

The intellectual climate of the late nineteenth century was especially hospitable to a man of Mach's multifarious talents. It was a time of extraordinary ferment in a whole range of disciplines, many of which were not so clearly distinguished from each other as they are today. The new science of psychology, in a variety of different guises, was adding a new dimension to studies in the other sciences. Fechner's psychophysics, Herbart's mathematical psychology, and Wundt's experimental psychology (still sailing under the flag of philosophy) had revolutionized the thinking of an entire generation. Impressionist painting, heavily dependent on Helmholtz and Fechner for its theoretical development, had drawn attention to the importance of the senses for an understanding of the world around us, while literary realism emphasized the subjective nature of human experience by restricting its scope increasingly to the point of view of a single observer. An interdisciplinary era that valorized both subjective experience and the life of the senses had begun.

Conducted in this favorable atmosphere, Mach's university studies were thoroughly characteristic of the period. Though his unorthodox education had left him with some ground to make up—he was forced to teach himself calculus, for example— , he was nonetheless able to take courses on mathematical physics and photographic optics, to mention just two of the fields that proved decisive in the later development of his thought. His practical skills enabled him, while still a student, to construct laboratory apparatus necessary to prove the Doppler effect (the changing pitch of a sound, such as a train whistle, as it moves towards or away from the hearer), which was at that time still a matter of lively controversy in the scientific world. Having received his degree, he became a university lecturer, essentially a private position whose modest income consisted of the fees paid by individual students to attend a given series of lectures. In accordance with his training, his first courses were on Fechner and Helmholtz. A handbill from the period announces, for example, "Popular Lectures for Ladies and Gentlemen on Acoustics as a Physical Basis for the Theory of Music" and proceeds to elaborate a sequence of lectures on Helmholtz's theories, to be illustrated by demonstration experiments.[3] Though he would have preferred to plunge immediately into scientific experiments of his own, these early lecture courses built the foundation of a good deal of his later work. When he finally did have an opportunity to do laboratory work, the subject he took up, significantly enough, drew on his knowledge of physics, physiology, and psychology. It was a study of the labyrinth of the inner ear.

Even at this very early stage of his career, Mach was in many ways a harbinger of developments to come. The idea for his first original experiment had come, just as his father had taught him, from close observation of experience. But unlike his father's observations, Mach's were not made in field or farmyard: they were made in the course of that quintessential late nineteenth-century experience, a train ride. Noticing that trees and chimneys seemed to swerve from the vertical when the train rounded a curve, Mach began to wonder whether this might not be due to the fluid inside the ear. Having received a research grant from the Vienna Academy, he investigated his hunch by calling forth another skill acquired during his early training: his carpentry and practical knowledge of mechanics. This apparatus he constructed was an enclosed rotatable chair that may be seen as a sort of prototype of today's flight simulators. With the aid of this device, he was able to prove that the sensation of motion derives from the movement of the fluid in this semi-circular canals. William James refers to this experiment in his *Principles of Psychology* (1980), [4] and Edwin G. Boring, writing in 1929, comments that the book in which Mach published the results of his study, *Theory of the Sensation of Motion* (1875) would have sufficed to "bring him into the body of psychologists."[5] Most of his contemporaries still considered him a physicist, however. Although in 1864 he had been appointed professor of mathematics at the University of Graz, he received the chair of experimental physics at the German University of Prague as early as 1867, when he was still only twenty-nine. During this period, he experimented extensively on optics and acoustics, work that was crucial for his later psychological studies.

One of Mach's early studies on vision drew attention to a phenomenon that still bears his name: Mach bands, narrow strips of light that are either too bright or too dark and appear on the line of demarcation between areas of greater or lesser intensity. Close observers are familiar with the fine bright line that can often be seen separating light from shadow. This was the phenomenon that Mach investigated in a series of experiments during the late eighteen-sixties with an adaptation of the color wheel familiar to present day students of optics. At this stage of his career, when he was not able to afford expensive equipment, the use of this simple apparatus had obvious advantages. But in terms of his later interests, the most important aspect of this experiment was not merely that it helped to explain a puzzling optical phenomenon. More significant was his argument that, although the phenomenon can be photographed and thus may at first blush to appear to be "objective," it results from neurological inhibition. In other words, both the rotating light and dark patches on the color wheel and any photograph taken of them must be seen by the eye; measuring devices independent of the human eye would not be able to detect the "Mach bands." In 1928, Georg von Békésy discovered similar subjective phenomena in auditory reception, but not until the nineteen-fifties did electrophysiological techniques become sufficiently advanced for these to be demonstrated empirically.[6]

In 1881, when Mach attended a conference on electricity in Paris, he heard a talk that provided the inspiration for the experiments in ballistics that were later to be revived by modern aerodynamics. A Belgian artillerist spoke about the sound effects created by bullets traveling through the air at high speeds: whereas at lower speeds the only sound heard was that of the bullet being fired, at high velocities there was an additional sound which he hypothesized might be caused by masses of compressed air borne along ahead of the projectile. In his tests of this theory, Mach's technical expertise again came to the fore. By means of an ingenious apparatus, Mach was able to take photographs of the air turbulence set up by high speed bullets and demonstrate that, when the projectile exceeds the speed of sound, a shock wave is created which we hear as a distinct report.[7] This work, though consigned to oblivion for many years and not resurrected until the age of supersonic aircraft, has made Mach's name a household word.

The results of Mach's ballistic experiments were published in 1910, but in the meantime, he had already distinguished himself in more theoretical domains. *Die Geschichte und die Wurzel des Satzes von der Erhaltung der Arbeit* (History and Origin of the Principle of the Conservation of Energy), a theory of knowledge based on mechanics and the physics of heat, had already appeared in 1872 and *Die Mechanik in ihrer Entwicklung historisch-kritish dargestellt* (Science of Mechanics), also heavily weighted towards theory of knowledge, in 1883. But the most influential book, whose impact was by no means limited to the world of science, was his *Beiträge zur Analyse der Empfindungen* which appeared in 1886 and which, considerably expanded and with the word "Beiträge" dropped from its title, ran through four more editions between 1900 and 1906. This was the book to which Hermann Bahr was referring when he wrote his essay "Das unrettbare Ich" in 1904. It had just appeared in a substantially revised version of which Mach himself was clearly very proud, since he took the trouble to send a copy across the seas to his colleague at Harvard, William James.[8]

At first glance the *Analyse der Empfindungen*, replete with carefully drawn line diagrams, looks too much like a science textbook to excite the furor described by Bahr in his essay. It is, after all, basically a study of sensory impressions and how they come about: a study of "colors, sounds, temperatures, pressures, spaces, times, and so forth."[9] It was essentially an eminently readable introduction to the psychology of vision, hearing, spatial perception, and the like. But its opening pages contained some remarks that were destined to throw its readers into panic and disarray. A self-portrait drawn with one eye closed illustrated Mach's new view of the self.[10] A curved line framing the picture turns out to represent his eyebrow, nose, and handlebar moustache, the only parts of his head visible from the one-eyed vantage-point. We see Mach's high-buttoned waistcoat, his right arm poised to draw the very picture we have before us, his legs extending before him on a chaise longue. The drawing includes the window, bookshelves, and floor of the left-hand side of his study. Mach's point is that the self is identical with this perspective: the visible parts of his body and the objects in his field of vision are equally parts of his "self." What this meant, as he spelled it out in the accompanying text, was that both "self" and "body" are merely handy labels for things that do not, in fact, exist as discrete units. There is no essential difference between the body on the chaise longue and the parts of the study that surround it, no dividing line between the inner and the outer world, between subject and object.

Mach recounts an experience in which he first recognized that he was no more than a "single mass of sensations, only somewhat more strongly cohering in the self."[11] Like free-floating particles, the sensory perceptions are sometimes more, sometimes less related to the perceiver. Mach goes on to argue that what we call "I" is no more than a sum of sense impressions received: when I see something green, for example, all that happens is that the impression "green" occurs in combination with a collection of other impressions. "The ego is not a definite, unalterable, sharply bounded unity."[12] Taking up an idea first enunciated by Lichtenberg, Mach declared that it is going too far to translate the Cartesian "cogito" as "I think": "we should say 'it thinks,' just as we say 'it rains'." In other words, he argues, "the self is unsalvageable."[13]

This was of course the most disconcerting of the ideas Mach put forward in his *Analyse der Empfindungen*. Although this view of the self was to have the most widespread influence on the culture at large, Mach's aim in this book was to present a far more encompassing epistemological theory. Although he had been decisively influenced by Kant at the early age of fifteen, Mach had since then turned away from the notion of the "thing in itself." Similarly, within the domain of what is accessible to knowledge, he now turned away from the notion of a contrast between "appearance" and "reality." Since all we have is the evidence of our sensory perception, with what justice do we claim that the bent pencil in a jar of water is "really" straight? What permits us to give this priority to tactile, rather than to visual impressions? In a lengthy comparison of the various sensory perceptions and their relation to each other, he showed that we generally tend to give more credence to the tactile alone than to any other sense. What is tangible is what we usually mean by "real." "Owing to the singularly extensive development of mechanical physics," he explained, "a kind of higher reality is ascribed to the spatial and the temporal than to colors, sounds, and odors; in accord with which, the temporal and spatial links of colors, sounds and odors appear to be more real than the colors, sounds, and odors themselves."[14] Thus Mach argued against the usual distinction between objective and subjective reality.

In so doing, he had returned in part to a philosophy first propounded by Berkeley. Although Mach acknowledged his debt to Berkeley's subjective idealism he insisted on certain distinctions between his position and that of his English predecessor. For one thing, Berkeley had maintained that the elements of sensory perception depended on God; Mach, by contrast, eliminated God from his system. For another, Mach by no means emphasized the subjective component of experience. For him, the main fact of sense-perception was what he called the "elements": "The primary fact is not the ego, but the elements (sensations)."[15] These elements were constantly changing, forming and reforming themselves into different complexes. His theory emphasized this flux in a way that was thoroughly characteristic of the late nineteenth, not of the eighteenth century. Finally, Mach did not wish to discredit what he described as "naive realism." He argued that, whatever philosophy we might hold in the abstract, we might be obliged to abandon it temporarily when pursuing some particular practical purpose. "No point of view has an absolute *permanent* validity. Each has an importance for one given end."[16] This was a substantial modification of Berkeley's views. Nonetheless, it failed to convince those of his detractors, notably Lenin, who claimed that Mach had simply plagiarized British empiricism.[17]

In his later writings, Mach continued to develop the ideas he had put forward in the *Analyse der Empfindungen*. Although he suffered a stroke in 1898, his output was considerable. Typing with one finger of his left hand and instructing his son, Ludwig, in how to conduct those experiments which he still wished to undertake, he devoted the rest of his life to developing his unique synthesis of philosophy, psychology, and physics. There were periods of days on end when he and his son disappeared into their laboratory, where they scarcely slept or ate while working on a problem. A good deal of this work consisted in elaborations of earlier work. He put together his lectures on the philosophy of science under the title *Erkenntnis und Irrtum* (1905, Knowledge and Error), collected and expanded his *Populär-wissenschaftliche Vorlesungen* (1910, Popular Scientific Lectures), wrote the first half of his *Principien der physikalischen Optik* (1912, Principles of Physical Optics), and worked on his *Kultur und Mechanik* (Culture and Mechanics), which appeared posthumously in 1915.

Increasingly, this work began to develop ideas which can be seen as forerunners to Einstein's theory of relativity: indeed, Einstein acknowledged the influence of Ernst Mach, who, he declared in 1916, "clearly recognized the weak points of classical mechanics and was not very far from requiring a general theory of relativity—and all of this almost half a century ago!"[18] Mach repeatedly argued against Newtonian physics. He explained that "absolute space and absolute motion . . . are pure products of thought, pure mental constructs, that cannot be produced in experience."[19] In this same vein, Mach inveighed against the common assumption that anything physically measurable—"the reduction of all physical measurements to such units as the centimeter, the gram, and the second"[20] —must necessarily be more "objective." Any attempt to arrive at measures independent of the observer and his senses is inevitably in vain, he argues. Here was the linchpin of Mach's entire system of thought: that it is impossible to eliminate the subjective element from scientific inquiry. Implicitly and explicitly, his published work declares over and over again that the study of physics is indissoluble from the study of sensory perception.

Though in all these ways the exponent of advanced views, Mach did have his blind spots. The most notable of these was his resistance to atomic theory. Here it is important to distinguish between what was termed "atomism" at the time and what we now understand by atomic theory. Like Wilhelm Wundt, his forerunner in the field of experimental psychology, Mach believed that the world was made up of "elements." For Mach, these elements consisted in sensory perceptions which, as they cohered more firmly in one spot or another, made up what we are accustomed to think of as "selves." Contemporaries frequently referred to this type of view as "atomism," since it posited a world somewhat like a pointillist painting. Atoms, in the modern sense of the word, were another thing altogether. Mach's rejection of this physical theory was entirely consonant with his view that the only reality was the reality of the senses. If we couldn't see atoms, then they simply didn't exist. At best, they were just as much a mental construct as the "thing in itself," a notion he had resisted equally vehemently from his student days. But his rejection of atomic theory involved him in debates with contemporaries that were much more vehement than his arguments with the neo-Kantians.

Mach was by no means the only thinker in the early part of the century who rejected metaphysics and adhered to what was then called "neutral monism," the notion that there was no distinction between appearance and reality and that everything was made up of one single "stuff." Mach's aim, indeed, throughout, was to eliminate dualisms and create a "science which, embracing both the organic and the inorganic, will interpret the facts that are common to the two departments."[21] But to argue against the new atomic physics was much less acceptable, and with his increasing illness and infirmity, it isolated Mach decisively from his scientific colleagues. It involved him in particular in some unpleasant arguments with Max Planck, who denounced him vehemently as a "false prophet." Much hurt by Planck's attacks, Mach struck back, claiming that the belief in atoms had become a sort of religion and that "the physicists are well on their way to becoming a church."[22] "If the belief in the reality of atoms is so essential to you," he continues in his reply to Planck, "then I will have nothing more to do with the physical way of thinking, then I do not want to be a real physicist, then I will forego any scientific esteem, in short, then I decline with thanks any participation in the community of believers; freedom of thought is much dearer to me."[23] The bitter character of these debates between two famous men cast a distinct shadow on the final years of Mach's life. From our present standpoint, it is easier to understand why Mach was so insistent in his rejection of atoms. In terms of his own theory of scientific "economy"—a kind of Occam's razor effect that permits those scientific theories that explain reality in the most compact way to win out over others in a kind of theoretical battle for the survival of the fittest—the notion of atoms was a superfluity that had to be cast aside. We should not mistake "intellectual machinery" for reality, he argued.[24] The notion of atoms seemed to him to undermine the monistic principles that were the very basis of his thought.

In order to understand Mach's complex position on the threshold of modern science, his peculiar combination of retrograde and revolutionary ideas, we need to understand his own view of the work he was doing.

While it may seem from today's point of view that Mach was now a physicist, now a philosopher, now a psychologist, his own view was that all of his work, whether experimental or theoretical, was laying an essential epistemological foundation for science as a whole. Thus it is entirely fitting that what made the greatest stir during his lifetime — at least before the debates about the reality of atoms broke loose — was his notion that sense impressions are all. One did not have to read far into the *Analyse der Empfindungen* to discover how radical the consequences of such a view might be. Unlike most other philosophers, Mach wrote simply and clearly, and knew how to illustrate his theses with convincing examples. His public lectures, furthermore, did much to aid the spread of his ideas. Mach was much more than a scholar or a scientist: he was a figure very much at the heart of contemporary Austrian culture.

As far as philosophy is concerned, Mach's influence was strongest in Vienna and Prague, but through Richard Avenarius, a philosopher who propounded similar ideas, it also spread to Zurich. Outside the German-speaking world, Mach's ideas were mainly transmitted by William James, who, having studied briefly in Germany, was steeped in the new psychologies.

The Vienna Circle, a group of young thinkers and writers, was one of the main vehicles that carried Mach's ideas into the popular domain. This group, which thought of itself as quintessentially modern, picked up and developed in its own way two main ideas from Mach's philosophy. The first was that of the "unsalvageable self" discussed in Bahr's retrospective essay,[25] the second a related notion that ordinary language had become invalid.

Bahr's essay is perhaps the best introduction to the first of these problems. In the guise of an autobiographical narrative, Bahr traces the development of Machian ideas and their reception by a relatively innocent young person. His starting point is the recognition that all experience is subjective; this is followed by the even more disconcerting discovery that the word "I" is "no more than an empty name."[26] The destructive influence of these ideas on a sensitive young soul is painted in vivid colors. Ultimately, however, the young person of Bahr's essay finds a way out of his dilemma, a way that gives new validity to the self and its needs by simply accepting as real what may be no more than a set of mental constructs. Insofar as we need these constructs, Bahr's narrator argues, they are true for us. The essay concludes with a decision to go on living as if there were no problem at all: "and so the sun continues to rise, the earth is real, and I am I."[27]

In suggesting this solution, Bahr was in fact merely spelling out the implications of Mach's own views. To respond to criticism that the *Analyse der Empfindungen* encouraged what amounted to solipsism, Mach wrote a new foreword to the fourth edition in which he explained that this was far from his intention. Both here and in a number of passages sprinkled throughout this edition, Mach argued that accepting his phenomenalism need not necessarily involve changing one's daily life: for practical purposes, it was perfectly sensible to act as if words like "self" and "body" were real entities rather than simply convenient labels for what is not at all so distinct. Appearing in 1904, this new edition with its prefatory warning was clearly the motivation of Bahr's 1904 essay. Doubtless because of this new material Mach sent a copy of the fourth edition to William James, who read it through very carefully, marking the passages that argued in favor of common sense and pragmatism and against those critics who had accused the book of nihilism.[28]

The implications of Mach's views for the theory of language were developed primarily by two influential Austrian figures. One of these was the philosopher of language, Fritz Mauthner, who had heard Mach's lectures in Prague during the early eighteen-seventies when he was still a young man. Like Mach, he believed that sense-perception was the basis of all knowledge. But in contrast to Mach, Mauthner tended to believe in solipsism: he questioned, for example, the possibility of any genuine communication, since the sense-experience of any given individual is not the same as that of any other. For Mauthner, language, especially in its social context, was essentially a game played according to rules.[29]

An even more skeptical view of language was presented by Hugo von Hofmannsthal. Having attended Mach's courses in Vienna, Hofmannsthal had absorbed some of his principal ideas at an early age; his poetry, which he began to publish at nineteen, testifies to this early reception of Mach's notion that the world consists in sense-impressions. By the turn of the century, however, Hofmannsthal had gained a certain distance from the Machian world view. His well-known text, *Ein Brief* (1902, A Letter), a fictive missive from Lord Chandos to Francis Bacon, describes through an ingenious temporal displacement what is in fact a contemporary problem. Frequently misunderstood as the statement of his own despair rather than as an analysis of symptoms from which he had already freed himself, the Chandos-Letter presented a vivid description of the kind of malaise to which a certain way of reading Ernst Mach might give rise. He depicted an experience in which self and world begin to break into fragments and in which, as a consequence, language itself "crumbles like mouldy mushrooms in one's mouth."[30] If traditional terms like subject and object must be abandoned as inadequate representations of reality, how can we possibly construct sentences in the familiar way? The fictive letter concludes by postulating the development of an entirely new language that would be free from the constraints of traditional categories; but to conceive such a language would take us beyond the bounds of what we can imagine within the system of existing language. It would only be, as Hofmannsthal's character Lord Chandos argues, a language "in which silent things speak to me."[31] This perceptive analysis of the dilemma into which Mach's views led if taken literally was itself, however, just as susceptible of misreading as Mach's *Analyse der Empfindungen.* Though in fact a fictive point of view, Hofmannsthal's Chandos-Letter was misunderstood as an expression of his personal despair; and so it combined with Mach's book on sensory perception to fan the flames of an increasing despair about the reality of the self and the validity of language.

It is not really surprising that Hofmannsthal's fictional letter was read in this way. His poetry and lyrical dramas were, after all, deeply indebted to Mach's way of thinking, although even quite early in his development he modified what he had learned from Mach by a perspective gleaned from other contemporary psychologists whose work was quite unlike Mach's. Throughout most of his literary career, for example, Hofmannsthal was fascinated by the phenomenon of split or multiple personality about which he had read in the French, English, and American psychological studies of his day. Like Mach's book on sense perception, these, too, reinforced a belief in the essential instability of the self that pervades all of Hofmannsthal's writing. But the most obvious influence of Ernst Mach can be seen in the impressionistic effects characteristic of Hofmannsthal's poetry. His well-known "Ballade des äußeren Lebens" (Ballad of the Outer Life), which begins with the word "and" and continues with a drifting, loosely linked series of images seen from no particular point of view, is typical of this mode, in which reality has not clearly defined contours and life does not appear to move towards any specific goal. Even in its final moment, where it attempts to gather this fragile concatenation of images into a single word, "evening,"[32] it singles out the very moment most beloved of the impressionists, the time of day where all forms begin to blur and become indistinct.

Later, Hofmannsthal came to regard this kind of indeterminacy, not as a general condition of life, but as a particular phase only. He called this phase "pre-existence" and defined it as that period of our lives—the whole of our childhood, in his view—where self and other are not yet distinctly separated. Seeing himself increasingly as a cultural critic, he began to perceive the dangers of languishing in aimless indeterminacy, a posture that had by then become quite fashionable. In a series of somewhat cryptic notes to himself entitled *Ad me ipsum* (1916-1929), he set forth his new system which was to show the way out of the flux of "pre-existence" and into a clearly defined social role. His play *Der Schwierige* (1921, The Difficult Man) is an excellent example of this system in action, turning as it does on the conversion of an indecisive and difficult man to marriage and participation in a regular life sanctioned by social convention.

Like Hofmannsthal, Arthur Schnitzler, another member of the "Young Vienna" group, also absorbed and took issue with Mach's ideas. His early plays, a loosely connected sequence arranged around a flighty young narcissist named Anatol, poke fun at the notion of the "unsalvageable self" even as they also demonstrate it. His development of stream-of-consciousness technique in his narrative, *Leutnant Gustl* (1900, Lieutenant Gustl), illustrates, among other things, his dependence on Mach's belief in the primacy of sensory perception. In a number of his early stories, he explored the problem of solipsism that seemed to have been raised by Mach's psychology, taking a critical stance to a position that would see reality as "all in the mind." Much closer to the real Mach is his presentation of a world in which subject and object, illusion and reality, are inextricably intertwined. His short stories from the eighteen-nineties are especially good examples of his attempt to transpose the Machian world view into fiction.

But despite the brilliance with which he succeeds in presenting the impressionistic aspect of Mach's thought, Schnitzler's reception is also a critical one, although the angle of his critique is very different from that of Hofmannsthal. Mach's psychology extended only so far as was necessary to provide an epistemological basis for science. Thus, although Mach defined his central term "sensation" to include not only sense impressions, but also feelings, memories, and hallucinations, he says very little about the latter in his writings. But as a doctor who spent his day working with patients, Schnitzler was naturally very interested in all these things. His stories and plays alike reflect this broadening of scope. Schnitzler's medical training had, after all, taken place in the Vienna of the early eighteen-eighties, and he was clearly well read in the whole range of new psychologies with their emphasis on problems of consciousness. But it was his day-to-day contact with real human beings that gave his writing a dimension going well beyond any simple transposition of psychological theory into art. Any attempt to reduce Schnitzler's work to one specific psychology or another would be a gross simplification.

So multiply refracted were the new psychologies, so very much a part of the general atmosphere of the time, that it is sometimes difficult to pinpoint the exact source of views that turn up in writers like Schnitzler. Another contemporary, Rainer Maria Rilke, is a case in point. While there is no evidence that he was familiar with the work of Ernst Mach, remarkably similar ideas can be seen in his works, not only in his early poetry, whose impressionism can be charged in large measure to turn-of-the-century fashion, but also in his novel *Die Aufzeichnungen des Malte Laurids Brigge* (1910, The Notebooks of Malte Laurids Brigge), where something much closer to Mach's presentation of sensory perception can be detected. "I'm learning to see," declares the fictional writer Malte,[33] turning the whole city of Paris into an experiment in perception in which subject and object are interpenetrable: "There is no roof over me. It rains into my eyes."[34] In his novel Rilke registers the anxieties provoked by the Machian perspective or something very like it in their full intensity.

Several years earlier, Franz Kafka, who had come into contact with Mach's ideas through his high school biology teacher,[35] had presented what amounts to a spoof on the notion that the self is "unsalvageable" in his first attempt at narrative fiction, *Beschreibung eines Kampfes* (Description of a Struggle) (1903-4). Here a man in a church tries to rescue his dwindling sense of self by praying so demonstratively that he will "acquire substance,"[36] as he puts it, by existing in the eyes of others. Not accidentally, it is precisely this figure who gives voice to questions about the validity of language that closely resemble those articulated in Hofmannsthal's Chandos-Letter. But in general, Kafka appears to have been more heavily influenced by other contemporary psychologists. Apart from this amusing vignette, Mach never surfaces again in his writings.

Of all the Austrian authors, Robert Musil was the most strongly influenced by Ernst Mach.[37] His dissertation, *Beitrag zur Beurteilung der Lehren Machs* (Towards an Evaluation of Ernst Mach's Theories) (1908), written under the aegis of Mach's Berlin adversary, Carl Stumpf, purported to be a critique of Mach's theories on "economy" in science, but was in fact an exposé of a discrepancy between Mach's belief that there were such things as "laws" of physics and his refusal to believe in the reality of self and body. In his dissertation, Musil convincingly showed that "the elements (of physics) that occur in laws are conceptual not sensible, as Mach indeed admits"; hence Mach involved himself in a contradiction when he claimed the existence of physical laws, but not the existence of an experiencing subject. While Musil's dissertation pointed to this rift in Mach's argumentation, his novels and stories were heavily dependent on Mach. *Die Verwirrungen des Zöglings Törleß* (1908, Young Törless), written simultaneously with the dissertation, bears Mach's imprint most clearly. The protagonist Törless is in effect both a young Mach and a young Musil. Just as Mach discovered Kant's *Prolegomena* at the age of fifteen and was profoundly impressed by it, so Törless, puzzled by the phenomenon of imaginary numbers, is instructed by his mathematics teacher that the answer to his questions can be found in Kant's philosophy. For Musil himself, it was Mach's *Populär-wissenschaftliche Vorlesungen* that played the decisive role in his intellectual development. When he came upon them in 1902 (at not quite so young an age as fifteen — he was twenty-two at the time), he wrote in his diary that the book had fallen into his hands at precisely the right moment.[38]

Young Törless's experiences correspond quite closely to certain views of Ernst Mach. In particular, his concern about what he calls a "gap in the causality of our thinking"[39] can be traced to Musil's study of Mach's theories of scientific economy. Similarly, Törless's apprehension of infinity in an unguarded moment when he seems to see it looming threateningly out of the sky resembles the experience recounted by Mach himself in a footnote to his *Analyse der Empfindungen* in which he felt overwhelmed by a "single mass of sensations." Törless's reflections on the problem of unreal numbers are an almost direct transposition of Mach's "neutral monism": though imaginary, these numbers can be used in calculations just like ordinary numbers, thus suggesting that there is no essential distinction between reality "out there" and the reality of the mind.

Mach's philosophy, in particular his monism, continued to play an important role in Musil's thinking, and can be shown to underlie the "daylight mysticism" of his uncompleted novel *Der Mann ohne Eigenschaften* (1930-1938, The Man without Qualities). Like Mach, the protagonist of this vast narrative project is a physicist turned philosopher; although the title identifies him as a "man without qualities," he is shown to be something much more like "qualities without a man." Mach's concept of sense-impressions that adhere only loosely to make what we call the self can be detected again and again throughout the novel. Mach's abolition of any distinction between subject and object posited by Mach is first demonstrated in the novel through the madman and murderer Moosbrugger, but it is soon revealed to extend also to rational characters like the protagonist. Embedded in five of twenty chapters that Musil read in proof on his deathbed is a discussion of contemporary psychology that makes almost explicit reference to the Machian position. In an essay which his sister finds lying about in a drawer, the protagonist, Ulrich, gives an extensive summary of three different psychological trends of his day. "There are psychologies of self," he writes, "and there are psychologies without self."[40] He spends several pages exploring the implications of Mach's position (the "psychology without self") and attempting to develop some new theories from it. Beyond these more or less direct allusions to Mach, however, Musil's novel is important for its analysis of Machian philosophy within the framework of contemporary cultural history. Through his critique of Austrian politics with its dithering ineffectiveness, he suggests that the egoless, objectless world of Ernst Mach had its direct parallel in the insubstantial culture all around him.

Since Musil's novel portrays turn-of-the-century Austria, it is only natural that it is so heavily indebted to Mach. Although Mach was still vividly present to Musil on his deathbed in 1942, his philosophy had long since ceased to be a force to be reckoned with in the world at large. Nonetheless, his ideas still continued to be a shadowy presence through the thoughts of other philosophers. They were transmuted in a number of different ways. William James, who shared with Ernst Mach his aim of writing so as to be readily understood, was one of the principal points of entry. But James, though essentially agreeing with Mach that subject and object were merely handy labels to distinguish what was perhaps not really separate and distinct, tended to emphasize the obverse of Machian theory. James argued that, since we tend to see the self as something separate and continuous, we might as well, for all practical purposes, regard it as being so. The difference between their two positions was not in fact very great, but in tipping the balance in this way James took much of the anxiety out of a philosophy that questioned the very underpinnings of our existence.

Largely under the influence of his readings in James and his colleague Ralph Barton Perry, Bertrand Russell, having at first vehemently attacked the "neutral monism" of Mach and his followers, came in the nineteen-twenties to accept a point of view very close to it. In a 1927 account of what he now called his "logical atomism," Russell declared that "both mind and matter are structures composed of more primitive stuff which is neither mental nor material." He acknowledged his debt to Mach and James, among others, in his development of this new position. To be sure, this was not to be his final position, but it dominated his thought for almost twenty years. Wittgenstein, too, though at first openly inveighing against Mach, ultimately came to share certain of his views. His theory of "atomic facts," developed while he was at Cambridge in a kind of reciprocal relationship with Russell's "logical atomism," is one example.

In more recent times, however, the influence of Mach's philosophy has receded and he is primarily known for his contributions to physics. Yet for Mach, the two were never really distinct. Again and again, he argued against what he saw as a false separation between "bodies and motions of bodies" on the one hand and our "sensations" or sense-impressions of these bodies on the other.[41] For him there was "no real gulf between the physical and psychical."[42] A physics without a theory of knowledge to support it was for him unthinkable. His willingness to question what seem to be some of the most obvious givens of natural science was what enabled him to develop ideas that were in so many ways ahead of his time. In an era dominated by positivism, Mach gave new meaning to the notion of scientific objectivity, thus setting a number of other thinkers on a track that was to revolutionize science in the most sweeping way. One of the most famous of these, Albert Einstein, located Mach's importance, his "true greatness," in his "incorruptible skepticism and independence."[43] In all his ventures, experimental or theoretical, Mach aimed, as he expressed it himself, to substitute a "freer, fresher view" for accepted forms of thought.[44] If this laid him open to attack from almost every quarter, it also stimulated a rethinking of received opinion that revitalized an entire epoch. His name deserves to be restored to the list of those who ushered in the modern age.

Notes

1. *Zur Überwindung des Naturalismus. Theoretische Schriften 1887-1904*, ed. Gotthart Wunberg (Stuttgart: Kohlhammer, 1968), pp. 183-192. Also in Hermann Bahr, *Dialog vom Tragischen* (Berlin: Fischer, 1904), pp. 70-101.
2. For my account of Mach's early life, I am indebted to the following two studies: Floyd Ratliff, *Mach Bands: Quantitative Studies on Neural Networks in the Retina* (San Francisco: Holden-Day, Inc., 1965), esp. pp. 7-36; and John T. Blackmore, *Enst Mach: His Work, Life and Influence* (Berkeley: University of California Press, 1972).
3. Blackmore, p. 203.
4. William James, *Principles of Psychology* (New York: Macmillan, 1890).
5. Edwin G. Young, *A History of Experimental Psychology* (New York: Appleton-Century, 1929), p. 390.
6. For more information on Mach bands, including recent experiments on the phenomenon, see Ratliff, *op. cit.*
7. Ratliff gives a good account of these experiments, along with a useful diagram (pp. 16-19).
8. This volume is now in the Houghton Library at Harvard University.
9. Ernst Mach, *Analyse der Empfindungen*, 4th ed. (Jena: Gustav Fischer, 1904), p. 1.
10. *Ibid.*, p. 15.
11. *Ibid.*, p. 24.
12. *Ibid.*, p. 19.
13. *Ibid.*, p. 20.
14. *Ibid.*, p. 6.
15. *Ibid.*, p. 19.
16. *Ibid.*, p. 30.
17. See Ratliff, p. 24. Paradoxically, the only book-length study in German concerning Mach's influence on contemporary literature appeared in East Germany: Manfred Diersch, *Empiriokritizismus und Impressionismus* (Berlin: Rutten und Loening, 1977).
18. Cited according to Ratliff, p. 31.

19. *Die Mechanik in ihrer Entwicklung historisch-kritisch dargestellt* (Leipzig: Brockhaus, 1883), pp. 222-223.
20. *Analyse der Empfindungen*, p. 280.
21. *Ibid.*, p. 83.
22. "Die Leitgedanken meiner naturwissenschaftlichen Erkenntnislehre und ihre Aufnahme durch die Zeitgenossen," cited in Ratliff, op. cit., p.33.
23. Ibid.
24. *Mechanik*, p. 483.
25. For a more detailed account of this problem, see my forthcoming book, *The Vanishing Subject: Empiricism, Impressionism and Literary Modernism*.
26. *Zur Überwindung des Naturalismus, op. cit.*, p. 192.
27. *Ibid.*
28. See Judith Ryan, "American Pragmatism, Viennese Psychology," *Raritan*, VIII: 3 (Winter 1989), 45-54.
29. On Mauthner, see Katherine M. Arens: *Functionalism and Fin-de-siècle: Fritz Mauthner's Critique of Language* (Bern: Lang, 1985).
30. Hugo von Hofmannsthal, *Gesammelte Werke. Erzählungen. Erfundene Gespräche und Briefe. Reisen* (Frankfurt: Fischer, 1979), p. 465.
31. *Ibid.*, p. 477.
32. *Gesammelte Werke. Gedichte, Dramen I*, p. 16. English translation by Michael Hamburger in *Poems and Verse Plays*, ed. M. Hamburger (New York: Pantheon, 1961), p. 33.
33. *Sämtliche Werke* (Frankfurt a. M.: Insel, 1966), vol. VI, p. 710.
34. *Ibid.*, p. 747.
35. Peter Neesen, *Franz Kafka und der Louvre-Zirkel* (Göppingen: Göppinger Arbeiten zur Germanistik, 1972).
36. Franz Kafka, *Sämtliche Erzählungen*, ed. Paul Raabe (Frankfurt am Main: Fischer, 1970), p. 227.
37. Claudia Monti, "Mach und die österreichische Literatur," *Akten des internationalen Symposiums Arthur Schnitzler und seine Zeit* (Bern: Lang, 1985), 263-283.
38. Blackmore, p. 188.
39. *Die Verwirrungen des Zöglings Törleß, Gesammelte Werke,* (Reinbek: Rowohlt, 1978, 2nd ed. 1981), vol. 6, p. 135.

40. *Der Mann ohne Eigenschaften, Gesammelte Werke* vol. 4, p. 1160.
41. *Analyse der Empfindungen*, pp. 36-37.
42. *Ibid.*, p. 58.
43. Cited according to Ratliff, p. 7.
44. *Analyse der Empfindungen*, p. 25.

Bibliography

Works by Ernst Mach

Die Geschichte und die Wurzel des Satzes von der Erhaltung der Arbeit (Prague; 1872, 2nd ed. Leipzig: Barth, 1909)
Die Mechanik in ihrer Entwickelung historisch-kritisch dargestellt (Leipzig: Brockhaus, 1883)
Beiträge zur Analyse der Empfindungen (Jena: Gustav Fischer, 1886; 2nd rev. and augmented ed.: *Die Analyse der Empfindungen und das Verhältnis des Physischen zum Psychischen* (Gustav Fischer: Jena, 1900)
Populär-wissenschaftliche Vorlesungen (Leipzig: Barth, 1896)
Die Principien der Wärmelehre, historisch-kritisch entwickelt (Leipzig: Barth, 1896)
Erkenntnis und Irrtum. Skizzen der Psychologie der Forschung (Leipzig: Barth, 1905)
Kultur und Mechanik (Stuttgart: Spemann, 1915)
Die Principien der physikalischen Optik, historisch und erkenntnispsychologisch entwickelt (Leipzig: Barth, 1921)

Works in English Translation

History and Root of the Principle of the Conservation of Energy, trans. P.E.B. Jourdain (Chicago: Open Court, 1911)
The Analysis of Sensation and the Relation of the Physical to the Psychical, trans. C.M. Williams, rev. and aug. S. Waterlow (Chicago: Open Court, 1914; re-ed. Dover: New York, 1959)
Popular Scientific Lectures, trans. T.J. McCormack (Chicago: Open Court, 1975)

Knowledge and Error. Sketches on the Psychology of Enquiry, trans. P.
   Foulkes and T.J. McCormack (Boston: Reidel, 1976)
*The Principles of Physical Oprics. An Historical and Philosophical
   Treatment*, trans. J.S. Anderson and A.F.A. Young (London:
   Methuen, 1926; New York: Dover, 1953)

Studies of Ernst Mach in English

Boring, Edwin G., "Kulpe, Mach and Avenarius," in *A History of
   Experimental Psychology* (New York: D. Appleton-Century,
   1929), pp. 389-393.
Bradley, J., *Mach's Philosophy of Science* (London, 1971)
Cohen, R.S. and Seeger, R.J., *Ernst Mach. Physicist and Philosopher*
   Boston Studies in the Philosophy of Science (Dordrecht: Reidel,
   1970).
Mises, R.von, *Positivism. A Study in Human Understanding,* trans. J.
   Bernstein and R.G. Newton (Cambridge: Harvard University
   Press, 1951).
Musil, Robert, *On Mach's Theories*, trans. Kevin Mulligan, introd. G.H.
   von Wright (Washington: Catholic University of America Press,
   1982).
Ratliffe, Floyd, *Mach Bands: Quantitative Studies on Neural Network
   in the Retina* (San Francisco: Holden-Day, 1965).
Ryan, Judith, "American Pragmatism, Viennese Psychology," *Raritan*
   VII: 3 (Winter, 1989), 45-54.
Weinberg, C.B., *Mach's Empirio-pragmatism in Physical Science* (New
   York, 1937).

Selected Studies on Ernst Mach in German

Diersch, Manfred, *Empiriokritizismus und Impressionismus* (Berlin:
   Rutten und Loening, 1977).
Monti, Claudia, "Mach und die österreichische Literatur. Bahr,
   Hofmannsthal, Musil." *Akten des internationalen Symposiums
   Arthur Schnitzler und seine Zeit* (Bern: Lang, 1985), pp. 263-283.

Musil, Robert, *Beitrag zur Beurteilung der Lehren Machs und Studien zur Technik und Psychotechnik* (Reinbek bei Hamburg: Rowohlt, 1980)

Fritz Mauthner

Elizabeth Bredeck

In a chapter of his autobiography called "First Language Studies"
Fritz Mauthner (1849-1923) declares that his fascination with language
stemmed directly from the circumstances of his childhood. His background does not determine or explain specific arguments advanced in his
philosophical works, but the description of that background nonetheless
merits attention, since Mauthner's situation is that of many Jews in the
Austro-Hungarian Empire during the later nineteenth and early twentieth
centuries:

> Indeed, I don't understand how a Jew who was born in one of the
> Slavonic lands of the Austrian Empire could avoid being drawn to
> the study of language. In those days he learned to understand three
> languages all at once: German as the language of the Civil Service
> of culture, poetry and polite society; Czech as the language of the
> peasants and servant girls, and as the historical language of the glo-
> rious kingdom of Bohemia; a little Hebrew as the holy language of
> the Old Testament and as the basis of Jewish-German jargon
> (*Mauscheldeutsch*) which he heard not only from the Jewish hawk-
> ers, but occasionally also from quite well-dressed Jewish business-
> men of his society, and even from his relatives. . . . Moreover, the
> mixture of quite dissimilar languages in the common Czech-
> German jargon (*Küchelböhmisch*) was bound to draw a child's
> attention to certain linguistic laws.[1]

Franz Kafka tells of similar experiences while growing up in Prague, and
Mauthner's account has been cited in connection with Rainer Maria Rilke
and Karl Kraus, among others.[2] But while his situation typifies that of the
Austrian Jew, it is not restricted to this one group; rather, Mauthner's

Beiträge zu einer Kritik der Sprache (1901-02, *Contributions Toward a Critique of Language*) documents the more general phenomenon of "Austrian language consciousness" we have come to associate with such works as Hugo von Hofmannsthal's *Ein Brief* (1902, *A Letter*) and Robert Musil's *Die Verwirrungen des Zögling Törleß* (1906, *Young Törless*).[3]

Mauthner's skepticism links him with other poets and philosophers who experienced a "language crisis" at the turn of the century, yet at the same time, it also sets him apart because his skepticism is so extreme. Gershon Weiler captures this radicalism well when he observes:

> The sceptic has frequently been but a figure of straw whom philosophers invented in order to show that their own arguments are immune to the criticism of a *possible* sceptic. For example, Professor Ayer in *The Problem of Knowledge* repeatedly refers to 'the sceptic' who might say this or that. Mauthner is a genuine sceptic and to my knowledge, the only philosopher who not only might have said all the things that Ayers's man of straw is made to say, but in fact said most of them. Mauthner's philosophy of language is thus committed to definite positions in psychology, linguistics, epistemology, logic and even history.[4]

Approaching the *Kritik* from a different, socio-historical angle, one of Mauthner's contemporaries arrived at a similar conclusion about his distinctive quality: "One might consider him a philosopher of the bourgeois class that has come to an end. But actually he stands above his class in that he has no illusions; he draws every logical consequence."[5] Mauthner would have appreciated the "tribute" since his primary goal in the language critique was to destroy illusions, "to prove to the owners of lovely words that in reality they posses nothing."[6] His relentless attacks on "word fetishism" and his insistence on the inadequacy of language to provide knowledge earned Mauthner an early reputation as a nihilist, but the label is one he himself rejected. Though critique of language admittedly unmasks or destroys former idols, argues Mauthner, it does so in the name of liberation; it should not be feared as a threat but welcomed as a sorely needed form of philosophical therapy.

Born in Bohemia, Mauthner considered himself neither an Austrian nor a Czech, but a German. A Jew by birth, he saw himself at times as an atheist, at other times as an agnostic. Though a professional drama critic and feuilletonist for over twenty-five years, he held that professional journalism degraded language. A "genuine sceptic," he nonetheless embraced a form of mysticism; and writing at the time of the "linguistic turn," which aimed to restore to philosophy a foundational status vis-à-vis other disciplines, Mauthner saw the history of philosophy as the "self-destruction of metaphors," and described philosophy as a discipline about to give way to psychology.

Mauthner was born on 22 November 1849 in Horzice (Hořitz), a small Bohemian town used briefly as a headquarters by the King of Prussia and Bismarck after the battle of Königgrätz (1866). Though Horzice was officially Czech, the local dignitaries at the time were "either Germans or those who proudly spoke some German" (*Erinnerungen*, 11), and Mauthner's father Emmanuel belonged to this group: the owner of a small weaving factory, he came from a highly assimilated upper-class Jewish family and insisted that German be spoken by his children at home. When Mauthner was five years old, his family moved to Prague, where his father felt the children might receive a better education; after two years of private tutoring with his siblings and three cousins he spent three more years at the *Klippschule*, a private Jewish school. Mauthner considered the decision to send him to the *Klippschule* an insidious "crime;" he felt he should have entered a *Gymnasium* directly. Almost sixty years after the fact he felt no differently. On the contrary, he claims bitterly and insistently in his memoirs that the "theft" of these three years was an offense against him that left deep and permanent scars.

Insulted and bored by much of the schoolwork, Mauthner was disappointed upon finally entering the *Piaristenkollegium* to find that the situation was not significantly better. He transferred five years later to the *Kleinseitner Gymnasium*, which enjoyed a better reputation and also appealed to Mauthner's growing German nationalist sentiments, since it was supposedly "ruled by a German spirit" (*Erinnerungen*, 81). During his student years at the University of Prague (1869-1873) he studied law at the insistence of his father, and participated actively in the *Lese- und Redehalle der deutschen Studenten Prags* ("Hall of Lecture and Discourse for German Students") founded in 1848. At a time when relations between German and Czech factions became increasingly hostile, Mauthner belonged to the delegation of Prague students who went to Strassbourg in 1872 to "convey greetings from the oldest German university to its youngest sister" (*Erinnerungen*, 172). Mauthner first attempted to write a critique of language during these years, but no record of this early version remains. Having slowly learned that the problems he confronted had as much to do with epistemology or theory of knowledge as they did with language, he began to read Kant: embarrassed by the naiveté of what he had written, he destroyed the manuscript. Not until twenty years later did he begin to write what ultimately became his *Kritik der Sprache*.

As a student Mauthner read Schopenhauer and Nietzsche avidly, and in 1872 he attended a series of lectures by Ernst Mach. In view of this background it may strike the modern reader as odd that he emphasizes his lack of philosophical training when describing the development of his views on language and knowledge. He explains, however, that his exposure to Nietzsche came not in philosophy seminars but in the *Redehalle*. He also read Schopenhauer on his own and was appalled that in a philosophy course he took on the concept of the will Schopenhauer was not even mentioned. As for Mach, at the time of his lectures in Prague he was "still considered a physicist rather than a philosopher,"[7] and Mauthner admits that he saw the connections between Mach's thinking and his own only some thirty years later when Mach reminded him of the lectures.[8] Those who had a more immediate impact were Otto Ludwig, Friedrich Nietzsche and Otto von Bismarck.

In Mauthner's view, each of these three "mentors" practiced language critique of sorts in the respective fields of aesthetics, philosophy and politics. In his *Shakespeare-Studien* Ludwig compared Schiller unfavorably with Shakespeare, and his criticism of Schiller's *schöne Sprache* (beautiful language) prompted Mauthner to think about language first as a medium of artistic expression and then as an instrument of knowledge. As Mauthner later argues in greater detail, the shortcomings of language as an instrument of knowledge derive from its failure to refer precisely to reality, yet in this same lack of direct correspondence between word and object lies the effectiveness of poetic language. That each word suggests not a single, distinct meaning but a multiplicity of meanings plays an integral role in the conveyance of mood, which for Mauthner is the essence of the literary work.

While Ludwig's criticism of Schiller prompted Mauthner to think about "word superstition" (*Wortaberglaube*) in aesthetics, Nietzsche influenced his conception of language by way of history. In Nietzsche's *Vom Nutzen und Nachteil der Historie für das Leben* (1873, *On the Use and Abuse of History*) Mauthner and his fellow students of the *Redehalle* found an answer to the historicism pervasive in nineteenth-century thought. Drawing on Nietzsche's statement that "insofar as historical laws exist, the laws are worth nothing and history is worth nothing," they attacked the fairly young discipline of linguistics for what in their opinion was an excessive reliance on "laws" in order to explain historical change in language: "There in a single catchword we had the antidote for the historical sickness. The history of humankind is without reason, is irrational, is a history that depends on contingencies (*eine Zufallsgeschichte*); there are no historical laws . . . (and) if there are no historical laws, there are also no laws in the history of language" (*Erinnerungen* 223). Mauthner continues his diatribe against the word superstition of historical-comparative linguists in volume two of his *Kritik der Sprache*, and he employs the concept of *Zufall* or contingency in another key context as well. In volume one of the critique, which will be discussed in more detail, he develops the notion of contingency in connection with an empiricist-evolutionist theory of knowledge.

Bismarck's influence differed from that of Ludwig or Nietzsche insofar as it came not from a written text, but from his personality. Half-joking, Mauthner contrasts Bismarck's *Realpolitik* to Kantian Idealism, and he expresses his admiration for the Iron Chancellor as a doer rather than a talker by comparing him with Faust: "Language-critical thinking learned from Bismarck the same thing that Bismarck had learned from Goethe: in the beginning was not the word, in the beginning was the deed. Knowing is knowing in words (*Wortwissen*). We have only words, we know nothing" (*Erinnerungen,* 220). Mauthner's high regard for Bismarck not only affected his philosophical thinking, but also influenced a specific decision he made several years after leaving the university. Trying to decide where to move, he chose Berlin over Vienna (his mother's preference) in the hope that someday he might hear Bismarck in person in the *Reichstag*.[9]

While still in Prague Mauthner had begun to work as a drama critic, and he continued in this field after moving to Berlin in 1876, but his real interest lay in writing of a different sort. As a student he had written poetry and had even published his *Revolutionssonnette* at his own expense. He had also tried his hand at drama, and before leaving Prague he saw his one-act play "Kein Gut, kein Mut" performed. However, it was with a collection of literary parodies called *Nach berühmten Mustern* (*After Famous Models*) rather than with a "serious" literary effort that Mauthner achieved recognition in 1879. The success of the parodies together with Mauthner's reputation as a critic and essayist led to the publication of several of his earlier literary works, but none of these enjoyed the same popularity as his satirical pieces.[10] Though he continued to write parodies, novels and novellas until the mid-1890s, in his lifetime he was known more widely for his theater criticism and essays, while more recent interest in Mauthner has focused exclusively on his philosophical works. One critic has even proposed that *because* he failed to become a great poet, Mauthner turned to philosophy.[11] Whether the relation between the philosophical and literary works is quite so straightforward is debatable; still, Mauthner's frustrated literary ambitions help explain at the very least his lifelong ambivalence toward the profession of journalism.

Before publishing his language critique Mauthner lived in Berlin for twenty-five years with his wife Jenny (née Ehrenburg) and their only child Grete, born in 1878. In addition to his activities as theater critic for the *Deutsche Monatsblatt* and later the *Berliner Tageblatt* Mauthner contributed book reviews and feuilletons to other newspapers and journals including *Die Zukunft, Schorers Familienblatt* and *Das litterarische Echo*.[12] Thus, when volume one of his language critique appeared in 1901, it came as a surprise to Mauthner's readers, colleagues, and acquaintances alike. The surprise was calculated: though he had been working on the critique since approximately 1893, Mauthner had mentioned the project only in correspondence, and only one excerpt had been published before the work appeared in book form.

The critique met with mixed reviews, and on the whole Mauthner was disappointed with its reception. He complained that it was not reviewed widely enough, and he felt that academic philosophers were particularly hostile toward the *Kritik der Sprache* since it had been written by an outsider rather than one of their own. Mauthner's disappointment was not altogether warranted; although some critics indeed dismissed him as a dilettant, his work received enthusiastic reviews as well.[13] Reassurance came also from Ernst Mach, who in a letter expressed confidence that the language critique would find an audience, but also cautioned Mauthner to be patient: "Slowly but surely your work will have an effect. The 'guild intellectuals' (*Zunftgelehrten*) are rather slow, ponderous creatures of habit. Ten to twenty years of rumination make no difference to them. Some of what seems like malice to a person of a livelier temperament is due in large part to this ponderousness" (*Selbstdarstellung*, 140). Mauthner saw that his status as a journalist did not help promote his work among academic philosophers. Yet by concentrating on the personal issue he minimized another factor of equal, if not greater, importance for the reception of the *Kritik*, namely, the arguments pursued in the work. As Weiler correctly notes, Mauthner "was radically out of step with the word-

realism of Husserl's increasingly influential phenomonology"
(*Mauthner's Critique*, 319), and as a result, it took even longer than Ernst
Mach had predicted for his work to receive serious critical discussion.[14]

The tradition with which Mauthner aligns himself most consistently
in the *Kritik* is that of empiricism. He acknowledges intellectual debts to
Kant, Locke, and Hume, and sees his work as the continuation or even
completion of their inquiries into the possibility of knowledge. Though he
compares himself with these three philosophers Mauthner also stresses his
divergence from them, and does so with his notion of the "contingent
senses" or *Zufallssinne*. Starting from the dictum "Nihil est in intellectum
quod non prius fueri in sensu," he outlines a fairly traditional-sounding
skeptical thesis about the limits and accuracy of empirical knowledge, but
then gives the argument an evolutionistic turn. He holds that the senses
are contingent on human needs and have undergone modifications over
time that correspond to shifts in those needs and interests. Therefore
sense data reflect what is useful, whereby utility by no means implies
accuracy. On the contrary, Mauthner presents the filtering, organizing
activity of the senses as a process of distortion.

Out of his skepticism about knowledge through the *Zufallssinne*
grows his thesis that language provides only *Zufallsbilder* or "contingent
images" of the world. He describes sense information as raw material that
must be processed before it qualifies as knowledge, and in his view the
process marks not only the beginning of cognition, but also the initial formation of words and concepts. "Language" thus refers to more than artic-
ulate speech. It is the very medium in which mental pictures of reality are
created; according to Mauthner, it is synonymous with reason or *Vernunft*
and also with the work of memory.

In Mauthner's work the notion of a gap between the sensible and the
intelligible is introduced already with the thesis of the *Zufallssinne*, and
the gap widens twice: first, when sense data become ordered or schema-
tized in language (here understood in the psychological, mentalistic
sense), and a second time when "translated" into the language shared by
members of a linguistic community. Mauthner contends that because no
two people have the same perceptions or thoughts, what they are able to
express by means of their communal language is virtually worthless. He
admits that the "misrepresentations" are adequate for the demands of daily
life but at the same time does not conclude that knowledge beyond the
shifting perspectival kind would be unnecessary or impossible. He retains
instead the premise that knowledge consists of accurate representations of

reality, and thus almost inevitably arrives at skeptical conclusions about the ability of language to provide such knowledge.[15]

Mauthner's theory of language has strong implications for his views on linguistics, philosophy, and poetry and on the relations between these different forms or genres of discourse. As noted earlier, he criticizes certain trends in nineteenth-century linguistics, and the criticism derives from his conception of all discourse as "metaphorical." Linguists, he argues, can make no special claim to scientific status for their discipline because their explanations of phenomena, like any other construct of language, are only approximations or hypotheses. While his immediate goal in volume two of the *Kritik* is to redefine the scope of linguistics, the questions Mauthner raises when polemicizing against then-current theories reflect broader concerns as well. When questioning the distinction between *Natur-* and *Geisteswissenschaften*, for example, he points to linguistics as a discipline that might be considered a natural *or* a human science, depending on one's definitions. He then goes on to dismantle the distinction between the two general types of disciplines and argues that we must dispense with the notion of "scientific" status altogether.

He views logicians with the same skepticism as linguists, calling their desire to "view the ordering of chaos in our thinking as 'science' a form of self-deception" (*Kritik* 3, 299), and he insists that an appeal to logic will not help philosophy retain its traditional status as a foundational discipline for all others. Philosophy in Mauthner's view is still primarily epistemology but it has lost its former authoritative voice. Philosophy, as critique of language, can analyze the terminology and unreflected assumptions of other disciplines as well as its own. But because the analyses are not carried out in any sort of metalanguage even language critique can provide no "true" knowledge.

At the beginning of the *Kritik* Mauthner points to the limitations of his work by admitting that language plays a double role: it is the vehicle of the critique, but also the object of study. But the full extent of the problem becomes clear only when Mauthner has developed his argument about the inadequacy of language as an instrument of knowledge. Given this position, one is forced to ask how he can still claim that language critique performs the task of liberation from what he calls "word fetishism" and *Logokratie*. To be consistent with his own skeptical viewpoint, Mauthner would presumably be unable to make any truth claims for his work and might even see himself reduced to silence. Though he discusses silence and mysticism, however, Mauthner does not remain silent. He asserts that critique in its purest form would be laughter, not silence. Moreover, he describes his own work as "articulated laughter" (*Kritik* 3, xi, 632) and maintains that his critique makes a genuine contribution to the discussion of problems of language and knowledge.

To support this claim Mauthner turns away from the psychological individualistic aspect of language and focuses on its social dimension as a means of communication. In this context he introduces the metaphor of a social game (*Gesellschaftsspiel*) and implies that if his critique is to be of any use, he too must participate in the game: "This critique of language would also like to contribute a small new alteration to the social game of knowing. It is the most worthless of all worthless things . . . so long as it remains my possession. It can only become slightly real if other players accept it, if others adopt the train of thought in the critique of language" (*Kritik* 1, 39). Recognizing that his work has value only if it is read and discussed by others, Mauthner paradoxically acknowledges the very "power" of language he would like to eliminate.

He often refers to the tyranny of language in connection with the images of social game and rules in order to stress the injustice that accompanies power. The language of the group determines that of the individual, but it is the language of the herd, which in his estimation has nothing to do with language as the object of his critique (*Kritik* 1, 39-40). The derisive attitude toward language in its social setting seems to complement Mauthner's notion of language as psychological process, but his statements about the purpose of the critique give the argument a new dimension that suggests the need to rethink the split between private and public language according to their respective "values." Naming the individual as the locus of (epistemological) value is itself a gesture that reflects social or communal agreement; the implied community in this case consists of philosophers writing before and at the same time as Mauthner, who likewise concentrate on the individual subject when theorizing about knowledge. Mauthner's characterization of the critique as a whole makes the same point about dependence on a community more explicitly. The very act of writing the critique might be seen as an admission, even an affirmation on his part of the importance of the social over the psychological aspect of language. Despite his radical nominalism he too remains subject to the social force of language: "I teach liberation of human beings from language as an unsuitable tool of knowledge; but I have no idea how one could free oneself from the power of language over morals, customs, commerce, life. For even lack of morals is merely a new custom, a new form of commerce, the tyranny of a new language."[16] To borrow a phrase from Richard Rorty, psychological process in Mauthner's work gives way to social practice; the epistemological model of "confrontation" is inscribed within one of "conversation."

Mauthner continues the conversation in two additional large works, both published during his lifetime: a two-volume *Wörterbuch der Philosophie* (1910- 1911, *Dictionary of Philosophy*), and *Der Atheismus und seine Geschichte in Abendlande* (1920-1923, *Atheism and its History in the Western World*). In both works he pursues the notion of power in language. The aim of the dictionary, as Mauthner explains in a lengthy introductory essay, is to trace the history of individual terms or concepts central to philosophy. By outlining the changes in meaning that terms undergo when translated or even used by different philosophers writing in the same language Mauthner argues once again that meanings are anything but stable and that, because there are no fixed referents in language, there is no true knowledge. Because Mauthner's nominalism skews the perspective decidedly, the dictionary is not always entirely reliable as a reference work. Nonetheless, individual articles contain a wealth of historical information, and together with the introduction they provide condensed versions of arguments in the *Kritik* and thereby a useful overview of Mauthner's positions.

The four-volume *Geschichte des Atheismus* likewise reflects Mauthner's conviction that linguistic meaning is a matter of usage and that usage changes over time. The title of the work suggests that a shift in focus from philosophy to religion and history has occurred, but the work is less of a departure from earlier concerns than it may seem initially. In his autobiographical writings Mauthner links his religious doubts as a child and an adolescent with his growing interest in language, though he admits that when he began speculating about the existence of God, he probably did not perceive any connection (*Selbstdarstellung*, 131). With the *Geschichte des Atheismus* he connects the two kinds of inquiry explicitly. He aims to prove that belief in "God" as anything more than a word is a form of word superstition and approaches his task in a way that recalls the *Wörterbuch der Philosophie*:

> If I must admit that this book is essentially a history of a word, the negative word-history of the gradual devaluation of the word 'God,' then I must not ignore the language that these writers used; I mean, naturally, not the different national languages, but their vocabulary,

strictly speaking their logic, independent of idiom.[17]
In addition to these two major works Mauthner published short monographs on Aristotle, Spinoza, and Schopenhauer. He also wrote the first
(and only) volume of his memoirs and edited several volumes in a series
called *Bibliothek der Philosophen* (*Library of Philosophers*). The series
was discontinued at the beginning of World War I after only four years;
the volumes on which Mauthner worked were on Jacobi's
Spinozabüchlein, Agrippa von Nettesheim, and the nineteenth-century
philosopher of language O. F. Gruppe.

By this time Mauthner was no longer living in Berlin. His wife
Jenny had died suddenly in 1896 and he suffered from insomnia, severe
headaches and eye problems. After publishing the *Kritik der Sprache* he
had continued to work as a journalist for several years, but in 1901 he
resigned from the *Berliner Tageblatt* after a quarrel with the editor. He
returned to work for the newspaper two years later, however, and although
anxious to leave the city permanently by this time, he stayed in Berlin
until his daughter Grete's marriage in 1905. Again suffering from depression and extreme nervousness, Mauthner took a lengthy vacation in
Teneriffe early in the year, but once back in Berlin the nervous condition
returned. After a brief visit with relatives in Vienna, he moved to Freiburg
im Breisgau in October.

In his correspondence Mauthner describes the decision to leave
Berlin as a matter of life and death, and writes that he wanted nothing
more than a cloistered atmosphere in which be might pursue his "quirky"
study of language philosophy (*meine sprachphilosophischen Schrullen*).
In the small university town of Freiburg he found such an atmosphere and
was generally more content than he had been in Berlin. He studied mathematics and natural sciences at the university, became a member of the
Kant Society, and thereby came into contact with Hans Vaihinger, founder
of the society and author of *Die Philosophie des Als-Ob* (1911, *The
Philosophy of the As-If*). Mauthner reviewed Vaihinger's book in 1913 and
included "Als ob" as a separate entry in the second edition of his
Wörterbuch der Philosophie: after praising the work's historical part he
takes issue with Vaihinger's theoretical distinction between hypotheses
and fictions. Vaihinger does not recognize the full extent of his thesis in
Mauthner's opinion "because, despite several gestures in this direction, he
could not or would not convince himself that it is a question of language
critique, and that all important linguistic concepts (*Begriffe*) , or perhaps
all concepts, are essentially fictions. . . . for this reason it will never be

possible to distinguish clearly the contrast between hypothesis and fiction" *(Wörterbuch* 1, 41-42). As the passage makes clear, Mauthner's skepticism about Vaihinger's distinction reflects his own radical nominalism. But while somewhat critical of Vaihinger, he still acknowledges a strong affinity with him and reviews the fourth edition of *Die Philosophie des Als-ob* in 1920.[18]

During the four years he spent in Freiburg he also became acquainted with Martin Buber, and at Buber's request wrote a volume on language for the series *Die Gesellschaft. Sammlung sozialpsychologischer Monographien (Society. Collection of Socio-psychological Monographs).* In *Die Sprache* (1907, *Language*) Mauthner touches on issues including recent efforts to establish Esperanto as an international language, the notion of a mother tongue or *Muttersprache,* and the discipline of *Völkerpsychologie.* In contrast to the *Kritik,* this volume concentrates on language as a social phenomenon. It also looks forward the *Wörterbuch der Philosophie* in two specific instances where Mauthner traces the history of the term "element" and examines loan translation in such sentences as "Today is Friday, the 18th of January in the year 1907" *(Die Sprache,* 62-65; 74-78).

Mauthner was not altogether satisfied with his new, seemingly idyllic lifestyle, since he suffered from the very solitude he had sought—and found—in Freiburg. After several years he met Hedwig Straub (1872-1945), who became both a personal companion and a driving force behind his second major work, the *Wörterbuch der Philosophie.* Straub, a doctor who had spent the previous ten years among Beduin tribes in the Sahara, reported that she had carried the *Kritik* with her on camelback through the desert and so even before meeting Mauthner personally had felt a spiritual kinship with him. In 1909 the two moved to Meersburg on Lake Constance, and were married in 1910.

During the years in Meersburg Mauthner published the *Wörterbuch der Philosophie* and *Geschichte des Atheismus,* both discussed above, and he also returned to writing fiction. In 1913 he published a novel entitled *Der letzte Tod des Gautama Buddha (The Final Death of Gautama Buddha)* and in 1914 the satirical *Gespräche im Himmel und andere Ketzereien (Conversations in Heaven and Other Heresies).* Five years later his six-volume *Ausgewählte Schriften (Selected Works)* appeared, which included novels, novellas, and the early parodies of *Nach berühmten Mustern* that had established his reputation as a satirist. Of all Mauthner's literary efforts both before and during his final years in

Meersburg, *Der letzte Tod des Gautama Buddha* is the only work to have received much attention from later critics, since this novel can be situated and interpreted most easily in the context of Mauthner's philosophical works. It contains a fictional account of the views on mysticism developed most fully in volume four of the *Geschichte des Atheismus.*

Already in the *Kritik* Mauthner discusses silence and mysticism as possible outcomes of language critique as he understands it. The article on mysticism in the *Wörterbuch der Philosophie* expands on this discussion, but only in his later works does Mauthner try to develop his own particular form of mysticism. In an effort to differentiate himself from such figures as Meister Eckhart he refers to his own concept as "godless mysticism," but whether Mauthner articulates something with this term that differs fundamentally from other forms of mysticism seems doubtful. The designation "godless" replaces two others used in the *Wörterbuch*, "nominalistic" and "skeptical" mysticism; as Weiler points out, Mauthner "uses the term purely negatively; his mysticism does not imply any assertion about the existence of any entity whatever" (*Mauthner's Critique,* 294). While he does not posit a union with the divine, his "godless mysticism" still leaves room for the notion of unification or non-differentiation: "For on one point monism and mysticism agree: in a feeling of yearning for unification, for becoming one. Of what? Of one's own Ego. With what? With the non-Ego" (*Geschichte des Atheismus* 4, 427).

The mystical dimension of Mauthner's thought was one of the first aspects of his work to receive attention in a number of different contexts including works by Gustav Landauer and Gustav Sack. The anarchist/socialist Landauer was a friend of Mauthner and had helped prepare the manuscript of the *Kritik* while serving time in Tegel prison. During this time (August 1899-February 1900) Mauthner also commissioned him to translate Meister Eckhart into Modern High German. In letters from this period Landauer notes similarities between Eckhart and Mauthner, and in *Skepsis und Mystik* (1903, *Skepticism and Mysticism*) he expands on the comparison, aligning Mauthner not only with Meister Eckhart but also Max Stirner and others, and he declares:

> The history of world-views, of philosophies and religions alike, might be divided into two camps: on the one side, those who quickly contented themselves with something positive: the priests and founders of philosophical systems as the better ones, and the clerics (*Pfaffen*) and philosophy professors as the not-so-good ones; on the

other side, those who passionately desired peace (*Ruhe*), but were pacified by nothing: the heretics, sectarians and mystics.[19]

Like Landauer, Gustav Sack states in his essay "Moderne Mystik" (1913) that feelings of union with God and dissolution of the self are common to the experiences of all mystics regardless of their particular historical circumstances. At the same time, however, Sack distinguishes Mauthner from the more general revival of interest in mysticism at the time, which he criticizes sharply as a form of escapism.[20] More will be said shortly about Sack's literary reception of Mauthner, but before moving away from the topic of mysticism we should look at one more of Mauthner's contemporaries whose work also links theory of knowledge with mysticism: Ludwig Wittgenstein.

In the *Tractatus logico-philosophicus* (1921) Wittgenstein takes very different stances from Mauthner's on such issues as the possibility of scientific knowledge, and he distances himself explicitly from Mauthner with the now familiar statement: "All philosophy is a 'critique of language' (though not in Mauthner's sense)."[21] Their differences derive from Mauthner and Wittgenstein's respective views of language and can be characterized with the help of a metaphor used by both thinkers. Wittgenstein asserts in the *Tractatus:* "Language disguises thought. So much so, that from the outward form of the clothing it is impossible to infer the form of the thought beneath it, because the outward form of the clothing is not designed to reveal the form of the body, but for entirely different purposes" (*Tractatus* 4.002).

Mauthner likewise discusses the relation of language to world in terms of ill-fitting clothes, but in his version of the analogy "thought" occupies the spot often occupied by "language"; it refers to the clothes rather than the wearer. "Language" too receives a new referent and becomes the fabric from which thought is fashioned: "It is thinking (*das Denken*) that 'fits' reality like a bad coat; language differs as little from thinking as the fabric from which the clothing is made differs from the clothing itself. If a piece of clothing fits me badly, it is not the fabric that is to blame"(*Kritik* l, 193) .

Unlike Wittgenstein, who maintains that congruence actually does exist between reality and language (in the form of logical propositions, not in its everyday colloquial sense), Mauthner holds that the gap can never be bridged. Despite this major difference, however, the *Tractatus* and Mauthner's *Kritik* both end with a turn toward mysticism that suggests a closer relation between the two thinkers than one might suspect initially. For Mauthner the premise that some unmediated and extralinguistic mode of experience exists leads to a mystical yearning or *Sehnsucht* for that kind of experience, which is equated with true knowledge or *Erkenntnis*. Wittgenstein in contrast proposes that scientific knowledge is possible. But after working through his supporting arguments he admits that this kind of knowledge is not comprehensive; something still eludes it, which may ultimately be more important than any information provided by science: "We feel that even when all *possible* scientific questions have been answered, the problems of life remain completely untouched. . . . There are, indeed, things that cannot be put into words. They *make themselves manifest*. They are what is mystical" (*Tractatus* 6.52, 6.522).

How well Wittgenstein knew Mauthner's *Kritik* is a question with no clear-cut answer,[22] but in general critics agree that similarities between the two emerge more clearly as one moves away from the *Tractatus* and looks instead at such later works as the *Philosophical Investigations*. Here the notions of language game (*Sprachspiel*) and meaning as use recall Mauthner's discussion of conventionalism in ordinary language. In addition Wittgenstein's description of critique of language as a kind of "therapy" that helps us recognize many philosophical problems as problems of language seems to echo Mauthner, who asserts that philosophy is "nothing more and nothing less than critical attention to language" (*Kritik* 1, 705).

The differences between Mauthner and Wittgenstein are as important as their similarities, however, and should be mentioned lest it sound as though the *Philosophical Investigations* and Mauthner's *Kritik* come to identical conclusions. In the earlier discussion of the *Kritik* a conflict between the mentalistic and social dimensions of language was noted that is never entirely resolved in the *Kritik* or in Mauthner's later writings. He recognizes and in effect demonstrates that knowledge of any "reality" unmediated by language-as-thought is impossible, but at the same time wishes it were otherwise, and he retains the notion of ineffability, if only in the form of desire or yearning for something whose existence he knows cannot be proven. Wittgenstein, in contrast, rejects the notion of a private language (*Privatsprache*) in his later works. Focusing on spoken language or "language as use," he moves beyond the dilemma that Mauthner never entirely overcomes.

While specific points of comparison between Mauthner and Wittgenstein have been addressed by a number of critics, the more general question of Mauthner's influence is a difficult one to answer, primarily because his critique of language is one text of many published around 1900 that thematize language as an instrument of knowledge. Thus it is not always easy to pinpoint his work as a specific source of influence. For example, Hofmannsthal owned a copy of the *Beiträge zu einer Kritik der Sprache,* and his correspondence with Mauthner suggests that he had read the *Kritik* when he wrote *Ein Brief.* Yet even Martin Stern, who published their correspondence, does not go so far as to name Mauthner as the sole, or even primary, influence on Hofmannsthal.[23] To do so one would have to ignore the fact that Hofmannsthal had attended lectures by Ernst Mach prior to writing the Chandos letter, for example, or that by this time he was familiar with Nietzsche, whom he described as the clear air in which his thoughts crystallized.[24] This is not to say that we can dismiss Mauthner's impact altogether or view him purely as a mediator between Nietzsche, Mach, and Hofmannsthal; but it does suggest the kind of complications involved in tracing the literary reception of Mauthner's ideas.

The task is easier when it concerns authors who *do* name Mauthner specifically. These writers include Gustav Sack, Christian Morgenstern, and Samuel Beckett. After Sack's death in 1916 his widow wrote to Mauthner that he had spent much of 1913-1914 reading the philosopher's works in the Munich State Library,[25] and Sack himself noted in the preface to his novel fragment *Paralyse:* "The reader . . . will occasionally come across borrowings . . . from Fritz Mauthner's *Wörterbuch der Philosophie.* To preserve the unity of the text before me and not disrupt the illusion, I will not refer to the borrowing in a footnote each time" (*Gesammelte Werke* 1, 38-39). His novel *Ein verbummelter Student* (1917) likewise attests to his familiarity with Mauthner: its protagonist, like Hofmannthal's Lord Chandos, experiences a rupture between language and reality (although, unlike Chandos, he explicitly summarizes the main points of the *Kritik der Sprache*). A book-length study on linguistic skepticism in Sack's work explores their relation in greater detail.[26] Christian Morgenstern's name has also been linked with Mauthner's; he apparently knew the *Kritik* as early as 1906 when he was writing many of his *Galgenlieder,* and Leo Spitzer drew explicit parallels between motifs in these poems and concepts in Mauthner's work.[27] Mauthner called Morgenstern's work a continuation of his own *(Selbstdarstellung,* 140), and once again Spitzer played a role by drawing Mauthner's attention to this aspect of Morgenstern's writing. As in Hofmannsthal's case, Nietzsche must also be taken into consideration when assessing Morgenstern's linguistic skepticism; he figures prominently in Alfred

Liede's discussion of Morgenstern as a writer of so-called *Unsinnspoesie*.[28]

Outside German literature Samuel Beckett's work offers the best-known instance of Mauthner's impact. Beckett became familiar with the *Kritik* in 1932 through James Joyce and in the late 1970s still acknowledged Mauthner's importance for him. Yet only in a 1980 article by Linda Ben-Zvi did the link first gain closer attention, perhaps in part because Mauthner's works are still unavailable in English translation.[29] Taking this relative inaccessibility into account, Ben-Zvi gives a helpful eight-point summary of arguments in the *Kritik* that figure in Beckett's writings[30] and summarizes their connection as follows: "By placing language at the heart of the *Critique,* subsuming under it all knowledge, and then systematically denying its basic efficacy, Mauthner illustrates the possibility of using language to indict itself. The same linguistic centrality and nullity lie at the core of Beckett's works" ("Limits of Language," 183).

Notably, when the issue of Mauthner's influence on literary figures arises, attention focuses almost exclusively on his general philosophical positions, not on his essays on literary and cultural trends around the turn of the century. If these essays are discussed, they are treated quite separately from arguments in the *Kritik* and *Wörterbuch* and their literary reception. By divorcing the drama critic and journalist from the philosopher of language, critics take their cue from Mauthner himself, who always considered his philosophical writings a more important contribution than any of his journalistic work or literary efforts. Nonetheless, the absence of any attempt to link these aspects of Mauthner's oeuvre is particularly noticeable in such works as Eschenbacher's *Fritz Mauthner und die deutsche Literatur um 1900* (1977). Just how close the connections are between his skepticism and his assessment of individual writers and movements remains to be seen; thus far only Mauthner's interest in Naturalism has been documented in any detail.[31] Of particular interest for future work might be such articles as his "Fin de siècle und kein Ende" (1891), "Die Allerjüngsten und ihre Artistenlyrik" (1898), and the collected essays in *Zum Streit um die Bühne* (1893).[32] Aside from these texts his correspondence with writers including Hermann Bahr, Gerhart Hauptmann, and Alfred Döblin might also shed light on Mauthner's involvement as a journalist in the literary and cultural developments of turn-of-the-century Berlin and Vienna in relation to his philosophical works.

Mauthner's last years were not without controversy. In 1919 an article written on the occasion of his seventieth birthday mocked the local Catholic pastor for visiting Mauthner occasionally "since he could not have him burned as a heretic." The letter enraged the priest, since it also listed among Mauthner's good deeds the fact that, when his maid gave birth to an illegitimate child (ostensibly his), Mauthner baptized the infant before it died.[33] Initially the priest's anger was directed at the author of the article, but when volume one of *Der Atheismus und seine Geschichte in Abendlande* was published in 1920, Mauthner himself became the primary target of attack. The priest urged the city council to revoke Mauthner's honorary citizenship, which for legal reasons was impossible, and continued to attack him on through the year.

From 1920 to 1923 Mauthner was in increasingly bad health. He suffered from arteriosclerosis and had a nervous breakdown in 1922. After spending the first few months of 1923 in the hospital he died on June 29, having lived long enough to correct proofs for the *Geschichte des Atheismus*. His funeral was conducted by a friend and non-denominational minister, Jacobus Weidenmann; it evoked protest from some local residents who thought it inappropriate to hold a service for an avowed atheist in the Lutheran church, and thus echoed the furor of the preceding years concerning both Mauthner as a person and his final work on atheism. In all fairness, however, it should be noted that while the work was predictably attacked by the church in Germany, it met with a more favorable reception in Switzerland, leading Mauthner to joke in a letter: "Oddly enough, it [the *Geschichte des Atheismus*] has found its best audience among religious-social ministers in Switzerland. I may yet be elected a minister."[34]

After his death a campaign to establish a Fritz Mauthner Academy was begun, but it was revealed as a hoax in 1925 when the organizer fled to the United States with the 25,000 *Reichsmark* that had been raised. Mauthner's hundredth birthday was celebrated in 1949 in Meersburg in 1949; it remains to be seen whether the "Fritz Mauthner Day" announced by Christian Morgenstern and scheduled for the year 2407 ("Grand Spectacle! . . . Main Event: Shooting of the Word 'World History' by Ten Sharpshooters from Ten German Tribes. . . . Cold Buffet!") will actually take place.[35]

Notes

1. Fritz Mauthner, *Erinnerungen. I. Prager Jugendjahre* (Munich: Müller, 1918, *Memoirs. I. Youth in Prague*), 30; henceforth cited as *Erinnerungen*. The passage is quoted here in J. P. Stern's translation; cf. Stern, "'Words Are Also Deeds': Some Observations on Austrian Language Consciousness," *New Literary History* 12 (1981), 509-527.

2. See J. P. Stern, "'Words Are Also Deeds'" 515, on Walter Muschg and Hans Weigel, who cite the Mauthner text in reference to Kafka and Kraus respectively. For more on Kafka in this connection, see for example Christoph Stölzl, *Kafkas böses Böhmen. Zur Sozialgeschichte Prager Juden* (Munich: Edition Text + Kritik, 1975), and on Rilke, Peter Demetz, *René Rilkes Prager Jahre* (Düsseldorf: Diedrich, 1953), esp. 201-205. A discussion of Mauthner's attitudes toward Judaism is found in Gershon Weiler, "Fritz Mauthner: A Study in Jewish Self-Rejection," *Yearbook of the Leo Baeck Institute* 8 (1963), 136-148.

3. Here I agree with J. P. Stern, who notes that "the situation he [Mauthner] describes may well be specifically Jewish in its intensity, but mutatis mutandis it applies beyond the reach of any racial criteria—it is, in this respect too, an Austrian problem" ("'Words Are Also Deeds,'" 516). See also Mauthner's article "Skepticism and the Jews," *The Menorah Journal* 10, no. 1 (1924), 1-14, where be contests that his philosophical outlook is uniquely Jewish.

4. Gershon Weiler, *Mauthner's Critique of Language* (Cambridge: Cambridge University Press, 1970), 3-4; henceforth cited as *Mauthner's Critique.*

5. F., "Fritz Mauthner," *Rote Fahne*, 1 July 1923, quoted by Joachim Kühn, *Gescheiterte Sprachkritik* (Berlin: de Gruyter, 1976), 293: "Man könnte ihn als Philosophen der bürgerlichen Klasse ansehen, die am Ende ist. Darin freilich steht er über seiner Klasse, daß er sich selbst absolut nichts vormacht, sondern unbekümmert jede Konsequenz zieht."

6. Fritz Mauthner, *Beiträge zu einer Kritik der Sprache* (Stuttgart/-Berlin: Cotta, 1901-1902) l, 665; henceforth cited as *Kritik.*

7. "Fritz Mauthner" in *Die Philosophie der Gegenwart in*

Selbstdarstellungen (2nd ed. Leipzig: Meiner, 1924), 129; henceforth cited as *Selbstdarstellung (Self-portrait)*.

8. See Katherine Arens, *Functionalism and Fin-de-siècle. Fritz Mauthner's Critique of Language*, Stanford German Studies 23 (Frankfurt am Main/Bern: Lang, 1984), chapter four on Mach and Mauthner; also the extensive footnote in Elisabeth Leinfellner, "Zur nominalistischen Begründung von Linguistik und Sprachphilosophie: Fritz Mauthner und Ludwig Wittgenstein," *Studium Generale* 22, no. 1 (1969), 213 (n. 7).

9. In this respect—as in many others—Mauthner resembles many German (and Czech) Jews of the Wilhelminian era; see for example Peter Gay, "Encounter With Modernism: German Jews in Wilhelminian Culture" in his *Freud, Jews and Other Germans* (Oxford: Oxford University Press, 1978), 93-168.

10. For a more detailed treatment of Mauthner's individual literary works, parodies and essay collections, see Joachim Kühn, *Gescheiterte Sprachkritik*, 130-174; 181-189.

11. Two examples from Joachim Kühn's *Gescheiterte Sprachkritik* may suffice: "Eine Integration von Sprachskepsis und Dichtung ist ihm . . . nicht gelungen, und er weicht deshalb auf eine philosophische Argumentation aus" (3); "Sein philosophisches Werk gibt Mauthner den Mut, das, was er fünfundzwanzig Jahre lang getrieben hat [den Journalismus], als nichtig beiseite zu schieben, nicht anders als seine Dichtung. Die *Kritik der Sprache* sollte der Anfang eines neuen Lebens sein" (199).

12. Cf. Joachim Kühn, *Gescheiterte Sprachkritik*, 174-199 for an overview of Mauthner's career in journalism; also Kühn's bibliography for a complete listing of Mauthner's articles.

13. See ibid 223-225 on the mixed reviews of the *Kritik*; also Gershon Weiler, *Mauthner's Critique*, 319-322, and Walter Eschenbacher, *Fritz Mauthner und die deutsche Literatur um 1900* (Frankfurt am Main/Bern: Lang, 1977), 117-130; henceforth cited as *Mauthner und die Literatur um 1900*.

14. Kühn notes an additional reason that Mauthner's work received little recognition even after phenomenology's dominance had begun to wane: as the work of a Jewish author, the *Kritik* was deliberately ignored in the 1930s (*Gescheiterte Sprachkritik*, 223).

15. Mauthner is not alone in making this assumption; on the contrary, his presuppositions about what constitutes "ideal" knowledge indicate his rootedness in Western philosophical traditions as clearly as

any of his more explicit statements of indebtedness to his philosophical "ancestors." See Richard Rorty, *Philosophy and the Mirror of Nature* (Princeton: Princeton University Press, 1979) on the notions of knowledge as "confrontation" and of philosophy as epistemology dominant since the time of Descartes and Kant respectively. The metaphors of visual perception used in reference to epistemology likewise rest on a long tradition discussed by Rorty, this time one which is traceable to Plato.

16. Fritz Mauthner, *Die Sprache* (Frankfurt: Rütten und Loening, 1907), 84.

17. Fritz Mauthner, *Der Atheismus und seine Geschichte im Abendlande* (Stuttgart/Berlin: Deutsche Verlagsanstalt, 1920-1923) 2, 376, quoted here in Gershon Weiler's translation; cf. *Mauthner's Critique,* 307-318 ("An Application of the Critique of Language: Intellectual Historiography"), also Gershon Weiler, "Fritz Mauthner as an Historian," *History and Theory* 4, no. 1 (1966), 57-71.

18. The initial three-part review appeared in the *Berliner Tageblatt* 42 (10, 17 and 25 March 1913). Mauthner's review of the fourth edition appeared in *Das neue Deutschland* 9, no. 1/2 (October 1920) , 6-11.

19. Landauer, *Skepsis und Mystik. Versuche im Anschluß an Mauthners Sprachkritik* (Berlin: Fontane, 1903; 2nd ed. Cologne: Maracan-Block, 1923, rpt. Münster/Wetzlar: Büchse der Pandora, 1978), 46. See Joachim Kühn, *Gescheiterte Sprachkritik,* 209-210 for excerpts from Mauthner and Landauer's correspondence during Landauer's imprisonment.

20. Gustav Sack, "Moderne Mystik" in Sack, *Gesammelte Werke in zwei Bänden,* ed. Paula Sack (Berlin: Fischer, 1920), 2, 290-294; here 290.

21. Ludwig Wittgenstein, *Tractatus logico-philosophicus* (London: Routledge & Kegan Paul, 1974) , 4.0031.

22. In most cases, discussion simply concentrates on points of correspondence between Mauthner and Wittgenstein. Weiler, however, takes up the question: noting that the three most specific points of comparison between the *Tractatus* and the *Kritik* involve images occurring in the first thirty pages of Mauthner's text, he proposes that Wittgenstein read the first part of the *Kritik* carefully, then read only parts that interested him (*Mauthner's Critique,* 299).

23. Martin Stern, "Der Briefwechsel Hofmannsthal-Mauthner," *Hofmannsthal-Blätter* 19-20 (1978), 21-38. The earliest mention of a possible influence that I am aware of occurs in Gustav Landauer's

Skepsis und Mystik; cf. also Kühn, *Gescheiterte Sprachkritik*, 20-29 on Hofmannsthal's *Ein Brief.*

24.	Hugo von Hofmannsthal, letter to Arthur Schnitzler, 13 July 1891; excerpted in *Nietzsche und die deutsche Literatur*, ed. Bruno Hillebrand (Tübingen: Niemeyer/dtv, 1978), 1, 77.

25.	Letter from 3 July 1917; quoted by Walter Eschenbacher, *Mauthner und die Literatur um 1900,* 134.

26.	See Karl Eibl, *Die Sprachskepsis im Werk von Gustav Sack*, Bochumer: Arbeiten zur Sprach-und Literaturwissenschaft 3 (Munich: Fink, 1970); also Kühn, *Gescheiterte Sprachkritik*, 29-38.

27.	See Alfred Liede, *Dichtung als Spiel. Studien zur Unsinnspoesie an den Grenzen der Sprache* (Berlin: de Gruyter, 1963), 1, 332.

28.	Ibid., 1, 254-349. See also Joachim Kühn, *Gescheiterte Sprachkritik*, 38-42, and Friedrich Hiebel, *Christian Morgenstern. Wende und Aufbruch unseres Jahrhunderts* (Bern: Francke, 1957).

29.	Ben-Zvi, "Samuel Beckett, Fritz Mauthner, and the Limits of Language," *PMLA* 95 (1980), 183-200; henceforth cited as "Limits of Language."

30.	"Limits of Language," 187-188: "1. Thinking and speaking are one activity. 2. Language and memory are synonymous. 3. All language is metaphor. 4. There are no absolutes. 5. The ego is contingent; it does not exist apart from language. 6. Communication between men is impossible. 7. The only language should be simple language. 8. The highest forms of a critique of language are laughter and silence."

31.	See Joachim Kühn, *Gescheiterte Sprachkritik*, 189-195, "Mauthners Kampf um den Naturalismus."

32.	Fritz Mauthner, "Fin de siècle und kein Ende," *Das Magazin für Litteratur* 60, no. 1 (3 January 1891), 13-15; *Zum Streit um die Bühne. Ein Berliner Tagebuch*, Deutsche Schriften für Litteratur und Kunst, 2. Reihe H. 5 (Kiel/Leipzig: Lipsus und Tischer, 1893); "Die Allerjüngsten und ihre Artistenlyrik," *Berliner Tageblatt* 27, no. 623 (8 December 1898), 1-2: "I. Die graue Theorie;" *Berliner Tageblatt* 27, no. 636 (15 December 1898), 1-2: "II. Stefan George."

33.	For this and other information about Mauthner's final years in Meersburg, I have relied on Joachim Kühn, *Gescheiterte Sprachkritik*, 267f.

34.	Letter to Auguste Hauschner, 21 March 1922; in *Briefe an Auguste Hauschner,* eds. Martin Beradt and Lotte Bloch-Zavřel (Berlin: Rowohlt, 1919), 238; cited in Kühn, *Gescheiterte Sprachkritik*, 272.

35.   The "advertisement" was written by Morgenstern in 1908, and is
      printed in full in Kühn, *Gescheiterte Sprachkritik*, 41-42.

Bibliography

Ia.   Works by Fritz Mauthner in German

Beiträge zu einer Kritik der Sprache. 3 vols. (*Sprache und Psychologie,
      Zur Sprachwissenschaft, Zur Grammatik und Logik*). Stuttgart (vol.
      3 Stuttgart/Berlin): Cotta, 1901-1902. 3rd ed. vols. 1-3 1923. Rpt.
      Hildesheim: Olms, 1964-1969; Frankfurt/Berlin/Vienna: Ullstein,
      1982.
"Die Herkunft des sprachkritischen Gedankens." *Die Zukunft* 12, no. 47
      (1904), 10-23. Rpt. in *Erinnerungen. I. Prager Jugendjahre*, 200-
      222.
Aristoteles. Ein unhistorischer Essay.   Berlin: Bard und Marquardt (Die
      Literatur 2) , 1904.
Die Sprache. Frankfurt: Rütten und Loening, 1907.
Wörterbuch der Philosophie. Neue Beiträge zu einer Kritik der Sprache.
      2 vols. Munich: Müller, 1910-1911. 2nd ed. 3 vols. Leipzig:
      Meiner, 1923-1924. Rpt. (1st ed.) Zurich: Diogenes, 1980.
Erinnerungen. I. Prager Jugendjahre. Munich: Müller, 1918.
Der Atheismus und seine Geschichte im Abendlande. 4 vols.
      Stuttgart/Berlin: Deutsche Verlagsanstalt, 1920-1923.
Muttersprache und Vaterland. Leipzig: Dürr und Weber, 1920.
"Fritz Mauthner." In *Die Philosophie der Gegenwart in Selbst-
      darstellungen*. Ed. Raymund Schmidt. Leipzig: Meiner, 1922, 3,
      121-144. Rpt. 1924, 123-145.
Gottlose Mystik. Dresden: Reißner, n. d. (1924) . Excerpts from *Wörter-
      buch der Philosophie, Der letzte Tod des Gautama Buddha* and
      Der Atheismus und seine Geschichte im Abendlande; compiled by
      Hedwig Mauthner.
Die drei Bilder der Welt. Ein sprachkritischer Versuch.   Ed. Monty
      Jacobs. Erlangen: Verlag der philosophischen Akademie Erlangen,
      1925 (posthum.).
Sprache und Leben. Ausgewählte Texte aus dem philosophischen Werk.
      Ed. + intro. Gershon Weiler. Salzburg/Vienna: Residenz, 1986.

Briefe an Auguste Hauschner. Eds. Martin Beradt, Lotte Bloch-Zavrel. Berlin: Rowohlt, 1929 (82 letters, 1883-1922).

Landauer, Gustav. *Sein Lebensgang in Briefen.* 2 vols. Ed. Martin Buber. Frankfurt: Rütten und Loening, 1929 (excerpts from 24 letters to Landauer, 1908-1919).

Stern, Martin, ed. + intro. "Der Briefwechsel Hofmannsthal-Mauthner." *Hofmannsthal-Blätter* 19-20 (1978) , 21-38 (12 letters, 1892-1907).

Thiele, Joachim. "Zur 'Kritik der Sprache'. Briefe von Fritz Mauthner an Ernst Mach." *Muttersprache* 76 (1966), 78-86 (7 letters, 1895-1906).

II.   Works by Fritz Mauthner in English

Aristotle. Trans. Charles D. Cordon. New York: McClure, Phillips, 1907.

"Scepticism and the Jews." *The Menorah Journal* 10, no. 1 (1924) , 1-14.

III.   Secondary Works in English

Arens, Katherine M. *Functionalism and Fin-de-siècle. Fritz Mauthner's Critique of Language.* Bern/Frankfurt: Lang (Stanford German Studies 23) , 1985.

——."Linguistic Skepticism: Towards a Productive Definition." *Monatshefte* 74 (1982) , 145-155.

Bredeck, Elizabeth. "Critique of Language and the Language of Critique. Fritz Mauthner's *Beiträge zu einer Kritik der Sprache.*" Diss. Univ. of Virginia, 1987.

——."Fritz Mauthners Nachlese zu Nietzsches Sprachkritik." *Nietzsche-Studien* 13 (1984), 587-599.

——."Historical Narrative or Scientific Discipline? Fritz Mauthner on the Limits of Linguistics." In *Papers in the History of Linguistics.* Eds. Hans Aarsleff, Louis G. Kelly, Hans-Josef Niederehe. Amsterdam/Philadelphia: Benjamins (Studies in the History of the Language Sciences 38), 1987, 585-593 .

——."The Retreat of 'Origin' as the Emergence of 'Language.' Fritz Mauthner and the Language of Beginnings." In *Theorien vom Ursprung der Sprache.* Eds. Wolfert von Rahden, Joachim Gessinger. Berlin/New York: de Gruyter, 1989, 1, 607-626.

Janik, Allan, and Stephen Toulmin. *Wittgenstein's Vienna.* New York:

Simon and Schuster, 1973, 121-133 .

Johnston, William M. *The Austrian Mind. An Intellectual and Social History 1848-1938*. Berkeley/Los Angeles/London: University of California Press, 1972, 196-199.

Stern, J. P. "'Words Are Also Deeds': Some Observations on Austrian Language Consciousness." *New Literary History* 12 (1981), 509-527.

Weiler, Gershon. "On Fritz Mauthner's Critique of Language." *Mind* 67 (1958), 80-87.

——. "Fritz Mauthner: A Study in Jewish Self-Rejection." *Yearbook of the Leo Baeck Institute* 8 (1963), 136-148.

——. "Fritz Mauthner as an Historian." *History and Theory* 4, no. 1 (1966), 57-71.

——. "Fritz Mauthner." In *The Encyclopedia of Philosophy*. Ed. Paul Edwards. New York/London: The Macmillan Company and Free Press, 1967, 5, 221-223 .

——. *Mauthner's Critique of Language*. Cambridge: Cambridge University Press, 1970.

IV.   Major Studies in German

Eschenbacher, Walter. *Fritz Mauthner und die deutsche Literatur um 1900*. Bern/Frankfurt: Lang (Europäische Hochschulschriften Reihe 1: Deutsche Literatur und Germanistik 163), 1977.

Gustafsson, Lars. *Sprache und Lüge. Drei sprachphilosophische Extremisten. Friedrich Nietzsche, Alexander Bryant Johnson, Fritz Mauthner*. Trans. Susanne Seul. Munich: Hanser, 1980.

Haller, Rudolf. "Sprachkritik und Philosophie. Wittgenstein und Mauthner." In *Sprachthematik in der österreichischen Literatur des 20. Jahrhunderts*. Ed. Institut für Österreichkunde. Vienna: Hirt, 1974, 41-56.

Kühn, Joachim. *Gescheiterte Sprachkritik. Fritz Mauthners Leben und Werk*. Berlin/New York: de Gruyter, 1975.

Leinfellner, Elisabeth. "Zur nominalistischen Begründung von Linguistik und Sprachphilosophie: Fritz Mauthner und Ludwig Wittgenstein." *Studium Generale* 22, no. 1 (1969) , 209-251.

Leinfellner-Rupertsberger, Elisabeth. "Sprachkritik und Atheismus bei Fritz Mauthner." In *Von Bolzano zu Wittgenstein. Zur Tradition der österreichischen Philosopie*. Ed. J. C. Nyíri. Vienna: Hölder-Pichler-Tempsky (Schriftenreihe der Wittgenstein-Gesellschaft

12/Teil 2), 1986, 173-182.

Müller, Heinz. "Fritz Mauthners Stellung in der Geschichte der Philosophie." Diss. Greifswald, 1966.

Weibel, Peter. "Philosophie als Sprachkritik. Sprachkritische Epistemologie in Österreich um 1900." *Manuskripte* 79 (1983), 64-73.

For a complete bibiography of Mauthner's works and all secondary literature up to 1975, see Kühn, *Gescheiterte Sprachkritik*, 297-362.

Rosa Mayreder

Harriet Anderson

A recent commentator has identified "Oedipal tension" and the "rebellion of the sons against the fathers" as a generalized phenomenon of Vienna around 1900.[1] It is seen as having its roots in the failure of late nineteenth-century liberalism, which caused the young people of Vienna in the 1870s to affirm a new "Dionysian art and populist politics"[2] against the overly rational and analytic premises of the fathers. The artistic avantgarde of the 1890s then, it is claimed, broke this forged link between culture and politics to become preoccupied with the nature of modernity and the life of the psyche, these being epitomized by the "modern malady" of the "dissolution of the ego"[3] and the apolitical flight into the interior. However, although necessarily schematic, such an analysis is nevertheless symptomatic of a widespread omission. For nowhere is there mention of the rebellion of the daughters, those supporters of the radical women's movement who, like their also largely neglected social reformist brothers,[4] did maintain the link between culture and politics, who did not succumb to apolitical introversion but continued to strive for a regeneration of the social fabric partly in the name of those seemingly exhausted values of the Enlightenment under the motto "Through insight to freedom and happiness."[5]

The following is an attempt to help correct this omission by offering an analysis of the life and writings of Vienna's most significant rebellious daughter, the feminist agitator and theorist, writer and artist Rosa Mayreder (1858-1938). A biographical approach has been chosen, one which profits from the exceptional wealth of autobiographical material available.[6] Mayreder constantly stressed the subjective nature of her work, claiming in the introduction to one of her collections of essays: "I freely confess that I only present a subjective world view, a fragment, which is limited by my own experience of people and books and not least

of myself.'"7 By placing Mayreder's writings in a biographical framework
it is hoped that the simultaneity of her activities—political engagement,
theoretical reflection, imaginative writing—will emerge, while at the same
time revealing the tensions between and within her life and the various
aspects of her achievement; her rebellion remains in many ways a product
of the culture of the fathers. Mayreder's place in the context of the world
will thus also be indicated: to a large extent she belongs to the liberal
social reformers while also making an original contribution to the artistic
avant-garde of the 1890s. And conversely, it is hoped that such a wide-
ranging if highly compressed study will in turn help to illuminate that context of early radical feminism as a heterogeneous cultural movement with
roots in the intellectual trends of its time and the pervasive pluralism in the
thought and cultural activity of Vienna around 1900.

Mayreder's family constellation was in many ways typical of her
generation. Her wealthy father Franz Obermayer, keeper of a highly popular public house and simple restaurant in the heart of the city, was the
embodiment of the self-made man of the economic boom of the mid-nine-
teenth century. A product of 1848 politically, he is presented by Mayreder
in her childhood memoirs as being almost a tyrant with regard to women.
Yet true to his liberal respect for learning, he was anxious to give both his
sons and daughters the best education available according to his conventional notions of what this might mean. Thus Rosa Obermayer enjoyed
(or endured) French, music, and drawing lessons in addition to attending
one of the young ladies' colleges of the city. Rosa's mother was also in
many ways a typical product of her social context. According to
Mayreder's account, her mother's marriage was largely one of conve-
nience in which she played the role of willing slave to her husband's
demands. 8 Yet there were also unconventional sides to Rosa's upbringing. Franz Obermayer may have been in some respects a patriarch in the
old manner, but he was willing to indulge his obviously highly intelligent
daughter's appetite for reading, giving her the collected works of Richard
Wagner —at her own request —as a Christmas present in 1874. Latin and
Greek lessons were not refused her after some struggle, and significantly
psychology was added to her courses at school at Rosa's own request.

This greater intellectual curiosity was reflected too in Rosa's first
attempts at writing—parodies of school teachers and other juvenilia and
also in her early awareness of women's disadvantagement, which came to
the fore in 1873. This was combined with a belief in her gifts as a writer
and with a strict regime of self-improvement and cultivation of individ-

uality and exceptionality, in which an important aid was her diary begun in April 1873. Through self-discipline Rosa hoped to rise above average womanhood and thus to justify her rejection of convention and her sense of heralding a new femininity, "for it was clear to me," she remarked with hindsight, "that I had the right to trespass beyond the boundaries of feminine duties only if I was a 'phenomenon.'"[9] Mayreder stresses in her autobiography that there were no external influences such as financial need or a model to emulate, which might have led her to emancipatory ideas.[10] She saw them instead as being the "symptom of a particular state of culture, yes, the symptom of a particular stage of human development."[11] Although it is possible to interpret this remark in general evolutionary terms, as intended by Mayreder, it is also possible to read it in a historically more accurate way, for Mayreder was indeed a symptom of her culture through her participation in the avant-garde intellectual climate of the time. This was mediated above all by her reading and friends, for these young people were in many ways typical representatives of Viennese Wagnerianism and the reception of Nietzsche of the 1870s, eagerly joining the attitude of protest against the ruling conventions of their parents.[12] Even if there were no role models, it was an atmosphere conducive to an emancipatory awareness. It was Mayreder's contribution to apply that awareness to the situation of women.

The circle of friends was important in another way also, for it was there that Rosa first heard of a young man, Emil, said to be an "homme vièrge," a trait which caused her to idolize him. This first experience of sexual idolization, Mayreder later claimed, made such a decisive impression on her that it determined her experience in sexual matters for the rest of her life.[13] It was also among this circle of friends that Rosa met her future husband, Karl Mayreder, later professor of city planning and a distinguished architect, whom she married in 1881. Problems soon arose which, however, Mayreder regarded as necessary, confiding to her diary: "As it has become clear to me that all happiness emerges out of the resolution of painful conflicts, how can I complain about these conflicts,"[14] thus applying one of the tenets of her thought to her life. She still stood by her adolescent creed of the freedom of the individual, another leitmotif of her philosophy, and it was this which was to be the basis of the marriage. It was agreed that each partner would give the other the freedom of full personal development, an agreement which was successfully put to the test between 1887 and 1889 when Rosa found herself attracted to another man. It was, however, an attraction which brought little happiness, reinforcing a dualism she had first felt as an adolescent, that between the intellectual and the elemental. This dualism was to become a characteristic of her anthropology.

In the late 1880s Mayreder became involved with a new circle of friends centered around the exotic Marie Lang. Members of this group included Rudolf Steiner, later the founder of the anthroposophic movement, and the composer Hugo Wolf. A close intellectual friendship developed with the former, for both were great admirers of Goethe's philosophy of nature and eager readers of Nietzsche and Max Stirner. Mayreder was, however, more open to the then fashionable theories of materialism than Steiner, a difference of thought which was to mark the different paths the two were to take and led to a personal estrangement.[15] Although in later years Steiner could talk of Mayreder in the highest terms in his autobiography, [16] her diaries reveal a lack of mutual esteem. Steiner did, however, help her to find a forum for the pieces she was writing in the early 1890s by putting her in touch with publishers. Most of these early minor publications were later included in independently published works.

The friendship with Wolf also resulted in a publication of the text of Wolf's only opera, *Der Corregidor,* the librettist being Rosa Mayreder. The collaboration, which did not begin until 1895, five years after completion of the text because Wolf initially rejected it, extended beyond a mere working relationship, as documented in Wolf's impulsive letters to his maternal friend. [17] Mayreder took on the function of adviser and confidante, helping Wolf through the trials and tribulations of everyday life. Although Wolf was on second thought enthusiastic about the libretto, the critics on the whole were not and the opera remained a source of injury for the rest of Mayreder's life.

Two years before the Wolf collaboration, in October 1893, Mayreder had already stepped into public life in a very different capacity: as committee member of the General Austrian Women's Association, the radical wing of the Austrian women's movement, founded in January of the year. It was the only bourgeois women's group in Vienna at that time which aimed to subvert the status quo and attended to a wide range of issues from women's political rights, the reform of women's education, and their working conditions to the double standards of sexual morality. In January 1894 Mayreder drew attention to the Association by giving a talk attacking the state regulation of prostitution, which she saw to be inefficient and hypocritical in its methods and a degradation of women in its conception, indulging for men what was forbidden for women. Her criticism was particularly outspoken, even for the notoriously radical Association, and her proposed solution, the general acceptance of concubinage (as well as increased employment opportunities for women) encountered opposition among the Association's member. Indeed, Mayreder's position in the Association was altogether ambiguous and her feelings ambivalent. She felt torn between the life of practical politics and that of the mind, increasingly considering herself unsuited to the former, yet driven by a sense of duty.

Mayreder was active in the 1890s in various spheres: as feminist agitator, as librettist, as writer of both fiction and theoretical essay; some of those essays which were later to be incorporated into her major work of feminist theory were conceive in the early 1890s. With regard to her imaginative writing, 1896 saw the appearance of her first independently published work, *Aus meiner Jugend* (From my Youth), a collection of three novellas, which, as Mayreder commented in letters, really did originate in her youth,[18] being the result of her adolescent need to express her thoughts. [19] All three novellas revolve around the theme of romantic love, the substance of conventional "women's literature," and are replete with the standard ploys of such texts: long-lost children, thwarted lovers, prodigal sons, concealed identity, and a *deus ex machina* figure. They are set in an unspecified context and conjure up the atmosphere of a Biedermeier idyll without any reference to wider political or social problems. Their interest lies in the fact that they are the first published expression of some major themes Mayreder was to develop at greater length in all her work, these being embedded here in a traditional framework which was later to be discarded. The uniting theme is that of the often strained relations of the individual to socially dominant norms, a theme which deeply concerned the young Mayreder, "Sonderlinge" ("Cranks"), for example the final novella in the collection, presents three figures, who in their own eyes are "normal" while regarding the others as cranks, thus indicating the force of the subjectivity of perception, another of Mayreder's dominant concerns. It draws on the Romantic literary tradition of the clash between the stolid philistine and the bohemian individualist (with Nietzschean airs) to deal openly with the conflict between the desire to fit into the social framework and the longing to follow the demands of the heart which might run contrary to the prevailing norms. Wendelin Traugott represents in his own eyes the impeccable bourgeois, the principle of reasonableness and correctness, whose life goes awry when he falls in love for the first time, only to be finally restored to social respectability by his obedience. Friedrich, on the other hand, represents the opposite pole: the young idealist who in true Romantic fashion flies in the face of bourgeois convention to seek rebirth in folk culture and later spurns the masses and recognizes the impotence such an attitude condemns him to. In the last resort both, it is very discretely hinted, suffer from their extreme adherence to the one point of view or the other; a synthesis, it is implied, between reason and emotion, conformism and individualism, is the ideal, whereby however it is the second element in each pair which is to lead.

The struggle and suffering of the individual in the face of social conventions are also taken up in the other novellas. The title story particularly focuses on the conventions surrounding the traditional young lady's upbringing. The fostered ignorance of sexuality and its role in human emotions is shown to lead to a lifelong loneliness: the narrator, Malwine, loses her fiancé through her blind adherence to the social mores of girls' innocence. And in the third of these novellas, "Der Letzte" (The Last in the Line), the problem of Oedipal tension, touched on in "Sonderlinge," is developed into another aspect of the clash between the individual and adherence to norms. Gandolf rejects his ne'er-do-well, tyrannical father and the commandment to honor one's parents, pointing out the injustice of such a commandment, while the count finally chooses to do his filial duty in the conflict between the demands of his father and those of his heart. Yet again the claims of the heart are shown in both cases to lead to personal happiness, and Mayreder firmly stands on this side.

This theme of the assertion of the individual against the tyranny of norms is taken up again in *Übergänge* (Transitions), which appeared one year after *Aus meiner Jugend* (three of the sketches had been previously published[20]). As the title suggests, many of the "psychological sketches"[21] which make up the collection deal with persons trying to cross over from one social form, that of convention, to another form perhaps more personally fitting. The collection thus represents a step beyond the critical beginnings of *Aus meiner Jugend* towards an attempt to offer possible methods of escape from social limitation, yet in contrast to the earlier volume without the almost obligatory happy ending of trivial literature. "Drei Briefe" (Three Letters), for example, tells of a woman's attempt to follow her feelings in the face of social conventions which place honor above love, how she is spurned by her lover who obeys those norms, and how her final capitulation involves donning a laughing mask to hide her pained face. The "philosophical badinage"[22] "Adam und Lilith" (Adam and Lilith) also deals with the strength of these social-sexual norms and the impotence of those who attempt to evade them. In this case it is the intellectual women, the independent Lilith as opposed to the docile Eve, the woman who dares to be more that the spare rib of the old Adam, who sharply criticizes the demands for female ignorance in sexual matters and declares her wish for a friendship with a man rather than a sexual relationship. Yet this vignette has a pessimistic ending, too, for the narrator makes it clear that the male sexual drive will finally triumph over all good resolutions when the flame of love has died, leaving only the grey ashes of mundane reality. Both an intransigent social order and a divisive natural one are shown to thwart the individual seeking a new space for personal development.

Another constraining force, that of the subjectivity of perception, a concern indicated in "Sonderlinge" is in *Übergänge* extended to the erotic and also political subjective idols and given a trenchant critical edge. "Sein Ideal" (His Ideal) clearly indicates how the idealization of an erotic object can be so strong that neither the idealized object nor the idealizing subject are able to escape the force of the ideal. Male idealization of woman merely leads to her being unable to be anything but an ideal, under which men are shown also to suffer while at the same time they tenaciously cling to precisely that idealization, unable to reconcile it with reality. The same force of subjective perception is shown regarding the political context in "Der Klub der Übermenschen" (The Club of the Supermen), which in addition to being a satire on the contemporary reception of the Nietzschean superman ideal by an uncritical youth, indicates the ease with which the strong can psychologically manipulate the weak and how the toppling of old idols merely leads to the erection of new ones without changing the fundamental attitudes.

In these sketches Mayreder displays a heightened awareness of the workings of the human psyche, its capacity for self-delusion and subjectivity of perception, the latter seen also in some of her nature descriptions, in which the physical landscape is a reflection of the protagonists' mental landscape.[23] The greater concern for subjectivity, the workings of the unconscious and of human drives is combined with an awareness of the hidden—often erotic—tentions in the patriarchal family constellations[24] and also with a tentative skepticism about language, for the male lover in "Adam and Lilith" is made to declare: "We will make ourselves understood only with difficulty, madam. We are discussing in two different languages and neither of us understands the other's."[25]

These concerns bring Mayreder very close to her Viennese contemporaries, for they too were interested in plumbing the depths of the psyche and in investigating the hidden erotic. As in their work this interest is reflected in experimentation with narrative techniques. Thus Mayreder adopts an impressionistic associative style[26] with interior monologue which reports a chain of thoughts in which the authorial voice retreats into the background to give way to a figurative narrator,[27] or to an authorial narration where one figure's inner life dominates and all events are seen in relation to that psyche.[28] *Übergänge* then represents Mayreder's step away form the insipid conventions of women's literature towards a combination of the aesthetics of the avant-garde of her cultural context with a critical concern above all for the individual's fruitless search for a new social-sexual order.

The pessimism displayed in *Übergänge* did not, however, deter Mayreder from continuing her political engagement, in particular with regard to the question of prostitution and the campaign against its tacit support by the state. In the year of the volume's publication she reacted critically to the insulting non-treatment of a petition she largely drafted for the abolition of state regulation, forcefully defending her point of view.[29] In this productive year she also co-founded an art school for women and girls, the aim of which was not to pamper the bourgeoisie's need for "a harmless occupation for young ladies to fill in the time between leaving school and becoming engaged"[30] but to train women in art so that they could earn a living. Mayreder herself rose above the average dilettante level to exhibit in Vienna and abroad. In addition she wrote in the summer of 1897 *Diana und Herodias* (Diana and Herodias), which had to wait until 1937 for private publication. This "mythical play" is significant in that it deals with the theme of polarity and synthesis, seen earlier in *Aus meiner Jugend* to be a concern of Mayreder's with regard to the individual, transferred to the cosmic whole and a mythical setting. In this short drama the positive and negative poles in nature are identified with the mythological and biblical figures of Diana and Herodias respectively, these corresponding to the pagan affirmation and the Christian denial of nature, which turn out, however, to be two different manifestations of the same phenomenon. This is a view which was not given expression in the discursive works until the early 1930s. The early date of writing and the misleading date of publication of *Diana und Herodias* thus indicate that Mayreder's intellectual development was not one from social concern and feminist engagement to mystical metaphysics, as might be imagined from merely looking at a list of publication. Political engagement, social concern presented in imaginative and discursive literature, and also a metaphysical world view run parallel, forming interweaving strands in Mayreder's life and works.

The activities of the 1890s continued for Mayreder on all three fronts. Political engagement was expressed in the foundation and for a short time co-editorship of *Dokumente der Frauen* (Documents of Women), a radical women's journal of high intellectual quality launched in March 1899, which, however, Mayreder decided to leave in October of the same year because of disagreements among the editors. This contretemps strengthened Mayreder's feelings that public agitation was not her metier and that her writing was more important, both to herself and to the women's cause.

Indeed, Mayreder's greatest imaginative contribution to the concerns of the women's movement can be found in *Idole. Geschichte einer Liebe* (1899, Idols. Story of a Love). It is a contribution made not by presenting role models but by sensitively demonstrating how insidious the social constraints on women's lives can be. This novel tells the story in her own words of Gisa, a girl of good family, trapped in the feminine role of career, who, for lack of other socially legitimated means, attempts to escape her stifling milieu through her phantasies of love for the work-obsessed and hyper-rational Dr. Lamaris. The theme of the sexual idol, noticed in some of the sketches of *Übergänge*, is thus made the dominant one. Gisa's idolization, which leaves her like the needle of a compass, helpless in the face of the attractive force,[31] is, as the title suggests, joined by other idolizations: that of the cavalier and womanizer von Zedlitz, who has an ideal image of woman which places her on a pedestal, that of Nelly, Gisa's acquaintance, who supports the cliché ideal of the strong man, while Lamaris adheres to that of the racially pure and healthy woman who will promote the genetic quality of the human race. These three forms of sexual idol are shown not to harm their idolizers because they separate love and desire. Only Gisa suffers as her ideal attempts to combine the two and to map out a new form of sexual relationship based on communion. As Gisa explains to an uncomprehending Nelly, her ideal is a man with a woman's heart: "A man who has everything which distinguishes men, forcefulness, determination, knowledge, and at the same time is full of devotion, tenderness, gentle ardour... How else would a boundless communion be possible...?"[32] Yet Gisa's idol is shown to have feet of clay, to be what Mayreder was to call a dyscratic man, one who is incapable of uniting love and the erotic drive, remaining trapped in his excessive intellectuality. Zedlitz on the other hand represents the opposite pole, what Mayreder was in her essays to call the primitive man, while Nelly and Gisa also represent a polar pair, the former being the undifferentiated woman, the female counterpart of Zedlitz, and the latter the synthetic, differentiated one, who can find no fitting place in her social context. Gisa is left in the confines of her milieu, her idol remains an ideal. As in *Übergänge* the attempt to find a new form of sexual relations runs aground on the rocks of reality.

Mayreder's leitmotifs of a concern for freedom, of personal development, human psychology, in particular the subjectivity of perception and the sexual idol, and her tendency to see polarities and posit a synthesis are thus carried further here than in her previous works. The fourth leitmotif, a critique of language, is also developed in *Idole,* and it is Mayreder's treatment of this which causes the novel to represent an original contribution. This she achieves by investigating the relationship of gender to language, an aspect her contemporaries ignored. Gisa attempts to find an alternative to the dominant masculine semantics, one which can verbalize what is shown to be her specifically feminine fantasy, but is thwarted in this attempt: "In love—ugly words, words which I could not gladly accept. They conjured up strange images, they did not belong to me. I searched for other words, for more intimate, penetrating, subtle words, but found none."[33] Patriarchal semantics are revealed as an inadequate vehicle of communication of authentic, specifically feminine experience. The murmuring of the feminine soul of "incomprehensible... What one can say does not go deep enough. The depths cannot be articulated."[34] Gisa's experience of idolizing love appears to be her path to finding a new language and also self-revelation. "That which had been dumb in me acquired a language; I could give expression to everything which happened inside me. To break the long silence of my soul was a pleasure without compare... I was richer, stronger, freer. I had only then become completely myself."[35] Yet this self-fulfillment is immediately compounded by the semantics of public reality, which labels the private reality "fantasies": "And my foolish heart became intoxicated with these fantasies which were so sweet and so full of promise." Denied the male objective reality of the professional, public world, Gisa's reality must be private, that of her idolization. Yet this is exposed as too fragile to withstand the outer world and the public semantic code: "You must remain silent, dreams of the lonely soul. You wonderful, playful soap bubbles, you must not be touched by words.":[36] It is tears, not words, which might be the real communicators, as Gisa opines on seeing Aunt Ludmilla cry over a sprig of lilac: "I felt that I would never ask her about the story with the lilac. It was perhaps the most beautiful moment of her lift, the only moment of happiness, of elevation above the mundane—but if she had recounted it with her well-bred remarks and petit-bourgeois phrases, it would have been destroyed forever. She had recounted it as she silently wept over the blossoming sprig. And can one communicate the most intense moments of life in any other way?":[37]

Yet only women in the novel search for an alternative semantics. The men remain trapped in the semantics of public reality, of everyday convention, and thus of non-communication, largely out of fear: "One never has one's words quite within one's control," Lamaris explains, "as soon as one speaks, one says more than one wishes.":[38] Words say both too much for men and too little for women, whereby the specifically feminine experience is condemned to silence. Gisa's dream of communion between the sexes remains also a dream of a common language.

The theme of the sexual idol can find a biographical correlate in Mayreder's own adolescent idolization of Emil. Her next published work, *Pipin. Ein Sommererlebnis* (1903, Pipin. A Summer Experience), can also find sources in Mayreder's life. As she remarked in a letter, the "very problematic book... leads the reader into a bizarre milieu in which I was involved years ago," adding self-deprecatingly, "and will probably be unpalatable and incomprehensible to all those who have not belonged to a similar circle.":[39] This milieu is almost certainly that around Rudolf Steiner and Marie Lang, for *Pipin* is among other things a satire on the theosophical and mystical quirks of a group of holiday-makers in a mountain resort, and ironically critical of the uncritical Wagner and Nietzsche reception *en vogue* in such groups in the late nineteenth century, in which Mayreder had eagerly participated. The Wagnerian cult of emotion over reason is caricatured in the shape of one of the party, Dr. Kranich, as is the claim of the precedence of the intellect over emotion, a position which is embodied by Elmenreich, an apparent misanthrope with Nietzschean traits, and which leads him to a Schopenhauerian pose of world negation. Spiritual regeneration, the 'back to nature' movement, the glorification of the Middle Ages as practised by the mystical Hermit of Mount Alvernia, and the "cult of the master" similar to that of the young Wagnerians of the 1870s and 1880s are exposed as elements of a bad farce under which the simple peasantry of the region suffer. This leads Mayreder to introduce a note of class consciousness very rare in her works. She makes clear how the city-bred tourists exploit the native inhabitants of the region and remain outsiders, this being indicated also by the two very different views of nature: for the peasants it is brutal, for the tourists an exotic backdrop.

The autobiographical elements are further reinforced by Mayreder's remark that the novel is a soliloquy in which the different facets of her own personality are personified in the figures of the novel.[40] Her own division between the intellect and emotions seen to be plainly articulated in the diaries of the 1880s thus finds here a literary form. True to being a conversation with herself, Mayreder in the form of letters and diary entries allows the female narrator to present the characters largely through what they say, with little narrative interruption. Indeed, this narrator deliberately refuses the narrator's role, preferring that of the observer instead: "For what do we discover of the fate of those who live beside us? Something occurs; but it is not the same for all who experience it. Each one acts according to his hidden motives, follows his secret goals, and the observer interprets the external signs. The inside of the event remains invisible and incommunicable: it must be guessed at as one solves a puzzle. Therein lies a danger of life but also its magic. Those who have learned that will prefer it if the observer does not become a narrator."[41] By this narrative technique Mayreder underlines the dominant theme of the subjectivity of perception, which she here extends beyond that of the subjective sex idol to the discrepancies between self-perception and the perception of and by others in general. Yet no authoritative picture of the characters and events is presented by the narrator. The reader is left to guess at the solution to the puzzle.

In the same year that *Pipin* was published, Mayreder officially renounced her position in the General Austrian Women's Association after a series of bitter differences of opinion concerning its integrity. At the same time she was composing sonnets, starting to write what was to become the mystery play *Anda Renata,* and above all, finishing the collection of essays which was published in 1905 as *Zur Kritik der Weiblichkeit* (A Survey of the Woman Question). It was this work which made Mayreder's name as a leading commentator on the woman problem both at home and abroad. She saw her concern with a theoretical basis to feminism not as an admission of the failure of active political agitation but as feminist engagement in a form better suited to her talents.

In this volume the themes already noted in Mayreder's imaginative writing are developed on a theoretical level. Her leading theme of the primacy of self-determination in her face of social norms, found in *Aus meiner Jugend, Übergänge* and *Idole,* also forms the starting-point here. In the first essay of the collection "Grundzüge" (Basic Traits) Mayreder launches a witty and trenchant attack on those male commentators who professed to generalizable insights on the nature of "woman"; she reveals her criticism to female commentators on the essence of femininity in the essay "Frauen und Frauentypen" (Women and Types of Women). Propagated vision of "true femininity" are male constructions, she claims in two further essays, "Der Kanon der schönen Weiblichkeit" (The Canon of Beautiful Femininity) and "Das subjektive Geschlechtsidol" (The Subjective Sex Idol), the abstract complementation of the psychosexual constitution of the male beholder. Yet this abstraction must be fought by women: "They must fight against woman as idol if they want to assert their right in the world as real persons," Mayreder proclaim. "That means emerging from a state of passivity and breaking the silence about themselves..."[42]

The cultivation of a type as against a fully individual personality also comes under fire in her discussion of traditional girls' education in "Familienliteratur" (Family Literature), for Mayreder recognizes that conventional femininity is largely a construct created by and for the   benefit of men. "According to it [the conventional view of femininity] woman is merely a means to an end - firstly, to the satisfaction of man, secondly, to the production of men . . . Woman is not to possess inherent value as an independent personality, to be an individual in her own right."[43]

This recognition of the norms surrounding femininity causes Mayreder to distinguish between real and ideal femininity and thus to consider the question of the relationship between sex and character. She thereby joins several of her contemporaries, notably Otto Weininger and Sigmund Freud. Mayreder explicitly takes issue with the former in her opening essay. She appreciates the emancipatory potential of the first part of Weininger's weighty work *Geschlecht und Charakter* (1903, *Sex and Character*), in which he suggests that all human beings possess different amounts of masculine and feminine plasma and thus varying amounts of masculinity and femininity, an attempt, as Mayreder sees it, to avoid stereotypic generalizations according to biological sex and to acknowledge the infinite variety of individual development. However, he fails in this attempt, she notes, when he moves to the second part of his investigation. There he deals with exactly those generalizations in his descriptions of the sexual types of pure masculinity and pure femininity, precisely because his hypothesis of sex gradation offers no absolute criteria of masculinity and femininity. Weininger then reverts to the most crude misogyny, reinstating the phallus as the carrier of all that is positive and failing, claims Mayreder, to see that the tasks of sex psychology will remain unsolved so long as biological difference is thought to extend to every aspect of the personality.[44] Mayreder characteristically posits a dualist view also, her dualism being, however, not that between masculinity and femininity, but between sexuality and the personality. Each human being is made up of a core masculinity or femininity, according to biological sex, a core which Mayreder calls teleological (or primitive) sexual nature and defines as the individual's psychic adaptation to his or her function as a reproductive agent. In addition, each individual possesses mental features which are not sex specific but "human" features which make up the individual personality. Mayreder interprets this dualism in evolutionary terms, seeing the majority of people as being dominated by their primitive sexual nature and therefore on a lower evolutionary level than that minority of differentiated persons whose individuality is highly developed. This minority embodies the ideal of "Mensch," the human being who combines masculine and feminine features and therefore includes the feminists, claims Mayreder in her essay "Die Tyrannei der Norm" (The Tyranny of the Norm), for feminists are women who dare to flout social convention in order to follow the inner voice of the personality. In that essay she expands this idea—and echoes her adolescent thoughts—to claim that progress in general, as seen in the case of the women's movement, is initiated by the avant-garde of such exceptional individuals without whom society would remain caught in tradition as represented by the conservatism of the masses. Both elements are necessary for a healthy society: the elements of innovation in the direction of increased personal freedom from norms and the elements of tradition. Social progress is brought about by the masses' gradual assimilation of new norms introduced by the innovative elite, which lead to greater personal freedom, but which also correspond to the needs and abilities of the masses. Thus progress takes the form of the gradual absolute elevation of the average type. It is, however, never the case that the majority can liberate itself from an obedience to norms; it is the norms which must change.

In practical terms as far as women are concerned this process of evolution implies breaking with the idea that femininity can be realized in legitimate motherhood alone—while illegitimate motherhood is hypocritically condemned—and recognizing that the cult of motherhood is a ruse by bourgeois society to convince women of the rightness of a renunciation of their own self-fulfillment: "We all know, women are not supposed to be or do anything themselves; instead, they are supposed to 'raise' their sons to become that which they themselves were denied."[45] Childrearing cannot be equivalent to independent intellectual activity, Mayreder claims, for a child is not the work of its parents but a product of nature with its own individuality.

Mayreder concludes her collection by presenting her vision of the ideal (implicitly heterosexual) pair, in which she draws on the Romantic tradition epitomized by, for example, Friedrich Schlegel's *Lucinde* (1799), of two individuals incorporating the best of conventional "masculine" and "feminine" qualities (Mayreder does not question the appropriateness of such genderizing) who are joined together in comradely harmony, in an exchange of souls based on mutual intellectual enrichment. Each is a fully rounded personality in his or her own right, managing to unite the claims of sexuality with those of the personality to achieve a happy synthesis.

Mayreder's essays thus pick up the main ideas already encountered in her imaginative works. The claims of the individual are again asserted: Mayreder's distinctive tendency to think in dualisms is also present, as is her probing of human psychology and assertion of the strength of subjectivity. Nor is the concern for language absent; terms such as "female honor" and "the glories of motherhood" are exposed by Mayreder to be covers for the hypocrisy of bourgeois morality, and her de-masking of contradictory definitions of "woman" in "Grundzüge" extends her discussion of the limitations of language and its questionable relationship to the world of referents. Yet in some contrast to her imaginative works she gives less weight in her essays to the tenacity of women's oppression, privileging the future-orientated perspective. This indicates what is perhaps the main weakness of Mayreder's theoretical discussion: her neglect of the material context and her exclusive emphasis on the primacy of nature and 'natural' individual gifts. According to Mayreder, differentiated individuals are born, not made[46] a view no doubt supported by her own exceptional position in her family. She thereby, however, opens herself to a highly elitist attitude that there is a minority of individuals selected by a constantly evolving nature to be its heralds as well as denying the possibility of individual psychosexual development as, for example, Freud suggested. In her eagerness to assert the value of the individual in the face of normative generalizations, Mayreder establishes a new ideal, the personality, and espouses an anti-egalitarian Romantic cult of the great individual. The original emancipatory intention has been found to be incompatible with equality and instead nature is appealed to as the instigator of the emancipation of a minority.

The essays of *Zur Kritik der Weiblichkeit* represent in many ways a radical critique of patriarchy, presenting an outline of the psychology of gender relations and its basis in misrelations in power. They break with established images of womanhood to present the ideal of an individualized femininity which harmonizes intellect and sexuality. How far, however, Mayreder remained trapped in the Christian-Romantic tradition of the intimate connection between love, life, and suffering and how far she still considered pain to be the path to insight and the development of the female personality above all can be seen from her diary entries concerning her second extra-marital love affair from 1902 to 1909. Mayreder obviously attached great importance to this largely unhappy episode, for over 1,000 pages of her diary are dedicated to it alone. She clearly saw that the relation from her side was not based on intellectual companionship, as idealized in the essays, but on sexual attraction. The object of her infatuation was a dyscratic man (to use Mayreder's own terms) who regularly visited prostitutes without any qualms, a fact which deeply troubled Mayreder, not surprising in view of her outspoken attacks on the institution of prostitution and the social-sexual system which underpinned it. Indeed, she continued to speak publicly against the system of regulation even during this period. To judge from the diary entries, it appears that her emotions took on a symbolic significance. She believed that the joy and the suffering this episode gave her were the sources of her productivity, comparing this to the pleasure and pain connected with the birth of a child: "One cannot be fruitful without pain," she asserted, "the life of the mind is like the life of the body: out of pleasure and out of pain emerges everything that is born."[47] She seems to have almost masochistically enjoyed the suffering her passion brought her, seeing this as the path to increased insight into the human soul.

In her diary entries for this period Mayreder revels in the emotional ups and downs of this relationship, recording every detail with an almost obsessive precision. It seems as though love and suffering take on the roles of surrogates for life, for Mayreder omits mentioning the wealth of other activities she was engaged in during these years. Yet in addition to completing *Zur Kritik der Weiblichkeit* she was finishing her sonnet cycle

Zwischen Himmel und Erde, published in 1908, composing more fabulous tales (Fabeleien) to add to those already published,[48] and drafting the drama *Anda Renata.* And of course she was running her house, fulfilling her family and social duties and on top of this undertook with her husband a journey to the Near East of several months' duration. The affair slowly petered out and by the autumn of 1909 the diaries are concerned with other themes. *Zwischen Himmel und Erde* thus came to be seen as her monument to this episode so full of conflicts, a direct response to her personal experiences.

It is a fitting monument, for it tells from the woman's point of view the story in four parts of the growth and death of a love affair in which the subjective sex idol rules again and turns out once more to be an illusion without foundation in reality. In the first part, which describes the growth and flowering of love, the conventional ideas of romantic love later to be given discursive expression (although already indicated in *Zur Kritik der Weiblichkeit*) are celebrated in traditional Romantic images, giving way in the second section, which describes the period of stable love. Again these present ideas, probably largely modelled on some of Goethe's poetry, which were to find discursive expression only much later in Mayreder's theodicy *Der letzte Gott* (The Last God): the element of Becoming as central to Being and the role of suffering as the path to personal growth. The poetic voice comes to see the element of fantasy in her image of her lover but is unwilling to renounce that dream, preferring to think of him in the "sunlight of poetry";[49] but she is then forced to recognize the inevitable deception of the sexual idol. Mayreder's discursive ideal of the pair united in companionship is thus again relativized, as indeed is the Romantic cult of love to which she apparently adheres in the first two parts. And indeed, the relativization is indicated at the very beginning, for the prefatory sonnet to the whole cycle clearly communicated the double-edged nature of Eros, "the malicious sweet god... the crafty one, whom no heart escapes/ As long as the forces of life abide there."[50] Romantic love is glorified but at the same time undermined, exposed as an illusion.

The claim to personal confession Mayreder made regarding *Zwischen Himmel und Erde* applies also to the next volume she completed, *Fabeleien über göttliche und menschliche Dinge* (Fables on Divine and Mortal Things), completed by 1911 but not published until 1921 after the manuscript had been peddled from publisher to publisher. Many familiar themes (apart from that of sex relations) crop up here: the all-pervading dualism of life which must reach a synthesis for harmony, the subjectivity of perception and question of identity, the role of language. They are, however, clothed in a very different guise than in Mayreder's previous works. These fabulous tales form the most original contribution to Mayreder's oeuvre as a writer of imaginative literature by presenting the themes of "Philosophenspäße," philosophers' jests in the style of fantastic realism. With overtones of Nietzsche[51] Mayreder explains in her preface to the collection that her fables are playful attempts to deal with those problems which philosophers have considered with seriousness and the claim to objective validity, suggesting that the philosophical systems of Western thought are themselves fables, systems which combine the real and the invented and are full of contradictions. Mayreder's aim is to subvert the status of those systems, to combat the encroachment of the hegemony of reason over the imagination and the objective over the subjective, and so to lead to a new evaluation of the imagination, subjectivity and also playfulness as elements of philosophy. Thus in "Ein Zwist" (A Quarrel) Darwinian theories of evolution, Schopenhauerian negation of the world, and Christian dogma are spoofed as the clamorings of puppets on a turntable, while in "Die Schätze des alten Zauberers" (The Treasures of the Old Magician) the dominant ideologically-loaded concepts of Western civilization are manufactured by magic powders: "There was a black crystalline powder that produced an atmosphere of piety and belief; a red granular one, that was for freedom and equality . . . a sky-blue round one brought in a whiff of enlightenment, humanity and progress; a yellow sharp-cornered one, that filled the air with class consciousness...."[52] The serious intention takes refuge behind the playfulness, as if Mayreder in this volume wished to relativize the earnestness with which she had once received and propagated these ideas and intellectual trends.

Yet through the playfulness emerges the earnestness of the themes dealt with. "Der Wiedergeborene" (The One Born Again) clearly preaches the ideal of the union of opposites in the figure obviously drawn from Wagner's work[53] of Jesus Apollo, the synthesis of the Christian and the pagan, the divine and the human, heaven and earth. The Apollonian and the Dionysian, life and death, embodied in two Grecian gods and the natural landscape are shown to cohabit in "Einsame Gegend" (Lonely Place), just as love and hate are two side of one god in "Ein Zwist." The theme of the synthesis of dualisms observed in all Mayreder's works here breaks out of the context of literary realism and analysis to take on a mythological dimension. It is as if Mayreder, through choosing the playful voices of gods, legendary figures, and fairies, allows herself the license to break with the constraints of imaginative writing. Thus the limitations of language, dealt with in a very different manner in *Idole*, are transcended in the *Fabeleien* by Mayreder's surrealist concretization of images, just as the problem of identity and self-perception, which is described in *Pipin* as the splitting of the subject into spectator and actor is in 'Grotesk-Pantomime' (Grotesque Pantomime) made a disturbing reality. In this collection Mayreder takes her claim of the primacy of subjectivity to extreme lengths by abandoning the various conventions she obeys in her other works to give herself the liberty to present the concerns which mark her thought with force and also humor, untrammelled by any notions of earnest realism.

Mayreder's extra-marital passion did not destroy the marriage, for Karl Mayreder took on the role of comforter and adviser. It was put under a far greater strain from 1912 onwards through Karl Mayreder's mental illness, which took the form of severe depression, withdrawal, and also in the first phases aggression towards his wife. Karl Mayreder's condition lasted until his death in 1935 in spite of seeking the help of fifty-nine doctors, including Alfred Adler and Sigmund Freud. The latter suggested that Karl felt dominated by his wife, a diagnosis which enraged Rosa, who saw this as evidence of the prejudices still prevalent against intellectual women. Yet Freud's diagnosis was probably to some extent correct. Rosa Mayreder seems to have been incapable of liberating herself from the ideology of lasting romantic married love, which dominates her later work on the subject even when it was so obviously contradicted by her own reality. This blow meant a personally difficult time which was aggravated by the hardships imposed on the civilian population by the First World War. Both these events seem to have reinforced her belief in the primacy of the strong individual, the first showing her again the need for her own strength of personality and the second the need for strong public leaders. Her comments in her diaries on the politics of war read like the practical political application of the theories of *Zur Kritik der Weiblichkeit*. Thus for example, echoing her thoughts presented in "Die Tyrannei der Norm," she recorded on 15 November 1918: "I do not believe in the 'people' as a power which can bring order into the world, I believe only in great personalities, bearers of a powerful will placed in the service of high ideas". As in her essays, she insisted on the driving force of the irrational and instinctual over any material concerns.

Yet Mayreder, as was the case with her concern for the women's movement, did not confine herself to theoretical pronouncements but sought to combine these with an albeit ambivalent political engagement. She thus adhered to a position of feminist pacifism although she was skeptical as to the real influence such ideas could have, a doubt which also parallels that concerning the women's movement twenty years earlier. In 1915 she joined what later became the International Women's League for Peace and Freedom and co-founded the Austrian branch of this organization in December 1919, remaining its nominal president. The goal of this organization was to combat all forms of war, exploitation, and oppression and to bring about social, political, and economic equality for all without regard to sex, race, class, or religion.[54] But again the picture of May-reder's official engagement is misleading, for her conviction of her unsuitability for public office, which had become clear as a result of her experiences with the General Austrian Women's Association, had not dwindled.

Mayreder's pacifist writings[55] indicate however that a change of thought concerning women had taken place, probably as a result of World War I. There she maintains that as destroyer of the life women have brought forth and nurtured, war is the absolute expression of the primitive masculine instinct for aggression[56] and therefore an atavistic phenomenon. Cultural progress, which implies the liberation of woman from her subordinate social position, can be achieved only through a reevaluation of the status of feminine values by putting these into the foreground. Mayreder stresses that this is the task of the women's movement: to promote those feminine values which implicitly offer an alternative to a civilization based on power and aggression. She thus reinstates the undifferentiated feminine in contrast to her presentation of it in *Zur Kritik der Weiblichkeit*.

Mayreder's experiences in the women's movement continued to occupy her in another way also, for they offered the basis of a lecture she gave in 1917[57] the only woman to do so to the left-wing Vienna Sociological Society (founded in 1907 by Rudolf Goldscheid, Karl Renner, Max Adler and others) on the typical course of social movements. She identifies three stages, seen in terms of organic growth and decline rather than resting on a materialist basis. The first, the stage of the idealists and martyrs, is marked by the birth of leading ideas but also powerlessness due to the lack of understanding for them on the part of the masses. This ushers in the second, organizational phase, during which the leading ideas are adapted by gifted popularizers to meet the needs of the masses. However, this phases degenerates into a struggle for power in which the ideology is abused in order to gain mass support. This is the third, imperialistic phase. Yet new leading personalities, idealists, can emerge and bring forth a new social movement which will in turn follow the same organic pattern of growth and decline. This scheme was in essence not new, for Mayreder had already indicated in letters [58] that she considered power and pure ideology to be incompatible, and it demonstrates once again her faith in organic evolution over revolution.

The horrors of the war caused Mayreder, however, to question this faith. She recorded sadly in her dairy on 26 October 1916: "Perhaps the hardest thing intellectually speaking which the war brought me is the collapse of my belief in human progress.... For someone who learned to look at the world from the point of view of progress alone, this recognition opens up a ravine into which the meaning of life tumbles and disappears." This new pessimism found expression in the writing of her childhood memories. It was an immersion and in some respects idealized past which helped her to flee dismal reality, giving her a sense of stability in the midst of the fragility of daily life. Yet a new tone of world-weariness set in and also an awareness of the conflicts found by a writing woman with domestic duties: "I have over all these years learned," she exclaimed, "to struggle unperturbed with my unfavorable circumstances and have acquired a kind of mental gymnastics in order to keep my concentration for my work but how much energy and invention have nevertheless been drained from me all my life by external circumstances!"[59]

Yet, although the external circumstances had taken a decisive turn for the worse and her interest in the subject was waning, Mayreder did manage to complete *Geschlecht und Kultur* (Sex and Culture), the sequel to *Zur Kritik der Weiblichkeit*, which she had been working on for about twelve years prior to publication in 1923. These essays document the change already indicated in Mayreder's pacifist writings, from a positive attitude to masculinity (as shown in *Zur Kritik der Weiblichkeit*) to a more negative one and a correspondingly higher evaluation of primitive femininity, and also her interest in the connections between sex, gender, and culture. Mayreder in this second essay volume joins fellow neo-Romantics[60] to assert that contemporary civilization is one-sided, which for her means one-sidedly masculine: aggressive, characterized by excess, the lack of leading ideals, and the domination of technology. This lamentable modern state of affairs Mayreder explains by saying that women have been excluded from the making of this technological civilization. It is thus in need of feminine culture, characterized by organic growth, receptivity, and above all harmony between the external circumstances of life and spiritual and intellectual ideals, the former serving the later. Only through this feminine counterweight can human wholeness be restored, values and ideals be reasserted in the face of a one-sided civilization of scientific specialism, materialism, and excessive productivity and activity, epitomized, claims Mayreder, by the metropolis. Women are to enter public life, to endow it with their specifically feminine qualities which, according to Mayreder, derive directly from woman's reproductive function but, as was the case for the women's movement, only those differentiated women with a consciousness of independence, that is, the feminist minority. For the majority the home and family will remain the most fitting context. This is woman's cultural mission.

Woman is helped, Mayreder suggests in "Die Krise der Väterlichkeit" (The Crisis of Fatherliness), another essay of the collection, by the gradual demise of patriarchy. Fatherhood is no longer legitimated by authority or the concept of property, as was formerly the case, but by emotions, the instinctual bonding of the father to offspring. The traditional legitimation of the pater familias is an anachronism, Mayreder claims, for women's growing economic independence, the youth movement, and also changes in family size have undermined his status, as have, more importantly, the growth of a consciousness of individuality and personality on the part of women and children. With this last point Mayreder openly takes issue with Freud's theory of the Oedipus complex, suggesting that social rather than sexual jealousy mark the relationship between father and son.

This development to a consciousness of personality and away from a concept of property is fundamental to Mayreder's exposition (also in this volume) of the cultural evolution of the male and female erotic. According to Mayreder, each developed by means of a dualism ideally to reach a harmonious synthesis at the highest levels of personal and evolutionary development. Thus the male erotic developed from the primitive orgiastic enjoyment of impersonal sexuality through Judaeo-Christian asceticism to attain the union of eroticism and asceticism in the differentiated man, while the female erotic evolved out of the concept of the female body as the property of the male through the idea of sacramental marriage as the only legitimation of a sexual relationship for women to the third stage of the autonomous female personality who disposes over her body as she thinks fit. Yet Mayreder is skeptical of whether either ideal has been achieved by more than a minority of individuals and is sharply critical of the contemporary move towards the rationalization of sex expressed in the eugenicist movement of, for example, Christian von Ehrenfels, as the privileging of reproduction leaves no room for the assertion of individuality in sex and therefore love. Mayreder offers in this volume the theoretical formulation of the ideas of love presented in *Zwischen Himmel und Erde* and clung to so tenaciously in her own life. She identifies seven such ideas, including that the lover is reborn in love, sheltered, protected, and completed by the other, declares the union based on love with the will for it to last to be the highest form of heterosexual union, and stresses that the ideas are not mere illusions but realizable. Her earlier insights in *Zur Kritik der Weiblichkeit* concerning the subjective sex idol and put into a literary form in her novels and sonnets have been submerged. It is as if the actual realization of her earlier insights in the form of the difficulties in her own marriage proved to be unacceptable and that she took refuge in the Romantic ideal. Mayreder's claim to writing experience must therefore once again be relativized, for here, too, as already seen in the case of her second extra-marital affair, there is an explicit tension between written expression and experience.

During the 1920s Mayreder remained a public figure. Her fame reached its peak on the occasion of her seventieth birthday, when she was awarded the honorary citizenship of Vienna and found herself celebrated by a special performance of *Der Corregidor* as well as being the recipient of a *Festschrift*.[61] Yet she felt increasingly isolated and misunderstood, her childhood memoirs and also the final version of *Anda Renata* having been rejected by numerous publishers. Although she professed to having lost her faith in the principle of progress during the War, she was in the early 1930s still able to write *Der letzte Gott,* the work foreshadowed forty years earlier by *Diana und Herodias.* This work, like both *Zur Kritik der Weiblichkeit* and *Geschlecht und Kultur,* is dominated by the idea of upward evolution, which works, according to Mayreder, by means of the characteristic polar dynamic between instinct (nature) and intellect (spirit), the latter leading the former to a higher level. In contrast to these other two works, however, in *Der letzte Gott* Mayreder adds another element to the process of evolution: suffering. Through suffering, she claims, echoing sentiments already expressed in her diaries many decades earlier and reinforced by the tragedy of her marriage, man can achieve deeper insight and be purged, thus reaching a higher stage of human development. The patterns of these ideas are already familiar. *Der letzte Gott* represents a step into new territory in that it takes ideas out of the context of sex psychology and the discussion on gender and culture to place them in a metaphysical context. At the same time Mayreder clearly displays her intellectual heritage. Apart from that of Christianity's metaphysics of suffering seen to be so powerful in her own life, the influences on Mayreder's thought can be identified as a critical reception of Darwinism for Mayreder does not share the Darwinists' creed of adaptation of their reduction of man to merely another link in the secularized "Great Chain of Being" and above all of Goethe's and the Romantics' philosophy of nature, particularly Schelling's philosophy of the all-embracing nature of evolution with its basic principle of polarity.

Der letzte Gott had a gestation period of about forty years, a feature shared by the Faustian drama *Anda Renata*, the first part of which was finally published in 1934. This represents the literary summing up of several long-standing trains of thought. The drama is set in the seventeenth century at the time of the persecution of the witches, whom Mayreder considers to be forerunners of emancipated women, and presents the various stages of suffering and error the female Faust figure, driven by the desire for insight and personal freedom, must go through in order to reach self-knowledge and therefore liberty. Anda is to learn that the higher level of being she strives after can be reached only through the overcoming of the baser instinctive elements by means of love. Thus her *rites de passage* include betrayal by her sexuality incorporated by the demon of sensuality and death, Aschmedai, and the idolization of a man unworthy of her, as well as her spiritual death from which she rises again, strengthened through the pure love of another man, to enter the realm of ideas where the female personality can live unrestricted. It is a journey of experience shrouded in the trappings of mystical symbols taken from Freemasonry, Christianity, alchemy, German mysticism, and called a "mystery play," for, as Mayreder explains in her epilogue, it is to indicate the final secrets of existence and turns to the metaphysical. [62] Yet as Anda's second reality after her resurrection is clearly a metaphysical dream reality located between heaven and earth, the fully developed personality and the ideal of love remain restricted to higher spheres, and again Mayreder's literary treatment remains pessimistic.

This tendency, which has been seen to dominate Mayreder's literary writing, makes itself perceptible also in her next work, written in 1937, a set of sonnets put into the mouth of the same Aschmedai as figures in

Anda Renata. He jocularly criticizes man for not acknowledging humanity's divine position as the incarnation of the divided god of good and evil and for not striving to achieve a higher level of existence through recognition of the polarity and the necessary synthesis of the world's forces. It is thus largely a paraphrase of the ideas of *Der letzte Gott.* Yet the use of the demonic voice again relativizes Mayreder's own discursive writing, for can the demon of sensuality and death be a sincere advocate of evolution? A diary entry of April 1937 gives perhaps some indication, for there Mayreder records that her despair had taken refuge in the humor of Aschmedai. Mayreder had lost her belief but still retained her lifelong need to concern herself with religion, which for her meant the belief in evolution. The sonnets proved to be her final work, for she died in January of the following year.

There can be little doubt that Mayreder's main significance for studies of Austrian culture lies in her work produced around 1900, particularly in the position she occupied in the women's movement and the contribution she made to the discussion on the "woman problem" in both her theoretical and her imaginative writing. Her contribution is original through its eclectic union of sharp insights into the workings of sexual politics with intellectual trends of the second half of the nineteenth century: the Enlightenment-Kantian ideal of self-determination and the individual combined with a belief in evolution and a liberal *laissez faire* trust in the regulating powers of nature, a Romantic creed of the dualist dynamic of nature and its resolution in synthesis as well as a neo-Romantic elitism, cult of the great personality, subjectivity, and the emotions.

Mayreder was, however, not only a product of a German-speaking intellectual environment, but also a product of a particularly Viennese one, and she joined her modernist contemporaries in several respects. She too privileged the psychological over the material and joined the flight from party politics which often accompanied this attitude. Like many of her contemporaries, she also turned to a questioning of personal identity and the subjective nature of perception, experimenting with literary techniques to convey the hidden workings of the human psyche. This concern for the hidden found expression also in the interest for the erotic, the recognition of its importance as a driving force of human behavior and also in the call for its liberation from the misformations caused by hypocritical bourgeois morality. Language too—its unreliability, inadequacy, and exploitation by social convention—is a common theme.

Yet Mayreder not only shared the concerns of her modernist

contemporaries; she also makes an original contribution by breaking with their male-centered, openly or latently misogynist views to privilege women, their psyche, their perception, their relation to language and also their special relation to a morality made by and for men. Unlike some of her Viennese contemporaries, Mayreder did not see ideal femininity and particularly its "pure" form, the prostitute, as the expression of untamed sexual freedom which was to act as the ultimate "Other" to man's rationality, the source of his inspiration but to remain firmly excluded from positions of political power. On the contrary, Mayreder was concerned to bridge the gulf between masculinity and femininity, which had been artificially widened in different ways by both the culture of the fathers and that of the rebellious sons by means of the concept of the human personality, which is to be harmonized with sexuality and thus contribute to the regeneration of human society.

This belief in regeneration indicates that Mayreder's Viennese context is not only that of modernism but also that of social reformism, the inheritance of the Enlightenment-liberal tradition and the stance adopted by a number of intellectuals in Vienna around 1900. Mayreder's belief in natural evolution combined with the power of leading ideas is characteristic of this attitude. Her original contribution lies again in her break with the male monopoly and deceptively gender-neutral viewpoint to apply these views to women's special and otherwise ignored concerns; she considered women to have a central role to play in the ascent of society, above all in the reform of sexual relations and the morality governing them.

Mayreder as feminist agitator, writer, and theorist takes up a unique position as the only woman of turn-of-the-century Vienna to be prolific on all three counts. A study of her life and works enriches the by now canonic view of the Viennese fin de siècle by adding the perspectives of early feminist thought and writing. It thereby indicates that that culture was not only one of decadent, introverted apoliticism. There was also a culture of courageous opposition to the status quo in the name of the rights of the also female individual. Any study of that culture owes Rosa Mayreder a place in its pages.

Notes

1. See Carl E. Schorske, "Generational Tension and Cultural Change: Reflections on the Case of Vienna," *Daedalus. Journal of the American Academy of Arts and Sciences*, 107, no. 4 (1978), 111-122.
2. See William J. McGrath, *Dionysian Art and Populist Politics in Austria* (New Haven: Yale University Press, 1974).
3. See Schorske, 115.
4. On social reformism in Vienna around 1900 see Ingrid Belke, *Die sozialreformatorischen Ideen von Josef Popper-Lynkeus (1838-1921) im Zusammenhang mit allgemeinen Reformbestrebungen des Wiener Bürgertums um die Jahrhundertwende* (Tübingen: Mohr, 1978).
5. This was the motto of the radical General Austrian Women's Association. See Allgemeiner Österreichischer Frauenverein, *III. Jahresbericht* (Wien, 1896), p. 7.
6. See Rosa Mayreder, *Das Haus in der Landskrongasse. Jugend-erinnerungen*, ed. Käthe Braun-Prager (Wien: Mensa, 1948); Rosa Mayreder, *Mein Pantheon. Lebenserinnerungen zweiter Teil*, ed. Walter Beck (Dornach: Anthroposophischer Verlag, 1988); Rosa Mayreder, *Tagebücher 1873-1937*, ed. Harriet Anderson (Frankfurt: Insel, 1988). See also the numerous letters from Rosa Mayreder and the Rosa Mayreder-*Nachlaß* in the Manuscripts Department of the Vienna City Library.
7. Rosa Mayreder, *Geschlecht und Kultur*, p. IV.
8. See Rosa Mayreder, *Das Haus in der Landskrongasse*, p. 86.
9. Ibid., p. 159.
10. Ibid., p. 173.
11. Ibid.
12. For a more detailed account of Mayreder's first readings of Wagner and Nietzsche see Rosa Mayreder, "Von Wagner zu Nietzsche. Ein Jugenderlebnis," *Die Glocke*, 2, no. 29/30 (February 1936), 8-15.
13. See Rosa Mayreder, *Das Haus in der Landskrongasse*, p. 222.
14. Diary 19 November 1881 (not included in Rosa Mayreder, *Tagebücher*).
15. See Rudolf Steiner, *Briefe* ed. by Edwin Fröböse and Werner Teichert (Dornach: Selbstverlag, 1953-1955), vol. 1, pp. 128-136: vol. 2, pp. 70-73.

16. See Rudolf Steiner, *Mein Lebensgang* (Dornach: Philosophisch-Anthroposophischer Verlag, 1925), pp. 107-109.
17. See Hugo Wolf, *Briefe an Rosa Mayreder*, ed. Heinrich Werner (Wien-Berlin-Leipzig: Rikola, 1921).
18. Letter to Auguste Fickert, 12 December 1895 (Manuscripts Department Vienna City Library, I.N. 70889/14).
19. Letter to Auguste Fickert, 24 December 1895 (Manuscripts Department Vienna City Library, I.N. 70889/15).
20. These were: "Lilith und Adam," *Neue Deutsche Rundschau (Freie Bühne)*, 5, no. 1/2 (1894), pp. 264-277 (under the pseudonym of Eremo); "Der Klub der Übermenschen," *Neue deutsche Rundschau*, 6, no. 3/4 (1895), pp. 1212-1228; "Mit dreizehn Jahren," *Neue Revue*, 7, no. 1 (January - June 1896), pp. 83-87 and pp. 117-122.
21. Rudolf Steiner, "Rosa Mayreder," *Die Gesellschaft. Halbmonatsschrift für Litteratur, Kunst und Sozialpolitik*, 16 (1900), vol. 2, no. 2, p. 80.
22. Hugo Wolf, *Briefe an Rosa Mayreder*, p. 21.
23. See, for example, "Das Stammbuch," *Übergänge*, pp. 58-75.
24. See, for example, "Eine blaue Schleife," *Übergänge*, pp. 90-105.
25. Rosa Mayreder, *Übergänge*, p. 250.
26. See "Unter blühenden Bäumen," *Übergänge*, pp. 1-8.
27. See "Die Amsel," *Übergänge*, pp. 76-89.
28. See "Mit dreizehn Jahren," *Übergänge*, pp. 37-57; "Halb tragisch," *Übergänge*, pp. 106-127; "Sein Ideal," *Übergänge*, pp. 197-217.
29. See *Zur Geschichte einer Petition gegen Errichtung öffentlicher Häuser in Wien. Protokoll der Frauenversammlung vom 20. Februar 1897 im alten Wiener Rathaus* (Wien 1897), pp. 6-19.
30. Rosa Mayreder, *Das Haus in der Landskrongasse*, p. 195.
31. See Rosa Mayreder, *Idole*, pp. 67-68.
32. Ibid., p. 49.
33. Ibid., p. 53.
34. Ibid., p. 28.
35. Ibid., p. 34.
36. Ibid., p. 52.
37. Ibid., pp. 123-124.
38. Ibid., p. 160.
39. Letter to Oskar Grohe, 21 November 1902 (Department of Manuscripts, Vienna City Library, I.N. 128.900).

40. Diary, 14 March 1905 (not included in Rosa Mayreder, *Tagebücher*).
41. Rosa Mayreder, *Pipin*, p. 15.
42. Rosa Mayreder, *Zur Kritik der Weiblichkeit*, p. 260. All translations from this volume are my own.
43. Ibid., pp. 200-201.
44. Ibid., pp. 30-33.
45. Ibid., p. 78.
46. Ibid., p. 83.
47. Rosa Mayreder, *Tagebücher*, p. 90.
48. These included "Drachentöter. Eine Fabelei," *Magazin für Litteratur*, 66, no. 33 (August 1897), col, 998-1002; "Erster Versuch," *Magazin für Litteratur*, 69, no. 1 (January 1900), col. 17-23; "Der Stiefvater," *Die Gesellschaft*, 16, no. 2 (April 1900), pp. 87-96; "Der Schatten", *Magazin für Litteratur*, 69, no. 38 (September 1900), col. 947-952.
49. Rosa Mayreder, *Zwischen Himmel und Erde*, p. 68.
50. Ibid., p. 1.
51. See Friedrich Nietzsche, *Zur Genealogie der Moral*, III, §12.
52. Rosa Mayreder, *Fabeleien*, p. 73.
53. See Richard Wagner, *Die Kunst und die Revolution*, in *Gesammelte Schriften* (Leipzig: Fritzsch, 1871-1881), vol. 3, p. 50.
54. See Internationale Frauenliga für Frieden und Freiheit, *15 Jahre Frauenliga. Tätigkeit und Organisation 1915-1930* (Wien: J. Steinmann, 1930), inside front cover.
55. These include "Der Haager Frauenkongreß im Lichte der Frauenbewegung," *Neues Frauenleben*, 27, no. 5 (May 1915), pp. 98-101; "Die Frau und der Krieg," *Internationale Rundschau*, 1, no. 10/11 (December 1915), pp. 516-527; "Die Frau und der Internationalismus," *Neues Frauenleben*, 28, no. 2 (February 1916), pp. 25-32; *Die Frau und der Internationalismus* (Wien: Frisch 1921).
56. See Rosa Mayreder, "Der Haager Frauenkongreß," p. 99.
57. See Rosa Mayreder, *Der typische Verlauf sozialer Bewegungen* (Wien: Anzengruber, 1917; second edition Wien: Braumüller 1926).
58. See letter to Auguste Fickert 14 September 1899; 22 September 1900 (both Department of Manuscripts, Vienna City Library, I.N. 70891/14 and I.N. 70892/6 respectively).

59. Diary 26 March 1925 (not included in Rosa Mayreder, *Tagebücher*)
60. See, for example, Ferdinand Tönnies, *Gemeinschaft und Gesellschaft. Grundbegriffe der reinen Soziologie*, second edition (Berlin: Curtius, 1912).
61. See *Der Aufstieg der Frau. Zu Rosa Mayreders 70. Geburtstag am 30. November 1928 als Ehrengabe dargebracht vom Verlag Eugen Diederichs in Jena*, ed. by Käthe Braun–Prager (Jena: Diederichs, 1928).
62. See Rosa Mayreder, *Anda Renata*, p. 245.

Bibliography

Works by Rosa Mayreder in German

Der Corregidor. Mannheim: Heckel, 1896.
Aus meiner Jugend. Drei Novellen. Dresden: Pierson, 1896.
Übergänge. Novellen. Dresden: Pierson, 1897.
Die Abolitionisten-Föderation. Wien: Plant, 1898.
Idole. Geschichte einer Liebe. Berlin: S. Fischer, 1899.
Pipin. Ein Sommererlebnis. Wien: Heller, 1903.
Zur Kritik der Weiblichkeit. Jena: Diederichs, 1905.
Zwischen Himmel und Erde. Sonette. Jena: Diederichs, 1908.
Der typische Verlauf sozialer Bewegungen. Wien: Frisch, 1921.
Fabeleien über göttliche und menschliche Dinge. Wien: Anzengruber, 1921.
Sonderlinge. Berlin: Hilger 1921. Reprint of a novella from *Aus meiner Jugend*.
Geschlecht und Kultur. Jena: Diederichs, 1923.
Askese und Erotik. Jena: Diederichs 1926.
Ideen der Liebe. Jena: Diederichs 1927.
Mensch und Menschlichkeit. Wien: Braumüller, 1928.
Die Krise der Ehe. Jena: Diederichs, 1929.
Der letzte Gott. Stuttgart: Cotta, 1933.
Anda Renata. Wien: Krey, 1934.
Gaben des Erlebens. Sprüche und Betrachtungen. Darmstadt: Darmstädter Verlag, 1935.
Diana und Herodias. Ein mythisches Spiel. Privately printed, 1937.
Aschmedais Sonette an den Menschen. Privately printed, 1937.
Das Haus in der Landskrongasse. Jugenderinnerungen. Ed. Käthe Braun-Prager. Wien: Mensa, 1948.

Mein Pantheon. Lebenserinnerungen zweiter Teil. Ed. Susanne Ker-
kovius. Dornach: Anthroposophischer Verlag, 1988.
A list of articles by Rosa Mayreder is included in Rosa Mayreder,
Tagebücher. 1873-1937. Ed. Harriet Anderson. Frankfurt: Insel,
1988.
In addition a number of selections from the works of Rosa Mayreder have
appeared:
Krise der Väterlichkeit. Ed. Käthe Braun-Prager. Graz-Wien: Stiasny,
1963.
*Zur Kritik der Weiblichkeit. Ed. Hanna Schnedl-Bubenicek. Munchen:
Frauenoffensive, 1982.*
Rosa Mayreder. Oder wider die Tyrannei der Norm. Ed. Hanna
Bubenicek. Wien: Böhlau 1986.
Tagebücher. 1873-1937. Ed. Harriet Anderson. Frankfurt: Insel 1988.

Works in English Translation

A Survey of the Woman Problem. Zur Kritik der Weiblichkeit, translated
by Herman Scheffauer. London: Heinemann, 1913.

Secondary Works in English

Harriet Anderson, "Beyond a Critique of Femininity. The Thought of
Rosa Mayreder, 1858-1938. Dissertation, University of London,
1985.
William M. Johnston, "Rosa Mayreder. Connoisseur of Woman's Role"
in *The Austrian Mind* (Berkeley: University of California Press,
1972), pp. 156-158.
Mary-Ann Reiss, "Rosa Mayreder. A Pioneer of Austrian Feminism,"
International Journal of Women's Studies 7 (1984), pp. 207-216.

Major Studies in German

*Aufbruch in das Jahrhundert der Frau. Rosa Mayreder und der
Feminismus in Wien um 1900.* Catalogue of the Historisches
Museum der Stadt Wien. Wien, 1989.
Herta Dworschak, "Rosa Obermayer-Mayreder. Leben und Werk."
Dissertation, University of Vienna, 1949.

Rosa Mayreder 1858-1938. Mitteilungen des Instituts für Wissenschaft
    und Kunst, 44, no. 1 (1989)
Edith Prost, "Weiblichkeit und bürgerliche Kultur am Beispiel Rosa
    Mayreder-Obermayer." Dissertation, University of Vienna, 1983.
Hanna Schnedl-Bubenicek, "Grenzgängerin der Moderne. Studien zur
    Emanzipation in Texten von Rosa Mayreder,' in *Das ewige Kli-
    schee. Zum Rollenbild und Selbstverständnis bei Männern und
    Frauen*, ed. Autorinnengruppe der Uni Wien. Wien: Böhlau, 1981,
    pp. 179-205.
———, "Pazifistinnen. Ein Resumee zu theoretischen Ausführungen und
    literarischen Darstellungen Bertha von Suttners und Rosa May-
    reders," *Wiener Beiträge zur Geschichte der Neuzeit*, 11 (1984),
    96-113.

Rainer Maria Rilke

Donald A. Prater

René Karl Wilhelm Johann Josef Maria Rilke (1875-1926), held by
many to be the greatest lyric genius of our century, was born on 4
December 1875 in Prague, the capital of Bohemia, a province of the
Hapsburg Empire of Austria-Hungary. Then the second largest state system of Europe, this vast amalgam of different races and languages, held
together under the rule of an aged King-Emperor, was not yet seriously
stirred in the provinces by the sentiments of national self-determination
which would result in its fragmentation after 1918: but the segregation of
the minority German-speaking "upper classes" from those lower orders
who were of different tongue was particularly marked in Rilke's Prague—
a "double ghetto" whose stifling atmosphere he was glad to escape at
twenty-one and to which he was afterwards always reluctant to return.
This "dark childhood,"[1] as he later recalled it, was not lightened by the
stiff, conventional manner of his father, now a railway official after ten
years in the army, or by the over-solicitousness of a mother who had
always wanted a daughter (even dressing her René as a girl) and whose
exaggerated piety as compensation for her unhappy marriage was enough
to turn him against the outward forms of religion.

Hoping for an army career for his son more successful than his own,
his father sent him at eleven to a cadet school in Austria, harsh surroundings for one hitherto so sheltered, and a traumatic experience he never
fully overcame. But he did surprisingly well in spite of frequent illness;
even more surprisingly he began to write verse. Finally persuading his
father that the army life was not for him, he was transferred at sixteen to
the commercial Academy at Linz. The relative freedom there encouraged
him in what he was beginning to recognize as his true vocation, poetry,
and some of his efforts already saw publication in Vienna journals. But
the freedom also led to an escapade with a girl, which culminated in their

running away together. Though he was soon brought back, the escapade was an eloquent gesture of refusal to follow the conventional path laid down for him. Thanks to a subvention from his uncle, who, lacking a son, saw in him a successor in his law practice, he was allowed private tuition in Prague to prepare him for university law studies. This gave him an opportunity which he seized with both hands. Rooming with relatives, for his parents were now separated, he was free, while diligent in his academic work, to plunge into a literary life, in contact with editors throughout Austria and Germany, sending his pieces to leading literary lights in Prague and Vienna and bringing himself to notice wherever he could. He tried his hand at everything, not only lyric poetry, of which he had now assembled a volume seeking a publisher, but also prose in stories and sketches, and attempts at drama. A first real love affair, deeply-felt but soon over, brought him his first patron: Valerie von David-Rhonfeld, at eighteen attracted to the budding poet, found the money to ensure the publication of his *Leben und Lieder* (1894, Life and Songs), a collection of verse on standard themes in imitative style, which gave little promise of his later powers. She also helped with support of the next volume, *Larenopfer* (1895, Offerings to the Lares), evocations of Prague in its German and Czech past and present, more mature and a notable advance in sharp observation.

That he was determined to make his mark as a writer and poet rather than embark in the more conventional career his family hoped for, became even clearer when he entered the university in Prague. Despite his uncle's death the allowance continued for him, and instead of reading law he chose history of art and of literature, also philosophy, subjects which afforded him an even wider range of literary and artistic contacts and gave full rein to his cultivation of both established masters and young "modern" artists. He published a journal of his own to be distributed free, *Wegwarten* (1895-1896, Wild Chicory), which saw but three numbers during its brief lifetime, but served his idealistic purpose of spreading culture to the masses and also as a vehicle for bringing his own work to the notice of the literary establishment. He wrote reviews and articles, helped with anthologies of translations from the Czech, secured a performance of his play, an abysmally naturalistic drama entitled *Jetzt und in der Stunde unseres Absterbens. . .* (1896, Now and in the Hour of our Departing. . .), and assembled yet a further volume of verse, pressing as well, though unsuccessfully, for the creation of a "free theater" in Prague for the production of modern works. But he longed for the still greater freedom which a move to the center of his native language, to Germany itself, could give: and with his father's reluctant consent he transferred to the University of Munich in the autumn of 1896. That his self-confidence was not as great as he would have wished, however, is evident from one of his very few autobiographical works, the novella *Ewald Tragy*, written a year or so later and never published during his lifetime: the story of the departure of a young man to Munich, longing to shake free of the constrictions and incomprehension of his family and to prove himself, yet torn by love for his father and still in doubt. "People ask [my father]: 'What is your son?'. . . What can he say? *Only* a poet? That's simply ridiculous. . . I lie awake sometimes the whole night. . . and torment myself with the question: 'Am I worthy?'"2

Yet, away from the more provincial atmosphere of Prague, in touch both with admired poets of the older generation, like Richard Dehmel and Detlev von Liliencron, and with like-minded contemporaries, he began to feel his hopes justified. The "Glorious year of 96,"3 as he called it, was marked by the publication of his third volume of verse, *Traumgekrönt* (1897, Crowned with Dreams). It showed a quieter and more assured lyrical touch and more originality. "You will see I am succeeding in what I wanted," ran the dedication to his father: "the sun himself comes to give me gold— not to the professor or the judge, but to your grateful, loyal son, the poet!"4 He pursued a conscious apprenticeship to his craft as a writer, the number of his stories already enough for publication in book form, his plays showing greater sensitivity and less of the crass naturalism of his earlier efforts. At the same time he missed little of the Munich social and cultural scene and was confident enough during the Christmas vacation to give a talk in Prague on Liliencron, to raise funds to relieve the older poet's distress. Notable above all was a cycle of poems he wrote now, "Christus. Elf Visionen"(1959, Eleven Visions of Christ), which remained unpublished more than twenty years after his death: not only in the strength of its poetic utterance, but also in the formulation of the ideas on religion which he held all his life— rejecting Christ as intermediary between himself and God, accepting him as great but still only human.

His meeting in May 1897 with Lou Andreas-Salomé was to prove the catalyst and seal for good his determination to live his life exclusively as poet and writer. The striking beauty of this thoroughly "liberated" scorner of convention, the formidable intellect of the former philosophy and theology student of Zürich, cast spell enough to make him abandon his studies and follow her on her return to Berlin in the autumn. Though strongly attracted and convinced of the powers he would show, she resisted his wooing, as she had that of Frierich Nietzsche much earlier, and indeed that of her professor husband, Andreas, with whom she maintained a firmly platonic relationship. Rilke's passion was overwhelming: "Tear out my eyes: I still can see you," he wrote to her one day in Munich,

> Stop up my ears: I still can hear you,
> Without feet I still can walk,
> Without a mouth still plead to you.
> Break off my arms: I'll grasp you yet
> With my heart as with a hand,
> Tear out my heart, my brain afire
> I'll carry you still in my blood——[5]

and there were certainly moments when she came close to surrender. But she was fully fourteen years older than he, and, as he came to realize, she was not prepared to abandon herself to him and give up the satisfying life of freedom she contrived to lead. Nevertheless, her powerful influence was enough not only to make him change his name from the precious-sounding "René" to the "plain fine German" of "Rainer," but also to bring out in the many poems he wrote for her a sincerity of expression hitherto lacking in his lyrics, and to encourage him in his exalted view of the poet's mission.

He had succeeded in finding a publisher for his volume of stories, *Am Leben hin* (1897, The Stream of Life); his Munich verse, still in his earlier style, appeared at the turn of the year *(Advent,* 1897); and *Zwei Prager Geschichten* (1899, Two Prague Stories), a sympathetic depiction of the Young Czech nationalist movement, like the autobiographical *Ewald Tragy* (1929), symbolized the final break with his homeland. He had adopted, like Lou, a simple vegetarian lifestyle (which he was to continue all his life), and though still a long way from financial independence, he could hope for a "winter of work" in Berlin, with Lou at his side and gaining through her the entree to the wider literary world of Berlin.

So, at first, it proved to be. With her he joined the select circle at Stefan George's ceremonious readings, met the dramatist Gerhart Hauptmann, the publisher Samuel Fischer and his revered "master" Dehmel. Soon he was deep in the study of the Italian Renaissance. His poems for her, forming a cycle in his notebooks *Dir zur Feier* (1959, A Festival for You), never saw publication in his lifetime, and many were destroyed out of discretion, but after a long visit to Florence and north Italy in the summer of 1898 he collected a counterpart, *Mir zur Feier* (1899, A Festival for Myself), his "first serious, ceremonious book,"[6] as he wrote to George, and indeed the first he would later acknowledge as of any worth. Viareggio was the inspiration for a lyrical drama, *Die weiße Fürstin* (1920, The White Princess), illustrating a basic element in his outlook: the concept of death as simply an unseen part of life, like the dark side of the moon—in form and content a marked contrast to his earlier plays. In a white leather volume impressed with Florentine lilies he began a diary for Lou: a vivid expression of the impact of his experience of the Renaissance and its creators, and setting down his thoughts on art, that "vaulting arch high above the people"[7] which was more and more to characterize his work, an act of creation in itself with no thought of popularity or of earning.

The return to Lou with this offering was to be for him a pilgrimage "deep into her soul, where it becomes a temple."[8] Instead, he found her cool towards his ardent wooing. Forced now to accept that they could never again be lovers, he found he could rationalize the cruel disappointment by keeping her still before him as an ideal, as only one of many goals to be striven for on his "road towards final fulfilment in a rich existence."[9] To set him alone on that road, Lou took the wise course of suggesting that he first accompany her and her husband on the visit they planned to her Russian homeland in the spring of 1899. The prospect gave him new heart: he began immediately to learn Russian, completed *Mir zur Feier,* and even enrolled at the University of Berlin for the coming summer term, for lectures on the history of art and classical poetry. The experience of the journey was everything he hoped for. The Orthodox Easter festival, the Russian spring, encounters with artists like Leonid Pasternak and Ilya Repin, a meeting with Tolstoy, study of religious art— all seemed like the culmination of what he had found in Florence. Russia itself was like his true homeland. He returned feeling he had gained in courage with a new plan to his life. Absorbed now completely in things Russian, he found his creativity restored: in less than two months he completed "Die Gebete" (The Prayers), to be the first part of his *Stundenbuch* (1905, *The Book of Hours*); *Die Weise von Liebe und Tod des Cornet Christoph Rilke* (1906, *Lay of the Love and Death of Cornet Christoph Rilke*); and *Vom lieben Gott und Anderes* (1900, *Stories of God*).

These three works were in due course to bring him a wider recognition than anything he had so far achieved, and for many who find his later works esoteric and difficult they will always represent the essential Rilke. "Die Gebete," in the final *Stundenbuch* entitled "Vom mönchischen Leben" ("Of the Monastic Life"), a long cyclic poem, expresses in the mouth of a Russian ikon-painting monk the concept of God Rilke had evolved from his Italian and Russian journeys: as a mystery rather than a revelation, as One still to be constructed by the artist, by the poet, indeed by all mankind:

> We are building Thee, with tremulous hands,
> and we pile atom upon atom.
> But who can complete Thee,
> Cathedral Thou?[10]

Not only the ultimate creator, but also a creature still to be formed; "neighbor God" existing in all things, yet still "ripening" like a tree towards an ever-distant maturity, still being created by the artist and truly existing only in him:

> What will you do, God, when I am dead?
> I am your pitcher (what if I should break?)
> I am your drink (What if I should perish?)
>
> You lose your meaning when I am no more.
>
> What will you do, God? I am afraid.[11]

A paradox indeed, which has no part in any orthodox religion: yet the myriad images, at once mystical and concrete, in which it is expressed, the soaring rhythms of his poetic mastery, make it convincing even to the orthodox. *Vom lieben Gott,* "Tales told to adults for children" as they were subtitled, expresses the same notion in more lighthearted prose: a God who may be omniscient but is not all seeing, who takes fright at his image in Michelangelo's marble but is restored to joy with the realization that He is in the sculptor too, each at work in mutual creation.

The *Cornet's* theme is quite different. Inspired by a laconic note in an old document of the death in 1664 of a young officer named Rilke in the Austrian campaign against the Turks in Hungary (son of a noble family the Prague Rilkes had hoped in vain to claim as their ancestors), it is a romanticized account in an easy flow of highly poetic prose of the lad's ride to his first and last experience of love and war — one night of love, an heroic death in the following dawn. It proved to be Rilke's most popular work with sales of over 300,000 before his death in 1926: it was said to be in every German soldier's knapsack in the First World War.

The "Russification" of his life with his progress in the language, attempts at translations and an essay on Russian Art, was intensified by a second visit to Moscow with Lou in the spring and summer of 1900, followed by an extensive journey throughout European Russia and the Ukraine. He felt more and more like a native of the country, his enthusiasm carried indeed to an excess which gave Lou some concern for his stability in the life of his own away from her which she wanted for him. After their return a stay of a few months among the artists' and writers' colony at Worpswede, near Bremen, seemed at first to give him the change he needed: a sense of community with like-minded people of his own age and acceptance among them as a poet in his own right, with the added attraction there of the budding artists Paula Becker and Clara Westhoff, and the feeling growing that to settle here with a wife like one of them would be ideal for his work. Yet, although his notebook accumulated many more poems than he had been able to write in Russia, by October he was back in Berlin, and before the year was out he was tormented by deep depression, uncertain where to find a support to replace that of Lou.

Abruptly he sought it in Clara Westhoff. Nearly three years younger than Rilke she showed great promise as a sculptor: marriage with her, he felt, would give them both the opportunity for developing their work, independently yet against the background of a real home. They married in April 1901 and set up house near Worpswede. Modest as it was, they still managed only with their parents' support. The rash venture proved difficult to sustain, but the first year was unclouded and for Rilke productive. Three of his earlier stories were published in November under the title *Die Letzten* (1901, The Last of their Line), and he completed another, as well as the long series of poems to form the second part of the *Stundenbuch* - "Das Buch von der Pilgerschaft" ("The Book of Pilgrimage"). This was a distillation of what he had gained from the Russian experience, the words those of the same "who knelt / Before Thee in the habit of a monk,"[12] and even weaving in the poem he had written long before to Lou ("Tear out my eyes, I still can see you"); but there was a subtle change of emphasis:

> The hamlet is but transient, a point
> Between two vast expanses, frightened in its bodings,
> A way past houses only, no path up.
>
> And those who leave the village wander long,
> And many die, it may be, on the road.
>
> Deep in the night, I dig Thee out, like treasure,
> For all the riches I have seen
> Are but poverty, poor substitute
> For Thy beauty which is still to come.
> But the way to Thee is fearful long,
> And, long untraveled, obscured to us.[13]

It was a premonition in fact of what his own life would bring: not the stability of home and family, but the hard road of the pilgrim.

For it was soon clear to him that not only were their uncertain incomes inadequate, but also that, even if they were to find patrons, his cherished notion of marriage as a "guardianship of each other's solitude"[14] was unworkable. With reluctance he accepted a commission for work to order: a monograph on the Worpswede artists, completed during the spring of 1902 *(Worpswede,* 1903) and he was already considering a move to Paris for them both, leaving their baby Ruth, born in December 1901, with Clara's parents, when a further assignment came to confirm this idea. Paris, where each could concentrate on their work alone, would give Clara the chance of benefitting from Rodin's advice: and the commission for him to write a monograph on the great sculptor sealed their decision.

He had meanwhile the satisfaction of seeing his next volume of verse in print, *Das Buch der Bilder* (1902, *The Book of Images*) dedicated to Gerhart Hauptmann — a selection from his production of the previous three years, combining Russian themes, his "songs to the maidens" Clara and Paula, a macabre requiem for a friend of Clara's. The book's overriding impression is one of melancholy rather than the joy of *Mir zur Feier* — the melancholy of childhood, of the "last of a line," his mood of depression before his marriage, and as a coda come the often-quoted lines:

> Death is great.
> We are his
> With laughing lips.

When we think to be in the midst of life,
He dares to shed his tears
Deep in our hearts.[15]

But financial need would not make him compromise over a work of art,
and he insisted on a costly production in a severely limited edition.
Neither this book nor *Worpswede* brought him much money: and only
through articles and reviews could he scrape enough together to set off
alone for Paris in August 1902, leaving Clara to close up the house and
join him later.

II

In a small room in Paris he found the solitude he had longed for, a
place for real work, in spite of the almost terrifying first impression of a
city full of the sick and dying. From Rodin, indulgent and helpful with
material for the monograph, he learned an important lesson — that his
own art should be pursued with the same patient application as that of
sculpture, not simply left to sporadic inspiration. He was not lacking in
the obsessive dedication that Rodin showed: his problem was how to follow the Master's advice, "il faut toujours travailler, rien que travailler,"
"patience is everything, patience and work". Most of his verses that
autumn were mood-images still: of the contrast between city streets and
the Worpswede moorland, of the summer's end when "he who has no
house will never build one now, And if he is alone will long remain so;"[16]
and these he would keep for a later enlarged edition of the *Buch der
Bilder*. But his new ambition began to bear fruit with the first of the fine-
ly-chiselled works which he would rightly call "New Poems," marvellous
renderings of observation which could stand alone, like sculptures: the
panther pacing his cage in the Paris zoo, the bars gliding past his weary
eye till he feels there are a thousand of them and beyond them nothing.

Soft padding steps of supple strength,
turning and turning in so small a space,
are like a dance of power round a centre
where a strong will lies benumbed.

But now and then the curtain of the eyelid
lifts soundlessly—. An image enters then,

runs through the quiet tension of the limbs,
reaches the heart—and ceases to exist.[17]

Clara arrived in October 1902; she lived apart from him as they had
agreed, and was soon working steadily. They managed to keep their heads
above water, she with support from home, he with editing work for his
Berlin publisher: but he still found it hard to force his Muse, and felt he
must escape to Italy in the spring. In Viareggio further "Prayers" came to
him rapidly to form the third part of the Stundenbuch, "Das Buch von der
Armut und vom Tode" (The Book of Poverty and Death)— prayers for
redemption from the "deep terror of the sprawling cities," where all is
false and where the unnatural life brings man to an unnatural death:

O Lord, grant each his own, his death indeed,
the dying which out of that same life evolves
in which he once had meaning, love, and need.

For we are but the leaf and just the skin.
But that great death which each one has within,
That is the fruit around which all revolves,[18]

and continuing in praise of poverty, "a great inward splendour", lauding
"the poor man's house like an altar-shrine" and St. Francis of Assisi,
"great evening-star of poverty."[19]

Finished the following year, these were verses of great evocative
power, and with the earlier "Monastic" and "Pilgrimage" cycles formed an
organic whole; like them, however, they were an exalted transmutation of
experience, this time of the great city, falling short still of the "thing of
art" created from observation, in the example of Rodin. After a brief further stay in Paris he and Clara resolved to return to Germany. There in
long letters to Lou he described his failure to attain his ideal, the failure to
present "longings and fears as things," converting what he had observed
into works of art—letters, however, which in their vivid depictions of
Paris, "great edifice of suffering,"[20] themselves began to form the "thing"
he would eventually make of it all, his novel *Die Aufzeichnungen des
Malte Laurids Brigge* (1910, *The Notebook of Malte Laurids Brigge*). A
move to Italy again, this time to Rome, might, he felt, show him the way,
and they arrived there in September 1903.

In modest separate quarters near the Borghese Gardens, their work
made some beginning. Rilke, encouraged by the proposal of the newly-

established Insel Verlag in Leipzig for a new edition of *Vom lieben Gott*, under the title of *Geschichten vom lieben Gott* (1904, *Stories of God*), began now the prose work, conceiving it originally as a sort of sequel, though it was to turn out quite differently in the novel of *Malte*. With the composition of this "firm consecutive prose," and of three more "New Poems"— "Geburt der Venus" ("The Birth of Venus"), "Orpheus. Eurydike. Hermes" and "Hetärengräber" ("Courtesans' Graves")— he seemed to have made a step forward, and many other projects were in his mind. But Italy's appeal faded quickly; and he was glad to accept an invitation to Sweden, organized by Ellen Key, the writer and educationalist who had long admired his work and done much to publicize it in the Scandinavian countries. Leaving Clara back at Bremen, where she had better opportunities for commissions, he crossed to Sweden in June 1904, to stay for several months at Borgeby Gård, near Malmö, as the guest of Ernst Norlind, artist and writer, and his fiancée, and later near Gothenburg with Jimmy Gibson, industrialist and literary enthusiast, and his wife Lizzie. This hospitality, with in the case of the Gibsons financial help, was the prototype for the life he was henceforth to lead: a poet of steadily-increasing renown and estimation, never well-off but housed by sympathetic patrons and enabled to pursue the perfection of his work in conditions of solitude when he preferred. A chance meeting with Luise, Countess of Schwerin after his return to Germany at the end of the year brought him a similar invitation to her château at Friedelhausen, near Giessen, and the introduction to her family, with the prospect of a visit to their villa in Capri.

After a reunion with Lou, now in Göttingen, and a stay in Berlin for a brief resumption of university studies, he was enormously encouraged to receive a warm letter from Rodin— "words of friendship and support for your spirit as a worker"[21]— and he decided to visit him again in Paris in the autumn. Invited then to stay at Meudon, he found the Master ready to devote many hours to him and soon offering him a paid post as his secretary, the first time Rilke had something approaching normal security in his life, and the opportunity he needed to "learn how to work," to "learn everything I lack."[22] He gained in assurance and confidence: gave lectures on Rodin in Dresden and Prague; returned then to Meudon; saw the *Stundenbuch* through the press with the Insel Verlag; and at last, alongside his secretarial work for Rodin which took up more time than expected, he succeeded in the steady, patient work of the kind he had aimed for, in further "New Poems." They were sometimes on classical and biblical themes; but the "Buddha" illustrates perhaps best his new departure:

He seems to listen. Stillness, things remote . . .
We stop, and they no longer reach our ear.
He is a star. And others of great note,
Unseen by us, are ranged about him near.

Oh, he is all. In truth, are we in wait
for him to see us? Can such a need he feel?
Were we to bow down here before him, kneel,
he'd stay withdrawn, indifferent to our fate.

For that which casts us at his feet
in him for long millennia has turned.
He who forgets what we have learned,
and learns, where we can but admit defeat.[23]

He had not yet been able to take up again the prose of *Malte*. When he came back to Meudon after further lectures on Rodin in Germany in the spring of 1906, interrupted by the need to go to Prague on the death of his father, the drudgery of Rodin's correspondence began to irk him, and he longed to be free for the work he now felt capable of. His liberation came, quite unexpectedly, in May, when Rodin, following a trivial misunderstanding, abruptly dismissed him. The loss of the small income and of the presence of the Master was more than compensated for by his relief at being once more truly alone, back in a simple room in Paris; and he began by finalizing for his earlier publisher the new edition of the Cornet and an enlarged version of the *Buch der Bilder*— tasks which had to be cleared before turning to *Malte* and the "New Poems," more of which now started to flow in almost a flood. Both of these books were destined for the Insel Verlag, with whom he had agreed upon more satisfactory terms and who were energetically promoting his works.

Paris was now "the bright, the silken,"[24] for him, no longer a city of terror but of joy. His work prospered, with the absorption daily of new impressions in the Louvre, in galleries, the Cluny Museum, the zoo: learning not just to wait until "the things in their power made something of one, but to forestall them."[25] More wanderings followed, however: to Belgium with Clara and Ruth, where a chance meeting with Rodin offered hope of reconciliation; to Friedelhausen again; then to Capri for the winter at the invitation of Alice Faehndrich, Luise von Schwerin's sister. Here in admirably solitary quarters he found inspiration in "Improvisationen aus

dem capreser Winter" ("Improvisations from the Capri Winter"), something like a new *Stundenbuch,* he thought, away from the manner of the
"New Poems" and so remaining unpublished; but he also with Alice's
help made a translation of Elizabeth Barrett Browning's *Sonnets from the
Portuguese.* Paris, however, remained his goal, now he knew what it
could give him, and he was back there by May 1907.

In July he was to send off to Anton Kippenberg, the new director of
the Insel Verlag, the final selection of *Neue Gedichte* (1907, *New Poems*).
These were no longer the expression of inner mood but its reflection in
"things," the Paris parks, a rose-window, animals in the zoo, a beggar.
Typical is the well-known "Das Karussell" ("The Merry-Go-Round") he
had often watched in the Luxembourg Gardens:

> Complete with roof and shadow it rotates
> a little while, bearing its gallant band
> of gaily coloured horses from the land
> that lingers long, ere it capitulates.
> Though yoked to carriages some of them pant,
> they one and all have courage in their faces;
> with them a lion, red and savage, paces,
> and now and then, all white, an elephant.
>
> Even a stag, as in the forest, too,
> but with a saddle, solemnly advances,
> strapped on its back a little girl in blue
>
> And on the fearful lion, grasping tight
> its teeth and lolling tongue with tiny hand,
> intrepid rides a little boy in white.
>
> And now and then, all white, an elephant.
>
> And as the horses gallop by, it chances
> a girl, too big for such pretending,
> out of the cavalcade, with charm unending,
> lets stray this way one of her random glances—
>
> And now and then, all white, an elephant.

So it pursues its purposeless careering,
revolving only, eager to be done,
a red, a green, a grey receding, nearing,
a little profile, hardly yet begun.
And sometimes, this way turned, a smile appearing,
a blissful smile, too dazzling, too endearing
to waste on breathless make-believe and fun.[26]

Many poems were of observation once removed, as it were: Christ in the garden of Gethsemane, an echo of the "Visions;" the departure of the Prodigal Son (like his own from Prague); classical and biblical subjects seen in a new light. All were characterized by his endeavor to follow Rodin in creating a "Kunstding," a "thing of art" more definite than its model: in his words to Clara, from "pursuing an experience to the very end beyond which no-one can go," to a work of art as "the most final expression" of its uniquéness. [27]

"I am on the way to becoming a worker," he told her. The completion of the volume had gone so well that he promised Kippenberg a second, aiming to finish it in a "summer of work" the following year. The winter passed with further public appearances, in Prague (depressing as always) for readings from his own work, and in Vienna, where a highly appreciative audience heard both the talk on Rodin and extracts from the *Neue Gedichte* and even from his first drafts of *Malte*, followed by a restful day in Venice. Expected in Capri again in the spring, he kept his stay there short. His preoccupations over securing a firmer financial basis for his future were meanwhile relieved: not only did Kippenberg guarantee regular advances against the coming works, but also Samuel Fischer offered him a substantial sum for a year's support without seeking any promise of works for his own house. With such assurances, and then a reconciliation with Rodin, who later became his neighbor in the old Hôtel Biron (one day to become the Rodin Museum), his return to Paris this time was therefore incomparably more hopeful.

His undertaking for the Insel Verlag prospered accordingly. By August 1908, in a productive flow, the second volume of poems— *Der neuen Gedichte anderer Teil* (1908, *New Poems II*)— was completed: a few earlier poems not included in first volume but the majority newly-written, among the most remarkable "Archaischer Torso Apollos" ("Archaic Torso of Apollo").

Though we've not known his unimagined head
and what divinity his eyes were showing,
his torso like a branching street-lamp's glowing,
wherein his gaze, only turned down, can shed

light still. Or else the breast's insurgency
could not be dazzling you, or you discerning
in that slight twist of his loins a smile returning
to where was centered his virility.

Or else this stone would not stand so intact
beneath the shoulders' through-seen cataract
and would not glisten like a wild beast's skin;

and would not keep from all its contours giving
light like a star: for there's no place therein
that does not see you. You must change your living.[28]

With these poems felt he had achieved greater depth in his "things of art," greater distance. The last line of the "Apollo," at first sight obscure, signified in fact the end for him of this phase in his poetic production. If there should one day be a third volume, as he wrote to Kippenberg, there would have to be a further similar "enhancement in ever greater conversion of reality," achieving of itself "a more limpid validity of all things."[29] Settling now in earnest to the second commitment, the prose of Malte, he came more and more to realize that this work, distillation of his experiences in different form, must be finished, worked out of his system, before he could "change his life" and attain that higher plane of lyrical expression. Malte must die, if Rilke was to survive for greater things: "Only through him can I get on, he stands in my way."[30]

It took him nearly two more years to reach this point. His resolve was weakened by failing health but restored by a journey through Provence in the autumn of 1909, and finally justified in January 1910 after he had had to give up his rooms in Paris, when he dictated the manuscript during a stay with Kippenberg in Leipzig. The result, *Die Aufzeichnungen des Malte Laurids Brigge*, was remarkable by any standard. In stark contrast to the "things of art" of the *Neue Gedichte,* these disconnected jottings of a young Danish poet, last scion of an aristocratic family, despairing and finally perishing in a Paris garret, came as an unconventional and esoteric composition which has surprised many of Rilke's admirers. For some its mannered prose and "purple patches" are too far a cry from the beauty and vigor of his verse: but for others, notably Laurence Durrell, it is "densely packed with the matter of poetic observation," its very formlessness bringing "an unrationalized order into the chaos around him."[31] For Rilke, it was the closest he ever came to autobiography: Malte is the same age, lives in Paris at one of his actual addresses, describes the horrors of the city's sick, poor and dying in the words of his own letters. The hypersensitiveness to his room-neighbors, his nameless fears and recollections of childhood anxieties, the mother's game of treating him as a girl, are all Rilke's experiences. And some even of what is imagined is Rilke as he wished he might have been: the last of a noble line, his mother loving and understanding as his own had never been. Malte's reading in French and Russian history is Rilke's, and in theme after theme of his musings— death, poverty, non-possessive love, the Prodigal Son who "did not want to be loved"— Malte is expressing Rilke. But his aim was to make "a thing out of his fears," so as to overcome them: and he always insisted the book was not to be seen as a gospel of despair, but to be "read against the current." Its success or otherwise in the market place was a matter of indifference to him.

The publisher, however, was confident. His generous advances to the poet (fully justified, in the event) made possible journeys of great importance to him, before he finally returned to Paris in the spring of 1911: to Berlin, Rome, Venice, and especially to Duino near Trieste and Lautschin in Bohemia, two of the grand homes of Princess Marie von Thurn und Taxis, who was to prove a benevolent patron, a firm friend with the commonsense advice he always needed. After *Malte* he had written to Kippenberg, "Everything can really begin":[32] but in these wanderings he searched in vain for the new beginning, even in a tour through North Africa (Algeria, Tunisia, Egypt), in spite of the powerful impressions gained from the souks of Tunis and the antiquities of Sakkara and Karnak. A return to his self-contained life in Paris and the "fallow writing-desk"[33] there seemed his only hope.

III

Circumstances seemed to favor him at last: he was once more in the familiar surroundings of the rue de Varenne, alone in the city which he always regarded more than any other as home, and this time with an assured, if modest, income from the publisher whom he was glad to guide now on his first visit to Paris. "Work" of a sort certainly began: correspondence, of course, and translations— the prose of Maurice de Guérin's *Centaur* (*Der Kentauer*, 1911), an anonymous sermon *The Love of Mary Magdalene* (*Die Liebe der Magdalene*, 1912), and the sonnets of Louize de Labé the sixteenth-century poetess of Lyons *(Die vierundzwanzig Sonette der Louize Labé,* 1917). Significantly, however, what attracted him in both these latter works was the theme he had made so much of in *Malte*: "intransitive love" that asked none in return. Outwardly nothing was lacking for him: it was an inner need that remained unsatisfied, the longing for that perfect partner, some "future beloved" who could be the complement to his solitude and the prop to his work. Without her, real inspiration obstinately failed:

> Like a door that will not stay closed,
> so time and again as I sleep
> the embrace looses hold. O nights of trouble . . . [34]

And he fell back on travel yet again: to Germany, to Lautschin at the Princess's invitation; to Weimar, where for the first time his antipathy to Goethe was overcome; even for a while to rejoin Clara and his daughter Ruth in Munich, where they had now settled with better prospects for Clara's work; finally, in October 1911, to Duino again, where the Princess suggested he should stay on alone after her departure at the end of the year. By this time he was almost desperate at his inability to get "down on the bedrock of work,"[35] even to the extent of considering psychoanalysis. The problem found expression in verses to Lou, and in long "confessions" to her by letter, in the end agreeing with her that analysis would not bring a solution:

> Why should I eject myself,
> while, it may be, your influence falls upon me,
> lightly, like moonlight on a window-seat?[36]

Yet, even while penning these confessions, he began to produce: the thirteen poems forming *Das Marienleben* (1913, *The Life of the Virgin Mary*). As it proved, this was a "little mill" driven by a greater stream. For, only a few days later, in January 1912, as he paced the bastions of the castle through a powerful wind, came the voice of inspiration:

"And if I cried, who'd listen to me in those angelic orders?"[37]-- the beginning of the First Duino Elegy, to which a second was quickly added, fragments of three more, and the opening lines of what he could already see as the last.

"The fearful thing about art is that the further one advances in it, the more it commits one . . .   to the almost impossible," he had written to Lou. The Elegies were to be that commitment, the celebration of the mission he had embraced,

> Because beauty's nothing
> but the start of terror we can hardly bear,
> and we adore it because of the serene scorn
> it could kill us with. Every angel's terrifying,

and they were to culminate in its jubilant praise:

> One day, when this terrifying vision's vanished,
> let me sing ecstatic praises to angels saying yes!
> Let my heart's clear-struck keys ring and not one
> fail because of a doubting, slack, or breaking string.
>
> . . .   And then how dear
> you'll be to me, you nights of anguish.[38]

The end he could already see, not yet what had to lead up to it. The beginning, however, the first two Elegies, came fast: a distillation, dense and elliptical in its allusions, of his experience of the conflict between the poet's mission and the demands of life:

> All that was your charge.
> But could you live up to it? Weren't you always
> distracted by hope, as if all this promised
> you a lover?

Despite his longing for such another, some "future beloved," he still felt profoundly that this should not be:

> Isn't it time our loving freed
> us from the one we love, and we, trembling, endured:

as the arrow endures the string, and in that gathering momentum
becomes more than itself. Because to stay is to be nowhere.[39]

Singing to the angels, "almost deadly birds of my soul," he was hymning
the perfection for which the poet must strive:

> spaces of being, force fields of ecstasy, storms
> of unchecked rapture, and suddenly, separate,
> *mirrors*: each drawing its own widespread
> streaming beauty back into its face, [40]

giving and receiving in perfect non-dependence, in human terms seemingly attainable only by those who die young, or by those great lovers whose
love no longer depends on its object. It was a goal he spent his life trying
to reach.

> Didn't the caution of human gestures on Attic steles
> amaze you? Weren't love and separation placed
> on those shoulders so lightly. . .

> All we can do is touch one another like this. The gods
> can press down harder on us, but that's the gods' affair.[41]

These verses were the subconscious expression of his determination, after long months of despairing introspection, to heal himself: to
devote himself to his mission and to hope that one day he could resolve
the fatal conflict "between life and the great work." Clara in fact was at
this time seeking their divorce (a project which in the end they failed to
carry through, though they never lived together again). Once Ruth's
schooling was assured with the aid of good friends, he was content to let
her go her own way, intent himself on finding the silent helpmate who,
understanding, would "protect his solitude."

His stay in Duino lasted fully six months and was followed then by
Venice, where he had the good fortune at last to meet Eleonora Duse, the
great actress to whom he had dedicated *Die weiße Fürstin* so many years
earlier. She was now retired, and unlikely, he realized, to achieve a come-
back, least of all with that ethereal and anachronistic vehicle. After an
autumn return to Duino he set off for Spain, for the Toledo of El Greco,
hoping— in vain— that these stimulating surroundings would renew the

creative flow, and finally for the majestic rocky landscape of Ronda. Here, although the "tiny snapped-off fragment"[42] of the Elegies was not at first resumed, at least a "Spanish Trilogy" and some verses in the line of the *Neue Gedichte* helped to raise his spirits, watching the shepherd in his daily task,

> as he moves about, sun-tans and with measuring sling-shot
> mends the hem of his flock where it grows ragged.[43]

Ronda seemed to him an heroic landscape in direct communion with the Whole, with what he called the invisible realm of the angels, where life and death were made one. He was reminded of earlier experiences of such communion as he had himself had in Capri and Duino, the feeling of "passing through to the other side of nature" and looking back on it as if over his shoulder, "Experiences" which he set down in the third person in his notebook: "He recalled too . . . how, if he bore it long enough, everything was so completely taken up in the clear solvent of his heart that the taste of all Creation was was in his being."[44] And he began then to rediscover for a while the "inwardness" of the Elegies, bringing to final form what was to form the Sixth, on a theme only dimly seen in Duino: the celebration of the Hero, whose death is not as we conceive it, merely the opposite of life, but the very fruit of life, the unseen dark side of a single Whole:

> Oh, we glory in our flowering, and so we come to
> the retarded core of our last fruit already betrayed.
> In a few the surge of action rises so strongly that,
> when the temptation to bloom touches the youth
> of their mouths, of their eyelids, like gentle night air,
> they're already standing and glowing with full hearts;
> only in heroes, perhaps, and in those destined to die young,
> those in whom death the gardener has twisted the veins
> differently. They plunge ahead of their own laughter
> like the team of horses in front of the lovingly
> chiselled reliefs of the conquering king at Karnak.[45]

With this renewal of hope, he was loth to leave Ronda, but finally the cold drove him back to Paris in February 1913 - helped as usual by extra allowances from Kippenberg to tide him over the expenses of his reinstallation there. There were at first many distractions, with old acquaintances passing through, and new ones, such as André Gide and Romain Rolland, being made; but he set to work, as usual, with translations, continuing that of the Louize Labé sonnets and beginning the letters of yet another of his gallery of "great lovers," the Portuguese nun Marianna Alcoforado. He found he was even able to develop some drafts on the themes of the Elegies. Kippenberg had every reason to be satisfied with his author, when he came to visit, taking with him the completed translations and bringing out soon afterwards the *Marienleben* and the first Insel edition of *Das Buch der Bilder.* He had now acquired the rights to all Rilke's earlier works and was planning not only a new edition of the *Rodin,* but also a selection of his *Erste Gedichte* (1913, *First Poems*). Yet the "turning inward" the poet sought still eluded him.

It was only after further travel— a "cure" at Bad Rippoldsau, a visit to Lou in Göttingen,and a stay at Heiligendamm on the Baltic coast— that he could feel it imminent, with verses coming to him in the new tone the Elegies had initiated, at the very limit of the expressible:

> Behind the guilt-free trees
> old Fate is slowly forming
> her taciturn face.
> Wrinkles travel thither . . .
> Here a bird screams, and there
> a furrow of pain
> shoots from the hard sooth-saying mouth.
>
> Oh, and the almost lovers,
> with their unvaledictory smiles!—
> their destiny setting and rising above them,
> constellational,
> night-enraptured. . . .[46]

When he returned to Paris in October he felt ready to "spin himself into his cocoon," "imitating the days in Duino," and completed the Third Elegy begun there— self-analysis again, as Lou had recommended, and influenced by their talks on the theories of Freud:

> To sing about someone you love is one thing; but, oh,
> the blood's hidden guilty river-god is something else.

Known to her only from a distance, what can her lover,
even, say about the lord of passion, who often out of
loneliness, before she could comfort him, often as if
she didn't exist, raised his godhead, oh, who knows from
what depths, came streaming, and incited the night to riot.
Oh that Neptune of the blood and his terrible trident!

Look, we don't love like flowers
with only one season behind us; when we love
a sap older than memory rises in our arms. . .
. . . inside us we haven't loved just some one
in the future, but a fermenting tribe; not just one
child, but fathers, cradled inside us like ruins
of mountains, the dry riverbed
of former mothers . . . [47]

Still the treatment under his own prescription somehow lacked the
hoped-for effect. By the turn of the year a discontent with his apparently
aimless existence in Paris mounted: he felt he was failing to find the way,
not only to the "Angel," but also to the longed-for companion.

You who never arrived
in my arms, Beloved, who were lost
from the start . . .
. . . All the immense
images in me— the far-off, deeply-felt landscape,
cities, towers, and bridges, and unsuspected
turns in the path,
and those powerful lands that were once
pulsing with the life of the gods—
all rise within me to mean
you, who forever elude me.

. . . An open window
in a country house—, and you almost
stepped up, pensive, to my side. . . .

And sometimes, in a shop, the mirrors
were still dizzy from your presence, and startled, gave back

my too-sudden image. Who knows?
perhaps the same bird echoed through both of us
yesterday, separate, in the evening. . .[48]

"If God has understanding," he wrote to Princess Marie, "He will let me
find a couple of rooms in the country, where. . . my Elegies can howl at
the moon as they will. . . and just the one person, that sisterly being (alas,
alas!) who would take care of the house and have no love at all—or so
much love that she would ask nothing except to be allowed to be there,
active and protective, on the borders of the invisible."[49] Till such a provi-
dential dispensation should come his way, he would have to stay where he
was, digging over "all the soil of the heart,"[50] but no longer looking to
find love. Strange to feel, he confided to his notebook, that he might
never experience that which he needed.

He had hardly written these words of resignation, when a letter
arrived from Vienna which seemed to give them the lie. Magda von
Hattingberg, a talented concert-pianist, writing in admiration of the
Geschichten vom lieben Gott, said she fervently longed to express it for
him in her music: and seizing with both hands this prospect, heaven-sent
as he thought, of being freed from his despair, he began to write almost
daily to this "'Benvenuta," "dear heart," "loving sister," to whom he could
speak "as though to the clouds and the deeps of my heaven." New life
breathed in his daily work, as he completed his translations of Gide's
Return of the Prodigal Son (1914, *Die Rückkehr des verlorenen Sohnes*),
started on the sonnets of Michelangelo and wrote an essay on Lotte
Pritzel's puppets; but it was in the letters to Magda, a flow of poetic prose
he had not known since the night of the *Cornet*, and in the poems to her in
the train on his way to their first meeting in Berlin, that he found his true
expression.

Can you imagine how for years
I've travelled thus, strange among strangers?
And now at last you take me in, to home.[52]

But it was not to be. He quickly saw that his "indescribable hopes"
of having at last found "the right relationship to another" had been
deceived again, and he did not need Princess Marie's advice, when he
took Magda to visit her in Duino in April 1914, to realize that this was one
more "beloved lost from the start." Back in Paris in June he found expres-

sion for the problem of his life in verses entitled "Wendepunkt" ("Turning-point"):

> For a long time he attained it in looking.
> Stars would fall to their knees
> beneath his compelling vision.
>
> Towers he would gaze at so
> that they were terrified:
> building them up again, suddenly, in an instant!
> But how often the landscape, overburdened by day,
> came to rest in his silent awareness, at nightfall.
>
> For there is a boundary to looking.
> And the world that is looked at so deeply
> wants to flourish in love.
>
> Work of the eyes is done, now
> go and do heart-work
> on all the images imprisoned within you; for you
> overpowered them: but even now you don't know them.
>
> Learn, inner man, to look on your inner woman,
> the one attained from a thousand
> natures, the merely attained but
> not yet beloved form.[53]

This was the turn, he was convinced, that must come if he was to survive, but for which he felt he must first find a doctor— not an analyst— who could resolve the paralyzing conflict between body and spirit. With the idea of consulting a doctor friend in Munich, and as so often before of seeking Lou Salomé's advice and comfort, he set off for Germany in July 1914. He had no inkling that in a matter of weeks the outbreak of the First World War would not only bring to an end the life of freedom to travel he had always enjoyed and cut him off from Paris, but also condemn his Muse to four weary years of virtual sterility.

With Germany and Austria, for neither of which he had ever felt patriotism, ranged now in war against Russia, his spiritual homeland, and France, his adopted home, he might have been expected to fall into even deeper depression. Strangely enough, however, the first weeks of August found him at one with the herd, stirring himself to celebratory verse to the god of war in "Fünf Gesänge" ("Five Hymns"),— the first time this intensely individual poet had expressed a profound *shared* emotion:

> For three days, is it true? Am I really hymning the horror,
> really that god whom as one of the olden times,
> distant and only remembering, I was wont to believe and admire?
>
> he stands. He transcends. And we? We merge into one together,
> into a new kind of being, mortally animate through him.
> So too *am* I no more. Out of the general heart
> My heart is beating in tune—[54]

It was a brief moment only: he very soon began to "encapsulate" himself against the immense outside force which had made a mirage of his "turning-point." Through the four years that followed he was only inter-mittently capable of resuming his true work in spite of material help from his many friends and well-wishers, and his search for the companion he needed for its support continued unrewarded.

Already in the autumn of 1914 a liaison with the painter Loulou Albert-Lazard raised his hopes again, but it had to end the following year with the same realization of failure. "Ausgesetzt auf den Bergen des Herzens," as he wrote in a memorable poem for her, he longed for, yet feared, this "exposure on the mountains of the heart":

> Look, how tiny down there,
> look: the last village of words, and, higher,
> (but how tiny) still one last
> farmhouse of feeling. Can you see it?
> Exposed on the cliffs of the heart. Stoneground
> under your hands. Even here, though,
> something can bloom; on a silent cliff-edge
> an unknowing plant blooms, singing, into the air.
> But the one who knows? Ah, he began to know
> and is quiet now, exposed on the cliffs of the heart.
> While, with their full awareness,
> many sure-footed mountain animals pass
> or linger. And the great sheltered bird flies, slowly,

circling, around the peak's pure denial.—But
without a shelter, here on the cliffs of the heart. . . .[55]

With Loulou, as with Magda, he was fated to remain "without a shelter."
While awaiting the inevitable call to the Austrian colors in 1915, he found
refuge with friends in Berlin and Munich. The funds from Kippenberg
continued, augmented by the gift of a large sum, made anonymously by
the philosopher Ludwig von Wittgenstein, so materially he had few worries. His call-up, when it finally came in January 1916, brought him, after
only a few weeks of the parade ground, to the safe haven of the Vienna
War Archive, where he joined other writers in propaganda work— and
even from this he was released the following summer and could return to
Munich.

Before this brief interlude of military service, he had been able to
continue his Michelangelo translations and had written a few remarkable
poems, notably "Der Tod" ("Death"):

There stands death, a bluish distillate
in a cup without a saucer. Such a strange
place to find a cup: standing on
the back of a hand. One recognizes clearly
the line along the glazed curve, where the handle
snapped. Covered with dust. And HOPE is written
across the side, in faded Gothic letters.
The man who was to drink out of that cup
read it aloud at breakfast, long ago. . . .

O shooting star
that fell into my eyes and through my body—:
Not to forget you. To endure.[56]

Death for him signified "life as a whole, the completeness of life"; its
demand on us is "to understand our earthly existence as simply one side of
being."

Now I'll speak, no longer be an awed
pupil facing their Examinerships.
Now I'll say 'Blue sky', I'll say 'Greensward',
and may the spirit taking it from my lips
turn it to eternity's account [57]

he wrote too at this time; and in such a "good, powerful rush of work" he even felt he could turn again to the cycle of the Elegies, writing the Fourth. Its theme, unsurprisingly against the background of war, was bitter and negative: man's inability in his dividedness of mind to surrender to the unseen forces whose instrument he is, and whose purposes alone give meaning to his life.

> O trees of life, when does your winter come?
> We are not in harmony, our blood does not forewarn us
> like migratory birds'. . . .

> we never know the
> actual, vital contour of our own
> emotions—just what forms them from outside.

A puppet is better than "these half-filled human masks": "it at least is full".

> I'll put up with the stuffed skin, the wire, the face
> that is nothing but appearance. Here, I'm waiting.
> Even if the lights go out. . .
> I'll sit here anyway. One can always watch. . . .

> am I not right
> to feel as if I must stay seated, must
> wait before the puppet stage, or rather,
> gaze at it so intensely that at last,
> to balance my gaze, an angel has to come and
> make the stuffed skins startle into life.
> Angel and puppet, a real play, finally.
> Then what we separate by our very presence
> can come together. And only then, the whole
> cycle of transformation will arise. . . [59]

But the Elegy ends in praise of childhood: if we could regain the child's open and undivided consciousness, we should be able to play our parts

in the infinite, blissful space between world and toy. . . .
Murderers are easy to understand. But this: that one can contain
death, the whole of death, even before
life has begun, can hold it to one's heart
gently, and not refuse to go on living,
is inexpressible.[60]

The military interlude, however, brought him sharply down to earth,
and for the remaining war years— in the country in Westphalia, in Berlin
and back again in Munich— he found he was incapable of resuming the
glorious flow. Invitations to give readings and talks in Switzerland
offered the hope at last of a breakout from this sterility, and in June 1919
he was finally able to accept: traveling not, like so many others appalled
by the chaos in Germany, as an emigrant, but fully intending to return in
the autumn after his speaking engagements.

IV

In Switzerland, as in Germany, there were many admirers and contacts of his friends, to make him welcome with accommodations and to
smooth his path through the bureaucratic jungle of residence permits, so
that he was able to enjoy to the full the feeling of freedom offered by this
neutral land. Thanks to their aid, he traveled it extensively— Zürich,
Geneva, the Grisons, Berne— and his reading tour of the German-speaking area in October and November 1919 scored a remarkable success, the
selections of verse, prose and translations suitably adapted to each different audience. In earlier years, passing through on his way to Italy, he had
almost disdained Switzerland's scenic marvels, which seemed to him too
contrived and unreal. Now with the entree he had to its old-established
families and their houses, he felt that he was penetrating to its true core—
and what was more, that it was here he might perhaps find the permanent
refuge needed for his work. A return to Munich in fact looked problematical now that he rated as a foreigner there; and having become effectively
a stateless refugee, following the break-up of the Austro-Hungarian
Empire, he decided early in 1920 to apply for a Czechoslovak passport,
his birthplace being now the capital of that new country. Loans from
friends tided him over, until later that year the stabilization of the German
mark made it possible for Kippenberg to remit funds from his healthy
account with the Insel; and he was able to stay for some months in suitable

solitary conditions, though still without any renewal of inspiration, in the country house of the Burckhardt family near Basel.

Two relationships he formed in this first year proved of great importance for him. The artist Baladine Klossowska, whom he had known before the war, was living in Geneva separated from her husband, also a painter and writer on art: and in their shared reminiscences of Paris the attraction he felt for her soon quickened to love. Though "Merline," as she was called, knew from his frequent letters that he must remain alone if he was ever to complete the Elegies, her growing passion for him could not be denied; for his part he could not withstand this new call to love, sending her roses and gifts,—even if he suspected that she too was "lost from the start" and no more likely than her predecessors to fill the role of undemanding mistress. The true helpmate he really needed he had found in Zürich at the outset of his tour: Nanny Wunderly, energetic and vivacious chatelaine, wife of a tannery owner and cousin of the Reinhart brothers in Winterthur, wealthy businessmen and art lovers, and herself with decided taste in art and literature. With endless patience she responded to his almost daily letters of self-analysis and recollection, and gave him a material support he had never before known, fulfilling every request and tirelessly shopping for him. With sure instinct he called her from the first his "Nikê"— goddess of victory— for it was to her that he would owe his final victory, not only in poetic achievement, but also over his sense of rootlessness and lack of an identity.

Not the least of her services was to find for him apparently ideal surroundings: the exclusive use for several months into 1921 of a friend's small country chateau north of Zürich, Schloß Berg am Irchel, with everything provided he could possibly need, including a silent servant, and surrounded by a little park. Here at last he felt he could settle to work. At first, of course, the reams of outstanding correspondence; then a light-hearted preface in French to a series of drawings of cats by Merline's talented younger son Baltusz (now of world fame as an artist). Suddenly then a series of poems came to him, "dictated" as he imagined by a former inmate of the chateau. *Aus dem Nachlaß des Grafen C.W.* (1950, *From the Literary Remains of Count C.W.*), as he called these smoothly-rhymed quatrains— "done I should think rather like knitting"[61] —the work was little more than a stimulating game and remote from the dense style of the Elegies. But it represented a step forward, and soon after, at the turn of the year, an elegy on the theme of childhood began to form, linked for him perhaps with the final passages of that completed in 1915:

Don't let the fact that childhood has been, that nameless
bond between Heaven and us, be revoked by fate.
Even the prisoner, gloomily dying in a dungeon,
it has sat by and secretly nursed to the end, with its timeless
hold on the heart. For the sufferer,
when he staringly understands, and his room has ceased to reply,
because, like all other possessions around him
feverish, fellow-suffering, it's curable,—even for him
Childhood avails, for purely
its cordial bed blooms among nature's decay. . . .

But anxiety!—Learnt all at once in that disconnexion
formed by us, by insolid humanity: draughtily
jerks itself in through the cracks: glides up from behind
over its play, to the child, and hisses
dissension into its blood—the swift suspicions that later,
always, only a part will be comprehensible, always
some single piece of existence, five pieces, perhaps, but never
Combinable all together, and all of them fragile.
And forthwith splits in the spine the twig of the will,
for it to grow into a forked doubting branch,
grafted on to the Judas-tree of selection.[62]

He had thought that with Merline the conflict between love and
work had been resolved, for she had been strong enough to respect his
need to be alone at Berg. But, although he withstood the temptation to
visit her, he could not resist spreading himself on paper in words of love,
imploring her to help him "in this heroic way," but still assuring her that
his love filled "all the distance between us. . . everything you breathe is
my love. . . "[63] It was no wonder that she could not hold to her resolution,
and summoned him to her side when she lay ill. His hopes of these ideal
surroundings thus proved illusory, and in any case he could enjoy them
only temporarily. In renewed depression he set down an impersonally-
written record of his failure to measure up to the trial, *Das Testament*
(1974, *The Testament*), a collection of fragmentary reflections and
extracts from drafts of letters, "random leaves" put together by "the writer. . . because in these insights into his singular fate a will is expressed
which will remain *his last*...." Its burden was the recognition that solitude
must remain his only love, and that "for a spirit which finds fulfillment in

such conditions, the state of *being loved* will perhaps always turn out a misfortune," the true mission always lost sight of.[64]

All the same, in this relentless delineation of his "non-achievement," he had made, if not *the* work, at least *a* work, a "thing out of his fear," and— as with *Malte*— succeeded in this detached way in gaining distance from a harrowing experience. The very process seemed to clear away the despair he had expressed; for on leaving Berg in May 1921 he set out deliberately on the search for another such refuge, still with Merline at his side, unwilling to renounce the dream that physical love need not be resisted and that she would be willing to withdraw if the Muse should summon him. Princess Marie, when she arrived on a visit, had her doubts, as she had had with Benvenuta. But she was quite convinced that his Elegies would one day be finished, and he must not, as he was half-inclined to do, publish them in their fragmentary form. Their search began to look vain, until by chance at the end of June a property for rent was found— the little tower of Muzot, a mile or two above Sierre in the Valais, countryside that reminded him powerfully of Provence or Spain. With admirable promptitude Werner Reinhart said he was ready to meet the initial rental for Rilke, who by the end of July, was installed there. Its practical drawbacks were many, but they were quickly overcome by his friends, not least by Merline, who moved in with him for a while, and by Nanny Wunderly, who helped to furnish the place, funded its budget and later found a housekeeper. Merline, this time firmly resolved that the disaster of Berg should not be repeated, left him there alone in November, and he was ready, despite his qualms, to look forward to a winter of work (deep in the workings of his mine, as he put it to Kippenberg).

It was the first time he had enjoyed real security of tenure, Reinhart having renewed the lease and already planning to purchase the property. His confidence grew, as the first months passed in clearing away his correspondence and in the encouragement from reading the verse of Paul Valéry, another who had lived long in silence before producing his great poetic works. His "letter-factory" must grind on, he wrote to Nanny Wunderly, "for only on the other side comes the valley of real solitude and then, beyond, the ascent to the mountain range of work." The dogged perseverance suggested by his metaphors of mountain or mine could not of course suffice: all he could do with this routine work— letters, transcriptions from his reading, translations— was to ready himself in the hope of a renewal of the inspiration of earlier days:

> Patience, patience
> patience dans l'azur,
> chaque goutte de silence
> est la chance d'un fruit mûr!

he quoted from Valéry to the Princess: "if I could have a hope like that for my silence."[65]

Early in February 1922, his patience was suddenly justified. To his own surprise, the lyrical outburst which began was not a continuation of the Elegies but the sequence of *Die Sonette an Orpheus* (1923, *Sonnets to Orpheus*), a memorial to a young girl of whose early death he had just learned. Their transcription completed for her mother, he took up the Elegies, and in a few days the cycle was finalized, he thought. It had been a "storm of spirit and heart," he said, writing at once to Kippenberg with the good tidings[66]: but the storm was not yet over. The Tenth was almost completely rewritten, and then an entirely new Fifth appeared to replace the earlier, giving the work what he could feel was its definitive form, with, finally, a second cycle of the Orpheus sonnets, the whole completed in just three weeks, and the "broken-off surfaces" in his life at last rejoined.

From its inception in Duino the shape of the Elegy cycle had been clear in his mind, a progression from the limitations of the human condition to affirmation of man's place in the Whole, from the celebration of the "terrifying" Angel to that of the "consentient" Angel. But it was only in the absolute solitude of Muzot that he had been able to find the progression from lament to praise: at first not in the missing Elegies but in the Sonnets, whose symbol was Orpheus, the god of poetry:

> Erect no memorial stone. Let the rose
> bloom every year to remind us of him.
> Because it's Orpheus. His metamorphosis
> is in this, and this. No other name
>
> should trouble us. Once and for all,
> when there's song, it's Orpheus. . . .[67]

In highly concentrated images the sonnets muse on many of his preoccupying themes: love, death, childhood, the joys and inadequacies of our earthly existence. Predominant however is praise:

Over what's passing and changing,
freer and wider,
your overture is lasting,
god with the lyre.

Pain's beyond our grasp,
love hasn't been learned,
and whatever eliminates

us in death isn't secret.
Only the song above the land
blesses and celebrates.[68]

And that praise was the key to unlock the door to his elegiac cycle. From
the joyous mood of the "spring" sonnet,

"Earth, lucky earth on vacation
play with the children now. We long
to catch you, happy earth. The happiest will win—"[69]

sprang the Seventh Elegy, the celebration of human existence— "Being
here is glorious"— and the assertion of man's potential to attain the intensity of Being that is the Angel's:

. . . Pillars, pylons, the Sphinx, the cathedral's striving
grey thrust out of its crumbling or alien city.
Wasn't it a miracle? Oh, Angel, marvel. That's us,
us, 0 great one. . . [70]

The door stood open now to the rest, the progress from lament to joy in
man's ability to attain the Whole. The Eighth, in counterpoint to the affirmation of the Seventh, again stressed his limitations:

All other creatures look into the Open
with their whole eyes. But our eyes,
turned inward, are set all around it like snares. . . [71]

and the Fifth, last to be written, the even more transient life of the traveling acrobats, assembled on their "threadbare carpet" to suggest the ulti-

mate loneliness of man. But in the Ninth he answered the question "Why have to be human?"[72] "We are here *once* each, . . . *once* and no more," but it is our ability, and the poet's vocation, to express the things of this earth, "to say them in a way that the things themselves/ never dreamed of existing so intensely," that makes possible the transformation of the material world into the invisible Whole:

> Earth, isn't this what you want: to resurrect
> in us invisibly?. . .
> What's your urgent charge, if not transformation?
> Earth, my love, I will.
> . . . Supernumerous existence
> wells up in my breast—

to an infinite realm in which being and non-being are one.[73]

Rilke seemed here to have found his way instinctively to the Buddhist conception of an external and an inner world as merely two sides of the same fabric, all its threads interwoven into a net of endless, mutually conditional relations, and to have anticipated in a striking way the modern conception in physics of the universe as a dynamic web of inseparable energy patterns (in April 1922, regretting his ignorance of Einstein's discoveries, he had written "it may be that exclusion from what is happening in mathematics and the natural sciences will bar one for ever from the intrinsic flavor of the fruit to be ripened in the uncertain climate of our century").[74] And he had been led to reject his earlier version of the Tenth Elegy, which had held only lament for the "nights of anguish," writing it anew to show the complementarity of sorrow and joy in the journey beyond the half-life of earth's Vanity Fair to the realm of "supernumerous existence":

> But if the endlessly dead awakened a symbol in us,
> perhaps they would point to the catkins hanging from the bare
> branches of the hazel-trees, or
> would evoke the raindrops that fall on to the dark earth
> in the springtime.

And we, who have always thought
of happiness as *rising*, would feel
the emotion that overwhelms us
whenever a happy thing *falls*.[75]

The Elegies and Sonnets— " of the same essence,"[76] as he always
maintained— were Rilke's supreme achievement, the culmination indeed
of a life devoted solely to poetry. His remaining years, which thanks to
Werner Reinhart's generosity he was able to spend in Switzerland at
Muzot, could not do other than represent a reaction after this great effort.
He continued certainly to produce, and now more and more frequently in
the language of his adopted country, French, with cycles of poems in
which Paul Valéry found a "strange grace. . . giving me a direct and ines-
timable impression of your pure and deep poetry."[77] Merline, established
in Paris, where he was more than content to leave her, helped arrange the
publication of two of these works: *Vergers suivis des quatrains valaisans*
(1926, Orchards, with the Valais Quatrains) and *Les Fenêtres* (1927,
Windows). For his cycle on "Roses," for which Valéry provided a preface,
he dealt himself with a bibliophile publisher in the Netherlands: *Les
Roses* (1927, *Roses*). In his own language his production was less formal-
ized: single poems, often occasional but still of considerable power, continuing his exploration "at the edge of the unsayable," and venturing
towards the ultimate in synaesthesia, at the "borders of sensuous perception":

"Gong" (1925)

Not meant for ears. . . : boom
that like a deeper ear
hears us, the seemingly hearing.
Reversal of spaces. Draft
of inner worlds outside. . .

duration squeezed out of motion,
star re-cast. . . : gong!. . .

wine on invisible lips,
gale in the pillar that bears,
rambler's fall to the path,
our treason to all. . . .: gong!

"Idol" (1923)

> God or goddess of the sleep of cats,
> devouring deity that in the dark
> mouth crushes ripe eye-berries,
> grape-juice of seeing grown sweet,
> everlasting light in the palate's crypt. . . [78]

Often, however, his verses carried a melancholy burden, reflecting the physical reaction which had followed the great effort of the Elegies, and which increasingly turned in these years to a real, if enigmatic, illness, two stays in the clinic of Valmont above Montreux during the winters of 1923 and 1924 failing to yield a diagnosis. With a visit to Paris in January 1925 he hoped the change of scene to these familiar surroundings might bring healing powers. He stayed on until June, but it was clear that his hopes were vain: the former attraction of the city had anyway faded in comparison with that of his settled existence in the tower of Muzot, and his physical condition steadily worsened. It was ironic that, with his pre-eminence now everywhere recognized, and his material well-being and a comfortable income assured, he should feel himself on a downward path, assailed by a malady the doctors could not identify or alleviate, even after a further sojourn in Valmont during the first months of 1926.

The change in him was well illustrated when a letter from the Russian poet Boris Pasternak told him of another admirer, Marina Tsvetayeva, living as an emigrée in Paris, her verse "true and genuine as none of us in the USSR today will ever write."[79] He wrote at once to this unknown, as he had so often before reacted to similar chance introductions, sending her the Elegies and sonnets with the dedication:

> We touch each other. With what? with beat of wings,
> with distances themselves we touch and meet.
> Alone *one* poet dwells—sometimes the one
> who bears him comes toward his *former* bearer;[80]

and her reply began a series of letters that were nothing less than a dithyramb of love. He felt himself drawn to her as he had once been to Magda von Hattingberg, this time however in the instinctive confidence that she was his equal (an instinct which has been amply confirmed by posterity): and he was moved to address to her another Elegy in the summer of 1926, celebrating the affinity in their poetry and the union of praise and lament in the poet's (and lover's) mission:

> Oh, the losses into the All, Marina, the stars that are falling!
> We can't make it larger, wherever we fling, to whatever
> star we go! Numbered for all time are the parts of the Whole.
> Neither can one who falls diminish the sacred number. . . .

> Waves, Marina, we're sea! Depths, Marina, we're heaven.
> Earth, Marina, we're earth, we're thousand times spring, we're soaring
> larks an outbreaking song flings to where eyes cannot see.

> Praise, my dearest, let us be lavish with praise.
> Nothing belongs to us. . . .

> Gods long ago discovered
> how to juggle with halves. We, drawn into the cycle,
> filled ourselves out to a whole like the disc of the moon.
> Even in time of wane, in the weeks of gradual turning,
> none could ever again help us to fullness except,
> lonely, that walk of our own over the slumberless landscape.

But, unlike earlier days, he soon tired of the effort of such correspondence after the burst of inspiration was over, and the relationship faded as quickly as it had come into being.

That summer and autumn much of his verse revealed a melancholy, almost a sense of farewell: it was "life slowing down," he wrote in a poem in French,

> c'est la vie au ralenti,
> c'est le coeur à rebours,
> c'est une espérance et demie:
> trop et trop peu à son tour. . . [82]

By November, his friends were shocked at his wasted appearance and evident fatigue, and he returned once again to the clinic at Valmont. This time there was no doubt of the diagnosis: an acute myelogenous leukemia, then as now incurable. Though everything possible was done, he grew progressively weaker under the torments of septicemia-like outbreaks on skin, mouth and nose, a "day and night hell," as he wrote in one of his last letters,[83] which, creative to the end, he was able to describe in a final penciled entry into his notebook:

> Now come, the last that I can recognize,
> pain, utter pain, fierce in the body's texture.
> As once in the mind I burned, so now I burn
> in you: the wood resisted, long denied
> acceptance to the flame you blazed at me,
> but now I feed you and in you I flare. . . .
> What burns there, so transmuted, is that I?
> Into this fire I drag no memory.
> To be alive, alive: to be outside.
> And I ablaze. With no one who knows me. . . [84]

He was released from his suffering at last on December 29, 1926, and was laid to rest, as he had wished, in the little cemetery at Raron high above the Rhône valley, one of the first places to bring him the "wind and light"[85] of the countryside where he had achieved his greatest work, and symbolically at the linguistic frontier where French and German meet. The headstone there stands inscribed with the verse he had written for it in his Will:

> Rose, oh pure contradiction, delight
> in being nobody's sleep under so many
> eyelids.[86]

As a less enigmatic epitaph for the life and work of this remarkable poet may perhaps stand the lines from his own favorite among the sonnets to Orpheus:

> Be ahead of all departure, as if it were
> behind you like the Winter that's just passed.
>
> Be here among the vanishing in the realm of entropy,
> Be a ringing glass, that shattered as it rang.
>
> Be—and at the same time know the implication
> of non-being, the endless ground of your inner vibration,
> so you can fulfil it fully just this once.[87]

Notes

1. *Briefe 1892-1904* (Leipzig: Insel, 1939), p. 37.
2. Sämtliche Werke (see Bibliography) III: p. 512 ff. (hereafter referred to as *SW*).
3. As Note 1: p . 28.
4. As Note 2: p. 550 f.
5. *Rilke/Lou Andreas-Salomé, Briefwechsel* (Frankfurt a. M.: Insel, 1975), p. 26.
6. As Note 1: p. 62.
7. *Tagebücher aus der Frühzeit* (Frankfurt a. M.: Insel, 1973), p. 46.
8. Ibid., p. 65.
9. Ibid., p. 119.
10. *SW* III: p. 316.
11. Ibid., p. 334.
12. *SW* I: p. 307.
13. Ibid., p. 323.
14. *Briefe und Tagebücher aus der Frühzeit* (Leipzig: Insel, 1933), p. 108.
15. *SW* I: p. 477.
16. Ibid., p. 398.
17. Ibid., p. 505.
18. Ibid., p. 347.
19. Ibid., pp. 343, 347, 356, 366.
20. As Note 5: p. 67.
21. *Briefe 1904-1907* Leipzig: Insel, 1939), p. 81.
22. As Note 5: p. 209.
23. *SW* I: p. 496.
24. As Note 21: p. 138.
25. *Briefe 1906-1907* (Leipzig: Insel, 1930), p. 46.
26. *SW* I: p. 530.
27. As Note 25, p. 279 f.
28. *SW* I: p. 557.
29. *Briefe an seinen Verleger* (Wiesbaden: Insel, 1949), p. 47.
30. *Briefe 1907-1914* (Leipzig: Insel, 1933), p. 54.
31. 'Malte Laurids Brigge', 1962.
32. As Note 29, p. 98.
33. Ibid., p. 115.
34. *SW* II: p. 379.

35. *Briefe an Sidonie Nádherný von Borutin* (Frankfurt a. M.: Insel, 1973), p. 136.
36. *SW* II: p. 40.
37. *SW* I: p. 685.
38. As Note 5: p. 241; *SW* I: pp. 685, 721.
39. *SW* I: p. 686 f.
40. Ibid., p. 689.
41. Ibid., p. 691 f.
42. As Note 5, p. 279.
43. *SW* II: p. 45f.
44. *SW* VI: p. 1040 f.
45. *SW* I: p. 706.
46. *SW* II: p. 61 f.
47. *SW* I: pp. 693, 696.
48. *SW* II: p. 79.
49. *Briefwechsel Rilke/Marie von Thurn und Taxis* (Frankfurt a. M.: Insel/Zürich: Niehans & Rokitansky, 1951), p. 345.
50. Notebook, January 1914 (qu. Joachim W. Storck, Diss. 'Rainer Maria Rilke als Briefschreiber', Freiburg i. B. 1957, p. 133).
51. *Briefwechsel mit Benvenuta* (Esslingen: Bechtle, 1954), pp. 27, 44.
52. Ibid., p. 147.
53. *SW* II: p. 82 ff.
54. Ibid., p. 88 f.
55. Ibid., p. 84 f.
56. Ibid., p. 103 f.
57. Ibid., p. 438.
58. Letter to Frau Jaffé, 14 Nov. 1915, qu. Schnack: *Rilke Chronik* (Frankfurt a. M.: Insel, 1975). p. 517.
59. *SW* I: p. 697 ff.
60. Ibid., p. 699 f.
61. *Briefe an Nanny Wunderly-Volkart* (Frankfurt a. M.: Insel, 1977), p. 349.
62. *SW* II: p. 130 ff.
63. *Rilke et Merline, Correspondance* (Zürich: Niehans, 1954), p. 125 f.
64. *Das Testament* (Frankfurt a. M.: Suhrkamp, 1975), pp. 12, 39.
65. As Note 49, p. 686.
66. As Note 29, p. 410.
67. *SW* I: p. 733.
68. Ibid., p. 743.

69. Ibid., p. 744.
70. Ibid., pp. 710, 712.
71. Ibid., p. 714.
72. Ibid., p. 701.
73. Ibid., pp. 717 f., 720.
74. Letter to Jean Strohl, 13 Apr.   1922 (Schweizerische Landesbibliothek).
75. *SW* I: p. 726.
76. *Briefe aus Muzot 1921-1926* (Leipzig: Insel, 1935), p. 333.
77. Letter of 20 Mar. 1924 (qu. Schnack, p. 908).
78. *SW* II: pp. 185 f.
79. *Rilke/Zwetajewa/Pasternak, Briefwechsel* (Frankfurt a. M.: Insel, 1983), p. 77.
80. Ibid., p. 105.
81. *SW* II: p. 271 ff.
82. Ibid., p. 684.
83. As Note 61, p. 1171.
84. *SW* II: p. 511.
85. As Note 61, p. 1192.
86. *SW* II: p. 185.
87. *SW* I: p. 759.

Bibliography

I.   *Works by Rainer Maria Rilke in German*

Sämtliche Werke, Vols. I-V, 1955-1966. (Also in a Werkausgabe, identical but in 12 volumes).
Tagebücher aus der Frühzeit, 1973.
Übertragungen, 1975.
     (All above ed. Ernst Zinn; Frankfurt a.M.: Insel Verlag).
Das Testament, ed. Ernst Zinn. Frankfurt a.M.: Suhrkamp Verlag, 1975.
Briefe, ed. Rilke-Archiv Weimar, 14-15. Tsd. Frankfurt a.M.: Insel Verlag, 1980.

II. *Works in English Translation*

Selected Poetry (bilingual text, tr. Stephen Mitchell). New York: Random House, 1982.

Selected Poems (tr. Robert Bly). New York: Harper & Row, 1981.

Poems *1906-1962* (tr. J.B. Leishman). London: Hogarth Press, 1976.

Poems 1912-1926 (tr. Michael Hamburger). Redding Ridge: Black Swan Books, 1981.

Duino Elegies and the Sonnets to Orpheus (bilingual text, tr. A. Poulin, Jr.) Boston: Houghton Mifflin, 1977.

Duino Elegies (bilingual text, tr. J.B. Leishman and Stephen Spender). London: Chatto & Windus/Toronto: Clark Irwin, 1975.

The Book of Hours (tr. A.L. Peck). London: Hogarth Press, 1961.

Poems from the Book of Hours (tr. Babette Deutsch). New York: New Directions, 1975.

Holding Out, poems (tr. Rika Lesser). University of Nebraska at Omaha, 1975.

Visions of Christ (tr. Aaron Kramer). Boulder: Colorado University Press, 1976.

From the Remains of Count C.W. (tr. J.B. Leishman). London: Hogarth Press, 1952.

Correspondence in Verse with Erika Mitterer (bilingual text, tr. N.K. Cruikshank). London: Hogarth Press, 1953.

Requiem for a Woman, and Selected Lyric Poems (tr. Andy Gaus). Putney, Utah: Threshold Books, 1981.

Possibility of Being, Selection of Poems (tr. J.B. Leishman). New York: New Directions, 1977.

The Roses and the Windows (tr. A. Poulin, Jr.) Washington: Grey Wolf Press, 1979.

Where Silence Reigns, Selected Prose (tr. G. Craig Houston). New York: New Directions, 1978.

The Notebook of Malte Laurids Brigge (tr. John Linton). London: Hogarth Press/Toronto: Clark Irwin, 1972.

Selected Works. Vol. I, Prose; Vol. II, Poetry (tr. J.B. Leishman). London: Hogarth Press, 1976.

Rodin (tr. Robert Firmage). Salt Lake City: Peregrine Smith, 1979.

Nine Plays (tr. K. Phillips and J. Locke). New York: Ungar, 1979.

Selected Letters 1906-1926 (tr. R.F.C. Hull). London: Macmillan, 1946.

Other translations in:

Mood, John L.: *Rilke on Love and Other Difficulties*. New York: Norton, 1975.

III.   *Secondary Literature in English*

Butler, Elizabeth M.: *Rainer Maria Rilke*, New York: Octagon Books, 1973.

Butler: "Rilke and Tolstoy." *Modern Language Review*. London, Vol. 35, No. 4, 1940.

Casey, Timothy J.: *Rainer Maria Rilke, a Centenary Essay*. London: Macmillan Press, 1976.

Heller, Erich: *The Disinherited Mind*. Essays in Modern German Literature and Thought, London: Bowes & Bowes, 1975.

Heller: *The Poet's Self and the Poem*. London: Athlone, 1976.

Mason, Eudo C.: *Rilke*. Edinburgh/London: Oliver & Boyd, 1963.

Modern Austrian Literature. University of California, Riverside, Vol. 15, No. 3/4, 1982 (Special Rilke Issue).

Morse, Benjamin J.: "Rainer Maria Rilke and English Literature." *German Life & Letters*, New Series, I, No. 3, April 1948, pp. 215-248.

Morse: "Rainer Maria Rilke and the Occult." *Journal of Experimental Physics*, July 1945, Oct. 1945 and Jan. 1946.

Prater, Donald A.: *A Ringing Glass— the Life of Rainer Maria Rilke*. Oxford/New York: Oxford University Press, 1986.

Rose, William and Houston, G. Craig (ed.): *Rainer Maria Rilke, Aspects of his Mind and Poetry*, with intro. by Stefan Zweig. London: Sidgwick & Jackson,   1938.

Thurn und Taxis, Marie: *Memoirs of a Princess* (tr. Nora Wydenbruck). London: Hogarth Press, 1959.

Wydenbruck, Nora: *Rilke, Man and Poet*. Westport, Conn.: Greenwood Press, 1972.

Zweig, Stefan: *The World of Yesterday, Memoirs of a European*. Lincoln: University of Nebraska Press, 1964.

IV.   *Major Studies in German*

Albert-Lasard, Lou: *Wege mit Rilke*. Frankfurt a.M.: S. Fischer, 1952.

Andreas-Salomé, Lou: *Rainer Maria Rilke*. Leipzig: Insel, 1928.

Bassermann, Dieter: *Am Rande des Unsagbaren, neue Rilke-Aufsätze.* Berlin/Buxtehude: Hübener, 1948.

Bassermann: *Der andere Rilke.* Bad Homburg: H. Gentner, 1961.

Černý, Vaclav: *Rainer Maria Rilke, Prag, Böhmen und die Tschechen.* Prag: Artia, 1966.

Fuerst, Norbert: *Rainer Maria Rilke in seiner Zeit.* Frankfurt a.M.: Insel, 1976.

Gebser, J.: *Rainer Maria Rilke und Spanien.* Zürich: Oprecht, 1946.

Guardini, Romano: *Zu Rainer Maria Rilkes Deutung des Daseins.* o.O.: Köpper, 1948.

Holthusen, Hans Egon: *Rainer Maria Rilke in Selbstzeugnissen und Dokumenten.* Hamburg: Rowohlt, 1976 (105.-108. Tsd.)

Kassner, Rudolf: *Rainer Maria Rilke, Gesammelte Erinnerungen 1926-1956.* Pfullingen: Neske, 1976.

Kim, Byong-Ock: *Rilkes Militärschulerlebnis und das Problem des Verlorenen Sohnes.* Bonn: Bouvier, 1973.

Kippenberg, Katharina: *Rainer Maria Rilke, ein Beitrag.* Wiesbaden: Insel, 1948.

Leppmann, Wolfgang: *Rilke, sein Leben, und sein Welt und sein Werk.* Bern/München: Scherz, 1981.

Mason, Eudo C.: *Rilke, sein Leben, und sein Werk.* Göttingen: Vandenhoek & Ruprecht, 1964.

Osann, Christiane: *Rainer Maria Rilke, der Weg eines Dichters.* Zürich: Orell Füssli, 1941.

Prater, Donald A.: *Ein klingendes Glas— das Leben Rainer Maria Rilkes.* München: Hanser, 1986.

Salis, J.R. von: *Rilkes Schweizer Jahre.* Frankfurt a.M.: Suhrkamp, 1975.

Simenauer, Erich: *Rainer Maria Rilke, Legende und Mythos.* Bern: Haupt, 1953.

Solbrig, Ingeborg/Storck, Joachim W. (hg.): *Rilke heute, Beziehungen und Wirkungen,* Bd. I, Bd. II. Frankfurt a.M.: Suhrkamp, 1975, 1976.

Ullmann, Regina: *Erinnerungen an Rilke.* St. Gallen: Tschudy, 1945.

Zech, Paul: *Rainer Maria Rilke, der Mensch und das Werk.* Dresden: Jess, 1930.

Zweig, Stefan: *Abschied von Rilke, eine Rede.* Tübingen: Wunderlich, 1927.

Peter Rosegger

Dean Garrett Stroud

Soon after Peter Rosegger's death in 1918 his long-time friend and fellow author Emil Ertl was walking through the Graz city park during a heavy rain storm. Because of the downpour the normally crowded park was deserted at the noon hour except for one man. A street worker was sitting on a bench holding an umbrella above his head to shield the book he was reading from the rain. Ertl noticed that the worker was engrossed in a book by Rosegger. For Ertl, it was magnificent to see "how this simple man from the common people (*Volk*) had submerged himself in the content of the volume to the extent that he neither saw nor heard anything that was going on around him. He did not notice...the rain that was soaking his clothes."[1]

Ertl's anecdote illustrates the immense popularity that Rosegger's works enjoyed during his lifetime and for a number of years thereafter. It has been suggested that no author was as widely read at the time.[2] The major reason for Rosegger's acceptance by readers was his intention always to write with such people in mind as the worker whom Ertl observed in the city park. He considered it his calling to write for people without education and sophistication rather than for literary critics and university professors. Throughout his life he referred to himself simply as a "writer for the common people"(*Volksdichter*), a writer for those people in society whom other writers either ignored or discounted, for it was from such people that he had come. In spite of his avid reading of the literary canon, honorary doctorates from the universities of Heidelberg, Vienna, and Graz, and the nomination for the Nobel Prize for literature in 1910, Rosegger never abandoned his fierce identity with the rural inhabitants (*Bauern*) of his native region.

Rosegger's enduring allegiance to rural people and their way of life was based on his personal experience of that life, an experience which he always valued as the most positive and worthwhile period of his life. Unlike Franz Innerhofer, whose miserable childhood on an Austrian farm has made him a major representative of "negative regionalism" (*Anti-Heimatliteratur*)[3] Rosegger represents a "positive regionalism" that resulted primarily from the favorable memories of childhood he carried with him when he left the farm for the city. His unusual experiences during those early years became an abiding source of material and inspiration for the rest of his life, and he never tired of telling stories from the period, often to crowed auditoriums of listeners throughout the German-speaking world. Because of the vital role that his childhood and early adulthood plays in his work, more than a passing knowledge of the author's formative years is necessary to appreciate his intentions as a writer and essayist, his place in Austrian literature, and his contribution to the genre of the village story.

Rosegger's Formative Years

Rosegger, the eldest of seven children, was born on 31 July 1843 to Laurenz and Maria Roßegger in their farmhouse, the "Kluppenegger-Hof," in the hamlet of Alpl near Krieglach in the Austrian state of Styria. The next day the child was baptized and christened Peter Kettenfeier, according to the tradition of naming children after the saint on whose day they received the sacrament. From the beginning the boy had little time for play or for gazing into the Alpine countryside because the difficult farm work made it necessary for him to work long hours. In an autobiographical essay he remembered not only the beauty of the countryside but the less pleasant aspect of life as well:

> When I found myself upon this earth, I was a boy on a beautiful mountain, where there were green meadows and many forests. . . . Working from early morning until late at night was the expected routine, even for me. And if I happened to be playing with stones, or dirt, or sticks somewhere in the pasture, I was always anxious that my father's voice would call me to come right away to do some chore.[4]

Charlotte Anderle, Rosegger's contemporary biographer, views the author's childhood even more grimly: "He learned to endure cold in snow storms when he was sent on errands, he learned to overcome fatigue and sleepiness when he spent nights at wakes or at the bedside of the dying reading to them. The harshness of daily farm life early on acquainted him with suffering, sickness, misery, misfortune, and death."[5]

Although life on the farm was not easy for the boy, Rosegger always placed the less attractive elements of that existence in the broader context of the loving and spiritual support he received from his parents. Though poor in material terms and without formal education, their influence on Rosegger had a tremendous effect on him and his work. From them he took his conservative model of the ideal family. When Rosegger wrote of his admiration for the "patriarchal peasant family," he generally was referring to the family unit as he remembered it from his childhood. This picture had his father as the farmer (*der Bauer*) who guides the work on the farm based on his intimate knowledge of nature, trusting in a merciful God to work the miracle of the harvest, his mother as the farmer's wife (*die Bäuerin*) whose spiritual strength and whose firm love hold the family together by keeping an eye on the daily details of reality in the country. Not just any man or woman would do, but a man like his father and a woman like his mother. Of all the stories in which this model is found the most detailed presentation occurs in the novel *Erdsegen* (1900, Earth's Blessings). What prevents this image from deteriorating into a cliché in Rosegger's better fiction is the vivid characterization that deconstructs the stereotype as well as the author's realization that reality seldom conforms to desire.

Rosegger's father appears to have been somewhat mystical, living more in the "Kingdom of God than in the visible world."[6] For eighty-two years, according to Rosegger's account, his father accepted life as it came to him, never complaining of hard work, ruined crops, disease, or life's tragedies. Although he witnessed the death of several children and his wife, he accepted such events as the mysterious workings of a loving God. Placing little store in pleasure, wealth, or power, the father preferred the company of the poor, the disadvantaged, and children to that of other farmers and workers who gathered at the village inn or neighborhood tavern (p. 23). With the exception of the story "Um Vaters Wort" (For Father's Attention) this is the image of the father that is sustained throughout Rosegger's collection of stories based on his childhood, *Waldheimat* (1877, My Forest Home).

The boy's mother, the daughter of a charcoal burner, often delighted the child with her stories of the forest (p. 13). Never in any of Rosegger's writings is there a critical word about this woman, whom he viewed as the personification of a boundless, selfless, and divine love that only mothers have, or ought to have, for their children (p. 13). As a wife she is usually supportive of her husband but not afraid to oppose him when she thinks his actions are wrong or unchristian (p. 14). Her Christianity was as simple and practical as her husband's was mystical: hard work, kindness toward others, and trust in God (p. 15) . From her Rosegger took his concept of a Christianity based on kindness rather than dogma.

What little formal education Rosegger received as a child was from the local schoolmaster, Michel Patterer. Having lost his teaching position as a result of the 1848 revolution, Patterer came to the mountains around Krieglach-Alpl much like a beggar looking for work. Traveling from farm to farm, the man taught the local children in exchange for food and shelter. Rosegger's attendance, however, was sparse because of having to work on the farm and because ill health plagued him throughout life. Yet this teacher served the author as the model for the protagonist in his first and most popular novel, *Die Schriften des Waldschulmeisters* (1875, The Writings of a Country Schoolmaster).

Rather than going to school the young Rosegger preferred to stay at home and read during the night. He would borrow religious books from neighbors and villagers, which he would read aloud in an attempt to imitate the High German he heard on Sundays. For a while it was believed that the boy would study for the priesthood, but the family's poverty made it impossible to pay for formal education, ("Lebensbeschreibung," p. xi). Unable to study and too physically weak to work on the farm, Rosegger became apprenticed to a tailor at the age of seventeen. With his master, Ignaz Orthofer, the youth traveled throughout the district working in various farmhouses and staying with the families day and night until their tailoring needs were satisfied. In this way the young man quickly acquired first-hand knowledge of life on some sixty-seven farms. From the extended farm family he learned local customs and legends, heard stories and songs, and saw the interaction among the different members of these small self-contained communities. On the roads and in the villages he enjoyed a contact with peasant society that most writers of village stories were never able to experience. Later he wrote that he considered these years as his "university years," although he never "studied" these people, preferring instead to live with them in good and bad times.[7] This experience as a member of peasant society sets Rosegger's village narratives apart from the usual village stories of his day.

During his apprenticeship (1860-1864) Rosegger began writing poems and short fiction based on the world he saw around him. These first efforts found little acceptance among the farmers and peasants because they harbored a mistrust of words and often viewed reading and writing as a waste of time: "...many a peasant, thumbing with crooked fingers through the pages, would utter this verdict, 'far better to work well and hard for your master or your father there at home than to scrawl this nonsense'"(*Weltleben*, pp. 70-71). Looking back on that period, he saw that it was a "sad and lonely time" and that he was misunderstood by those around him (p. 71). However, he continued to write, collecting motifs and anecdotes that would provide much of the material for his more mature works.

In 1864 Rosegger sent a number of his poems to Adalbert Svoboda, editor of the Graz newspaper "Daily Post" (*Tagespost*). Several months later Svoboda wrote that he judged the work to have sufficient merit to warrant serious attention and further development. The newspaper editor became Rosegger's benefactor and friend, and he brought the young poet from the mountains to the city. Through the editor's efforts the young man received an apprenticeship in a bookstore in Laibach. Shortly after his arrival there he suffered his first major bout of homesickness, a malady that would afflict him for the rest of his life. After only nine days in Laibach the young Rosegger returned to Graz, where he was enrolled by Svoboda in the Academy of Trade and Industry. This was the only formal education that Rosegger ever received. For four years he devoted himself to academic subjects; then he left the school determined to be a professional writer. While a student, he enjoyed the city with its theaters and concerts, but he always felt like an outsider among other students: "...just as I had earlier had the feeling that I didn't fit in with farm boys, now it came to me that I didn't fit in any better with the sons of merchants, bankers, and industrialists" (*Lebensbeschreibung*, p. xvii). There was always something of the misfit in Rosegger's nature that comes through in much of his fiction as an inability on the part of his protagonists to adapt to their surroundings.

Along with the inability to adjust to new surroundings there is a melancholy in much of Rosegger's fiction that came from an overwhelming sense of loss on his part. After leaving the farm he always carried with him the feeling that he had left the world as it should be and had entered a world in desperate need of reform. Time, not distance, had destroyed Rosegger's paradise. After the death in 1916 of August Brunnlechner, a friend since his student days, Rosegger confessed in a letter: "I have my own kind of faith in the return of all that is past, so that a person's life constantly repeats itself and brings back from time to time what has been lost in a new form without our remembering times that we experienced with each other."[8] It is obvious that the letter contains more desire for the past than confidence in its eventual return. In spite of Rosegger's popular reputation as an optimistic writer his life was dominated by an overwhelming sense of loss that colored much of his fiction. Two major experiences in his life account in large measure for this melancholic side of Rosegger: the loss of the family farm and the death of his first wife.

In 1868 Rosegger's parents, overburdened with debts, were forced to sell the farm at auction. It had been in the family's possession for at least four generations, perhaps even longer. In a letter to Brunlechner, Rosegger lamented the forfeiture of the homestead: "I have no home (*Heimat*) anymore. Yesterday my brother wrote that my father's home had been sold, that strangers now live in it. . . .it was only a poor hut, but for me...it meant more than a golden palace. . . . I am a stranger on the earth"(Janda, p. 60). Although the letter may strike the modern ear as overly sentimental, the pain of a person deprived of emotional security is apparent. In the same letter Rosegger went on to say that only in that house had he experienced something approaching idyllic serenity. From the early letters and from his autobiography it is clear that the farm functioned as a spiritual anchor in Rosegger's life, a place where he could always go to find direction, orientation, and assurance that his life had meaning and worth.

Four years after the loss of the farm Rosegger met his first wife, Anna Pichler. They married the following year and had their first child, a son, in 1874. From the letters in which he mentioned his wife it is evident that the young writer was deeply in love with this woman from the city who was interested in village stories and dialect verse. Soon after the birth of their daughter in 1875 his wife died, leaving the writer terribly stricken with grief. In the autobiographical novel *Heidepeters Gabriel*(1881) Rosegger recounted in loving fashion their short life together.

Rosegger as Journalist

Largely in an attempt to deal with his despair over his wife's death Rosegger began publishing the periodical *Heimgarten*(The Backyard) in

1876. As he wrote in a letter from January of that year, he needed a purpose in his life in order to move beyond his grief.[9] Although his wife's death played a major role in his decision to begin the journal at that time, there was another reason for the type of magazine he wanted to publish. Rosegger had always wanted to have an impact on people's thinking. He wanted to influence their opinions on religion and politics as well as to offer them entertaining stories about peasant life. As he stated in a letter to Brunlechner, a writer should be "a priest and a prophet of the eternal spirit: here he should comfort, calm, lift up, inspire; there he should warn, caution, scold, shatter" (Anderle, p. 38). A monthly journal offered the ideal means to bring his views to bear on burning social issues, religious controversies, and literature. It also served as a convenient vehicle for the presentation of his fiction to the reading public.

As one can see from Rosegger's zeal to speak the truth as he understood it, Rosegger never intended *Heimgarten* to be just another popular family-oriented periodical that avoided controversy for the sake of commercial success. So opposed was he to such journals that he refused to refer to *Heimgarten* as a family publication (*Familienblatt*); in his mind these were nothing more than mindless entertainment. Rosegger preferred instead the term "people's journal" (*Volksblatt*) to describe his concept of the journal (Eckle, p. 15). In the first issue Rosegger informed the readers that it was to be a periodical offering not only selected stories, descriptions, and images of the peasant's life and culture, but also observations and opinions about world events and current issues.[10] It was to be a forum for his personal views about those issues which touched directly the lives of the peasant class regardless of how popular or unpopular they may be (Eckle, p. 16). Thus the magazine quickly became a personal portrait of Rosegger's life and development over some forty years. This personal tone set *Heimgarten* apart from its competition (Eckle, p. 101)

Heimgarten was never as widely read as other family journals of the day. For example, the family-oriented publication *Die Gartenlaube* had some 6,000 subscribers in its first year and after after seven years had reached a readership of 100,000 in 1863. In contrast, *Heimgarten* began with 4,000 subscribers and in time reached 6,000 (Eckle, pp. 96-97) .With the exception of peasants, who hardly read anything from the the outside world, its readers came from all segments of society, as Rosegger noted indirectly in the publication's twentieth year:

The peasant reads neither poetry, nor novels, nor village stories. At best, he has his Christian house book, his fairy tales, his almanac; and even in these he reads very little. In the last few years workers have begun reading the political publications of their party. The overburdened businessman has no time to read, neither does the officer. . . the professor does not read literature unless he is a literature professor, and then he reads very few of the new books. Our reliable readership is and remains, however, just these circles, and in them there are a few people who refuse to become hardened by their daily occupations but rather maintain a spirit for the ideal (quoted in Eckle, p. 93).

While the majority of the journal's readers were from Styria, *Heimgarten* found subscribers throughout Austria and Germany and as far away as America.

Perhaps what the periodical's varied readers had in common with its editor was a faith in what Rosegger always referred to as "the Ideal." By this he seems to mean nineteenth-century humanism in its broadest terms. But for him this humanistic ideal was centered in the notion that human beings were engaged in a struggle between their animal nature, as defined by Darwin's concept of the survival of the fittest, and their spiritual nature, as defined by tolerance. All of his life Rosegger fought against his inclination toward pessimism to hold on to the belief that humanity was destined by its creator to leave its physical form behind and be united with God in a spiritual union that would complete the creation. In a *Heimgarten* essay on religion he wrote: "The human being is really a magnificent creature. All the earthy happiness that he can imagine means nothing to him. And all the earthly unhappiness that he must bear he bears only because he knows that it purifies, strengthens, and ennobles him on his path toward perfection. He wants to go even higher than all the powers of earth and all human cunning can lift him."[11] Rosegger felt that when humanity reached the heights to which its creator called it, human beings would experience the essential unity of all people regardless of nationality, race, religion, creed, sex, or any other barrier society had erected. This unity could be experienced in certain moments by everyone who remained sensitive to what people had in common rather than being swayed by what divided them. Beyond political creeds and social differences lay the final experience of death, and this common fate could act as a force for unity even among the most opposite camps in society: "We are all human beings, even the Social Democrats, and yes, even the capitalists.

Above us all looms a fate that makes no distinction between rich and poor, great or small. There come times in which we all feel this one-ness, and in such times we are at our best and are our happiest."[12]

Happiness was the goal of life for Rosegger. However, happiness in his opinion had nothing whatsoever to do with wealth, possessions, rank in society, education, or health. Happiness could never come from outside a person but had to come from within. Peace of heart, which was Rosegger's personal definition of happiness, lay not in what one had or in what one experienced in life but rather in one's subjective attitude toward life's events:

> It is not events themselves that upset us, rather it is the way in which we view them. In and of itself the loss of material goods is nothing terrible, for we see many people living perfectly happy lives who never possessed these things. But our belief that the loss is terrible causes us worry and fear.—Never tell yourself: "I have lost some-thing," because you never really possessed it, it was only loaned to you for a while, and to give it back means also to return the worries and responsibilities that went with it....[13]

The perspective that people brought to the events of their lives determined reality far more than the external factors over which one had little control. For Rosegger it was the ability on the part of human beings to select the perspective through which they saw life that provided meaning to life. This power to see one's existence through a positive or negative light lay within the reach of every person, and the way it was used could bring hap-piness to the poorest of peasants or misery to the wealthiest of capitalists.

In an article entitled "Which Viewpoint Ought We To Give Our Children" Rosegger went into great detail about the perspective he consid-ered vital for children to receive from their parents if they were to lead happy, productive lives. Once again he stated his conviction that "human contentment or discontentment depended in large measure on the view-point" (*Weltanschauung*) that people held of life in general.[14] Using the metaphor of eyeglasses, he emphasized simply and graphically his belief that one could select how one saw the world just as one could select which pair of glasses one wanted to use. In the first years of life, he wrote, parents had the power to shape the way their children would view life. According to him, the parents' most important duty was to give their chil-dren a perspective that showed them a world that was beautiful and good rather than one that was ugly and unjust. This goal, Rosegger believed, could be accomplished first by parents and then later by teachers through an emphasis on the positive and beautiful aspects of life: "Children ought to hear of beauty, goodness, and greatness. The human past is so filled with great advances—I don't mean the advances of armies in wars and the destructive deeds of victorious generals, not the intrigues of land-hungry princes and such things by which they want to "shape" our youth—I mean the spiritually enriching and fortunate deeds of noble human beings"(p. 825).

The deeds that the author had in mind were the moments in history, music, art, and literature when tolerance triumphed over bigotry and hatred. If there was one common characteristic of great human beings, then it was tolerance, for it reflected divinity (p. 826). Tolerance of those who were different needed to replace the glorification of war because "the idea, for whatever reason, that human beings may kill innocent human beings must gradually be extinguished from the human race" (p. 827). By exposing children to the great and beautiful episodes of history parents and teachers could show their children where patriotism ended and prejudice began (p. 827).

As editor of *Heimgarten*, Rosegger wrote a number of articles addressing the problem of nationalism and patriotism in which he tried to combat growing jingoism. In Rosegger's mind patriotism had positive and negative sides. In the positive sense patriotism meant a love for one's homeland that expressed itself in a feeling of unity with all who lived in that land and a willingness to place the good of one's country before one's own good. This unity was founded on a common language and tradition that gave one the sense of belonging to a large family, a family whose safety and well-being determined the nature of work and, in times of national danger, sacrifice. Yet Rosegger feared that this "noble, fruitful, positive nationalism" had been perverted in his day.[15] Instead of something good patriotism had become a force of evil and a breeding ground of prejudice that based the love of one's country on the hatred of other countries. The author blamed not only the politicians for this distortion but the poets as well. Through them love of country had become the "sickness of our time" (*Zeitkrankheit*) that must be eradicated from Europe (p. 830).

During the First World War Rosegger wrote articles supporting Austria's military efforts. At times he seems to have been caught up in the zeal to defend the nation's honor that swept much of Europe. Yet there are also several articles from his hand which suggest he continued to work for peace and the reconciliation of Europe. In a 1916 essay, for example, he reminded his readers that one of his biographers was a Frenchman. In spite of the war and the hatred against France that was being preached on every side he still considered Bulliod a friend whose welfare was important to him. Then he returned to his life-long theme of unity among nations: "It is not impossible that the French farmer stands closer to the German farmer than he does to the Parisian lawyer or newspaper writer, for the same occupation tends to bind people closer together than does politics. And because my French friends and I see our common calling in the reconciliation of people, perhaps we will soon find our way back to each other."[16]

To a large extent Rosegger's ability to write such an editorial calling for international reconciliation in a time of war stemmed from the religious view of life that he carried with him from his childhood in the countryside. As a child he experienced God's presence as much in nature as in the church, and his observations of nature led him to the conclusion that God was inclusive rather than exclusive. Throughout his life the author loved to climb mountains, for, viewed from any mountain top, the world revealed itself void of the national borders human beings were taking so seriously. If God formed the natural world without such boundaries, then these lines drawn by politicians, kings, and popes were artificial and misleading.

In an important *Heimgarten* article on religion Rosegger referred to the experience of mountain peaks in order to illustrate the dangerous limitations of that human perspective which took pride in the differences among nations and people. Until people rose above such notions as "homeland" and "nation" to a universal humanism, they could not experience God.[17] According to Rosegger, it was the duty of religion to lead people to the universal acceptance of all races, for nothing less did justice to the God religion claimed to serve.

When religion encouraged the spiritual development of people, then Rosegger accepted it as authentic regardless of its label. "Whenever I find a good heart sensitive to what is good and beautiful," he wrote, "I view that as revelation of the Holy Spirit."[18] In addition to such sensitivity he believed that an essential part of any religion had to be a sense of wellbeing that remained firm even in the midst of suffering. This inner security represented for him "peace of heart" (*Frieden des Herzens*). He regarded it as the goal of each individual life to find its own path to the inner security that would offer support in a chaotic world. Religion could be of tremendous benefit in this regard only if it was what Rosegger termed "pure" religion rather than the "pro forma" sort that attracted so many adherents. For him pure religion was "the longing and searching for a divinity" that was eternal rather than temporal and that reflected the spiritual harmony of the universe by not surrendering a single creature to loss or death; the practice of this kind of religion was the humble devotion to this ideal regardless of pressure from contemporary forces advocating the supremacy of any one religion, race, or nation. (*Himmelreich*, p. 85)

While Rosegger was convinced that pure religion was available to anyone who looked for it in the right manner, he regarded the organized Church as an obstacle that more often than not hindered the seeker. It is interesting that Rosegger's fictional account of the life of Christ was written as a frame novel, thus illustrating the subjective nature of authentic religion. In this novel, *I.N.R.I: Frohe Botschaft eines armen Sünders* (1905, I.N.R.I: The Good News of a Poor Sinner), written after a *Heimgarten* essay on Christ was censured by the authorities, a condemned man awaiting execution writes a personal version of the gospel after a representative of the Catholic Church refuses to bring him a New Testament.[19] Drawing upon childhood memories of his mother's account of Bible stories, the man has a vision of Christ coming to him in his cell. It is not the Christ of dogma in whom one must believe but the Christ of the poor, the suffering, and the lost. As the narrator describes the vision, the reader receives an important insight into the author's faith: "Such is the mystery of the Savior's eternal power, that he is for each individual human being exactly the Christ whom that person needs" (p. 35). The work reflects Rosegger's faith that, as long as it was the Christ of love in whom one trusted, then each human being could safely call upon his or her personal idea of Jesus, and it would be the correct one (p. 35). When scholars were ruthlessly searching for the historical Jesus, Rosegger, true to form, went in the opposite direction and insisted upon the historical Jesus becoming the Jesus of personal faith, released both from the clutches of historians and priests alike (p. 35).

Christianity could best help people in their quest for contentment in the midst of strife by emphasizing the gospel of Christ rather than the diversive dogma that separated the Catholic and Protestant branches of the faith (*Himmelreich*, p. 53). This basic tenet of Rosegger's religious faith was underscored not only in his novel about Christ but also in numerous *Heimgarten* essays and fictional accounts. He felt strongly that Catholics and Protestants could unite in a common ministry of love. All they had to do was relegate the teachings that divided them to a secondary place in their expression of Christianity. By concentrating on what they had in common, namely the Christ of love, they could become a powerful force for good and change in the world rather than yet another force dividing human beings from each other. Although he was raised a Roman Catholic and remained a member of that church throughout his life, he worked tirelessly to reconcile Catholics and Protestants, going so far as to become the chief force behind the establishment of the first Protestant church in Styria.[20] In a number of fictional narratives, he expressed poetically the image he had of a unified Christianity working with peasants in their daily struggle for survival, purpose, and dignity.

Rosegger as Apologist

While *Heimgarten* remained an important forum for Rosegger to convey his thoughts on society, religion, politics, and literature, it served another function as well. In the pages of his journal the essayist and author opened a window for his readers into a world that for the most part was otherwise closed, the world of the Austrian peasant. Unlike so many writers of the day who wrote about peasant life from an outsider's perspective, Rosegger wrote from an insider's point of view. When he described life in the village or on the farm, he was writing about a way of life he had experienced firsthand. It was not only a life that he knew, it was one that he loved, valued, and honored. Rosegger made a great effort to reveal the many facets of village life and to defend that way of life from detractors and critics. His concern to be an apologist for village life formed a bridge between his fiction and non-fiction, for there are elements of both the essayist and author in every piece of writing from his hand.

It is difficult for the modern reader to appreciate how isolated the peasant's world was in Rosegger's time. For most people living in the cities rural society represented a distant, remote, and somewhat suspicious way of life. Like Appalachian society in the United States, the Austrian peasantry was foreign and strange to the average burgher of the Empire. Therefore thinking about peasant life was dominated by prejudice, stereotypes, and inaccuracies. The village and farm were seldom viewed as a diverse community of individuals but as a monolithic society of uneducated and uncouth people. In a *Heimgarten* article from 1889 the author characterized the urban dweller's view of country folk this way: "What is more repulsive than rural people in the villages and farm huts? Raw, dumb, belligerent, impudent, violent, indecent, superstitious, bigoted, dirty! If you encounter a peasant, then you have to hold your nose three steps in front of him and four steps behind him. If you step into a peasant's room, then you can be struck dead on the spot because of the diseased air."[21]

Rosegger's response to such prejudice was to insist that those holding such views acknowledge the humanity of the peasant in its negative and positive aspects. In the same article the author refused to stop with the above list of unfavorable traits in his fictional rebuttal to the urbanite's complaint against country folk. He went on to make the list of sins inclusive of non-peasants as well: "Why haven't you listed more? Why haven't you listed all of the sins and crimes and shortcomings and revolting things that occur in the world? For all of these as well you can find among human beings, to whom—in the widest sense of the word—even we belong" (p. 39). Yet Rosegger insisted that there was another side to the peasant's world, a side that was closed to the outsider who came into the village with feelings of superiority. The more realistic perspective on country life was attained only by those who came to the countryside prepared to encounter people no better and no worse than themselves. This attitude, which opened the peasant's world to full view, Rosegger called "the art of humanity" (p. 40).

When one entered the village with a receptive attitude, one was prepared to find no such thing as a "peasant," but rather a collection of human beings who differed from each other in the same manner that people in urban settings differed from each other: "You have to have known them in all their different types and activities, if you are to judge and evaluate them"(p. 41). He never wrote about that world to ridicule it, to complain about its poverty, or to show its misery apart from its abundance. He never desired to make the people who lived there appear better than they were but rather as they were: "If an author wants to offer peasants for public view, then they have to be authentic peasants, but they should be dressed in their Sunday best. The exception to this rule, of course, is those who have no Sunday best to be dressed in."[22]

Rosegger as Writer of Village Literature

During his student days at Graz Rosegger happened upon the writings of Adalbert Stifter. If Rosegger found much of his material and many of his themes in his background in Krieglach-Alpl, he may well have discovered his tone in Stifter. All of his life Rosegger remained a devotee of his fellow Austrian, reading his entire works some eight times over a forty-year period.23 In 1912 Rosegger expressed his love for Stifter's works: "I read him because of the quiet greatness of his rural nature, because of the peaceful grandeur of his characters, because of the blessed divine peace that covers his world. Only in my later years did I go beyond the superficial quietness, the lovely smallness of daily life (*Kleinleben*) to discover the great passion, the dark tragic fate. the unbending defiance, the panting desire that at times lie hidden behind the mild peaceful form" (p. 325). In Stifter's novels and stories lay the filter through which Rosegger learned to pass his own experiences. Passion, desire, and defiance were filtered through the "quiet greatness" and "peaceful grandeur" of simple characters who bent to nature but not to fashion. This "gentle law" (*das sanfte Gesetz*) of nature became for Rosegger a "battle line against the current direction in literature, art, and general philosophies."24 Although Stifter's direct influence on Rosegger's style, motifs, and themes may be seen in a number of early stories from *Waldheimat* (1877, Forest Home) and in the opening of *Jakob der Letzte* (1889, The Last Jacob), Stifter's most enduring legacy is discernible in Rosegger's fiction in the celebration of quiet heroes and simple events of daily peasant life. Rosegger found in Stifter a kindred spirit whose writings validated both his own experiences as a human being and his basic intentions as a writer.

Rosegger's best stories about peasant life are found in the *Waldheimat*, a collection of narratives based on his childhood in and around Alpl. These stories, written over a number of years for *Heimgarten*, were published periodically in book form beginning in 1877. In the definitive edition of his works that Rosegger edited shortly before his death, the *Waldheimat* narratives account for four of the forty volumes. Covering the years from 1848 to 1870, the collection is divided into four parts, each reflecting a chronological period of the author's life starting with early childhood and running through his student days in Graz. In the very first stories the narrator introduces the reader to the sense of history and tradition that permeates the entire collection by retelling events that happened to Rosegger's grandfather and parents on the farm long before his birth. A feeling of permanence about the farm is thus evoked that makes the eventual loss of the homestead years later all the more tragic.

The autobiographical nature of *Waldheimat* is somewhat misleading. Although the stories do recall Rosegger's youth, his family, life on the farm and in the area around Krieglach and Alpl, it was never the author's intention to render realistic descriptions of his early life. To appreciate these stories fully readers must be aware of the importance memory plays in Rosegger's understanding of writing. In the forward to the first collection of stories he warned against taking events too literally:

> It is one of our mind's divine attributes that we can more easily forget past misfortune than past joy, that in remembering these joys cleanse themselves more and more from the cinders of hardship until they stand like a heavenly altar, even for the old "child." One calls them dreamers, these people who love to look back into the past. Yet we fail to consider that they are guarding over a treasure in a state of dreamlike happiness. It is a treasure that cannot be lost or destroyed as long the soul lives in which it rests. (Hausbuch, p. 9)

Memory had for Rosegger more to do with the present than with the past in that it revealed far more about an individual's present situation that about previous experiences. Memory was a treasure that neither contemporary circumstances nor time could destroy; a treasure that bestowed joy on those who watched over it. But it was a treasure created in the present, not retrieved from the past.

In an essay on memory Rosegger underscored the dominance of the present over the past by considering the literal meaning of the German word for memory (*Erinnerung*). For him it meant entering into one's depths, a going into ones's center (*Einkehr in sein Inneres*). He stated that, when someone wrote a piece entitled "The Memories of my Life," most readers assumed that the person was offering detailed descriptions from the past that had been preserved in that person's mind. But Rosegger questioned the validity of this assumption, maintaining that such attempts to revive what was dead were doomed to failure. The mind's inability to retrieve the past as it really had happened made all such accounts suspect. Because remembering meant for Rosegger entering into the present self, not going back into the past, the act of recalling past experiences vividly revealed the authentic self, the true personality, and represented a new life experience. This experience, because it was subjective, could not be subjected to life's external circumstances and events. Regardless of how terrible life became for a person, what happened outside in the world had "little importance compared to one's inner life"(Hausbuch, p. 343).

When writing about his childhood and early youth, Rosegger was therefore selectively recalling various episodes that illustrated certain principles and values that he deemed important for the present. He was writing about the world as he saw it rather than about life as it had once been "in the good old days." In this sense the stories became to some degree socially critical narratives that invited readers to view society from a different perspective. That perspective was more often than not that of a human being concerned with the erosion of community and with modern society's alienation from nature.

In the vignette "Was bei den Sternen war" ("What Stars Mean"), for example, the reader senses the family's intimate ties to nature as Peter quizzes various members of the farm community about the significance of the stars and their relationship to people. Through the responses of his parents, farm hands, and others the narrator offers a number of explanations for the stars, ranging all the way from a scientific account to a superstitious one.[25] In each account the person links the stars' meaning to a personal experience that tells more about the individual than about the stars. Only Peter lacks this intimate link to the heavens, and at the end of the story the boy is standing alone outside the farmhouse contemplating the night sky and the many interpretations he has heard. When his grandmother comes to tell him that his mother has just given birth to a boy, Peter has the experience that can connect his life to the stars. Having just seen a falling star, the young narrator tells his grandmother, "it's not true that stars fall from the sky, those are really angels that fly from heaven with new babies" (p. 132)

Peter's comment about stars falling from the sky refers to an earlier episode in the story. One evening Peter finds his grandmother sitting outside the house looking up at the sky. She also offers an interpretation of the stars; informing Peter that every person has either a lucky or unlucky star. When that person dies, her or his personal star falls to earth. She points to hers and tells him that it is already beginning to fade; soon she will die. When Peter wonders aloud if hers has been a lucky or unlucky star, she pulls him to her breast and whispers: "Of course it was a lucky star, you lovely child, of course it was!"(p. 130). This short exchange between grandmother and grandson touches upon a major theme in *Waldheimat*: death as a natural part of life. The boy says nothing sentimental about not wanting her to die, and the old woman does not avoid the topic. Rather than an occasion for fear, death presents the opportunity to measure the quality of one's existence as the grandmother does when asked about her star.

Death serves the same function in one of the best known stories in the *Waldheimat* collection, "Wie der Meisensepp gestorben ist" (How Sepp Died"). In this account the young narrator is called away to read to Sepp from a religious book. As the boy sits with the man and his family, the reader becomes aware of the living conditions among the poor and gains insight into local folklore about death. But the focus of the story remains on Sepp. Narrated without pathos, the narrative reveals the dying man's quiet courage.[26] Like Peter's grandmother contemplating the stars, the man easily accepts death because he has accepted life. The memory of Sepp's death becomes an ever present reminder of spiritual values that aids the narrator later in life when he is tempted to forget those basic principles he learned at Sepp's bedside. In this way Rosegger's memory of childhood and the collection of stories in *Waldheimat* had more to do with how he wanted to live in the present than with an attempt to flee into a Golden Age.

Rosegger's shorter fiction, of which *Waldheimat* ranks among the best, provides the reader with an unforgettable picture of village life in Austria during Rosegger's lifetime. The motifs that arise in these stories reflect the daily events in the village: crime, courtship, marriage, sickness, death, poverty, family concerns, religion, and military service, to name but a few. Beyond these the reader learns of customs and practices of country people and follows village life throughout the year in its observance of holidays. The problems confronting the farmer, his wife, the farm workers, the elderly, and the poor are presented in vivid detail. One learns of the social problems that affected the community and of the ways in which the people of the area attempted to deal with them. In a typical village story by Rosegger the reader receives a picture of the rural community as a network in which each member is related in some sense to all the others. More often than not the plot revolves around the disruption of this structure by people who allow self-centered concerns to blur their obligations to their neighbors.

Rosegger often portrayed the breakdown in the social structure with humor, as in the story "Als Hans der Grete schrieb" ("When Hans Wrote Grete").[27] When Grete, an illiterate stable maid, receives a letter from Hans, who is away in the army, she faces the problem of finding someone to read it to her. By describing her unsophisticated manner of viewing the world, the narrator prepares the reader to accept both Grete's naiveté and the implausible ploy on which the story depends. In her haste to learn the letter's content she makes the mistake of going to another servant girl for help who is secretly in love with the same young man. The protagonist seeks this particular girl's aid because she has seen the other woman using a prayer book during church services and reasons that she must understand print. But her rival is also illiterate; it is false pride rather than knowledge or piety that places the prayer book in her hands. Christle, the antagonist, knows that Grete's guardian, who can read, is opposed to Grete's loving a soldier. Using her cunning to lead the curious lover into a trap, she tells Grete that if the old man, who is hard of hearing, reads the letter aloud, he can not understand its content. When the guardian reads the love letter, he learns Grete's secret and forbids her having any further contact with the boy. She must now overcome his opposition by her strength of will. In this narrative Christle represents the individual in the social structure whose pride and self-will prevent her from aiding a neighbor. Because of the story's humorous nature the plot backfires, and the ending is positive. Through such accounts of farm life Rosegger communicates the impor- tance of literacy for every member of the rural community without allow- ing this didactic concern to weigh unduly on the narrative's structure.

In general Rosegger's shorter fiction deals with daily life in the vil- lages and countryside by concentrating on the characteristics of rural life that pertain to an isolated community of human beings who have little contact with outsiders. In stories like the one above the tensions arise because of relationships within the community. In his shorter works Rosegger limited himself more often than not to love stories, humorous tales, and narratives that centered on eccentric characters. In such narra- tives Rosegger functioned as a folklorist as an author.

Rosegger and the Decline of the Peasantry

Another side of Rosegger's fiction presents the peasant's world as a community in crisis. In these stories the author showed his readers a way of life that was endangered from outside forces over which the peasant had little or no control. While many of the plots Rosegger employed may appear far-fetched today, for the most part they reflected accurately the social conditions facing rural communities during the writer's lifetime. Here Rosegger wrote as a social activist concerned with problems of the day. In doing so he ran the risk of having his works lose their relevancy once the issues had passed from the stage.

According to Rosegger's point of view, the overriding issue of his time was the disappearance of the peasantry. During the author's literary period the peasant's world was in irreversible decline. He wanted to use his influence as a writer to halt this decline by demonstrating the quality of life available to those living in the country and by depicting the darker side of city life. This mission, if one may use that term, made Rosegger a conservative writer and thinker in the sense that he wished to preserve a way of life he deemed valuable. Knowing full well that once life as he had experienced it as a child was gone from the scene it would be lost forever, he devoted a great deal of his writing to a positive presentation of country living. This way of life began to disintegrate after the exeration of the peasants in 1848 from their dependence on large landowners. Although the intent was laudable and the action long overdue, it caught the peasants unprepared for such a drastic change.

As Anderle observes, land reform replaced one dependency with another. She goes on to explain, "In place of being dependent on large landowners, the new bondage resulted from ongoing indebtedness due to large transfer fees and ever higher taxes, which ended more often than not in the forced auction of the farm, causing the family to lose both home and possessions" (Anderle, p 97). To gain title to his land the farmer had to pay the landowner one third of the land's value outright, while the government paid the other two thirds. But one third of the government's payment was passed on to the farmer as a special tax. To this tax the state added monetary taxes that replaced former payments in goods (*Robotleistungen*). As if this were not burden enough, the government placed an unreasonably high evaluation on the land, inflicting further hardship on the farmer (Hackl, p. 131). Rosegger experienced the effect of land reform in the loss of his family's farm in 1866, one of many victims. In 1800 there were some seventy farms in and around Alpl and Krieglach; by 1890 there were only eight (Anderele, pp. 100-101).

One of the major consequences of these changes was a massive flow of peasants from the countryside into the cities. Because farms were failing, farmers and laborers were forced to seek employment in the industrial areas of the country. In numerous articles Rosegger attempted to stem the flood by pointing out reasons to remain on the farms even in desperate times. Although he criticized the state's mistakes and callous behavior, he also attacked the shortsightedness and greed of country people who thought that paradise lay in the urban centers and their factories. "Whatever one wants to say about this," he wrote, "the cause that today...the farmer wants to move to the city is not the drive for spiritual betterment but the greed for material glitter, for power, and for money."[28]

This desire, more often frustrated than not by the poor working conditions in the cities, originated in a dissatisfaction with the simple living conditions and few wants that characterized rural life. For Rosegger the luxuries offered by the city were "superfluous" and only made one more dependent on a dangerous consumerism that sought only to satisfy artificial needs and manufactured desires (*Höhenfeuer*, p. 19). One major disadvantage to city life, as Rosegger saw it, was the impersonal working conditions in both factories and private homes. Even if life in the country was harsh, it offered a sense of community that was lacking in the metropolitan centers.

Although Rosegger could address the social situation in positive terms, he could vividly describe its tragic consequences, as he did in the novel *Jakob der Letzte* (1889, The Last Jacob), which has been recognized as one of the most important representations of the social-political conditions facing rural people in the second-half of the nineteenth century.[29] The novel's background lay in yet another result of the land reform laws: the purchase of farms by wealthy city dwellers for hunting purposes. After buying a farm, they would turn the land into private game reserves for their own amusement. Rosegger was horrified by this practice, both as an advocate of animal rights who opposed hunting for sport on moral grounds and as a defender of the beleaguered farmer, whose land would produce wildlife instead of crops. According to Rosegger, the idea for the novel came in a conversation on this topic with a hunter: "On the 29th of June 1886 I argued with a hunter in an inn in Krieglach who said: 'The stupid farmer in Styria has to be exterminated. Styria is not for farms but for the hunt'" (*Hausbuch*, p. 398).

In *Jakob* Rosegger became far more aggressive and less humorous in his defense of the peasant class. By telling the story of Jacob he addressed the status quo in such a way that broke from the tradition of village literature represented by Ludwig Anzengruber, Rosegger's popular contemporary and friend. Anzengruber believed that the emergence of the agricultural-political problems signaled the end of village literature. According to Azengruber, literature had no business offering solution to these rural problems.[30] Rosegger, however, regarded literature as a powerful vehicle for social change.

Writing in the forward to *Jakob*, Rosegger acknowledged that he felt himself personally affected by the decline of the farmer and stated explicitly his literary intentions: "The book should show what happens in people's hearts when they cut themselves off from the land."[31] To accomplish this, Rosegger wrote his most dramatic novel in which conflicting viewpoints about the agricultural crisis battle each other until the small village is destroyed and the land turned into a game reserve. The action builds to a powerful climax, in which Jacob commits suicide rather than sell the farm that has belonged to the family for generations.

Most of the people in the area want to sell their land to the forester, who is buying it for an unknown businessman. Yet Jacob feels that if the largest land owner of the village (*der Großbauer*) refuses to surrender to the temptation, the remaining farmers will find the courage to remain on their property as well. When he argues his case, Jacob touches on a major theme in village literature, the notion that a community is a community only if everyone holds together in times of crisis. For village authors like Rosegger the homeland (*Heimat*) is a place of shared values that cement individuals into a larger whole. This sense of belonging also reaches back into the past, as Jacob makes clear when he tells the land owner, "Neighbor, remain with us. Your ancestors were born and died on this land..." (p. 43). After another farmer is forced by back taxes to sell his farm, he becomes "a stranger in the house of his fathers" (p. 56). To cut one's self off from one's past and from one's homeland is to turn the world into a strange, unfamiliar, insecure place.

For Rosegger, the tragic irony of the rural situation lay in the inability of apparent wealth to make one truly wealthy, and of independence from one's past or neighbors to make one free. By selling their lands the farmers in the novel accomplish the opposite of their intentions; they fall deeper into slavery. By trying to free themselves they give up their spiritual center, the purpose that anchors their daily life in a universal whole. They not only lose their land but also their meaning in life. Now with money they are afraid for the first time in their lives that someone can take something of value from them. They exchange security for fear.

Jacob, Rosegger's protagonist, refuses to sell because he knows the spiritual wealth he possesses as a man who lives close to nature and therefore close to God. The farmer understands his work in the field to be a form of worship. In the sowing of seed and the harvesting of grain he finds the miracle of God's love enacted in nature's death and resurrection (p. 166). The cycle of seasons, the changes they bring, and the inability of human beings to command rain to fall or storms to cease becomes for Jacob a sacred parable that teaches the greatest lesson in life: authentic humility before one's creator (p. 167).[32] As with the biblical Jacob, Jacob Steinreuter experiences a mystical ladder into heaven when he sits in meditation on the altar made of the stones he and his ancestors have cleared from their land (p. 168).

Time and time again Rosegger returned in his writings to the theme of the spiritual significance of farming. By working the fields and observing the laws of nature the farmer experienced God more directly than worshippers in a church. The religious nature of life on a farm set farming apart from all other occupations and professions in the author's mind. Nowhere did Rosegger express this more clearly than in *Erdsegen*. In this epistolary novel a journalist takes a year's leave of absence from his newspaper in the city to live on a farm. As time passes he learns to see in the elderly farmer a priest whose acts are sacred.

For Rosegger then the agricultural crisis had spiritual ramifications as well as economic ones. If farmers were more than willing to sell their land and move to the city, where they faced an even more uncertain future than on the farm, then the problem was ultimately a moral and spiritual one (*Bauertum*, p. 20).

The road from the village led in the other direction too. Not only were country people leaving rural areas for the city, city dwellers were entering the countryside, bringing with them attitudes and practices that questioned the conservatism, independence, and spirituality of village life. The railroad brought a demand for wood that resulted in the wanton destruction of forests (Anderele, p. 98). With this influx from the cities came the technological and materialistic *Zeitgeist* that ruled Europe in the second half of the nineteenth century (Hackle, p. 132). Factories sprang up, and farm workers became factory workers without leaving the area. The new standard of worth was money rather than produce and handcrafted goods. When country people wanted to live like city people, Rosegger knew that the village as he had experienced it was doomed.

The destruction of the village from outside forces formed the basis of the *Heimgarten* narrative "Das zugrundegehende Dorf" (October, 1884, "The Destroyed Village"). The author, however, developed this theme in far greater detail in the novel *Das ewige Licht* (1896, Eternal Light). Uniting two of his favorite narrative forms, the epistolary and the Robinsonade, Rosegger related the story of a young Catholic priest, Wieser, whose bishop sends him to a remote parish in the mountains as punishment for his having published liberal essays in a church periodical. While the priest describes village life and his reflections about events in the parish, the reader follows the hamlet's rapid decline as it opens itself more and more to the industrial age and the negative influence of insensitive tourists.

Like farming, Rosegger viewed community in spiritual terms. When the people of Torwald lose their sense of belonging and cease to feel any responsibility for the welfare of the village, they lose more than their community, they lose their souls as well. They cut themselves off from God when they cut themselves off from their neighbor's need, they sever their ties to nature when they see the forests in material terms, and their lives become shallow when they become consumers of goods for which they had previously no need. Once industry enters the village, Wieser becomes aware of his inability to alter events, for the people have caught the disease of individualism and materialism introduced by outsiders. Tormented by his helplessness and inability to summon the villagers back to their spiritual roots, the priest loses his mind and dies a broken, disillusioned man (p. 281).

In both *Jakob* and *Das ewige Licht* Rosegger acknowledged that the destruction of peasant life as he had known it was a fait accompli. Both protagonists fail to reverse events, and both die in despair, refusing to live in a world void of community and empty of spiritual values. Like his fictional heroes, Rosegger recognized his inability as an author to reverse events. The most he could do was chronicle the decline of a way of life, to describe for posterity what was being destroyed. This recognition on his part is not only evident in the fate of Jacob and Wieser, but also in the title of his next collection of stories: *Idyllen aus einer untergehenden Welt* (1899, Idylls from a World in Decline).

Two Favorite Motifs

The incident of the tourists lost in the cave outside Torwald which concludes the first part of *Ewiges Licht* illustrates a major motif in Rosegger's writings, that of living entombment. The motif is employed as a means of testing character. In novels such as *Der Gottsucher* (1883, God Seeker), *Martin der Mann* (1889, Martin the Man), and many short works the reader finds the major characters caught in snowstorms or lost in caves. While entombed they must face the smallness of human beings before the great forces of nature; they confront their own shortcomings and emerge as new people or ignore the lesson and emerge unchanged, as in the case of the seven spelunkers.

In Rosegger's only novel of historical fiction, however, the motif undergoes an important change. *Peter Mayr: Der Wirt an der Mahr*

(1893, Peter Mayr: Innkeeper on the River Mahr) has the hero using nature as a weapon. Mayr, a supporter of Andreas Hofer's revolt against the Bavarians in 1809, flees to the mountains to escape capture. In hiding he experiences an avalanche which gives him the idea "of uniting with nature to defeat the enemy."[33] Drawing the French and Bavarian troops into an ambush, the Tyrolian forces cause an avalanche which kills a number of them.

Although the novel presents the Tyolian viewpoint, the narrator shifts perspectives at this point in the narrative from that of the Austrians to that of a young Bavarian officer. As the man admires the countryside and listens to a Tyrolian flutist, he wants to lift his hat in salute to the beauty of the music, never suspecting that the song is a dance of death signaling the hiding Austrians of the enemy's approach. By shifting narrative perspective the narrator shows the humanity of the enemy, thereby lifting the novel above the trivial treatment of national military heroes to glorify war.

This incident becomes the psychological turning point of the novel; Mayr is tormented thereafter by his deed. He has nightmares about the avalanche and cannot tolerate the rushing noise of mountain streams. At this point Mayr leaves again for the mountains, where he voluntarily entombs himself in a cave. There he is arrested. Before the military judge Mayr refuses to speak in his own behalf, as if accepting the guilt for the death of the soldiers (the battle occurred after Austria signed a peace treaty). Determined not to lie, he goes willingly to his death.

According to this use of the familiar motif, nature stands as the revelation of God that can teach and humble human beings, but it is a violation of the natural order to transform its forces into weapons or to use nature in the service of limited and often self-serving ends. Mayr's sin against nature consists of not learning anything more from his entombment than how to destroy life.

Into this historical novel Rosegger wove another narrative which relates the love story of two peasants, Tonele and Hanai. Although they are secondary characters, their story ranks as one of Rosegger's finest literary achievements, for in it he again demonstrated how well he could bring to life the simple cares, problems, loves, and hates of country folk.

Tonele represents the outsider, who does not belong to the area. He is not tied down to the region by family or by employment, so he is free to roam the countryside, coming and going as his care free will directs him. Love for Hanai rather than loyalty to the homeland keeps bringing him back to the district. Unlike many authors of regional literature (*Heimatkunst*) Rosegger often makes the outsider the hero of his narratives, thereby strongly criticizing the mistrust of outsiders that marks much village literature as nationalistic. Not place of origin but character becomes the standard by which human beings are to be judged, and it is to Hanai's credit that she recognizes this principle.

Rosegger's Place in Austrian Literature

There are several reasons that Rosegger has fallen between the cracks of literary attention. In an enlightening essay on Rosegger and Germanists, Uwe Baur suggests that Rosegger's absence from the canon of serious literature may lie in the fact that Rosegger viewed himself as a *Volkserzieher*, a writer for the common people who seeks to educate as well as entertain.[34] By electing this understanding of literature, Baur maintains, Rosegger placed himself in the tradition of "bourgeois enlightenment" at a time when literature was being designated either as "serious" (*Hochliteratur*) or as "entertaining" (*Volksliteratur*). Serious literature, according to Baur, represented the concerns and interest of the aristocracy, who by virtue of their class enjoyed the luxury of an education, while the lighter literary efforts were aimed at the literate members of the lower classes. Serious village literature sought to bridge this gap by offering works that had merit and were entertaining at the same time. Baur places Rosegger firmly in this tradition. (pp. 15-16).

Baur's essay is certainly helpful in explaining Rosegger's reception or lack thereof in recent German studies. Most of the secondary literature available on Rosegger illustrates Baur's major points. Germanists often view him as a representative of trivial literature, by which most mean a representative of the village literature that was popular in the nineteenth century. They hold that the values expressed are irrelevant or unacceptable for our time. However, some contemporary critics are rediscovering Rosegger as a spokesman for environmental concerns.

With his anti-city and anti-industry stance Rosegger was an outspoken environmentalist who wrote extensively about nature, conservation, and the dangers of pollution. An example of Rosegger's stance on pollution is found in an oft quoted *Heimgarten* essay from 1906:

> The cause of this misery, as of so many, is again industry. It is too large and it eats away everything. It devours not only country peo-

ple, but their forests and drinks away their water. What it leaves behind, it spoils so much that even the original inhabitants of our waters, fish, must die. Industry uses up timber for construction, timber for charcoal, timber for paper, and everything near this consumption is choked by smoke. Industry, that is already changing our political and social conditions, will also alter our green homeland, making of it a moon landscape.[35]

It is not difficult to understand why many supporters of the "Green" movements in politics consider Rosegger one of them.

Yet another rediscovery of Rosegger comes from those scholars who reject the dichotomy between serious and trivial literature in favor of literature as a historical and social product which throws light on daily life in former times (culture with a small "c"). For literary historians, sociologists, psychologists, linguists, and folklorists Rosegger becomes a valuable resource (Baur, p. 21).[36] For them his works may well accomplish one of the major goals he set for himself: to open the door onto a closed society so that readers might find among the villages and farms human beings with a culture of their own, who faced the common problems of existence in their particular way, and who had something of importance to relate to those who lived outside their world.

Conclusion

After the Second World War village literature fell into disrepute largely because of the "Blood and Soil" (*Blut und Boden*) tradition of the National Socialists. In an effort to move beyond that era all village writers, especially those like Rosegger who had been used by the Nazis on a highly selective basis, were painted with the same brush. The community of scholars quickly dismissed Rosegger as a representative of a literature whose time had passed. Yet this rejection was often done without closely examining his works. His village stories reach beyond the narrow confines of the Austrian countryside to embrace universal themes. To his credit Peter Rosegger wrote from the perspective of liberal humanism, which emphasizes spiritual values over material ones.

Rosegger's intention as an author was to use village literature as an inclusive rather than exclusive genre. If he wrote about prejudice in the village against the outsider, then it was in part because he knew full well that prejudice also existed beyond the confines of the village. He believed that the village offered any writer all the material one needed to relate the joys and tragedies of human existence. Peasants were different from people who lived in the city, but aside from the superficial aspects of their character that made them interesting or colorful to bourgeois readers they were human beings with the same fear of death, longing for love, and desire for happiness that all humans share. They prayed to the same God, suffered from the same diseases, and stood in need of the same spiritual values as any person living in any metropolitan center. This was the foundation of Rosegger's humanism, and it served as the basis for his literary efforts as well.

Rosegger's literary achievement rests on his ability to write about universal concerns through the narrow setting of the village. As he wrote in a defense of village literature, his characters spoke without ever consulting a conversational lexicon, never took vacations to Italy to view the art museums, and could not conjugate the verb "work." Neither were they able to discuss the latest literary sensation that had every one in the capitol excited. But in the end that was not what he found interesting about people. What interested him was their humanity in its tragic and joyous manifestations (*Höhenfeuer*, p. 213). This interest combined with his love for telling a good story makes his work worthy of any reader's consideration.

Notes

1. Emil Ertil, *Peter Rosegger: wie ich ihn kannte und liebte* (Leipzig: Staackamnn, 1923), p. 220.

2. James p. Sandrock, "The Vision of Rural Life in German *Heimatliteratur*, in *Iowa State Journal of Research*, Vol. 49, No. 2. Pt. 2 (November 1974), 208.

3. Gerald A. Fetz, "Franz Innerhofer" in *Major Figures of Contemporary Austrian Literature*, edited by Donald G. Daviau (New York: Peter Lang, 1987), pp. 237-265.

4. Peter Rosegger, "Lebensbeschreibung des Verfassers: Von ihm selbst," in *Die Schriften des Waldschulmeisters*, Vol. I of *Gesammelte Werke von Peter Rosegger: Vom Verfasser neubearbeitete und neueingeteiltete Ausgabe*. 40 Vols. (Leipzig: Staackmann, 1922-1926), p. VIII. Further references to this article appear in the text. Further references to theis edition appear in notes with volume number and abbreviated citing of title.

5. Charlotte Anderle, *Der andere Peter Rosegger: Zeitkritik und Vision im Spiegel des "Heimgarten" 1876-1918*, (Wien: Österreichischer Agrarverlag, 1983), p. 23. Further references to this work appear in the text.

6. Peter Rosegger, *Mein Welteben*, (München: Staackmann, n.d.) p. 23. Futher references to this work appear in the text.

7. Peter Rosegger, *Das große Rosegger Hausbuch*, ed. Hubert Lendl, (München: Staackmann, n.d.), p. 9. Further references to this text appear in the text.

8. Otto Janda, *Peter Rosegger: Das Leben in seinen Briefen*, (Graz: Böhlau, 1948), p. 321. Further references to this work appear in the text.

9. Elisabeth Eckl, *Peter Rosegger als Herausgeber der Zeitschrift "Heimgarten"*, diss. University of Vienna, 1948, p. 1. Further references to this work appear in the text.

10. Peter Rosegger, *Heimgarten* 1, No. 1 (1876), p. 1.

11. Peter Rosegger, *Heimgarten* 15, No. 9 (1891), p. 679. Further references to this article appear in the text.

12. Peter Rosegger, *Heimgarten* 19, No. 5 (1895), p. 376. Further references to this article appear in the text.

13. Peter Rosegger, *Höhenfeuer*, Vol. 30 of *Gesammelte Werke*, p. 124. Further references to this work appear in the text.

14. Peter Rosegger, *Heimgarten* 3, No. 11 (1879), p. 832. Further references to this article appear in the text.

15. Peter Rosegger, *Heimgarten* 23, No. 11 (1899), p. 829. Further references to this article appear in the text.

16. Peter Rosegger, *Heimgarten* 41, No. 1 (1916), pp. 56-57.

17. Peter Rosegger, *Heimgarten* 9. No. 3 (1884), p. 192.

18. Peter Rosegger, *Mein Himmelreich*, (München: Staackmann, n.d.), p. 53. Further references to this work appear in the text.

19. Peter Rosegger, *I.N. R.I.: Frohe Botschaft eines armen Sünders*, Vol. 38 of *Gesammelte Werke*, p. 18. Further references to this work appear in the text.

20. For Rosegger's relationship to Judaism, see Wolgang Bunte, *Peter Rosegger und das Judentum* (New York: Olms, 1977).

21. Peter Rosegger, *Heimgarten* 14, No. 1 (1889), p. 38. Further references to this article appear in the text.

22. Peter Rosegger, *Heimgarten*, 34, No. 11 (1910), p. 867.

23. Franz Hasling, "Ein Herold Adalbert Stifters: Roseggers fünfzigjähriges Wirken für die Anerkennung von Stifters Gesamtwerk,"

Oberösterreische Heimatblätter, 2 (1948), p. 324. Further references to this article appear in the text.

24. Rudolf Latzke, "Roseggers Bekenntnis zu Stifter," *Adalbert Stifter Almanach*, 1947, p. 99.

25. Peter Rosegger, *Waldheimat* (München: Staackmann, n.d.), pp. 127 ff. Futher references to this work appear in the text.

26. Sandrock, *Heimatliteratur*, p. 209.

27. Peter Rosegger, *Geschichten aus der Steiermark*, (München: Staackmann, n.d.), p. 91. Further references to this work appear in the text.

28. Peter Rosegger, *Heimgarten*, 5, No. 8 (1881), p. 614.

29. Karl Wagner, "Roseggers *Jakob der Letzte* und die zeitgenössische Diskussion der Agrarfrage," in *Fremd gemacht?: Der Volksschrifter Peter Rosegger*, ed. Uwe Baur, Gerald Schöpfer, und Gerhard Pail. (Wien: Böhlau, 1988), p. 90.

30. Rudolf Latzke, *Peter Rosegger: Sein Leben und sein Schaffen* Vol. I (Weimar: Böhlau, 1943), p. 187.

31. Peter Rosegger, *Jakob der Letzte* (München: Staackmann, n.d.). Further references to this work appear in the text.

32. On Rosegger's understanding of humility, see Dean Stroud, "Idyll as Possibility: Rosegger's Humanism" in *Modern Austrian Literature*, 21, No. 2 (1988), 23-40.

33. Peter Rosegger, *Peter Mayr: Der Wirt an der Mahr*, (München: Staackmann, n.d.), p. 213. Further references to this work appear in the text.

34. Uwe Baur, "Peter Rosegger in der Wissenschaft" in *Fremd gemacht?*, p. 13. Further references to this article appear in the text.

35. Peter Rosegger, *Heimgarten* 30 (1906), p. 506.

36. See, for example, James R. Dow and James P. Sandrock, "Peter Rosegger's *Erdsegen*: The Function of Folklore in the Work of an Austrian *Heimatdichter*." *Journal of the Folklore Institute*, 3 (1976), 227-239.

Bibliography

I. Works by Rosegger in German

The definitive edition of Rosegger's works were edited by the author toward the end of his life and were published in a forty volume set over a four year period following the author's death. This set is no longer in print but is available in a number of libraries throughout the United States of America and Europe. This edition is cited first, but the major portion of the bibliography indicates those works that are currently commercially available. The volumes, all published by Staackmann without copyright date, are listed in the order in which they originally appeared during the author's lifetime.

Gesammelte Werke von Peter Rosegger: Vom Verfasser neubearbeitete und neueingeteilte Ausgabe. 40 vols. Leipzig: Staackmann, 1922-1926.

Die Schriften des Waldschulmeisters.

Waldheimat: Erinnerungen aus der Jugendzeit.

Heidepeters Gabriel: Eine Geschichte in zwei Büchern.

Volksleben in Steirermark: in Charakter- und Sittenbildern dargestellt: Das Haus.

Volksleben in Steuermark: In Charakter- und Sittenbildern dargestellt: Das Jahr.

Der Gottsucher: Ein Roman.

Jakob der Letzte: Eine Waldbauerngeschichte aus unserer Zeit.

Der Schelm aus den Alpen: Allerlei Geschichten und Gestalten. Schwänken und Schnuren.

Peter Mayr, der Wirt an der Mahr: Eine Geschichte aus deutscher Heldenzeit.

Wanderungen in der Heimat.

Das ewige Licht: Erzählung nach den Schriften eines Waldpfarrers.

Mein Weltleben oder wie es dem Waldbauernbuben bei den Stadtleuten erging.

Erdsegen: Vertrauliche Sonntagsbriefe eines Bauernknechtes: Ein Kulturroman.

Mein Himmelreich: Bekenntnisse, Geständnisse und Erfahrungen aus dem religiösen Leben.

Weltgift: Roman.

Die Abelsberger Chronik.

Die Försterbuben: Roman aus den steierischen Alpen.

Das Buch von den Kleinen.

Heimgärtners Tagebuch.

The following works are new collections originally published under different titles.

Als ich zum Pflug kam.
Novellen I: Liebes- und Heiratsgeschichten.
Novellen II: Von jungen und alten Leuten.
Novellen III: Wundersame Begebenheiten aus alter Zeit.
Das große Rosegger Hausbuch, ed. Hubert Lendl.
Tiergeschichten.

II.   Works in English

Forest Schoolmaster, trans. E.F. Skinner. London: Putnam, 1901.
God Seeker. London: Putnam, 1901.
A Tale of Old Styria, trans. E.F. Skinner. London: Putnam, 1901.
The Earth and the Fullness Thereof, trans. E.F. Skinner, London: Putnam, 1902.
I.N.R.I. A Prisoner's Story of the Cross, trans. Elizabeth Lee. London: Hodder and Stoughton, 1905.
The Eternal Light. London: Unwin Fisher, 1907.
My Kingdom of Heaven, trans. Elizabeth Lee. London: Hodder and Stoughton, 1907.
The Forest Farm: Tales of the Austrian Tyrol. London: A.C. Fifield, 1912.
Freedom; or Peter Mayr, Landlord of the Mahr, trans. Mary Dougherty. Dublin: M.H. Hill, 1913.

III.   Selected Secondary Works in English

Dow, James R. and James p. Sandrock. "Peter Rosegger's *Erdsegen*: The Function of Folklore in the Work of an Austrian *Heimtdichter*." *Journal of the Folklore Institute*, 3 (1976), pp. 227-239.
Stroud, Dean. *The Sacred Journey: The Religious Function of Nature Motifs in Selected Works by Peter Rosegger*. Stuttgart: Akademischer Verlag, 1986.
____."Idyll as Possibility: Rosegger's Humanism," *Modern Austrian Literature*, 21, No. 2 (1988), 23-40.

IV.   Major Studies in German

Anderle, Charlotte. *Der andere Peter Rosegger: Zeitkritik und Vision im Spiegel des "Heimgarten" 1876-1918.* Wien: Österreichischer Agrarverlag, 1983.

Baur, Uwe and Gerhart Pail, ed. *"Fremd gemacht?": Der Volksschriftsteller Peter Rosegger.* Wien: Böhlau, 1988.

Bunte, Wolfgang. *Peter Rosegger und das Judentum.* Judaistische Texte und Studien, Vol. 16. New York: Olms, 1977.

Janda, Otto. *Peter Rosegger: Das Leben in seinen Briefen.* Graz: Böhlau, 1948.

Latzke, Rudolf. *Peter Rosegger: Sein Leben und sein Schaffen: Der junge Rosegger.* Weimar: Böhlau, 1943.

_____.*Peter Rosegger: Sein Leben und sein Schaffen: Der ältere und der alte Rosegger.* Graz: Böhlau, 1953.

Ferdinand von Saar

Kurt Bergel*

"Every individual life is a piece of world history."[1]

Ferdinand von Saar (1833-1906) was not a fashionable writer during his lifetime. He never produced a bestseller. Yet, when his seventieth birthday was celebrated, virtually every reputable Austrian writer contributed to a congratulatory volume,[2] in which a critic wrote that Saar had secured for himself a "first place in contemporary literature."[3] A few years later the writer Richard Schaukal remarked that Saar "remains our [i.e. Austrian] only novelist."[4]

Saar has never been widely known in the German-speaking world, especially outside of Austria, nor particularly in the English-speaking countries. Translations of his works into English are practically non-existent. It is the aim of this essay to bring Ferdinand von Saar to the attention of American and English readers and thereby to rescue this unjustly ignored poet from oblivion. He was not strikingly original or brilliant nor the founder of a "school" or movement, but his poetry is rich in emotion and his novellas abound in living portraits of fascinating characters as well as in word paintings of Austrian rural and urban scenery. He was a highly observant, although not always profound, describer of human lives, a subtle pre-Freudian student of the psyche, a charitable commentator on our frailties, and above all a virtuoso of empathy.

The almost seventy-three years of Saar's life comprise a period of many changes and much restlessness in the Hapsburg empire. It extends politically from Prince Metternich's reaction anywhere in the first half of

*The writer wishes to express his gratitude to professors Alice R. Bergel and Dorothy Augustine for translating all the texts by Saar used in this essay (with one exception). He also wants to thank them for critically reading his manuscript.

the nineteenth century through the revolution of 1848 to the struggle between renewed reaction and cautious liberalism. Nationalism forced Austria's withdrawal from most of Italy and led to her expansion in the Balkans. Just a few years after Saar's death that expansion brought about the First World War and the dissolution of the multi-national Austro-Hungarian monarchy. Saar's lifetime extends culturally from the "Biedermeier," the world of an inward-looking apolitical middle class, through a growing scientism and philosophical materialism to a realistic and naturalistic art and literature. It ends with the impressionism and subjectivism of the *fin de siècle*.

As a fourteen-year-old student Saar saw clashes of workers and soldiers during the March revolution. As a young officer he participated in the Italian Campaign of 1859, and as a mature poet he witnessed the industrialization of his country and the modernization of its capital. The architectural metropolization of Vienna, especially the erection of modern apartment houses and representative cultural and municipal buildings along the Ringstrasse, the city's main boulevard, was comparable to the approximately simultaneous work done by Baron Haussmann in Paris; both reflected the growing wealth and self-confidence of the rising upper middle class in the last third of the nineteenth century. Saar often wrote about these changes in his works and generally looked at them with regret and nostalgia. It is not only as the poet of the *Wiener Elegien* (Viennese Elegies) that he called himself the "Viennese elegist."

I. SAAR'S LIFE

"I well know what it is/To bear life's burden at a tender age/ And not to have a whole, a real youth. / Whatever one achieves in later years, /One feels betrayed for having lost the best."[5]

Ferdinand von Saar was born in Vienna on 30 September 1833. All his grandparents were members of the lower nobility. Four months after the boy's birth, his father died from a heart attack at the age of thirty-four, and his mother was forced to move with her baby into her father's house. Ferdinand knew poverty throughout his childhood and much of his early adult life. Since the poet later repeatedly refused to write his memoirs because, he said, most of his experiences had found their way into his writings, we will not go wrong in reading many passages as fragments of an autobiography. Thus we may well hear the lines above from his first play as Saar's personal confession . The boy attended various schools in Vienna, of which one—the Schottengymnasium—was a prominent high school where clerics were the instructors. To judge from the whimsical description in his *Pincelliade*, Saar was a less than enthusiastic student, who found the Latin and Greek drills particularly odious.

Saar was only sixteen when, apparently urged by his guardian, he entered the army. The family's poverty and the tradition of military service among the nobility must have been decisive factors. Many years later Saar gave a bitter-humorous parody of military life in his *Pincelliade*. Love affairs seem to have led to debts, unpaid debts to arrests and brief prison sentences. As army life became more frustrating, the poetic gift in Saar asserted itself more firmly. In his biography of Saar Anton Bettelheim published a letter in which the young soldier wrote to his mother that he intentionally allowed himself to be imprisoned for unpaid debts in order to have more time for work on a play that was then on his mind.[6] He did not enjoy his life in the army because he was not a soldier at heart, but his novellas show how he later used many of the landscapes and people he encountered during those years as raw material. His very first novella, *Innocens,* for instance, takes place in a fort outside of Prague, where he had once served and which is described minutely in the story.

His decision to leave the army at the age of twenty-six is not well documented. That he had never freely chosen a military career, that he had advanced only to the rank of second lieutenant ("Unterleutnant"), that he had nothing to look forward to in the army but a humdrum life of poverty and boredom, and above all that since boyhood he had had a strong desire to be a writer—all these reasons led to his decision to leave the army.

His literary apprenticeship imposed great hardship on the young man. He suffered intense poverty for years, was almost constantly in debt, and, as mentioned, was sometimes even in debtors' prison . But with determination and encouragement from a few friends he wrote his first plays and found a publisher. In 1865 he published *Hildebrand,* the first part of his tragedy *Emperor Henry IV,* and his first novella, *Innocens.* The second part of the tragedy, *Henry's Death,* followed two years later. The monetary rewards were insignificant. Sometimes his humor helped him a little: "What a pity that not a single one of the nine Muses has any inclination for cooking so that she could once in a while feed one of her hungry disciples. That would help me a lot right now."[7]

Saar's greatest disappointment, however, was that no theater was

interested in attempting a performance of his historical tragedy. It was a
critical rebuff which also precluded potentially large financial rewards.
Lack of popular success, poverty, the difficulty of complete concentration
even in a quiet suburb like Döbling near Vienna, disappointment in a love
affair, and the declining health of his beloved mother led around 1865 to a
crisis in Saar's life. Reduced self-confidence slowed down the progress of
two plays (*Thassilo* and *The Two De Witts*) and a novella (*Marianne*); this
crisis fed on itself for about seven years.

"But for the grace of God there goes Saar!" the poet may well have
exclaimed as he created the character of Bracher in *Tambi* (1882).
Although Bracher was modeled after a playwright called Bachmayer,
there was enough of Saar in the character to read *Tambi* as a semi-autobi-
ographical novella. Like Saar, Bracher early attracted attention with a
serious play. Likewise both writers then suffered a crisis of creativity,
which, however, in Bracher's case led to a disintegration of personality
and finally to suicide. Saar, writing a decade after he had overcome his
crisis, must have looked at Bracher's fate with a shudder at what might
have happened to him and with gratitude for what he was able to achieve
instead.

The year 1872 became a turning point. Saar began to receive support in a variety of forms from a number of generous aristocratic patrons.
The death of Saar's mother in that year made it possible for him to accept
an invitation from Princess Elizabeth von Salm-Reifferscheidt to take permanent residence in her castle at Blansko in Moravia. There the poet
found a congenial atmosphere for concentrated work. In the thirty-four
years that remained to him Saar spent more time at Blansko than anywhere else. There the forty-seven year old Saar married Melanie Lederer,
who had translated his novella *Marianne* into French.[8] The marriage was
happy, but soon Melanie fell seriously ill. Convinced that her illness was
incurable, she took her own life after a marriage of only three and a half
years. Saar's letters give evidence of how deeply he suffered from this
loss.[9]

A few months after his wife's death, Saar wrote the poem
"Melanie." In it he sees his wife in a dream and tries to comfort both of
them by saying that they can still live with each other in spirit. The poem
then continues:

> Again you mind our little house
> You tended once with loving hand,
> Adorn the cell of this your poet

Whom none, like you, did understand....
Our covenant became more strong
As, through the years,we strove and won.
Enduring what the world allowed
To happen to us made us one.
And only now that here are gathered
My songs, so dearly loved by you,
Our bond receives its consecration—
As long as they live, you do, too.[10]

Princess Marie zu Hohenlohe, the wife of one of the highest officials at the imperial court, the Princess zu Salm, Josephine von Wertheimstein, and others not only opened their grand mansions to Saar, but also helped him pay his debts and guaranteed him a modest but secure existence for the second half of his life. He never earned a living from his writings. Once forced by necessity to lead an austere life, he continued this lifestyle even when he could have afforded some comfort. He was, however, always generous in helping others.[11]

The difficulty of being the frequent guest of wealthy patrons is mentioned in one of the letters which comprise the first novella, *Marianne,* completed after Saar had overcome his crisis:

Easter is past, dearest Fritz, and gradually the salons of the capital are closing. Oh, how often in the course of this winter have I thought of you and the quiet university town, where you with a small group of enthusiastic students live entirely for your scholarly work, while I, chased around in circles by invitations and social obligation, could not find any rest and concentration, any regular activity. And with all that one is nothing and cannot be anything to all the people who open their glittering reception halls to you! When I would return late at night from some splendid party to my remote suburb, ill-humored and weary, then this confounded idleness always troubled me sorely, and more than once I resolved to break off all relations into which, through my sudden literary successes, I had slid against my will. But how could I have carried out this decision without being downright inconsiderate, without hurting the feelings of people who with the best intentions of being useful by promoting my interests had introduced me into the most prominent circles? And thus nothing was left to me, except sticking it out to the end, for better or for worse.[12]

Perhaps the most important patron and friend in Saar's life was Josephine von Wertheimstein, partly because of her unusual personality, partly because of the nature of her salon in what Saar called the "Golden House," and partly because of the members of her large family, all of whom occupied important positions in the social and cultural life of Vienna. Generations of writers from Grillparzer, Bauernfeld, and Wilbrandt to Hugo von Hofmannsthal were attracted by this lovely and noble lady. In her "salon" this important institution in the cultural life of nineteenth-century Europe found its Austrian equivalent.

Unlike most of the men and women who were drawn into the orbit of the "Golden House" in Döbling, Saar became virtually a member of the family. On birthdays and holidays he appeared in person or sent a letter. He often presented congratulatory verses, as he put it in 1872 in a poem for Josephine's name day, "in order to join in my own way those who in quietly rejoicing tenderness ("in stillaufjubelnder Zärtlichkeit") approach you with fervent good wishes" (III, 55-58).

As Saar grew older, he became increasingly free of financial worries through private and public support. He received an annual ministerial stipend, an annual gift from the Emperor, and a pension from the Schiller Foundation. Yet even in the last decade of his life, when he was widely recognized as a national treasure, he could not have lived on the income that his writings produced.[13]

The elderly Saar received many public honors, of which the poet enjoyed greatly his appointment in 1902 to the Austrian House of Lords ("Herrenhaus").[14] In his last years Saar suffered from poor health. He had to undergo an operation which could improve his condition only temporarily. We find many passages like this one in the letters of those last years: "I really don't know what to do any more—and if my old servant were to fall ill, I would be completely helpless, for a stranger—even if it were a schooled nurse—could not do as much for me as this person who is so familiar to me. If only I'll not get bedridden! So far I am still on my feet."[15] In 1906 his pains grew so severe that he decided to end his life, as his wife had done for the same reason almost exactly twenty-two years earlier. On 23 July 1906 Saar shot himself with his old army pistol; he died on the following day. As he had wished, he was buried in the Döbling cemetery in the city of his birth. The prophecy of his Viennese Elegy was fulfilled: "And where my cradle once stood, will in the end be my grave."[16]

II. THE PLAYS

Saar's life was rich in paradoxes. His failure as a playwright and his success as a writer of novellas were exactly the opposite of what the poet expected. In his generation most writers strove for success on the stage. Other novelists, such as Gottfried Keller and Marie von Ebner-Eschenbach, also made serious attempts to become successful playwrights. It was not sufficient that even a personality like Grillparzer praised Saar's *Emperor Henry IV,* that many lesser judges considered it a remarkable first play, and that even a modern reader is struck by the nobility of its language and the dramatic vigor of some scenes. The play has never been performed on any stage. Saar's other plays *Die beiden de Witt* (The Two De Witts), *Thassilo, Tempesta,* and *Eine Wohltat* (A Good Deed) did not fare much better. One may generalize that in his dramas and lyrical poetry Saar largely followed a tradition whereas as a writer of novellas he pointed ways into the literary future. Today his plays are out of print, but his novellas are reprinted again and again. I will, therefore, devote more space here to the novellas than to the dramas.

One can well understand that the confrontation of two strong historical personalities, the Holy Roman Emperor Henry IV and Pope Gregory VII, and conflicting principles the struggle for hegemony between State and Church would attract a novice playwright like Saar, just as it later attracted another devotee of historical drama, Ernst von Wildenbruch. Moreover, the relationship of Church and State was still, or again, a problem in Austria and was soon to lead in Germany to the *Kulturkampf,* the struggle between Bismarck's government and the Catholic Church.

Here is how Saar's Gregory in a conversation with a church dignitary envisions the place of the church:

> You're wroth with me because with iron fist
> I exercise the pow'r bestowed by God.
> I want the Church as ruler of the world,
> And rule she can't with gentleness and love.
> A diff'rent realm you have staked out for her
> In those too playful waking dreams of yours.
> Dreams are but shadows, and they will not hinder
> My moving forward on my chosen path:
> But should you ever cross me with one act—
> Then woe to you! Before you'd bat an eye,
> I'd smash you.[17]

It is Henry's political dilemma that he faces an ambitious Pope in Italy and rebellious princes in Germany. When Gregory excommunicates the Emperor, the princes renounce their feudal obligation. Thus Henry is forced to cross the Alps barefoot in the winter and to kneel as a penitent in the court of the castle of Canossa, begging the Pope to rescind his ban. Here is part of Henry's monologue:

> And why must I stand thus and bear this shame?
> Why do I not return to Reggio,
> Where waiting for me are the Lombard Lords,
> And lead an army 'gainst this silent fort,
> And drag the Pope as captive home with me,
> Exhibiting this monster everywhere?
> Why not? Because tame caution counsels me
> To fake a meekness which I do not feel.
> With his free will he must revoke the ban,
> With his free will return to me the crown.
> An act of force, interpreted as crime,
> Would forge a new sword for my en'my's use.
> Indeed, I've slid downhill so far by now
> That I cannot regain my father's throne
> Except through vicious lies and through dissembling,
> As loathsome to my frank and open nature
> As to my naked hand the poisonous
> And clammy breed of toads.[18]

The following scene between Pope and Emperor may be more successful theatrically than dramatically. It is night; Gregory appears high up on the parapet of the castle, speaking to Henry far below him in the courtyard. The Pope accuses the shivering man in the snow of only feigning penitence. A real head-on duel between the two world-historic ideas never occurs. This failure of the potentially pivotal scene is perhaps the play's main weakness.

Saar's interest in psychological motivation is evident in this early work. One might almost say that Gregory's austerity is seen in a pre-Freudian light. In a scene with the pious and beautiful countess Mathilde, the mistress of the castle of Canossa, the Pope accuses her of not having sufficiently suppressed her sensuousness, he sends her away to pray and fast until the "sinful reddishness" has disappeared from her cheeks. He tells her to scourge her body, but after she has left, he imagines in a sadistic fantasy that he himself scourges her:

Gregory (looking after her with a distraught expression):

Hand me the whip'—Oh, how her lovely form
Is writhing under my ferocious blows!
The snow-white back contorts in wildest pain—
Her blood spurts up into my burning face,
And, bending down, I kiss her bleeding wounds.
                    (Startled)
My passions ruling me!—who's talking there?
                    (Looking around)
Who's here and sees me thus? There's none but me,
Alone I'm here, and I am my own master.[19]

This outbreak of perverted sexuality in the austere Pope is explained only later when he confesses to Mathilde that as a young priest he loved her but that her love for the young Henry embittered his life. This portrayal of the Pope alone would explain why this play had no chance of being performed in Catholic Austria or in any of the Protestant states of Germany with sensitive Catholic minorities.

The next play, *Die beiden de Witt,* 1875 (The Two De Witts), deals with two stalwart defenders of Dutch republicanism facing the rising monarchic ambition of the House of Orange, while *Thassilo* (1886) deals with the problem of particularism and national unification, an especially burning issue to an Austrian of the 1860s and 1870s. Saar chose as his hero a Bavarian prince who tried in vain to protect his country's independence from Charlemagne's expansionism.

Saar's dramatic protagonists are noble losers rather than tragic heroes, interesting throughout, in a few instances temporarily successful, like Henry IV, but all ultimately vanquished. They are all loyal to a principle and to themselves, Henry to the idea of the dignity of the empire, Thassilo to the rights of traditional local sovereignty, the de Witts to the Dutch republic, and Louis XVI (in an interesting fragment) to the constitution which he has sworn to uphold. Thassilo and Louis are Hamletlike procrastinators. Such a hero is dramatically acceptable on the stage only if he is colorful enough to sustain our interest throughout an evening of delayed action . This is not the case with Thassilo, a much less profound character than Hamlet. It is difficult to write a play about a figure whom history passed by. While Saar was not successful as a playwright, he has left behind plays which are full of dramatic encounters and poetry.

II. THE POETRY

Saar was an eminently subjective poet. His experiences and thoughts, his observations and warnings, his joys and pains are the sources and the subject matter of his poems and novellas. Objective portraits in poetic form were foreign to Saar, as were poems that primarily reflected abstract thought and knowledge ("Bildungsgedichte"). A few of his poems are among the best in the German language, and most are of a respectable quality; all are the fruits of a warm heart, a great sensitivity, and empathy with the suffering of others: the poor, the ugly, the despised. His poetic work is firmly embedded in the tradition of German poetry from Goethe to Lenau and Geibel. Some of it, no doubt, sounds conventional today.

Saar's subjectivity, while universally acclaimed as appropriate for poetic expression of feeling or nature, is not as unquestioningly accepted when opinion and meditation intrude. The following poem is one of the very few by Saar that was translated, although shortened, into English before those in this essay.

Girls Singing

Spring-time: in the evening shade
I was strolling through the vale—
All at once before me strayed
Gentle sounds across the dale.

I drew nearer; all serene
Two were sitting hand in hand—
Maidens as by day are seen
Working in the furrowed land.

And their faces both were brown
From the kissing sunbeams' glow;
Underneath each ragged gown
Bare a sun-burnt foot would show.

But they sang, their heads held high,
Songs that from their bosoms sprang
To the stars that lit the sky,
Sang, and knew not how they sang.

Thus they sang the old, old lays
All of love, its joy and pain,
Heedless, seeking no one's praise,—
Through the wide and lonely plain.[20]

"Herbst" (Autumn) must be ranked among the very best of Saar's poems. Its atmosphere reminds one a little of Goethe's *"Wanderer's Night Song."*

Autumn

Mild and sunny season, whose
Woods are painted, cast in hues
More lovely than the blooming rose,
Autumn gently glows.

Storm and stress no longer rail;
Sounds of longing wane and fail.
Now the calm of soft repose
Deep fulfillment knows.

And yet, one hears a rustling sigh—
Scarcely breathed; muted, shy—
Curling through the leaves, lamenting:
It is ending.[21]

A critic has observed that without the last stanza the poem would be more unified.[22] This seems a purely formalistic judgment; the third stanza, adding a melancholy note and symbolic quality, is particularly characteristic of Saar. On the occasion of his sixtieth birthday Theodor Gomperz honored Saar at the house of his sister Josephine von Wertheimstein with an address in which, referring to this poem, he spoke of the autumnal maturity of the poet's work.[23]

Quite touching is "An eine junge Holländerin"[24] (To a Young Dutch Lady). This is truly a diary page. Written in Rome in the fall of 1873

(Saar's only vacation trip abroad), it describes a chance meeting with a lady in the waiting room of the railroad station. No words are exchanged. The poet sees in the Dutch lady's eyes a longing that all the sights of Rome have not satisfied. Suddenly he feels a passion rising up in him and a certainty that through this woman he could find all the happiness that he had always, without success, been hoping for. The departure signal calls her to her train. In his mind he follows her north through Italy and Germany to Amsterdam, while he is about to leave for southern Italy.

Often Saar's poems give us impressions of casual insignificant occurrences which to the sensitive poet take on an unexpected emotional or symbolic meaning. For instance, "Die Nonnen" (The Nuns): two nuns come to the poet's door to collect donations for poor orphans. One is an older woman with a tired face. "The other, slender, graceful like a doe, her shyly lowered eyes are filled with woe." Her charm moves the poet, the young nun blushes, but they do not exchange a word.[25]

Over many of Saar's poems lies a mist of sadness and deep melancholy, a sense of personal insufficiency which drives the poet into loneliness. "Unmut" (Ill Humor) seems like an echo of the Book of Ecclesiastes and many a baroque poem: "Surely, surely, all is vain, all is fraud and sham—"[26] In the poem "Der Säulenheilige" (The Stylite) Saar speaks of a man who, like the holy penitents of a bygone age, stands on a high column. He suffers the burning sun in the summer and the icy chill in the winter. What moves his heart deeply he can see only from afar. He stands there for many years; the temptation of ending his life by a leap is great, but he shrinks back from this last step.[27]

Compassion with the poor and weak is a major topic in Saar's work. Often the weak are children; "Die Kuh"[28] (The Cow) is an example. The poet takes a walk through the fields. It is an autumn day and he enjoys the refreshing air. Suddenly he sees a cow running away and a little girl trying in vain to stop the animal. A haggard old man shouts at the girl and curses her for her "carelessness." Then suddenly, "lightly dancing, as only cows do," the animal returns to the barn, "ending the girl's misery." "But for me," adds the poet, "the beautiful day was spoiled." There is a refreshing unpretentiousness in this idyllic anecdote written in lightly flowing iambic pentameters.

Saar's poems contain many portraits of women. One type of "modern woman," whose coming Saar found regrettable, was a brilliant but unfeeling person portrayed in the poem "Stella."[29] She is a gorgeous beauty whose appearance and knowledgeable conversation captivate everyone. She is all "brain" and "nerves," but "no heart beats in her tender breast."

> Deep in your secret core you are excited
> Hearing that Master's *Tristan and Isold'*,
> Yet have you never truly been ignited
> By what is deeply felt: man's word of gold.

Thus the ultimate question for Saar is not how true to tradition or open to new ideas a woman or a man is but what integrity of human feeling a person has.

When Saar observed attacks against unnatural social mores and institutions, he could ridicule the more radical forms of women's emancipation. His satire could be witty and even sharp. In the *Wiener Elegien* he observes two "modern" girls:

> Fullest freedom of love you promise—while you and your girlfriend
> Walk with a swagger and sport hair lacking grooming and chic.
> Back of her weighty brow I can see she's eagerly pond'ring
> How the whole genus of men can from the planet be swept.[30]

Saar's political insight is generally not profound but rather conventional. In a letter to Theodor Gomperz he speaks of his "denseness in political matters" ("bei meiner Begriffsstutzigkeit in rebus politicis").[31] Yet his pessimism, especially with regard to the prevailing trends of the last quarter of the nineteenth century, gave him a prophetic sense of the brittleness of his culture and political conditions. His poem "Bismarck's Tod" [32] (Bismarck's Death), for instance, while conventionally praising the statesman's strength, ends with these somber lines: "the Reich's further destinies still rest darkly in the future's lap," words quite unexpected in a poetic necrologue and therefore almost prophetic twenty years before the collapse of the German Empire.

At a time when commercialism had not yet invaded and engulfed the giving of presents to the degree we find today, the congratulatory poem by poets and would-be poets was a treasured gift. Sad events—deaths and funerals—were likewise occasions for the making of poems or speeches. Saar wrote many, and quite a few found their way into his *Collected Works*. The names of those who were thus honored in life and death read like a Who's Who of Saar's biography. Not only birthdays and other special occasions in his circle of friends but also official festivities increasingly stimulated Saar's poetic activity. As he received special gifts and honors from the Emperor, Saar honored Franz Joseph and Empress Elisabeth with works from his pen on such memorable days as the imperial couple's silver wedding anniversary; a festival play *An der Donau*[33] (On The Danube) was performed in the court Opera Theater with great success on 24 April 1879. The four poems Saar wrote on the fiftieth anniversary of Franz Joseph's ascension to the throne in 1898 owe their existence to the whim of the calendar and may not be works of great literary value, but they are witnesses to Saar's patriotism and loyalty to the Monarch to whom the young cadet had sworn allegiance half a century earlier. More importantly, they document how representative a figure Saar had become in his country. At the time of his death, ten years before that of his Monarch, Saar had become virtually the Emperor's and the Monarchy's unofficial court poet.

Throughout his life Saar believed in poetry and art in general as the noblest human undertaking. Bettelheim reported about a never-published series of sonnets in which the young army lieutenant expressed his faith that art ennobles man, overcomes meanness and crudeness, and leads to the highest human values.[34] One is reminded of the idealization of music by the young composer in Hofmannsthal-Strauss's *Ariadne auf Naxos*. It is striking how often the word "heilig" ("holy" or "sacred") appears, especially in the poems of the younger Saar, almost always in connection with art. Even the older poet's "Gefasst"[35] (Ready) ends with the sentence: "To you, oh holy art, did I devote my life" With such words Saar, as writers of German Romanticism had done before him, raised the aesthetic to a quasi-religious sphere. The word "heilig" also appears frequently when nature is described: we hear of a forest that is "sacredly silent," "the summer's holy earnestness," "the creation's holy traces,"[36] and many more references. A sort of pantheistic emotion pervades this poetry.

Saar speaks much of his suffering and bad luck, but his biography reveals neither paranoia nor weakness. We also read much about the need for perseverance; the poet admonishes himself in his verse to be strong so that he can fulfill his poetic mission. One could print such poems and document each one with a parallel letter. The poet begins his "Gebet"[37] (Prayer) with the assurance that in spite of all the suffering he has endured his "tortured heart" has remained "strong and unconquered." He turns to the "eternal powers," praying to be allowed to complete his work. Yet at the last moment the poet is overcome by doubt: will his struggle perhaps end in defeat? In the spirit of stoic resistance to fate is the poem "Mahnung" (Exhortation),[38] in which he advises the reader to turn suffering into a source of deeper self-awareness. Marie von Ebner-Eschenbach wrote to Saar: "Your wonderful poem 'Exhortation' has delighted all those who have a heart for poetry".[39]

The elderly Saar undertook three large poetic works, of which he completed two: *Wiener Elegien* (Viennese Elegies) and *Hermann und Dorothea*. *The Pincelliade* remained unfinished. The fifteen elegies published in 1893 surpass the other works both in terms of inherent worth and of critical and popular acclaim. Here is the first elegy in the meter of the original:

> Hail, I see you again, you shimmering town on the Danube,
> Which already for years only in passing I'd touched.
> Warmly a rural home did surround me, while sternly the Muses
> Ordered collectedness—thus, yielding, I banished myself.
> Now in the ev'ning of life when my labors are almost completed,
> Mem'ry is driving me back, longing is driving me back.
> True, you are no more the city you used to be; time e'er passing
> Ran in an altering course over your houses and streets.
> Old things familiar to me and to which my soul was attachèd
> Vanished; a stranger I've been long to the race living now.
> Still from yon mountain, the Kahlenberg, is the air blowing
> Which as a child I did breathe, which me to manhood did shape.
> Vestiges still can the eye perceive of long elapsed days,
> And they fill with nostalgic delight gently the old poet's heart.
> Therefore my greetings to you! I am yours henceforth and forever,
> You never missed me before, yet do you clasp me in love.
> Listen, I'll sing you a song, the most faithful I of your children,
> And where my cradle once stood, will in the end be my grave.[40]

In this work Saar truly becomes Vienna's *poeta laureatus*. Lament over the loss of the city as he knew it as a pupil and a young man is balanced by the praise of the eternal Vienna. This balance is achieved with great skill. For whenever the historical perspective prevails, the poet regrets the triviality and ugliness of urbanization. But where he follows the cycle of changes during the year, each season with its own attraction and ending with the resurrection of life at Easter time, he forgets the city's and his own old age and celebrates Vienna as it partakes in the eternal renewal of nature: "And in the cycle of life, life is preserving its youth."[41] This mixture of emotions, according to the German aestheticians of the eighteenth century, men like Abbt and Jacobi, characterizes elegiac poetry.[42] Such a dichotomy of feeling we find here. But Saar's feelings are well matched by very precise observation. There is almost a Baedeker quality in this cycle; we may well describe the poems as realistic elegies.

Die Pincelliade, published as a fragment in 1897, is a humorous epic, a satire on army life and human frailty. Pincelli is a tight-fisted army tailor and soldier who falls head over heels in love with a woman of poor reputation. He insists on marrying her, and to the delight of the soldiers their marriage bed is inadequately separated from the soldiers' beds in the large dormitory by a curtain. Let us hear Saar in quite a new tone:

> To whom God loves he gives as special favor
> A faithful wife, which happens to but few;
> The rest of us have here on earth to savor
> The opposite exactly, sadly true.
> Into one body man and wife do grow,
> They say; but with their souls such is not so.
> They end up feeling clearly: they are twain,
> And soon there turns up number three, a swain.[43]

For a while Sofka remains a faithful wife, but when a young, attractive new recruit appears, she cuckolds Pincelli, who is still too smitten with her to take any action. In fact, when her young lover is transferred to Italy, she persuades her husband to move there also, in the hope of finding the young soldier. All this is told with an uninhibited and for its time a bold wit. Overly sensitive or prudish critics have expressed their displeasure.[44] Saar's unexpected ability to write with broad humor and in witty rhymes as befits a mock epic is admirable, even though the work is unfinished and the freshness of the beginning is not quite maintained throughout.

Hermann and Dorothea (1902) is called an "Idyll in Five Cantos." The glow and peace of a wonderful sunset settled on Saar when he wrote this work of his old age. The Homeric and Goethean hexameters demanded and permitted broad strokes of the pen: idealized young lovers guide their destinies to a happy end. There are no great depths and "modern" psychological twists. It is as if Saar, who with age had become more pessimistic and less confident in man's freedom of will, enjoyed creating strong, self-confident, and yet sensitive and lovable people here, in contrast to his other characters.

Just as Gottfried Keller in *Romeo und Julia auf dem Dorfe* (Romeo and Juliet in the Village) transferred Shakespeare's setting of Italian Renaissance patricians to the world of contemporary Swiss peasants and acknowledged this indebtedness by the choice of title, Saar changed the setting of Goethe's story of Alsatian refugees to the world of late nineteenth-century Moravia with its nationality struggle between German-Austrians and Slavs:

> Stored was the harvest already in granaries holding the riches,
> And the sparkling gold of the summer began to turn paler;
> Colorless in the surroundings the stubble-fields
>   shimmered; the roses
> Had on the thorny shrubs of the borders matured into berries,
> And from the scaffolds there rose, aromatic, the scent of the fodder.
> Also that time came around for the feast
>   which the folks of the township,
> Germans, who lived thereabouts ev'ry year
>   came to hold for support of
> Schools in Moravia, Bohemia, with funding provided by Vienna
> So that the sound of their tongue should
>   remain alive for the children.[45]

Saar further strengthened his ties with Goethe's work by having his Dorothea recite from Goethe's work on the occasion of a German festival, thereby giving his Hermann a sense of the girl's nobility and patriotic feeling. However, Goethe's epic is far less a celebration of patriotism than it appears to those Germans in Saar's idyll, a German-Austrian epic written by a poet who, because he had lived in Moravia for so long, knew personally how embattled German culture and political dominance in those areas of the empire were less than two decades before they became part of Czechoslovakia.

IV. THE NOVELLAS

There is no doubt that of Saar's work his novellas have survived best, at least in the German-speaking world. Small and large collections have appeared since 1945. Therefore one would also expect that any awakening interest in Saar among English-speaking readers would begin with his novellas or short stories.

Twenty-six of Saar's thirty-two novellas are "link and frame" stories ("Rahmenerzählungen"); a narrator, generally an "I," meets someone whose story is then disclosed to him. Sometimes there are two narrators when it is unlikely that the primary narrator could have had access to the whole story. One would have to analyze the function of the narrator or narrators in each novella individually, but a rough generalization would suggest that a narrator adds an ambivalent quality to the narrative. As an "eye-witness" he adds a quality of objectivity within the framework of fiction, and on the other hand the story is subjectively tinged by the narrator's personality, purpose, and prejudices. Hence this device causes the story to float in the twilight zone between pretended objectivity and real subjectivity. Saar published novellas over a period of forty years. I propose to delineate the changes in his outlook by sketching some comparisons between his first and last, *Innocens* (1865) and *Die Pfründner* (1905, The Poor House Folk). In the first of these (like his first drama a remarkably good work for a beginner), the narrator, obviously Saar in service as a young officer in the Wyschehrad citadel outside Prague, meets Innocens, a priest who lives a secluded life and serves a little church within the citadel. Innocens is an enlightened priest who spends his free hours with scientific studies, and he and the narrator become good friends. Before the narrator leaves the citadel to go with his regiment to Italy, where the war of 1859 has just begun, Innocens tells him the story of the great crisis of his life. Years ago he had fallen in love with a young girl, and only after an inner struggle did he regain the strength to remain faithful to his priestly vow. Resignation is the theme of this story. The ideally drawn priest finds happiness by serving his chosen profession; he remains true to himself by exercizing his free will in overcoming his temptation. There prevail in this novella harmony and optimism, the belief that man can shape his destiny. The work is rooted in a prerealistic romanticism. My own criticism would be only that the speeches are a little too formal and stilted.

How different is *The Poor House Folk*, one of a series called *Tragik des Lebens* (1906, Tragedy of Life). Karl Schirmer, once a well-to-do businessman but now impoverished, and Rosi Weigel, once his maid, meet again in the poorhouse after many years of drifting apart. Both of them have had unhappy marriages and lives, Karl because he is a weak-willed and easily intimidated man. Years before he had loved Rosi but, unable to make a decision, had failed to end his marriage to an unloved and unloving woman. Now he and Rosi dream of a life together. Quite unexpectedly Karl is informed that he has become the beneficiary of a family trust. The chance of escaping the hated poorhouse now seems real. But then Karl is so provoked by his roommate, an envious bully, that a fight ensues in which Karl is fatally wounded. Rosi dies years later in a "house of charity."

In *Innocens* we find no evil or even low-spirited character. In the late novella, on the other hand, the good-natured but not very bright main characters try in vain to maintain themselves against a crowd of hateful, envious, and jealous people. The poorhouse is a shark pool in which a quasi-military hierarchy gives an ex-convict the power to boss his roommates. Human weakness and strength are seen as innate or results of experiences over which people have no control, while chance plays a large role for good or evil. Illness and poverty are powerful and cruel forces. Like European literature, Saar has traveled in forty years from a prerealistic to a naturalistic age and style. The stilted speech of Innocens has given way to conversations in dialect.

Marriage to the "wrong person" appears so frequently in nineteenth-century fiction that one might say that society almost programmed many men, and particularly women, to lasting unhappiness. Trivial circumstances often lead to the wrong marriage. The heroine of *Marianne* (1873) and her sister marry early in order to escape from their parental home, which a quarrelsome stepmother had come to dominate. Society, which had no place for a respectable woman outside her parents' or husband's home, forced girls into bad marriages. Marianne's husband is an unimaginative and humorless pedant. When she meets the writer A., the author of the letters which comprise the story, a warm friendship develops.

Marianne, like some of Saar's most attractive women, is not very educated but has a rich spontaneity of feeling, sometimes unfulfilled. Marianne admits to A. that she is ashamed of her ignorance: "You are wrong," I exclaimed, overwhelmed by the simple grandeur of this confession, "you are wrong, Mrs. Dorner! For you have preserved that spontaneity which in women is more delightful than all knowledge of the earth!"[46] This echo of Faust's conversation with Gretchen—there is another such echo in *Ginevra* (1892)— must not blind us to the fact that Saar's late-born Gretchen does not have the health of her Storm-and-Stress predecessor; Marianne suffers from a weak heart, and several other of Saar's women characters show pathological traits; Ludovika in *Die Geigerin* (1877, The Violin Player) and Elsa in *Geschichte eines*

Wienerkindes (1892, Story of a Viennese Child) are only two examples.

A. knows that Marianne loves him, but, like Innocens, he chooses resignation. That evening A. writes: "I stayed behind in the dusk, alone with my feelings in which pain and bliss were wondrously interwoven." This mixture of contradictory emotions dominates *Marianne* and many of Saar's other novellas. Determined to respect the integrity of Marianne's marriage, A. accepts a call as librarian in a remote castle. On the night before his departure, he and Marianne dance together. And now finally they allow their passion to express itself in the ever-accelerating waltz:

> I drew Marianne to me; I bent my head toward her; my mouth brushed against her hair, her forehead. She let it happen and looked at me, smiling. And more and more closely we held each other; our cheeks, our lips touched; our breaths flowed into one. Thus did we glide along,—ecstatic, blissfully intoxicated— between heaven and earth. Suddenly it seemed to me that she was stumbling. My arms wanted to support her; but I myself was tottering. She slid slowly down my side, her head hanging backwards, her eyes staring vacantly. A sudden horror tore at my heart; I heard shrieking all around me and the music breaking off with a shrill dissonance; I saw people rushing toward us from all sides—the room began to turn, and I lost consciousness.[47]

When A. regains consciousness, he learns that Marianne has died.

Saar is particularly good at the portrayal of characters and landscapes. He is obviously more a man of the eye than of the ear; references to painters and sculptors appear frequently, those to musicians rarely. Since the famous painter August Pettenkofen was a cousin of Saar's, we may assume that the poet had perhaps inherited an observant and artistic eye. [48]

Saar's fiction turns up quite a few eccentric characters whose anomalies the writer describes with detached amusement or pity. *Leutnant Burda* (1887, Lieutenant Burda) deals with an officer whose *idée fixe* is his firm belief that a certain princess, a member of the highest nobility, reciprocates his love for her. What is to the reader clear evidence that the princess is quite indifferent toward Burda "proves" the opposite to him. His wishful dreaming leads him into ever deeper jungles of self-deception. His desire to impress his princess gets him involved in a conflict with his comrades which is bound to end in several duels. Burda faces them with valor; it may have been the courage of Don Quixote who took on whole armies.[49]   Burda is mortally wounded in the very first of these duels.   On his deathbed he wonders for a fleeting moment whether the love of the princess was only his illusion, but he dies with his belief intact.   On the day of his funeral the newspapers publish the announcement of the Princess's engagement.

An eccentric of a different sort is the Italian-born captain in *Conte Gasparo*, (1897, Count Gaspar), who combines an "unusually strong attraction to the female sex" and "a not very outstanding intelligence," an ironical understatement.   These qualities lead him into many embarrassing situations that provide scenarios for Saar's sense of humor and wild irony, rare in his novellas.   We read that the captain with his forget-me-not-blue eyes and fox-red moustache is smitten with the wife of the barber in a Moravian garrison town and that he "was seen in the barber shop more frequently than the growth of his beard and hair required."[50]   The unmartial Count wins short victories in bedrooms but loses his modest possessions and his will to live in the long run.   Yet we cannot deny our sympathy to this likable man with his grotesque absence of common sense.   Eventually he falls so far that a shot from his army revolver seems to him the only way out of his dilemma.

We are amused and satisfied at the same time when a lecherous older man's unwelcome sexual advances are frustrated.   The inspector in *Der Brauer von Habrovan* (1901, The Brewer of Habrovan), who has long planned to seduce the pretty young brewer's wife, seems close to satisfying his desire.   From a favorable but uncomfortable position in a tree he watches her undress in her bedroom.   We can appreciate the inspector's feelings when he suddenly sees a beermaker with a goatish appearance sneak into the bedroom, where he is received amorously by the woman.   All the frustrated man can do is to throw a handful of sand against the window of the "sinners."

A very subtle, one might almost call it a philosophical, type of humor pervades *Herr Fridolin und sein Glück* (1894, Fridolin's Good Luck).   Fridolin is a servant in a castle, who has risen in the service of the count through honesty, talent, adaptability, and industriousness until he is indispensable to his master.   He seems happy in his marriage even though his energetic wife Katinka keeps a careful eye on him when he drinks with his friends in the local inn.   The narrator, who knows him as a dutiful and unemotional man of common sense, is therefore quite surprised one day to hear Fridolin tell the story of his past: as a younger man he fell in love with Milada, a girl who gained so much power over him that she forced him to propose marriage. Since she had served time in a penitentiary, Fridolin could not marry her and keep his job in the castle. The couple agreed to elope and to emigrate to America. All the plans were made, but Milada did not appear at the appointed place and time. Instead Fridolin received a letter saying that she had decided to accept a marriage proposal from an older man. Feelings of love, jealousy, and relief alternated in Fridolin. In the long run it was mainly relief. The tale ends with the narrator's ironic remark that Fridolin's story "did, to be sure, not prove the power of his passion, but that of his luck."[51]

The story at first poses as a serious philosophical discussion about human luck. Schopenhauer, Saar's favorite philosopher, is quoted as saying that "the so-called lucky people only seem to be lucky or are so only by comparison." The exceptions are rare and serve as a sort of "decoy bird" (Lockvogel).[52] There is humor when after this serious introduction the poet proceeds to tell the story of this down-to-earth valet, who reminds one at times of Figaro without that factotum's rebelliousness. Humorous also is how Fridolin, who confesses to have been before his marriage "what in women one calls a virgin,"[53] is manipulated by women, first by Milada, who almost derailed his good luck, then by the Countess, who arranges his marriage to Katinka, and then by Katinka herself; and yet Fridolin does not emerge as a dupe. The spirited tale bears its dark philosophy lightly.

From the eccentric to the alienated is only a short step. *Seligmann Hirsch* (1888) is the story of an elderly Jew whose loud and obtrusive behavior makes him a disagreeable nuisance to everyone. It is a tribute to Saar's skill that in the course of the story he arouses our sympathy for the rich but lonely man, as we learn how his daughter treats him like a King Lear and his ambitious son openly shows that his Polish-born father embarrasses him in the upper-class circles into which he is moving. Years after the narrator has met Hirsch an acquaintance tells him at a charity ball that Hirsch committed suicide. He points out a baron as the extremely rich son of the old man and, as a beautiful young girl dances by, he remarks: "Voilà: the granddaughter of the late Seligmann Hirsch."[54] Most stories by Saar have a sad or tragic end; *Marianne, Tambi,* and *Seligmann Hirsch* are the rule, *Innocens* and *Fridolin* the exception. Saar motivates his characters' downhill road with great care. The general Jewish destiny, the discrepancy between wealth and the little training in living with it gracefully, and the generation gap created by different degrees of social and cultural assimilation explain much of Seligmann Hirsch's ruin.

Likewise social decay, as we encounter it in *Die Troglodytin* (1889, *The Troglodyte*), is also well motivated. Maruschka Kratochwil is the daughter of a drunkard who, heavily in debt, loses his modest cottage; the family, abandoned by the community, settles in a cavernous depression in the forest. Maruschka is neglected, never learns how to work, and is finally sentenced to a year's service in the penitentiary for theft. When she is free again, a young forester who is attracted by her beauty helps her to find work, but she soon quits. Begging and roaming the woods is her idea of the good life. She contrives to meet the forester in the woods and tries to seduce him. Attracted and repelled, he resists. When a house in the village burns, the suspicion of arson falls on her. The court acquits her, but the mayor manages to have her committed to a year's forced labor because her "incorrigible aversion to work" allegedly makes her "a danger to public morality and general safety."[55] After a year Maruschka returns to the village as a changed woman: "The once strong and slender figure had taken on an unhealthy bloated heaviness and in her pale puffed-up face lay that indescribable feature of dreary dullness which is characteristic of most inmates of penal institutions."[56] Filled with a desire for revenge against the mayor and with resentment against society, Maruschka really sets fire to the mayor's house, and other houses catch fire too. At the edge of the forest, overlooking the burning village at night, the forester and Maruschka meet again:

At the same moment we felt a terrible, hot gust of wind which sent us both staggering; the trees behind us moaned and groaned, and new flames darted out of the dying fire. "Ha, ha," she cried with shrill laughter. "You see, Heaven is on my side! It is burning again—it is burning!" ... She shouted with wild joy, pulled out the bottle, and drank greedily, her head bent backwards and her arms raised high. "Yes, now they will fry—all— all who got me into the workhouse. Oh, how I suffered there! I don't want to work, I don't like to work, I can't work, and whoever forces me to is my enemy; I'll hate him, and I'll kill him!" Like a brandy-drunk maenad she began to dance around me in clumsy, ugly leaps. I grabbed her roughly and forced her to stand still. ... She threw herself down and writhed at my feet. "Or, no, rather kiss me!" she cried, jumping up. "Do you think I don't know that you liked me? That you were in love with me? Yes, in love! At that time—don't you remember?

You were ashamed, and that's why you didn't follow me like a dog. That's why you didn't snatch me up in your arms. Do it now that everything is over! You must!" Like a wildcat she jumped up and clung to me as if she wanted to strangle me, while her thirsty lips sought mine. "Come," she gasped, come with me into the forest! There it is night—no one sees us—come! come!" Still furiously embracing me, she tried to drag me along with her. I made all possible efforts to free myself— it did not work; I would have had to use utmost force. And in spite of all my disgust and loathing, in spite of the fear of her that now gripped me, I felt a sudden rush of my blood, my senses threatened to get confused.[57]

Fleeing the police, the desperate girl disappears in the woods. She is not captured. In the following spring her frozen corpse is discovered as the snow melts.

In order to show the wide range of Saar's psychological portraits we turn from this gypsy-like arsonist, perhaps his most primitive character, to Klothilde von Gunthersheim in *Schloß Kostenitz* (1892, The Castle of Kostenitz), perhaps his most morally sensitive woman. We move from a hovel in the ground to a refined castle. The young Baroness and her middle-aged husband, retired from high government service, live in a happy marriage. Their quiet idyllic life is disturbed when soldiers are garrisoned in the village near the castle and the Baron reluctantly consents to offer quarters to their officer, Count Poiga. Klothilde is disquieted to discover, especially after she has observed the cavalry captain's virtuoso horsemanship, that the self-assured manliness of the young, handsome Poiga has impressed her. One day in the castle park the Count, with the skill of the experienced lady's man, tries to force his attentions on Klothilde. She flees in horror and accuses herself of perhaps having unintentionally encouraged the man's desires. As she tells her husband what has happened, she speaks of herself almost as though she had violated her marriage bonds. She falls ill; the physician diagnoses a brain fever. She dies a few days later.

Klothilde's moral sensitivity is equaled by her husband's. As he ponders his sudden misfortune, he wonders whether by marrying a much younger woman he had not started the chain of events that led to her death. Yet, if he had not married her, another would have. Who can say that she would have been happier?   What does one ultimately know? "Yes, a human life cannot be calculated in all its possibilities."[58]

Saar originally meant to call this novella *Baroness Clotilde*.[59] By changing the title the author indicated his intention of giving more than just the story of his heroine, namely the biography of a castle from 1849 to almost the end of the century. After Klothilde's death the Baron donates his castle in his last will to the local village "for the establishment of beneficial public institutions." After twenty-five years a rich industrialist acquires and modernizes the property: "A new, more solid, self-confident generation"[60] now lives at Kostenitz. The surrounding locality has also changed: from a feudal village with a rural population has grown a town which benefits from the handsome price that the nouveau-riche industrialist paid for Kostenitz.

As Saar unfolds this miniature history, he reaches the limit of a novella and almost produces what he always said was beyond his ability, a novel. When he rejected suggestions to write a novel, he generally said a novelist had to have an analytic talent which he found missing in himself.[61] His weakness or lack of interest in this respect may be described as an inability or lack of desire to accumulate and organize large amounts of historical, sociological, and other materials, to interrelate many characters, and to portray major characters in breadth and depth. His goal was to seek brevity and precision, true virtues of the writer of novellas. A detailed analysis of each of his works of fiction would show how every sentence has its proper place in the whole. Saar does not engage in the luxury of making detours.

In the last decade of his life Saar was very productive. As he grew physically more infirm, suffering from illness of the eyes and the intestines, he wrote more and more easily. However, his last novellas are all pessimistic stories of human decay, misery, self destruction, and ugliness. *Die Brüder* (1901, The Brothers) contains a thoroughly wicked character. *Der Burggraf* (1899, The Castle Count) lets us trace the decline of a retired officer to utter poverty and sickness, a man who displays a strange mixture of bigotry, "boundless aristocratic arrogance," and "an unbelievable lack of self-respect."[62] *Der Brauer von Habrovan* (1901, The Brewer of Habrovan) is the story of a man who is so shaken by his doubts of whether his child is really his that he ends his life by suicide.

In all of these late novellas Saar reveals a growing interest in the darker side of the complex psyche. This after all was the decade in which Freud wrote his first major work. *Die Heirat des Herrn Stäudl* (1902, Mr. Stäudl's Marriage) is a case in point. A man on trial for having strangled his wife tells the judge that he had never been much interested in women but that when he was promoted to be head gardener of an estate he got married mainly because he thought it was appropriate for a man in his position. When this seemingly unemotional and conventional man believes that his wife has betrayed him, he strangles her in a paroxysm of jealousy, hatred, and lust. That he expects the jury to find him innocent adds an almost humorous note.

In a letter to his patroness, Princess Marie zu Hohenlohe, Saar wrote: "Every one of my novellas represents a piece of contemporary Austrian history. It is quite incomprehensible that critics have not noticed this—or at least have not stressed it."[63] Complaints about this indifference of the Austrian public to his work are a leitmotiv in Saar's letters. He sounds like a disappointed lover, but he never gave up wooing his countrymen with his writings. Students of Austrian cultural history can easily make their own lists of Austrians who suffered from their countrymen's indifference or hostility from Mozart to Freud.

V. SAAR'S WELTANSCHAUUNG AND PERSONALITY

Velle non discitur (Seneca)

The intellectual and artist in the modern class society is uncertain of his social position, but Saar was even more so, floating between classes. He tasted the life of a pauper and in later life was associated with high nobility. Having been born into the lower nobility and having joined the officer corps at an early age, he would never identify himself with the lower class to which, at least as a young man, he belonged economically. In his attitude toward the proletariat and the dispossessed of all varieties he expressed the noblesse oblige of an aristocrat and the compassion of a Christian, a man whose vivid imagination made him capable of empathy with all those in material and spiritual distress.

Novels and novellas that dealt with workers were still fairly uncommon in Austria when *Die Steinbrecher* (*The Stone Breakers*) appeared in 1874. Saar clearly states why he wrote it. He says that most of those who travel over the Semmering line will never bother to think of those hard-working men and women who built it "without enjoying the blessings of progress themselves." He has not written, he says, in order "to paint in glaring colors the hard life of these pariahs of society or to describe what role the so-called fifth estate might be playing in the future but only "to show how sorrow and pleasure move every human heart and that the great tragedy of the world is everywhere reenacted in a small way."[64] Depending on one's point of view, one may praise Saar for raising his proletarians to the level of human beings all of whom are ultimately alike in ecstasy and suffering. Or one may criticize the poet's conservatism for watering down the specific social substance of working class existence in the generalities of "human" feelings.

Saar was intensely aware of growing social tensions that industrialization brought in its wake. He knew the lot of seasonal workers who suffer intense deprivation much of the time. The following poem is an example:

Night Scene

The man who goes alone there
Has neither roof nor bed.
He spreads his things about him
On corners dim instead.

Beside him on the sidewalk
Neatly, he thinks, are spread
A row of grimy bottles
And meager bits of bread.

From time to time he stretches
His fingers numb with chill
Above a seething stew-pot—
The night is raw and still.

And soon there comes a-marching
With heavy steps and sad
A throng of shivering people—
Folk, hungry and ill-clad

Of those who eat and drink here,
Beware, my friends, beware.
The bread that here they're breaking
Feeds pain, distress, despair.

The wine that they toss down here,
It is an evil brew
Which in their brains' confusion
Turns into anger's stew.

Beneath the loathsome kettles
Glow coals whose force unfurled
Will spread the sparks of hatred,
Igniting all the world.[65]

Saar is aware of the possibility of a social revolution; he had lived through the socio-political revolution of 1848 even though he was too young to understand what was going on. Perhaps, however, the poet was naive to expect revolutionary action from the *lumpenproletariat* which he described in this poem. Marie von Ebner-Eschenbach wrote to Saar that she especially liked those of his poems which, like *Night Scene,* have "a socialist hue."[66] We may, however, question her choice of the word "socialist" in this context.

In contrast to this explicit description of what threatens the social order, unrest from the lower classes is sometimes merely implied in Saar's poems. The alienating dullness of menial work is shown without any commentary by the writer in the following poem:

The Brick Factory

Far-flung dreary wasteland stretches—
  Dirty-yellow water puddles—
Lonely does the furnace smoke-stack
  Rise above the rotten woodsheds.
Sallow people, as if kneaded
  From the sallow loam, the soil,
Which they dig in, do in silence
  Year by year their dreary labor:

Filling empty bins and buckets,
  Mixing, treading, smoothing, planing,
Thus repeating, stern and sullen,
  Sameness of the brick forever.

Wearily pass by the hours;
  Melted into dust and heat
Or dissolving into mire,
  Here the world seems at an end.[67]

How the economic system estranges man from nature and his fellow man is told in a very simple poem, "The Strawberry."[68] The poet describes a child who picks strawberries but suppresses a desire to eat a few in order to earn a little more from selling them. The green-grocer pays as little as possible for the strawberries, and they are finally eaten by the well-to-do. Thus, says the poet in the last stanza, even the generous gift of loving nature becomes merchandise and is perverted to serve the greed for profit.

A Count Erwin appears in *Dissonanzen* (1900, Dissonances) and in *Die Familie Worel* (1905, The Worel Family). In both stories he discusses socialism. While the Count in the earlier story talks about socialism in an arrogant and even hostile tone, he speaks with much empathy about it in *Die Familie Worel*. Referring to the labor dispute in progress between his own family as employers and their workers, he assures his conversation partner that even a small wage increase could wipe out any profit. He continues: "But perhaps there is no need for profit. For it is only the workers who keep the enterprise going—and why should they have to provide profit to the Roggendorfers through their labor? They could take over the plant themselves and carry on."[69] Has the Count, to some extent Saar's spokesman, changed his mind between 1900 and 1905? Hardly. The difference is motivated by the context of the two passages. In *Dissonanzen* we find Erwin in a discussion with a scholar who takes the socialist position, which Erwin opposes. In *Die Familie Worel* we hear about a labor dispute, and the structure of the plot forces the writer to put some defense of the workers into the Count's mouth since he is their only available advocate. But there is more here: Saar and the Count were essentially conservative, but, like the English Tories or Bismarck, they felt a certain obligation as aristocrats toward the lower classes. This attitude may represent partly a carry-over from feudal morality, partly a political strategy to forestall social and political unrest. In any case, it is remarkable that a member of the Austrian House of Lords had enough imagination to have a fictional character defend the position that workers could run factories by themselves.

Saar was not a systematic thinker but a poet given to meditation on human destinies and ultimate purposes. Although trained in a Catholic school, conventional religious views did not satisfy him. He was greatly influenced by the scientific thinking of his times and traced the causes of his characters' actions as far back as he could. He believed that physiological studies would eventually enable us to understand the motives of our actions, which are partially veiled from view. In this spirit Saar chose Seneca's words, "Velle non discitur" ("Willing cannot be learned"), as the motto of his drama *Tempesta* (1881). Again and again this question of causation puzzled and even tormented him. Here, as an example, is the end of his *Geigerin* after the talented musician has drowned herself:

> "So tell me," he continued, "how it came about that this lovely girl, equipped with all the good qualities of her sex, which others know so well how to take advantage of, threw herself away on unworthy men; how it came about that, in a ridiculous reversal of conditions, she was trying to take care of those whose duty it was to take care of her—until, still so young, she ended her life so miserably. Why was she not as clever and good as her sister Anna, now a happy wife and mother? Why was she not as clever and bad as her sister Mimi, now traveling the world as a chanteuse, showered with gold and diamonds? Why? That is the great question which neither our philosophers and moralists nor the stilted characters of our modern playwrights know how to answer. It will not even be solved when the physiologists know how to trace every thought, every word, every action to a corresponding fiber of the brain, to this or that twitching nerve, and to the more or less perfect function of a certain organ. But once it is recognized that man is nothing but a mixture of mysteriously working atoms determining his fate from the embryonic state on, then, I believe, it will be realized that, in spite of all intellectual achievements it is better not to live!"—[70]

The knowledge that there are hidden links in the causal chain leads to a moral, not merely an intellectual, obligation to abstain from superficial judgment. Here is a passage referring to the compulsive woman-chaser, Count Gasparo: "The world, in a hurry to judge, might call him an old weak-brained Satyr, but I, who always secretly took pride in penetrating more deeply into the soul of a person, I could not allow myself to judge this way."[71]

The question, why did this happen?—why do some people master the complexity of life while others are crushed by its forces—a question insistently asked in the work of Saar—is in the novellistic realm the same problem which philosophers and theologians from Jeremiah and Job through Leibniz and Hegel to the thinkers of our own age have kept pondering: the problem of theodicy. What emerges from Saar's conviction that man's actions are largely removed from his free will is a pessimistic world view; its basis was probably laid in his childhood, youth, and early manhood when poverty, an unfulfilling army life, and literary failures were Saar's lot. Early in his life an encounter with Schopenhauer's writings seems to have given focus and intellectual dignity to Saar's attitude based on experience and observation. Living in an increasingly crisis-ridden age, suffering from what he sees as his country's decline, and distraught over his own misfortune—the early death of his wife after a short happy marriage and his long illness—the older Saar became ever more deeply pessimistic. Saar showed a melancholy which, according to Alfred von Berger, is "the heritage of all the more profound and more sensitive spirits in Vienna, which allegedly is so merry and jovial."[72]

But there was also another Saar; life-loving, fond of fun and the pleasures of life. Early photos show him as a handsome, dashing man.[73] Friends relate how merry and playful he could be when he felt at home, especially with children, and how on festive days he improvised plays and all kinds of humorous entertainment.

It is only consistent that a determinist would follow the principle that to understand all means to pardon all. Saar, however, set up ideal moral goals with old-fashioned rigor. In his poem, Höchstes Ziel (Highest Aim),[74] he says that man should strive and struggle to understand his own self; he who has not successfully practiced self-recognition cannot judge another; much evil in this world flows from self-deception.

A determinist is inclined to believe that we judge others too harshly. After Dr. Trojan, the unlicensed physician in the novella Dr. Trojan, has escaped through suicide what to him would be worse punishment, Dr. Hulesch remarks: "In any case, the punishment here was greater than the crime. But who knows whether that is not always the case."[75] Here we see in one sentence Saar's humane personality, a man lenient with others yet demanding of himself. In the same spirit he addresses in free rhythms a warning word "to the strong ones," to those who enjoy power and the goods of the world:

Thus never may cross your lips
The horribly thoughtless word of the Pharisee:
"Through your own fault."
Lovingly rather extend your helping hands
And raise those whom they yet can reach,

So that they may walk among you,
Blissfully grateful.[76]

Notes

1. Ferdinand von Saar, *Sämtliche Werke in zwölf Bänden,* hrsg, von Jakob Minor, (Leipzig: Max Hesses Verlag, n.d. (1908)), VIII, 51. All quotations in this essay are translations from this edition. The Roman numeral refers to the volume, the Arabic numeral to the page.

2. *Widmungen zur Feier des Siebzigsten Geburtstages Ferdinand von Saar's,* hrsg. von Richard Specht, (Wiener Verlag, 1903).

3. Ella Hruschka, "Ferdinand von Saar." *Jahrbuch der Grillparzer-Gesellschaft,* 12. Jahrgang, (Wien, 1902), p. 138.

4. Richard Schaukal, "Ein Meister der Novelle," *Das literarische Echo,* XVI, (May 1906), 1114.

5. F.v. Saar, *Heinrichs Tod,* V, 130.

6. I. 29.

7. Letter from Saar to his friend, Friedrich Marx, 26 April 1869, as quoted in Ferdinand von Saar, *Marianne,* kritisch herausgegeben und gedeutet von Regine Kopp, (Bonn: Bouvier Verlag, 1980), p. 73.

8. Ibid. p. 124.

9. Letters to Princess Marie zu Hohenlohe of 31 July 1884, and 5 June 1885, as quoted in *Fürstin Marie zu Hohenlohe und Ferdinand von Saar: Ein Briefwechsel,* hrsg. von Anton Bettelheim, (Wien, 1910) (hereafter cited as Hohenlohe Correspondence with dates of letters and no pagination).

10. II, 156 f.

11. Letters to Theodor and Elise Gomperz in this writer's possession.

12. VII, 75f.

13. I, 172.

14. ib.

15. Letter by Saar to Elise Gomperz of 31 July 1905, in the possession of this writer.

16. IV, 11.

17. V, 26.

18. V, 82.
19. V, 80.
20. Translated by Margarete Münsterberg and published in *The German Classics*, edited by Kuno Francke, Albany, N.Y., 1914, vol. 18, p. 292. This is the only text by Saar in this essay which was not translated by Alice R. Bergel and Dorothy Augustine for this publication. The original poem is entitled "Die singenden Mädchen" (II, 34f.).
21. II, 33.
22. Robert Mühlher "Ferdinand von Saar, Ein österreichisches Dichterleben zwischen Vormärz und Moderne," *Jahrbuch der Grillparzer-Gesellschaft*, Dritte Folge, elfter Band (Wien: Bergland Verlag, 1974), p. 58.
23. I, 142.
24. II, 96ff.
25. II, 171.
26. II, 45.
27. II, 48f.
28. II, 130f.
29. II, 142f.
30. IV, 23.
31. Letter of 18 February 1906, in the collection of this writer.
32. III, 68.
33. II, 201-213.
34. I, 24f.
35. II, 117f.
36. II, 19; II, 20; II, 30.
37. II, 52f.
38. II, 51f.
39. Marie von Ebner-Eschenbach's letter to Saar of 24 November 1876, as quoted in *Briefwechsel zwischen Ferdinand von Saar und Marie von Ebner-Eschenbach*, hrsg. von Heinz Kindermann (Wien: Wiener Bibliographische Gesellschaft, 1957).
40. IV, 11.
41. IV, 15.
42. Theodore Ziolkowski, *The Classical German Elegy*, (Princeton,,

1980).

43. IV, 98.
44. An example is R. Latzke in Nagl-Zeidler-Castle, *Deutsch-österrei-chische Literaturgeschichte*, (Wien, 1930), vol. III, p. 1089.
45. IV, 43.
46. VII, 93.
47. VII, 105.
48. VII, 115f.
49. IX, 68.
50. X, 207f.
51. X, 58.
52. X, 11.
53. X, 46.
54. IX, 115.
55. IX, 151.
56. IX, 154.
57. IX, 151ff.
58. IX, 338.
59. IX, 275.
60. IX, 345.
61. I, 159f.
62. XI, 76.
63. Letter of 8 February 1889, in Hohenlohe Correspondence.
64. VII, 114.
65. II, 178f.
66. Letter of 19 January 1882, as quoted in *Briefwechsel zwischen Saar und Ebner-Eschenbach.*
67. II, 36f.
68. II, 37.
69. XII, 12.
70. VII, 196f.
71. X, 231; similar ideas are raised in XII, 50 and IX, 337f.
72. Alfred von Berger, *Buch der Heimat* (Berlin, n.d. [1910]), vol. II, p. 316.
73. The third volume of Ferdinand von Saar, *Das erzählerische Werk,*

(Wien: Amandus-Verlag, 1959), reproduces five photos from different periods of the poet's life.

74. II, 122f.
75. X, 199.
76. II, 76f.

Selected Bibliography

I.   *Works by Ferdinand von Saar in German*

Kaiser Heinrich IV. Ein Deutsches Trauerspiel in zwei Abteilungen,
    I. *Hildebrand* (1865). II. *Heinrichs Tod* (1867).
Innocens (1866).
Marianne (1873).
Die Steinklopfer (1974).
Die beiden de Witt. Trauerspiel in fünf Akten (1875).
Novellen aus Österreich (*Innocens, Marianne, Die Steinklopfer, Die
    Geigerin, Das Haus Reichegg*) (1877).
Tempesta, Trauerspiel in fünf Akten (1881).
Gedichte (1882, 2. Auflage 1888).
Drei neue Novellen (*Vae Victis, Der Exzellenzherr, Tambi*) (1883).
Thassilo. Tragödie in fünf Akten (1886).
Eine Wohltat. Volksdrama in vier Akten (1887).
Schicksale (*Leutnant Burda, Seligmann Hirsch, Die Troglodytin*) (1889).
Frauenbilder (*Ginevra, Geschichte eincs Wienerkindes*) (1892).
Schloß Kostenitz (1892).
Wiener Elegien (1893).
Herbstreigen (*Herr Fridolin und sein Glück, Ninon, Requiem der Liebe*)
    (1897).
Die Pincelliade. Ein Poem in fünf Gesängen (1897).
Nachklänge. Neue Gedichte und Novellen (*Doktor Trojan, Conte
    Gasparo, Der Sündenfall*) (1899).
Camera obscura (*Die Brüder, Die Parzen, Der Burggraf, Der Brauer von
    Habrovan, Dissonanzen*) (1901).

Hermann und Dorothea. Ein Idyll in fünf Gesängen (1902).

Österreichische Festdichtungen (1903).

Camera obscura (Zweite, um fehlende Stücke vermehrte Auflage: *Außer Dienst, Die Heirat des Herrn Stäudl, Der Hellene*) (1904).

Tragik des Lebens (*Die Familie Worel, Sappho, Hymen, Die Pfründner*) (1906).

Sämtliche Werke in zwölf Bänden. Im Auftrag des Wiener Zweigvereins der Deutschen Schillerstiftung mit einer Biographie des Dichters von Anton Bettelheim herausgegeben von Jakob Minor. (Leipzig: Max Hesses Verlag, o. J. (1908)).

Das erzählerische Werk. Gesamtausgabe, Hrsg. von Josef Friedrich Fuchs. (Wien: Amandusverlag, 1959), 5 Bände.

Requiem der Liebe und andere Novellen. Hrsg. und eingeleitet von Hans-Heinrich Reuter (= Sammlung Dieterich Nr. 220). (Leipzig: Dieterich, 2. Auflage, 1965).

Fürstin Marie zu Hohenlohe und Ferdinand von Saar: Ein Briefwechsel. Hrsg. von Anton Bettelheim. (Wien: 1910).

Briefwechsel zwischen Ferdinand von Saar und Marie von Ebner-Eschenbach. Hrsg. von Heinz Kindermann. (Wien: Wiener Bibliophilen-Gesellschaft, 1957).

Ferdinand von Saar: Briefwechsel mit Abraham Altmann. Kritisch herausgegeben und kommentiert von Jean Charue. (= *Ferdinand von Saar, Kritische Texte und Deutungen.* Hrsg. von Karl Konrad Pohlheim. Erster Ergänzungsband). (Bonn: Bouvier Verlag Herbert Grundmann, 1984).

Briefe an, von und um Josephine von Wertheimstein. Ausgewählt und erläutert von Heinrich Gomperz, 1933. Für die Drucklegung neu bearbeitet und hrsg. von Robert A[dolf] Kann, 1980-1981 (= Österreichische Akademie der Wissenschaften. Phil.-hist. Kl., Sitzungsberichte, 390. Bd.).

II.   *Works by Ferdinand von Saar in English*

"The Stonebreakers," in Patten, William, ed., *Short Story Classics*, vol. III (New York: Collier, 1907).

"The Troglodyte," translated by Marie Busch, in: *The World's Classics*, vol. 337 (London: 1928).

"Girls Singing," translated by Margarete Münsterberg, in: Francke, K., ed. *The German Classics*, vol. 18 (New York: about 1914).

III.   *Secondary Works in English*

Daviau, Donald G., "Herrmann Bahr to Ferdinand von Saar: Some Unpublished Letters," *Monatshefte*, (November 1961), 285-290.

Hodge, James Lee, *The Novellen of Ferdinand von Saar: Anticipations of Twentieth Century Literary Themes and Techniques*, Dissertation (Typescript). (Philadelphia: Pennsylvania State University, 1961).

Plater, Edward M. V., "Ferdinand von Saar's *Schloss Kostenitz*," *Modern Austrian Literature*, vol. 16, no. 2 (1983), 19-35.

IV.   Major Studies in German

Aspetsberger, Friedbert, "Die Typisierung im Erzählen Ferdinand von Saars," *Zeitschrift für deutsche Philologie*, Bd. 87, Heft 2 (Mai 1968), 246-272.

Berger, Alfred von, "Meine Beziehungen zu Ferdinand von Saar" (=A.v.B., *Buch der Heimat*, Bd. 2, pp. 255-269 (Berlin: o.J., [1910]).

Bettelheim, Anton, *Ferdinand von Saars Leben und Schaffen* (Leipzig: Max Hesses Verlag, o.J. [1908]). (This is vol. 1 of the *Sämtliche Werke* listed above. It is the only comprehensive biography of Saar).

Haberland, Detlef, "Ferdinand von Saar und das Judentum," *Cosmographia Spiritualis*, Bonn 1984, pp. 17-51

Hruschka, Ella, "Ferdinand von Saar," *Jahrbuch der Grillparzer-Gesellschaft*, Jg. 12, pp. 77-139 (Wien: 1902).

Kretzschmar, Hadwig, *Ferdinand von Saar. Eine Zusammenstellung der seit seinem Tode erschienenen Ausgaben seiner Schriften und der Literatur über ihn und sein Werk.* (=Bibliographische Hefte. Hrsg. von Bibliothekar-Lehrinstitut des Landes Nordrhein-Westfalen, Heft 4; Köln: 1965).

Latzke, Rudolf, "Marie von Ebner-Eschenbach und Ferdinand von Saar," in *Deutsch-Österreichische Literaturgeschichte*, Hrsg. von W. Nagl, J. Zeidler und E. Castle, Bd. 3, pp. 1036-1091 (Wien: 1935).

Minor, Jakob, *Ferdinand von Saar, Eine Studie* (Leipzig und Wien: 1898).

Mühlher, Robert, "Ferdinand von Saar. Ein österreichisches Dichterleben zwischen Vormärz und Moderne. Mit einem ungedruckten Brief

Saars," *Jahrbuch der Grillparzer-Gesellschaft*, Dritte Folge, ll. Band (Wien: Bergland Verlag, 1974), pp. 11-72.

Polheim, Karl Konrad, ed. *Ferdinand von Saar: Kritische Texte und Deutungen*.

Bd. I *Marianne*, ed. Regine Kopp (Bonn: Bouvier, 1980).

Bd. II, *Die Geigerin*, ed. Heinz Gierlich (Bonn: Bouvier, 1981).

Bd. III, *Seligmann Hirsch, ed. Detlef Haberland (Tübingen: Niemeyer*, 1987).

Bd. IV, *Innocens*, ed. Jens Stüben (Bonn: Bouvier, 1986).

Polheim, Karl Konrad, Hrsg., *Ferdinand von Saar: Ein Wegbereiter der literarischen Moderne* (Bonn: Bouvier, 1985).

Felix Salten

Lore Muerdel Dormer

Felix Salten, born Siegmund (Zsigi) Salzmann, known to many as the author of *Bambi*, by fewer as the early friend of Schnitzler and Hofmannsthal and the archenemy of Karl Kraus, left an oeuvre of reviews, essays, novels, novellas, and plays so voluminous that *Das große Groner Wien Lexikon* calls it "nearly impossible to survey."[1] And just as most of his works were forgotten, many facets of his biography became so obscure that to this day major encyclopedias give faulty information, even about the date of his death.[2]

The only thorough dissertation, by K. Riedmüller, which researches Salten's life and works, and two others dealing with specific areas of it were never published.[3] This study hopes to provide the first accurate biography of Salten as his life intersected those of more famous contemporaries during a highly decisive period of European political and cultural history and also to examine his most important works.

Born 6 September 1869 in Budapest, Salten was brought to Vienna when he was four weeks old. References to his difficult childhood and youth in several biographies seem to make him kin to the many half-illiterate immigrants arriving in Leopoldstadt and struggling to climb to fortune or social prominence. In contrast, the Salzmann ancestors had been rabbis for many generations, and the wealthy, renowned family of his mother, Maria Moskovia, from whom he seems to have inherited his love of art and music, had connections to Hungarian nobility (W). The problems Salten's family encountered stemmed from the mercurial nature of his engineer father Phillip, whose ill-conceived business enterprises never worked out (R).[4]

The family settled in the suburb of Währing, where the little boy, second youngest of eight children, attended elementary school. The first of Phillip's financial set-backs had already occurred in Hungary, so they lived among the poor. however, since the parents' marriage was very close and the children were loved, Salten's early childhood still held happy memories (W). At that time his father saw the future of the Jews in their international cultural integration and did not believe in any religious education for his children (W), so Siegmund, the only Jewish pupil in his class, became completely absorbed in the Catholicism of his surroundings (R). This experience accounts for his ability to describe later in his Viennese stories religious happenings with true insights. However, after he transferred to the Gymnasium [university preparatory school], he became aware of his Jewishness, proud of its traditions, and later an admirer of Theodor Herzl, the founder of Zionism.

Following a conflict with one of his teachers, Salten left the Gymnasium after only three grades and never returned. His family's fortunes were also at their lowest ebb: the Saltens had been evicted from their apartment and had to lodge in hotel rooms (R). So at age sixteen, with the help of an uncle, young Siegmund found work with the Phoenix insurance agency, and together with an older brother Emil was able to rent an apartment for the family. But the job turned out to be very boring for him. He started to write short stories and poems during his work, hiding them under a blotter, and peddled his creations after hours to several Viennese newspapers. Annoyed with the family's absorption in his older brother's poetic writings, he secretly started publishing under several pseudonyms, the most successful among them Felix Salten, which eventually became his legal name.

After losing his position with Phoenix, Salten started to make his living as a journalist for different papers. While working on the editorial staff of *An der schönen blauen Donau*, he me Arthur Schnitzler, who introduced him to his friends Richard Beer-Hofmann and Hugo von Hofmannsthal. Soon Salten became a regular of their well-known circle of Café Griensteidl.

All published correspondence of the Young Vienna group—Leopold von Andrian, Hermann Bahr, Richard Beer-Hofmann and Arthur Schnitzler—testifies to the fact that Salten attended many of their planning sessions and social events.[5] His journalistic connections and theater reviews played an important part in the advancement of their ideas. On 7 July 1891, together with Schnitzler and Hofmannsthal's father, he was among the first executive committee of the association *Die Freie Bühne*, which, like Otto Brahm's theater in Berlin, had been modeled after the théâtre libre in Paris (R).

As the fame of the Young Vienna group increased, so did the circle of its enemies, the most prominent being their one-time member Karl Kraus, who in 1897 took the demolition of the Café Griensteidl as the opportunity for his famous attack on his peers in *Die demolirte Litteratur*. Kraus's satire was particularly hard on Salten, whom he pictured as a copycat of his aesthete friends and incapable of good style in his writing: "An upstart of manners who has copied his literary table companions in everything and owes to them his knowledge of the most important gestures. . . he never needed to go far for new literary themes. He always wrote about that which his famous friends had in their works. . . Sorely tried in the service of journalism, the writer has been able to retain his individuality to this day. He still succeeds with the undiminished vigor of his youth in confusing the dative and accusative."[6]

Severely offended, Salten cornered and bodily attacked Kraus, deepening an enmity that would accompany him through many years, as seen in numerous issues of *Die Fackel* (The Torch).[7] Kraus's deep-seated hostility may well have been rooted in envy: he was small in stature and had failed as an actor; while he later found ardent followers among young existentialist and appreciation for his evenings of recitations, he was at first an outsider of society. In contrast, Salten, handsome and elegant far beyond his means, played the man about town, so secure in his manners that he became a friend and trusted confidant of the imperial dukes of the Toscana line (R,W).

This tendency to high living pushed Salten deeply into debt. Added to his own financial problems were obligations taken over from his father's bankruptcy and care for two illegitimate children (R). For several years he worked frantically for several newspapers, most importantly the *Wiener Allgemeine Zeitung*, to increase his output of reviews, their wordiness and repetitiousness a testimony to his being paid by the column. However, Salten's work for *Die Zeit* was important in gaining the breakthrough for the ideas of Jung-Wien; for example, his necrologue for Emile Zola on 30 September 1902, characteristic of his vivacious style, won him the respect of his colleagues: "What is poetry? They all assured us: a monster [meaning Zola] has crawled out of the sewers of the metropolis. Later, however, the following generation grasped the [true] meaning: A poet had descended into the depths of existence"(W). Salten also effectively supported the cause of modern art, particularly the work of Gustav Klimt.

A marked change occurred in Salten's personal life with his marriage in 1902 to Ottilie Metzl, a Burgtheater actress who had been fired because of Salten's attack on the director Paul Schlenther. She seems to have combined understanding for his work and tolerance for his episodes of violent temper with talent for domestic management, and she helped him to overcome his most catastrophic financial crisis: the stillborn attempt to establish the cabaret *Zum lieben Augustin*: "Around the turn of the century at the Theater and der Wien I experienced with a cabaret performance the greatest flop of my existence and the most striking demonstration of my unpopularity with the Viennese press. Maybe some of the harsh criticism dealt me was not completely unjustified. However, because of me Franz Lehár appeared for the first time on the stage, in a duet; in addition, Frank Wedekind, playing the lute, sang his classical *Brigitte B*. and other [works]. The *Neue Freie Presse* wrote: 'A certain Mr. Wedekind sang songs of idiots for idiots' "(W). An ill-conceived business contract with his two financial backers left Salten alone to shoulder the ensuing debts (W).[8]

In 1906 Salten accepted a leading position as editor for the *Berliner Zeitung* and the *Morgenpost* where his talent at managing news came into its own. When word of the big San Francisco earthquake arrived after working hours and the printers refused to set type, he accomplished the task himself. However, after a time in the Prussian capital he came to dislike the police state of William II and returned to Vienna and a better position with *Die Zeit* (R).

The years up to World War I brought success with the publication of his stories and his essays on important personalities of his time, with performances of his plays, the Bauernfeld-Prize in 1912, and happy domesticity (his children, Paul and Anna-Katherina, were born in 1903 and 1904). In her memoirs[9] Brigitte Fischer, the daughter of his friend and early publisher Samuel Fischer, tells fondly of her childhood holidays with Salten's family and his special gift of relating to children. Her parents, particularly her mother Hedwig, a talented musician, enjoyed his companionship and his congenial, enthusiastic personality during their times together in Berlin and later during summers at the Berghof in the Vienna woods.

When the war began, Salten, already contributing part-time to the *Neue Freie Presse*, was working for the *Fremdenblatt*, Emperor Franz Josef's favorite source of information, and was thus exempted from military service. He joined the friends of his youth, Hofmannsthal and Bahr, in supporting the war effort, all satirized by Karl Kraus in his superdimensional drama *Die letzten Tage der Menschheit (The Last Days of Mankind)*.10

Salten was not blind to the atmosphere at court: He was a trusted friend of the Archduke Leopold Ferdinand, the brother of Louise of Saxonia-Coburg, whose flight with her lover in 1902 had created an international sensation. The author had followed the pair in his press reports and had written articles in Louise's defense. Yet in spite of his detailed knowledge of aristocratic cabals he stayed loyal to Franz Josef (R).

However, his articles for the *Neue Freie Presse* show his growing understanding for the uniqueness of this war, in which personal heroism was replaced by the battle of the armament industries, and for its threat to all levels of civilization: Even while he still waved the flag of triumph in 1915 ("Wiedererobert, [Retaken], *Neue Freie Press*, 6 June 1915), he deplored the loss of young life: if mankind could become truly sensitive to all the unhappiness and suffering, "no one would ever start a war" (*Neue Freie Presse*, 4 April 1915). In 1917 he touched upon the tremendous changes which had occurred since the beginning of the war, that summer's experience "like a thunderstorm clearing the air." But then "no one was capable of imagining that we should be looking back to these first days from a distance of 3 years and would still be at war. . . . A daemonic role in this war is played by modern technology. . . the tremendous danger of its instruments has become a seductive lure" (*Neue Freie Presse*, 29 July 1915). And in the summer of 1918, he once more reflects on the summer of 1914 and the great loss since then: "Human work can accomplish much in four years. But one single hour of artillery fire, a group of airplanes dropping bombs, can destroy the work of four years. Destruction is as fast as lightning, human work as slow as a germinating seed. For four years, work has stopped, destruction is rampant. Summing up is easy, but the result is too monstrous to comprehend" (*Neue Freie Presse*, 28 July 1918).11

While his friends mourned the loss of the empire, he seems to have been more profoundly disturbed by the devastation the war had wrought on the culture of the Western world during a time of isolation among its foremost proponents. He clearly expressed these sentiments in a contribution to the *Neue Freie Presse* of 2 February 1919, written as a fictitious letter to an American friend: "For years, we have known of each other only what the general-staff reports told us. The representatives of the mind, to which you now want to turn, men of arts and science, have lived, thought, worked, and created for years in two different worlds, and each of these separated worlds was only a fragment of that large world which once before encompassed all work of science, every research activity of the mind, all beauty of artistic creation as a whole. . . . These two groups of peoples, together the leaders and builders of the world, have been forced for five years to live without each other. . . . even though it betrays their mutual task in this world. This is unprecedented and irresponsible."

Even during a time of hunger, epidemics, and political upheavals, Salten's feuilletons for the *Neue Freie Presse* and *Fremdenblatt* far from being the frothy creations often associated with the genre, testify to his efforts to assist in the rebuilding after the war. He demanded artistic freedom and the financial resources to return to nightly stage performances and pointed out the special need to preserve the best of art, music, and theater in this now so small relic of the former empire. (*Fremdenblatt*, 25 December 1918, 5 January 1919). For those who now return from the battlefield to school he wants the support and understanding of the educational authorities. Reflecting on a student rally (*Neue Freie Presse*, 22 December 1918) he demanded careful rethinking of the educational structure and new emphasis on the value of education: "The old government went to ruin because of its sin against the mind. Only if it relies on the [powers of the] mind will the new government be able to attain a happy existence. Formerly education was suspect. . . . not necessary for a career. Today, we experience the consequences: the missing leaders. . . . In the future, it must once again count for an honor, at least for a recommendation, to be an educated human being. It is one of the most important tasks of the new government to support this goal."

During the 1920s and early 1930s Salten was at the height of his career as a journalist: the *Neue Freie Presse*, Vienna's leading newspaper, now became his main employer, and he was made editor of the Sunday feuilleton, a great honor. On 6 September 1929 his sixtieth birthday, he received the congratulations of his writer friends: Richard Beer-Hofmann, Max Brod, Sigmund Freud, Gerhart Hauptmann, Hugo von Hofmannsthal [apparently written ahead of time, before Hofmannsthal's death on July 15], Arno Holz, Heinrich Mann, Thomas Mann, Arthur Schnitzler, and Friz von Unruh, among others, published in the 1930 *Jahrbuch* of the Zsolnay Verlag, which also issued a jubilee edition of his collected works. Honored was a writer filled "with most fruitful curiosity," a person of great sensibility and empathy but still of splendid independence of thought. Salten's most treasured gift may have been that of his home town: in recognition of his services to the City he was made an honorary "Bürger" [citizen] of Vienna (R).

Most importantly, a new direction in Salten's writing brought him world-wide recognition: from his earliest youth he had been a passionate hunter, but when he became more mature—most likely also under the impression of the excessive slaughter seen in Austrian imperial hunting photos—Salten grew deeply concerned with the treatment of animals and the protection of wildlife.[12] So, while nearly all works of his friend Schnitzler still dealt with the past era, Salten wrote fewer Austrian stories after the end of the war and turned to the description of nature.

Bambi, the life-story of a fawn who develops into a proud stag among his woodland friends, serialized in 1922 in the *Neue Freie Presse* and first published by Ullstein in 1923, became an international best-seller because it was related to the world-wide "back to nature" movement. People of all war-weary countries, deeply aware of the "struggle for survival" and longing again for innocence and simplicity, found their emotions reflected in Salten's book. It was widely translated and unfortunately completely typecast its author. Salten's journey to America in 1930 with a group of colleagues, at the invitation of the Carnegie Foundation, solidified his international standing: celebrated as the author of *Bambi*, he met many leaders from all fields of public and artistic life and was received at the White House.

Salten's great concern for international communication led to his eager participation in a new authors' association:[13] The P.E.N. Club had been founded in 1921 on English initiative by Amy Dawson Scott. Its first international president John Galsworthy, the well-known author of the *Forsyte Saga*, had been able to attract a world-wide following. In 1923, Arthur Schnitzler first headed the newly founded Vienna chapter, and in 1928 Felix Salten assumed the presidency. He became the leader of many festive social gatherings, all ridiculed by Karl Kraus, and organized P.E.N.'s 1929 international congress in Vienna (R).

This continued interest in P.E.N. contributed fatefully to the most severe crisis of Salten's life in connection with the 1933 international P.E.N. conference, held May 25-28 at Ragusa—now Dubrovnic—in Yugoslavia. The congress convened shortly after the German Nazi government had assumed power on 30 January 1933. Organized by the newly founded Ministry of Propaganda under its cunning leader Josef Goebbels, and spurred on by the rivalry between the two student associations, the DSt [Deutsche Studentenschaft] and the NSDStB [Nationalistischer

Deutscher Studentenbund], the takeover of the universities had started in the "Aktion wider den undeutschen Geist" [Action Against the Non-German Spirit]. On 10 May in Berlin and several other cities, the carefully orchestrated demonstrations were followed by burning the books of many Jewish and leftist writers. However, not all universities complied: both universities of the state of Württemberg, the university of Tübingen, and the Technische Hochschule of Stuttgart, refused to participate.

At the time of the Ragusa conference things were still very much in flux, and the German delegation used the confusion to depict the book-burning as the action of an extreme Nazi faction. Right from the start the representatives of the individual chapters were divided concerning the proper course of action in response to the events in Germany. In the end the faction demanding immediate action won out, and the conference climaxed in a heated confrontation, followed by the walkout of the Nazi delegation.

Salten, continuously reappointed to the presidency of the Vienna chapter, headed the Austrian delegation. The assignment was ill-fated from the start: since 1932 the Vienna chapter had been dominated by its right wing under Friedrich Schreyvogl, and it had pledged all its delegates to absolute political neutrality. In addition, Grete von Urbanitzki, who shared with Salten the leadership of the Vienna delegation, was an early Nazi follower, a party member, and had already shown her support of the new Nazi government in a letter to the international headquarters of P.E.N. To add further to Salten's problems, John Galsworthy had died on 30 January 1933, and the politically more militant Herbert G. Wells was now international president. Salten was devoted to his late friend and took as his legacy Galsworthy's stand of absolute neutrality for P.E.N. in all political matters, a policy which had been established during times of frequent political changes.

As reports of the conference—a significant share of them unconfirmed rumors—appeared in the international press, Salten was seen as a traitor to his race in having sided with the Germans and was accused of disloyalty because the books of his late friend Arthur Schnitzler were among those on the pyre.

The cynical remarks of his longtime enemy Karl Kraus were particularly crucial in creating this Salten image: the issues of *Die Fackel* in 1933 dealing with the Ragusa conference were not released then because of Kraus' fears for his informants in Germany. But his comments resurfaced as part of his collected works in the volume *Die dritte*

Walpurgisnacht[13] published by Heinrich Fischer (1952-1955), just as the former exiled writers were working to reestablish the literary life of Vienna. They worshipped Karl Kraus and uncritically accepted his judgement of Salten. One example of several: Salten was pictured as naive and disloyal to his race in having stated at the conference: "I am a Jew, and in Germany I have never been questioned concerning my racial origins." Kraus cleverly took this quote out of context. Salten, rising from his front row seat, had shouted during the tumultuous departure of the Germans: "I said that I had always and everywhere professed to be a German Jew, that my prior existence in friendly relationship with German poets and writers had been possible without questioning each others' racial origins. The assembly could appreciate my emotions regarding the present situation in Germany. In spite of it I had tried to make it possible for the German delegates to remain at the congress because of my loyalty to the tenets of the P.E.N. club which were now endangered."

Recent studies have attempted to investigate the events of Ragusa more objectively,[14] establishing that Salten was definitely no Nazi sympathizer and in contrast to Grete von Urbanitzki had not joined the German walkout. However, he had opposed the confrontational policy of Herman Ould, who had brought matters to a head in his famous two questions, asking "whether it were true that the Berlin P.E.N. chapter was taking away the membership rights of members with Communist or similar leanings and was thus violating one of the basic rules of P.E.N. to stay out of politics." Ould's wording of the second questions was unfortunate, because the conference was not obviously deeply involved in politics. These and other clumsy parliamentary procedures enabled the Germans to declare that their leaving the conference was not a political protest but one concerning "breach of protocol," and through their clever tactics they acquired a much larger, politically motley, crew of followers.

Salten had supported an earlier resolution sponsored by Belgium but rarely mentioned in secondary literature, which seemed to have succeeded in bringing the German delegates to account for the actions of their new government. But at the same time it had tried to prevent a direct confrontation with them. Salten explained in his defense that he had favored this milder resolution, hoping to shelter those writers in Germany whose livelihood was at that time in immediate danger. A friend of two major Jewish publishers, Samuel Fischer and Paul Zsolnay, both deeply involved in the literary output of Austrian writers, Salten had recognized the threat to their publishing empires better than many of his colleagues.

Moderation in order to gain time could still be justified in 1933, for because of the well known disunity in its ranks, the survival of the new government in Germany was for many observers still in question: in the spring of 1933 Hitler's hold on power was not yet absolute, a fact literary historians seem to have long overlooked: it took another year, the murder of Ernst Röhm and his faction on 30 June 1934, the death of Hindenburg on 2 August, and the oath of allegiance by the armed forces to Hitler alone on 6 August 1934, to establish National Socialism for the duration.

In the aftermath of the Ragusa conference, Salten was exonerated at the General Assembly of the Vienna P.E.N. chapter on 28 June 1933, but a declaration of solidarity with the German colleagues—worded to be even "milder" than the Belgian resolution at Ragusa—started the break-up of the chapter: Robert Hohlbaum, Conte Corti, Franz Spunda, and Mirko Jelusich left the club. In the following months it lost more and more of its members who sympathized with the new German powers. As Hilde Spiel pointed out in her description of the time,[15] it was often difficult to clearly identify the fronts during the Dollfuß and Schuschnigg regimes. Salten who had acted as caretaker of P.E.N. Vienna, was unable to prevent the break-up of the chapter, and he finally joined his publisher Zsolnay in leaving the club.

The politically turbulent times coincided for Salten with those of personal tragedy: in 1937 the death of his son Paul, a cutter in the young film industry, following a car accident (W) and, after the German take-over in 1938, the loss of his job with *Neue Freie Presse*. Salten's spendthrift ways may have saved his life: after marching into Vienna, the Germans were in the habit of confiscating the houses of wealthy Jews and sending their owners to concentration camps, where few of them survived. Salten had never managed to save enough to buy a home, and when the Germans came to his rented house, Pepi, the resolute longtime family housekeeper, was able to fend them off (W). In addition, Salten's many friends in America seem to have used the influence of the U.S. embassy to protect him (R). However, without income of any kind Salten, like all Jews remaining in the city, found himself in more and more humiliating circumstances (W). Finally, his daughter, a Swiss citizen by marriage, was able to arrange his emigration to Switzerland; Salten, his wife, and Pepi settled in Zürich, where he lived for the rest of his life. References to a time of emigration in America—New York and Hollywood—in important sources of documentation[16] are incorrect: Salten's trip to America in 1930 was his only journey to the New World (W).

His permit to settle in Switzerland prohibited work for newspapers, magazines, radio, and even lectures at universities. While the author's publishing firm Zsolnay eventually returned his rights, his new publisher Müller would accept and reissue only animal stories (W). So his Viennese tales and essays were forgotten, and his important novel *Ein Gott erwacht* (A God awakens)[17] conceived during the turbulent last year in Vienna, was never published.

The great success of Walt Disney's film version of *Bambi* in 1941 brought no direct financial reward for Salten. He had sold the motion picture rights in 1933 to the producer Sidney Franklin, who passed them on to Disney.[18] However, the film led in turn to new issues of the book, and the success of *Bambi* enabled Salten to sell several less perfect animal stories.

While Salten spent his exile in reasonable comfort—his daughter had been able to bring most of his valuable furniture and his important files to Switzerland—his grief over the loss of Vienna and of his prestige as a well-known cultural leader changed his once sparkling personality to that of a taciturn old man, particularly after the death of his wife in 1942 (W). But he never became bitter and especially enjoyed his relationship with children and the many letters they wrote to him in celebration of his seventy-fifth birthday (R,W). In a public address at a memorial service for his friend Max Reinhardt in Zürich,[19] he recalled once more the splendors of the past, but he died on 8 October 1945 without having seen Vienna again.

Several popular encyclopedias cite 1947 as the year of Salten's death, a sign of astonishing negligence.[20] Certainly these two additional years of life would have helped the author to defend himself against the severe and largely undeserved criticism by the powerful Kraus faction and to obviate the fateful consequences to his literary reputation. Salten's life and works need reevaluation. His characterization of Carl Torresani in one of his essays on well-known contemporaries could be applied to himself: "One could now say: `He was a gifted author of trivial literature [Unterhaltungsliteratur], a swift writer of stories, high-spirited, and amusing.' One could write down all these words of a literary necrologue, could stress, however, that he certainly did not possess a superior talent, for artistic creation. . . . But that would mean to fall short pedantically in appreciating the gifts of a very vibrant personality."[21]

The best of Salten's essays, stories, and plays on Vienna await rediscovery, and many more deserve translation. The knowledge of his works should make it possible to allot him his rightful place in Austrian literary and cultural history.

B. Works

In the *Festschrift* published in honor of Felix Salten's sixtieth birthday Hugo von Hofmannsthal describes him and his writing with special sensitivity: "We do not see him struggling to formulate a special passage, a metaphor, a caption. Immediacy of life itself, rhythm which springs from emotion, give power to his style. . . stronger than the design of the characters, stronger than the invented plot is his empathy with youth, with old age, with illness, with health, empathy for pride, power, misery, animal existence."[22]

The term "animal existence" celebrates the internationally known author of *Bambi*, but its inclusion in Hofmannsthal's reflections also touches upon important characteristics of Salten's work: he looks at the world with the eyes of a born hunter: his attention aroused, he stalks his prey and relates the action in vivid spontaneity. He is at his best, often even better then his more famous friends, where he relates careful observations, weakest where he has to invent. Thus Salten's special contributions to the literature of Jung-Wien are his closeness to life and the vivacity of his style.

Carefully structured and polished craftsmanship of writing was not Salten's main concern, and no special maturation process seems to be noticeable in his works. Some of the author's earliest essays and stories are among his best.[23] For this reason they will not be discussed in chronological order but in their thematic interrelationship and their link to contemporary, particularly Viennese, literature and society. The select bibliography at the end of this chapter contains the most important publishing dates.

1. Reviews

In his profession as a journalist Salten wrote numerous articles which were reprinted in many different papers—the majority of them theater reviews in Vienna—not for a select group of connoisseurs but for the general public. Salten seems to have understood how to converse with his readers: his judgment was sought and valued, most of all in his home town.

In her recent thesis on Salten's theater reviews, Ingrid Kunz identified "the closeness of each individual work to life" as the most important criterion of Salten's evaluations.[24] Instead of giving a merely intellectually founded critique, the reviewer has to confer this interrelationship of art and life on his reader, and he needs to reorient his own evaluation of art continually on life itself. While Salten admired Naturalism, which had rediscovered actuality and brought new impulses to acting, directing, and stage design, he required more of the dramatist: his work should also show life in greater intensity and bestow on his audience concepts of timeless value which the author called "erhöhtes Leben" (heightened life).

Salten has been criticized for his lack of cutting commentary, by most considered a necessary tool of any reviewer, but his craft cannot be understood without the setting in which it developed and to which most of his reviews relate: the Vienna Burgtheater. In 1922 Salten defined its ancient tradition and the development of a special characteristic style at the "emperor's own theater."[25] It became an institution which in its excellence could withstand the rise and fall of diverse movements and directors, the only German language stage to be compared to the Comédie Française.

The Viennese public was very knowledgeable. News about the theater and the lives of actors and actresses was uppermost in everyone's interest, inexpensive standing room tickets were affordable for many, and general expectations were awe-inspiring. Beginners needed encouragement, and Salten helped advance many careers. But he also engaged several times in fierce journalistic battles with directors who, in his opinion, did not measure up to preserving the valued tradition, to renewing it in a nurturing manner, and who did not take proper care of the talented artists in their charge.

Of all directors Salten most admired Max Reinhardt and his unique gifts: he appreciated a genius who could grasp the innermost core of a poetic work, reveal its significance, and draw from it effects never realized before: "No one equaled him [Reinhardt] in discovering the talent of an actor and continuing in guiding him to surpass himself in searching for his most hidden innate capabilities. No one but Max Reinhardt perceived in his own musicality so faultlessly the musicality of every poetic work. No other possessed the masterful creativity to make a given stage setting an integral part of the action." Reinhardt in turn appears to have been so appreciative of Salten's support that on occasion he delayed the first night of a play when Salten was out of town.[26]

Salten's ideas of reviewing can best be found in the preface to his collected essays, *Geister der Zeit*, (1924, Modern Movers and Shakers) and in *Dialog vom Kritiker* (1921, Dialogue of a Critic), a conversational introduction to volume 1 of *Schauen und Spielen*[27] (1921, Viewing and Performing), his own selection of reviews and some essays on famous artists and writers in two volumes.

Most important in the first volume are Salten's critiques of dramas by Schnitzler and Wedekind. His reflections on *Frühlings Erwachen* (*Spring's Awakening*), performed for the first time in Vienna but known for fifteen years in print, testify to the validity of his judgment in stressing Wedekind's specific contributions to modern drama. Outstanding among the discussion of five dramas of Schnitzler—*Der Ruf des Lebens*, (*The Call of Life*), *Der einsame Weg* (*The Lonely Way*), *Zwischenspiel*, (*Intermezzo*), *Das weite Land*, (*The Vast Domain*), and *Der junge Medardus*—is the review of *Der einsame Weg*; starting with a motto taken from Hofmannsthal's famous play *Gestern* (*Yesterday*) Salten's concomitant reflections on the circle of Jung-Wien represent one of its most moving documents. "It [the drama] contains the legacy of a generation which has given to literature many great and important works of beauty. It will give witness that it was. . . marvelous to live in this world, but that it was... not easy at all to exist at a time when feelings of friendship and love were shy and sparse. . . without happy impulses of giving. . . It was a time which spoke very much, maybe too much, of death, but it had forgotten the word, taken from Oscar Wilde, . . . 'the mystery of love is greater than the mystery of death.'"[28] The five critiques of dramas by Gerhard Hauptmann are not from his Naturalistic period for which he is now best known, because Salten could identify better with Hauptmann's later works. Reviews on the famous Scandinavians Ibsen and Strindberg and on Wilde, Shaw, and Tolstoi round out the volume.

The second volume—many of it essays on minor authors and plays—is of lesser importance for those interested in Austrian literature except for a review of Hofmannsthal's play *Jedermann* (*Everyman*), now performed traditionally at each Salzburg Festival. In a more thoughtful way than Karl Kraus's thematically related and better-known treatise on the *Welttheaterschwindel* (World Theatre Swindle).[29] Salten questions here the transposition of a medieval play into their time without sharing its inner commitment and shows that even the friends of Hofmannsthal's youth had problems in accepting the creative changes in his work after the turn of the century.

A stylistic bridge between the report of a journalist and the form of the essay can be seen in Salten's two travelbooks. *Fünf Minuten Amerika*[30] (*Five Minutes of America*), describing his one (and only) trip to the United States in 1930, shows him at his vivacious best in meeting new people in new surroundings. His thoughtful observations—examples are descriptions of the wide-open West, the slaughterhouses of Chicago, a visit with Henry Ford in Dearborn, the problems with prohibition, and race relations in the South—represent valuable documentation, even for Americans themselves.

Equal attention should be given to the author's travelbook on Palestine, *Neue Menschen auf alter Erde* (*New Men on Ancient Soil*).[31] Published in 1925 and written from a Zionist's point of view, it gives an informed account of the conditions in the country after the first settlers took over, of their expectations, ideals, and their great contrasts in education and national background. Anyone interested in understanding the present conflict between Jews and Palestinians could profit by reading this book.

2. Essays, Novellas, and Novels

In connection with his work Salten met many important figures of his time. His essays should be rediscovered, and quite a few deserve translation. Many readers used to the concise, carefully balanced masterpieces of his contemporaries might find Salten at first lengthy and often repetitious. But, just as in brass rubbings many not clearly directed strokes finally result in startling likeness, he creates surprisingly vivid pictures. An outstanding example is his essay on Lueger, the well-known mayor of Vienna,[32] which represents a prophetic case study of a Hitler-like character. In his charismatic charm interlaced with brutality, this demagogue sensed the lack of leadership in the lower classes during the 1880s and 1890s among the misery and overcrowding of the suburbs: "There comes this man and slaughters—after all his other tricks went astray—a Jew in front of the howling masses. On the speaker's podium he verbally slaughters him, verbally stabs him to death, tears him apart, and throws him as a sacrifice to the people. This is his first monarchical-clerical action: to direct the general discontent towards the Jewish ghetto, where it may let off steam. A thunderstorm has to cleanse the decayed air of Vienna. He lets it descend on the Jews. . . and everyone draws a breath of relief."[33]

Of equal importance for historians is, in the same collection, Salten's essay on the founder of Zionism who deeply influenced the writer's spiritual development (movingly expressed in two chapters of the Palestine travelbook).[34] His sensitive description of Theodor Herzl's complex character can enhance even a specialist's understanding of the movement and the roots of its future troubles.

Unfortunately not included in later editions of Salten's essays, the best in *Geister der Zeit*, is his early collection *Wiener Adel* (1905, The Viennese Nobility),[35] which paints a daring picture of decay at the highest levels of society. In "Zwei Typen" he pictures in "Graf Sandor" the nobleman who callously plays to the sensation-seeking of the masses, and in "Fürst Metternich" the political schemer: "From the imperial court down to the lowest levels of society, he recognized the black-yellow [imperial colors] character and used it, yes, he really was the man who shaped this trend in Austrian character—amiable violence, cynical treachery, friendly malice, and sincere unreliability—into a firm system."[36] The essay "Paläste" featuring some of the most beautiful residences in Vienna, points out the fact that these locations in town, just like all most desirable wooded lands, mountains, lakes, rivers, and hunts, belong to Austrian nobility and to a church for which the time of the Counterreformation was "a splendid business enterprise" and which considers it sinful to change the status quo.[37]

"Erziehung" (Education) shows the dominance of the Jesuits and the famous boarding school of the Theresianum in shaping the minds of the young aristocrats. Salten, to avoid a brush with the censor, carefully quotes an older source in condemning the education of the imperial princes and its sad consequences: "The inability to think and act independently, the lack of the courage to be truthful, just, and loving. Thus the princes, even those gifted by nature with the most favorable character attributes, later become pawns in the hands of plotting cliques or scheming minions."[38] The essays "Hofball" (Court Ball) and "Gewehr heraus!" (Present Arms!) describe imperial surroundings, especially the old emperor Franz Josef, with skill resembling the use of a film camera, and in "Das österreichische Antlitz" (The Austrian Face), the title feature of another collection,[39] Salten summarized for all, astonished by the impact of this seemingly dull personality on so many for so long, why the Austrian monarchy remained intact in spite of all obvious degradation. "How familiar this face is to us. . . even our fathers never knew another picture of an emperor, and when we were little boys, this face looked at us when we sat for the first time in our classroom. Now our children grow up and go to school, and they too are confronted by the same face in its solemn frame. . . these two. . , a monarch and a face, are from our earliest childhood on so insolubly merged that now it will be impossible for us to separate them anymore, whatever may happen [in the future]."40

Important essays on art and music in the collection *Geister der Zeit*, are those on "Gustav Klimt" whom Salten supported during a critical phase of his development, the exhibit of the Secession in 1903, on "Gustav Mahler," "Caruso" and on several well-known conductors. Also remarkable are the author's portraits of two famous Viennese writers, "Peter Altenberg" and "Ferdinand von Saar." He discovered behind Altenberg's well known peculiar habits a unique new style and contribution to the literature of Jung-Wien. The essay on Saar is courageous in the discussion of his and Adalbert Stifter's suicides as part of their vulnerable and troubled personalities.

However, the most creative influence on Salten's writing of essays and stories stemmed from his work as a reviewer of plays, his daily association with the stage. While his descriptions of "Alexander Girardi" and "Eleonora Duse" are excellent, the optimal example of his actors' portraits may be his essay on "Josef Kainz" a close personal friend, whom he pictures in several of his finest roles as Romeo, Tasso, Fiesco, and Don Carlos, summarizing: "He always stood higher than all his characters, was always richer than all his works. . . He could just as easily have become a painter, a poet, or a sculptor. For in the depth of his being he was an artist, not just an actor. His human nature was most closely meshed with his artistic genius, it was the color of his blood, the mainspring of his instincts, the fine tuning of his nerves."41

Salten was married to an actress and had an insider's knowledge of many lives connected with the stage. The best of his tales—in length and structure short stories, novellas, and short novels—deal with the fates of actresses. The author is completely realistic in setting their private lives apart from public morality: their lovers, aristocrats or rich businessmen, surround them with the luxuries—clothes, jewels, horse and carriage, beautifully furnished houses—which are needed for public image. But, as Salten shows in the title character of his best known short novel *Olga Frohgemuth* (1910),42 in the double standard of his time this past is difficult to overcome if such a liaison involves the highest levels of society. In her childhood, Olga, the daughter of a teacher at a Gymnasium [university prep school] had met Prince Emanuel Ferdinand when he had visited his teacher during his student days. While the Prince was away, she had become a famous "Soubrette," a singer of Operettas, beloved by all Vienna for her beauty and charm. Olga's triumphs were secretly shared by her mother, but she had been cast out by her father as a "fallen woman." After Emanuel Ferdinand's return the couple fall in love, as it seems for life, until he hears of her former liaisons, in her eyes simply a part of her advancement and not to be compared with her feeling for him. He is not able to overcome his disappointment and leaves town. In her despair Olga "wills" herself to die. Like the grief stricken Prince, her father sees too late what he has lost in the narrowness of his thinking. The novel is flawed by too much sweetness in the descriptions of Olga's beauty, her happiness, and her dying.

Much better is *Mizzi*, (1932).[43] In contrast to his friends, who generally show young girls of the working classes as "süße Mädel" (sweet girls) in the social sphere of their aristocrat lovers, Salten stresses the lower origins of Mizzi and makes them an integral part of his plot. She is an outstanding beauty who, not from artistic interest but solely to liberate herself and her mother, a widowed washerwoman, from desperate poverty, asks brashly for a theater audition. In spite of her lack of education and training Mizzi succeeds by "playing herself." Her fame rising, she accepts and dismisses her moneyed lovers with the same pecuniary goal in mind but in strict adherence to her own standards of fairness. One of them, Erwain, an aristocrat-businessman, falls deeply in love with her, and when she expects a child, he makes her his wife. Touched by his devotion, she leaves the stage and for six years completely blends into his wealthy background. But during an outing to the "Heurigen" [new wine] she meets Poldi Wiesinger, a folksinger, and discovers that she had never felt entirely at home in upper-class society. Leaving her husband and young son, she obtains a divorce and with the settlement money buys a country inn, where she serves their guests and Poldi sings for them, their household including her mother, Herr Ebensberg, a retired actor, and later Kathi, a young widow. When Mizzi discovers that Poldi and Kathi have become lovers, she stays true to her warning, once given to Poldi: "If you are ever unfaithful to me, watch yourself, or you'll croak like a dog!" She prepares a poisoned pie, serves it to all but the old actor, stoically watches their death, and joins them in the end. "Herr Ebensberg later told the story which no one could invent."[44]

The collective volume of the Jubilee Edition titled *Mizzi* also contains ten fairly short stories. They were originally published as a novel *Künstlerfrauen* (Artists' Wives) and show the domestic life of artists' couples with a superb gift of insight into their various problems. Here too either husband or wife often comes from a farmers' or workers' background. Among the best is the humorous study on "Die Schauspielerin Elisabeth," (The Actress Elizabeth), a famous actress whose writer husband has fallen in love with, and married, her stage personality but finds himself privately with a "cleaning-demon" housewife: "She abandoned herself when she stood up there on the stage, and what was she not able to give of her unused riches! But then she quickly submerged herself again into commonness. . . tied herself to life where it was mechanical, handy, and most obviously purposeful."45 Equally witty is the story of "Tini Holms Aufstieg" (Tini Holm's Advancement). Tini, also of humble origins, beats the rich businessman-father—sponsor of her career who wants her to invigorate the life of his languid heir—at his own game and wins a husband as well.

"Das Manhard Zimmer" (The Manhard Room),46 a story not reprinted in the Jubilee Edition, should have been included because it uses a well-known Viennese setting in a new original way: Heinrich, its main character, is a hotel headwaiter in charge of all chambres separées. Over the years he has observed the actress Johanna Manhard coming to her special room with her lovers: the first one, who taught her fine manners, and all the others who nevertheless testified to her style and good taste in people. They both have aged in their respective roles and as Heinrich has saved enough to go into business for himself, he approaches her during one of her visits. The story ends with the promise of their future life together.

Of novellas not related to the stage, three deserve special attention. The first, "Philippine erobert ihr Eigentum" (Philippine Regains Her Possessions),47 pictures the manifold complex problems in high society during the break up of the multinational empire. At the beginning of World War I, Philippine, illegitimate daughter of a Habsburg magnate, saves her large landholdings in Serbia by selling them fictitiously to a local banker who pretends after the end of the war to have truly bought the estates. The spirited young woman has to use a clever but dangerous ruse to win back her lands. Philippine's toughness, hidden behind a delicate "Madonna face," exemplifies Salten's tendency to stress the strength and tenacity of the lower classes, who are able to revitalize the often degenerate nobility.

The stylistic mastery of the second story, describing the shabby poverty of old age and the barrenness of spinsterly life, can be traced to particularly close observation: the novella "Die Geliebte des Kaisers" (The Emperor's Beloved)[48] and the essay "Mauerbach" in the collection *Das österreichische Antlitz*[49] share their setting. At the former Carthusian monastery in Mauerbach a part of the church was walled off and subdivided into two stories of dormitories for destitute old people, while the altar and its surroundings remained intact. Even the sacred ceiling figures the decorations were shared by the upper dorm, which had a window overlooking the sanctuary. In the story Hofrat Lehmgruber brings his sister Johanna, who has spent all her working days as "servant" for his family, to this poorhouse to die. After a conversation with a cynical inmate Johanna has to face the truth of her complete abandonment: "she was like a tree branch which, sawed off, lies on the ground and dies of its wounds. . . ." In Johanna's inner vision all her former life disintegrates, and, lonely and desperate, she creates her own legend surrounding the tombstone of the emperor Friedrich der Schöne at the church. When she hears that his remains have long since been removed to a different place, her shock and grief lead to her death. But in the apotheosis of her last vision the emperor, joined by the ceiling figures of angels and saints, claims her for his own.

The third story, *Die kleine Veronika*,[50] also relates to the genre of the essay. Readers unfamiliar with the local dialect cannot fully appreciate the little masterpiece *Wurstelprater* partially written in Viennese dialect and accompanied by seventy-five photos by Dr. Emil Meyer.[51] They are compensated by reading the novella in which this "people's part" of the famous park provides the setting for the turning point of the story: Rosi, a prosperous Viennese prostitute, has invited Veronika, her godchild, raised in poverty, to celebrate her confirmation at St. Stephen's in Vienna. All inhabitants of the brothel have worked together in creating an atmosphere of respectability for their unsuspecting young guest. After the solemn ceremony the girl enjoys the traditional Fiaker ride, and their arrival at the Wurstelprater seems the culmination of her bliss. But there, where—as described in the essays—happiness turns into drunken brawl, where the children's Punch-and-Judy theater stands next to show booths with monstrosities, where honest citizens are quickly deceived by carnival shysters, Rosi's façade of respectability begins to crumble: they meet several of her customers, and their party ends in mutual drunken dissipation. Veronika finds herself in bed with the youngest man, and her innocent reaction at awakening is interpreted as a calculated game. Abruptly and cruelly sent home, Veronika is overwhelmed by her inner confusion, shame, and pain. She leaves the train and ends her life in the Danube. The end of the novella reminds one of Gottfried Keller's well-known *Romeo und Julia auf dem Dorf*, (*A Village Romeo and Juliet*), but the carefully structured plot has merits, and the main theme, a young girl's loss of virginity, is handled with sensitivity and tact.

Unfortunately, Salten's creative attempts are led astray when he transposes the same theme into mythical or historic settings. In "Der Schrei der Liebe" [meant is a woman's outcry at climax] and to a lesser degree in "Die Gedenktafel der Prinzessin Anna" (The Memorial Tablet of Princess Anna)[52] his treatment of this topic seems to cross the boundaries of good taste.

The author appears to show greater skill in creating outright pornography: During a blossoming of the genre in the 1960s and 1970s, the preface in a pirated edition of *Josefine Mutzenbacher*[53] ascribed the novel to Salten and praised his accomplishment. While he never admitted his authorship, it is now definitely established. The novel's subtitle, "life-story of a Viennese prostitute," is misleading: it begins with Josefine's fifth year and describes in the form a memoir written in her later years her progression into prostitution from her earliest incestuous experimentations up to her first sex-for-pay, not at a brothel but from a home base in the suburbs, where her father functions in the double role of lover/pimp. We see Josefine driven by an inborn sexual hunger and note her continuous enjoyment of its satiation. Many contemporary works speak of the threat and tragic consequences of the ever present exposure to syphilis. But the novel never mentions any precautions or any worries about pregnancies and abortions. Characteristic of all adults and children involved is the nearly complete absence of scruples or regrets. Even the act of confession is used to further sexual proclivity and the lasciviousness of the clergy. The story clearly represents the wish-fulfillment of any client who is thus contributing to a woman's livelihood and her bliss at the same time, and it brings Salten close to the opinions of Karl Kraus, who regarded prostitution as "a woman's inborn drive."[54]

An easily overlooked aspect of the novel affirms modern research on major causes for incest and child abuse: Josefine grows up in extreme poverty at an overcrowded tenement house (Mietskaserne). She, her parents, and her two brothers share one small room and a kitchen, and among her earliest sexual initiations she describes molestations by several

"Bettgeher," workers on night shift who rent her parents' bed during the day.

The same crowded living situation, a bed even in the kitchen, is shown again in *Martin Overbeck*,[55] a novel of the twenties, pure "Unterhaltungsliteratur" in its fairytale ending but important in picturing the surroundings of the workers (even their unionization), which the rich hero shares in order to win his heroine. He learns to value their honest camaraderie and, after an accident at work, their selfless charity.

Salten was unique in the circle of Jung-Wien because of his complete familiarity with the life of the lower classes. Having shared their milieu during the severe deprivation of his early years, he made no attempt to idealize it. He had escaped, and his voluminous production, quantity often before quality, his love of luxury, and his enjoyment of gift giving and entertaining point to his rejection of poverty and his efforts never to slip back into it again.[56]

While critics of his time praised Salten's historic novels and novellas, readers interested in Jung-Wien will much prefer his contemporary works. Exceptions are those historic tales which seem to express concerns of his own time or which in their subject were unsuitable for modern stories. Examples are "Herr Wenzel auf Rehberg" and "Der Hund von Florenz."[57]

Salten was a close friend of several imperial dukes, especially of Leopold Ferdinand of Toscana, and had detailed knowledge of the tragic fate of Louise von Coburg, Leopold's sister. When her fight with her lover created an international sensation in the press, he became deeply involved and tried to help her in his journalistic reporting. In 1905 he anonymously published *Bekenntnisse einer Prinzessin* (Confessions of a Princess),[58] believed by some to be her diary. He later wrote several versions of a drama about her. These experiences had shown the author that privileged positions at court were exceedingly dangerous and often morally destructive. In *Herr Wenzel auf Rehberg und sein Knecht Kaspar Dinkel* (Herr Wenzel of Rehberg) these ideas are moved back into the time of emperor Charles V., to whose court in Augsburg Wenzel, a Bohemian knight of lower nobility, is called by a powerful relative. On the way he is assisted by Kaspar, an army wagoner, whom he likes and intends to take into his service. after his arrival in Augsburg, Wenzel is taken to attend the emperor's meal, a scene the author uses to depict Charles as a degenerate, willful despot. Taken up with court duties, Wenzel fails to hire Kaspar and meets him again on the march into war when he observes Charles' anger at the slow progress of the wagons. Caned by the impatient emperor, Kaspar, who does not recognize his attacker, slashes Charles' face with his whip. Rehberg tries to prevent the wagoner's hanging and seems to succeed, but he discovers that Kaspar, before being freed to his service, has to have his nose and ears cut off. Kaspar, unable to endure this shame, asks for mercy, and Rehberg shoots him to death. Burdened by guilt, Wenzel leaves the imperial court and returns home: "How does it come about, I thought, what atmosphere is there [at court] that I became bad, a boaster, caught up in vanity and unfaithfulness. . . . This lowly fellow happened to raise his arm and at the same time he tore the veil from the Emperor's face who was thus revealed to me as a small and miserable human being. . ."[59]

In the second novel, *Der Hund von Florenz*, (The Hound of Florence) which could be told only in a historic setting, a quote from the hermit of Amiata, "If you are poor here on earth you must be a dog for one half of your life, then you will be permitted to spend the other half as a human being," is exemplified in the fate of a poor Viennese sculptor of Italian descent. He is so consumed by his longing to reach true artistic perfection at his father's school in Florence that, observing a dog trotting beside the archduke's coach as he departs on a journey to Italy, he wishes to join them: "If I could only be myself every other day. . . then I would like to be that dog and go along on the journey."[60] Through a magic spell, which the author has to construe somewhat laboriously, Lukas' wish is granted. His experiences on the way to and in Florence changing daily from man to dog, culminate in disaster because the man becomes the archduke's rival in a love affair with Claudia, a beautiful courtesan. The dog attacks his master, whom he watches embracing Claudia, and is stabbed by the angry archduke. The next day the man is found seriously wounded in front of Claudia's door. The spell is now broken, and the story's open end pictures Claudia trying to save Lukas' life.

The stylistic merits of the novel are more obvious when it is seen in relationship to Salten's animal stories, to which one half of it belongs: While *Bambi*, *Perri*, and their minor companions once made the author world famous, they now survive mainly in their Disney versions. In his otherwise enthusiastic preface to the English edition of *Bambi* John Galsworthy may have touched upon one of the most important reasons for the book's lack of durability: "I do not, as a rule, like the method which places human words in the mouths of dumb creatures."[61] Had Salten's animal stories—in their plot and choice of vocabulary—been focused on small children into whose world of wonders talking animals belong, had the style of *Florian*, the life of a Lippizaner horse during the last years of the Austrian empire, been changed into a youth book similar to the author's earlier study of the emperor Maximilian,[62] they might still be in print today. Their creator, while now often condescendingly judged for these attempts, would be a well acknowledged writer in a modern field of literature.

Bambi succeeded because its author shared a popular movement of the 1920s when a childlike view of nature was still possible for the average reader. In the meantime the progress of photography, particularly the development of the telecamera, which permits the closest unobtrusive observation of animals in their own realm, has radically changed our point of view.

In contrast to these works *Der Hund von Florenz* still appeals to modern perception because on the days belonging to the dog the man reacts with him and in him, and we appreciate Salten's exceptional grasp of animal existence, which he shows also in some adult shorter sketches describing his experiences with animals. Examples from the collection, *Gute Gesellschaft. Erlebnisse mit Tieren* (Good Company. Experiences with Animals)[63] are "Mein Falke" (My Falcon) and "Mieze aus dem See" (Kitty from the Lake).

3. Drama

Salten's great gift of spontaneity at the same time prevented his becoming a successful playwright. He lacked the tenacity and most likely the ideologically unifying view of the world which we detect in the works of successful modern authors of evening-filling, carefully structured dramas. But he collaborated in the creation of libretti for several operettas, in the translation of plays, and, in his style so congenial to the new medium, he became involved in the production of films. This area of his work, including the films of some of his novels, deserves detailed documentation, which is still missing.

His best known three-act drama *Der Gemeine*, (The Private [Soldier])[64] replays Büchner's *Woyzeck* theme in a very minor key showing the love (to Marie, a Viennese folksinger), rebellion, and the catastrophic end of Josef, formerly an architectural draftsman, who was forced into military service as a common soldier. Large sections of the play are written in dialect. Similar to Schnitzler's famous story *Leutnant Gustl*

(*None but the Brave*), the action stresses the willfulness and arrogance of the Austrian officers' corps; censorship delayed the play's performance in Vienna until 1919.

More unified in their structure are Salten's one-act plays, published in sets of three to parallel a three-act drama but not necessarily related in content. From the collection *Kinder der Freude* (Children of Joy),[65] two plays have survived well: In *Auf der Brücke* (On the Bridge), Frau von Kirchhoof cures her son Fritz, well on his way to ruining his life over an infatuation with the actress Sylvia Felsenbach, by revealing that she and Sylvia went to school together. *Lebensgefährten* (Life Companions) represents the dramatization of one of the studies in *Künstlerfrauen* on Katharina Kron and her fate as the wife of a famous, now aging actor who still nurtures liaisons in his self-centered vanity but is completely insensitive to her life and the sacrifices she has made in caring for him and their two children.

Most effective on stage could be *Auferstehung* (Resurrection) from the collection *Vom andern Ufer* (From the Other Shore).[66] The plot is somewhat confusing, but the fine points of its human interaction are carefully worked out and result in superb comedy, meeting the demand of the genre to contain hidden tragedy. Konstantin Trübner, a wealthy bachelor seemingly on his deathbed, had married his former mistress Marie, whom he had not seen for nine years, in order to legitimize their 12-year-old daughter Lotti. The play starts with Konstantin's miraculous recovery and the ensuing complications: Leopold Schenck, a piano teacher who during the years since Marie's separation from Konstantin had become her companion and a "father" to Lotti, is not willing to give her up and—just one of many humorous stabs at the hypocritical aspects of morality—cannot live with her anymore because she is now a "married woman." He had been looking forward to marrying her as a respectable "widow with child." To complicate matters further, Konstantin's present mistress Daisy, having graciously arranged the deathbed marriage, has already made her plans without Konstantin: she has had success in her recent play and signed a contract to go to Berlin; also, as the play reveals, she was secretly involved in an affair with Konstantin's best friend. Konstantin sees that his "resurrection" has caused nothing but problems. So he decides to leave them all, taking with him half of his fortune and bequeathing the other half to Marie and Lotti. To his friend he gives his watch, and to Daisy, who had already shown that she can cope with life supremely well, he leaves nothing: "If someone is reborn, he does not

take the same wife, nor the same friend, nor the same mistress. . . that
would be truly inept!"

Salten's one-act plays deserve a second look. Some were adapted for the radio, i.e., *Lebensgefährten* (W), and nearly all of them would
be excellent on television. They should be considered by directors of
small theaters in search of new plays and could provide superb thought-
provoking material for student performances at German departments
abroad.

Notes

A.   Biography

1.   Ed. Felix Czeike, (Wien/München/Zürich: Fritz Molden, 1974),
      pp. 284 f.
2.   Examples are: October 8, 1945 in the source above; October 8,
      1947 in *RoRoRo Autorenlexikon*; October 8, 1947 in *Großer
      Brockhaus*; October 8, 1945 in *Kröner Deutsches Dichterlexikon*.
3.   Kurt Riedmüller, *Felix Salten als Mensch, Dichter und Kritiker*,
      Dissertation, Wien, 1949; Graziella Zambrini, *Felix Salten als
      Kritiker und Jugendschriftsteller*, Tesi di Lauria, Universita
      Commerciale Luigi Bocconi [Milan], 1957; Ingrid Kunz, *Felix
      Salten als Theaterkritiker zwischen 1902 und 1910*, Lizentiatarbeit,
      Zürich 1983.
4.   Unless mentioned otherwise, all information concerning the biogra-
      phy of Felix Salten is based on the chapter "Der Mensch Felix
      Salten" in Riedmüller's dissertation. The typescript—most of its
      contents verified by family documents—was given to me by
      Salten's granddaughter Lea Wyler on October 5, 1987 in Zürich.
      During our conversation Mrs. Wyler added details about Salten's
      life and later sent me the transcript of a radio broadcast [Radio DRS
      Studio Zürich, Lea Wyler, *Bambis Vater. Eine Collage über Felix
      Salten, erzählt von seiner Enkelin*] which contained additional
      unpublished documents and episodes connected with Salten's biog-
      raphy. Her help is gratefully acknowledged. Information from
      Riedmüller and Wyler is indicated in the text by (R) or (W) respec-
      tively.

5. See as examples: Hugo von Hofmannsthal—Arthur Schnitzler, *Briefwechsel* (Frankfurt am Main: S. Fischer, 1964); Hugo von Hofmannsthal—Richard Beer-Hofmann, *Briefwechsel*, (Frankfurt am Main: S. Fischer, 1972); Hugo von Hofmannsthal-Leopold von Andrian, *Briefwechsel*, (Frankfurt am Main: S. Fischer, 1968). See the index in each work.

6. (Wien: A Bauer, 1897), pp. 21-25.

7. Gustav H. Bäuml und Franz H. Bäuml, "Namensverzeichnis zu Karl Kraus *Die Fackel*," *Modern Austrian Literature* Vol. 9, No. 1 (1976), p. 60.

8. Max Burckhard, "Jung-Wiener Theater Zum lieben Augustin" in *Die Zeit*, 23 November 1901. Somewhat better fared Max Reinhardt's enterprise "Schall und Rauch" (Kleines Theater) 1902 in Berlin which combined cabaret with the performance of one act plays, some of Salten's included. Leonhard M. Fiedler, *Max Reinhardt* (Reinbek bei Hamburg, Rowohlts Taschenbuch, 1975), p. 37.

9. Brigitte Fischer, *Sie schrieben mir* (München: Deutscher Taschenbuch Verlag, 1981), pp. 76 ff.

10. (München: Kösel, 1964) (*Gesammelte Werke*). First published in 1922.

11. Translations by the author. Thanks to Gregor Ackermann in supplying from his Salten documentation these and all following press reports.

12. See his "Brief an Galsworthy," written as a preface to *Gute Gesellschaft* (Berlin/Wien/Leipzig: Paul Zsolnay, 1930), pp. 9 f. Galsworthy had stressed three major problems: Vivisection, hunting, and the imprisonment of wild animals. Touching is Salten's attempt to overcome his hunting urge as described in some of his later stories.

13. For the history of the PEN Club, the congress of Ragusa, and the subsequent history of the Vienna PEN chapter, see Klaus Amann, *PEN—Politik. Emigration. Nationalsozialismus. Ein österreichischer Schriftstellerverband* (Wien/Köln/Graz: Hermann Böhlaus Nachfolger, 1984). Amann contains an extensive bibliography for further study of the complex events and, particularly in his last chapters, a detailed account of the denazification of the literary community in Vienna. For details on the "Aktion wider den undeutschen Geist" and the book burning, see Hans-Wolfgang Sträz,

"Die geistige SA rückt ein" in *10. Mai 1933. Die Bücher-verbrennung in Deutschland und die Folgen*. Hrsg. Ulrich Walberer (Frankfurt am Main: Fischer Taschenbuch, 1983).

14. (München: Kösel Verlag, 1952/1955).

15. Hilde Spiel, *Die österreichische Literatur nach 1945. Eine Einführung; Kindlers Literaturgeschichte der Gegenwart*, Vol. V (Frankfurt am Main: Fischer Taschenbuch Verlag, 1980), p. 21.

16. A few examples are: Spiel, p. 13; *RoRoRo Autorenlexikon*. Hrsg. Manfred Brauneck (Reinbek bei Hamburg: Rowolt Taschenbuch Verlag, 1984), p. 512; *Meyers Enzyklopädisches Lexikon*, (Mannheim: Bibliographisches Institut Lexikonverlag, 1977).

17. The novel deals with the return of the god Apollo to earth. The first version was completed 1938 in Vienna, but changes appear to have been made in exile.

18. Letter of February 26, 1988, by David R. Smith, Archivist, Walt Disney Archives, Burbank, California. His help is gratefully acknowledged.

19. *In Memoriam Max Reinhardt*, Schriftenreihe des Schauspielhauses Zürich Nr. 1 (Zürich/New York: Verlag Oprecht, 1944), pp. 25-30.

20. See note 2 above.

21. *Geister der Zeit. Erlebnisse* (Berlin/Wien/Leipzig: Paul Zsolnay, 1924), pp. 208-211.

22. Hugo von Hofmannsthal, *Reden und Aufsätze III. 1925-29. Gesammelte Werke in 10 Einzelbänden*. Hrsg. B. Schoeller, I. Beyer-Ahlert in Beratung mit R. Hirsch (Frankfurt am Main: Fischer Taschenbuch Verlag, 1980), p. 230. This and all following translations are the author's.

23. May be still under the critical influence of his friends. As letters and accounts show, they often read and criticized each other's works.

24. Kunz, [see note 2], pp. 87-92.

25. *Das Burgtheater. Naturgeschichte eines alten Hauses* (Wien/Leipzig: Wiener Literarische Anstalt, 1922).

26. *In Memoriam* [See note 19], p. 29 f.; *Czernowitzer Morgenblatt*, May 19, 1925: "Max Reinhardt hat die Werfelsche Premiere [*Juarez und Ferdinand* im Theater an der Josefstadt] verschoben, bis Felix Salten nach Wien kommt." Salten's reviews were also very important in establishing the international fame of the Salzburg Festival.

27. (Berlin/Wien/Leipzig: Zsolnay, 1924), (Wien/Leipzig: Wila, 1921).

28. Ibid., p. 179.
29. See: Kari Grimstad, *Mask of the Prophet, the Theatrical world of Karl Kraus* (Toronto/Buffalo/London: Univ. of Toronto Press, 1982), pp. 195 ff.
30. (Berlin/Wien/Leipzig: Zsolnay, 1931).
31. (Berlin/Wien/Leipzig: Zsolnay). This direct report of Zionists' concerns is far superior to Salten's attempt to create a "hero" for them in his sentimental retelling of Samson's and Delilah's story: *Simson, das Schicksal eines Erwählten*. Part of Zsolnay's Jubilee Edition, 1929.
32. *Geister der Zeit*, pp. 174-186.
33. Ibid., p. 178.
34. See: *Neue Menschen auf alter Erde*, pp. 100-105 and 166-175.
35. (Berlin/Leipzig: Hermann Seemann Nachf., 1905).
36. Ibid., pp. 9-11.
37. Ibid., p. 16.
38. Ibid., pp. 23-25.
39. (Berlin: S. Fischer, 1909).
40. Ibid., pp. 267 f.
41. *Geister der Zeit, Erlebnisse*, p. 108.
42. Best accessible in the Jubilee Edition of the Paul Zsolnay Verlag, *Der Schrei der Liebe* (1928), pp. 303-420.
43. Jubilee Edition, *Mizzi* (1932), pp. 9-49.
44. Ibid., p. 49.
45. Ibid., pp. 259-275; quote on p. 274. *Tini Holms Aufstieg*, pp. 393-405.
46. In *Die Wege des Herrn* (Wien: Deutsch-?sterreichischer Verlag, 1911). Dramatized in *Schöne Seelen* (not accessible to the author).
47. In: *Mizzi*, pp. 73-114.
48. Jubilee Edition, *Die Geliebte des Kaisers* 1929, pp. 397-451.
49. (Berlin: S. Fischer, 1909), pp. 169-179. As the manuscripts were not accessible, it is not certain if essay or story were written first. The publication date can not be used as information, some of Salten's stories and essays had long stages of "incubation."
50. *Der Schrei der Liebe*, pp. 9-108 and 109-183.
51. (Wien/Leipzig: Verlag Hermann Seemann, 1905).
52. *Der Schrei der Liebe*, pp. 9-108 and 109-183.
53. (München: Rogner und Bernhard, 1969).
54. Nike Wagner, *Geist und Geschlecht, Karl Kraus und die Erotiker*

der Wiener Moderne (Frankfurt am Main: Suhrkamp Verlag, 1982), p. 161: "Ohne Rücksicht auf soziale Termination nennt er [K. Kraus] die Prostitution einen Naturtrieb." See also the links to Otto Weininger in Wagner's chapter III: "Eros und Logos," pp. 132 ff.

55. *Martin Overbeck, der Roman eines reichen jungen Mannes* (Berlin/Wien/Leipzig: Zsolnay, 1927).

56. Compare his essay *Ich wünsche mir Reichtum* in: *Die Dame im Spiegel* (Berlin: Ullstein Verlag, 1920), pp. 105-115.

57. *Die Geliebte des Kaisers*, pp. 9-82 and pp. 83-290.

58. (Wien/Leipzig: Wiener Verlag, 1906).

59. Ibid., p. 79 f.

60. Ibid., p. 103.

61. Translated by Whitaker Chambers (New York: Simon and Schuster, 1928).

62. *Florian, das Pferd des Kaisers*, (Berlin/Wien/Leipzig: Zsolnay Verlag, 1933); *Kaiser Max, der letzte Ritter* (Ullsteins Jugendbüdner, Berlin: Ullstein Verlag, 1913).

63. *Gute Gesellschaft*, pp. 23-34 and pp. 145-155.

64. (Wien: Wiener Verlag, 1901). The play was first staged 1902 in Berlin. Censorship prevented its performance in Vienna until 1919.

65. (Berlin: S. Fischer, 1917), pp. 69-142 and pp. 143-204.

66. (Berlin: S. Fischer, 1908), pp. 109-174.

Felix Salten, Selected Bibliography by Gregor Ackermann

I.   Works by Felix Salten in German

Der Hinterbliebene. Kurze Novellen. [Wien:] Wiener Verlag Rosner, 1990.

Der Gemeine. Schauspiel in drei Aufzügen. Wien: Wiener Verlag, 1902.

Die Gedenktafel der Prinzessin Anna [Wien:] Wiener Verlag, 1902.

Gustav Klimt. Gelegentliche Anmerkungen. Wien & Leipzig: Wiener Verlag, 1903.

Die kleine Veronika. Novelle. Berlin: Foscher, 1903.

Das Buch der Könige. München & Leipzig: Georg Müller, [1905].

Der Schrei der Liebe. Novelle. Wien & Leipzig: Wiener Verlag, 1905.

Wiener Adel. Berlin & Leipzig: Hermann Seemann Nachf., [1905].

Herr Wenzel auf Rehberg und sein Knecht Kaspar Dinckel. Berlin: Fischer, 1907.

Die Geliebte Friederich des Schönen. Novellen. Berlin: Marquardt, [1908].

Künstlerfrauen. Ein Zyklus kleiner Romane. München & Leipzig: Georg Müller, 1908.

Vom anderen Ufer. Drei Einakter. Berlin: Fischer, 1908.

Das österreichische Antlitz. Berlin: Fischer, [1909].

Mein junger Herr. Operette in drei Akten von Ferdinand Stollberg [d.i.: Felix Salten]. Musik von Oskar Straus. Berlin: Felix Bloch Erben, [1910].

Olga Frohgemuth. Erzählung. Berlin: Fischer, [1910].

Reiche Mädchen. Operette in drei Akten von Ferdinand Stollberg [d.i.:Felix Salten]. Musik von Johann Strauß. Wien: Karczag & Wallner, 1910.

Wurstelprater. Mit 75 Originalaufnahman von Emil Mayer. Wien, Leipzig: Brüder Rosenbaum, [1911].

Das Schicksal der Agathe. Novellen. Leipzig: Insel-Verlag. 1911.

Die Wege des Herrn. Novellen. Wien: Deutsch-Österreichischer Verlag, [1911].

Die Gedenktafel der Prinzessin Anna. Der Schrei der Liebe. Zwei Novellen. München: George Müller, 1913.

Gestalten und Erscheinungen. Berlin: Fischer, 1913.

Kaiser Max der letzte Ritter. Berlin: Ullstein, 1913.

Das lockende Licht. Pantomine in vier Bildern. Berlin: "Harmonie-" Verlagsgesellschaft für Literatur und Kunst, 1914.

Das stärkere Band. Drei Akte und ein Epilog. Berlin: Felix Block Erben, 1915.

Abschied im Sturm. Novelle. München: Albert Langen, [1915].

Die klingende Schelle. Roman. Berlin, Wien: Ullstein, 1915.

Prinz Eugen der edle Ritter. Berlin & Wien: Ullstein, 1915.

Kinder der Freude. Drei Einakter. Berlin: Fischer, 1917.

Der alte Narr. Novellen. Berlin: Rudolf Mosse, [1918].

Im Namen des Kaisers. Eine historische Erzählung. Leipzig, Wien: Lyra-Verlag, 1919.

Die Dame im Spiegel. (Bilder, Buchschmuck und Einband nach Zeichnungen der Gr fin Christine von Kalckreuth). Berlin: Verlag Ullstein, 1920.

Schauen und Spielen. Studien zur Kritik des modernen Theaters. 2 vols. Wien, Leipzig: Wiener Literarische Anstalt, 1921.

Das Burgtheater. Naturgeschichte eines alten Hauses. Wien, Leipzig: Wiener Literarische Anstalt, 1922.

Bambi. Eine Lebensgeschichte aus dem Walde. Berlin: Ullstein, 1923.

Der Hund von Florenz. Wien, Leipzig: Herz-Verlag, 1923.

Geister der Zeit. Erlebnisse. Berlin, Wien, Leipzig: Zsolnay, 1924.

Bob und Baby. Zeichnungen von Anna Katharina Salten. Berlin, Wien, Leipzig: Zsolnay, [1925].

Neue Menschen auf alter Erde. Eine Palästinafahrt. Berlin, Wien, Leipzig: Zsolnay, 1925.

Schöne Seelen. . . Lustspiel in einem Akt. Mit einem Nachwort von Julius Ferdinand Wollf. Leipzig: Reclam, 1925.

Martin Overback. Der Roman eines reichen jungen Mannes. Berlin, Wien, Leipzig: Zsolnay, 1927.

Der Schrei der Liebe. Novellen. Berlin, Wien, Leipzig: Zsolnay, 1928.

Simson. Das Schicksal eines Erwählten. Roman. Berlin, Wien, Leipzig: Zsolnay, 1928.

Fünfzehn Hasen. Schicksale in Wald und Feld. Berlin, Wien, Leipzig: Zsolnay, 1929.

Die Geliebte des Kaisers. Novellen. Berlin, Wien, Leipzig: Zsolnay, 1929.

Gute Gesellschaft. Erlebnisse mit Tieren. Berlin, Wien, Leipzig: Zsolnay, 1930.

Teppiche. Allen Freunden dieser unentbehrlichen Gewebe. Wien: Emanuel Fischer, 1930.

Freunde aus aller Welt. Roman eines zoologischen Gartens. Mit 16 Tiefdruckbildern. Berlin, Wien, Leipzig: Zsolnay, [1931].

Fünf Minuten Amerika. Berlin, Wien, Leipzig: Zsolnay, 1931.

Auf Tod und Leben. Die Liebesgeschichte der Prinzessin Louise von Koburg. Berlin-Wilmersdorf: Felix Block Erben, [1932].

Mizzi. Novellen. Berlin, Wien, Leipzig: Zsolnay, 1932.

Florian. Das Pferd des Kaisers. Berlin, Wien, Leipzig: Zsolnay, 1933.

Kleine Brüder. Tiergeschichten. Wien: Zsolnay, 1935.

Die Jugend des Eichhörnchens Perri. Wien: Zsolnay, 1938.

Bambis Kinder. Eine Familie im Walde. Zürich: Albert Müller, [1940].

Renni der Retter. Das Leben eines Kriegshundes. Zürich: Albert Müller Verlag, [1941].

Kleine Welt für sich. Eine Geschichte von freien und dienenden Geschöpfen. Zürich: Albert Müller, Verlag [1944].

Djibi, das Kätzchen. Rüschlikon-Zürich: Albert Müller Verlag, [1945].

II.   Works Ascribed to Felix Salten

Die Bekenntnisse einer Prinzessin. Wien & Leipzig: Wiener Verlag, [1905].

Josefine Mutzenbacher, oder Die Geschichte einer Wienerischen Dirne, von ihr selbst erzählt. [Wien:] o. Verl., 1906.

III.   Works in English

The Love of Life. Adapted by Joseph H. Nube. Chicago: 1910.

Moral Courage. (The Gravity of Life.) A play. in: *Fifty More Contemporary One-Act Plays.* Selected and edited by Frank Shay. New York: Appleton, 1928, pp. 453-463.

Bambi. A life in the Woods. Foreword by John Galsworthy. Translated by Whittaker Chambers. New York: Simon & Schuster, 1928.

The Hound of Florence. Translated by Huntley Paterson. New York: Simon & Schuster, 1930.

Fifteen Rabbits. Translated by Whittaker Chambers. New York: Simon & Schuster, 1930.

Samson and Delilah. Translated by Whittaker Chambers. New York: Simon & Schuster, 1931.

The City Jungle. New York: Simon & Schuster, 1932.

Florian, the Emperor's Stallion. Translated by Erich Posselt and Michael Kraike. Indianapolis: Bobbs-Merrill, 1934.

Perri. Translated by Barrows Mussey. Indianapolis: Bobbs-Merrill, [1938].

Prisoner Thirty-three. A Fantasy of Today. Translated by Hildegard Nagel. - [n.p., n.d.].

Bambi's Children. The Story of a Forest Family. Translated by Barthold Fles. Indianapolis, New York: Bobbs-Merrill, 1939.

Renni, the Rescuer. A Dog of the Battlefield. Translated by Kenneth C[arlyle] Kaufman. Indianapolis, New York: Bobbs-Merrill, [1940].

A Forest World. English text by Paul R[obert] Milton and Sanford Jerome Greenburger. Indianapolis, New York: Bobbs-Merrill, (1942).

Good Comrades. Translated by Paul R[obert] Milton. Indianapolis, New York: Bobbs-Merrill, [1942].

Djibi. The Story of a Cat. Translated by Raya Levin. London: Pilot Press, 1946.

The Memoirs of Josephine Mutzenbacher. Translated by Rudolf Schleifer. North Hollywood: Brandon House, [1967].

IV.   Secondary Works in German

Kurt Riedmüller, "Felix Salten als Mensch, Dichter und Kritiker," Phil. Diss. Wien 1949.
Graziella Zambrini, *Felix Salten als Kritiker und Jugendschrifsteller*. Tesi di Laurea. [Milano:] Universita Commerciale Luigi Bocconi. 1957.

Gregor Ackermann is presently working on a complete bibliography of Salten's numerous works.

Arthur Schnitzler

Gerd K. Schneider

Arthur Schnitzler's comments "on the pulls and tugs of sex are as up to date as the latest Hite Report, and probably more reliable,"[1] stated Walter Goodman, theater critic of the *New York Times,* in his review of *Romance/Romance,* a musical based on Schnitzler's *Die kleine Komödie* (*The Little Comedy*) and Jules Renard's *Pain de Ménage.* This show, called the "littlest big musical Off Off Broadway,"[2] was so successful that it was moved uptown from the Actors Outlook Theater in May 1988. It was performed until January 1989 in the newly restored Helen Hayes Theatre, the former Little Theatre at 240 W. 44th Street, which had staged as its second play in 1912 Arthur Schnitzler's cycle *The Affairs of Anatol* with John Barrymore in the leading role. There it played *vis-à-vis* the continuously sold-out *Phantom of the Opera,* one of Andrew Lloyd Webber's multimillion dollar megamusicals. Although *"Romance/Romance* may lack the powerful effects of Broadway's multimillion dollar extravaganzas, . . . it certainly provides more charm and warmth than those overpriced and overproduced monsters."[3] This remark by Martin Schaeffer not only indicates dissatisfaction with extravagant spectacles, but also testifies to the enduring appeal of Schnitzler's works.

Arthur Schnitzler, the author of *Die kleine Komödie,* was born on 15 May 1862 in Vienna, the first child of the laryngologist Johann Schnitzler (1835-1893) and his wife Louise Markbreiter (1840-1911), a physician's daughter. The family was Jewish, but for Arthur Schnitzler Jewishness was only a question of race and not one of religious commitment. After graduating with distinction from the Viennese *Akademisches Gymnasium* in 1879, he enrolled in the School of Medicine, receiving his medical degree in 1885 and serving as an intern at the Vienna *Allgemeine Krankenhaus* (General Hospital) until 1888. By that time he had published a few articles and poems in the journals *An der schönen blauen*

Donau and the *Deutsche Wochenschrift* as well as articles and book reviews in the professional field; these medical articles appeared in the *Wiener Medizinische Presse* and the *Internationale Klinische Rundschau*. Instrumental in encouraging him to write fiction was Olga Waisnix, a married woman with three sons, whom he had met in 1886 while vacationing with his family in Reichenau and with whom he had a platonic love affair. Schnitzler followed her advice and in 1886 submitted a few of his aphorisms and short stories to publishers. In 1888 he became assistant to his father at the *Allgemeine Wiener Poliklinik* (General Viennese Polyclinic), where he remained until his father's death in 1893.

Between 1888 and 1893 Schnitzler worked on *Anatol* and *Die kleine Komödie*, two comedies which are related thematically. *Anatol* (1893; *Anatol*), a cycle of seven one-act plays, is held together by the title figure, a young bachelor who is described by Dvorak as "the melancholy brooder who passes through life unable to accept its reality and [who] is unsuccessful in attempting to create a satisfactory one of his own. From the first to the last Anatol remains the true impressionist who seizes the moment but cannot bear the total weight of the picture it paints. The unsettling aspects of reality compel him to remain immersed in a world of dream and appearance."[4] Anatol's *alter ego* is his friend Max, whose rational, down-to-earth, sometimes cynical comments frequently contradict Anatol's highly subjective, impressionistic statements. The American premiere in 1912 with John Barrymore was a success. Later performances were viewed more critically; as Stephanie Hammer reports, "the play came increasingly to be dealt with as either a curio or a farce."[5] As proof Hammer quotes from the Seattle Repertory's flyer describing the 1936 production of this play:

> From the city of the aristocrats—Vienna—comes . . . *The Affairs of Anatol*. Gaiety and sophistication, as well as airy humor abound in the three subtly charming—but aimless—episodes which comprise the play. Each episode deals with one of Anatol's 'affairs' which [sic] although Anatol would be the last to admit it, nearly always turn to his advantage. He fancies himself an irresistible Don Juan and is in and out of love with singular regularity. Yet none of his setbacks affect his unimpressionable ego. You'll thoroughly enjoy his laugh-provoking difficulties (65).

The book edition in the United States was also received enthusiastically, but the reviewer for the *New York Times* made it quite obvious that these scenes were not intended for young people. In his review titled "Dialogues for Adults" the more puritan American attitude toward the 'Human-All-too-Human' can be clearly seen: "It is true that Schnitzler's work is sophisticated. He deals with life as he sees it and banters gaily with many things which our Anglo-Saxon prejudices are in the habit of wailing over or completely ignoring. There is nothing of the Puritan in his composition. But it is impossible to read this sequence of dialogues without admitting that the man is, in his genre, an artist and a thinker."6

The second play in this cycle, *Weihnachtseinkäufe* (A Christmas Present), is especially important because here Anatol introduces the concept of the *süße Mädel*, or the 'sweet girl', the type Schnitzler described in his autobiography as follows:

> The prototype of Viennese womanhood with a bewitching figure made for dancing; with lips… made for kissing; eyes luminous and full of life, dressed simply, a *grisette* type—she sways a little when she walks, is lithe and unconcerned. Her voice is clear; she speaks vibrantly and naturally in the vernacular, and what she says is said as only she can say it—has to say it—that is to say, high-spiritedly and with slight touch of haste. We're only young once, she says, with an unconcerned shrug, and is thinking: we shouldn't miss anything… and this is discernment washed by the light colors of the south. And with all of this a curious air of domesticity… The usual brothers and sisters, all living with their parents, the gossipping neighbors, every now and then an opening phrase, and then again a quite folksy melody…. 8

The type of the *süße Mädel* we meet also in the *Kleine Komödie* (1895). Alfred von Willemer is an Anatol-type who is independently wealthy, suffers from *ennui*, and passes his time in coffee houses and seducing women. He poses as a struggling poet in order to experience real romance outside his social class. His female counterpart is Josefine Weninger, a wealthy demimondaine, whose lover had just left her. She masquerades as a poor seamstress, portraying the type of the *süße Mädel*—with apparent success. Both meet and predictably fall in love. Their illusion of a happy romance outside the pretense of their social class does not last long—exactly nineteen days and nights. The disclosure of their true identities is a relief for both of them since their masquerades had imposed some hardships on them; both had given up their luxurious lifestyle by drinking cheap wine and making love in a bedroom with painted rather than papered walls. In the end the reader, or the audience, is left with the impression that the "Little Comedy" covers up the "great tragedy" of their empty and boring lives and their inability to experience a feeling of real love, which Schnitzler defined later as being there for someone else. This selfless attitude toward the other person we find in Christine, a so-called *süße Mädel,* the main character in *Liebelei* (1896; translated as *Light-O' Love, Playing with Love,* and *Flirtations).* The man she loves, Fritz, who also has an affair with a married woman, expresses to his friend Theodor his view on women as follows: "You have no idea how I've longed for such tenderness without melodrama, for someone so sweet, so quiet, someone kind to me, someone who can help me recover from these endless tempests and martyrdoms."[10] Theodor agrees with him and summarizes for his friend the ideal situation for the young men of the social class to which they both belong:

> That's it, you're right! Recovery. That's what it's all about. They're here to help us recover. That's why I'm not in favor of these so-called interesting women. Women aren't meant to be interesting, they're meant to be pleasant. You must look for your happiness where I've already looked and found it, where there are no big scenes, no dangers, no tragic complications. Where the beginning has no particular difficulties and the end has no torment. Where you take your first kiss with a smile and say good-bye with touching emotion—[12]

The title *Liebelei* is ironical because in this play we have those elements which Theodor dislikes: big scenes, dangers, and tragic complications. Fritz gets killed in a duel with the husband of the woman with whom he had an affair; Christine, to whom Fritz meant her whole life, runs away, and her father fears that she will never return. She does not fit the pattern of the *süße Mädel* because she does not believe, as Richard Alewyn, notes, in the "Wiederholbarkeit des Unwiederholbaren" (the repetition of the unrepeatable). Finding herself excluded from the social and inner life of her lover, her tragedy then lies, as Stern points out, "not in Fritz' death in the duel, but in Christine's realization that she meant nothing to him: that *nothing* meant anything to him: and that she gave herself, all she was, to this nothing. The tragic conclusion lies in her realization of an absolute betrayal."[13] At the end she stands, as Swales remarks, " in absolute isolation, an isolation that is totally unbearable because her being can exist only in relationship to another fellow being. Christine has loved in a void; she cannot and will not continue to live in that void."14

People who can live in that void, which they continuously try to overcome through sexual unions, are shown in *Reigen* (1900; translated as *Hands Around* and *La Ronde*). This work, written by Schnitzler in the winter of 1896-1897, was published in a private printing with a preface stating that Schnitzler did not intend to make this play publicly available because of possible misinterpretations. It has been termed by many critics a 'danse macabre,' in which ten persons are doubly linked by sex. In the first scene a street walker has sex with a soldier, then come the soldier and a parlormaid, followed by the encounter of the parlormaid with a young gentleman, whose sexual liaison with a married woman is succeeded by the sporadic nightly ritual of husband and wife. The husband continues the circle by seducing a '*süßes Mädel*,' who passes on to the poet, whose get-together with an actress is followed by the combination of actress and count. In the last coupling we see the count with the prostitute from the beginning. The translators of this play remarked in the 1929 private printing for 'Members of the Schnitzler Society': "All stratagems of sex are uncovered not through the curious observations of a faunic mind, but through the finer eyes of a connoisseur of things human. The Puritan fanatic with his jaundiced inhibition or the moral ideologist with his heart of leather may toss the book aside resentful because of its inherent truth. The philosopher of human life, taking the larger aspect of this drama, will close it with the serene smile of understanding."15

Schnitzler proved right with his pessimistic prediction that this work would be misunderstood. The polemical reviews of the play were based less on its artistic merits than on the Jewish background of its author. In Berlin and Vienna nationalistic and anti-semitic groups caused a theater scandal during the performances, and the director and actors of the Berlin theater were taken to court. The trial, which lasted from 5 November to 18 November 1921, ended with the acquittal of the defendants. In his summary the attorney for the defense emphasized the racial overtones of this trial: "For the defense it is important to state that this trial is indeed not a battle against the *Reigen* but one against the Jews, that *Reigen* was used only in order to bring about an anti-semitic action."16

To avoid any further disturbance Schnitzler decided to withhold this play from the stage in Germany and Austria. Not until 1982 could *Reigen* be seen again in these two countries. In New York State, where the English translation appeared in 1920, it was banned by John S. Sumner, Secretary of the New York Society for the Suppression of Vice. Because one New York bookstore owner had this work in stock, charges were brought against him in 1929. The case was dismissed, however, with the following ruling: "Although the theme of the book is admittedly the quite universal literary theme of men and women, the author deals with it in a cold and analytical, one might even say scientific, manner that precludes any salacious interpretation. A careful scrutiny reveals not a single line, not a single word, that might be regarded as obscene, lewd, lascivious, filthy, indecent, or disgusting with the meaning of the statute."[17]

The tragedy for the characters in *Reigen* is that they cannot find what they are continuously looking for: real love and total commitment. The same lack of total commitment we find in the figure of Fedor, a character in Schnitzler's first full-length play *Das Märchen* (1891; The Fairy Tale). This work is based on his relationship with the actress Mizi Glümer, a woman he passionately loved. Despite his great love for her, he did not marry her because he was unable to overlook her unfaithfulness. In his diary he noted: "I cannot marry her. It is impossible for material reasons, and I confess that I am still too much of a coward to live in Vienna with her as my wife.—I don't have to explain this further—everything is already contained in *Das Märchen*."[18]

Schnitzler describes in *Das Märchen* the fate of the actress Fanny Theren, who has had two lovers before she meets Fedor Denner, a young poet and a seemingly liberated person who, contrary to the rigid rules of society, argues that one should not consider this type of girl as inferior. Fanny's hope is crushed when she finds out that he unfortunately does not have the strength to live up to his high ideals and act independent of social opinion. Just as Fedor Denner was unable to shake off the chains of social convention, Schnizler could not persuade himself to take the final step and marry Mizi. Psychologically he could not overcome her past, and Fedor's words at the end of the play also express the conflict Schnitzler suffered: "And there is no kiss chaste enough—and no embrace scorching enough, and no love eternal enough, to extinguish the old kisses and the old love. What was, is!—that is the deeper significance of events!"[19]

The three versions of this play show Schnitzler's recognition that any problem has more than one solution and his aversion to any one-sided dogma. In this respect he exemplifies Nietzsche's concept of perspectivism. The world, as this poet-philosopher has stated many times, is capable of being interpreted from many perspectives. The result of this

Weltanschauung is the death of dogma because the world has an infinite number of interpretations. This conviction carries with it the great danger of nihilism and chaos since there is no longer a focal point to which one can refer, not even the seemingly "indestructible" I. Schnitzler is similar to Nietzsche inasmuch as he also has a tendency to view a problem or issue from various angles.

It would be wrong, however, to interpret Schnitzler fully as a perspectivist; for there are some issues on which he is not flexible. A case in point is *Professor Bernhardi* (1912; *Professor Bernhardi*). Bernhardi, director of the Elisabethinum Clinic in Vienna, refuses permission for a priest to administer the last rites to one of his female patients who is in a euphoric state and unaware of her impending death. This case is reported to the authorities, and Bernhardi, who is Jewish, finds himself subjected to anti-semitic attacks. Bernhardi has the unshakable conviction that it is his professional and human duty to reduce suffering and pain in any way he can. The same strong attitude we find in the figure of the priest, who has an equally unshakable belief in his mission. Although neither man is willing to compromise his position, Schnitzler shows in this play that understanding between opponents is possible, provided they are true to themselves and their calling. With this play Schnitzler hit a raw nerve. His criticism of the anti-semitism led the Austrian censors to bar performance of the play in 1913. It was performed again after the collapse of the monarchy in 1918, and many critics considered it among Schnitzler's finest plays.

In *Freiwild* (1898; *Free Game*) Schnitzler takes up another social problem which was of great concern to him: the fight of the individual against the social convention of dueling. The title *Freiwild* refers first to actresses in summer theaters who were considered "free game" for officers stationed in nearby garrisons. These actresses were expected by tacit agreement between the director of the theater and the audience not only to perform on stage but also to serve as companions to the military visitors. Anna Riedel, an actress, refuses to obey these game rules because she is in love with Paul Rönner. Lieutenant Karinsky, who considers Anna his "game," offends her and gets slapped by Paul. Karinsky challenges Paul to a duel, which Paul rejects as a matter of principle; Paul now also becomes "free game" because Karinsky, to save his "honor," has to shoot him down. Schnitzler's concern here was not so much the duel itself but, as he wrote in a "Rundfrage über das Duell" (Poll Concerning Dueling), the obligation to fight a duel. Schnitzler was very much opposed to any kind of societal pressure, which he criticizes in this play and other works dealing with the convention of the duel: in *Liebelei, Das weite Land (The Vast Domain)*, and the fragment *Ritterlichkeit* (Chivalry).

A recurring motif in Schnitzler's works is the interfusing of illusion and reality. This is the common element running through three of his one-act plays which premièred at the famous Burgtheater in 1899: *Der grüne Kakadu (The Green Cockatoo)*, *Die Gefährtin (translated as His Mate and His Helpmate)*, and *Paracelsus (Paracelsus)*. *Der grüne Kakadu* is set within the time frame of the French Revolution of 1789; the title is the name of an inn where actors play social outcasts to the amusement of the aristocratic audience. The audience does not know that the drama will soon become reality in the streets of Paris; the very actors who play the revolutionaries will in a few hours take part in the real revolution. The political event is interwoven with the personal love affair of Henri, the main character of this play. He announces that this will be his last performance because he intends to live with Léocadie, whom he has just married and who he knows has had an affair with the Herzog von Cadignan. Henri is willing to put Léocadie's past behind him and start a new life in the country. What Henri does not know is that the duke still is his wife's lover, a fact known to most of the audience. Henri's improvisation as a criminal, passionate, and jealous husband who pretends to have murdered the duke, is illusion to him but appears as truth to his friends, who advise him to go into hiding until the revolution is over. Henri thus learns of his wife's infidelity and, when the duke enters, converts stage illusion into reality by killing him. This murder at the dawn of the revolution makes him a hero in the eyes of his fellow actors, but in the blending of reality and illusion the whole revolution becomes questionable: if actors are revolutionaries, then the reverse is also true and the fictional nature of the proclaimed ideological basis becomes apparent.

We find a similar blending of reality and illusion in the other two one-act plays, *Paracelsus* and *Die Gefährtin*. Paracelsus is too sure of his wife's fidelity and when his wife is put into a hypnotic trance, he must learn that she had desired other men although she did not have a lover. He should therefore be cautious about taking her faithfulness for granted. Pilgrim, the husband of the recently deceased Eveline in *Die Gefährtin*, discovers his wife's unfaithfulness after her death. He is not too dismayed since he was an older man and had preferred his work to her; he can understand that she had sought satisfaction elsewhere. What does surprise him is that his wife's lover was engaged to another woman and that his wife had known of her lover's other attachment. This knowledge did not hinder Eveline from continuing her relationship with her paramour. At the end it becomes apparent that Pilgrim had not known his wife's real character at all. To all three of these plays, which are characterized by the illusory nature of reality and the real nature of illusion, the often-quoted lines of *Paracelsus* apply: "There flow together dream and waking time. Truth and deception. Certainty is nowhere. Nothing we know of others, of ourselves no more; We always play—and wise is he who knows."20

The first translation of these plays by Horace B. Samuel in 1913 evoked the following comment of the reviewer:

> The three one-act plays in this volume are characterized by an altogether unusual amount of detail, not entirely subordinated to the main theme. *The Green Cockatoo*, recently performed by the Stage Society, is an extreme example of this elaboration. There is a play within a play, and the internal drama is allowed to expand, and finally to envelop all the characters. *The Mate*, while its humor is distinctly Schnitzler's, is almost like Strindberg in the succession of ignoble revelations. *Paracelsus* also introduces a secondary theme which embraces in the end the whole action; and here, as often elsewhere, Schnitzler makes use of the device of hypnotism on the stage, which he employs with extraordinary effect. The personality that emerges from these plays is pleasant, and, if a trifle cynical, has something of the geniality of Anatole France. 22

A play within a play with the internal drama expanding is found also in *Leutnant Gustl* (1900; translated as *None But the Brave*). Written entirely in the form of an interior monologue, the reader can look into this young lieutenant's mind with all his prejudices and bigotry. The external event which triggers these impressionistic associations is simply told: Gustl, who is given a ticket to a concert he does not enjoy, argues with a baker who, standing before him in a queue before the cloakroom, grabs his sword, and insults him. Gustl cannot cope with the baker because he does not want to cause a scene; thus, according to the military code of honor, he must now commit suicide or resign from the army. The chance incident sets in motion the psychological drama, which exposes the lack of values in Gustl. The frightened Gustl wanders all night through Vienna preparing to end his life. In the morning, when he learns that the baker has died from a stroke, a burden is lifted from him. The entire experience is forgotten, and at the end Gustl remains exactly the same as he was at the beginning; the experience of the night and the insight into his own shallow, vain self are a thing of the past.

Schnitzler succeeds here in laying bare not only the officer's innermost personal thoughts, but also the superficial values of an Austrian officer, whose vanity and conceit can be regarded as representative of a typical army officer's mentality at that time. This feature was recognized by a reviewer in 1926 who remarked: "[Gustl] is made to stiletto his own vitals. And behind him Schnitzler does not let us forget the emptiness of the whole military class of which this one individual is supposed to be representative."[23] Another critic concluded that *Leutnant Gustl* has an underlying tone of a savage satire on the professional military officer:

> Young Gustl's half-baked opinions and stubborn dogmaticism are imperceptibly but inexorably indicated. Schnitzler makes clear that Gustl is the fine flower of a ridiculous and untenable position: that a resort to force is the confirmation of a lofty and upright nature, and the only way to establish truth. The brass buttons and gold braid are left very little glamour when Schnitzler has finished with Gustl, the braggart and café bully, the coward with the chip on his shoulder. [24]

Schnitzler's criticism of the military mentality was well understood in his time; at a court martial he was charged with defamation of the army and stripped of his commission as a reserve lieutenant. This judgement was welcomed especially by the nationalistic and anti-semitic press; in their denunciations they discredited Schnitzler as a writer: "Schnitzler, the literary Jew . . . trashy literature . . . Shameful work . . . We say 'our army' . . . because it is a thoroughly Aryan one, therefore, strictly antithetical to Jewish nature and fundamentally despised by the Hebrews."

The same social criticism that we have in *Leutnant Gustl* we can also detect in Schnitzler's unshakable conviction that politics and politicians are suspect. Schnitzler, a pacifist, believed that wars cause senseless slaughter. He presented his views in the pamphlet *Über Krieg und Frieden* (1939, *Some Day Peace Will Return*) published in *Aphorismen und Betrachtungen* (1967, *Reflections and Aphorisms*). One example is the following, written in 1915:

> The thesis of Clausewitz that war is nothing but politics by different means is witty, therefore half-true, therefore dangerous, therefore

nonsense. So is the dictum that war is a necessity and that therefore one must not oppose it. Plague and cholera too are "necessities." Only the fact that we do oppose such alleged necessities makes us really human beings. And, in any case, defending oneself is also a necessity... The only indubitable possession of man is his life ... Compulsory military service, however, is the most monstrous violation of the one indubitable possession of man.

Schnitzler continues his satire of military life in *Spiel im Morgengrauen* (1927, *Daybreak*). In this novel Lieutenant Willi Kasda wants to help a comrade in financial straits. First he wins at the gambling table, but then his luck runs out, and he finds himself in the same predicament as the friend he thought to help. He now turns to his uncle, the only person who can assist him. However, his uncle's younger wife, Leopoldine, controls the purse strings, and it is she who will decide his fate. Ironically, it was she with whom Kasda many years before had spent a night and, not sensing that she loved him, he had paid her for her services. Leopoldine now agrees to spend another night with him, but instead of paying his debt she leaves him the same denomination banknote he left her. Kasda sends this note to his fellow-officer, but unable to pay his own debts, he obeys the honor code of the Austrian army and shoots himself, unaware that Leopoldine will send the amount he needs later. He is thus more consistent than Gustl, who does not have the courage to act in accordance with the prescribed code of military honor. Kasda's death can be seen, however, as poetic justice. He is punished for a deed he had forgotten but that had a powerful impact on the life of the other person, in this case Leopoldine, who appears to be acting here almost as the executrix of a higher fate. In this story as in other works by Schnitzler there are occurrences beyond human comprehension which cannot be explained through human logic. An American reviewer praised the book: "In this book Schnitzler shows himself, as usual, to be a clever literary craftsman. The plot moves smoothly and inexorably to its painful conclusion... In its implied criticism of an entire social caste it... makes one look forward hopefully to the full-length novel *Theresa* which is announced for the spring." [27]

Therese (1928 *Theresa*) chronicles the life of a woman who is the daughter of an Austrian officer and a Hungarian princess. After she leaves home, she becomes a governess in Vienna, where she has various affairs during the next few years but with little personal involvement. She is a passive lover "merely succumbing, rather wearily, to numerous adventures, none of which result in any permanent attachment." [28] A few times she has the opportunity to find happiness, but one of her lovers commits suicide and another dies from a heart attack. She is left alone save for her son, whom she curses before he is born. This son turns out to be a criminal, blackmailing his own mother. While trying to rob her, he injures her so badly that she dies. Before her death she requests that her son not be punished too severely: "He is innocent. He has only repaid what I did to him. He must not be punished too severely." [29] *Therese* is a work of social criticism, and also one in which, as in *Spiel im Morgengrauen,* some mysterious higher order punishes severely those who transgress against an inherent universal moral law. Therese understands this situation at the moment of her death when she discovers her love for the son at the moment he has become "executor of an eternal justice."

Other works dealing with the fate of women include *Frau Bertha Garlan* (1900, *Bertha Garlan*), *Frau Beate und ihr Sohn* (1913, *Beatrice*) and *Fräulein Else* (1924, *Fräulein Else*). All of the women in these works belong to the Viennese upper middle class and, as Agnes Jacques has pointed out, "intellectually these three women are strikingly similar—they are able to view their anguish with detachment, impersonally and without illusion." [30] Bertha Garlan, a middle-aged woman, whose husband has been dead for three years lives with her young son in a small provincial town, earning a living by giving piano lessons. She is still attractive and is pursued by Klingemann, the local Casanova, and also by her brother-in-law. She and Frau Rupius, who is married to an invalid, travel to Vienna, where Frau Rupius apparently has an affair and Bertha Garlan meets Emil, a famous virtuoso whom Bertha knew from earlier years. Emil spends one night with her and despite Bertha's desire to see him again soon, he offers her an opportunity to spend only one night with him at six-week intervals. This suggestion Bertha rejects, and all of a sudden she realizes that not love had motivated her to spend the hour with Emil but "the desire of the moment." This insight brings the awareness that she had committed a sin; she sees a parallel between herself and Frau Rupius, who is dying from an abortion: "It would only be a justified punishment of heaven, if she were to perish for her dishonor just like the poor woman [Frau Rupius]." In Bertha there is now an unquestionable certainty that she is to die: "She sensed the immense injustice in the world, that the desire for bliss has been instilled in woman just as in man; but that this becomes sin in woman and demands atonement if the desire for bliss is not at the same time the desire for a child."

Beate in *Frau Beate und ihr Sohn* is also a middle-aged woman, a widow of eight years, who tries to break off a love affair between her seventeen-year old son and the Baroness Fortunata, a former actress in her husband's acting group. A little later she finds herself in the same situation when she has an affair with her son's nineteen-year old friend Fritz. When her son learns of this, ironically from the Baroness, he cannot face the world any longer. Beate feels betrayed because her young lover's bragging about his affair has reduced her experience to a dirty joke; thus she and her son drown themselves. Schnitzler prepared the reader for this passionate side of Beate, which does not suddenly spring into existence but has always been there. Beate, who had been a faithful wife to her actor-husband, found satisfaction for her varied erotic desires by imagining to be someone else: "In her early girlhood had she not wished to be the wife of the actor because union with him offered the only possibility for her to live the decorous life which her bourgeois upbringing had intended for her, and at the same time to lead the wild adventurous existence for which she longed in her secret dreams?"[31] Max A. Egloff in 1926 came to the conclusion that "*Beatrice* is a story which many will immediately applaud and later condemn. Only in retrospect will it appear as the exaggeration that it is, and this display of Herr Schnitzler's profound psychological insight transform itself into magnificent exhibitionism."[32]

Fräulein Else, like *Leutnant Gustl,* is written in the form of an interior monologue. This enables the reader to experience everything that concerns Else directly. Else, who is staying with some family members at a Swiss summer resort inn, receives a letter from her mother asking her to help her father. He embezzled 30 000 Gulden from a trust fund and has to restore it or go to prison; this amount is later raised to 50 000. Else's mother suggests to her that she solicit the help of Dorsday, a middle-aged wealthy art dealer. Else swallows her pride and asks for the assistance. Dorsday promises his help provided he can see Else in the nude for a short while. Else is now in a state of great confusion—she loves her father and wants to help him, but her sense of decency is equally strong. Her attachment to her father is also mixed with resentment because his embezzlement has placed her into this shameful situation in the first place. She goes to her room, takes her clothes off, puts on a fur coat, and goes to the music room, where someone is playing Schumann's *Karneval*. She finds Dorsday among other guests, lets her coat drop, and thus fulfills the condition set by Dorsday. She then loses consciousness and is carried to her room, where she later takes an overdose of sleeping pills. Before she dies, she experiences a moment of metaphysical bliss, hearing the music of the spheres, which puts her in harmony with herself and the world, including a reconciliation with her father. "The writhings of the girl's soul," Amy Loveman remarked, "the decision and indecision that alike tear her, the final shift of emotion from Else to those around her while she is still maintained as the medium through which the feelings of all are reflected, are conveyed with a directness that is as highly charged as it is effective. From start to finish the story moves with absolute certainty. Its technique is flawless." [33]

A highly personal theme for Schnitzler was the problem of aging, which is portrayed in *Dr. Gräsler - Badearzt* (1917, *Dr. Graesler*), which he had included with *Frau Beate und ihr Sohn* and *Casanovas Heimfahrt* (1918, *Casanova's Homecoming*) in an anthology entitled *Die Alternden* (The Aging). The seriousness of this concern is reflected in the diary entry of 23 April 1900: "I have a growing fear of becoming old, an immense need for tenderness, to be loved, adored, admired. Only this relieves me occasionally of my feeling of anxiety." Four days later he wrote in his diary: "There is only *one* experience—that is: getting old. Everything else is adventure."

The principal character in *Dr. Gräsler* is a middle-aged bachelor physician whose sister has just passed away. Afraid of spending the rest of his life alone, he is psychologically prepared to enter marriage, which is not an easy decision for him because of his lack of self-confidence, especially in his conduct toward women of his own social class. First he meets Sabine, a beautiful and upright woman who is living with her parents at the spa. Despite her obvious willingness to marry him he is too timid to take the final step of asking her. He returns to his home town, where he meets Katharina, a common store clerk, with whom he spends a few weeks of sexual bliss before he decides to approach Sabine again. Rejected by her, he returns to Katharina prepared to marry her but discovers that she is dying of scarlet fever. He ends up marrying the woman whose small daughter he treated for the same disease with which he infected Katharina. His marriage is based not so much on love but on his growing old; as Edwin Muir commented in *The Freeman* on 27 February 1924, it is "the final capitulation of a gentle soul to life as it is. As such it is unbearably sad; yet, since everything in Schnitzler's novels has an enigmatic ring, it is not entirely sad. One feels that the continuity of life will return, on a level of lower vitality it is true, but in the form in which it can best be borne by the protagonist, and not without a measure of solace." [34]

While *Dr. Gräsler* has a certain enigmatic ring to it, *Casanovas Heimfahrt* is far more dramatic. It is one of Schnitzler's masterworks, which in the first eleven years went through forty-nine editions. This novella, as Gabriela Annan remarked, is "about the humiliation of old age as suffered by the decrepit Italian adventurer."[35] Schnitzler portrays the aging adventurer's return to his beloved city, Venice, which he had to leave because of his political leanings. Waiting for the permission of the city's authorities to enter his birthplace, he stays with an old acquaintance and meets the young and beautiful Marcolina, who possesses everything he has always wanted in a woman. He is almost beside himself with the desire to be close to her, a desire increasing in intensity after he observed Lorenzi, a younger version of himself, leaving Marcolina's bedchamber. He beats Lorenzi in a cardgame, knowing that the young lieutenant cannot pay his gambling debt, and then proposes that Lorenzi exchange places with Casanova so that the old adventurer can spend the night with Marcolina. Lorenzi agrees and Casanova, entering Marcolina's room in the dark, experiences a bliss he has never known. In the morning Marcolina finds out that she has been deceived, and he reads in her eyes "the word which to him was the most dreadful of all words, since it passed the final judgement upon him: old man." When he leaves her room, he is confronted by Lorenzi, whom he kills in a duel. The conclusion leaves open who has the better fate since Casanova has to spend the rest of his life working as a spy for the authorities he has always despised. Casanova might have enjoyed a better fate if he had not insisted that Lorenzi pay his gambling debt in the form he had. Casanova experienced foreboding but his passion was stronger than his altruism.

The publication of this work in the States aroused considerable controversy. It was banned until 1930 when Magistrate Maurice Gottlieb threw out the suit brought against the book by the New York Society for the Suppression of Vice, declaring that "the book must be measured by living standards of our own time, not by those of the mid-Victorian era. He hailed Arthur Schnitzler as one of the world's greatest writers and characterized *Casanova's Homecoming* as an incontestable contribution to literature."[36]

A theme Schnitzler treated numerous times is the subconscious workings of the sexual and psychological desires in a marital situation. In *Traumnovelle* (1926, *Rhapsody*) these subconscious desires and fears are presented in masterful compact form. Fridolin and Albertine, a seemingly happily married couple, talk about their unfulfilled erotic opportunities, and it becomes clear that below the surface of their conventional marriage strong desires and mutual distrust present a danger to their union: "The business of living is honeycombed with countless corridors through which slide the instinctive desires, the half-awakened madnesses, the colored romanticisms, the appalling sex demands that make up the conglomerate soul of an individual."[37] Schnitzler places Fridolin in situations where he has an opportunity to experience his erotic fantasies, but it becomes apparent that Fridolin's moral restraints and his love for Albertine keep him from living out his desires with someone else. At the same time, Albertine enjoys sexual freedom and erotic bliss—not in reality but in a wild erotic dream which reveals her secret desire and cruelty and also, mysteriously, contains many elements of Fridolin's nightly adventure, including her husband's ethical stand. Dream and reality mingle, as in many of Schnitzler's works, and finally the couple understands the fragile nature of their relationship. To Fridolin's question of what they should do now, Albertine replies: "I think that we ought to be thankful to fate that we have come unharmed out of all our adventures, whether they were real or only a dream . . . I sense that the reality of one night, not even the reality of an entire life is at the same time its innermost truth."

The last work Schnitzler published during his lifetime was *Flucht in die Finsternis* (1931, *Flight into Darkness*.) Central characters of this novella are two brothers, Otto, the psychiatrist, and Robert, who is slowly losing his mind. Robert had asked Otto to kill him if madness were ever to befall him, and Otto had reluctantly agreed to do so. Recognizing his insanity, Robert now lives in constant fear that Otto will make good his promise. Persecution mania sets in and Robert, misinterpreting the signs of brotherly love and affection as hostile, kills his brother. Three days later Robert is found dead. In this gripping story the physician Dr. Leinbach has told Robert that death is actually non-existent because all the dying live out their past lives in the last moment of their remembered life; since this last moment contains another last moment, "Hence, dying itself was nothing different from eternity in accordance with the formula of a mathematical progression."[38] Robert ponders this "Logik des Metaphysischen" (logic of the metaphysical) and concludes: "If that explanation were correct, one would not know how many times one had lived through any one experience, nor did it matter, since one was condemned to live through all his experiences an infinite number of times."[39]

Robert's explanation of being condemned to an eternal life differs sharply from Johanna Wegrath's decision in *Der Einsame Weg* (1904, *The Lonely Way*) to commit suicide. She does so because she accepts the idea of eternal recurrence, which gives her another chance to be together with Sala, the person she loves and who she knows will die soon. Both aspects of eternal recurrence, the positive life-affirming one and the pessimistic-nihilistic one, show again Schnitzler's fusion of life and death. In addition they indicate that he grew more pessimistic as he grew older; if one is *condemned* to an eternal life, one loses one's freedom, which Schnitzler considered one of the most precious commodities of human existence.

Arthur Schnitzler cannot be interpreted within the narrow framework of any one system, psychoanalysis included. Although Schnitzler and Freud were contemporaries living in the same city and sharing the same professional interest, Schnitzler does not fit the psychoanalytical mold, nor any other dogmatic framework. His perspectivism, noted in many of his works, is the result of his honesty and skepticism, which later turned to pessimism. He believed that human beings are beset by sometimes contradictory values which testify to the all-comprehensiveness and interconnectedness of the "Human-All-Too-Human" world. In the drama *Das weite Land* (1911, *The Vast Domain*) one of the characters expresses Schnitzler's basic philosophy as follows: "Shouldn't you have observed what complex subjects we humans basically are? We can accommodate so many things at the same time—! Love and deception . . . Faithfulness and infidelity . . . Worship for one and desire for another or others. We try to create order within ourselves, as best we can, but this order is truly only something artificial... The natural state... is chaos... Yes... , the soul... is a vast domain, as a poet once expressed it." [40]

One can also find this quotation in his autobiography, *Jugend in Wien* (1968, *My Life in Vienna*), where he refers to *Das weite Land* and remarks: "Feelings and reason may sleep under the same roof, but they run their own completely separate households in the human soul." [41] Nietzsche once referred to these 'modern' people as "Dividuen" (dividuals) in contrast to the traditional notion of men and women as "individuals." The dividuality of man also makes it difficult to achieve a very close union with a partner or partners; people may discover sooner or later in life that the person they loved was not worthy of their affection, that their most intimate feelings were based on a delusion because their partner was really a stranger. Once this truth is known, "there will be," as Oskar Seidlin so aptly stated it, "no outcry to herald it. A world may collapse, all that a human being has loved and lived for may be buried under the landslide of a shattering revelation, the ground upon which one stands may tremble and give, but all we hear is the faltering of a voice, a muffled breathless stammer, a brief choked silence. And yet, we do not doubt for a second that in this stammer, in this moment of silence a human life is breaking to pieces. Tragedy engulfs us, but the conversation flows on, *sotte voce,* in Schnitzler's inimitable *sotte voce.*"[42] As long as these human tragedies remain with us, Schnitzler's works will be read and appreciated because behind their elegant and polished style an aspect of the vast domain of the human soul and man's loneliness becomes visible. This is as true today as in Schnitzler's own time.

Notes

1. Walter Goodman, "Stage: 'Romance Romance,' Two Plays, *New York Times* 17 November 1987: C 15.

2. Walter Goodman, "A Small-Scale Romantic Musical Moves Uptown." *New York Times* 2 May 1988: C 15.

3. Martin Schaefer, "Romance/Romance," *Backstage* 20 May 1988: 38-39.

4. Paul F. Dvorak, Introduction to *Illusion and Reality. Plays and Stories of Arthur Schnitzler,* translated and introduced by Paul F. Dvorak (New York, Berne, Frankfurt am Main: Peter Lang, 1986), p.xvii.

5. Stephanie Hammer, "Fear and Attraction: *Anatol* and *Liebelei* Productions in the United States," *Modern Austrian Literature,* Special Twenty-Fifth Anniversary Issue, 19, no. 3/4 (1986), 65.

6. Anon., "Dialogues for Adults," *The New York Times* 13 August 1911, 496.

7. Arthur Schnitzler, *Jugend in Wien. Eine Autobiographie* (Wien, München, Zürich: Molden, 1968), p. 114.

8. Arthur Schnitzler, *My Youth in Vienna,* translated by Catherine Hutter, foreward by Frederic Morton (New York, Chicago, San Francisco: Holt, Rinehart and Winston, Inc., 1970) , pp. 92-93.

9. Arthur Schnitzler, "Liebelei," in *Gesammelte Werke. Die Dramatischen Werke,* I (Frankfurt am Main: S. Fischer Verlag, 1962), 219.

10. Arthur Schnitzler, "Flirtations," in A. S., *Plays and Stories,* edited by Egon Schwarz and foreword by Stanley Elkin (New York: Continuum, 1982), p.6.

11. "Liebelei," 219.

12. "Flirtations," p. 6.

13. J. P. Stern, "Introduction," in A. S., *Liebelei, Leutnant Gustl, Die letzten Masken*, ed. J. P. Stern (Cambridge: At the University Press, 1966), p. 15.

14. Martin Swales, *Arthur Schnitzler. A Critical Study* (Oxford: Clarendon Press, 1971), p. 198.

15. F. L. G[laser] and L. D. E[dwards], "Introduction," *Hands Around [Reigen]. A Cycle of Ten Dialogues by Arthur Schnitzler.* Authorized Translation. Number 618 of 1475 copies (New York: Privately Printed for Members of the Schnitzler Society, 1929), p. xiii.

16. Wolfgang Heine, Ed. *Der Kampf um den Reigen. Vollständiger Bericht über die sechstägige Verhandlung gegen Direktion und Darsteller des Kleinen Schauspielhauses* (Berlin: Rowohlt, 1922), p.164.

17. "When Judges Disagree," *The Publisher's Weekly*, xxiv, no. 116, 14 December 1929, 2758.

18. Arthur Schnitzler, unpublished diary entry of 15 September 1892.

19. Arthur Schnitzler, "Das Märchen, *Die Dramatischen Werke*, I, 198.

20. Arthur Schnitzler "Paracelsus." *Die Dramatischen Werke*, I, 498.

21. Arthur Schnitzler "Paracelsus," in *The Green Cockatoo and Other Plays.* Tr. Horace B. Samuel (Chicago: A.C. McClurg, 1913), p. 121.

22. Anon., "*Schnitzler (Arthur), The Green Cockatoo and Other Plays*, translated by Horace B. Samuel," *The Athenaeum* (London) 31 May 1913: 599.

23. Anon., *None But the Brave* (Arthur Schnitzler), *The Saturday Review of Literature* 4 December 1926: 399.

24. Anon., "Schnitzler's Surgery [review of *None But the Brave*], *"New York Times Book Review* 24 October 1926: 31.

25. *österreichische Volkspresse* 30 June 1901, quoted by Otto P. Schinnerer, "Schnitzler and the Military Censorship: Unpublished Correspondence," *The Germanic Review*, 5 (1930): 245: translation of this passage in part by Robert O. Weiss, in Arthur Schnitzler, *Some Day Peace will Return. Notes on War and Peace*, edited, translated and introduced by Robert O. Weiss (New York: Ungar, 1972), pp. 4-5.

26. Arthur Schnitzler, *Gesammelte Werke. Aphorismen und Betrachtungen*, ed. Robert O. Weiss (Frankfurt am Main: S.

Fischer Verlag, 1967), pp. 205-206.   Translation by Robert O. Weiss in *Some Day Peace will Return*, pp. 54-55.

27. Rose Lee, "Schnitzler's Tragedy has a Light Touch," *New York Time Book Review* 27 November 1927, 5.

28. A.W.G. Randall, "A New Schnitzler," *The Saturday Review of Literature* 21 July 1928: 1953.

29. Arthur Schnitzler, "Therese," in *Gesammelte Werke. Die Erzählenden Schriften*, II (Frankfurt am Main: S. Fischer, 1962), p. 880.

30. Arthur Schnitzler, *Beatrice*, translated by Agnes Jacques (New York: Simon and Schuster, 1928, p. iii.

31. *Beatrice - A Novel*, pp. 12-13.

32. *The Saturday Review*, 15 May 1926: 785.

33. Ibid., 23 November 1925: 335.

34. *The Freeman*, 27 February 1924: 596.

35. *The New York Times Review of Books*, 21 July 1983: 16.

36. *Publisher's Weekly*, 27 September 1930: 1532.

37. *The New York Times Review of Books*, 27 March 1927: 5.

38. Arthur Schnitzler, "Flucht in die Finsternis," in *Gesammelte Werke. Die Erzählenden Schriften*, II (Frankfurt am Main: S. Fischer, 1962), p. 917.

39. Ibid. p. 913.

40. Arthur Schnitzler, *Gesammelte Werke. Die Dramatischen Werke*, II (Frankfurt am Main: S. Fischer, 1962), p. 281.

41. Arthur Schnitzler, *Jegend in Wien*. eds., Therese Nickl and Heinrich Schnitzler (Wien, München, Zürich: Molden, 1968), p. 274.

42. Oskar Seidlin, "In Memoriam Arthur Schnitzler: May 15, 1862-October 21, 1932," *The American-Germanic Review*, XXVIII, iv (1962): 4.

Selected Bibliography

I.   Works in German

A.   Bibliographies

1879-1965: Allen, Richard H. *An Annotated Arthur Schnitzler Bibliography*. Chapel Hill: University of North Carolina Press,

1965. 1965-1977: Berlin, Jeffrey B. *An Annotated Arthur Schnitzler Bibliography.* München: Fink, 1978. For subsequent years see *Modern Austrian Literature.*

B.   Works

Gesammelte Werke in zwei Abteilungen. Die Erzählenden Schriften, 1-3. Berlin: S. Fischer, 1912.

Gesammelte Werke. Die Theaterstücke, 1-4. Berlin: S. Fischer, 1913.

Der Geist im Wort und der Geist in der Tat. Vorläufige Bemerkungen zu zwei Diagrammen. Berlin: S. Fischer, 1927.

Über Krieg und Frieden. Stockholm: Bermann-Fischer, 1939.

Gesammelte Werke. Die Erzählenden Schriften, 1-2. Frankfurt am Main: S. Fischer, 1961-1962.

Gesammelte Werke. Die Dramatischen Werke, 1-2. Frankfurt am Main: S. Fischer, 1962.

Aphorismen und Betrachtungen. ed. Robert O. Weiss. Frankfurt am Main: S. Fischer, 1967.

Frühe Gedichte. ed. Herbert Lederer. Berlin: Propyläen-Verlag, 1969.

Meisterdramen. Frankfurt am Main: S. Fischer, 1971.

Meistererzählungen. Frankfurt am Main: S. Fischer, 1975: Zürich: Diogenes Verlag, 1975.

Gesammelte Werke in Einzelausgaben. Das erzählerische Werk in 7 Bänden. *Das dramatische Werk* in 8 Bänden. Frankfurt am Main: Fischer Taschenbuchverlag, 1977-1979.

Beziehungen und Einsamkeiten. Aphorismen. ed. Clemens Eich. Frankfurt am Main: Fischer Verlag, 1987. (Fischer Taschenbuch 5980).

C.   Published Posthumously: Poetic Works, and Autobiography

Entworfenes und Verworfenes. Aus dem Nachlaß. Ed. Reinhard Urbach. Frankfurt am Main: S. Fischer Verlag, 1977.

Jugend in Wien. Eine Autobiographie. Eds, Therese Nickl and Heinrich Schnitzler. Wien, München, Zürich: Molden, 1968: Berlin, Weimar: Aufbau, 1985.

Ritterlichkeit. Fragment aus dem Nachlaß. R. Schlein. Bonn: Bouvier, 1975.

Das Wort. Tragikomödie in fünf Akten. Kurt Bergel. Frankfurt am Main: S. Fischer, 1966.

"Über Psychoanalyse," ed. Reinhard Urbach. *Protokolle* 2 (1976): 27-284.

Zug der Schatten. Drama in 9 Bildern (unvollendet). Ed. Francoise Derré. Frankfurt am Main: S. Fischer, 1970.

Tagebuch 1879-1892. Ed. Werner Welzig, et al. Wien: Verlag der Österreichischen Akademie der Wissenschaften, 1987.

Tagebuch 1909-1912. Wien: Verlag der Österreichischen Akademie der Wissenschaften, 1981.

Tagebuch 1913-1916. Wien: Verlag der Österreichischen Akademie der Wissenschaften, 1983.

Tagebuch 1917-1919. Wien: Verlag der Österreichischen Akademie der Wissenschaften, 1985.

E.   Unpublished Material

Neumann, Gerhard & Jutta Müller. *Der Nachlaß Arthur Schnitzlers. Verzeichnis des im Schnitzler-Archiv der Universität Freiburg i. Br. befindlichen Materials.* München: Fink, 1969.

Welzig, Werner. "Im Archiv und über Briefen. Mitteilungen aus dem Nachlaß," in Hans-Henrik Krummacher, ed., *Zeit der Moderne.* Stuttgart: Metzler, 1984.

II.   Works in English Translation

1.   Narrative Prose

Beatrice: A Novel. Tr. Agnes Jacques. New York: Simon & Schuster, 1926.

Bertha Garlan. Tr. Agnes Jacques. Boston: Badger, 1913: New York: Boni & Liveright, 1918. Tr. J. H. Wisdom and Marr Murray. London: M. Goschen, 1914.

Casanova's Homecoming. Trs. Eden & Cedar Paul. New York: Thomas Seltzer, 1922: London: Brentano's, 1923: New York: Simon and Schuster, 1930: New York: Avon, 1948: London: Weidenfeld & Nicolson, 1954: London: World Distributors, 1959.

Daybreak. Tr. William A. Drake. New York: Simon and Schuster, 1927.

Dr. Graesler. Tr. E.C. Slade. New York: Thomas Seltzer, 1923: London: Chapman & Hall, 1924: New York: Simon and Schuster, 1930.

Flight into Darkness. Tr. William A. Drake. New York: Simon and Schuster, 1931.

Fräulein Else: A Novel. Tr. Robert A. Simon. New York: Simon and Schuster, 1925: *Fräulein Else.* Tr. F. H. Lyon. A. M. Philpot: 1925: London: Constable, 1929.

My Youth In Vienna. Tr. Catherine Hutter. Foreword by Frederick Morton. New York, Chicago, San Francisco: Holt, Rinehart and Winston, Inc. 1970.

None but the Brave [Leutnant Gustl]. Tr. Richard L. Simon. New York: Simon and Schuster, 1926.

Rhapsody: A Dream Novel. Tr. Otto P. Schinnerer. New York, 1927.

Some Day Peace will Return. Notes on War and Peace. Edited, translated and introduced by Robert O. Weiss. New York: Ungar, 1972.

The Mind in Words and Action. Preliminary Remarks Concerning Two Diagrams. Translated and introduced by Robert O. Weiss. New York: Ungar, 1972.

The Road to the Open. Tr. Horace Samuel. London: H. Latimer, 1913: New York: Alfred A. Knopf, 1923: London: George Allen and Unwin.

Theresa: The Chronicle of a Women's Life. Tr. William A. Drake. New York: Simon & Schuster, 1928: London: Constable, 1929.

2.   Dramatic works

Anatol. A Sequence of Dialogues. Paraphrased for the English stage by Granville Barker. London: Sidgwick & Jackson, 1911: New York: Mitchell Kennerley, 1911.

Countess Mizzi. Tr. Edwin Björkman. Boston: Little, Brown, 1907.

Free Game. Tr. Paul H. Grummann. Boston: Badger, 1913.

Gallant Cassian: A Puppet Play in One Act. London & Glasgow: Gowans & Gray, 1914. Tr. Adam L. Gowans: Boston: Leroy Philipps, 1921.

Hands Around: A Roundelay in Ten Dialogues. Tr. Keene Wallis. Illustrated René Gockings. New York: Julian Press, 1929. [Many other translations of this work exist.]

Light-O' Love: A Drama in Three Acts. Tr. Bayard Quincy Morgan. Chicago: Dramatic Publishing Co., 1912: also *Playing with Love.*

Chicago: A. C. McClurg, London: Gay & Hancock, 1914.
Playing with Love. Tr. P. Morton Shand. The Prologue to *Anatol,*
by Hugo von Hofmannsthal, rendered into English verse by Trevor
Blakemore. London: Gay & Hancock, 1914.
The Lonely Way. Tr. Edwin Björkman. Boston: Little Brown, 1904.
Professor Bernhardi: A Comedy. Adaptation in English by Mrs. Emil
Pohli. San Francisco: Paul Elder, 1913. [Abridged]: also
Professor Bernhardi: A Comedy in Five Acts. Tr. Hetty Landstone.
London: Faber & Gwyer, 1927: New York: Simon & Schuster,
1928.

III.   Secondary Works in English

Bailey, Joseph W. "Arthur Schnitzler's Dramatic Work," *Texas Review* 5,
no. 4 (1920): 294-307.
Behariell, Frederick J., "Arthur Schnitzler's Range of Theme,"
Monatshefte 43, no. 7 (1951): 301-311.
Carr, G.J. and Eda Sagarra, eds. *Fin-de Siècle Vienna.* Dublin: Trinity
College, 1985.
Lederer, Herbert. "Arthur Schnitzler's Typology. An Excursion into
Philosophy," *PMLA* 78 (1963): 394-406.
Liptzin, Sol. *Arthur Schnitzler.* New York: Prentice Hall, 1932.
Politzer, Heinz. "Arthur Schnitzler: Poetry of Psychology," *Modern
Language Notes* 78, no. 4 (1963): 353-372.
Reichert, Herbert W. and Herbert Salinger, editors. *Studies in Arthur
Schnitzler. Centennial Commemorative Volume.* Chapel Hill:
University of North Carolina Press, 1963.
Schinnerer, Otto P., "The Early Works of Arthur Schnitzler," *The
Germanic Review* 4 (1929): 153-197.
——."The Literary Appprenticeship of Arthur Schnitzler," *The
Germanic Review* 5 (1930): 58-82.
Schneider, Gerd K., The Reception of Arthur Schnitzler's *Reigen* in the
Old Country and the New World: A Study in Cultural Differences,"
Modern Austrian Literature, 19, nos. 3/4 (1986): 75-89.
Seidlin, Oskar. "In Memoriam Arthur Schnitzler: May 15, 1862-October
21, 1931," *The American-German Review* 28, no. 4 (1962): 4-6.
Schorske, Carl E. "Politics and the Psyche: Schnitzler and
Hofmannsthal," in C.E.S., *Fin-De-Siècle Vienna. Politics and
Culture.* New York: Random House, 1981. pp. 3-23.
Swales, Martin. *Arthur Schnitzler: A Critical Study.* Oxford: Clarendon
Press, 1971.

Tax, Petrus W. and Richard H. Lawson, editors. *Arthur Schnitzler and his Age. Intellectual and Artistic Currents.* (Symposium on 'Fin de Siècle'). Bonn: Bouvier, 1984. (Modern German Studies. vol. 13.)

Urbach, Reinhard. *Arthur Schnitzler.* Tr. Donald G. Daviau. New York: Frederick Ungar Publishing Co., 1973. (World Dramatists)

Viereck, George S. "The World of Arthur Schnitzler," *Modern Austrian Literature* 5, no. 3-4 (1972): 7-17.

Wiener, Marc. *Arthur Schnitzler and the Crisis of Musical Culture.* Heidelberg: Carl Winter, 1986.

Weiss, Robert O., "Arthur Schnitzler's Literary and Philosophical Development," *Journal of the American Arthur Schnitzler Research Association* 2, no. 1 (1963): 4-20.

Zohn, Harry. "Schnitzler and the Challenge of Zionism," *Journal of the American Arthur Schnitzler Research Association* 1, no. 4-5 (1962): 5-7.

IV.   Major Studies in German

Baumann, Gerhart. *Arthur Schnitzler. Die Welt von gestern eines Dichters von morgen.* Frankfurt am Main: Athenäum-Verlag, 1965.

Janz, Rolf-Peter, Klaus Laermann. *Arthur Schnitzler: Zur Diagnose des Wiener Bürgertums im Fin de Siècle.* Stuttgart: Metzler, 1977.

Just, Gottfried. *Ironie und Sentimentalität in den erzählenden Dichtungen Arthur Schnitzlers.* Berlin: Erich Schmidt, 1968. (Philologische Studien und Quellen. H. 42.)

Koerner, Josef. *Arthur Schnitzlers Gestalten und Probleme.* Wien: Amalthea, 1921.

Lindken, Ulrich. *Arthur Schnitzler: Aspekte und Akzente. Materialien zu Leben und Werk.* Frankfurt am Main, Bern [usw]: Lang, 1984. (Europäische Hochschulschriften. Reihe 1. Bd. 754.)

Melchinger, Christa. *Illusion und Wirklichkeit im dramatischen Werk Arthur Schnitzlers.* Heidelberg: Carl Winter, 1968. (Beiträge zur neueren Literaturgeschichte. 3. F. Bd. 7.)

Offermanns, Ernst L. *Arthur Schnitzler. Das Komödienwerk als Kritik des Impressionimsus.* München: Fink, 1973. (Kritische Information. 9.)

Perlmann, Michaela L. *Arthur Schnitzler.* Stuttgart: J.B. Metzlersche Verlagsbuchhandlung, 1987.

Reik, Theodor. *Arthur Schnitzler als Psycholog.* Minden, Westfalen: J.C.C. Bruns, [1913].

Rey, William H. "Arthur Schnitzler." In: *Deutsche Dichter der Moderne.* ed. Benno von Wiese. 2nd, rev. ed. Berlin: Erich Schmidt, 1969. pp. 237-257.

——.*Arthur Schnitzler. Die späte Prosa als Gipfel seines Schaffens.* Berlin: Erich Schmidt, 1968.

Scheible, Hartmut. *Arthur Schnitzler und die Aufklärung.* München: Wilhelm Fink Verlag, 1977.

Schnitzler, Heinrich, Christian Brandstätter, Reinhard Urbach, eds. *Arthur Schnitzler. Sein Leben, sein Werk, seine Zeit.* Frankfurt am Main: S. Fischer, 1981.

Seidler, Herbert. "Die Forschung zu Arthur Schnitzler seit 1945," *Zeitschrift für Deutsche Philologie* 95 (1976): 576-595.

Specht, Richard. *Arthur Schnitzler, der Dichter und sein Werk. Eine Studie.* Berlin: S. Fischer 1922.

Urbach, Reinhard. *[Arthur] Schnitzler-Kommentar. Zu den Erzählenden Schriften und dramatischen Werken.* München: Winkler, 1974.

Name and Title Index

Name and Title Index   469